Succeeding in Life and Career

Foundations of Human Studies

12TH EDITION

Frances Baynor Parnell

Wilmington, North Carolina

Publisher
The Goodheart-Willcox Company, Inc.
Tinley Park, Illinois
www.g-w.com

About the Author

Frances Baynor Parnell was a secondary family and consumer sciences teacher for 32 years and served as department chair. She is president of Natural and Family Resources, Inc., which provides opportunities to be involved in cultures around the world. She has conducted research and completed a project on work and family skills to supplement family and consumer sciences education programs in North Carolina. In addition to writing this text and its supplements, Frances coauthored the book *Guarding Your Own Mental Health in a Fast-Paced World*. She is currently coauthoring the book, *Attracting Birds in the Carolinas*, which is to be released in the spring of 2021. Further, Frances has written numerous articles for professional publications and has conducted many workshops and given frequent presentations.

Frances has also contributed her expertise and leadership to a number of professional and civic organizations, which have earned state and national recognition in areas of environmental concerns.

During her years of teaching, Frances has received such awards as the North Carolina Home Economics Teacher of the Year, the Outstanding Educator Award (from East Carolina University, where she received her BS and MS degrees), and the Frances Hutchinson Teacher of the Year Award from John T. Hoggard High School.

Most recently, both Frances and her husband were inducted into the Order of the Long Leaf Pine, honoring their contributions to education and conservation. This is the highest honor granted by the Office of the Governor of North Carolina to individuals who have shown extraordinary service to the state.

Reviewers

The author and Goodheart-Willcox Publisher would like to thank the following professionals who provided valuable input to this edition of *Succeeding in Life and Career: Foundations of Human Studies*:

Cassie D. Blackwelder
Family and Consumer Sciences Instructor
Leesville Road High School
Raleigh, North Carolina

Heather Clary
CTE Teacher, Fashion Design and Interior Design
Grand Oaks High School
Houston, Texas

Linda Cooper-Suggs
Family and Consumer Sciences Instructor
James B. Hunt High School
Wilson, North Carolina

M. Kathleen Goldman
Family and Consumer Sciences Instructor
Salem High School
Virginia Beach, Virginia

Jana Lucas
Family and Consumer Sciences Instructor
Stratford High School
Houston, Texas

Beryl T. McMillian
Family and Consumer Sciences Instructor
Green Hope High School
Cary, North Carolina

Yvonne Nixon
Family and Consumer Sciences Instructor
Liberty Junior High
Liberty, Missouri

Charlotte C. Penny
Family and Consumer Sciences Instructor
North Cobb High School
Kennesaw, Georgia

Brenda D. Samdahl
Family and Consumer Sciences Department Chair
First Colonial High School
Virginia Beach, Virginia

Linda Olsen Spruill
Family and Consumer Sciences Coordinator
Virginia Beach City Public Schools
Virginia Beach, Virginia

Yvonne Tomlinson
CTE, Family and Consumer Sciences, and Principles of Technology Instructor
Brenham High School
Brenham, Texas

Sharon Carter Underwood
Family and Consumer Sciences Instructor
Leesville Road High School
Raleigh, North Carolina

Contributor for Sewing Chapters
Joyce Honeycutt Wooten
Burgaw, North Carolina

Student Tools

Student Text

Succeeding in Life and Career: Foundations of Human Studies is an advanced comprehensive text designed to help students adjust to change, especially as they become young adults. Relationships and personal development, lifespan development, resource management, wellness and nutrition, personal finance, fashion and apparel, and housing and transportation topics help students build the skills necessary to manage life and career. Special features include *21st Century Skills, Healthy Living, Life Skills, Financial Literacy, Science Connection, Math Connection, Mental Health Awareness, Wellness Awareness,* and *Living Green.* The text stresses career readiness and introduces the 16 career clusters. Additionally, students gain hands-on experience building a portfolio by completing chapter projects. Likewise, critical-thinking activities, 21st century applications activities, and FCCLA activities at the end of each chapter help students develop leadership and college and career readiness skills. Special *Journal Writing* activities at the end of each chapter help students develop their reflective writing skills.

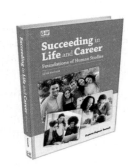

Workbook

The workbook that accompanies *Succeeding in Life and Career: Foundations of Human Studies* includes activities to help students recall, review, and apply concepts introduced in the book.

Online Learning Suite

The Online Learning Suite provides the foundation of instruction and learning for digital and blended classrooms. An easy-to-manage shared classroom subscription makes it a hassle-free solution for both students and instructors. An online student text and workbook brings digital learning to the classroom. All instructional materials are found on a convenient online bookshelf and accessible at home, at school, or on the go.

G-W Companion Website

The G-W Learning companion website is a study reference that contains e-flash cards and vocabulary exercises. The companion website is accessible from any digital device.

Online Learning Suite/Student Text Bundle

Looking for a blended solution? Goodheart-Willcox offers the Online Learning Suite bundled with the printed text in one easy-to-access package. Students have the flexibility to use the printed text, the Online Learning Suite, or a combination of both components to meet their individual learning styles. The convenient packaging makes managing and accessing content easy and efficient.

Instructor Tools

LMS Integration

Integrate Goodheart-Willcox content within your Learning Management System for a seamless user experience for both you and your students. LMS-ready content in Common Cartridge® format facilitates single sign-on integration and gives you control of student enrollment and data. With a Common Cartridge integration, you can access the LMS features and tools you are accustomed to using and G-W course resources in one convenient location—your LMS.

To provide a complete learning package for you and your students, G-W Common Cartridge includes the Online Learning Suite and Online Instructor Resources. When you incorporate G-W content into your courses via Common Cartridge, you have the flexibility to customize and structure the content to meet the educational needs of your students. You may also choose to add your own content to the course.

QTI® question banks are available within the Online Instructor Resources for import into your LMS. These prebuilt assessments help you measure student knowledge and track results in your LMS gradebook. Questions and tests can be customized to meet your assessment needs.

Online Instructor Resources (OIR)

Online Instructor Resources provide all the support needed to make preparation and classroom instruction easier than ever. Available in one accessible location, the OIR includes Instructor Resources, Instructor's Presentations for PowerPoint®, and Assessment Software with Question Banks. The OIR is available as a subscription and can be accessed at school, at home, or on the go.

Instructor Resources One resource provides instructors with time-saving preparation tools such as answer keys, editable lesson plans, concept organizers, and other teaching aids.

Instructor's Presentations for PowerPoint® These fully customizable, richly illustrated slides help you teach and visually reinforce the key concepts from each chapter.

Assessment Software with Question Banks Administer and manage assessments to meet your classroom needs. The question banks that accompany this textbook include hundreds of matching, true/false, completion, multiple choice, and short answer questions to assess student knowledge of the content in each chapter. Using the assessment software simplifies the process of creating, managing, administering, and grading tests. You can have the software generate a test for you with randomly selected questions. You may also choose specific questions from the question banks and, if you wish, add your own questions to create customized tests to meet your classroom needs.

G-W Integrated Learning Solution

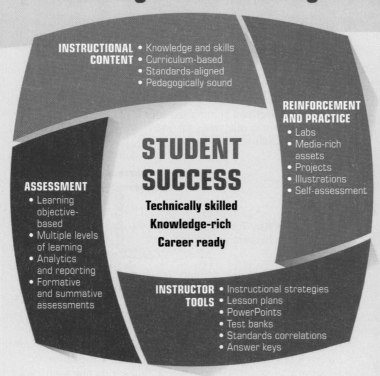

INSTRUCTIONAL CONTENT
- Knowledge and skills
- Curriculum-based
- Standards-aligned
- Pedagogically sound

REINFORCEMENT AND PRACTICE
- Labs
- Media-rich assets
- Projects
- Illustrations
- Self-assessment

STUDENT SUCCESS

Technically skilled

Knowledge-rich

Career ready

ASSESSMENT
- Learning objective-based
- Multiple levels of learning
- Analytics and reporting
- Formative and summative assessments

INSTRUCTOR TOOLS
- Instructional strategies
- Lesson plans
- PowerPoints
- Test banks
- Standards correlations
- Answer keys

The G-W Integrated Learning Solution offers easy-to-use resources that help students and instructors achieve success.

▶ **EXPERT AUTHORS**
▶ **TRUSTED REVIEWERS**
▶ **100 YEARS OF EXPERIENCE**

EMPLOYABILITY SKILLS · TECHNICAL SKILLS · ACADEMIC KNOWLEDGE · INDUSTRY RECOGNIZED STANDARDS

Organized for Successful Learning

As you prepare for adult roles in managing your life and career, the knowledge and skills you gain from this text will help your future success. *Succeeding in Life and Career* is a contemporary, comprehensive text that presents concepts that are vitally important to your success in the workplace and in life.

Sections in an easy-to-read format present the main themes in each chapter.

Reading Prep offers quick, easy activities that help you develop reading and literacy skills, as well as engage with the chapter content.

Concept Organizers challenge you to present chapter information in logical ways.

Companion Website activities extend learning beyond the classroom and include a variety of vocabulary exercises using the Key Terms and an interactive glossary.

Objectives summarize your learning outcomes for each section.

Key Terms help you define and expand your vocabulary.

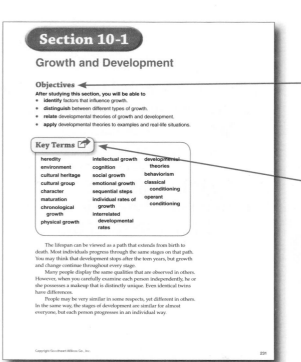

Activities Maximize Learning Impact

It is important to assess what you learn as you progress through the text. Multiple opportunities are provided to confirm your learning as you explore the text content. End-of-chapter *formative assessment* activities include the following:

Core Skills activities link to academic subjects and skills, including reading, writing, speaking, listening, history, math, science, and social studies.

Portfolio Builder projects guide you in developing a portfolio of your best work throughout this course. Learning the basics about portfolio development will help compile an effective portfolio for future employment.

Critical Thinking questions challenge you to use your higher-level thinking skills when reviewing chapter concepts.

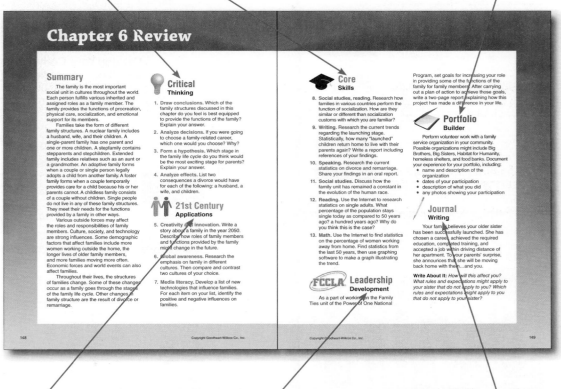

21st Century Applications activities help prepare you for real-life scenarios as a student, family member, citizen, and member of the workforce. These activities encourage learning and innovation skills; life and career skills; core subject skills; and information, media, and technology skills.

FCCLA Leadership Development activities encourage leadership development through Family, Career and Community Leaders of America activities and competitive STAR Events. Each activity enhances your classroom learning and emphasizes family and consumer sciences concepts.

Journal Writing activities offer real-life scenarios to help you apply text concepts and expand your reflective writing skills.

Reading Review questions at the end of each section help you check your comprehension of key text concepts.

Engaging Features Promote 21st Century Skills

Practical information helps prepare you for the future. Engaging special features add realism and interest to enhance learning in every chapter.

feedback to your friend. This will continue to help build your friend's self-concept. At the same time, a true friend will do the same for you.

Mutual Respect

Mutual respect means each person regards the other with honor and esteem. People in positive relationships do not expect each other to agree on everything. Neither person tries to force an opinion or idea on the other. They respect each other's right to differ. They respect each other for who they are.

Building mutual respect between teens and adults is sometimes a challenge. Some teens feel threatened by the experience and maturity of adults. They think adults judge them unfairly. On the other hand, adults fear that teens believe adults are not in touch with current youth culture.

Teens and adults both need to feel they are valued by one another. Teens can benefit by seeking wisdom from adults. Likewise, adults can be inspired by the enthusiasm of youth. Such worthwhile exchanges can help teens and adults build mutual respect and develop positive relationships.

Trust

Trusting people means having confidence in them. In a positive relationship, you must trust the other person. However, you must also prove that you are trustworthy. You must be careful not to betray the confidence that is vested in you. You must be able to keep secrets. You must not laugh at friends who share serious concerns with you. You must not encourage others to participate in activities that are not in their best interests.

Trust in a relationship can be fragile. If you give advice that backfires, you may not be trusted in the future. When advice is sought, it may be better to help friends view situations from several different perspectives. Allow them to analyze the possible alternatives and choose their own plan of action.

Openness

Openness in a relationship refers to an atmosphere in which people feel free to share their thoughts and feelings. You must create this atmosphere for people with whom you relate. You must make them feel comfortable about opening up to you.

You must also be willing to open up to others. No one can second-guess what you think or feel. People cannot meet your needs unless you tell them what your needs are.

Reliability

People in positive relationships must be reliable. If you say you will do something, people must be able to count on you to do it. If you say you will be somewhere, people must be able to depend on you to be there.

21st Century Skills

Integrity. Monique works on confidential reports. She is careful not to share any of the information she knows with people outside of her company.

Analyze and Solve

List people in the community with whom you have developed or can develop positive relationships. Explain benefits that might come from networking with these people.

21st Century Skills addresses qualities that lead to success in the workplace.

Analyze and Solve helps you develop problem-solving, critical-thinking, and decision-making skills.

Serving Your Community fosters concern, appreciation, and involvement with the community, emphasizing your role as a citizen.

do your work for you. On the other hand, do not assume that you can get along without your coworkers. Most jobs are a team effort. If you show consideration to coworkers, they will be likely to cooperate with you.

Benefits of Positive Relationships

Positive relationships produce many benefits. Research has shown that relationships can affect a person's physical and emotional well-being. People who maintain positive relationships have fewer physical illnesses. They are also less prone to diseases and tend to live longer. Their emotional well-being is enhanced because they know people care about them. They can share their problems and thereby reduce the stress of daily living.

Positive relationships also provide social benefits. You are more likely to go places and get involved in activities when someone can join you. Your present relationships can serve as bridges to future relationships. Your social circle will expand as you meet new people.

Economic well-being can be a benefit of positive work relationships. People who relate well on the job are likely to enjoy their work. This will encourage them to stay on the job. They will increase their chances of being promoted and getting more pay raises.

Qualities Needed for Positive Relationships

As you read earlier, positive relationships do not happen automatically. Both people involved must work to develop key qualities that form the basis for positive relationships. These qualities include a positive self-concept, mutual respect, trust, openness, and reliability.

Positive Self-Concept

As you have read, a positive self-concept means that you see yourself as worthwhile. Confident people who care for others may anticipate that others will care for them in return. In addition, when others see that you think highly of yourself, they are likely to think highly of you as well. They may realize that they would enjoy forming a friendship with you.

A positive self-concept usually results from positive feedback. Therefore, an important part of friendship is providing positive

Serving Your Community

Investigate local programs focused on encouraging and helping older adults who live alone to socialize with others. Research why these programs are so important. Ask about volunteer opportunities for teens.

Healthy Living

Friendships and Emotional Health

Everyone needs friends. Positive friendships are important to emotional health. Characteristics of true friends include people
* with whom you feel you can talk about anything
* who make you feel peaceful just by being with them
* with whom you can have fun—even when you are not doing anything special
* to whom you can tell a secret and know it won't get spread around
* who understand and support you whether you're feeling up or down

Healthy Living focuses on ways you can maintain a healthy lifestyle.

Jetta Productions/Photodisc/Getty Images

Many schools, especially private schools, require students to wear uniforms. The uniforms of exclusive schools often serve as symbols of prestige. Some public school systems require students to wear uniforms as an antiviolence measure. Wearing uniforms sends a message that all students belong to the same "team." This results in less competition and more cooperation among "team members." Uniforms keep fashion from being an issue so students can focus more on learning.

Some groups do not have specific uniforms. However, they use certain colors or symbols to identify their members. For instance, members of sororities and fraternities often own garments with Greek letters representing the names of their organizations.

Many people show group identity simply by yielding to the influence of their peers. Your peers form an informal group. By wearing the kinds of clothes your friends wear, you are showing you are a member of that group. Jeans and T-shirts are typical attire of many teen peer groups.

19-1
These uniforms are worn by students at a high school in the state of Washington.

Life Skills

Clothing for Special Needs

Some people, such as older adults or people with disabilities, have special clothing needs. Older people may choose more casual, comfortable clothes for their daily activities. Easy care is another important factor. People with disabilities may want clothes that are stylish, yet easy to get on and off. Elastic waists and knit fabrics allow both comfort and ease of movement. People with physical limitations or low vision also need simple fasteners and larger openings.

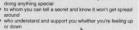

Life Skills provides additional information that will help you develop life skills in a variety of areas.

Complex Concepts Presented Simply

The easy-to-understand presentation of complex concepts helps you build essential skills for managing your life at home and in the workplace.

Financial Literacy features help you develop money-management skills.

Financial Literacy

Types of Taxes

Taxes collected for government services can be classified in the following ways:
- *Progressive taxes:* as the item being taxed increases, the rate of tax increases. For instance, income tax is a progressive tax. The more you earn, the higher is the percentage of tax you pay.
- *Direct taxes:* those charged directly to the people who are to pay them. Sales tax is an example of a direct tax.
- *Indirect taxes:* are included in the price of taxed items. Excise tax is an example of an indirect tax.

How do taxes affect citizens? Consider the following examples involving the purchase of gasoline and antifreeze, both costing $3.50 a gallon:
- Excise tax of 20 cents a gallon is *included* in the price of the gasoline. Therefore, you will have to pay $3.50 for a gallon of gasoline.
- A sales tax of 6 percent is *added* onto the price of the antifreeze. A gallon of the antifreeze will cost you $3.71.

Science Connection features link chapter content to the field of science.

Science Connection

Generating Energy with Biomass

Wood once provided all the energy needed for heating homes and cooking. Today it is used in fireplaces, but this is a minor use. Burning wood is restricted in many areas because the smoke contains pollutants. Industries that convert wood to paper, chemicals, and building products use wood waste to produce their own steam and electricity.

Crops like corn and sugar are fermented to produce the transportation fuel called *ethanol.* Another such fuel, *biodiesel,* is made from oil extracted from soybeans. Although in limited supply, these new types of fuel will become more available in the future.

Solid waste is considered biomass if it is the type that rots, such as food scraps and lawn clippings. (Trash also contains glass, metals, and plastics, which are not biomass.) Burning this waste generates steam and an ash by-product, often used for roads. When the waste is placed in a landfill, it releases a gas that can be converted to a fuel source.

Math Connection expands the chapter content related to math. Specific examples demonstrate step-by-step calculations essential to life and career.

Math Connection

Determining Quantities

Kristen read that Americans create an average of 4.4 pounds of trash daily. She wants to know how much trash her class of 24 students creates in a year. She can do this by multiplying the average number of pounds by the number of students.

4.4 pounds × 24 students = 105.6 pounds per day

Then she would multiply the daily number of pounds by the number of days in a year (365).

105.6 pounds per day × 365 days = 38,544 pounds per year

Mental Health Awareness connects chapter content to mental health topics and shows how mental health can affect multiple areas of life.

Wellness Awareness encourages you to explore health and wellness topics related to chapter content.

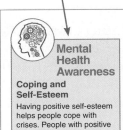

Wellness Awareness

Research instances where children who were neglected emotionally developed physical health problems. What is the link between mental/emotional health and physical health?

Mental Health Awareness

Coping and Self-Esteem

Having positive self-esteem helps people cope with crises. People with positive self-esteem have a strong sense of self-worth and are less prone to self-criticism and unreasonable guilt. They are confident about their ability to accept new responsibilities. They are also likely to acknowledge how they have grown by meeting new challenges.

Living Green offers easy tips to incorporate environmentally friendly habits into your daily life.

Living Green

You want to meet new people, but where do you start? Consider working on a gardening or recycling project in your school or community. While helping the environment, you can cultivate friendships as well.

Brief Contents

Contents

Unit Four

Parenting, Child Care, and Guidance

Unit Five

Wellness and Nutrition

Unit Six

Personal Finance

Unit Seven

Fashion and Apparel

Unit Eight

Housing and Transportation

Features

 Career Spotlight

Financial Literacy

Healthy Living

Life Skills

Math Connection

Mental Health Awareness

Science Connection

Join Student Organizations

You may be familiar with many student organizations at your school. Some exist specifically to help you and other young people learn the skills they will need in the work world. These organizations are known as Career and Technical Student Organizations (CTSOs). Joining one or more of these organizations can benefit you in many ways:

- develop skills for employability and career success, such as leadership, cooperation, responsibility, and creativity
- practice skills in planning, communication, and teamwork
- build friendships with peers who share similar values and goals
- learn how to network with peers and professionals

As part of a CTSO, you will have access to in-depth, profession-related knowledge. Staff, organization leaders, and teachers can provide you with valuable insights you will need on your career path. The U.S. Department of Education recognizes 11 CTSOs. Two relate most to the content of this text.

Family, Career and Community Leaders of America (FCCLA)

FCCLA is a student led intra-curricular organization that promotes personal growth and leadership development through Family and Consumer Sciences education. As the only in-school student organization that focuses on careers that support the family, FCCLA is an ideal companion to courses in your school's Family and Consumer Sciences program.

Involvement in FCCLA offers the opportunity to

- participate in activities and events at local, state, and national levels
- develop leadership and teamwork skills
- help others through community service projects
- prepare for future roles in your family, career, and community

STAR Events—Students Taking Action with Recognition

Students compete in events that test their leadership and career preparation skills. Students participate in cooperative, individualized, and competitive events. Topics include career investigation, entrepreneurship, job interviewing, and event management.

For additional information, visit the organization's website at fcclainc.org.

SkillsUSA

SkillsUSA is an organization of students preparing for careers in trade, technical, and health services. Students may compete in the SkillsUSA Championships at the local, state, and national levels. SkillsUSA emphasizes not only those qualities necessary to begin a successful career, but also the importance of lifelong education and training. Check out the organization's website at www.skillsusa.org.

Career Discovery

Human Services

Are you a "people person"? Are you motivated to improve the lives of others? Perhaps a career in human services is the best choice for you.

Human Services Pathways

Early Childhood Development and
  Services
Counseling and Mental Health
  Services
Family and Community Services
Personal Care Services
Consumer Services

Jeanette Dietl/Shutterstock.com

Education and Training

If you are passionate about learning and like being in a school or academic setting, you may enjoy a career in education and training.

Education and Training Pathways

Administration and Administrative
  Support
Professional Support Services
Teaching and Training

Fuse/Thinkstock

Career Spotlight: Career Counselor

- **Description.** Career counselors help people begin their careers, enter a new career field, or return to work after a period of absence. Counselors often help clients evaluate their interests, aptitudes, and abilities. They help clients create or strengthen their résumé, build job search skills, and plan education and training goals. They may also help professionals navigate career choices and opportunities within their field. Career counselors may work in schools, colleges and universities, career centers, or in private organizations.
- **Education and training.** Requirements vary, but many states require career counselors to have a master's degree in career counseling, or a master's degree in counseling with a focus on career development. Licensing or certification is often required; internship experience is often preferred.

- **Skills and personal qualities.** Career counselors must have the desire to help people secure employment and succeed in the workplace. Strong interpersonal, communication, organization, planning, research, and problem-solving skills are needed. Honesty, patience, and the ability to teach are also important qualities for career counselors.
- **Job outlook.** Job growth through 2028 is projected to grow faster than average for all occupations. Visit the *Occupational Outlook Handbook* online to learn more about a career as a career counselor.

Human Services

Career Spotlight: Preschool Teacher

- **Description.** Preschool teachers care for, guide, and teach children between the ages of three to five. They help children develop their reading, writing, language, social, math, and science skills. Teachers help meet preschoolers' physical, intellectual, and social-emotional needs through planned activities, play time, nap time, and meal or snack time. Preschool teachers help prepare preschoolers for kindergarten.
- **Education and training.** Requirements vary by state and facility. Some child care facilities may only require teachers to have a high school diploma or an associate's degree. Most schools, however, require teachers to have a bachelor's degree in early childhood education or a related field. Public schools also require licensing to teach. Many teachers earn a Child Development Associate (CDA) certification. A thorough knowledge of child development is critical.

- **Skills and personal qualities.** Preschool teachers must genuinely like children and desire to help them develop physically, intellectually, and socially-emotionally. Strong interpersonal, communication, critical-thinking, and problem-solving skills are essential. Patience, kindness, and creativity are also needed.
- **Job outlook.** Job growth for preschool teachers through 2028 is projected to grow faster than average for all occupations. Visit the *Occupational Outlook Handbook* online to learn more about a career as a preschool teacher.

Education & Training

Sources: States' Career Clusters Initiative, Bureau of Labor Statistics Career Guide to Industries

Chapter 1
Exploring Careers

Reading Prep

Read the chapter title and write a paragraph describing what you already know about the topic. After reading the chapter, summarize what you have learned.

Concept Organizer

Use a Y-chart to organize what you know about your interests, aptitudes, and abilities.

G-W LEARNING.com

Click on the activity icon to visit www.g-wlearning. com/comprehensive/8062 to access online vocabulary activities using key terms from the chapter.

Planning Your Future

Objectives

After studying this section, you will be able to

- **describe** how personality affects career planning.
- **relate** self-esteem to a positive self-concept.
- **contrast** needs and wants.
- **summarize** how values and standards shape career plans.
- **identify** ways to prepare for change.
- **explain** potential and how to achieve it.

Key Terms ⬈

personality	wants	perseverance
self-concept	values	resiliency
self-esteem	peers	potential
needs	standards	

Thinking about the future can be exciting, but it can also be scary. After you finish school, you will need to find work and make it on your own. Ideally, you will have an enjoyable job that pays well, a nice place to live, and occasional extras.

Does this sound too good to be true, or can this become your future? Some teens falsely believe a fulfilling life "just falls into place." However, nothing could be further from the truth.

Your life is too important to leave to chance, so start planning your future now. If you have already started, congratulations, but if not, it's never too late to begin. How do you get started? You begin by studying the qualities that make you unique and actions that help shape a satisfying future. You will explore career possibilities and learn how to identify the options that suit you. As you determine about your future place in the work world, you are taking steps toward building a successful life.

Knowing Yourself

To start planning your future, begin by understanding yourself. In what types of careers do you picture yourself? What are your needs, values, and standards? What type of personality do you have?

Personality

Personality is the total of all the behavioral qualities and traits that make an individual. These traits develop over time. Personality includes the way you feel, think, speak, dress, and relate to others, **1-1**.

Why is it important to understand your personality? Generally, people are attracted to careers that suit their personalities. Various types of work complement certain personalities more than others. You probably know classmates who are primarily social or primarily inquisitive. Social personalities do well in teaching and social work because they enjoy interacting with people. This is a key job responsibility in both cases. Inquisitive personality types, on the other hand, enjoy exploring ideas as scientists or news reporters.

1-1

The way you interact with your friends is a part of your personality that makes you unique.

fstop123/E+/Getty Images

Most individuals are more complex than the two distinct personality types identified. People generally possess various personality traits. For example, they can be both social and inquisitive. More types of work will appeal to those who possess a wider variety of personality traits.

Do you already know what your key personality traits are? You can learn your personality type by talking with your school counselor and taking an appropriate test.

Self-Concept and Self-Esteem

When you think about the future, in what careers do you imagine yourself? Your view of yourself is your **self-concept**. You began developing your self-concept or self-identity at an early age. This view is largely influenced by how people behave around you and how you interpret their behaviors toward you. Your view of yourself can be positive or negative.

When people show approval of you and your behavior, you react with positive feelings. Such feelings help you develop a *positive self-concept*. These feelings are also called *self-esteem*. **Self-esteem** is the sense of worth you attach to yourself. Taking pride in yourself and your accomplishments reflects self-esteem. If you feel that you are worthwhile, it will show in your relationships with others and the confidence you have in yourself.

When people possess self-esteem, they use their best judgments and make their own decisions. They know that others do not shape their sense of worth, so they pay little attention to negative comments. Their demonstration of responsible behavior makes them positive examples for others.

Having self-esteem does not mean everything you do will be successful. However, it helps you to keep a realistic view of your successes and failures. With self-esteem, you work harder at reaching your goals and fulfilling your responsibilities.

Sometimes people show disapproval, and when they do, you feel their dislike or rejection of you. Messages such as these tend to promote a *negative self-concept*. You may feel uncomfortable about yourself and avoid reaching out to others in fear of possible rejection. On the other hand, you may recognize some truth in the message and learn from it.

Every person receives some positive and some negative messages. However, it lies within the individual to filter out any unhelpful messages. Self-esteem gives a person the confidence to shape his or her own self-worth.

Needs Versus Wants

Understanding your needs helps you pursue everything you want in life. **Needs** are the basics required for living. All people have the same basic needs that must be met for proper growth and

Mental Health Awareness

Improving Self-Esteem

Everyone has days when they have feelings of low self-esteem. Here are some helpful tips for improving your self-esteem:

- Stop yourself from thinking over-critical thoughts. Instead, take a moment to start a *self-affirmation file*. Write a note about something positive in your life, put it in folder, and read it when you feel low. Also, add affirming notes you receive from others.
- Choose excellence over perfection. Trying to achieve perfectionism can be emotionally and intellectually draining. Strive for excellence and do your best.
- Learn from your mistakes. Everyone makes mistakes—it's all part of learning. Making a mistake and learning from it can make you stronger.

Financial Literacy

Do You Really Need That?

Do you buy the latest clothes and newest technology just to show them off to your friends? Do you buy things because they fill a real use in your life, or do you buy them to impress others? The key to making sound financial decisions is to know the difference between needs and wants. Do you know the differences between your own needs and wants?

Developing a sense of purpose and direction about your needs can help you avoid draining your resources. Knowing the difference between needs and wants can also help you to avoid debt.

development. Psychologist Abraham Maslow identified five levels of human needs that he prioritized as physical, safety and security, social, esteem, and self-actualization, **1-2.**

More needs are related to the psychological environment than to the physical environment. Realize, too, that physical needs are more urgent. They must be fulfilled before psychological needs can be considered.

Everyone has the same basic needs, but people have different wants. **Wants** are things people desire, but do not need. They are not necessary for survival, and life will go on without them. Wants make life more pleasant, though. The latest video game and attractive jewelry are examples of wants.

Basic food and shelter are clearly needs, but so is the employment that allows people to pay for those needs. Preparing yourself to have employable skills is a related need. When you are tempted to spend time with friends instead of study for a test, can you separate needs from wants? Doing your best as a student is a need at this stage of your life.

As you define your needs and wants, recognize that wants should not come ahead of needs. Establishing values and standards for your life will help you put needs ahead of wants.

Your Values

People satisfy their needs in different ways. If this were not so, everyone would eat the same kind of food and live in the same kind of house. Instead, life is full of variety. Each person has his or her own style of living. Each person's decisions and behaviors are different from those of anyone else. Factors that contribute to the differences between people include their values and standards.

Values are the beliefs, feelings, and experiences you consider to be important and desirable. Honesty, friendship, freedom, happiness, popularity, health, or education may be values you consider important. The combination of values you have and the importance you give each one makes you unique. Your values become a part of your personality.

Your values also affect your behavior. Consciously or unconsciously, they guide the decisions you make every day. If education is important to you, you might choose to spend an evening studying rather than watching TV. If adventure is something you value, you probably would choose an exciting hobby, such as snowboarding.

Living Green

Think before you buy any product. Consider the environmental impact of the use and disposal of the product. By buying only what you need, you will purchase less and create less waste in the future.

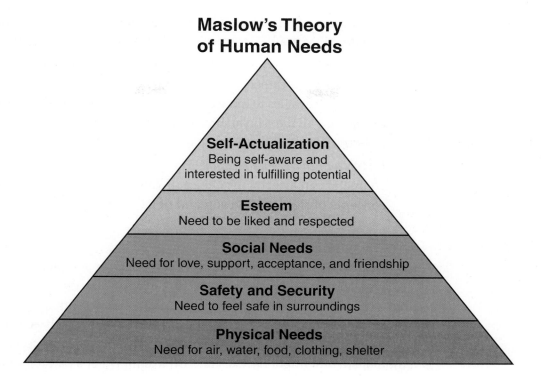

**Maslow's Theory
of Human Needs**

Self-Actualization
Being self-aware and
interested in fulfilling potential

Esteem
Need to be liked and respected

Social Needs
Need for love, support, acceptance, and friendship

Safety and Security
Need to feel safe in surroundings

Physical Needs
Need for air, water, food, clothing, shelter

You did not possess values at birth; they developed over time. All the experiences in your lifetime have contributed to your values. Your future experiences will also affect your values. Some values will become more important to you, while others will become less important. Your set of values will never be final. They will change just as you change.

1-2

According to Maslow, physical needs must be met before meeting other needs.

Factors Affecting Your Values

Many factors influence the development of your values.

- *Relationships with parents and other adults.* Your first basic values were learned from the people who cared for you as a young child—parents, family members, babysitters, and teachers. Children imitate people they admire.

- *Relationships with friends.* The people you meet, especially your friends and peers, influence what you consider important. (Your **peers** are other people in your age group.)

- *Relationship with children.* When people have children, their values often change. Being financially secure and having nearby schools for their children may take on new importance. Older adults may value living near their grown children and spending time with grandchildren.

- *Experiences and education.* Once you experience or study something, you decide if it will become a part of your values.
- *Needs.* Pressing needs can persuade you to adopt new values. For example, if your career choice requires expensive schooling, you will value opportunities to reduce the financial burden. One opportunity is to apply for all the scholarships you can. Another opportunity is working full-time for an employer that pays for courses taken to improve job skills.
- *Morals and character education.* The presence or absence of good character can affect your choice of values. These, in turn, affect your concepts of right and wrong and of good and bad.

Your Standards

There are many different kinds of **standards** or accepted levels of achievement. People have standards for their appearance and how well they perform certain skills. They have standards for the quality of their possessions. People also set different standards for themselves. For instance, one student might have a standard to correctly answer every test question. Another student might have a standard to simply get a passing grade.

Standards and Values

People's standards are related to their values. Their standards will be high for the items they highly value.

Like values, people acquire their standards through personal contacts and experiences. Therefore, people from the same culture, and especially the same family, often have similar standards.

Knowing your own standards and what you expect from life can help you understand yourself more fully. In a similar way, you can have a better understanding of other people if you notice what standards they apply to their lives.

Meeting Future Challenges

You often hear the saying *life is full of challenges*. All students your age face many of the same pressures, but there are ways to handle them. One way is to recognize that changes are coming and prepare for them. Another way to meet future challenges is to build inner strength and confidence. These challenges simply mean you are maturing and moving toward independence.

Prepare for Change

Change is a normal part of life. It can be uncomfortable to people uncertain about what lies ahead. Change, however, brings new opportunities and experiences, especially for teens preparing for a promising future, **1-3**. For those who make life and career plans, change can even be exciting and fun. Replace any fear of the unknown you might have with a commitment to learn how to deal with change.

1-3
You will face many changes, challenges, and opportunities throughout your teen years.

Gather Information

You can prepare for upcoming changes by finding out as much as possible about them. What information will help you adjust to the changes that lie ahead? Can you talk to someone who has already met those challenges? Check with your teachers and school counselor for advice.

Develop Skills to Adjust

With patience and practice, you can develop the skills you need to prepare for change. One important skill is **perseverance** or sticking to an action or belief even when difficult. When you carefully decide a course of action, never give in to the urge to quit, no matter how tempting. Pause long enough to remind yourself what needs to be accomplished and why.

Another skill that will help you cope with change is **resiliency**. This is the ability to adjust to setbacks and make changes that allow you to survive and thrive. Being resilient means to bounce back when something stands in your way. Keeping a positive attitude can help you find a way through hurdles you thought were impossible to conquer.

Remember that everyone gets discouraged from time to time, but you have the ability to move on. Always find a way to encourage yourself to keep moving forward.

Manage the Change

The completion of high school will be a time of great change for you. What career-related steps will you take? How will your schedule change? Will you still be able to see your friends and family?

Take one step at a time, and recognize what needs to be done to bring more certainty to every situation. The more you know about the changes you will experience, the more confidence you will have to face them.

Achieve Your Potential

Everyone is born with **potential**. This is the capacity to develop, succeed, and make further advances in life. You have the ability to make good choices and develop new skills to achieve whatever you want. You may experience temporary setbacks, but realize this happens to everyone. Maintain confidence in yourself and accept any challenges you face. Here are some recommendations for achieving your potential.

Be Realistic About Your Expectations of Yourself

Remember that no one is perfect. Know that you will do some things very well, but not everything. Others will excel in certain areas. Feel good about all your accomplishments and do not be afraid of failure. Failure can be beneficial if it forces you to take a fresh look at yourself.

Think about what went wrong and find a way to make a comeback. With that comeback, you can experience a sense of freedom that allows you to take new risks. You may find untapped inner resources as you tackle challenges head-on.

Develop Your Skills

Look for opportunities to develop your talents and abilities instead of sticking to "safe" activities you already do well. What type of skills will be needed for the career you want? Pursue activities that may relate to your future career. You can develop and strengthen your skills by joining a career and technical student organization (CTSO), such as Family, Career and Community Leaders of America (FCCLA).

Look for Positive Relationships with Others

Living in a negative psychological environment and maintaining a positive outlook is difficult. Therefore, try to surround yourself with positive people who support you. Everyone needs positive reinforcement to get through challenging times.

Spend Time Alone

All people need to devote time to thinking about their lives, hopes, and dreams. Spend some time alone, imagining yourself in your future career. For example, maybe you like to walk or ride a bike when you are feeling stressed. These activities can help you relax and see things more clearly.

Develop a Sense of Humor

Most importantly, develop a sense of humor. Learn to laugh at yourself without being embarrassed. A sense of humor can diffuse tense situations. It can take the sting out of cutting remarks and sarcasm. Finally, a sense of humor also makes others feel more comfortable around you.

21st Century Skills

Social skills. Andy has great job skills and is confident that he will succeed in his new job. Andy also realizes that although job skills are important, it's also important to have good interpersonal skills as he builds relationships with his new coworkers.

Reading
Review

1. Explain the relationship between self-esteem and self-concept.
2. Describe a person with a positive self-concept.
3. What is the difference between needs and wants?
4. List five factors that influence the development of a person's values.
5. Describe how standards are related to values.
6. How can resiliency help you cope with change?

Section 1-2

Career Planning

Objectives

After studying this section, you will be able to

- **explain** how your interests, aptitudes, and abilities relate to your career choices.
- **identify** the importance of a personal plan of study.
- **determine** factors to consider in making career decisions.

Key Terms

job	ability	internship
occupation	job shadowing	apprenticeship
career	cooperative	
aptitude	education	

You will hear the terms *job, occupation,* and *career* as you begin planning your career. Do you know their meanings? A **job** is one or more tasks, while an **occupation** is paid employment involving a job. An occupation, however, is often called a job. A **career** is a series of related occupations that show progression in a field of work.

Begin career planning by picturing yourself in the occupations that interest you. This helps you narrow the list of career possibilities and focus on your favorites.

Knowing Your Interests

One person's interests are not better than another's. Interests simply help define an individual and reflect that person's values. Career interests are grouped into three types.

- *Interest in people.* Do you like to work alone or as part of a team? If you enjoy being with others, you are suited for a career that focuses on interacting with people. Sales, counseling, and teaching are examples of people-oriented careers, **1-4**.

- *Interest in information.* Do you like to check details and make discoveries? If you like to find facts and share what you know, you would enjoy a career focused on information. Researching and reporting are examples of information-oriented careers.

- *Interest in tools and objects.* Do you like to work with your hands? If you do, a career that focuses on tools and materials could be ideal for you.

Many careers involve all three interest areas in various degrees. If you have trouble narrowing your interests, your school counselor can help by giving you one or more interest assessments.

1-4

People who prefer working with children might enjoy teaching in elementary school.

Knowing Your Aptitudes and Abilities

Most people have more than one **aptitude** or natural talent. These are areas in which you excel, develop your greatest skills, and generally find satisfaction. Aptitudes often relate to job success. For example, people with an aptitude for singing do it well even without practice. Because they enjoy singing, they also enjoy practicing. With more practice, they sing even better.

A person without an aptitude for singing may still be able to develop singing ability. An **ability** is a skill a person learns through practice. Someone without singing talent who practices often may achieve some success. That person is unlikely, however, to be as successful as one with natural singing aptitude.

The same is true in employment. People who perform a job using a natural talent often do it better and quicker than others. When you match yourself against your peers, in what areas do you excel? The activities you most enjoy are probably those you do best.

Your school counselor can identify your natural talents through aptitude and ability assessments. Keep in mind, however, the results will not give definite answers to career questions. The results will simply indicate your strong areas. That information will give you an idea of the kinds of careers that offer you the best chances for success.

Learning About Careers

Perhaps you thought a certain career was right for you, but learned more about it and changed your mind. That happens to many people. Learning that specific careers are wrong for you is valuable. That knowledge moves you closer to finding the right career. When researching careers, consider the industry, required education and training, and other factors to determine which career might be right for you.

The Career Clusters

An easy way to investigate careers is by exploring the *career clusters*, which are 16 groups of career specialties, **1-5**. Occupations within each cluster are similar or related to one another. The occupations within a cluster, therefore, require a set of common knowledge and skills for career success. These are called the *essential knowledge and skills*.

To find occupations relating to Family and Consumer Sciences, look in these career clusters:

- Agriculture, Food & Natural Resources
- Arts, Audio/Video Technology & Communications
- Education & Training
- Health Science

Sixteen Career Clusters			
Agriculture, Food & Natural Resources	Education & Training	Hospitality & Tourism	Manufacturing
Architecture & Construction	Finance	Human Services	Marketing
Arts, A/V Technology & Communications	Government & Public Administration	Information Technology	Science, Technology, Engineering & Mathematics
Business Management & Administration	Health Science	Law, Public Safety, Corrections & Security	Transportation, Distribution & Logistics

1-5

The career clusters represent different career areas.

- Hospitality & Tourism
- Human Services

Each career cluster is broken further into *career pathways*. These career subgroups often require additional or more specialized knowledge and skills. If one or two jobs in a career cluster appeal to you, it is likely that others will, too.

Programs of Study

A program of study is a menu that lists a sequence of courses and activities that prepare students for occupations within a certain career pathway. Customizing a program of study results in a *personal plan of study*. The plan shows the career direction you have decided and the courses and activities chosen to address your career-preparation needs. It eliminates the frustration of not knowing what you need to do next.

Postsecondary options such as degree programs and on-the-job training are included in the plan. It also shows the employment options available with further study and the professional associations to contact for more career information. Be sure to update your plan at least yearly, but more often if your goals change.

Career Information Sources

One of the best ways to find employment as well as general career information is to search government websites, **1-6**. You can search for open positions in your area or across the country. Many of the websites also provide tips for job hunting.

Your friends, relatives, neighbors, and other people in the working world are also good resources. Ask them about their jobs and how they chose their careers. This will help you learn about different jobs. What are the good and the bad points of their jobs? As you talk with others, consider which types of jobs you might enjoy.

Often students begin exploring career options through **job shadowing** programs. These give students knowledge of a particular career area through a one-day visit to a job. The student accompanies an employee to work and observes that person's activities. Job shadowing can help students gain a realistic understanding of a typical day on the job. It can also give them a better feel for their level of interest in pursuing a related career. Teens are sometimes given opportunities to shadow parents for a day to develop a deeper understanding of their work responsibilities.

Talking with a guidance counselor can answer your questions about career opportunities. He or she can tell you about the education and experience needed and suggest several schools that offer such programs. Counselors may even set up meetings for you with recruiters from various schools.

Most libraries, at school and in your community, are rich sources of career information. A good place to begin your research is the computer catalog system. Look under *careers*, *jobs*, or *vocations* for general information. If you are interested in a certain field, such as teaching, look under that topic.

Online Career Resources	
Source	**Internet Address**
CareerOneStop	www.careeronestop.org
Occupational Outlook Handbook, U.S. Department of Labor	www.bls.gov/ooh
Career Outlook, U.S. Bureau of Labor Statistics	www.bls.gov/careeroutlook
O*NET, The Occupational Information Network	www.onetonline.org
U.S. Department of Labor Employment and Training Administration	www.doleta.gov
USAJOBS, the official job site of the U.S. Federal Government	www.usajobs.gov

1-6

These websites are good places to start exploring career information.

Education and Training Options

Sometimes high school graduates obtain job experience by joining the military. Others may gain job experience by volunteering for the Peace Corps or a similar organization. Other high school graduates go on to schools of higher education to prepare for their careers.

Some careers require little training beyond high school, while others require extensive training or education. When planning your career, you will need to determine what further education is needed. There are a number of ways to acquire the education and training.

Work-Based Learning Programs

Work-based learning programs offer students an opportunity for job placement while still taking classes. A program coordinator works with the students and their worksites to make these work experiences successful.

Cooperative education prepares high school students for an occupation right after school through a paid job experience. Students generally go to school for at least half the day and hold a part-time position for the rest of the day.

Supervised learning opportunities at the postsecondary or college level are called **internships**. They offer paid or unpaid supervised practical work experience. Students enroll in internship programs much like they enroll in courses. They may work several days per week with a reduced class load, or work during the summer. Students generally receive college credit while gaining valuable work skills.

Occupational Training

Various types of occupational training can help you prepare for a career in a specific field.

Career and technical education (CTE) programs provide training at both the high school and postsecondary levels. CTE programs involve training for careers that require hands-on experience. Health science, automotive repair, and culinary arts are examples of CTE programs. These programs are usually available through high schools, career centers, community and technical colleges, and four-year universities.

Students who attend CTE classes during high school often receive a certificate for a specific job skill with their high school diplomas. Students who complete postsecondary training often receive a two-year degree or a certificate.

Another option for occupational training is an *apprenticeship program*. An **apprenticeship** is learning a trade or skill on the job under the supervision of a skilled worker, **1-7**. These programs may last several months or many years. Requirements for entering the programs vary among the states and different trades. Students usually must enter a legal agreement to work for the employer for a specified length of time in exchange for the training and instruction.

Colleges and Universities

You can obtain degrees from two-year colleges and four-year colleges or universities. Attending a community or junior (two-year) college leads to earning an *associate's degree*. Completing a program at a four-year college or university results in a *bachelor's degree*. For careers that require a higher level of education, students can study for another year or two to earn a *master's degree*. A doctoral degree, also called a

Mental Health Awareness

Happy Workplaces

Employers are adding workplace features and benefits to help improve employees' social and emotional well-being. Some employers have a generous vacation policy. Others pay for training and education to develop personal and professional interests. A few employers even have onsite bowling alleys and rock-climbing walls for challenge, relaxation, and socializing.

21st Century Skills

Negotiation. David feels as if he has reached a plateau in his career. He meets with his supervisor to negotiate a career track. His supervisor advises him to further his education to increase his chances of being promoted.

doctorate, often requires several years of additional study beyond a master's degree.

To find out about schools that offer the education and training you desire, talk with your guidance counselor. You may also want to explore schools of interest online.

Your counselor can help you find high school courses that earn credit toward a college program that suits your career direction. This will help you reach your career goals more quickly.

Certification and Licensing

Occupations that deal with people's lives, health, or safety often require certification or a license. *Certification* is a special standing within a profession as a result of meeting specific requirements. A *license* is a work requirement set by a government agency. Licensing requirements are similar or identical to the certification requirements, but carry the force of law.

Certification and licensing usually require the following:

- completion of an acceptable program of study
- minimum level of education or degree(s)
- completion of an internship and/or on-the-job experience
- minimum grade or score on a national exam
- continuing education

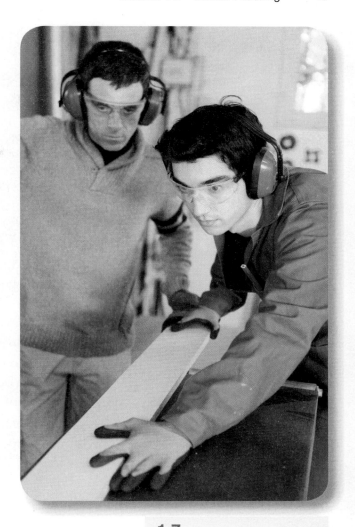

1-7
On the job, apprentices learn from a supervisor or skilled worker.

Certificates and licenses usually have expiration dates. Professionals may need to renew their credentials every few years.

Many professions require a commitment to lifelong learning. Continuing education even after a degree, certificate, or license is earned is called *lifelong learning*. Professionals often need to continue to learn and study to advance in their career or to keep up with their career and industry. Lifelong learning is a commitment to furthering your education and expertise.

The Employment Outlook

Knowing the future need for various occupations is important to your career research. The U.S. Department of Labor studies job trends and forecasts the employer demand for occupations in 10 years. New technologies are creating new jobs while making some traditional jobs obsolete.

Check the outlook for the occupations you are considering. For example, will there be more, about the same, or fewer jobs that need

Financial Literacy

Potential Income

Income is another factor to consider in your career choice. How much income do you want to earn? What is the income potential in your chosen career? Will it provide for personal and family needs?

When checking for a career's outlook, you can also check its wage trends. You will be able to find median wages for a recent year, as well as if the pay period is hourly or yearly. You may be able to find profiles for a particular state's trends, which will be even more helpful than looking at national trends.

your skills in 10 years? If the job outlook is good, the career area is growing and job opportunities will continue to increase. This means more jobs will be available to you.

Other Factors

When planning your career, there are other factors to consider. Some or all of these factors may be important to you.

- *Rewards.* People have different opinions on what job aspects qualify as a "reward." For some, frequent travel is a reward, while others consider it an annoyance. Many workers like a sameness to their schedules, but some people prefer constant variety. Each occupation presents conditions that some will like but others will not.

- *Employer location.* Find out where workplaces that employ people with your expertise are located. Are they conveniently located or close to you? Will certain employers require you to move to a new location?

- *Workplace conditions.* Is the work environment quiet or noisy? Is it near public transportation, or will you need a car? How long is the daily commute? Think carefully about your preferences.

As you plan your career, try to make choices that will give you the greatest satisfaction. In doing so, you are taking steps toward mastering your life and your career.

Reading
Review

1. Explain how a person's interests, aptitudes, and abilities affect his or her job satisfaction.
2. What are career pathways?
3. What is job shadowing?
4. What is the difference between an internship and an apprenticeship?
5. Most students receive a/an _____ degree after two years of study at a community college.
6. Explain how people can have different opinions on what qualifies as a job reward.

Section 1-3

Finding a Job

Objectives

After studying this section, you will be able to

- **describe** sources used to find job openings.

- **prepare** for a successful job interview.

- **list** the advantages and disadvantages of being an entrepreneur.

Key Terms

networking	references	entrepreneur
résumé	portfolio	cover letter

Once you have a career plan in mind, your next step is to find a job that fits it. Perhaps you would like to hold a part-time job while in high school. This can help you gain valuable skills and experience while you explore your career choice. Having a job provides some income and helps you sharpen your communication skills.

Finding a job takes work. You will need to make the effort to find job openings that fit your qualifications. Do not wait for an employer to come to you!

1-8

Family and neighbors can be great resources when you start your job hunt.

Finding Meaningful Employment

When looking for a job, consider as many sources of information as possible. Your teachers, school counselors, and parents may know some openings for you to pursue. Friends and relatives are often your most fruitful resources, **1-8**.

The process of connecting with the people you know is *networking*. **Networking** means developing contacts with people

Resources for Locating Jobs	
Resource	**Description**
Websites	Check potential employers as well as trade and professional associations.
Job Boards	Check job postings online and those in your school's career center.
Career Fairs	Talk with employer representatives to learn more about specific companies.
Print Resources	Find job listings in the classified ads of local, state, and national publications.
Employment Services	Public employment services are free services for finding jobs in the state and beyond. Private employment agencies are businesses that are paid to fill openings; some may charge you a fee.

1-9

These resources can help you identify job leads.

who may be able to find you a job. You will find that most people are happy to help you. There are social networks as well as business networks. In the world of work, however, people focus on finding jobs and learning new skills. These relationships can greatly impact career success.

Finding meaningful employment will probably require a time-consuming search, **1-9**. While you are networking, check other resources for finding job openings.

Professional and Trade Associations

Professional and trade associations can help you explore your career options. They also connect you with members who can help you establish your career. While still in school, you may be able to join one or more such organizations if they have student chapters.

Membership in such organizations can help you land your ideal job. Membership shows employers that you are serious about a career in a particular area. Many professional organizations also provide career-search help to their members.

Applying for a Job

If you want to work for a certain company, try a direct approach. You can visit the company and ask to fill out a job application, but sending a cover letter is usually preferred. Either way, you will need a well-prepared résumé.

Résumé

A **résumé** is a brief account of your education, work experience, and other qualifications for employment. It is a quick reference for the employer to determine if a person meets specific job qualifications. When you apply for a job, you submit a copy of your résumé, **1-10**.

Carefully prepare the design and content of your résumé. Some software programs create résumés that look professionally prepared. The appearance of a résumé may be as important as the information in it. A good résumé sparks the employer's interest in you. It should prompt the employer to ask you for an interview. As a teen, you may have no job experience to report. If so, focus on your volunteer activities as well as your interests and abilities. Make sure your résumé is free of spelling and grammar errors.

Provide *references* upon request. **References** are people who know you well and can vouch for your good work. Have at least three references ready to give to employers. The list should include their names, titles, work addresses, phone numbers, and e-mail addresses. Be sure to acquire each person's permission before adding his or her name to your list.

For your references, select people who are respected in the community. Teachers, counselors, employers, and religious leaders are ideal choices. Never name family members or personal friends since their opinions may be viewed as biased.

Omit information that is personal and has no bearing on your qualifications for the job. This includes your race, ethnic background, religion, gender, marital status, and disabilities. Equal opportunity laws prohibit employers from considering these facts in deciding whom to hire.

Wait at least 7 to 10 business days after you send your résumé to see if you receive a call from the company. If you do not, you may want to call to underscore your job interest.

Applying Online

Most companies today request applicants to submit their résumés electronically instead of by mail. This is especially true when a company

---

Terry C. Pinkham
204 Quail Run Road
Oak Park, TN 30241
(321) 555-4567

tpinkham@provider.com

Employment Objective	Day camp counselor
Education 20XX-present	Oak Park High School, Oak Park, TN
Work Experience	*20XX-20XX* Babysitter for two school-age children
	Summer 20XX Volunteered in church nursery with school-age children
Honors and Activities	Member of Family, Career and Community Leaders of America for two years
	Member of Spirit Club for three years
	Member of Student Council during junior year
	Member of choir for three years
	Member of National Honor Society for one year
	Student of the Week, Oak Park Center for Youth

References available upon request.

1-10

A résumé is a brief overview of your qualifications for employment.

posts an ad for the job opening online. They may ask for a résumé to be sent via e-mail or posted to a website.

To create an electronic résumé, save your résumé as "text only" without any formatting. Then review the file to make sure lines and headers break properly. Be sure to keep your formatted résumé saved in a separate file.

Employers may use electronic résumé files to search for key terms that match their descriptions of an ideal job candidate. This simple format makes the search easier for employers. It also makes it easier for key terms to be matched in your résumé so you come to the employers' attention.

Portfolio

A **portfolio** is an organized collection of your best and most creative work. It should give a balanced view of who you are as a potential employee. A portfolio provides a visible way to demonstrate your skills and achievements to those who might want to hire you, **1-11**.

Contents of the portfolio will vary, but should always include a copy of your résumé and any letters of recommendation. Keep your portfolio up-to-date. Add new items and replace others to make the portfolio relate to the requirements of the job you are seeking. Carefully label and date everything you include, and display the items neatly.

During job interviews, offer the employer an opportunity to review your portfolio. Be prepared to discuss any item included, highlighting only the main points. Always take your portfolio with you when you leave an interview.

Cover Letter

Your first contact with a potential employer will likely be a *cover letter*. A **cover letter** is a letter that introduces yourself and your résumé. You can make a lasting impression, so make sure your letter is neat. Use a standard format and font, and be sure to check spelling and punctuation. Consider having one or two people proofread your letter and recommend improvements. Make sure it is free of mistakes. Always include your résumé with your cover letter.

The letter should be brief, positive, and to the

1-11

Start preparing your portfolio now. Compiling your portfolio over time will make it easier to document your achievements.

Personal Portfolio

Include a copy of your résumé and as many of these items as possible.

- Transcript of completed courses
- National and state test results
- Recognitions and letters of recommendations
- Career/technical training records
- Evidence of involvement in extracurricular activities
- Outstanding school papers and projects
- Samples of graphs, charts, computer-assisted designs (CAD), or brochures produced by you using a computer
- Photos, newspaper clippings, web pages, videos, and other documentation of completed projects

point. Send the letter only to places at which you are truly interested in working. When responding to newspaper or online ads, be sure to follow the specific directions given.

Job Application

An employer will generally have you complete a job application before an interview. An *application form* requests your personal, academic, and employment information. Although some questions will duplicate your résumé, the employer will need a completed form for the company's records. Fill out the form carefully, **1-12**.

Interviewing

The *job interview* is a discussion between the job applicant and the person doing the hiring. The interviewer will want to know about your work skills, knowledge, and experience.

Be Prepared. Find out all you can about the job opening and the company. Research the products it sells or the services it offers. Talk to people who work there or know someone who does. Review your own qualifications for the job. Find out what type of questions are asked, **1-13**.

Look Your Best. First impressions are important. Look neat, clean, and dressed in business attire one step above what your future coworkers wear. Polish your shoes and neatly groom your hair and fingernails. If you wear makeup or jewelry, keep it subtle. Body piercings, tattoos, extreme hairstyles, and very tight or skimpy clothing may prevent you from getting the job you want.

Be on Time. Arrive at least 10 minutes early for your appointment. Tell the receptionist your name and the name of

Job Application Forms

Follow these guidelines when completing forms:
- Read the entire form first. Ask for clarification on any items that are not understood.
- Follow directions exactly.
- Write information neatly.
- Omit your social security number to protect your identity. Write *will provide if hired*.
- Include employment history dates for all jobs, even part-time jobs and volunteer work.
- Answer all questions with complete responses. Write *does not apply* or *N/A* as needed.
- To make changes, neatly draw a line through incorrect information and write it correctly.

1-12

Completing a job application is an important step in the job search process.

1-13

Be prepared to answer common interview questions.

Interview Questions

The interviewer will probably begin by saying, "Tell me about yourself." Then questions will follow:
- What are your least favorite subjects in school? Why?
- Describe your computer skills.
- What did you like, or dislike, about working on team projects?
- What types of work do you dislike doing?
- Tell me about a time when you made a serious mistake. What did you do?
- How would others describe your strengths and weaknesses?
- What would you like to be doing five years from now?
- What does success mean to you?

the person you are meeting. Listen closely if the receptionist corrects your pronunciation of the interviewer's name. Then wait patiently to be welcomed into the interviewer's office.

Greet the interviewer with a firm handshake. When you are offered a seat, sit up straight with feet flat on the floor. Look alert, maintain eye contact, and speak clearly. If you believe you can do the job, explain why. Practice answering common interview questions with a friend or family member so your responses reflect accuracy and enthusiasm.

The interviewer should bring up the topic of pay. If the job is available at a specific pay rate, your decision should be easy to make. Either you will accept or reject the rate. By rejecting a fixed rate, you reject the job.

If the pay level is flexible and the job appeals to you, you should say "salary is negotiable." This means you are willing to discuss pay after all the benefits and other features of the job are discussed.

Do not feel obliged during the interview to declare the specific pay you expect. You will want to consider all that you learn about company benefits and weigh everything accordingly. If the interviewer presses you to declare a salary level, state a range that is not excessive. You will not want to make the mistake of quoting a pay so high that the interviewer eliminates you from consideration.

After the Interview

After completing a job interview, send a *follow-up letter* right away using a standard business format, **1-14**. Thank the interviewer for his or her time and express your continuing interest in the position. This is your chance to clarify any points about your qualifications.

If the interviewer does not contact you as promised, follow up with a telephone call. When you make the call, be brief. Just say something like, "Good afternoon, Mr. Smith. This is (name) calling. I had an interview with you on (date). I am still interested in the position and wonder if you have made your decision." Whatever the interviewer's response, be as pleasant and positive as you were during the interview.

If you do not get the job, try not to be discouraged. Usually many applicants compete for the same job. Learn from this experience by evaluating what went well in the interview and what you would do differently. Then continue your job search. Try to be positive and think about all the other employment opportunities that may be better than the job you did not get.

Evaluate Job Offers

When considering a job offer, you will need to carefully consider the facts provided by the interviewer. Always use diplomacy when discussing sensitive topics.

- *Physical workplace.* Is the location convenient? Is the atmosphere conducive to your working style? Is public transportation conveniently located, or will you need a car?

Living Green

When you become employed, get involved in recycling efforts at the workplace. You might want to suggest that your company have a "green" committee that investigates ways the company can be an environmentally friendly workplace.

- *Work schedule.* Can you adhere to the work schedule? Is occasional overtime a requirement?

- *Income and benefits.* Is the salary or wage proposal fair? Will you receive benefits that are just as valuable as extra income? What are the policies for sick leave, vacation leave, and medical and life insurance? Will the employer pay for college tuition for studies related to your job responsibilities? Is foodservice provided? Is refrigerated storage available for sack lunches brought from home?

- *Job obligations.* Will you be required to join a union or other professional organization? If so, what are the costs? Is there reimbursement for these costs? Will meetings occur after work hours?

- *Job advancement.* Does advancement require additional degrees or certifications? What training program does the employer offer? How soon after demonstrating good performance can you pursue additional responsibilities?

204 Quail Run Road
Oak Park, Tennessee 30241
June 3, 20XX

Mr. C. L. Stone, Personnel Manager
Camp McGhee
106 S. Main Street
Oak Park, Tennessee 30241

Dear Mr. Stone:

Thank you so much for taking time to interview me yesterday.

I am excited about the possibility of working as a camp counselor during the summer. My interview made me more certain that this would be a good place for me.

I eagerly await your decision and look forward to hearing from you.

Sincerely,

Terry C. Pinkham

Terry C. Pinkham

1-14

Sending a follow-up letter after a job interview is a courtesy the interviewer will appreciate.

Making Job Changes

Whatever the reasons for leaving a job, you can grow from analyzing the pros and cons of a work experience. A positive attitude and a willingness to learn from mistakes can make your next job more productive and satisfying. A new job can offer a chance to begin again and put your experience to work.

When you leave a job, it is important to behave professionally. Most employers request at least a two-week notice that you will be leaving. Provide this notice in writing, giving the date of your last day on the job. If you desire, you can state the reason for resigning.

Avoid focusing on what you do not like about the job you are leaving. Instead, describe the challenges that attracted you to your new position. Remember that even unpleasant work experiences can provide chances to learn and grow as a professional. Be sure to thank your employer for the opportunities your present position offered.

Creating Your Own Job

Another option to finding a job is creating your own job. Many people fulfill their career goals by creating their own jobs rather than working for others. **Entrepreneurs** start and manage their own businesses. They also assume all risks and responsibilities. For many people, entrepreneurship is a rewarding and satisfying experience.

Entrepreneurship: Pros and Cons

Being an entrepreneur has both advantages and disadvantages. One main advantage is that you are your own boss. You make your own decisions, rules, and business policies. You can be as creative as you desire in trying new ideas. You create your own work schedule. If you manage your business well, you have the potential to make as much money as you want.

Being an entrepreneur has some disadvantages as well. Until the business develops a good reputation, entrepreneurs must work long hours on weekdays and weekends. Entrepreneurs must buy their own health and business insurance. They must find out what legal requirements apply to them and adhere. Often no profit is made in the first year. Most entrepreneurs live off their savings until their businesses start to make money. If you make a wrong decision, you cannot blame anyone else. Financial problems and poor management are two common reasons for failures of new businesses.

Getting Started

If you think you have what it takes to succeed as an entrepreneur, you can start at any time. Your business should be something you enjoy doing. Few people combine their interests, aptitudes, and abilities into a truly customized job. However, people who acquire the needed skills and work hard can achieve their goals.

Sometimes the hardest part is deciding what to do. You must study your interests, aptitudes, and abilities to make a good decision. The suggestions in **1-15** may spark your imagination. The examples listed in the table show only a few of the many ways students can earn money.

Sources of Help

The Small Business Administration's website answers many common questions and links to the state Departments of Commerce. Many regulations that affect small businesses are set by the states.

Your local chamber of commerce may also be able to help you check for local regulations. These sources may be free or require a small fee.

Mental Health Awareness

Personality and Entrepreneurship

According to the Five Factor Model, happy, successful entrepreneurs have five general qualities. One quality is emotional stability, or not given to excessive fear, anger, or anxiety. Another quality is agreeableness, or the ability to be approachable, flexible, and open to others' ideas. Extroversion, or the tendency to be outgoing and friendly, is also helpful. Entrepreneurs must also be conscientious, especially in meeting deadlines and keeping commitments. Finally, entrepreneurs should be open to new experiences.

Be an Entrepreneur

1-15

Have you ever thought about becoming an entrepreneur? If so, one of these ideas might appeal to you.

Gift Shopping Service

Don't have time to shop for those special gifts? Local teen will do your shopping for you! Gift wrapping and mail service also available. Hourly fee charged. 555-1212

Vacation Service

Going out of town? Let me take care of those routine household tasks. I can collect mail, care for pets, water plants, and do yard work—all for one low fee. Call for more details. 655-9881

Letter Addressing Service

Talented teen with neat handwriting. Will address wedding invitations, party invitations, and holiday greeting cards. Call for a free sample of my work. 656-6200

Baking Service

If you don't have time to prepare homemade baked goods you like, call me. I will bake and deliver your favorite breads and desserts. 555-3754

Fruit Basket Service

A thoughtful way to welcome houseguests or show a friend you care! Personalized fresh fruit baskets arranged and delivered for you. Local delivery to hospitals, hotels, or your home. Call for more details. 555-1492

Lawn and Garden Care

One-time or all-the-time yard care. Grass mowing, weeding, edging, planting, raking, or clean-up. Free estimates. 565-0321

Birthday Party Catering Service

Celebrate your child's birthday with no hassles! For one set fee, I arrange a party for up to 15 children. The fee covers your expenses, including the cost of the cake, punch, cups, napkins, favors, and entertainment. A variety of party themes available. 565-2387

From time to time, you will also need the advice of these professionals:

- A lawyer will make sure you fulfill all legal requirements.
- An accountant can handle or check your bookkeeping and tax-related records.
- An insurance agent will determine the amount and types of insurance you need.

These professionals can be expensive, but they limit your business risk and provide peace of mind.

Reading Review

1. A _____ is a brief account of your education, work experiences, and other qualifications for employment.
2. How many references should you submit to an employer upon request?
3. List five points job applicants should keep in mind about their behavior during an interview.
4. Explain the purpose of writing a follow-up letter after an interview. What points should the letter include?
5. List six factors to consider when evaluating a job offer.
6. List two advantages and two disadvantages of becoming an entrepreneur.

Chapter 1 Review

Summary

Planning your future begins with learning about yourself. Your self-concept begins to develop early and affects your self-esteem. As a unique person, you have needs, wants, values, and standards. Each one affects your behavior. The way you meet your needs, the values you adopt, and the standards you set for yourself have a great effect on your life. To meet challenges, prepare for change and work toward achieving your potential.

Learning more about your interests, aptitudes, and abilities is the next step in matching yourself to the right career. Many resources are available for gathering career information. Exploring the career clusters may help you choose your personal plan of study. In setting your career goals, consider the education and training you will need. Investigate whether you will need a license or certification. Analyze other factors, such as employment outlook. Making a career decision now will help you get started in reaching your goals.

Networking and other resources will help you find job openings. Applying for job openings may involve sending a résumé and cover letter, applying online, or applying in person. A job interview is your chance to make a favorable impression on the interviewer. After the interview, sending a follow-up letter is important. Another option in job hunting is to create your own job by becoming an entrepreneur.

Critical Thinking

1. **Summarize details.** Summarize ways you are influenced by each of the following:
   A. personality
   B. self-concept
   C. self-esteem

2. **Analyze information.** What advice would you give to a friend who makes this statement: "I really feel down! I'm the shortest one in gym class, my grades aren't that great, and I don't feel like I fit in!" Base your response on the principles of self-concept and self-esteem.

3. **Recognize values.** Describe how people might show they have the following values: beauty, love, security, adventure.

4. **Draw conclusions.** Why is evaluating your current interests, aptitudes, and abilities an important part of career planning?

5. **Summarize details.** Briefly summarize the factors you think will affect your career choices.

6. **Making inferences.** How can a person's self-concept impact relationships with family and peers? Create a graph or image to represent your response.

21st Century Applications

7. **Collaboration and communication.** In small groups, discuss Maslow's theory of human needs. How do the levels relate to each other? Then research metamotivation. Together, create a graphic representation of metamotivation in relation to the hierarchy of needs.

8. **Entrepreneurial literacy.** What recommendations would you make to a friend who is thinking of starting a business? Use information learned in the chapter as well as additional sources to form your response.

Core
Skills

9. **Writing.** Choose a career that interests you and write a career profile. Include the following information: nature of the work, places of employment, training and qualifications needed, advancement opportunities, typical salaries, and social and psychological factors related to this career choice.

10. **Speaking.** Role-play several different job interviews. As a class, evaluate each interview situation.

11. **Writing.** Write a follow-up letter to the interviewer in one of the role-play interviews described in the previous activity.

12. **Reading.** Research one career cluster of interest. What types of education and training are typically needed within this cluster? Then select one career within the cluster and examine education and training requirements. Do requirements differ on local, state, and national levels? How can professionals maintain their credentials?

13. **Math.** Using spreadsheet software, make lists of items you want or need. Then use the software to make a chart showing what percentage of the items are wants and what percentage are needs. Discuss the results illustrated by your chart in class.

14. **Writing.** Research E. G. Williamson and his impact on career counseling. Write a report discussing your findings and include a time line outlining his achievements.

Leadership
Development

Go through the steps of applying for a job as you participate in the Job Interview STAR Event. You will need to prepare a portfolio, complete a job application, and demonstrate interviewing skills.

Portfolio
Builder

When you apply for a job, an employer will often ask for references. A person who makes a good reference can comment on your character traits, such as fairness, respect, trustworthiness, responsibility, and citizenship. Ask at least three people you know to be references for you. Prepare a list of references that you can include in your portfolio. Include all the information identified in the chapter.

Journal
Writing

You need to earn money to attend the national meeting of the Family, Career and Community Leaders of America. You know how to bake, decorate cakes, and plan parties. You decide to start a temporary business.

Write About It: *How can you publicize your business? What personal qualities might help you succeed? How can this experience help you pursue a career?*

Chapter 2
Skills for Career Success

Reading Prep

In preparation for reading the chapter, think about what makes a person successful. How do people measure success? As you read, consider how the information in this chapter supports or contradicts your answers to these questions.

Concept Organizer

Use a T-chart to illustrate the characteristics of verbal communication and nonverbal communication.

G-WLEARNING.com

Click on the activity icon to visit www.g-wlearning.com/comprehensive/8062 to access online vocabulary activities using key terms from the chapter.

Qualities of Successful Employees

Objectives

After studying this section, you will be able to

- **identify** the qualities and skills needed for job success.
- **determine** the effects of technology on the workplace.

Key Terms

work ethic   telecommuting

What qualities are needed for job success? The same personal qualities that help you get a job can also help you keep it. Most employers look for certain qualities when they hire employees. They want employees who have skills to get the job done and work well with others. Most successful employees share many of these same qualities. As you read this section, think about the personal qualities you have now. Developing these qualities will increase your chances of being a successful employee, too.

Personal Qualities for Job Success

Several qualities are key factors in job success. Having a positive attitude, being dependable, being honest, and getting along well with others will contribute to your becoming a successful employee.

Positive Attitude

Your attitude plays a big role in your success on the job, **2-1**. It shows how you think and feel about other people and situations. A positive attitude will help you learn your job duties, work with others, and get ahead in your career.

If you have a positive attitude, you always try to do the best job possible. You accept your fair share of the responsibility without complaining. You accept criticism as a means of improving your job performance. You are willing to try new tasks. If you enjoy your work, you are more likely to do a better job. This makes you a more valuable employee.

A positive attitude helps you get along with others, too. People enjoy working with someone who is friendly and cheerful most of the time.

2-1

People who have positive attitudes are willing to tackle any job task.

Being courteous and showing respect for others are positive qualities to have.

Dependability

If you are dependable, your employer can count on you to be reliable and responsible. You get your work done and do not expect others to do it for you. You have a good attendance record and start work on time every day.

Honesty

Another personal quality of a good employee is being honest. Employers want employees they can trust. That means telling the truth, keeping any promises you make, and dealing with people fairly. Being honest also means putting forth your best effort on the job. You do the job you are assigned and do not waste time. Employers expect you to give an honest day's work for an honest day's pay.

Ethics

A **work ethic** is a standard of conduct for successful job performance. Your concepts of fairness, right and wrong, and good and bad affect your work ethic. A strong work ethic will help you achieve personal satisfaction. Successful employees work not only for the company but also for personal satisfaction. Chances are that your boss will not compliment you daily for your work. Consequently, you need to develop personal feelings of satisfaction from the work you do. You need to set high standards for your work and take pride in meeting them. In turn, personal satisfaction will make your work seem more important and more enjoyable.

Cooperation

An ability to work well with all people is important for job success. This means you can work with people of all ages, of both genders, and of different backgrounds. You show respect and courtesy to your boss, coworkers, and customers.

Part of getting along with others is working as a team member. To show others you want to be cooperative, you accept your share of the work. You make an effort to contribute to the group's goal. Each group member should feel free to make worthwhile contributions. Combining the special traits and skills of each person allows the group to achieve the best results.

Ethics. Elena is careful to never spread rumors. She believes that loyalty to her employer is important, thus she avoids destructive comments.

Good working relationships are based on respect for others' feelings. Follow directions carefully. Ask questions when you do not understand how to do a task. Do not expect your coworkers to do your work for you. On the other hand, never assume that you can get along without your coworkers. If you willingly cooperate with them, they will cooperate with you. Being friendly, respectful, and enthusiastic will help you become part of a team.

Good Appearance

Whether fair or not, others judge you by your appearance, either consciously or subconsciously. What you wear to work reflects how you feel about your work. Try to look your best every day because neatness shows respect for yourself and others.

Most employers enforce dress codes that list clothing styles and items inappropriate for the workplace. They know the importance of clothing to maintaining a businesslike atmosphere. Customers, too, expect business people to dress appropriately. They do not want to be served by workers who appear sloppy or dressed for some other occasion. Customers often take their business elsewhere if a company does not maintain businesslike surroundings.

Becoming a Professional

When you display all the positive qualities discussed, you are on the road to becoming a professional. A professional is an employee who keeps a courteous, conscientious, and businesslike manner. When companies hire new employees, they look for people who fit this description. They want to maintain a good public image and seek employees who share their concern.

Becoming a professional is not a goal reserved for certain careers. Any employee can be a professional, no matter what his or her job is. A professional is easy to spot, **2-2**. It is the person who demonstrates the following qualities:

- smiles and greets everyone pleasantly
- remembers and uses correct names and titles
- treats everyone with respect
- keeps a calm disposition
- avoids talking negatively about coworkers and customers
- wears appropriate clothing from head to toe
- chooses a becoming and conservative hairstyle
- avoids excessive use of perfume and cologne
- limits jewelry and makeup
- practices good hygiene
- uses proper etiquette

2-2

A well-groomed appearance and a pleasant smile are two clues that this person is a professional.

Professionals uphold the standards of the company and set positive goals for themselves. They avoid doing anything that disrupts the work environment. They focus on doing their jobs well and helping the company succeed.

Technology in the Workplace

Advances in technology have changed many aspects of life. Computer technology is used in every industry and in most classrooms and homes to make time-consuming and demanding tasks easier. As technology continues to change our world, people must adjust to new roles and responsibilities.

All jobs are affected by innovative technology. In factories, computerized robots perform the most dangerous and monotonous jobs efficiently. Sales teams receive records of purchases as soon as they are made anywhere in the company and can readily determine future inventory needs. In the workplace, people can use e-mail and video conferencing to stay in touch with coworkers and clients. See **2-3**. People can also use these devices to work out of their homes. This is called **telecommuting**.

With every technological device comes a need for specialists who can operate and service it. In some businesses, new job positions are created to fulfill these needs. In other cases, job roles are expanded to

Living Green

If you work with computers, set computers to energy-saving settings and shut them down when you are finished working. "Standby" settings will continue to draw power even when not in use. The U.S. Department of Energy recommends turning off a computer if it will not be used for 2 hours.

include new duties. Job expansion also creates a need for more education. People must have the knowledge and training necessary to operate new equipment.

There is great demand for people who excel in the use of today's technologies. Competition among employers for these skills increases the salary employees can command. The salary for a position will also increase as the education and duty requirements for the position increase.

Instead of being apprehensive about learning how to use new tools in their jobs, employees are advised to expect and welcome change. The latest innovations in technology soon become obsolete. Future changes may occur even more rapidly. Technological progress is occurring at an accelerating rate. Any new technology will probably lead to other new technologies. Workers must stay flexible enough to adopt new procedures and work methods.

As devices are developed to perform tasks more accurately, some jobs are eliminated. Thus, people can no longer prepare for one career or know what new technologies will affect their jobs in the future. Lifelong learning is essential for those who plan to hold wage-earning jobs during all of their productive years.

Occasionally technological changes bring some negative results. Physical ailments such as carpal tunnel syndrome increase with the growth of technology. Repetitive body motions can cause this work hazard over extended periods. Also, telecommuters who have limited opportunities for personal interaction sometimes feel isolation and loneliness.

Technology impacts every aspect of the workplace. It promotes greater speed, efficiency, and accuracy. However, competence with technology is just one of five skills that effective workers are expected to have. Employees with workplace know-how also need competence with resources, interpersonal skills, information, and systems.

Blend Images/Shutterstock.com

2-3
Through video conferencing and an Internet connection, people can work together online even when separated by long distances.

Reading
Review

1. List three qualities needed for job success. State some examples of each quality.
2. Why is a work ethic important to job success?
3. Using technological devices to work from home is known as _____ .

Section 2-2

The Communication Process

Objectives

After studying this section, you will be able to

- **improve** your listening and speaking skills.
- **begin** and **develop** conversations more easily.
- **use** several forms of nonverbal communication to communicate more effectively.
- **describe** the use of several types of electronic communication.

Key Terms

communication	active listening	manners
verbal communication	feedback	body language
	passive listening	personal space
nonverbal communication	rapport	
	reflection	

To develop good relationships with other people, you have to be able to communicate. **Communication** is the process of conveying information in such a way that the message is received and understood. Through communication, you can share ideas, opinions, and facts with others. In close relationships, you can also discuss and share your problems and feelings. See **2-4**.

Good communication is a skill you will use throughout your life. It is based on a mutual effort between people to understand one another. Speakers must try to make their messages relevant to the listeners. At the same time, listeners must open their minds to the messages being sent.

All forms of communication—speaking, listening, reading, writing, and body language—can be grouped into two different categories. The first is **verbal communication**, which involves the use of words. **Nonverbal communication** is the second category; this involves sending messages without words. In this section, you will learn more about these two forms of communication.

Verbal Communication

Communication skills are just like word processing skills or baseball skills. You can learn them, practice them, and improve them. The first steps in improving your verbal communication skills are learning to listen and to speak well.

Listening

Listening plays an important role in communication. A spoken message is worthless unless someone hears it and listens to it. *Hearing* and *listening*, however, have two different meanings. You hear many sounds all day long. Radios, kitchen appliances, cars, and airplanes are just a few examples. If you really listened to all these sounds, you would not have time to think about anything else. Instead, you have developed the habit of ignoring unimportant sounds. This is usually a good and helpful habit. If you are not careful, however, you may find yourself slipping into this habit more often than you should. You may be ignoring spoken messages that people are trying to send to you.

Dean Mitchell/E+/Getty Images

2-4

How much time do you spend every day communicating face-to-face with family, friends, classmates, and teachers?

Barriers to Good Listening

Recognizing what gets in the way of good listening can help you learn to overcome these barriers. The habit of ignoring sounds is just one barrier to good listening. Forgetting all or part of the message is a common communication barrier. Even if you listen to what is being said, there is a chance for a communication failure. Studies show that people remember as little as 25 percent of the information they receive through listening. People remember more when they see, read, or verbally repeat the message they hear. Listening by itself does not always ensure good communication.

Another barrier to good listening is not understanding the message being sent. The message a person sends to you may not be the same message you receive. The speaker may pronounce words differently if he or she is from a different part of the country. The speaker may use slang expressions or words that are unfamiliar to you. You may think the speaker is joking when he or she is serious. Even the tone of voice can change the meaning of what is said. These are just a few of the factors that can interfere with good listening.

Life Skills

Active Listening Tips

- *Ask questions to clarify the message.* This shows you are not only hearing what the speaker is saying, but also processing it.
- *Pay attention.* Use eye contact. Avoid daydreaming or letting your mind wander to other topics.
- *Be interested.* You will listen better if you have a sincere desire to know what the other person is saying and feeling.
- *Be patient.* Do not interrupt and take over the speaking role.
- *Keep the speaker in mind.* Expect the information to come from the speaker's background of experiences or point of view. Put aside your previous thoughts and biases.
- *Stay focused.* Some people are too busy thinking about what they will say in response to a speaker. As a result, they fail to listen to what is said.
- *Use reflection.* Repeat in your own words what you think was said. The receiver might say, "If I understand you correctly, you are saying…".
- *Listen to the speaker's tone of voice.* Sometimes the way something is said is just as important as what is said.

Become an Active Listener

Listening is important to good communication because you listen more often than you speak. With practice, you can develop good listening skills.

A good listener is an active listener. **Active listening** means focusing on the speaker's message and then providing feedback. **Feedback** lets the speaker know the message is getting through to the listener and how it is being received. The feedback can be a nod, a smile, a question, or a comment that lets the speaker know the message has been received.

Passive listening is hearing the spoken words, but not the meaning of the words. A passive listener does not respond to the speaker in any way. The speaker does not know if the message is being received or not.

Speaking

Speaking is the most widely used form of verbal communication. Speaking and listening are equally important in the two-way communication process.

You spend much of your day speaking with others. The way you speak affects your life in many ways. It affects your relationships with your family members and your friends. It affects your daily interactions with teachers, classmates, coworkers, and employers. Speaking clearly will help you express your thoughts, feelings, and ideas to others.

Have you noticed that some people have better speaking skills than others? You could listen to them for hours and not lose interest. With practice, you too can develop your speaking skills.

Developing Speaking Skills

How good are your speaking skills? Do you send clear messages when you speak to others? Do others interpret your messages correctly? The way you speak affects the impressions people form of you. If your skills need improvement, try using some of these techniques:

- *Keep the listener in mind.* Use words the listener will understand.

- *Keep messages short and simple.* Leave no room for confusion and you are more likely to be understood.

- *Be considerate of others' feelings.* Think before you speak. Avoid making comments that may hurt someone. If criticism is needed, try to make it constructive.

- *Be open and honest.* Do not expect people to read your mind.

- *Respect the listener.* Good rapport between a speaker and a listener aids good communication. **Rapport** is a relationship built on respect and sincerity.

Life Skills

How to Start a Conversation

- *Ask questions that require more than a yes or no answer.* Examples are, "What do you think about…?" "How do you feel about…?" Or, ask about the person's work, hobbies, or family.
- *Make a sincere compliment.* When people are complimented, they are likely to relax and begin talking.
- *Mention something you have in common with the other person.* Discussions of current events, movies, books, and sports events can keep a conversation going.
- *Discuss one topic.* Explore just one key point of common interest. A constant change of subjects may drive the other person away.

- *Be positive.* People enjoy listening to someone who has a positive outlook on life.

- *Check to see whether your message is being received accurately.* Questions such as "What do you think?" or "How do you feel about this?" will draw your listener into a speaking role. He or she will then use reflection to give you feedback. **Reflection** is when the listener repeats what he or she thinks the speaker said.

Nonverbal Communication

People communicate in many ways other than the spoken or written word. Communication that does not involve words is called nonverbal communication. The way a person looks, dresses, acts, and reacts are forms of nonverbal expression.

Your Appearance

Does your appearance send the message you want it to send? When people meet you, what is their first impression? People form their impressions of you based on the way you look. Often these judgments are made quickly. Before you say anything, your appearance is sending a message to them. Are you communicating a positive message about yourself?

Good grooming is one way to send a positive message. It shows you care about yourself and the way you look. Neat, clean clothes that fit well help create a positive image.

Mental Health Awareness

Cell Phone Attachment

Some people are so attached to their cell phones that they get anxious if they do not have access to them. Some signs of this unhealthy attachment are: checking a cell phone frequently, keeping the phone on hand at all times (including meals and after going to bed), struggling to concentrate on tasks or conversations, and imagining that a silent phone is vibrating when it is not.

Your Actions

The actions you take can send messages to others. For instance, **manners** are rules to follow for proper conduct. Using good manners sends the message that you want others to feel comfortable. In most cases, having good manners is as simple as being kind to others and using common sense.

Other actions will send the message that you care about people's feelings. Using the words *please, thank you,* and *excuse me* shows courtesy and respect to others. Sending a note of thanks, a card, or a text message to cheer someone up reflects thoughtfulness. Giving a gift on a special occasion tells people you are considerate. Using a pleasant tone of voice lets others know you want them to feel at ease.

Body Language

When you nod your head, shake your fist, or point your finger, you are communicating without words. With **body language**, you are using body movements, such as facial expressions, gestures, and posture, to send messages to others.

Although you are not using words, your messages can be crystal clear. The expression on your face can convey your mood before you even begin to talk. Direct eye contact with someone can convey honesty and straightforwardness. With a smile and a shake of your head, you can let someone know that you agree. With a wink, you can say "I like you." Some people use hand gestures to make their spoken messages clearer.

Personal Space

Your **personal space** is the area around you. When others enter this space, your reaction is a form of nonverbal communication. The way you allow people to use your personal space depends on the way you feel about these people. You may enjoy the closeness of a hug from a special person, or a whisper in your ear from another. A quick handshake may be as close as you wish to be with others. When a person enters your personal space you feel either comfortable or uncomfortable. Your behaviors reveal the way you feel.

Some people like to stay about an arm's length from each other when they speak. This is not always the case, however. People from some cultures like to stand closer when they speak. This closeness may make people in other cultures feel uncomfortable. An awareness of this cultural difference can help you avoid any misinterpretation of another's actions.

Life Skills

Body Language Around the World

Some communications are influenced by cultural diversity, so being aware of cultural differences is important. For example, in some cultures people are taught to never make eye contact with someone in authority. A friendly hug may also be off-limits. In large U.S. cities, people avoid making eye contact with anyone on the streets. While some specific body language does vary, a person from any culture is likely to understand gestures meaning *yes, no, come, stop, up, down,* and *thank you.*

Technology and Communication

Technology, the use of scientific knowledge for practical purposes, has led to many new ways for people to communicate with each other. No longer do you have to wait a week or more to receive a written response for a letter you sent. You can send a message around the world in an instant. It is possible to receive a reply equally fast. Though most people see many benefits to these methods of communication, others see some drawbacks. See **2-5** for some points to keep in mind when using technology to communicate.

Cell Phones

Cell phones provide two-way communication. Some cell phones are *smartphones*, or phones with apps, a camera, and access to the Internet.

Cell phones allow communication from wherever you are, which is particularly beneficial in emergency situations. Cell phones are often paired with global positioning devices to provide emergency assistance and information to travelers.

The use of cell phones can be disturbing to other people if used in public places. Though popular with students, many schools ban their use. If you use a cell phone, have consideration for the people around you when at school or in a public place. Ringing phones can be disruptive to others. Conversations on cell phones should not take place where other people can hear them. Also, it is inconsiderate to send text messages while carrying on a face-to-face conversation with another person.

Voice Mail

Voice mail allows callers to leave a recorded message for the recipient to listen to later. When leaving a voice mail message, there are certain courtesies you should follow.

- Speak clearly and distinctly.
- Give your name and telephone number.

Financial Literacy

Evaluating Cell Phone Plans

Cell phones and monthly rate plans can be purchased from a wireless service provider. Compare the costs and features of several different plans before making a selection. Be sure you understand your plan—if you use more minutes than are included, the costs can be high.

Pay-as-you-go phones are purchased with a certain number of minutes. When the minutes are used up, you can buy more minutes. This option can be more cost-effective than monthly rate plans for people who do not use their cell phones often.

2-5
When communicating electronically, follow these guidelines.

Electronic Communications Etiquette

- When using e-mail, grammar, spelling, and punctuation must be accurate, as in any written form of communication.
- Avoid using emoticons, such as :-) for a smile, in business communications. Use them in personal e-mail only.
- Don't use e-mail or text messaging to deliver sensitive information. A face-to-face or telephone conversation is better to prevent misunderstandings.
- Don't post personal information about others on social networking sites.

Analyze and Solve

In groups, discuss the advantages and disadvantages of text messaging. In what situations can text messaging be disruptive? In what ways does text messaging enhance or hinder communication?

Living Green

Many electronics contain hazardous material that can harm the environment if it enters the waste stream. When purchasing new electronic devices, make sure you recycle your old products. The Environmental Protection Agency provides information on recycling electronics on their website.

- Keep your message brief (30 seconds is ideal), but explain the reason for your call.
- Minimize the need for a call back if possible. For instance, if a meeting date has changed, give the date for the postponed meeting.
- Give the date and time.
- Let the person know the best time to reach you.

The Internet

Many people rely on the Internet to communicate to others anywhere in the world. Social media websites, blogs, and e-mail are examples of online communication tools. E-mail is regularly used in the workplace.

Conferencing is also a popular form of communication. Communication may be audio (with sound), visual, or audiovisual. Video conferencing involves seeing and hearing another person using a camera and the Internet. Extended family members who live distances apart find video conferencing to be an excellent way to stay in touch. Workplaces use video conferencing to conduct meetings and communicate with distance employees. *Webcasts*, one-way communication streams, are often used to broadcast information. *Webinars* allow professionals to interact online during a seminar, lecture, or presentation.

Be cautious about the information communicated to you online. When using the Internet for research, you will find an abundant amount of sources and information. Anyone can place any type of information online, whether that information is accurate and reliable or not. Therefore, when researching, focus on using reliable sources, such as websites created by the government, educational institutions, or credible organizations. Analyze each source thoroughly. Check the accuracy of information provided by unfamiliar sources. Also, make sure you monitor children when they are online. Children can accidentally wander into inappropriate sites.

Reading
Review

1. Name two barriers to good listening skills.
2. True or false. People are more likely to remember a message they hear if they do not repeat it verbally.
3. Briefly describe five techniques for improving speaking skills.
4. List four suggestions for starting a conversation.
5. Explain how nonverbal communication is related to your appearance.
6. List three electronic means of communication. Give an example of how each can be used to benefit communication.

Section 2-3

Communication in Relationships

Objectives

After studying this section, you will be able to

- **state** the importance of open communication in relationships.
- **list** ways to communicate positive feelings.
- **describe** barriers to communication.
- **suggest** methods for handling negative feelings.
- **give** tips for communicating in the workplace.

Key Terms

open communication	prejudice	role expectations
stereotypes	mixed messages	diverse

People often speak of **open communication**. This means a free flow of ideas, opinions, and facts among the people involved. They may not agree on everything, but they respect one another's point of view. They can have intelligent discussions about views that differ from their own. All ideas are treated with interest, curiosity, and respect.

Clearly communicating your thoughts and feelings is part of open communication. In this section, you will learn more about skills you can use to develop open communication in your relationships. These include communicating positive feelings, overcoming barriers, and handling negative feelings.

The Importance of Communication in Relationships

Open communication has many benefits, especially in personal relationships. It allows people to learn more about themselves and other people. It helps people express their feelings to their friends and family. Using it helps strengthen relationships. Overall, it can lead to richer, more satisfying relationships.

Rawpixel.com/Shutterstock.com

2-6

People who communicate their positive feelings enrich the lives of others.

Communicating Positive Feelings

Each person is responsible for his or her own happiness. Do you want to be happy? If so, you must work toward that goal. Thinking positively about most situations in life will help you be happy. Your positive attitude encourages open communication.

Good feelings are contagious. If you are a positive person and communicate this to others, they will feel happier, too. See **2-6**.

Barriers to Open Communication

Communicating with others is not always easy. Many barriers stand in the way of open communication. A few of the barriers are physical in nature, such as speech and hearing disabilities. However, most barriers to open communication are social or psychological. Understanding these differences can help you avoid them. Some of the most common ones are described on the following pages.

Stereotypes

One barrier to open communication is stereotyping. A person who **stereotypes** others has a set belief that all members of a group will behave in the same ways. Stereotypes put labels on groups of people. These labels may be based on a group's age, sex, race, or religion. For instance, some people may believe that all young men should participate in sports or all older people are forgetful.

Because every person is different, neither of the above statements can be true for all people within these groups. If you pay attention to stereotypes like these instead of accepting individual differences, you may misinterpret messages. To be a good listener, you must have an open mind. You must ignore stereotypes and give people the chance to communicate as individuals.

Healthy Living

A Positive Outlook

Use the following tips to communicate positive feelings:
- Whenever you meet someone, be the first one to say hello.
- Offer praise and compliments when they are deserved.
- Defend people who are the object of harmful gossip.
- Smile and look happy. Show your positive personality traits.
- Look others in the eye when you talk to them and speak clearly.
- Show concern for others by asking them about matters that are important to them.

Prejudices

Another barrier to open communication results from prejudices. **Prejudices** are opinions that people form without complete knowledge. They are usually based on a lack of facts and a lack of understanding. People with prejudices do not accept that others' beliefs can be different from theirs. Prejudices might include negative attitudes toward religions, races, cultures, nationalities, socio-economic groups, cities, geographic regions, or foods.

Many prejudices lead to negative behaviors such as name-calling. Prejudiced people may choose to avoid certain groups or individuals. They usually do not seek understanding or new meanings. They have already made up their minds. It is as if they are saying "I already know about that" or "I already know about your kind." These actions set up barriers and prevent good communication from taking place.

Here is an example of a man who had a prejudice toward certain foods. When the man took his date out to dinner, she ordered roast lamb. She soon realized he was embarrassed to be seen with a date who ate lamb. He did not eat meat and thought of it as unwholesome. He also felt prejudice toward her because she ate a food that he did not consider acceptable. Because of his prejudice, the couple never dated again. Such a prejudice toward people and objects—in this case food—hampers good communication.

Some prejudices come in the form of love. For example, parents are naturally proud of their children. They may think their son or daughter is the best looking, most talented, and most personable individual. This may be true, but such an attitude is usually padded with a little pride and prejudice. Loving people is important. However, maintaining an ability to be rational about all people and objects is important, too.

Mixed Messages

When a person's behavior contradicts their words or actions, they are using **mixed messages**. Listeners are forced to make assumptions as they receive the speakers' messages.

For example, a person may say he or she is telling you the truth, but avoids making eye contact or seems uncomfortable. Another example is the statement "Give me your honest opinion." Some people may really want your opinion. Others say this when they really mean "Tell me I am right. Support me in what I have done." You must decode the message according to the situation. Your clues may be the person's tone of voice, facial expression, or body language. See **2-7**.

21st Century Skills

Cross-cultural skills. Helen respects the cultural differences among her coworkers. She tries to explore and understand some of their traditions and customs.

2-7

Observing a person's body language is helpful in deciphering mixed messages.

Gender Differences

Sometimes, differences between males and females create some barriers to communication. These barriers may be related to role expectations. **Role expectations** are patterns of socially expected behavior. In other words, people learn to behave the way they think society expects them to behave. They also expect certain role behaviors from others.

Certain roles are associated with being male or female. For males, some of these roles include brother, son, boyfriend, husband, and father. Female roles include sister, daughter, girlfriend, wife, and mother. Both men and women also have expectations as to how the opposite sex should fulfill their roles. For instance, some husbands may expect their wives to cook and do household chores. A girlfriend may expect her boyfriend to pay for every date.

Role expectations can create confusion. This is because people do not always agree on the behavior for certain roles. Today, some of the barriers created by gender differences are diminishing. As society's view of male and female roles continues to change, people's views of role expectations will change, too.

When Negative Feelings Occur

Every person has negative feelings at times. When you hold back negative feelings, they may become stronger and more frustrating. You need to know how to vent your emotions. Even negative feelings can be communicated in a useful, constructive way.

Handling Negative Feelings

There are many ways you can resolve negative feelings. You must first wish to communicate effectively and be willing to take the first steps to resolving these feelings. As you read the following suggestions, think about yourself. Which of these guidelines would be most helpful for you?

- Discuss your negative feelings with the person whose behavior is bothering you. Do not complain to others until you have spoken with that person. People who are not involved in a problem usually cannot do anything about it.

- Keep a simple issue simple. Do not add other issues to it, building it up until it becomes a major problem.

- Do not reopen old issues that have already been settled.

- Discuss the problem without making nasty comments and accusations that would hurt the other person. Recognize your own faults and accept them. Do not blame them on others. Try to be pleasant rather than grouchy. Help people see that you like them, even though you do not like their behavior.

- Say what must be said and stop. Do not continue talking about one issue and repeating yourself.
- Try to end on a positive note. Make a positive comment about the person or the situation.

Communication in the Workplace

The communication skills you have learned to use in your personal life can help you communicate at work. The circumstances differ, however. You have known your family and close friends for a long time, and you have learned how to communicate with them. When you begin a job, you will meet many new people. In today's world, the workforce is likely to be very **diverse** (differing from one another). Workers differ by age, ethnicity, and gender. Increasing numbers of workers have disabilities. Due to the diverse nature of the workforce, communication can be more challenging. See **2-8**.

2-8

Clear communication in the workforce can be challenging, but it is necessary for a team to function well.

The goals of communication at work are to pass along information and to build effective work relationships. Different styles of communicating and different interpretations of communications can interfere with attaining both of these goals. People from different backgrounds may define problems differently. They bring their personal goals, priorities, and standards to their jobs. When diverse people form team-based work groups, disagreements may occur. It is important to remember that every person is different. That does not mean they are difficult. By thinking of someone as just different, you become less judgmental. You can be more open to their opinions and ideas.

Many of the effective communication techniques that you use in other settings can also be used on the job. In addition, the following points can be helpful:

- Keep conversations unrelated to work to a minimum. These prevent you and other employees from doing your work. Your personal life should be kept private. Workplace gossip should be avoided. Professionalism is expected of employees.

- Show courtesy to customers and clients. Do not keep them waiting while you finish a conversation with a fellow employee.

- Use good listening skills. Listen carefully when directions are given. Ask questions to prevent any misunderstandings.

- Use standard English at work, not slang. For example, say *yes* rather than *yeah*.

- Avoid telling jokes at work. Because of the diverse nature of the workforce, some people may be offended by an innocent joke.

- If misunderstandings occur, discuss them with the person involved. It is possible to respectfully disagree.

 **Reading**
Review

1. True or false. In open communication, people know each other so well that they agree about everything.
2. Give five examples of ways to communicate positive feelings.
3. A communication barrier based on opinions that people form without complete knowledge is known as _____ .
4. Identify five ways to communicate negative feelings.
5. How can you communicate to others effectively in a workplace setting?

Section 2-4

Conflict Resolution

Objectives

After studying this section, you will be able to

- **identify** some types and causes of conflict.
- **explain** possible negative and positive reactions to conflict.
- **describe** constructive and destructive methods of conflict resolution.
- **list** the steps in the conflict resolution process.
- **explain** the use of mediation.

Key Terms

conflict	compromise	mediation
scapegoating	conflict resolution process	peer mediator
negotiation		

Each person has a unique way of viewing and reacting to every situation. When people live and work closely, as they do in families, in friendships, and on the job, conflicts are bound to arise. A **conflict** is a struggle between two people or groups who have opposing views. The ability to resolve a conflict is an important skill in good communication.

Types of Conflicts

There are all types of conflicts. Some are small, such as a disagreement between two people over a trivial matter, **2-9**. You and a friend may disagree over where to go after school. Disagreements can grow into larger conflicts if the two people are not willing to reach an agreement peacefully.

Conflicts can also occur within families—between husbands and wives, parents and children, or among siblings. Again, the conflicts can be small and easily resolved. They can also be over important issues. Maybe you and your parents disagree about how late you should be able to stay out on weekend nights. Bringing up an issue that is causing a conflict is a good way to begin to deal with the problem. Listening to each other's views and talking about them can usually lead to good solutions.

Conflicts are not confined to interpersonal relationships. They can occur between larger groups—even entire nations. Throughout the world, there are nations that are at war with other nations. These, too,

2-9

Even good friends can have conflicts because they are together so much of the time. What is important is to choose a method of resolving the conflict that is fair to all.

are conflicts, but on a much larger scale. Many times the conflicts between nations are based on some of the same differences that cause conflicts between individuals. Differences in religious beliefs and practices are often at the core of many national conflicts. Disagreements over government policies can also lead to major disputes.

Causes of Conflict

Causes of conflict can be trivial or significant. It is important to take an objective look at the conflict and try to determine the cause. Knowing why the conflict occurred will likely help in resolving it. Many conflicts occur because of poor communication. Have you ever made arrangements to meet some friends, and they never showed up? You may have been really angry until you found out they never received your message, or they misunderstood where you were to meet. Many times a failure to communicate can be more serious. Has anyone ever said to you "If you had told me, all of this could have been avoided"?

Some conflicts result from specific situations. For instance, perhaps you and your friend both like the same boy. The situation could lead to a conflict between the two of you. Other conflicts are caused by personality clashes. If people have very different personalities, they could be on a collision course.

Conflicts often occur between parents and their children during the teenage years. The role of parents is to guide their children as they grow toward adulthood. Parents are responsible for their well-being until they are adults. The role of teens is to develop independence. They are anxious to be able to make decisions for themselves. Finding a happy medium between these opposing roles is often difficult. Parents and children often pull in opposite directions. Conflicts frequently occur during these tumultuous years.

Differences in values can lead to conflicts. Your values are important to you. If someone else does not have the same values as you, conflicts can arise. The degree of conflict depends on the importance of the value to you. For instance, your parents may think good grades are most important, while you think your performance on the volleyball team is most important. You want to spend time practicing when they want you to study more.

Some conflicts can be traced to cultural differences. For example, some cultures may value active and busy schedules. Other cultures may value a more relaxed pace.

21st Century Skills

Conflict resolution. Jackie and Kelly are coworkers with different personalities. However, they resolve their conflicts quietly and do not let them affect their work.

Reactions to Conflict

Conflict is normal. There will always be disagreements between people. It is how people react or respond to these disagreements that determines whether they ignite into major conflicts or just go away. Negative reactions can escalate conflicts and lead to hostility and personal attacks. Some even end in violence. Positive reactions can lead to solutions that both parties can accept. Many actually lead to personal growth.

Negative Reactions

Avoidance is a common reaction to conflict. Some people just walk away. This might be a good response if a person is concerned that an argument could escalate into violence. A cooling-down period might be good for everyone involved. In most cases, however, avoidance simply puts off resolution. It does not solve the problem. Instead, resentment builds up as the person tries to suppress hurt feelings. If this continues over a period of time, it can lead to an explosion of emotions when the person finally reaches a breaking point.

Some people attempt to resolve conflicts by blaming others. This is called **scapegoating**. The person blamed for the problem is the scapegoat. Everyone else is freed of the responsibility for the problem because they can blame this other person. This is not a resolution because no one tries to solve the conflict. The conflict goes on with both parties feeling it is "not my problem."

Some responses to conflict include arguing, becoming angry, and name-calling. When one person becomes angry and begins yelling, the other person is likely to become angry as well. Verbal attacks fly back and forth. People say hurtful things they often regret later. They feel belittled when their self-esteem is under attack. It is sometimes hard to forgive people when such outbreaks occur. An atmosphere of hostility prevails.

The most destructive reaction to conflict is violence. If tempers flare out of control, shoving, hitting, or pushing can result. Some people first experience hitting as children. They think this is an acceptable form of reaction because their parents hit them. They also see more violence portrayed in the media—on television and in movies. As they become older, they may use this same form of behavior. A violent reaction to conflict is never the answer. It can lead to child abuse, spouse abuse, or elder abuse. It can also lead to violence outside the home.

Positive Reactions

There are ways people can react to conflict that will help the situation. First, you can learn to control your emotions. Lashing out in anger usually solves nothing. You can also ask the other person to remain calm. Both people need to stop, take a deep breath, and quiet their emotions. See **2-10**.

Analyze and Solve

Form small groups to discuss and answer the following questions: Is peer pressure a big problem for teens? Do you agree that most peer pressure does not come from close friends? Have you seen peer pressure used as a scapegoat? Can you cite some instances? In what ways do teens deal with peer pressure? Summarize your group's responses and present them to the class.

2-10

Being calm and using humor are ways to soothe the heated emotions of a conflict.

It is also important to listen. Instead of shouting, stop and listen to what each person is saying. Focus on the real problem as you exchange views. Do not bring up other issues. Focus on the current conflict.

Try to remain neutral. Do not jump to a judgment before everyone has his or her say. Then you are ready to find a real solution to the conflict.

Learning to react positively when a conflict occurs is an important life skill that can lead to personal growth. It is a sign of maturity when you can control your emotions, listen to other viewpoints, and avoid jumping to conclusions. These skills will help you in your personal relationships as well as in work situations. Teamwork is stressed in today's workplace. You might someday be working closely with other employees in a work setting. Because conflicts will arise, reacting positively can lead to constructive resolution of these conflicts. An employer will recognize and appreciate your ability to handle conflict in a mature manner.

Constructive Methods for Handling Conflict

To resolve a conflict, each person has to assume responsibility for his or her feelings. The emotions you feel may be caused by others, but they belong to you. If you wish to lessen stress that occurs in conflict, you must be willing to resolve the conflict. Try these techniques for starters.

Use "I" Messages

Use "I" messages instead of "you" messages. This means you take ownership for your feelings. You state what you feel or think instead of criticizing the other person. Say "I think you are ignoring me" rather than "You are ignoring me". You might further say, "When I think you are ignoring me, I feel hurt. I do not like being ignored." As you express your feelings, you are taking credit for them.

"You" messages, on the other hand, come across as accusations. "You are ignoring me" places blame on the other person and may aggravate the situation. When taking ownership and saying "I think" or "I feel," you avoid accusing the other person of negative behaviors.

Learn to send "I" messages. For example, "When you tell so-called funny stories about me to my friends, I am embarrassed." Can you see in this example that you are assuming responsibility for your feelings of embarrassment? A "you" message sounds like an accusation. "You embarrass me when you tell your so-called funny stories about me to my friends." The "you" message places the blame on the other person.

Decide Who Owns the Problem

Whose problem is it? When a problem exists between two people, both own the problem. Even when one person creates the problem, he or she makes it a problem for the other. State your point of view in a way that will not create an argument. Seek feedback to determine how the other person is receiving your message. To avoid misunderstandings, use clarifying messages periodically, **2-11**. Try comments such as: "If I am hearing you correctly, you are saying that..." or "I think I heard you say..."

2-11

When resolving a conflict with another person, state your point of view calmly and clearly. Then ask for feedback.

Learn to Negotiate and Compromise

An important method for resolving conflicts is negotiation. **Negotiation** means communicating with others in order to reach a mutually satisfying agreement. Such an agreement usually involves a compromise. In a **compromise**, both parties agree to give up something. Each person gives up something of importance to obtain something else that also has importance.

Negotiation and compromise must be considered carefully. Some issues may be so important to you that you will be unwilling to negotiate and compromise. For example, you may not wish to compromise your moral views or spiritual views. For this reason, you will not enter into a negotiation that would require you to make a compromise. What is important is that you negotiate and compromise when it is appropriate.

The purpose of negotiation and compromise is to remove conflict. Four methods are commonly used.

- *You win/I lose.* The person who wins is happy with this compromise. However, you are likely to be unhappy about your loss. The conflict is likely to resurface at a future time.

- *I win/you lose.* This is the opposite of the above situation. You feel happy because you achieved what you wanted. However, the person who loses may not be happy about being the loser. This conflict is likely to resurface. One person had to compromise too much.

Mental Health Awareness

Benefits of Facing Conflict

Dealing with conflict constructively can improve social and emotional well-being, even if the conflict is not resolved. By expressing their views, the people involved gain better understanding of each other. They may learn new, creative ways to deal with problems, both personal and work-related. They may also learn not to be afraid of conflict and to accept people who are different from themselves.

- *I lose/you lose.* Negotiations apparently became very difficult this time. Both you and the other person are losers. So many compromises were made that neither person's wishes were met. No one is happy.

- *I win/you win.* This is the ideal way to resolve conflicts. You were able to negotiate in such a way that each achieved what he or she wanted. Neither person forced his or her ideas on the other. Neither was forced to compromise anything that was cherished. Those items that were lost were not highly valued, so there were no losers. Both are now happy winners.

You must recognize that some conflicts cannot be resolved. There are people who create conflicts and refuse to resolve them. Some people make unfair demands on others. If this happens, you may have to give up your responsibility toward resolution. You may have to recognize that the problem is not yours and leave it with the person who owns it.

In these situations, relations between the people involved will suffer. Perhaps the relationship is already weak. Remember that relationships are between at least two people. Sometimes every person has to be willing to stand alone. When efforts toward negotiation and compromise do not work, you can still feel you tried your best. In spite of the outcome, you have gained some experience from having tried to resolve the issue.

Use the Conflict Resolution Process

In some instances, a more formal process may be needed to resolve the conflict. The **conflict resolution process** is a step-by-step form of communication that allows conflicts to be worked out in a positive manner. The process should be used as soon as possible after a conflict occurs. This prevents anger and tension from building. It should also take place in private with only the individuals or parties involved present. Everyone needs to remain calm and be willing to listen to each other.

Life Skills

The Conflict Resolution Process

1. State the problem. All participants must have the opportunity to tell their view of what is causing the problem. Each person must listen carefully and stay focused on the main issue. All must agree on exactly what the problem is.

2. **List possible solutions.** The next step is to suggest all potential solutions. Think of as many solutions as possible even if some seem unworkable. An idea can sometimes spark a better solution. Everyone should be able to speak freely and without criticism.

3. **Evaluate each possible solution.** Take a closer look at the best possible solutions. Which ones do both parties like? Which ones seem to solve the problem? Use negotiation skills until a compromise solution can be reached.

4. **Pick the best solution.** Finally, both parties must agree to the best solution. It will not be a solution unless everyone is in agreement.

5. **Carry out the solution.** A plan should be made to carry out the solution. State what each party will do and when they will do it. Keep it simple. Also, decide what actions the parties will take if a conflict occurs again.

6. **Evaluate the results.** The process does not end until the solution has been put into action and the results are evaluated. If a conflict is still occurring, the process needs to begin again. Following these steps, where everyone involved is allowed to speak freely, should lead to satisfactory solutions. More serious and escalating conflicts can be avoided.

Mediation

Some efforts to resolve conflicts between parties just do not work without outside help. Mediation may be needed. In **mediation**, a third person is called on to help reconcile differences between the conflicting parties. This person is called a mediator. Through mediation, an attempt is made to settle the dispute and find a peaceful solution to the conflict. The opposing parties talk to each other with the help of the mediator. Mediators can assist in school, work, and even international disputes. They are often included in the conflict resolution process.

A mediator is sometimes needed to settle family disputes. Family members live under the same roof, share meals and living space, work together, and play together. Conflicts are bound to occur. The conflict resolution process can be used by family members to resolve their conflicts. The two family members can talk about the problem and find a solution acceptable to both. Sometimes mediation may be needed. Who becomes the mediator? Anyone who is not emotionally tied to the issue can become the neutral third party. When a mom and daughter have a strong difference of opinion, the dad or son might be the mediator who helps bring about a win/win solution.

Peer Mediation

Many schools use **peer mediators**. These are students who are trained in the conflict resolution process. They listen and act in an unbiased manner to help fellow students settle their differences. Peer mediators are selected for their leadership skills, emotional maturity, and interest in helping others. They are often preferred as mediators because students feel more comfortable with a peer, **2-12**. They may feel another student can understand their problems better than an adult. Hopefully, solutions can be found. When conflicts cannot be resolved, the parties involved may have to agree to disagree, but in a peaceful manner. This necessitates respect for all concerned.

SDI Productions/E+/Getty Images

2-12

Many students feel more comfortable in resolving conflicts when their peers provide leadership.

Violence: A Destructive Method of Handling Conflict

You have learned of constructive ways to deal with conflict. Is there such a thing as a destructive method of dealing with conflict? If a conflict is settled, how can it be destructive? The answer is if an act of violence is used. If physical force is used against another person or group that harms them to the point where they are completely subdued and afraid to speak up, then a destructive method of handling conflict has been used. The conflict is ended only because one person or party has been injured or even killed by another person or group.

Gangs often use this form of conflict resolution. It also happens within some families. It may take the form of spouse abuse, child abuse, or elder abuse. If conflicts arise, one family member may attempt to completely dominate another family member. Physical force is often used, but emotional abuse can be equally devastating. Suicide also falls into this category. A person may feel there is no way out and attempt suicide.

Remember that violence does not solve a conflict. Violence is costly to society in terms of tax dollars spent on criminals in prisons. It is also costly to people in terms of lowered self-worth and lost dignity in addition to physical pain and suffering.

Always strive for positive resolutions of conflicts where differences are settled peacefully and friendships and families are kept intact. Conflict resolution skills will benefit you throughout your life as they foster relationships, increase job productivity, and prevent violence.

 **Reading**
Review

1. State three possible causes of conflict.
2. Give an example of a negative reaction to conflict and an example of a positive reaction to conflict.
3. Why are "I" messages more successful than "you" messages in resolving conflicts?
4. Name the most ideal negotiation and compromise method.
5. List the steps in the conflict resolution process.
6. Why is mediation sometimes needed to resolve conflicts?

Chapter 2 Review

Summary

A positive attitude, dependability, honesty, and an ability to work with others will help ensure your success in the workplace. Staying up-to-date on changes in technology is key to staying competitive in the job market.

Developing your ability to communicate well will help you throughout your life. To do this, you will want to improve your verbal communication skills. As a speaker, you need to send clear messages. As a listener, you want to receive and understand messages.

Nonverbal communication is an important part of the communication process as well. As you talk with people, you will become aware of the many messages you receive through nonverbal communication. Your appearance, manners, and body language are just a few of the ways you convey messages without words.

Technology has led to new forms of communication. These include cellular phones, e-mail, and video conferencing. Remember to use these mediums of communication cautiously and courteously.

Recognizing common communication barriers such as stereotypes, prejudices, mixed messages, and gender differences helps people overcome them. Because of the diversity of today's workplace, communication in the workplace is especially important.

No matter how well people communicate, conflicts are still going to occur. There are many types and causes of conflicts, just as there are negative and positive reactions to them. Conflicts can best be resolved through negotiation and compromise. The conflict resolution process can also be used to resolve conflict. Mediation by a neutral third party is sometimes necessary. Violence is a destructive method of conflict resolution.

Critical Thinking

1. **Analyze priorities.** If you were an employer, what three qualities would you most want in an employee? Explain your answer in a written paragraph.

2. **Apply ratings.** How would you rate your verbal communication skills at school and at home? Based on your rating, what steps would you take to improve your listening and speaking skills?

3. **Analyze behavior.** Ask classmates to demonstrate desirable skills in communicating the following messages. Discuss each message after it is delivered. Tell why you think the speaker chose a certain phrase, speaking style, or tone of voice.
   A. Describe your favorite meal to your best friend.
   B. Describe your favorite meal to your grandparent.
   C. Ask a restaurant waiter to recook a hamburger that is too rare.
   D. Ask a salesclerk to recheck a sales slip that you think is wrong.
   E. Communicate with a four-year-old who wants to eat cookies just before dinner.
   F. Role-play a situation in which a talkative young man is dating a quiet young woman.

4. **Apply ratings.** Select and rank any four barriers to communication listed in this chapter. Use the number one as the most frequently observed barrier. Use the number four as the least frequently observed barrier. List some ways to overcome each barrier.

5. **Compare and contrast.** What in your opinion is the best way to resolve a conflict? the least desirable way to resolve a conflict?

21st Century
Applications

6. **Civic literacy.** Successful employees are also responsible citizens. Exceeding expectations is a way to be successful at school and in your career. Make a list of five things that you expect of yourself on a daily basis, such as being on time, completing tasks as assigned, or being courteous. For each of the things you expect from yourself, think about and record what you could do to exceed those expectations. What effect do you think exceeding your expectations has on your success?

7. **Flexibility and adaptability.** Employees sometimes have to be flexible and adaptable in responding to a new situation, problem, or issue in the workplace. For example, suppose you work at a clothing store. You usually work at the cash register and your coworker is usually on the sales floor assisting customers and making sure products are well-stocked. Your manager informs you that your coworker has called in sick. How might you respond to this situation to reflect flexibility and adaptability?

8. **Media literacy.** Use drawing software to illustrate the cycle of communication. Make sure to include speakers, listeners, and feedback.

9. **Information, communications, and technology literacy.** Create a video on successful communication strategies for student groups to use at school.

10. **Communication and collaboration.** Select a possible conflict between two students who are working together on a class project. Describe how the conflict could be resolved using each of the methods of negotiation and compromise. Create an electronic presentation or video, or role-play a scenario and present your project to the class.

11. **Social and cross-cultural skills.** In some cultures, some common gestures may carry different meanings. With a partner, role-play two scenes that involve the use of verbal and nonverbal communication. In the first scene, show an example of a miscommunication based on cultural differences in body language. In the second scene, show how the miscommunication can be resolved. What is the essential difference between the two plays/interactions?

Core
Skills

12. **Listening.** Improve your listening and speaking skills by having a conversation with another person about any topic. When one partner speaks, the other listens. Neither person may respond to any statement without first summarizing what the partner has said. Incorrect summaries must be clarified before the conversation continues.

13. **Listening, writing.** Interview a successful employee about his or her attitude, dependability, honesty, ethics, cooperation, and appearance on the job. Ask how these factors have impacted the employee's performance. Write a newspaper-style article on the qualities of successful employees. Use quotes from the interview in your article.

14. **Speaking.** Prepare a speech on a topic of interest and present it to the class. Have classmates critique your speech on the criteria listed in "Developing Speaking Skills."

15. **Social studies.** Research how stereotypes and prejudices are formed about different groups of people. Write a brief summary of your findings.

16. **Reading, history.** Study the causes of different wars. Could these conflicts have been avoided? Were any caused by a failure in communication?

17. **Social studies.** List lifestyle differences in cultures that could lead to conflict.

18. **History.** Describe examples of negotiation and compromise between nations. Discuss the individuals representing all parties and their qualifications as negotiators.

19. **Speaking.** Role-play the use of the conflict resolution process. Describe a hypothetical situation that might occur in your school where the conflict resolution process could be used. Have classmates take roles as the two groups in conflict. If your school has peer mediators, ask one of them to participate in the role-play.

20. **Writing.** What type of technological skills do you think will be most important in the workplace in 10 years? 20 years? Write a brief summary of your response. Support your claim with research and evidence.

Leadership
Development

As a part of working on the FCCLA's Focus on Children STAR Event, visit a child care center and observe the way teachers communicate with the children. Notice the way children communicate with one another. Write recommendations for eliminating any communication barriers you observe.

Portfolio
Builder

Electronic communication is fast and convenient. Many people don't think before they hit the "Send" button. Give examples of electronic communication pitfalls and prepare a list of guidelines to follow to avoid them. Document how electronic communication can both help and hinder a career. Add your list of guidelines to your portfolio.

Journal
Writing

You hear footsteps coming closer. You turn and see your best friend walk into the room. His shoulders are slumped and his arms are folded. One of his hands is clenched in a fist. He is frowning, and he avoids making eye contact with you.

Write About It: *What nonverbal messages are being sent? What would be your response to these messages?*

Chapter 3
Working in a Team

Reading Prep

Before reading this chapter, flip through the pages and make notes of the major headings. Analyze the structure of the relationships of the headings with the concepts in the chapter.

Concept Organizer

Use a three-circle Venn diagram to compare and contrast the different types of leadership.

G-WLEARNING.com

Click on the activity icon to visit www.g-wlearning.com/comprehensive/8062 to access online vocabulary activities using key terms from the chapter.

Section 3-1

Leadership and Teamwork

Objectives

After studying this section, you will be able to

- **explain** the roles of leaders and followers.
- **demonstrate** the qualities of effective team members.
- **identify** three types of leadership.
- **describe** five functions performed by group leaders.

Key Terms ⤴

team	autocratic leadership	laissez-faire
leader		motivation
follower	democratic leadership	brainstorming
diversity		tact

Throughout life, you will be a member of several groups. Your family is a group. Your classes are groups. You may also be involved with clubs, bands, sports teams, and choral groups.

Each member of a group can affect the success of group activities. Learning how to work with others will allow you to contribute to a group's effectiveness. In the process, you will develop positive relationships with your peers. Participating in group activities will also promote your social and emotional development.

Being a Team Member

A **team** is a group of people organized around a common goal. Every good team has leaders and followers. No team can exist with just one or the other. When team leaders and followers work toward the group's goal, they are practicing good teamwork.

A **leader** is a person who influences the behavior of others. Leaders take charge and help group members set and achieve group goals. Good leaders inspire the trust of their followers and respond to their teammates as friends. They involve all group members in planning, conducting, and evaluating group activities.

No person is a leader in all situations. A leader in the drama club may be a follower in the band. An athletic leader may be a follower on the yearbook staff. A business leader may be a follower in a social setting. You will be needed to lead in some cases and follow in others.

A **follower** is a person who supports a group by helping put goals into action. The best plans of any group will not yield results without the support of dedicated followers. Followers are needed to supply time, talents, energy, and other resources to achieve team goals. Followers take direction, but also help leaders determine the best course of action. Most people develop team skills by first assuming a follower role. They grow into leadership positions gradually as they develop self-esteem.

For a team to function effectively, leaders and followers must show a spirit of give and take. Followers must be willing to take a leadership role when their expertise is needed to achieve the team's goal. Likewise, leaders must recognize that sometimes a follower is better suited to temporarily take charge. When team members work well together, they do what needs to be done, no matter what titles they have. See **3-1**.

Both leaders and followers are needed to build strong teams at school, in the community, and in the workplace. Teams are especially important in the workplace. Consequently, employers try to hire individuals who have good teamwork skills.

3-1

Team members may alternate roles as leaders and followers, but they all work together to accomplish tasks.

monkeybusinessimages/iStock/Getty Images Plus

Qualities of Effective Team Members

Team members put the interests of the team first and always emphasize "we" instead of "me." They keep open minds and come to meetings willing to discuss all ideas. They expect others to have different ideas and opinions. They do not become offended when their ideas are criticized. They use humor whenever appropriate, but never in a way that offends someone. They do their share of work, complete assignments on time, and keep a positive attitude. Effective team members try to do what is best for the team.

Members of teams that operate effectively pay close attention when others speak. They do not interrupt the speaker when he or she is talking. They also do not make fun of a team member's idea or immediately dismiss the idea. Effective team members show respect and understanding toward other team members. They show support for team members and ask questions if an idea or solution seems unclear. Sometimes a language barrier exists, making it difficult for people to express ideas clearly. In this case, extra patience and understanding is needed by everyone.

Qualities of Committed Team Members

- Smile and use a pleasant tone of voice.
- Remain quiet until you have the floor.
- Think highly of every team member including yourself.
- Seek clarification when something is not clear.
- Be willing to compromise on issues that can be handled effectively in several different ways.
- Celebrate your team's successes and the ability of members to work well together.

3-2

These personal qualities are signs that members are committed to their group.

You will encounter people from other cultural backgrounds throughout life. This influence is the result of a multicultural society. Sometimes the term **diversity** is used to refer to the condition of a team whose members represent many different cultures. Diversity presents opportunities to share cultural traditions and customs. When everyone's culture is respected, individuals feel free to express opinions and views. The team benefits from the open, honest discussions. Often more and better ideas result.

On the other hand, diversity can create team conflict unless there is an effort to understand other cultures and a strong commitment to cooperation. Some additional ways to demonstrate team commitment are listed in **3-2**.

Opportunities for Leadership

Leaders are people who step up and take charge of a situation. They are needed at all levels of human organization. Countries, states, cities, businesses, schools, and clubs all need leaders. Your skills as a leader may be used in a number of ways, both now and in the future.

Right now, you may be needed to lead class discussions, club meetings, or athletic rallies. You may know a student who has personal problems and needs your encouragement to seek counseling. You may serve on a team headed by a weak leader and have some ideas for motivating the group.

If you become a parent later in life, you will be a leader to your children. You may serve a leadership role in your community and possibly run for an elective office. No doubt you will join community and social groups devoted to your interests and possibly hold leadership positions.

In the workplace, you will have many opportunities to lead. Unlike the past, when supervisors told workers what to do, today's workplace uses a teamwork approach. Employees are expected to work well as teammates and share the leadership role as assignments dictate. Group members must possess the teamwork skills of creative thinking, decision making, and conflict resolution. A leader must know how to organize and manage the team's resources. Participation in school clubs and organizations will help prepare you for leadership.

Types of Leadership

There are three basic types of leadership. The first type, **autocratic leadership**, demands the cooperation of others. The autocratic leader has full control of the group and makes all the decisions for the group. Autocratic leadership stresses meeting goals. It demands that team members perform as directed to reach goals. Autocratic leaders may seem harsh at times. However, their followers receive the satisfaction of knowing they have done more than they thought they could do. Some people would never try unless, in a kind but firm manner, a good leader says, "Do it."

Democratic leadership stresses the needs and wishes of individuals. The group discusses matters of policy. Members are encouraged to participate in decision making by voting.

In a democratic group, members have the power to select a leader to act in their best interest. They trust the leader to make good decisions for the group. If the leader fails to consider the group's wishes, however, the members have the power to choose a new leader.

The third type of leadership is called **laissez-faire**. Laissez-faire leaders play down their roles in groups. They are on hand only to serve as resources. Laissez-faire leadership allows true freedom. Members may do whatever they want to do. The group is not pressured to move forward on a schedule. An active group may fail to reach goals due to a lack of organization. In the end, members may feel that little has been accomplished in spite of their individual efforts.

All three types of leadership have good points. Autocratic leadership may be needed to help some people become productive and meet fixed deadlines. Democratic leadership takes advantage of members' ideas and provides the organizational structure to accomplish goals. Laissez-faire leadership fosters individual creativity, even though it may result in a low degree of productivity. See **3-3**.

The secret to involving all members is to know how and when to use all three types of leadership. You must vary your leadership style to fit the people in the group as well as the

3-3

Laissez-faire leadership works well in situations where group members need to use their creativity.

situation. Take care not to become a bossy autocrat. Do not get carried away with the laissez-faire style or your group may not accomplish anything. Democratic leadership usually works best, but you cannot expect it to work in every situation.

Effective Leadership

Leaders perform a number of functions in a group. They must set a good example, motivate followers, and guide group planning. Leaders also need to use tact and give recognition to those who deserve it.

Set an Example

When you are the leader of a group, you need to set an example for the other members. Although you have extra responsibilities as leader, you also have the responsibility of doing your share of the work. If you fail to participate, you set a poor example for your followers. They may see no reason to help with projects if you are not helping. They may also lose respect for you and begin to resent you.

On the other hand, you should not try to do all the work by yourself. If you are a good leader, you will get other people involved. Try to place all members on one or more active committees. Give others the chance to participate and have the satisfaction of being useful and needed. Involving more people will allow more work to be done and more goals to be achieved.

Another way you can set an example is by cooperating with everyone. Some large groups tend to divide into little groups of friends. You, too, may feel more comfortable working with your friends. However, you must remember that you are leading the entire group. You must go outside your usual circle of friends to include everyone. Your example will encourage others to work together for the good of the group.

Motivate Followers

As a leader, you may need to motivate followers to get involved in group projects. **Motivation** is a force that gives people a reason to take action.

Some people have *intrinsic motivation*. Their motivation comes from within themselves. They set many goals for themselves and willingly work to achieve those goals. Group members who are intrinsically motivated show enthusiasm. They never need to be prodded. Instead, they always look for ways to help.

Other people need *extrinsic motivation*. This motivation comes from a person's environment. Leaders can provide followers with extrinsic motivation by helping them notice their environment. A choir director may say the choral group sounds better when members are smiling. A scoutmaster may comment that the flowers in the city park need weeding. Such suggestions from leaders can motivate followers to take action. See **3-4**.

Living Green

Planting trees is good for the environment. Obtain permission to organize a tree-planting event at your school or community park. Ask student and community organizations to participate.

21st Century Skills

Leadership. Micah strives to keep morale high among his staff members. He knows that when morale is high, workers are enthusiastic about work and are willing to perform assigned tasks to meet goals.

3-4

This choir director uses extrinsic motivation to encourage his group to prepare well for a concert.

Mental Health Awareness

The "Apple" Effect

The saying, "one bad apple spoils the whole bag" can apply to team settings. One member can negatively affect others' efforts and enthusiasm and cause team members to adopt a negative attitude. Likewise, one person's strong positive attitude can benefit the team. Positive attitudes can cause feelings of cooperation, motivation, and enthusiasm.

Some followers are very willing to help but have no idea what needs to be done. Watch for these individuals and recommend tasks to them so they can enjoy being productive team members. Without positive direction, these people often get lost in confusion.

What about those who refuse to get involved? If you know their reasons, you may be able to motivate them. For instance, some people may not think they are capable of doing a job. You could help these people find tasks that better match their skills. This will allow them to develop more self-confidence.

Some people may refuse to get involved because they are too busy. They may have numerous other commitments. You might motivate these people to take on small tasks. This will allow them to participate without devoting a large amount of time. These people can take on larger tasks when their schedules are less hectic.

Guide Planning

Being involved in the planning motivates group members to participate. With careful planning, a group can successfully handle several projects and activities. Your role as leader is to guide the planning. Be sure the group thinks through a plan and is able to carry it out. Summarize thoughts frequently to ensure that all members understand the same meaning.

During a planning session, a leader can encourage a group to express ideas by brainstorming. **Brainstorming** is a group problem-solving method in which individuals offer all ideas that come to mind. It is a technique that requires rapid thinking and a constant expression of ideas. Some of the ideas will be really wild, but that does not matter. The goal is to develop many ideas, not a few well-planned thoughts. No one is allowed to criticize any ideas, so members offer them without fear of embarrassment. Later, the group decides which ideas to pursue, sometimes combining two or more brainstorming thoughts. The ideas that motivate the most members will be put into action.

Brainstorming has two benefits. First, the group is likely to find answers to its problems or challenges. Secondly, the opportunity to offer suggestions promotes member participation and motivation.

Use Tact

Successful leaders need to have tact. **Tact** is knowing what to do or say to avoid offending others. If being tactful is not one of your strong qualities, work on developing it. Tact will help you work with others without hurting them or making them angry.

Getting group members to do their share of tasks often requires tact. Most people like being *asked* to do something rather than being *told* what to do. Some leaders are afraid that if they ask followers to do something, the followers will refuse. Therefore, they just tell the followers what to do, even though this approach often causes friction. Eventually group members may not cooperate willingly.

Tact is necessary whenever you deal with people. Being kind and considerate is always appreciated. A smile with a pleasant tone of voice is important in all situations. This is true whether you are a leader or a follower.

Give Recognition

Leaders also need to give followers the recognition they deserve. Your encouragement can help bring out the best in others. When their efforts enable the group to reach a goal, give them the credit.

One way leaders can give recognition is with a sincere "thank you." People need to know their personal efforts are important and truly appreciated. The leader should take the time to congratulate the person in front of the group so everyone knows that individual efforts are noticed and valued.

Promote Cultural Diversity

One of the responsibilities of a group's leader is to promote cultural diversity. The acceptance of other cultures begins with an understanding of them. Therefore, a leader might encourage group discussion about cultural differences. The leader might also plan cultural activities, asking group members of differing backgrounds to plan the events. This will help bring down barriers in the group, enabling group members to work better together.

Reading
Review

1. True or false. A strong leader always performs as a leader, never as a follower.
2. Suggest five qualities of effective team members.
3. List and describe the three basic types of leadership.
4. A force that gives people a reason to take action is _____ .

Section 3-2

Organizations That Work!

Objectives

After studying this section, you will be able to

- **explain** how a group's constitution and bylaws act as guidelines for electing officers and holding meetings.
- **describe** how to use parliamentary procedure to run group meetings.
- **demonstrate** how a group can establish a goal around which programs and activities can be organized.

Key Terms

constitution	bylaws	parliamentary procedure

What makes an organization successful? Its purpose is a key factor. A group's purpose is its reason for existing. A group sets goals to help achieve its purpose.

Youth and Professional Organizations

One purpose of most youth organizations is to help prepare young people for their adult roles in society. Perhaps you are a member of such a group. Most schools offer a range of organizations that encourage student participation. As an adult, you may become involved in an organization that enhances your profession. The purpose of these organizations is to promote the career areas in which their members work. Professional organizations may achieve this purpose by funding research, offering scholarships, and sponsoring meetings to keep members updated.

Getting Organized

Organization is another factor that contributes to a group's success. Members know what to expect when a group follows set guidelines for electing officers and holding meetings. These guidelines are stated by the group's constitution and bylaws.

Living Green

Volunteer with a team of classmates to work on a recycling program in your community. Working together as a team will bring your group closer together. Using teamwork will help you accomplish environmental goals.

Many groups are local chapters of national organizations. All the chapters share the same purpose as the national organization. They also follow the same basic constitution and bylaws.

The **constitution** is a set of laws that govern an organization. In its simplest form, a constitution usually includes the following:

- name and purpose of the group
- membership requirements
- the group's officers, their duties, and the method of election
- basic meeting requirements, such as the number of people that must be present before a meeting can be held
- procedures for changing the constitution

Many groups also have bylaws that accompany the constitution. The **bylaws** are a set of specific rules that expand the constitution by giving more information. For instance, bylaws list the names and functions of committees. They state the order of business and any other information that is needed to make the constitution clear. The rules stated in the bylaws are more likely to need changing from time to time.

3-5

A group's constitution will describe the duties of the group's president and other officers.

Electing Officers

Your group's constitution and bylaws will state the officers to elect and their duties. Knowing the duties expected of various offices will help you nominate people qualified to handle the jobs if elected. See **3-5**.

Different groups nominate candidates for offices in different ways. Some groups simply accept nominations from the members during a business meeting. Other groups have interested persons submit requests to run for offices. Many groups have a nominating committee that prepares a list of candidates to present to the full membership. In every case, members vote to determine the winners.

In addition to officers, most groups need to elect or appoint chairpersons for the standing, or permanent, committees. Membership, publicity, and fund-raising committees are examples of standing committees. Your group's method for selecting chairpersons will be described in your bylaws. Some groups elect all

jsmith/E+/Getty Images

committee chairpersons. In other groups, the president or a committee appoints chairpersons.

Chairpersons are also needed for ad hoc committees. An *ad hoc committee* is one that is appointed to perform a specific task. When that task is completed, the committee dissolves. A committee to plan this year's homecoming float is an example of an ad hoc committee.

Holding a Meeting

Most groups follow guidelines to help them conduct meetings in an orderly fashion. The guidelines most often used by groups are called **parliamentary procedure**. Using parliamentary procedure, a meeting usually begins with a call to order. Then the minutes of the last meeting are read. The *minutes* are an official record of what took place at the meeting. The minutes are followed by reports from standing and ad hoc committees. Any unfinished business from the previous meeting is discussed next. Finally, the group discusses any new items of business.

Before a group can take action, members must vote. Before the vote, a motion must be made. A *motion* is a suggestion to take action. One group member makes a motion and another member seconds it. To *second* a motion means to show support for it. After a motion has been made and seconded, group members have an opportunity to discuss the motion. Under parliamentary procedure, the discussion must focus on the topic of the motion. Only one person can speak at a time. All members must be given an equal opportunity to state their opinions. During the discussion, a member may move to *amend*, or change, the motion. When the discussion is over, a vote is taken by raised hand, voice ("aye" or "nay"), or a written ballot. The group must follow the decision of the *majority*. Usually a majority equals half the total number of members present plus one.

Math Connection

Fundraiser Proceeds

The North High School FCCLA chapter raised money to help a homeless shelter. They raised $365.00 at a car wash and $270.50 at a bake sale. 243 students donated $2.00 each, and 332 students donated $3.00 each. How much did the FCCLA chapter raise for the homeless shelter?

Elijah, the group treasurer, determined the amount the group raised in the following way:

First, he multiplied the numbers of students and their donations.

$243 \times \$2.00 = \$486.00$

$332 \times \$3.00 = \$996.00$

Then to get the total, he added the amounts from above to the proceeds from the car wash and bake sale.

$\$365.00 + \$270.50 + \$486.00 + \$996.00 = \$2,117.50$

Choosing Effective Programs and Activities

Some people join organizations because they need outlets for their energy and ideas. Unfortunately, it seems there are never enough of these people. According to research, about 10 percent of the members in a typical group do most of the work. About 80 percent tag along and enjoy belonging to the group. The other 10 percent criticize and complain about what is being done.

As a leader, your job is to be sure to keep the interest of the active members and involve the others. If you succeed, your group will be doing better than most. As you work toward this goal, try not to let the criticism of a few members squelch your enthusiasm.

The key to keeping members involved is planning good activities. The activities of a group should be planned around one main goal for the year. The goal should relate to the personal needs and priorities of group members. It should make a difference in the lives of the members. Having one main goal provides a standard for measuring the group's progress throughout the year. It also creates a focus that builds interest.

A group's goal can be represented in every program and activity. For instance, your group's goal might be to improve communications. Programs could be built around ways to communicate with people. Emphasis could be placed not only on verbal communication, but also on body language, music, and poetry. A fund-raising project might be selling note cards or stationery. A related activity could be becoming pen pals with people of other cultures. You might sponsor a fashion show that features clothes that communicate. You could communicate food customs by preparing international dishes. Going on a picnic with preschoolers might help you improve your communication with children. Although the activities are varied, they all relate to communication. Questions that guide the selection of programs and activities appear in **3-6**.

Mental Health Awareness

Interactive Social Flow

Interactive social flow describes the satisfying experience of being part of a group where everyone works to achieve the group's goals. The communication, cooperation, and social aspect of contributing to a group can often feel more rewarding than reaching the same goal alone. These positive feelings increase enthusiasm for starting another project.

3-6

Asking these questions can help group members select worthwhile programs and activities for their organization.

Stay Within the Limits

All groups have to operate within limits. You have limited amounts of time and money to spend on activities. You have a limited number of members who can participate. In order to have a successful group, you must avoid planning projects that are beyond your resources.

Certain school rules often limit what a group can and cannot do. When planning programs and activities, it is important for your group to follow these rules. You should not do anything that jeopardizes your group's relationship with others. You want to keep on good terms with

Selecting Programs and Activities

- Is this program or activity consistent with the overall purposes of the group?
- Will it help us attain our goals?
- In what ways will members benefit?
- In what ways will others benefit?
- Will the program or activity be enjoyable?
- Can it be completed within a reasonable length of time?
- Will it provide opportunities for members to grow as individuals?
- Will all people who wish to work on this program or activity be permitted to do so?
- Will it be so difficult that members will become discouraged?
- Will this program or activity provide a break from the usual routine?

other groups in your school. You need to preserve the respect of school officials. You also need to maintain the support of the community.

If you have concerns about whether or not your group is operating within the rules, investigate before proceeding. Sometimes the limits can be stretched a bit to accommodate special situations. However, it is best to get approval in advance. Your group is likely to suffer negative consequences if it tries stretching the limits without permission.

There may be times when your group cannot do something you want it to do. Accept the facts. Part of learning about group participation is learning to cope with disappointments.

Publicize

You need to let people know about your group's exciting programs and activities. Your group should have a publicity committee to help get the word out. Publicizing your group's plans can also attract new members to the group. Publicity can help build support for your group in the community, too.

You may want to announce upcoming events in your school and local newspapers. If you plan something very newsworthy, you might want to contact local radio and TV stations. The yearbook is another important place to publicize school groups. If your group is part of a national organization, you might submit stories for their state and national publications. Once you start, you will find many interesting ways to publicize your group.

Evaluate Your Accomplishments

Make a point of evaluating your group's programs and activities. Check to see how much your group has accomplished toward achieving your goal. Groups that do not take time to do this miss one of the real satisfactions of work. You may be surprised at all you have done.

Evaluating your accomplishments can help you improve in the future. As you think back, try to remember some activities that sounded great but did not work. Discuss why those activities failed. Discuss how your group can prevent similar failures in the future.

Teamwork. Lee is a team member on a project. Lee's team works well together. They share information and motivate each other to work smarter.

Reading
Review

1. What is the purpose of most youth organizations?
2. List five types of information an effective constitution should include.
3. List two guidelines of parliamentary procedure.
4. What is the key to keeping members involved in a group?

Summary

Both leaders and followers are needed to create teams. An effective team is the result of committed members who put team goals first. Team members listen to others and are respectful of others' ideas. Through teamwork, members can develop leadership skills. Team settings are often diverse.

Leaders are likely to use a combination of autocratic, democratic, and laissez-faire leadership styles. Leaders are expected to set an example to motivate group members. They need to use tact and give recognition as they guide group planning as well.

As a teen, you may belong to one or more youth organizations. You may join a professional organization when you enter the workplace. These and all organizations need to follow some guidelines in order to be effective. Groups need to elect officers who will hold meetings and plan worthwhile programs and activities. Group events need to be publicized to generate interest and evaluated to improve future planning.

Critical Thinking

1. **Develop a plan.** Imagine you are the captain of the volleyball team that is selling candy to raise money. As an effective leader, explain how you might set an example, motivate followers, guide planning, use tact, and give recognition for this project.

2. **Apply processes.** Imagine that your Family, Career and Community Leaders of America chapter has a concern about traffic along Main Street where young children walk to school. Develop a plan that addresses this concern.

3. **Recognize alternatives.** What type of leadership would you recommend in each of the following situations? Explain your choices.
   A. Organizing the planting of a vegetable garden with a group of young 4-H members who have no prior gardening experience.
   B. Planning a fund-raiser for a local youth group.
   C. Serving as a campaign manager for a friend who is running for a seat on the student council.
   D. Teaching a new play to a football team.

21st Century Applications

4. **Social and cross-cultural skills.** You may have been taught to treat others how *you* would like to be treated. This is often referred to as the *golden rule*. Productively working with others who have a background different from yours may require that you learn to treat others as *they* wish to be treated. Conduct research online about cultural differences related to personal space, time, gestures/body language, and relationships with authority figures. Create a T-chart

that shows the cultural difference on the left side of the chart and ways you could adapt your interactions to account for that difference on the right side of the chart.

5. **Global awareness.** To become career ready, it is important to learn how to communicate clearly and effectively. You may need to communicate with people outside of your city, state, or country. Create an outline that includes information about the importance of working as part of a team, even when team members are not physically in the same place. Using your outline, make a presentation to your class about successfully working in teams.

6. **Creativity and innovation.** Being creative and innovative are two characteristics that many professionals possess. Whether you see problems as challenges or opportunities, creative thinking is often required to reach a solution. Many new inventions come from trying to solve a problem. Describe a situation in your life or in history in which a problem led to the creation of a new way of doing things or a new invention.

7. **Environmental literacy.** Work in small groups to write a plan to get your school involved with recycling paper. Use word processing or publishing software to create a newsletter promoting the plan.

8. **Flexibility and adaptability.** Assume you are the vice president of a volunteer group at your school. At today's meeting, the group will discuss how to organize a food drive. You remember that the president of the group left school early today due

to sickness. This means it is up to you to lead today's meeting. Create a brief plan outlining your steps to organize the group meeting. What type of leadership will you use? Will you involve other group members to help run the meeting?

Core
Skills

9. **Writing.** Write an essay on the leadership in a country of your choice. What type of leadership is being used? Provide examples that demonstrate this leadership style. Remember to cite any sources of information used in your report.

10. **Reading.** Read a biography or an autobiography of a famous leader. Share the story with your classmates. Work together to identify the leadership style he or she used most often. Also list the leadership skills the leader used to involve his or her followers.

11. **Speaking.** Take turns leading a class discussion. Have other students rate your speaking skills and give constructive criticism. Why are speaking skills important to leaders?

12. **Social studies.** Research a country with an autocratic type of leadership. Write a paper comparing and contrasting that leadership to the democratic leadership of the United States.

13. **Listening.** Ask permission to attend a meeting of a school club or organization. At the meeting, listen carefully and observe how the meeting

is run. What type of leadership is used? Is the parliamentary procedure followed? Then write a summary of your experience. Did the meeting run smoothly? Why or why not? Do you have suggestions for how the meeting could run more smoothly next time?

14. **Speaking.** Use presentation software to give a presentation on a group to which you belong or have belonged.

15. **Writing.** A *press release* is a written notice of an event that is given to a newspaper or other source for wide distribution. Press releases are short and include the *who*, *what*, *where*, *when*, *how*, and *why* of a story. Practice writing a fictional press release announcing an event for a school organization of your choice. Remember to reread and edit your press release. Then exchange your announcement with a classmate for critiquing. Place a final copy of your press release in your portfolio.

Leadership
Development

As your chapter prepares for the Parliamentary Procedure STAR Event, follow parliamentary law while running business meetings throughout the year.

Portfolio
Builder

Membership in a student organization can help you build self-esteem and develop a positive self-concept. If you are not already involved in a student organization, join one that interests you. If you are already active in an organization, volunteer to lead a special project. Document your participation for your portfolio, including:

- name, description, and logo of the organization
- dates of your participation
- description of your roles and responsibilities
- list of special projects or activities
- photo of an important project or activity

Journal
Writing

You are a member of the school beautification club. Members of the club voted to replace the worn draperies in the student lounge. Your club leader asked a small task force to research the group's options for raising funds. Once the membership discussed the options, the group voted on a fund-raising event.

Your leader then suggested group members get prices for ready-made and custom-made draperies. These prices were compared to the cost of materials for making the draperies yourselves. Group members met several times to discuss the possibilities. The group is meeting next week to vote on a final decision.

Write About It: *What type of leadership is being used? How would you feel about being a member of this group? What type of leadership, in your opinion, would best fit this situation? Give reasons for your choice.*

Career Discovery

Resource Management

Unit Two

Human Services

The Consumer Services Pathway within the Human Services career cluster includes careers that focus on helping people manage their resources. Bank tellers, insurance brokers, and real estate agents are a few examples of consumer services careers.

Human Services Pathways

Early Childhood Development and Services
Counseling and Mental Health Services
Family and Community Services
Personal Care Services
Consumer Services

Sanjay Deva/Shutterstock.com

Education and Training

The Teaching and Training Pathway within the Education and Training career cluster includes careers that work closely with others to advance their knowledge and skill sets. Human resources managers, training managers, teachers, and librarians are examples of education and training careers.

Education and Training Pathways

Administration and Administrative Support
Professional Support Services
Teaching and Training

Dragon Images/Shutterstock.com

Career Spotlight:
Real Estate Broker/Sales Agent

- **Description.** Real estate brokers and sales agents help people buy, sell, or rent a property. Although they can assist clients with commercial or residential properties, most sell residential property. Brokers and sales agents can serve buyers or sellers. They meet with clients to understand their property needs and how much they can afford. They also stay current on different types of financing options available, zoning, and fair housing laws. Real estate brokers are licensed to manage their own businesses, while sales agents must work for a broker. Most brokers and sales agents are self-employed, work irregular hours, and set their own schedules.
- **Education and training.** Real estate brokers and sales agents must complete real estate courses that are generally state-accredited to be eligible for licensure. Some states waive these courses if a licensure candidate has completed college courses in real estate. Licensing candidates must be 18 years of age, complete necessary real estate courses, and pass the licensing exam in their state.
- **Skills and personal qualities.** Real estate brokers must have strong interpersonal skills. They must be pleasant and show enthusiasm and trustworthiness to attract and keep clients. Real estate brokers and sales agents must be organized and able to work independently.
- **Job outlook.** Job growth through 2028 is projected to grow faster than average for all occupations. The demand is high because people use brokers and sales agents when looking for a home.

Human Services

Career Spotlight:
Human Resources Manager

- **Description.** Human resources managers plan, coordinate, and direct the human resources activities of a company. They are responsible for recruiting, interviewing, and hiring new staff, as well as serving as a link between a company and its employees. Human resources managers sometimes have to deal with difficult situations such as disciplining or firing employees. They also make sure employees receive correct compensation and benefits for their work.
- **Education and training.** Requirements vary, but most human resources managers are required to have a bachelor's degree in human resources, business administration, or a related field. They should also have several years of related work experience. Some employers may require a master's degree and certification.
- **Skills and personal qualities.** Human resources managers must enjoy working with others and solving problems and conflicts. Strong interpersonal, communication, decision-making, and problem-solving skills are essential. Sensitivity to others' problems, social awareness, and strong listening skills are also needed.
- **Job outlook.** Job growth is projected to grow faster than average for all occupations through 2028. Visit the *Occupational Outlook Handbook* online to learn more about a career as a human resources manager.

Education & Training

Sources: States' Career Clusters Initiative, Bureau of Labor Statistics Career Guide to Industries

Chapter 4
Learning to Manage

Reading Prep

Before reading this chapter, review the objectives for each section. Based on this information, write down five to seven items that you think are important to note while you are reading.

Concept Organizer

Make a T-chart with one column labeled *Material Resources* and the other labeled *Human Resources*. List resources you currently possess under each category.

G-WLEARNING.com

Click on the activity icon ↗ to visit www.g-wlearning. com/comprehensive/8062 to access online vocabulary activities using key terms from the chapter.

Section 4-1

Goals and Resources

Objectives

After studying this section, you will be able to

- **describe** the different types of goals.
- **identify** your resources, recognize their limits, and apply techniques to make the most of them.

Key Terms ↱

management	long-term goal	community resources
resources	visionary goal	
goal	material resources	natural resources
short-term goal	human resources	

You live in a busy world. You have to keep track of responsibilities, assignments, and deadlines. Keeping all these details straight is not always easy. Learning some management skills can help you maintain control of your life.

Management can be defined as wisely using what you have to achieve goals. The means used are called resources. **Resources** may be time, objects, services, or abilities.

Setting and Prioritizing Goals

Goals are the aims people consciously try to reach. When you reach one of your goals, you attain something you wanted and considered important. Your efforts will be rewarded with a feeling of satisfaction.

People set goals that reflect their values. Perhaps one of your values is physical fitness. You might set a goal of jogging one mile each day. Perhaps you value knowledge. You might set a goal of earning a degree.

Your goals help to make you unique. Even when you have the same values as someone else, your goals may differ. Some goals involve only yourself. Some involve your family and friends. Some involve groups, **4-1**. Some even involve people and organizations you do not know yet. For instance, you may want to work in the sales department of a large company, but you may not know at which company.

Short-Term and Long-Term Goals

You may have several goals at the same time. Some are **short-term goals**. You can reach these goals in an hour, a day, or even a week. Others are **long-term goals**. You may need several months or even several years to reach these goals.

Suppose you want to be the best high jumper in your state. This would be a long-term goal. As a freshman, you could join the track team. During the next four years, you could try to reach many short-term goals. You could work to get in good shape. You could set a goal of jumping a little higher each week. You could try winning the high jump events at track meets. Finally, you might be ready to reach your long-term goal. Perhaps you could win first place in the high jump event at the state track meet.

Visionary Goals

You may have a few goals that you do not really expect to achieve. These can be called **visionary goals**. Though you know you probably will not reach these goals, they are worthwhile. They can inspire you to do more than you thought you were capable of doing. They may also add some interesting experiences to your life.

4-1

Through teamwork, group members can accomplish many goals they might not achieve alone.

Suppose you had a visionary goal of winning an Olympic gold medal for high jumping. The effort you put into reaching this visionary goal could yield interesting experiences. This mental image could help you win a local meet. You might get the chance to talk to and work out with other prospective members of the Olympic team. You may even have the chance to compete in the Olympic games.

Fixed and Flexible Goals

Some goals are *fixed*. This means they are related to a specific date in time. For example, your term paper is due on a certain date. You must achieve your goal of finishing your paper by this date or receive a failing grade.

Other goals are *flexible*. They can be achieved at any time. For instance, you may be trying to achieve a goal of having $1,000 in your savings account. This can be done over a period of time with no particular end date. You can just keep saving until you have achieved your goal.

Steps in Setting and Achieving Goals

Have you thought about your goals? What careers interest you? What do you want from life? Setting goals is an important part of achievement. Goals give you a sense of direction. They add motivation to keep you moving forward.

The first step in setting and achieving goals is to make a list of what you want out of life, **4-2**. Be as honest with yourself as possible as you make your list. Be sure to include both short- and long-term goals. You may want to set some visionary goals for yourself, too. Just remember to keep them in their proper perspective. Do not feel disappointed if your visionary goals are never achieved.

The second step is to consider your values. Determine which ideals and objects are the most important. Make a list of them. How will they influence the goals you have listed? You will not want to give up what you consider important to achieve your goals. For instance, suppose owning a car was one of your goals. You could ask your parents to give you the money you need. However, if you value independence and personal achievement, you would find another way to reach your goal.

The third step is to list ways you could achieve your goals. Give yourself several options. Life continuously

4-2

Owning a house one day may be one of your life's goals.

Mental Health Awareness

Manageable Goals

Goals that are out of reach can add stress and anxiety. Keeping goals manageable helps you stay positive while pursuing them. Learn what you can reasonably expect from resources, such as money and help from others. Setting short-term goals and time frames for achieving those goals can also help you stay positive.

Innovation. Ben views mistakes as opportunities to learn and improve. He often reaches his goals by trying again and not giving up.

changes. You change, and the people around you change. Likewise, the situations and problems you face change. Having a few alternate plans is always a good idea.

Although you need to include options in your list, you should keep the list realistic. You should not count on luck to help you achieve your goals. You might win a huge sweepstakes, but your chances are not very good. You probably will have to find another way to achieve your goals.

The fourth step is to make some definite plans. Goals will not be reached unless specific steps are taken. Try to group some short-term goals with related long-term goals. Perhaps achieving some short-term goals will lead you closer to the achievement of your long-term goals. On the other hand, you may find you have to sacrifice some goals to achieve others. For instance, you may have to give up some free evenings to take courses at a nearby school. You may have to give up a summer vacation to earn money for a new car. You may have to delay marriage until you have become established in a career.

The final step in setting and achieving goals is to establish deadlines and rewards. *Deadlines*, or time goals, help you direct your efforts. They state what needs to be done first, what should be done next, and what can wait. A final deadline or time goal can help you work efficiently to get a job done.

Meeting Your Goals

When you meet a deadline, you deserve a reward. You can challenge yourself more fully when you know your efforts are worthwhile. Unpleasant tasks need special rewards. You can promise yourself a weekend vacation, a free afternoon, or a new shirt. The size of the reward is not as important as feeling good about completing the task and achieving the goal.

The key to success in setting and achieving goals is knowing yourself and what you want to accomplish. Some people do not know what they really want in life. They simply try a variety of activities. By keeping their options open, many find what is right for them. You can save yourself a great deal of time and frustration by trying to know yourself. You can do this by thinking about your values, your goals, and the methods you use to achieve your goals.

Recognizing Your Values and Standards

You tend to take actions that support your values and maintain your standards. Therefore, you need to recognize the values and standards that relate to your problem. They will affect the way you choose to reach your goal. For instance, if you think health and exercise are important, you might consider walking to the game. If you value convenience, you may ask a friend to pick you up. Suppose you have a high standard for promptness. You may not want to ride with a friend who cannot get to the stadium in time for the kickoff.

Determining Your Resources

The types and amounts of resources people have vary. Look at and try to assess your resources. This will help you determine which to use to reach your goal.

Material and Human Resources

Resources can be classified as material or human. See **4-3**. **Material resources** are not physically or mentally part of a person. They include time, money, possessions, and community resources.

Human resources come from within people. They include skills, knowledge, talents, energy, and people themselves. Athletic skill is a human resource that helps ballplayers achieve the goal of winning a game. Teachers are human resources that help students reach the goal of getting an education. Energy needed to walk is a human resource you could use to get to the game.

People do not always recognize the value of their human resources. These resources can often be used in place of material resources. For instance, sewing skills can be used instead of money to make clothes rather than buy them. Although fabric and sewing items cost money, they cost a lot less than a finished garment. Also, cooking skills can be used to prepare food at home instead of spending considerably more money to eat out.

Many times, human resources need to be used with material resources to reach goals. For instance, skill in operating a computer is a human resource. However, it must be coupled with the material resource of a computer in order to be useful. With this blend of resources, countless goals can be reached. You could write reports and calculate math problems to reach goals at school. You could send e-mail to reach communication goals. You could access information to achieve research goals.

Community Resources

Community resources are parks, schools, libraries, and other facilities that are shared by many people. Kitchen equipment and food supplies are material resources that could help you reach a goal of satisfying hunger. Public transportation is a material resource that could help you reach your goal of getting to the game.

Resources	
Human	**Material**
abilities	appliances
communication	car
creativity	clothing
dedication	fire and police protection
enthusiasm	food
flexibility	housing
interests	libraries
knowledge	money
optimism	parks
people	schools
skills	technology
talents	time

4-3

Both human and material resources can be used to meet goals.

Serving Your Community

Create an announcement prompting people to care for community resources in your area. Such issues as refraining from littering and writing graffiti can also be addressed. Obtain permission to post the announcement on the school's website, or make an announcement through the PA system or local radio station.

Natural Resources

Natural resources are taken from the land. Agricultural products, forest products, and fossil fuels are examples.

Resource Limitations

All people have a variety of resources. However, they have limited amounts of each resource. No one has an endless amount of money, time, energy, or any other resource.

The limits on resources will be different at different points in your life. For instance, the longer you work, the greater your income is likely to be. This means you will have more money available when you are older than you do now. On the other hand, as you get older, you are likely to have less energy than you do now.

In addition to being limited, many resources are *expendable*. In other words, they can be used up. For instance, a piece of paper is an expendable resource. It can be used to reach the goal of sending a letter. The piece of paper cannot be used again to reach a future goal of writing a report. See **4-4**.

Not all expended resources are gone forever. Some can be renewed. For instance, taking a nap or eating a snack can restore your energy. The piece of used paper can be recycled to make more paper.

Some resources are actually *expandable*. Solving problems, making decisions, and using skills, for example, tend to improve with use. In fact, they may weaken when not used.

4-4

Food is an expendable resource. It can be used only once to meet the goal of satisfying hunger.

Conserving Human and Material Resources

Knowing which resources are limited and which can be renewed or expanded can help you plan. You need to think about how future goals might be affected before deciding to use resources for present goals. You do not want to deplete a resource now if you will need it in the future. In your goal of getting to the game, taking public transportation would require money. Money is an expendable resource. If you have a goal of buying a gift next week, you might not want to use this resource now. Walking to the game might be a better choice since it requires energy—a renewable resource.

Flexibility of Resources

Resources are flexible. They can be decreased and increased in a number of ways. For instance, breaking your leg would temporarily decrease your athletic skill. Taking a computer class would increase your knowledge and skill with computers. Losing your job would decrease your income. Winning a contest would suddenly increase the amount of money you have available.

You cannot plan to win a contest. However, you can use various techniques to help you make the most of limited resources. These techniques include substituting, combining, and exchanging resources.

Substituting Resources

One resource can often be substituted for another because most goals can be reached in more than one way. People often substitute a plentiful resource for one that is more limited. Friendship, money, and energy are all resources. They could all be used to reach the goal of getting to the game. If you have too little money, you could substitute friendship or energy.

Combining Resources

Most goals are reached through the use of a combination of resources. For instance, walking to the game would require both time and energy. Riding with a friend would require the friend's car as well as the friend.

Family members often combine their resources. Together, a family unit has more resources than any one person in the family. Each family member can contribute human resources. Some members may cook; others may be able to repair appliances. All family members may contribute to cleaning and other home care tasks. Families often have an easier time meeting goals when they work together.

Exchanging Resources

Resources must often be exchanged to achieve a goal. Money is probably the resource that is exchanged most frequently. Money can be exchanged for a wide range of goods and services. Food, clothing, furniture, vacations, and the services of doctors, plumbers, and mechanics can all be obtained in exchange for money.

Money is not the only resource that is exchanged. People exchange time, energy, and skills, too. For instance, you might use your math skill to tutor your friend in exchange for a ride to the game. You might use your sewing skills and several hours of time to create clothes too expensive to buy.

Reading
Review

1. Wisely using resources to achieve goals is known as _____ .
2. Give an example of a short-term goal, a long-term goal, and a visionary goal.
3. True or false. Possessions are human resources.
4. What are three techniques that can be used to help make the most of limited resources?

Section 4-2

Decision Making and the Management Process

Objectives

After studying this section, you will be able to
- **explain** the importance of management skills.
- **outline** the steps in the decision-making process.
- **explain** the management process.

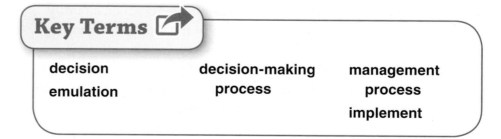

Key Terms

decision
emulation

decision-making
process

management
process
implement

The way you manage your daily life will greatly influence the quality of your life. You are the manager of your life. That means you are responsible for making the choices and decisions that will move you toward your goals. Management skills will help you solve problems and make decisions. By the decisions you make on a daily basis, you move closer to your goals. You move toward something you want to achieve—something that is important to you. If you are a good manager, you will be more likely to achieve the quality of life you desire.

Solving Problems and Making Decisions

A **decision** is a conscious or unconscious response to a problem or an issue. Whenever you make up your mind about what you will do or say, you are making a decision. Some decisions are made without thinking; they just happen. Some decisions are actively made after much thought. Either way, your values, goals, standards, needs, and wants will affect the decisions you make.

Making Routine Decisions

Some decisions seem simple. These *routine decisions* are made often and without much thought. For instance, you need to brush your teeth every morning. You probably do this when you first wake up or after you finish breakfast. You do it without thinking about the pros and cons. Habit causes you to make many daily decisions without even thinking about them. There are other ways to make routine decisions as well.

*Impulsive decisi*ons are made on the spot. You see something; you want it; you get it, **4-5**. Perhaps you are in the supermarket. A product promoter is serving bite-size portions of a new brand of pizza to shoppers. It looks good, so you pick up a portion and pop it into your mouth. You never asked yourself "should I taste this?" You just tasted it impulsively.

Emulation is a regular source of decisions for teens. **Emulation** means you do what most other people around you are doing. What do you wear to school? Students often dress like other students. If your school has an official uniform, you get up in the morning and put it on. If your school has an "unofficial uniform" such as jeans, sweatshirts, and athletic shoes, you probably emulate that dress code.

Creativity is the motivator for some decisions. You just want to do

Persuasion. Jeremy tries to improve morale at his company by suggesting ways to solve problems identified by his work team. He focuses on solutions to problems so his supervisor will be receptive.

4-5

People often buy items they see on an impulse.

something different. For instance, when Sara's family decided to spend more time together, she suggested an old-fashioned marshmallow roast.

Default is the act of not making a decision. For example, you could not decide whether to go to the movies or go to the dance. You ended up doing neither. You stayed home. By not deciding between the two options you had considered, you ended up making a decision by default.

Steps in Decision Making

Some decisions are more complex. Deciding whether or not to get a part-time job, making a career choice, or buying a car are examples. These will need to be made more carefully as many of these decisions tend to have long-lasting effects. When you have important decisions to make, the decision-making process can help you make the decisions that are best for you. The **decision-making process** is a set of logical steps to follow when making complex decisions.

1. *Define the problem or the decision to be made.* Be sure that you recognize the real problem and its importance to your life.
2. *Establish your goals.* Review your long-term goals and what you want out of life. Review the short-term goals you have set for yourself, too. Then establish new, additional goals related to the problem.
3. *Prioritize your goals.* List your goals in order of importance, placing the goals you want to accomplish most first on your list. Direct most of your efforts toward your major goals. Your less important goals can be put on a waiting list.
4. *Look for resources.* Make a list of everything available to you that will help you reach your goals.
5. *Identify alternatives.* Make a list of all the pros and cons of each alternative. Try to keep an open mind as you do this. Avoid letting any personal prejudices become stumbling blocks to progress. A good way to test alternatives is to ask yourself these questions:
   - Would I want to keep this decision a secret from others?
   - Will this decision hurt anyone (including myself) either emotionally or physically?
   - Can this decision have a negative influence on my goals?

   Answering *yes* to any of these questions means caution. You may want to reconsider the decision and choose another alternative.
6. *Make a decision.* If you have been guided by your most objective thinking, you will probably be happy with the decision you make. Decision making often involves taking risks. You may make some errors and create some conflicts. However, if you follow these steps, most of your decisions should produce good results.
7. *Carry out the decision.* After thinking through and making your decision, take action to carry it out. This can be a difficult step, but it is important. You must make the effort to follow through.

Living Green

Use the steps of the decision-making process in managing the upkeep of your room. Use the process in deciding which items, such as old clothes, sports equipment, or electronics, should be recycled, given away, or sold.

8. *Evaluate the results of your decision.* Once a decision is made and action is taken, the result cannot be changed. This is part of learning to take responsibility for your decisions by accepting the consequences. You can, however, benefit from past experience by using it to help you make a future decision. To do this, you need to evaluate your decision. That means looking back on your decision and judging its success. Did your decision solve your problem? Did the decision help you reach your desired goal? Are you satisfied with the results? Try to see what did or did not work. In evaluating your decisions, you learn from your mistakes as well as from your successes.

As you can see, the decision-making process can be applied to all kinds of decisions and problems. You can use it for important decisions you make every day. The steps can also be applied to more complex decisions such as those involving your education, your career, parenthood, or major purchases, **4-6**. These major decisions can impact your family, friends, society as a whole, and your future.

4-6

Using the decision-making process can help people make important decisions that impact life goals.

The Management Process

Management involves following a series of steps called the **management process**. This process helps you plan how to use resources to achieve goals. In some ways, the management process is similar to the decision-making process. The management process can be used by families and other groups as well as by individuals. It helps all members know what goals have been set and what plans are to be followed. Otherwise, group resources may not be used efficiently and group goals might not be met.

Planning

The first step in the management process is to form a plan. Begin forming your plan by deciding exactly what steps to take to reach your goal. Think about the best order for accomplishing the steps.

When working toward a short-term goal, like your goal to get to the game, this step may be brief. You might plan to check the bus schedule,

Analyze and Solve

Choose a real or imaginary problem. Write a paper explaining how you could use the decision-making process to solve the problem.

walk to the bus stop, and get on the bus. Long-term goals, however, will require more in-depth planning.

Organizing

For long-term goals, you should write down the steps of your plan for frequent review. Be sure to list everything you must do. Note people you must see and materials you will need. When you make a thorough plan, you are less likely to forget little details.

Determine standards for each step in your plan. This will help you know when you have accomplished the step to your satisfaction. Set deadlines, too. Deadlines keep you working toward the goal by preventing you from getting sidetracked.

Implementing

To **implement** a plan simply means to carry it out. Putting your plan into action is the next step of the management process. Again, this step may take little effort when working toward short-term goals. It would involve actually checking the schedule, walking to the bus stop, and getting on the bus.

For a long-term goal, you might want to divide large tasks into several smaller tasks that are easier to accomplish. Check off the items listed on your plan as you complete them. Try to honor the deadlines you set for yourself. This will give you a feeling of success.

Evaluating

You will probably find yourself evaluating each step in your plan as you complete it. You will check to see if you have met your deadlines and maintained the standards you set.

After you have completed all the steps in your plan, you will want to do a final evaluation. You might ask yourself the following questions: Were my goals reasonable? Did I use my resources as I had anticipated? Was I able to follow my plan? How can I improve when I do this again? Your evaluation might tell you that walking to and from the bus stop took more energy than you had planned. You might decide that next time you will do just as well to walk to the game.

Many people like to keep records of their evaluations that can be used for reaching future goals. Such records can make planning easier the next time.

Mental Health Awareness

Using Failure to Succeed

Fear of failure stops some people from trying again to reach their goal. If seen positively, however, failure can be a step toward success. For example, the chocolate maker Milton Hershey failed in his first two attempts at the candy business. After several years of working and refining his product, he established a company that became one of the biggest candy sellers in the world.

Reading
Review

1. Explain what it means to be the manager of your life.
2. List the eight steps in the decision-making process.
3. List the steps of the management process.

Section 4-3

Managing Your Time

Objectives

After studying this section, you will be able to
- **explain** the importance of time management.
- **list** some ways to help manage time.

Key Terms

time management   multitasking

Sometimes people remember exactly what they did yesterday or last week. At other times, they cannot recall. Was the time well spent, or was it wasted? Managing time is very important because once this resource is wasted, it is never regained. It is lost forever.

Why Plan Your Time?

Time management is the ability to plan and use time well. It is not a way to change time but to change people. Time management is really about self-management. By managing time, you accomplish more of what you want to do. This is the main reason for time management.

In addition, there are several other benefits of managing time. You meet your deadlines. You are ready to face each day's responsibilities. By managing time, you can put small periods of time to good use so none is wasted. You complete your short-term goals, work toward long-term goals, and even find time for visionary goals.

Short-Term Goals Are Met

Short-term goals are your immediate aims for today and this week. For example, you attend classes, do homework, and meet deadlines for term papers. You also do household tasks and possibly hold a part-time job. Fulfilling all these duties does not happen automatically. It is the result of managing time well.

Long-Term Goals Are Met

A long-term goal, such as choosing a career, takes more than a month or even a year to achieve. These goals require considerable thought and preparation. By dividing long-term goals into smaller steps, however, you can work on them gradually. As a result, you will be better prepared to make major life decisions when the time comes.

Some long-term goals involve perfecting skills and finding helpful resources to make decisions. Related activities include looking ahead to foresee and prevent problems that may stop you from reaching your goals.

Visionary Goals Are Addressed

Managing time allows you to dream, explore, and fit unexpected opportunities into your schedule. Staying ahead of deadlines can help you do this.

Preparing in advance for scheduled events gives you flexibility when unplanned opportunities suddenly arise, **4-7**. You can then adjust your schedule to take advantage of them without sacrificing your performance in other areas.

Steps in Time Management

Busy people who handle many tasks well make time management look easy. With practice, it can be. Time is managed in three steps: planning and organizing, carrying out the plan, and evaluating the results.

Planning and Organizing

Before planning actually begins, you need a clear work area. You also need to review your goals and values. Only then can you develop a to-do list and weekly plan.

Good planning begins with an organized work area. Not being able to grab a pencil and paper to record your thoughts will slow the planning process. It is important to have a neat workspace with storage for all your tools. Returning tools to their proper places will allow you to find them when needed.

- *Consider goals and values.* Consider where you want to direct your life and spend time on related activities. Occasionally you must skip some interesting activities to allow room for those most important to you.

- *Make to-do lists.* Activities that are not part of a routine should be added to a to-do list. Some people arrange their lists in priority order. Other people rank the must-do tasks A; the next-do tasks B; the should-do tasks C; and the can-wait tasks D. All A and B tasks are included in the day's plan. C and D tasks are handled as time allows.

4-7

This student stays up-to-date on her school assignments so she can avoid stress and maybe attend special events that are suddenly announced.

- *Create a weekly plan.* Map each day on paper so you can see which hours are filled and which are open. Look ahead to assignments due later in the month that should be started this week. Then take one day at a time, determining what to do on each day to be prepared for the next. Transfer items from your to-do list to the weekly plan, scheduling them to suit your needs.

Implementing

Now it is time to put your plan into action. Remember your standards of excellence. Think: "Do it well so it reflects the pride I have in myself."

Do not be afraid to think creatively. Find new ways to do old tasks. Creativity can help you implement your management plan and give you a greater sense of accomplishment.

Evaluating

Evaluation may be as simple as noting whether or not the plan worked. If you finish all the tasks scheduled for the day, you can begin working on tomorrow's. That will help you get ahead of your deadlines. If some tasks could not be completed, ask yourself why. Did you misjudge the amount of time needed for each task? This is quite likely to occur with your first few efforts at planning. With practice, you will be able to set more realistic deadlines.

Remember that a time management plan is simply a guide. It is not meant to be a perfect balance between available time and tasks to do. If you scheduled too few tasks one day, use your spare time well. If you fall behind in completing your A list, reschedule whatever you can for later.

Managing Time Wisely

To get started on managing time well, look for some helpers. See what tools are available to help you create your weekly plans. Then keep your plans on track by using strategies that help you use time effectively.

Using Time Management Aids

All you really need to get started is pencil and paper. Also, you will need a calendar to see the "big picture" so you can stay on schedule.

Visit an office supply store and browse the planners, calendars, and schedules. Also check the calendars and task lists that can be created by computer. Handheld electronic organizers are quite useful tools. Also consider the features of your cell phone. Some include a calendar for recording important dates such as due dates for projects and assignments. (Keep in mind your school's rules regarding use of cell phones in class.)

Experiment with several tools to see which work best for you. If you find what you need in one tool, your plans will be easier to manage. Use a tool that shows an entire week in a glance and allows you to easily add

Mental Health Awareness

Using Deadlines

Rushing to meet a deadline can result in stress and poor performance. Think twice, however, before pushing a deadline back. Fixed deadlines have an emotional benefit that helps you meet goals on time. Psychologists call this the "goal looms larger" effect. The closer you get to your goal, the more motivated you feel to reach it.

Wellness Awareness

Research the relationship between a well-nourished, rested body and a person's effective use of time.

new tasks. Do not get complex tools that require great effort to operate. This could cost you more time than it saves!

Using Time Management Strategies

Using time well is a skill that requires practice. Here are several strategies to help you reach that goal.

- *Steer clear of time wasters.* Do television programs or phone calls from friends sidetrack you from scheduled tasks? Discipline yourself to follow your plan as closely as possible.

- *Avoid procrastination.* Do you stare into space, only to realize later that too much time has passed? Make a point of starting each task in a timely manner.

- *Multitask whenever possible.* **Multitasking** means combining tasks or working on more than one task at a time. For example, you can combine family time with physical activity by encouraging family members to walk, bike, or run together. When cleaning up after meals, you might combine the chore with recreation. You can listen to the radio, watch TV, or socialize with family while you clean. Many tasks cannot be combined, but look for those that can be.

- *Break tasks into smaller steps.* In this way, time-consuming or complex tasks are much easier to do. Also, the satisfaction of crossing the finished steps off your list will motivate you to tackle the remaining steps.

- *Compensate for lost time.* Review your priorities, multitask when possible, and eliminate unnecessary tasks. This will help to get a schedule back on track.

- *Be prepared to use spare time.* Waiting to see a doctor or to take a sibling home from practice often lasts longer than expected. When you find yourself with spare time, be prepared to use it. If you go somewhere, always take a project along, such as a book to read or homework to do. See **4-8**.

With time management, you are in the driver's seat, determining the direction your life will take.

Energy and Task Management

Time is a limited resource and so is energy. All people have the same amount of time each day, but all people do not have

4-8

While waiting to be picked up after school, these students wisely use the time studying.

the same amount of energy. A time management plan must take into consideration the energy a person has to give. No amount of goal setting can force you to accomplish more than your body can handle.

Some students finish homework and go to bed at 11 p.m. Others must finish homework by 10 p.m. or they fall asleep. Do the students who go to bed earlier have fewer responsibilities? No. They may have more. How do they accomplish their tasks? They use time management techniques. They schedule their time well and avoid wasting it.

Sometimes you may feel inefficient and unable to do all you should. In these cases, ask yourself, "Am I getting enough sleep? Am I energized when I wake up in the morning?" Enough rest and recreation is needed for physical growth and for motivation to work. *All work and no play* is not a formula for healthy living. Rest and recreation should be included in your daily schedule.

Creativity is a helpful resource to use when you feel unable to keep up with your schedule. Look for shortcuts that take less time without cutting quality. Remember, you are in the driver's seat. When beginning a project, ask yourself, "How can I best accomplish this without sacrificing quality?" Consider your energy and ways to manage the tasks efficiently.

Managing Your Study Time

Study management begins by listening carefully to your teacher during class. Teachers often provide guidance on what portions of your text or assignment are most important. Paying attention in class can allow study time to be used more efficiently later.

Note taking is also an important study skill. Notes taken in class identify and clarify important points. They also remind you of what was emphasized in class. Notes are absolutely essential when information not included in your text is presented in class. Test taking becomes much easier when you have written notes from which to study.

To manage your study time at home, try to determine how you study best. Maybe this is at the dining room table or in your room at your desk. Try to work without the distractions of music or television. Once you have determined your best location for studying, map out time that you will use *only* for studying. Do not let yourself be distracted during this time by phone calls, visitors, or even other chores.

Balancing Personal, Family, Work, and Leisure Time

Balancing your time means making sure that everything you value is included in your schedule. Your obligations at school, home, and work absorb most of your daytime hours. Meeting these obligations also requires spending time with others and learning to communicate and work well with them. In addition, time must be devoted to physical activity, rest, and sleep—all of which your body requires.

21st Century Skills

Productivity. Kim's coworkers and supervisor appreciate that she is always on time for work and seldom calls in sick. Because she is at her workstation at the assigned time, productivity is maintained.

Besides these common activities, your values will prompt you to add others to the list. For example, you will want to spend some time helping others in need and beautifying your community. Satisfying your spiritual needs and practicing your religious beliefs is another important way to spend time.

Everyone has only 24 hours each day. To accomplish all the tasks that become a part of a busy schedule means managing yourself first. Then you can use your time to pursue your priorities.

Reading Review

1. Why plan for the use of time?
2. Which goals are addressed by a time management plan?
3. Name the three steps involved in time management.
4. Name four strategies for time management.

Section 4-4

Managing Your Money

Objectives

After studying this section, you will be able to

- **discuss** work compensation.
- **describe** the deductions taken from an employee's paycheck.
- **distinguish** between gross income and net income.
- **prepare** a personal budget.
- **list** ways to reduce flexible expenses.
- **explain** how a computer can be used to help manage money.

Key Terms ↗

budget	fringe benefits	fixed expense
hourly wage	gross income	flexible expense
salary	net income	

Money is an important resource. A **budget** is a plan to help you manage your money wisely. A budget will help you time your purchases so you can reach both short- and long-term goals. If you do not have a plan, it is easy to spend money on immediate wants without saving for future goals. The ability to plan purchases and stick with a budget is a mark of maturity.

Earning an Income

Employees who are paid a set amount of money for each hour they work earn an **hourly wage**. If they work more than 40 hours per week, they are usually paid overtime. *Overtime* pay is usually one and one-half times the employee's hourly wage. For instance, an employee who earns $8.50 per hour would receive $12.75 per hour of overtime pay.

In certain types of jobs, employees earn a salary. A **salary** is a set amount of money paid for a certain period of time. For instance, teachers sign a contract to do a specific job for a certain salary amount. To fulfill their contract, they spend time in and out of the classroom. Some full-time employees earn an annual salary, with the amount divided into equal payments during the period. If salaried employees in professional positions work more than 40 hours a week, however, they do not receive overtime pay.

Many full-time workers receive financial extras called **fringe benefits**. These benefits are provided by the employer in addition to the worker's regular paycheck. What types of fringe benefits can you expect when you work full-time? This depends on the company where you work. However, many companies offer the following benefits: health and life insurance, paid vacation time, paid sick days, savings plans, and retirement plans.

Understanding Your Paycheck

One of the benefits of employment is earning an income. When you receive your first paycheck, you may be surprised. The amount you were promised when you were hired will be different from the amount you

Math Connection

Calculating Overtime Pay

Jenny works as a store clerk. She is paid $11.50 per hour plus time and a half for overtime. The standard workweek is 40 hours. This week, Jenny worked 46 hours. What is Jenny's gross pay for this week?

First, calculate the pay for the first 40 hours.

$11.50 × 40 = $460.00

Then calculate the pay for 6 hours of overtime at 1½ times the normal hourly rate. Begin by finding the rate for one hour of overtime.

$11.50 × 1.5 = $17.25

Multiply the overtime rate by the number of overtime hours worked.

$17.25 × 6 = $103.50

Add the straight time to the overtime to determine the total gross pay.

$460.00 + $103.50 = $563.50

Financial Literacy

Taxes and Other Deductions

Your paycheck stub lists the various deductions your employer subtracts from your gross pay. Some, such as income taxes and Social Security taxes are mandatory. Other deductions are made with your permission.

- **Federal and State income taxes.** This tax money is the government's main source of income. The government uses the tax money to provide services, programs, and facilities to all citizens. The amount of tax taken out of your paycheck is based on how much you earn.
- **Social Security taxes.** This amount may be listed under the letters FICA (Federal Insurance Contributions Act). The federal government administers the Social Security program. It provides retirement, disability, and survivor benefits to eligible working citizens. Your contribution is a percentage of your earnings. Whatever you pay, your employer pays a matching amount for you.
- **Other deductions.** These may include health and life insurance, savings and retirement plans, union dues, and charitable contributions.

receive in your paycheck. Why do you not get to keep all the money you earned? A part of your earnings are deducted from each paycheck by your employer for taxes and other benefits. An important part of understanding your paycheck is knowing what comes out of your paycheck and where it goes.

Paychecks and Paycheck Deductions

The paycheck stub attached to your paycheck provides important information about your earnings and deductions. The total amount of money you earn *before* deductions is your **gross income**. The actual amount of your paycheck *after* deductions is your **net income**, sometimes called your *take-home pay*. Though payroll deductions vary for individuals, about two-thirds of a person's wages remain after deductions are made. The paycheck stub in **4-9** shows an example of earnings and common deductions.

4-9

As this paycheck stub shows, your net pay will be less than your gross pay.

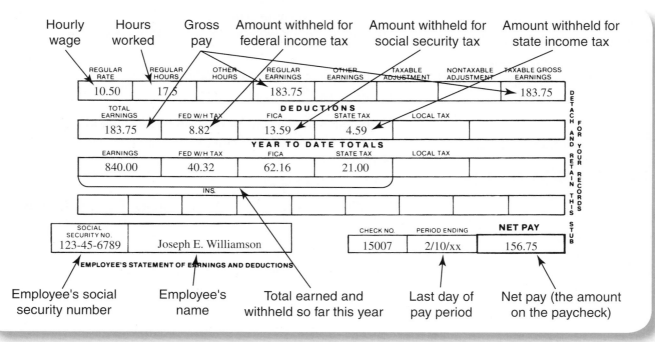

REGULAR RATE	REGULAR HOURS	OTHER HOURS	REGULAR EARNINGS	OTHER EARNINGS	TAXABLE ADJUSTMENT	NONTAXABLE ADJUSTMENT	TAXABLE GROSS EARNINGS
10.50	17.5		183.75				183.75

Hourly wage — Hours worked — Gross pay — Amount withheld for federal income tax — Amount withheld for social security tax — Amount withheld for state income tax

DEDUCTIONS

TOTAL EARNINGS	FED W/H TAX	FICA	STATE TAX	LOCAL TAX		
183.75	8.82	13.59	4.59			

YEAR TO DATE TOTALS

EARNINGS	FED W/H TAX	FICA	STATE TAX	LOCAL TAX		
840.00	40.32	62.16	21.00			

INS.

SOCIAL SECURITY NO. 123-45-6789	Joseph E. Williamson		CHECK NO. 15007	PERIOD ENDING 2/10/xx	**NET PAY** 156.75

EMPLOYEE'S STATEMENT OF EARNINGS AND DEDUCTIONS

Employee's social security number — Employee's name — Total earned and withheld so far this year — Last day of pay period — Net pay (the amount on the paycheck)

DETACH AND RETAIN THIS STUB FOR YOUR RECORDS

The Basics of Budgeting

Budgets are designed to reflect income and expenses for a given period of time. Many families prepare annual budgets. Some people prefer monthly budgets because most of their bills must be paid monthly. If you receive a weekly paycheck or a weekly allowance, you may find a weekly budget helpful.

Setting up a budget involves only a few basic steps. Once you learn these steps, you can develop a budget of your own. A sample weekly budget is shown in **4-10**.

Establish Financial Goals

The first step in developing a budget is to set goals for your spending. Your primary goal will be to meet all your commitments and pay for all of your basic needs. However, you are also likely to have financial goals to purchase certain items. You may have short-term goals for items you would like to buy soon. You may also have long-term goals for items you want to purchase in the future. Long-term goals often center on more costly items. Attaining such goals will require saving money over an extended period.

Once you determine your goals, list them with an estimate of each item's cost. This will help you budget money for basic needs in a way that allows you to save for goals. Keep in mind that your goals may change. Review your goals from time to time so you can make any needed adjustments in your budget.

Determine Sources of Income

The second step in making a budget is to list your sources of income. List the amount of money you receive from each source during the time period of your budget.

Income is all the money you receive. Most income is *earned income*. This is money received for working. It may be in the form of a salary, wages, tips, or commissions. Some income is *unearned income*. This includes interest on bank accounts, dividends on stocks, and money received as prizes or gifts.

When you record income, remember to count only your take-home pay. Any deduction from your paycheck is money already spent. Also, count only income that you are certain to receive. Income that might be available from overtime work or gifts should not be included.

Weekly Budget	
Income	
Allowance	$20.00
Babysitting	45.00
Total Income	$65.00
Expenses	
Fixed Expenses	
Lunch	$10.50
Savings	20.00
Flexible Expenses	
Entertainment	$15.00
Snacks & eating out	9.00
Clothes and accessories	10.50
Total Expenses	$65.00

4-10

A teen might use a weekly budget to balance income and expenses.

Living Green

Encourage family members to file their tax returns online, if possible. Filing online saves paper and time. Visit the IRS website for a list of authorized e-file options.

Estimate Expenses

The third step in developing a budget is to estimate your expenses for the time period of your budget. Make a list of items and services you buy and what they cost. This list will reflect your spending patterns. Later, you can review the list to see if you need to change your spending patterns.

Expenses can be divided into two general groups—fixed and flexible expenses. These groups are further divided into various budget categories according to your spending patterns.

Fixed expenses are items that cost set amounts that you are committed to pay. Included in this group are mortgage or rent payments, installment payments, insurance premiums, and pledged charitable contributions. Savings are also considered a fixed expense. If you do not make a commitment to save a certain amount, you might end up not saving anything.

Flexible expenses are costs that occur repeatedly, but which vary in amount from one time to the next. These expenses commonly include food, clothing, transportation, and recreation.

Compare Income and Expenses

The fourth step in developing a budget is to compare your income and expenses. If your income is greater than your expenses, you can put the extra money toward your goals. If your income equals your expenses, you will be able to meet all your commitments. However, you will not be able to work toward your goals. If your income is less than your expenses, you will not have enough money for your commitments.

If you are not able to meet your commitments, you must look again at your income and expenses. You must either increase your income or decrease your expenses. You may wish to take these steps even if your income and expenses are equal. This will allow you to have extra money to put toward your goals.

Write the Budget and Keep Records

Putting your budget in written form is the fifth step in budget planning. Written records will help you keep track of your spending and stay within your budget. When you set up a record-keeping system, keep it simple. The simpler your system is, the more likely you are to use it regularly and accurately.

Your written budget can be prepared in one of several styles. Choose the style that is easiest and most logical to you. You may decide to buy a record book and set up different accounts for budget categories, **4-11**. With this method, you allocate a certain amount of money to each category and keep a running balance. You can easily see just how much you can afford to spend. You can also see which expenses, if any, are getting too large.

Some people decide how much money they will need to cover their expenses for a month. They divide this amount by the number of paychecks they will receive during the month. Then they set aside the appropriate

Food Budget for March

Balance _____

Mar.	1	Budget allocation						400.00
	1	Lunch at deli					7.75	392.25
	3	Supermarket					54.20	338.05

Recreation Budget for March

Balance _____

Mar.	1	Budget allocation						75.00
	5	Movie for two					22.00	53.00

4-11

Listing purchases in a record book can quickly show how much money is left in each budget category.

amount from each check. They use the balance for goals or spending money. For instance, assume you need $1,000 a month for expenses. Suppose you receive four paychecks a month. Divide $1,000 by 4 to get $250—the amount to set aside from each check. Managing your money in this way takes a certain amount of discipline. You must train yourself not to use money set aside to cover expenses. Big-budget items such as annual insurance premiums require extra planning. Start preparing to pay them several months in advance. Set aside a certain amount from each paycheck so you will be ready when the premium is due.

Evaluate the Budget

Like any good planning process, the final step in planning a budget is evaluation. Evaluate your spending every few months to see how well you are following your budget. If you have money left over, be proud of yourself. If you overspent, try to find out why. Perhaps you allowed too little for certain expenses.

You may need to make adjustments in your budget. Perhaps you will want to increase your allotment in one category to more accurately reflect your spending patterns. However, remember that this will require you to reduce your allotment for another category to keep your budget balanced.

Financial Literacy

Reducing Flexible Expenses

If you want to cut down your flexible expenses, consider these points:

- **Food:** Cook at home instead of eating out. Cooking from scratch is less expensive than buying convenience foods.
- **Clothing:** Well-made, durable garments may cost a little more, but they need not be replaced often. If you know how to sew, make your own clothes or do your own repairs and alterations.
- **Transportation:** Instead of driving, car pool with friends, use public transportation, ride a bike, or walk.
- **Recreation:** The amount of money you spend depends on the types of activities you do. Evaluate recreation expenses in relation to other expenses. Then decide how much money you are willing to spend on recreational activities.
- **Other expenses:** Miscellaneous expenses can make or break your budget. Such expenses might include grooming products and services, school supplies, and gifts. Evaluate how much money you spend on these items.
- **Unexpected expenses:** Unanticipated expenses require an emergency fund to meet unexpected needs. These can include loss of income or health emergencies. It is wise to build a savings account with at least three months of income to meet these needs.

A budget is not a rigid schedule that must remain constant. When there is a need to change the budget, do so. Your budget should work for you, not against you.

Budgeting with a Computer

A computer with appropriate software can make money management and record keeping easier. A year-end printout can help you quickly complete income tax forms and plan a budget for the next year.

Most bills can be paid online. You can set up billing accounts to electronically deduct the payment amount from your checking or savings account. You can even set the transfer to happen automatically on a certain day each month. If you choose to pay bills online, take steps to protect yourself from identity theft. Make sure websites are secure before transmitting any personal or financial information.

A computer is also helpful for keeping track of investments. It can easily calculate figures for dividends, rates of return, capital gains, and depreciations. This saves time and improves accuracy when planning future investments.

Reading Review

1. Give three examples of fringe benefits.
2. Explain the difference between gross income and net income.
3. What are the six steps in developing a budget?
4. True or false. A fixed expense is an unpredictable expense that changes each month.
5. How can a computer be used to help manage money?

Chapter 4 Review

Summary

Learning to manage involves identifying your goals, recognizing your values and standards, and determining your resources. You can learn to use both human and material resources to reach your goals. Then you must form a plan, put it into action, and evaluate the results.

Managing your life also involves learning how to solve problems and make decisions. Some decisions are routine, while others are more complex. Using the decision-making process can help you make the best decisions for your life. To be an effective manager, you need to learn to use the management process. The management process involves planning, organizing, implementing, and evaluating.

One of the most important material resources to manage is time. By managing it well, you can achieve short- and long-term goals. You can even address your visionary goals. Using time management aids and strategies will help you manage your time wisely and effectively.

Managing your finances is another important part of resource management. In return for your hard work on the job, you receive a paycheck. Understanding what comes out of your paycheck is important for budgeting. A budget is a helpful tool for managing money to reach financial goals. To establish a budget, you must determine your sources of income and estimate your fixed and flexible expenses. After evaluation, you may find it necessary to reduce some of your flexible expenses to balance your budget.

Critical Thinking

1. **Evaluate resources.** State a long-term or short-term personal goal that you would like to achieve. What resources do you already have to help you reach that goal? What other resources will you need?

2. **Analyze relationships.** Discuss the relationship between material resources and human resources. How are they similar and how are they different? Then create a Venn diagram displaying the relationship.

3. **Recognize alternatives.** List some of your flexible expenses and give suggestions for reducing them. Write a brief plan describing how you can reduce these expenses.

4. **Apply knowledge.** How can organization and resource management help you maintain a level of professionalism in the workplace? Write a brief list of recommendations and tips for workplace success relating to time management, goal setting, and organizational skills.

5. **Assess technology.** Think of a decision you have faced recently. Make a list of any technological devices that served as resources or influenced the decision. (Examples include cell phones, computers, and video cameras.) Was the technology you used as a resource helpful? Why or why not?

6. **Analyze situations.** Your friend Adrian is involved in many activities. He is president of the school's volunteering group, a member of the soccer team, a member of the basketball team, and a writer for the school's newspaper. He also has a part-time job as a waiter and babysits his younger siblings on the weekends. Adrian is regularly stressed and his grades are falling behind. What advice could you give Adrian to help reduce his stress and better manage his responsibilities?

21st Century
Applications

7. **Productivity and accountability.** It is important to act as a responsible individual. For every action, there is a reaction whether it is immediately seen or not. There are positive and negative consequences for different actions and inactions. Make a list of five decisions you have made for which there were either positive or negative consequences. Put a plus sign (+) beside the positive outcomes and a minus sign (-) beside the negative outcomes. What could you have done differently that would have changed each outcome?

8. **Environmental literacy.** The Great Lakes represent 18 percent of the surface freshwater on the planet. Water, a natural and essential resource, is integral to human survival. Research the *Great Lakes Basin Compact* to learn the purpose of the compact. Analyze the information and identify the key features of the compact. Prepare an electronic presentation of your findings and share your findings with the class.

9. **Initiative and self-direction.** Create to-do lists and weekly plans over the next month. Then write a brief report on what you learned about how well you use time. Are there opportunities for more efficient time management in your schedule?

10. **Information, communications, and technology literacy.** Evaluate several types of apps used for maintaining a schedule. What are the pros and cons of each app? Would you use the app on a daily basis to manage your time? Write a brief review of at least three scheduling apps or programs explaining your answer.

Core
Skills

11. **Writing.** Write a biographical sketch of an imaginary person. Set a long-term goal for this person. Then set several short-term goals to help the person reach his or her long-term goal. Finally, list the resources the person could use to reach the goals.

12. **History.** Write a research report about a historical figure who had visionary goals. Describe ways this person worked to achieve his or her goals.

13. **Writing.** Your visionary goals are just as important as your short-term and long-term goals. Your visionary goals can guide your other goals. Write descriptively about one of your career-related visionary goals. Describe your job responsibilities, what a typical day on the job looks like, where you are living, with whom you are interacting, and how you were able to accomplish this visionary goal.

14. **Writing.** Write a short story about a family who learns to use the management process. Show how it improves their family life.

15. **Reading.** Read poetry written on the subject of time, such as Shakespeare's Sonnet XIX, *Devouring Time*, and John Donne's *The Sun Rising*. Why do you think classic poets wrote on the subject of time?

16. **Math.** Using spreadsheet software, prepare a weekly budget for yourself. Include your flexible and fixed expenses. After following it for two weeks, write an evaluation describing its usefulness. Also note any adjustments you would want to make in the budget. Only include income you are certain to receive.

17. **Math.** Research facts on the federal budget. How is the budget established? What factors are taken into account? Who must approve the budget? Does the federal government usually meet its budget? Why or why not?

18. **Listening.** Do an Internet search to find speeches made by successful individuals that tell how they became financially independent. Select one speech of your choice and listen to it in its entirety. Describe the line of reasoning, organization, development, and style the speaker used to prepare his or her information. Identify the target audience and the purpose of the speech.

19. **Speaking.** There will be many instances when you will be required to persuade a listener. When you persuade, you convince a person to take a course of action which you propose. Prepare for a conversation with a financial adviser at a bank to persuade him or her to allow you to take out a loan for $1,000.00. Consider how you would develop and structure your argument. Include a plan for how you will repay the loan.

 **Leadership**
Development

Discuss the similarities and differences between the eight steps of the decision-making process presented in the text with the five steps in the Planning Process developed by FCCLA. Use both methods with an upcoming decision at a FCCLA meeting. Compare the results and discuss which process worked best.

 **Portfolio**
Builder

Managing your time is important both as a student and when you have a career. Conduct a time study for yourself, writing everything you do and the time. This will help you determine how you spend your time. Perform an analysis of how you spend your time and write about how you can improve your time management skills. Add these to your portfolio. Analyze the schedule in terms of the following:

- What are your time wasters?
- Do you procrastinate?
- Are there tasks that could be combined?
- Could tasks be broken into smaller steps?
- How can you compensate for lost time?
- How can you make better use of spare time?

Journal
Writing

You think that you are not spending enough time with your family. Sometimes you hardly feel you know them. You would like to spend at least one hour with your family each day. However, you have many other important goals and activities.

Write About It: *How can you use the decision-making process to address this problem? What might be some of your resources? What might be some of your alternatives?*

Chapter 5
Community and Environmental Responsibilities

Reading Prep

Before reading this chapter, go to the end of the chapter and read the summary. The chapter summary highlights important information that was presented in the chapter. Did this help you prepare to understand the content?

Concept Organizer

Make an idea wheel with *Citizenship and Environmental Activities* in the center. In the spokes, identify opportunities for you to be involved in the community. Also include ways you can care for the environment.

G-WLEARNING.COM

Click on the activity icon to visit www.g-wlearning.com/comprehensive/8062 to access online vocabulary activities using key terms from the chapter.

Section 5-1

Citizenship

Objectives

After studying this section, you will be able to

- **explain** the importance of being an informed citizen and exercising your right to vote.

- **describe** the purpose of taxes.

- **consider** why community involvement is important to individuals, especially teens.

Key Term

volunteers

You are a citizen of your city or town, your state, and your country. As a citizen, you have certain rights and responsibilities. You have a right to enjoy the freedoms that are protected by laws. You have the responsibilities of becoming informed, voting, obeying laws, paying taxes, and protecting the environment. Fulfilling your responsibilities will help you protect your rights and the rights of others.

To Be Informed

You have a right to information about the world around you. You have a responsibility to use that information to be an informed citizen.

Laws and government policy affect how you live. You need to be aware of how new and revised laws and policies might affect your rights and the rights of others. For instance, a change in the education policy could affect the schools you attend. Factors in the economy can limit your ability to find a job and purchase goods and services. New environmental standards will affect the air you breathe and the water you drink. International events can alter your sense of security.

As an informed citizen, you can work to resist negative conditions and make positive changes. When you are knowledgeable, you can speak to other citizens about issues that concern you. You can write to your political leaders to express your views. By being informed, you can take steps to defend your rights. See **5-1**.

fizkes/iStock/Getty Images Plus

To Vote

Voting is both a right and a responsibility. It is a privilege to be able to help choose your government leaders. People in many nations do not have that freedom. It is your duty to cast your ballot on election days. If you do not vote, you will be letting other people choose your leaders for you.

If you are 18 years old and a United States citizen, you may register to vote. Make a point of learning how candidates stand on the issues. You will then be able to determine which candidate's views are most like yours. This will help you know how to cast your vote.

To Obey the Law

Although people sometimes complain about laws, life would be chaos without them. You have a right to the benefits that laws provide. You have a responsibility to obey laws that govern your behavior. For instance, you have a legal right to a public education. However, you also have a legal responsibility to attend school until you reach a certain age.

To Pay Taxes

Taxes are needed to create the type of society to which U.S. citizens have grown accustomed. Federal, state, and local governments collect taxes. Tax dollars are used to pay for national defense, postal services, health inspection services, and police and fire protection. Roads, parks, and schools are all funded by taxes.

As a citizen, you have a right to the services provided by tax dollars. You also have a responsibility to pay taxes. Monitoring the fairness of tax laws is both a right and a responsibility.

To Be Involved in Your Community

Taxes provide most of the public services needed, but never stretch far enough to cover everything. This is why volunteers are welcomed in many government and nonprofit agencies. **Volunteers** are people who provide valuable services by offering their time, talents, and energy free of charge.

People who become involved in their communities take pride in them. They enjoy knowing they make a positive contribution. Such contributions can make the community more beautiful, such as freshly painted park benches, litter-free sidewalks, and holiday decorations. Volunteering also makes a noticeable difference in people's lives. Examples include making food baskets for the needy and helping people learn to read.

Most communities have a roster of volunteer opportunities available. However, you might see a specific need and simply inform the people in charge that you want to fill it. Think about your interests and abilities in deciding where you want to devote your efforts. That will lead you to find a volunteer opportunity that matches your enthusiasm.

Volunteering can benefit you in more ways than you imagine. You learn more about your community and your neighbors. You meet new friends and receive the personal satisfaction of seeing that your help really matters. You also perfect your skills and can also gain new skills.

Volunteering can help you determine your career interests. By gaining firsthand experience in related areas, you can better decide which direction in life appeals most to you. For example, if your interests include working with children and oil painting, you could seek a job that includes both. Some possible jobs that merge these interests are likely found in community recreation programs and local child care centers. If your interests change, you can always shift to other types of volunteer work to explore new areas.

Your volunteer experience will be a valuable asset when you try to obtain your first job. See **5-2**. First-time job seekers who have no previous job experience to report can always list their volunteer work. Such work

Financial Literacy

Types of Taxes

Taxes collected for government services can be classified in the following ways:
- *Progressive taxes:* as the item being taxed increases, the rate of tax increases. For instance, income tax is a progressive tax. The more you earn, the higher is the percentage of tax you pay.
- *Direct taxes:* those charged directly to the people who are to pay them. Sales tax is an example of a direct tax.
- *Indirect taxes:* are included in the price of taxed items. Excise tax is an example of an indirect tax.

How do taxes affect citizens? Consider the following examples involving the purchase of gasoline and antifreeze, both costing $3.50 a gallon:
- Excise tax of 20 cents a gallon is *included* in the price of the gasoline. Therefore, you will have to pay $3.50 for a gallon of gasoline.
- A sales tax of 6 percent is *added* onto the price of the antifreeze. A gallon of the antifreeze will cost you $3.71.

Mental Health Awareness

Giving and Getting

People who give to the community get a lot back emotionally. Simply giving a compliment or volunteering can increase your feelings of happiness as well as strengthen social bonds. The emotional benefits you experience are greatest when you give freely and not from a sense of obligation or reward expectations. Spontaneous, anonymous giving can also add a special *feel good* bonus.

5-2

In addition to the job skills learned while volunteering, you also develop important interpersonal skills by working with the general public and cooperating with coworkers.

Serving Your Community

Organize an environmental club in your school or become involved in an existing club. Plan activities to increase environmental awareness, encourage conservation of resources, and improve the environment.

is just as important to employers as job experience gained in a paid position. Also, some of the people you help by volunteering may keep you informed of job openings in your field of interest. They can vouch for your ability to do a good job to a potential employer you may want to impress. They may even offer you a full-time job when you leave school.

Later, when you meet the age requirement, you may wish to serve on a local committee or run for an elective office. Most of the big issues affecting a community are resolved in the political arena. The many different roles of public service are important, and dedicated people are always needed to fill them.

To Protect the Environment

You are not just a citizen of a city, state, and nation. You are also a citizen of the world. As such, you have a right to live in a clean, healthy environment. You also have a responsibility to help keep your environment clean and healthy.

Protecting the environment means doing your part to help keep the air and water supply clean. It also means conserving the land and its resources.

Reading
Review

1. What requirements must a person meet to register to vote in the United States?
2. List five services provided by tax dollars.
3. State three results of volunteering that can help teens get a full-time job in the future.

Section 5-2

Caring for the Environment

Objectives

After studying this section, you will be able to

- **explain** the importance of a healthful environment.
- **identify** the causes of different types of pollution.
- **relate** how pollution affects people's health.
- **discuss** ways people can protect and build a healthful environment.

Key Terms

fossil fuels	**hazardous waste**	**recycle**
pollution	**toxic waste**	

Some of the most serious world problems threaten the environment. Limited natural resources, rapid population growth, and pollution are a few of these. People must think about how they use the environment. This includes how they affect the environment and what they can do to protect and preserve it.

5-3
The natural beauty of the environment can be preserved for future generations through the wise use of natural resources today.

A Healthful Environment

A *healthful environment* promotes good physical and mental health and enables people to reach their goals. It has clean air, unpolluted water, rich soil, a continuing supply of natural resources, and pleasant surroundings, **5-3**. The surroundings are spacious enough to allow individuals some privacy and room for recreation. A healthful environment also supports diverse plant and animal life.

Does such an environment exist only in secluded or primitive areas? Can it coexist with an advanced standard of living? Many people believe that, with care and effort, everyone can enjoy a healthful environment.

Factors Affecting the Environment

Two factors play major roles in the increase of environmental problems—rapid population growth and shrinking natural resources.

Rapid Population Growth

The human population is increasing at a rapid rate and living longer. This affects the environment. As the population increases, the available living space for each person decreases. Existing resources must be divided among more and more people. Food, one of these resources, is sometimes not available to some people.

A growing population needs more goods and services, and industries use more energy to provide them. As more goods are produced and used, solid waste is created. Ever-growing amounts of waste can mix with the air, water, and soil. Without controls, the end result is a polluted environment.

Shrinking Natural Resources

The earth has two categories of resources—renewable and nonrenewable. Understanding the difference is important. Plants and animals are *renewable resources*. These resources are replaced rapidly enough to provide people with a continuing supply.

If land continues to be fertile, plant resources can be renewed and even increased as people grow new crops each year. Healthy animals can also grow and reproduce. Some energy resources, such as the sun and wind, are also renewable. They will probably play a much greater role in supplying the energy needs of the future. Water is a renewable resource, too. Maintaining it in an unpolluted state, however, is difficult and costly.

Oil, coal, and natural gas are called **fossil fuels**. Their energy is derived from the partly decayed plants and animals that lived long ago. The earth's supply of fossil fuels is limited and replaced very slowly. Fossil fuels are therefore called *nonrenewable resources*. Minerals such as copper and gold belong in this category, too. When present supplies of these resources are depleted, no more will be available. The cost and availability of fuel supplies has been a source of tension among world powers.

Pollution

The environment greatly affects people's health. One unhealthful side effect of society is pollution. **Pollution** is harmful changes in the environment that make resources unclean or unsafe to use. Pollution occurs when people mismanage the air, water, or land. Pollution can also be caused by some natural sources. Substances that actually cause pollution are called *pollutants*.

Air Pollution

People must have clean air to breathe and remain healthy. Air pollution is linked to respiratory ailments, such as bronchitis, asthma, lung cancer, and other lung diseases. Pollutants are dangerous because they build up over time and may stay in the air. Long-term exposure to air pollution is especially harmful to young children, older adults, and people who are ill. Limiting the volume of pollutants that become airborne is the focus of many nations.

Smoking cigarettes and using pesticides also cause airborne pollutants, but the burning of fossil fuels causes the biggest problem. Industries and consumers use fossil fuels to run cars, produce heat and light, and power tools and equipment. Burning these fuels creates airborne pollutants, particularly carbon dioxide and carbon monoxide.

Living Green

Work with your family to set up a recycling area in your home or garage. Designate areas for paper, plastics, glass, metal, and electronics. This will keep items organized until they can be disposed of in an environmentally responsible way.

The Thinning Ozone Layer

Closely related to air pollution is the apparent weakening of the natural ozone layer in the stratosphere. The ozone layer filters ultraviolet radiation so less reaches the earth. Scientists think the layer is thinning, thus allowing more solar radiation to penetrate. Ozone-depleting chemicals are now banned in many countries.

Acid Rain

Acid rain is a term used to describe acids that fall from the atmosphere in either a wet or dry form. The acids are created from the emissions of electric power plants and motor vehicles, **5-4**. The chief cause is sulfur dioxide. Acid rain can pollute rivers, damage the surface of cars and buildings, and harm or kill plant and aquatic life. Efforts are underway to limit the use of the chemicals causing acid rain.

5-4

The generation of electricity is a major cause of acid rain.

Water Pollution

Water pollution is the accidental or careless addition of waste materials to rivers, lakes, oceans, and underground water supplies. Industrial wastes, sewage, and agricultural chemicals are the main causes. In recent years, oil tankers have spilled their loads into ocean waters. Some industrial plants have discharged lead, mercury, and other toxic waste. Untreated sewage causes problems in areas with inadequate sanitation systems. Rains wash agricultural

chemicals, especially fertilizers and pesticides, into nearby streams. Animal wastes from feedlots have seeped through soil, contaminating some water supplies.

Noise Pollution

Noise pollution is the excessively high sound level to which people are subjected in their everyday lives. Modern machines, such as jet planes and jackhammers, introduce dangerously loud noises to the environment. Amplified sounds from concerts also add to the problem. One of the major dangers of noise pollution is loss of hearing since constant exposure can damage it. Environmental Protection Agency (EPA) standards limit the noise level of newly built vehicles and equipment. Many communities enforce local rules to reduce loud, irritating noises in residential neighborhoods.

Hazardous Waste

Hazardous waste is a by-product of society that poses a danger to human health or the environment when not properly managed. Hazardous waste has at least one of four characteristics. It may ignite, corrode, chemically react with another material, or be toxic. **Toxic waste** can cause injury if inhaled, swallowed, or absorbed through the skin.

What can be done to reduce hazardous waste in the environment? Become an advocate of continued EPA monitoring of illegal dumping. Support community programs that inform the public about hazardous waste and provide collection sites for their proper disposal.

At home, make sure items requiring special disposal are handled appropriately. For instance, used motor oil, antifreeze, certain batteries, and empty pesticide containers should be taken to special collection sites. The products should not be placed with other household trash. Look for labels on paints, pesticides, solvents, and other consumer products that contain special disposal alerts.

How You Can Help

Individuals can play an important role in preserving and protecting the environment. They can learn how to use natural resources to achieve a better standard of living. They can recognize that misused resources lead to pollution and other negative consequences. Finally, they can make a strong commitment to maintaining the health of the environment.

Conserve Resources

One way you can help conserve natural resources is by recycling. To **recycle** means reprocessing resources to use them again. See **5-5**. Some recyclable items are aluminum cans, glass and plastic bottles, and paper. Old furniture and appliances can also be recycled.

Analyze and Solve

Imagine you are adapting this section to be studied by teens in another part of the world. What other topics would you want to add? What topics could you delete because they would not be applicable?

Take recyclable trash to recycling centers instead of throwing it away. Ask your friends to pitch in and do their part, too. Some companies will pay you for recyclable items, so you can earn money as you lessen pollution.

Old clothing is another recyclable resource. Give outgrown clothes to someone who can wear them or consider restyling them for yourself. In many instances, you can make new garments from old ones. Often there is enough fabric in adult garments to make clothing for children. Donate clothing you cannot use to charitable organizations that collect it.

Reduce Pollution

To reduce air pollution in your area, try walking, riding a bicycle, or taking public transportation. If you must drive, use the car efficiently by carpooling or combining several errands in one trip.

To reduce water pollution, avoid dumping waste on the ground or into bodies of water. Choose nontoxic cleaning agents and biodegradable detergents.

Do your part to reduce noise levels and help insulate your home from noise pollution. Carpeting, draperies, and acoustical tile deaden outdoor noise. If you are exposed to high noise levels on your job, protect your hearing by wearing ear protectors.

Carelessly tossed gum wrappers and soda cans may not seem like pollution. However, they create litter, which is a sign of mismanaging

5-5

Collecting materials for recycling instead of throwing them away helps conserve limited natural resources.

Living Green

When is the last time you looked up a phone number in a phone book? Opt out of receiving phone books, which often end up in landfills. Use your computer or other electronic devices to find current listings.

the land. Always keep the environment clean and dispose of your waste properly. Think of ways to make others want to stop littering and do their part, too.

Waste from product packaging takes up a lot of space in landfills. You can lessen the environmental impact of packaging by following the slogan *reduce, reuse, recycle*. Reduce the amount of packaging material you bring home by choosing products with minimal packaging. For instance, select unpackaged fruits and vegetables instead of produce sold on foam trays wrapped in plastic. Reuse empty product containers whenever possible. Use rechargeable batteries. Recycle as many product containers as possible. Glass, metal, paperboard, and many plastics can be recycled into other materials.

Learn how your community handles waste. Enlist the support of your parents and other adults to insist that local leaders use safe practices at all times. Join community groups that address environmental issues or help clean up problems. Write your legislators to express your views on pending environmental legislation. Much can be done to control pollution if each person makes an effort.

Make Responsible Decisions

Making responsible decisions regarding the environment can be challenging. For instance, one source says using plastic bags will save the trees used to make paper bags. Another source says paper bags will save the fossil fuels used to make plastic bags. Reusing your own cloth bags is the best choice here.

Many consumers end up making environmental tradeoffs. In other words, they exchange one resource to save another resource. As a citizen, you have a duty to carefully evaluate your choices to the best of your ability.

Seek out environmental information from reputable sources. Begin with information from the EPA and the sources linked to its website. The Agency's information is thoughtfully composed and reviewed by many experts. When some disagree with its opinion, consider whether they have something to gain personally by holding other views.

Math Connection

Determining Quantities

Kristen read that Americans create an average of 4.4 pounds of trash daily. She wants to know how much trash her class of 24 students creates in a year. She can do this by multiplying the average number of pounds by the number of students.

4.4 pounds × 24 students = 105.6 pounds per day

Then she would multiply the daily number of pounds by the number of days in a year (365).

105.6 pounds per day × 365 days = 38,544 pounds per year

Reading
Review

1. List five requirements for a healthful environment.
2. Name the two primary factors responsible for the increase of environmental problems.
3. Explain the difference between a renewable and nonrenewable resource.
4. Name four types of pollution.
5. List five ways for people to promote the health of the environment.

Section 5-3

Conserving Energy

Objectives

After studying this section, you will be able to

- **identify** renewable and nonrenewable energy sources.
- **discuss** ways you can help conserve energy at home.

Key Terms

solar energy	**wattage**	**lumens**
biomass		

Another important part of caring for the environment involves using energy wisely. *Energy* could be defined as something that gives a machine the power to perform an action. There are many different kinds of energy: light energy, heat energy, and electrical energy. Energy can be stored. The energy stored in gasoline is harnessed when an engine burns it. Energy stored in batteries can power tools and appliances.

People have many ways to supplement their own physical energy with energy from other sources. For example, they burn gasoline to run their cars, thereby saving the energy of walking or pedaling a bicycle. They use electricity to run a clothes washer, thereby saving the labor of washing clothes by hand. People also use energy to heat and light their homes and run household equipment. See **5-6**. There are two major sources of energy—nonrenewable and renewable.

5-6

Dams generate a large share of the country's electricity.

Innovation. Darnell is committed to caring for the environment. He leads the environmental committee in his workplace. Over the past few years, the committee has developed new ways for the company to reduce waste, increase recycling, and conserve energy.

Nonrenewable Energy Sources

Once current supplies of nonrenewable energy are used, no further supplies are available. This is why fossil fuels are classified as *nonrenewable resources*. Because they have been so affordable for so long, much of the world operates on fossil fuels.

These fuels are available in the liquid, gaseous, and solid states. Crude oil, often just called oil, is unrefined petroleum. It is a dark, thick liquid. Natural gas is a mixture of gases beneath the earth's surface, usually in petroleum deposits. Coal is the only solid fossil fuel.

Uranium ore is another nonrenewable energy source. It is used to provide nuclear power that is converted into electricity. Supplies of this energy source are limited and there are concerns related to the disposal of radioactive waste.

Renewable Energy Sources

Sources of energy that can be replaced are called *renewable energy sources*. These sources can produce additional supplies of energy in a relatively short period. However, producing a large supply of energy from these sources at an affordable cost may require more research and investment. Energy can be produced from five renewable sources—water, wind, solar, biomass, and geothermal.

Water

The energy of falling water can be converted into electrical energy called *hydroelectric energy*. The amount of power generated at a given plant is limited, but another plant built downstream can generate more power from the same water. As water evaporates and falls again as rain, water supplies are replaced. More flowing water allows the plant to generate more electrical power. This cycle is a renewable source of energy.

Building more hydroelectric plants is not likely. Most of the practical power-generating sites in the United States have already been developed. Building other sites could damage the environment.

Wind Energy

An average wind speed of about 14 miles per hour is needed to economically convert wind to electricity. Wind turbines can convert the energy of the wind into electrical energy, which can be stored in batteries and used as needed. Good wind sites are often located far from where most energy is needed. Wind energy is the fastest growing energy technology in the world. Good sites are abundant and the technology produces no pollution.

Solar Energy

The greatest renewable source of energy is the sun. Energy from this source is called **solar energy**. The sun's energy can be captured and used in several ways. Solar collectors absorb it to provide hot water for household use or for space heating. See **5-7**. Photovoltaic systems convert sunlight to electricity that may be used directly or stored in batteries for future use. Special reflectors focus sunlight into a fiber optic system to light the interior of buildings. Solar energy has two advantages: the supply is almost limitless, and it does not have harmful effects on the environment.

Biomass

Energy is stored in dry, decayed plant and animal matter called **biomass**. When burned, biomass produces heat and steam, both of which can be converted to electricity. Many types of biomass exist, but the three main types burned to create energy are wood, crops, and solid waste.

Geothermal Energy

Geothermal energy is derived from heat produced within the earth.

Analyze and Solve

Suppose you are planning to build a house and cannot use fossil fuels. Which of the renewable energy sources would you choose to supply power to your home?

5-7

A solar heat collector traps the heat of the sun to heat water and living spaces. As you drive through the countryside, look for solar farms that generate electricity for municipalities.

DiyanaDimitrova/iStock/Getty Images Plus

Science Connection

Generating Energy with Biomass

Wood once provided all the energy needed for heating homes and cooking.

Today it is used in fireplaces, but this is a minor use. Burning wood is restricted in many areas because the smoke contains pollutants. Industries that convert wood to paper, chemicals, and building products use wood waste to produce their own steam and electricity.

Crops like corn and sugar are fermented to produce the transportation fuel called *ethanol*. Another such fuel, *biodiesel*, is made from oil extracted from soybeans. Although in limited supply, these new types of fuel will become more available in the future.

Solid waste is considered biomass if it is the type that rots, such as food scraps and lawn clippings. (Trash also contains glass, metals, and plastics, which are not biomass.) Burning this waste generates steam and an ash by-product, often used for roads. When the waste is placed in a landfill, it releases a gas that can be converted to a fuel source.

This source of energy is readily available in certain geographic locations, where it is collected as steam to generate electricity. The United States leads the world in generating geothermal energy from power plants in the western states, Alaska, and Hawaii. Advancements in technology may lead to the ability to collect geothermal energy in more locations across the United States.

Energy in the Future

The energy picture for the future is clouded. Oil and natural gas supplies are heavily used and being depleted. Coal is one fossil fuel that is still abundant, but it presents some concerns. Unless properly controlled, the by-products of burning coal can add to air pollution.

Renewable sources currently account for only a small percentage of U.S. energy supplies. Renewable sources offer promise, but there are many challenges. Switching U.S. consumption away from fossil fuels requires public support as well as new processes and facilities. Greater investment in research and development is needed to make newer energy forms more available and affordable. Historically low fossil-fuel costs have discouraged those investments. Record-high prices for fossil fuels increase interest in the renewable fuels.

You Can Help Conserve Energy

An important goal for everyone is to reduce the use of fossil fuels. This goal is partly met by newer, energy-efficient appliances, which are designed to run on less energy. Another factor that affects energy use is how people live with and use their appliances. The checklist shown in **5-8** will help you discover ways to conserve energy in your own home. Using less energy can also lower utility bills.

Heating and Cooling a Home

More than half of the energy used by a household is for heating and cooling. A whole-house approach is the only way to lower the amount of energy used by the furnace and air conditioner. Controlling indoor

Serving Your Community

Develop a web page of energy-saving tips, devoting separate sections to specific appliances or activities. Be sure to cite your sources for various statistics, if any are used. Include links to helpful websites. Work with your teacher to post the information on your class or school website.

Residential Energy Checklist

The Home's Shell

- Are plants properly located around the house to provide a break against wind and unwanted sun?
- Are drapes and furniture located so they do not obstruct heating, air conditioning, or ventilation?
- Are exterior house doors closed quickly after use?
- Do you have double-pane windows or storm windows and doors?
- Are all doors and windows properly caulked and weather-stripped?

- Are draperies and shades closed at night, on cloudy days during the heating season, and on sunny days during the cooling season?
- Are draperies opened to admit sunlight on sunny days in the heating season?
- Is the attic well ventilated and insulated?
- Are the walls well insulated?
- Is the house shaded from the western sun?
- Is your home sealed from drafts? Is it free from cracks and holes?

Environmental Control

- Does your home have as much fluorescent lighting as possible?
- Is the fireplace damper closed when not in use?
- Are lights turned off when they will not be used for several hours?
- Are appliances turned off after use?
- Are ducts, radiators, or air conditioners closed off in unused areas?
- Are air ducts and hot-water pipes insulated in spaces that lack heating and cooling?
- Is the thermostat set at 65°F or lower during the heating season and at 78°F or higher during the cooling season?

- Is the thermostat turned back at night and when the house is empty?
- Are furnace and air conditioner filters kept clean?
- Is the air conditioning unit properly sized for your needs?
- Are windows and doors tightly closed while heating or cooling the home?
- Is an attic fan used in the summer?
- Is the water heater insulated or located in a heated space?
- Do you use natural ventilation as much as possible?
- Are radiators and other heating or cooling equipment clean and dust free?

Housing Selection

- If you live in an apartment, is it an "inside" apartment?
- If you live in a mobile home, does it have a "skirt"?

- If you live in an older home, has the plumbing, wiring, insulation, and chimneys been checked by experts?
- Is the den, game room, or family room oriented to the south?

5-8

Can you answer yes to these questions? If so, you are doing your part in helping to conserve energy.

5-8

(Continued)

Residential Energy Checklist, *Continued*

Appliance Use

- Are the refrigerator and freezer kept free of frost buildup?
- Is the refrigerator set at 40°F?
- Is the freezer set at 0°F?
- Is the cooking range turned off immediately after use or a short time beforehand?
- Are appliances clean and dust free (particularly cooling coils)?
- Is a timer used to avoid overcooking?
- Is the dishwasher's air-dry cycle used?
- Are dishes washed only when there are full loads?

- When washing clothes, is cold or warm water used in place of hot water as often as possible?
- Are clothes always rinsed with cold water?
- Is the lint screen cleaned after each dryer load?
- Do the members of your family limit water use when showering or bathing?
- Is an outside air conditioning unit located on the shady (north) side of the house?

temperature, sealing air leaks, and using appropriate window coverings are simple steps. Other steps include increasing the home's insulation, installing energy-efficient windows, and landscaping wisely.

Use a programmable thermostat to regulate temperatures that make sense for your family. Take into account the periods when less heated (or cooled) air is needed, such as when everyone is away or asleep. Set your thermostat as low in winter and as high in summer as is comfortable. Consider 65°F in winter and 78°F in summer. Wear layered garments so clothing can be removed or added as needed.

If indoor air is leaking outdoors, sealing these areas can lead to savings on your energy bill. Begin by sealing and weather-stripping all cracks and openings around doors and windows. Indoors, look for possible paths to the outdoors that streams of air may take and seal them. Examples include fireplace chimneys, electrical outlets, ceiling fixtures, and entrances to the attic. Also seal ducts that leak heated air into crawl spaces and other unheated areas.

Make sure all windows have draperies, window shades, blinds, or other window coverings that can be opened and closed. Let the sunlight in to warm a room, but block it for cooling. To let in the most sunlight, keep windows on south and west sides clean.

Adding insulation to a home built before 1980, if not done already, is probably a good long-term investment. Good insulation controls the movement of air and moisture into and out of the home. Some insulation additions are easy to make, while others may need an insulation expert. That person can measure how well your home's insulation compares to the recommendations for your region.

Single-pane windows, which are on nearly half of all U.S. homes, are big energy wasters. They should be covered with storm windows or replaced with double-pane windows of high-performance glass. In cold climates, gas-filled panes with "low-e" coatings reduce heat loss. In warm climates, windows should have one or more coatings that block the sun's rays.

Another way to better insulate a dwelling is through landscaping. Use trees, shrubs, and vines to help shield a home from sun, wind, and noise, **5-9**.

5-9

Trees and foundation plantings help insulate a home against heat, cold, and wind.

Water Heating

After the climate-control appliances, the single biggest energy user in the home is the water heater. It averages about 15 percent of the home's energy budget. Water-heating bills can be cut by using more energy-efficient appliances and less hot water.

There are several easy ways to cut back on hot water. Taking quick showers instead of baths and using aerating showerheads are two ways. Running the dishwasher and clothes washer only when loads are full is another. Insulating the hot water storage tank and first six feet of pipes saves energy, too. You can also lower the temperature setting of your water heater so less energy is needed to heat the water. Lowering it to 120°F should provide enough hot water for most families.

Using cooler water whenever possible spares the water heater from heating more water. For example, hot water is a must for washing dishes, but not for cleaning most loads of laundry. Cold and warm water are often effective for most clothes washer cycles. Cold water is appropriate for rinsing all types of laundry. Heavily soiled laundry, however, needs hot-water washes to get clean.

Homes with heated pools use considerable energy, perhaps doubling their water-heating bill. Because few households own pool heaters and pumps, they are not figured into the national averages.

Science Connection

How CFLs Work

CFLs, or compact fluorescent lamps, produce an energy-efficient type of light. To create light in CFLs, electricity is driven through a glass tube that contains small amounts of argon gas and mercury vapor. This creates invisible light that excites a *phosphor* (a luminescent substance) coating on the inside of the tube. The tube then gives off visible light. Because CFLs contain small amounts of mercury, do not throw them in the trash when they no longer work. You can recycle them at most home improvement centers. For more information on CFLs, visit the Energy Star website.

Lighting and Appliances

After considering furnaces, air conditioners, and water heaters, all other energy users average about 28 percent of the home's energy budget. This group includes lighting, appliances, and power-using equipment such as TVs and office machines.

- *Lighting.* Use energy-efficient lightbulbs, such as Energy Star approved LED lights or compact-fluorescent bulbs. They give off the brightness and color of traditional lightbulbs, but last much longer. Always use the lowest wattage lightbulb that gives adequate light for the specific need. **Wattage** indicates the amount of energy required to operate the bulb. The amount of light produced is stated in **lumens**. Both figures are usually labeled on packages.

- *Refrigerated Food Storage.* Open and close the door quickly to prevent the escape of cold air. Cover food containers before storing to prevent the release of moisture. Added moisture makes the refrigerator work harder. Keep refrigerator temperatures between 37°F and 40°F.

- *Other Kitchen and Laundry Appliances.* When loading the dishwasher, scrape off food scraps without rinsing to keep water use to a minimum. Use the dishwasher's air-drying feature when quick drying is not essential. When cooking, match the size of a pan to the heating element. Always use covers to hold heat in, especially when boiling water. When using the oven, cook several dishes at the same time. When washing clothes, adjust the water level to the size of the load. Dry heavier items such as towels separately from lighter items. Avoid overdrying laundry.

- *Home Electronics and Office Equipment.* For home electronics and office equipment, 75 percent of the energy they use occurs while turned off. Unplugging the items or plugging them into a power strip that is switched off stops this wasteful "leakage."

Shopping for Energy Efficiency

When shopping for appliances, electronics, and powered equipment, there are two prices to consider. The first is the purchase price, which is clearly labeled. The second is the operating cost. Operating cost is an important consideration, especially if you plan to use the item for many years.

Bright yellow *EnergyGuide* labels help you compare the operating costs of major appliances. These labels, developed by the

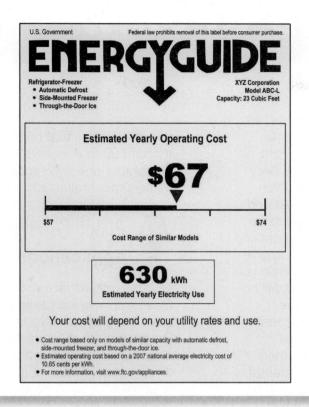

5-10

EnergyGuide labels help you compare the operating costs and energy use of appliances.

U.S. Department of Energy, appear on gas and electric appliances. They display each model's yearly energy use on a scale showing comparisons to the least-efficient and most-efficient models. Labels for refrigerators, refrigerator-freezers, freezers, dishwashers, water heaters, and clothes washers also show the average yearly bill for running the appliance. See **5-10**.

Another label to look for is the ENERGY STAR label, developed by the EPA. See **5-11**. This label appears in 40 product categories on only the most energy-efficient models. Besides appliances, the label appears on home electronics, office equipment, fluorescent lighting, windows, and even new homes. When products save energy, they deliver environmental benefits as well.

5-11

ENERGY STAR labels identify the appliances and other consumer products that use the least energy.

energy ENERGY STAR

US Environmental Protection Agency, ENERGY STAR program

Reading
Review

1. List four renewable energy sources.
2. What is preventing some renewable energy sources from being used more widely as fossil fuel replacements?
3. Name five ways you can help conserve energy in your home.

Chapter 5 Review

Summary

As a citizen, you have a responsibility to be informed, vote, and obey laws. You also have a responsibility to pay taxes and protect the environment. Performing these tasks will help you protect your personal and legal rights. Volunteering allows you to give back to your community. It can also help you gain experience and friendships that will be beneficial in getting a job in the future.

A healthful environment is one that promotes good physical and mental health and allows people to reach their goals. Pollution and other environmental problems are concerns that directly affect everyone's health. Each person must assume a responsibility for protecting the environment that supports all living things.

Conserving energy is an aspect of caring for the environment. By using less energy, the fossil fuels are spared. Every person must be willing to do his or her part. Knowing conservation issues helps people make energy-saving practices a habit.

Critical Thinking

1. **Analyze priorities.** What rights do you value most as a citizen? What responsibilities can you fulfill to help protect those rights?
2. **Judge actions.** Write a brief reaction to this statement: taxes should be abolished.
3. **Draw conclusions.** Should protecting the environment be a global effort rather than a local effort? Give at least three reasons in your explanation.
4. **Predict outcomes.** Which of the nonrenewable energy resources do you think the global community should try hardest to conserve? Which of the renewable energy resources do you think is most reliable?

21st Century Applications

5. **Leadership and responsibility.** Research ways citizens can fulfill roles as leaders in your community. Develop a list of leadership opportunities. Then select two to three opportunities of interest. What responsibilities come with each leadership role?
6. **Civic literacy.** Select two tax laws that generate funds for government services. Describe how the revenue generated from these taxes help contribute to the betterment of the community.
7. **Environmental literacy.** Visit an appliance store and record information on the EnergyGuide labels on refrigerators, freezers, dishwashers, and clothes washers. Use spreadsheet software to illustrate the energy efficiency and operating costs of various models.

Core Skills

8. **Writing.** Write a paper about your description of a healthful environment. What factors are included? What factors are absent?
9. **Science, reading.** Research one of the nonrenewable resources to learn how it is formed, where it is found, and what has been done to preserve it.

Can anything be used as a substitute for this resource? Take the time to identify and understand any technical terms used in your research.

10. **Science.** Research the use of wind energy in the world. Where is the largest wind-energy farm located in the United States? in the world? Report the number and size of the wind generators used in both locations as well as the amount of electricity produced.

11. **Math.** Use spreadsheet software to make a list of all the purchases you make in a week. Place the price of the items in one column, the amount of tax in a second column, and the totals in a third. Add the columns to see how much tax you have paid and how much your totals are as compared with the base costs of the items.

12. **Writing.** Create a class blog promoting resource conservation. Include information from this chapter as well as additional information from outside sources.

13. **Writing.** Social entrepreneurs are people who recognize major issues in a community or society and work to develop a solution or new system to address these issues. Research Anna Y. Reed and Eli Weaver and their impact on education and social reform. Write a report about their societal influences and create a timeline showing their major contributions.

Leadership
Development

Using a Community Needs Assessment as a part of your work in the Community Service program, plan activities to: honor local service members, host a blood drive, raise funds for a local food bank, support foster children, or teach technology skills to older adults.

Portfolio
Builder

You want your home and neighborhood to be a safe, secure place. With the help of your local police department, organize a neighborhood watch program. If one already exists in your neighborhood, join it. At meetings, take notes about home security issues in your area and how crime can be prevented. If the police department offers workshops on crime prevention topics, attend them. Add meeting notes and any workshop certificates to your portfolio.

Journal
Writing

You do not have an after-school job, but you know the importance of having work experience to list on college and job applications. You are considering doing some volunteer work in your community instead. This could be a fun and meaningful opportunity to help others while building an attractive résumé.

Write About It: *What factors should you consider in choosing the best volunteer options for yourself? How will you benefit from the experience now? How might volunteer work help you get a job later? How might it help you identify your future career goals?*

Relationships

Human Services

The Counseling and Mental Health Services Pathway within the Human Services career cluster involves working with people as individuals and as large groups to address social-emotional wellness. Sociologists, psychologists, and counselors are examples of careers within this pathway.

Human Services Careers

Early Childhood Development and Services

Counseling and Mental Health Services

Family and Community Services

Personal Care Services

Consumer Services

PeopleImages/E+/Getty Images

Education and Training

The Professional Support Services Pathway within the Education and Training career cluster involves helping people address problems and develop strategies to cope with and manage issues. Counselors, teachers, social workers, and advisers are examples of such careers. These careers are also considered Human Services careers.

Education and Training Pathways

Administration and Administrative Support

Professional Support Services

Teaching and Training

Wavebreakmedia Ltd/Wavebreak Media/Thinkstock

Career Spotlight: Sociologist

- *Description.* Sociologists study human society and the social behavior of large groups. They study cultures, organizations, and social institutions. Sociologists collect data about the attitudes, beliefs, and behaviors of different groups; analyze that data; and form research-supported conclusions. Most sociologists work in research institutions, colleges and universities, government agencies, or consulting agencies.
- *Education and training.* Most sociologists have a master's degree or Ph.D. in sociology. Master's programs in sociology either prepare students for a Ph.D. program or to enter the workforce. People with a bachelor's degree in sociology often find work in other fields such as social services, sales and marketing, and management.
- *Skills and personal qualities.* Sociologists must have strong analytical, communication, problem-solving, and critical-thinking skills. They should also have good reasoning skills and social perceptiveness. For sociologists who plan to teach sociology, instructing and speaking skills are also important.
- *Job outlook.* Job growth for sociologists through 2028 is projected to grow faster than average for all occupations. Visit the Occupational Outlook Handbook online to learn more about a career as a sociologist.

Human Services

Career Spotlight: Mental Health Counselor

- *Description.* Mental health counselors help people diagnose, manage, and treat mental and emotional disorders or issues. They may help individuals deal with family and relationship troubles, substance abuse and addiction, stress management, self-esteem, and other issues. Mental health counselors listen carefully and ask questions to help clients understand their problems. They also help clients develop skills and strategies to improve their lives.
- *Education and training.* Mental health counselors are usually required to have a master's degree in psychology, counseling, social work, or a related mental health field. They also need a license to practice. In addition, mental health counselors must complete annual continuing education classes.
- *Skills and personal qualities.* Mental health counselors must be compassionate and have the desire to help people. They must have strong interpersonal, listening, speaking, and organizational skills. They should also have good decision-making and critical-thinking skills.
- *Job outlook.* Job growth for mental health counselors through 2028 is projected to grow 22 percent, or much faster than average for all occupations. Visit the *Occupational Outlook Handbook* online to learn more about a career as a mental health counselor.

Education & Training

Sources: States' Career Clusters Initiative, Bureau of Labor Statistics Career Guide to Industries

Chapter 6
Understanding Families

Reading Prep

Scan this chapter and look for information presented as fact. As you read this chapter, try to determine which topics are fact and which topics are the author's opinions. After reading the chapter, research the topics and verify which topics are facts and which are opinions.

Concept Organizer

 Create a fishbone diagram including the different functions of the family. For each function, list details of ways your family fulfills these functions.

G-WLEARNING.com

Click on the activity icon to visit www.g-wlearning. com/comprehensive/8062 to access online vocabulary activities using key terms from the chapter.

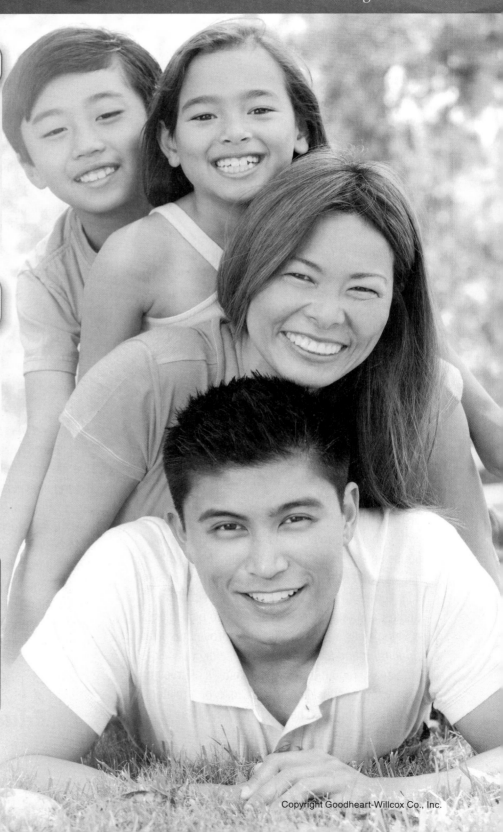

What Is a Family?

Objectives

After studying this section, you will be able to

- **describe** roles of family members.
- **name** functions the family unit performs for individuals and society.
- **analyze** how people with a single lifestyle meet their needs for the functions provided by families.

Key Terms

family   procreation   socialization

The family unit forms the foundation of society. Most people are raised in family settings. In these settings, they learn skills and share experiences that will shape the rest of their lives.

The term **family** can be defined in a number of ways. One common definition is: two or more people related by blood, marriage, or adoption. This definition emphasizes the structure of the family unit. Other definitions emphasize the roles, responsibilities, rights, and relationships of family members. For example, a family can be described as two or more persons committed to one another over time who share resources, responsibility for decisions, values, and goals.

What makes the family such an important unit? To answer this question, you must take a closer look at the roles family members fulfill. You must also consider the functions families provide for individuals and society.

Roles of Family Members

Each member of a family has special roles to play. Such roles include parent, child, spouse, sibling, and income provider. The behaviors expected of people in these roles vary from family to family. Many of your family roles were inherited when you were born. At birth, your sex determined your role as son or daughter, brother or sister, and niece or nephew. See **6-1**.

AJR_photo/Shutterstock.com

6-1

In this family, how many different roles can you identify?

Some of your family roles are assigned to you. You are expected to fulfill certain responsibilities as a result of assigned roles. For instance, if you are an older sibling, you may have to fill the role of caregiver to younger siblings.

Some roles are chosen. If you have talent in the kitchen, you might choose the role of family cook.

Functions of the Family

Through their various roles and responsibilities, family members form an interactive unit. This unit creates a healthful physical, mental, emotional, social, and spiritual environment for its members. The family unit also has a number of societal functions. Family functions include procreation, providing basic physical needs, socializing children, and providing emotional support to family members.

Procreation

One of the basic functions of the family is **procreation**, or the bearing of children. Parents have children to express their love for each other. They desire the experience of raising children and watching

Analyze and Solve

Research role overload in dual-career families. What are some strategies families can use to prevent role overload?

them grow into unique adults. They want their children to carry on the heritage and traditions of their family line.

The function of procreation assures the continuation of society. As children are born into families, the population is maintained. As the children become adults, they may find partners and decide to have children of their own. Their parents then become grandparents. As the youngest generation continues to procreate, the cycle continues.

Physical Care

When parents supply their children with food, clothing, and shelter, they are providing the function of physical care. This function also includes providing medical care and creating a safe and healthy environment.

Society helps families with the function of physical care. If parents cannot afford food, shelter, or medical care, public assistance and charitable programs try to meet those needs. If families face unsafe situations, police and fire departments can assist them.

Society is not set up to provide complete physical care for all people. Therefore, families serve a vital function by satisfying some of these needs themselves.

Socialization

Another important function of families is the **socialization** of children. This means teaching children to conform to social standards. As parents socialize their children, they act as authority figures in the home. In this role, they establish reasonable rules of conduct. Parents set limits that protect their children and teach them appropriate behavior.

Teaching children about their heritage is part of socialization. Children need to learn about their cultural background. Parents can share family traditions with children and help the children develop pride in their ancestral roots.

Education is also part of the socialization process. Parents provide infants and young children with general guidance and moral education. They act as role models and provide career training. Parents are also responsible for enrolling their children in formal education programs. As children get older, therefore, schools and other agencies assume part of the responsibility for socialization.

Emotional Support

Perhaps the most critical function of families in today's society is the emotional support of family members. No other social unit can replace the family for providing children with love and nurturing. Parents form a bond with their infant children. As children grow, parents are there to comfort children when they are sad. They can reassure children when they have doubts. They can forgive children when they make mistakes. See **6-2**.

Wellness Awareness

Investigate public health programs offering free or discounted medical care to children. Develop a list of programs available in your area.

Mental Health Awareness

Physical Needs and Trust

How well a family meets children's physical needs has a great impact on their sense of trust and security. According to Erik Erikson's psychosocial theory, children raised without their basic needs met often develop anxiety about themselves and the world in general. Witnessing parents struggle to provide basic care makes them fearful about the future. They may doubt their own self-worth. If these fears are not addressed, they can continue into adulthood.

Children are not the only family members who require support. Parents rely on their children to let them know they are loved and appreciated. Parents also count on support from each other. Some marriages are partner-centered instead of children-centered. Partner-centered marriages often provide stability in the home and create a secure atmosphere for all. Children as well as parents benefit from a family that is led by a strong partnership.

Single Living

Not all people live in families. Many adults are single. They may live alone or with roommates. These adults must find other resources to meet their needs for functions provided by the family.

People choose a single lifestyle for different reasons. Some single people want time to explore their own interests. Some people want the flexibility to travel. Some people want a single lifestyle while they finish their education or establish careers.

A single lifestyle is not always chosen. Widowed people are forced to accept a single lifestyle when their mates die. Likewise, people must make a transition to a single lifestyle when a divorce occurs. Some people who would like to be married struggle to accept a single lifestyle. Some of these people never find the right person to be a marriage partner. Others had a painful relationship in the past and are afraid to develop a new relationship.

Meeting Needs for Family Functions

Regardless of the reasons for their lifestyle, single people need the functions provided by families. They must find other means of meeting these needs.

Adult single people must work to earn a living and provide for their own physical care. They pay for their own housing. They buy their own food and clothing. They rely on physicians when they get sick. They turn to public agencies, such as police and fire departments, for help with their needs for safety.

Many single people have a strong network of friends. These friends serve as a source of emotional support. They provide love and encouragement when family members are not available. Some single people live with roommates. Roommates help share the expenses of food, housing, and other physical needs. They provide one another with a sense of security. They also help meet emotional needs by providing companionship. Although people in a single lifestyle do not live with family members, they often maintain close relationships with them. Visits, e-mail, and phone calls provide the family contact many single people require.

6-2

Helping children feel secure is one way parents provide emotional support.

Social skills. Tamika's coworkers admire her because she conducts herself in a respectable, professional manner. Her interactions with others are as positive as possible.

Reading
Review

1. What are the three ways family members get their various roles?
2. What are the four main functions of the family?
3. List three ways single people meet needs provided by families.

Section 6-2

Family Structures Vary

Objectives

After studying this section, you will be able to

- **describe** characteristics of various family structures.
- **name** six factors that can influence family responsibilities.

Key Terms

family structure	extended family	media
nuclear family	childless family	demographics
single-parent family	adoptive family	
stepfamily	foster family	

How would you describe a typical family? Your answer to this question is likely to differ from the answers given by your classmates. This is because there is no "typical" family. Some families have two parents and some families have one parent. Some families have stepparents and stepchildren. Some families have grandparents, aunts, uncles, and cousins. Some families have children and some families do not.

Family Structures

Family structure refers to the makeup of a family group. It is based on the relationships of the members in the family. Each basic structure is able to provide the main family functions for its members.

Nuclear Families

A **nuclear family** is a family group that consists of a man and woman and their children. This structure gives children the comfort and security of family ties with both parents. It gives them a solid base for the development of human relationships. The nuclear family also gives children a view of adult roles modeled by their parents.

Single-Parent Families

In the **single-parent family** structure, one adult lives with one or more children. The adult may be widowed, separated, divorced, or never married. The single parent must provide the functions of a family without the aid of a spouse.

Cooperation is the key to success in single-parent families. Each member should be aware of the needs and concerns of other members. When one family member has a problem, another member may be able to understand and offer help.

Stepfamilies

When a single parent marries, a **stepfamily** is formed. One spouse or both spouses have children from other marriages. Thus, the stepfamily structure includes the roles of stepparents and stepchildren.

In most cases, at least some of the family members were previously part of a nuclear family. They may have faced the crisis of death or divorce. Making the adjustment to a stepfamily may be stressful for them. To cushion this adjustment, each family member must try to be understanding and cooperative.

A stepfamily is usually a new experience for everyone involved. Each person brings his or her hopes and doubts into the family. New relationships form. Besides adjusting to each other, husbands and wives must adjust to each other's children. The children must adjust to a new parent as well as new brothers and sisters.

Extended Families

Extended family includes relatives other than parents and their children, such as grandparents, aunts, uncles, and/or cousins.

In many extended families, members offer one another support. Grandparents and other adults may help care for children in the family. Some middle-age adults have the responsibility of providing care to aging parents. These arrangements are more common when extended family members live nearby.

Adoptive and Foster Families

In **adoptive families**, couples choose to legally adopt another couple's child. Some couples adopt because they cannot have children of their own. Others choose to adopt in addition to having biological children.

In **foster families**, couples temporarily provide care for children from other families because their parents cannot. Some children remain in a foster family until they can be permanently placed with another family. Other children may return to their biological families.

Childless Families

Another type of family structure is the childless family. A **childless family** is a couple without children. Some childless couples are not able to have children and prefer not to adopt. Other couples choose not to have children.

People who do not have children may choose to interact with children in other settings. They might spend time with nieces or nephews. They might also do volunteer work with children in their community.

Cross-cultural skills.
Ron strives to hire people of diverse backgrounds. He believes that people of varied backgrounds can provide his company with new ideas and increase both innovation and quality of work.

Factors Influencing Families

Families are affected by outside forces, both good and bad. Parents try to take advantage of the positive influences to enhance the family's well-being. They also try, to the extent possible, to shield family members from negative influences.

Cultural Influences

Perhaps the strongest influence in shaping family structure is the cultural heritage of the individuals involved. Culture shapes a person's expectations for the different roles of various family members. The U.S. population includes people from cultures throughout the world. Therefore, newlyweds may have different expectations for their new life together if they come from different cultural backgrounds.

Respect for the extended family is a strong influence among people of many cultures. The benefits of a close extended family may include help with child care tasks. While the son or daughter raised in a tight-knit extended family may feel comfortable with this arrangement, his or her spouse may not.

The cultures that value extended families are also likely to emphasize family interests over the individual's. This may be expressed by the family deciding what career their son or daughter eventually pursues. A family-arranged marriage is another sign of a family that emphasizes family interests over the individual's. See **6-3**.

6-3

Couples contemplating marriage would benefit from meeting each other's families to experience their customs and values firsthand.

Healthy Living

Television Influences

Children and teens can learn from viewing high-quality TV programming. However, passively watching many hours of TV per day can have negative effects. Studies show that TV violence can cause children and teens to be more likely to hurt others, behave aggressively, and lack empathy. To counteract TV's negative influence

- limit TV viewing to one or two hours daily. No TV for children two and under.
- choose programs as a family. Talk about compelling issues and news events.
- participate in other family activities. Play games, go biking, or take a walk.

Societal Influences

Through the socialization process, parents teach children the do's and don'ts of society. The family interprets the standards of society to help children understand what behaviors are expected of them. By learning these important lessons through teaching and training, children understand how the standards apply to their lives. With parental love and support, children then grow into productive members of society.

In a democratic society, free expression is allowed and encouraged. Sometimes the ideas and values expressed are not consistent with what children learn from their families. Peers, for example, can strongly influence individuals to join group activities, for good or bad.

Advertising and other forms of media can also influence individuals to behave contrary to their training. **Media** are channels of mass communication, such as magazines, television, radio, and the Internet. These influences can convey beliefs, priorities, and standards of conduct contrary to a family's view of what is right and proper.

When negative influences from society begin to make an impact, parents are challenged to work harder in the role of socializing their children.

Technological Influences

Many of the time- and energy-saving tools and appliances used in homes are the result of technology. These devices help families manage their lives and interact with their children.

Telecommuting is also possible as a result of technology. Telecommuting allows parents to earn income while staying home. When parents work from their homes, they can tailor their schedules to include both roles of parent and income producer. As a result, they mesh the responsibilities of being a parent with those of being an employee, **6-4**.

One of the most important benefits of new technology is the ability to communicate easily with others. Using the Internet, family members living apart can stay in touch. They can share family photos and custom-made video clips, such as thank-you messages or birthday greetings.

Living Green

Technological advances in appliances and tools are increasing energy efficiency. As your family shops for appliances, encourage them to consider buying energy-saving appliances and tools. These appliances and tools will help conserve energy as well as save your family money on bills.

Broadcasts of holiday celebrations and family events help family members throughout the world share common experiences. Communication technology increases the ability of families to provide emotional support to distant members.

Demographic Factors

Many demographic factors indicate that families are changing. **Demographics** are statistical qualities of the human population. By checking demographics, many trends can be observed.

A major trend affecting the family is the high percentage of women working away from home. Historically, the man was the "breadwinner" while the woman tended to the home and family. Today the majority of mothers hold jobs outside the home. If fathers are also away at work, some outside help is needed to care for young children. Extended families are very helpful in this situation. With one or more other adults living with the family, someone may always be present to care for the children. Without this help, parents often share—with a babysitter, child care worker, or teacher—their responsibilities for providing physical care and socialization to children.

Another trend that impacts families is the growing population of older adults due to increasing lifespan. When older adults are healthy, they can lead independent lives. When their health begins to fail, their lifestyles must change, too. Older adults with physical or mental disabilities must be watched closely so they do not fall prey to accidents or safety hazards.

Another important demographic trend is the high mobility of the U.S. population. Compared to past generations, when moving once or twice was common, today's families move five or more times. Often they move so parents have better job opportunities. The move may benefit the family financially, but it can negatively impact members emotionally. Left behind are cousins, aunts, uncles, and grandparents that provided emotional support. Often they provided physical support, too, especially in helping with child care. In these situations, parents must fill the void created by moving away from beloved family members.

Economic Forces

Economic forces have much to do with a family's well-being. The absence of good jobs causes some families to leave familiar

6-4
Mothers of young children especially value telecommuting careers.

Mental Health Awareness

Social Media and Self-Esteem

Social media can be useful for sending updates and staying connected with distant family members and friends. Excessive use of social media, however, may be a sign of insecurity. Some studies show that people with low self-esteem may send hourly updates and post frequent selfies as a way to get approval and recognition.

surroundings, seeking opportunities elsewhere. Left behind is the family support system that helped in times of need.

If one salary does not satisfy family needs, one parent must work multiple jobs or both parents must earn incomes. In these cases, parents are often faced with finding alternatives for handling part of their child care responsibilities. When older children are present, more household and child care responsibilities are usually assigned to them.

World Events

Family development is influenced not only by events within the country, but also by world situations. People of the world are no longer isolated from one another. New communication systems make worldwide information readily available. Therefore, events that occur in one country become common knowledge around the world within minutes.

Social and political unrest in one area of the world can influence countries on the other side of the globe. Family members can be separated when there is a need to send military troops abroad. Natural disasters such as floods or earthquakes can devastate whole cities. After such events, families from distant countries may donate money, clothing, and food to assist the victims.

The family is no longer an independent economic unit. Families depend on global markets to satisfy needs for many products. For example, consider what happens when a war interferes with shipments of petroleum from oil-producing countries. Less fuel is available to drive cars and heat homes, causing prices to skyrocket. Families have little choice but to pay the higher prices. Often they must alter their lifestyles and postpone unnecessary purchases, too. Higher fuel costs eventually increase the prices of all goods and services, affecting everyone's pocketbook. This, in turn, influences the general economy. When the public has less spending power, companies respond by producing less and, thus, cutting jobs. Events in other parts of the world can have long-term effects on families in your area.

Living Green

World events, such as high fuel costs can affect a family budget. To avoid high fuel costs, consider walking to nearby destinations as a family. The physical activity is good for family members and allows you to spend quality time together.

Reading
Review

1. The makeup of a family group is called _____.
2. Identify six types of family structures and provide a brief description of each.
3. List six factors that can affect the responsibilities of family members.

Section 6-3

Family Structures Change

Objectives

After studying this section, you will be able to

- **list** the six stages of the family life cycle.
- **determine** the consequences of divorce.

Key Term

family life cycle

Family structures do not always remain the same. They may change as new members are added to a family or as present members leave. For instance, a nuclear family may become a single-parent family. Some of these changes occur as a result of the natural passage of time.

Family Life Cycle

While family structures vary, each structure includes basic stages of growth and development called the **family life cycle**. See **6-5**. Studying this cycle can help people prepare for the challenges that may exist in their own families.

6-5

Family life follows a series of stages as couples age and children come and go.

Family Life Cycle

Beginning Stage	Childbearing Stage	Parenting Stage	Launching Stage	Mid-Years Stage	Aging Stage
• Married couple without children	• Couple from birth of first child through birth of last child	• Couple with child(ren)	• Couple with child(ren) leaving home	• Couple with independent child(ren) living away from home	• Couple during retirement until death of both spouses

Stages in the Cycle

The family life cycle contains six main stages. The first stage is known as the *beginning stage*. Families in this stage consist of a married couple. While in this stage, couples make adjustments to marriage and form foundations for their future families. There may be many money pressures as couples try to establish a new home. There may be time pressures, too, as spouses try to build careers, finish a higher education, or perhaps do both.

During the years when a family is growing, it is in the *childbearing stage*. This stage includes the birth of the first child through the birth of the last child. This is a very busy period since attention to the child is full time. If a parent cannot stay home with the child, arrangements must be made so the child receives quality care. Whether a career couple hires outside help or one spouse stays home full time, there is often considerable money pressure.

The family continues to grow in the *parenting stage*. Parents provide for the children, while the children pursue their individual interests and school activities. This tends to be the most expensive stage of the family life cycle. Food and clothing costs increase as children grow. Having enough space for everyone to live comfortably may require remodeling the family home or moving to a larger one. School activities and sports often involve extra fees. Saving money for the children's college educations occurs during this period. Also, tension between the spouses can develop if there is no plan for handling the many housekeeping and child care duties.

The *launching stage* is when children begin to leave home and become independent of their parents. They may leave for college and continue after graduation in their chosen careers. Some may find jobs and move to their own housing; others marry and start their own families. However, today it is not unusual for adult children to return home at some point.

The launching stage is followed by the *mid-years stage* when all children have left and the couple is again independent. During this period, couples enter their peak earning years. They can spend more of their income on themselves instead of the children. They may do so by upgrading their homes or taking more frequent vacations. They may also become grandparents in this stage.

The final stage of the family life cycle is the *aging stage*. This stage begins at the time of retirement and continues until both spouses die. During this stage, one spouse may live alone after the death of the other. When the spouses are financially secure and enjoying good health, it is a very rewarding period. Time can be devoted to lifelong interests at whatever pace is comfortable. When problems begin to surface over finances and/or health, life can become unpleasant. Tensions may develop with other family members who try to offer assistance.

Variations in the Cycle

Families are unique and do not always fit a given mold. Many families have overlaps in the stages and substages of the life cycle. For example, a family may include a baby, school-age children, and teenagers all at one time. A family may launch an older child while a preschooler is still at home.

Sometimes many years separate the stages of a family's life cycle. For example, a couple may have a teenager before their second child is born. This family experiences the qualities of both the childbearing and parenting stages.

As individuals progress through the stages of the family life cycle, they are faced with different roles and responsibilities. Roles change as family members grow older. For example, in the beginning stage, a man has the role of husband and provider. In the childbearing family stage, he takes on the additional role of father, **6-6**. In the aging stage, he no longer has the role of provider and may have to accept the role of widower.

6-6

A man takes on a new family role with new responsibilities when he becomes a father.

Divorce

Changes in family structure are not always the result of time passage. A change from a nuclear family to a single-parent family is often the result of divorce. Divorce is common in today's society. Many couples decide they have problems and differences that cannot be resolved. They believe they would be happier living apart, so they get a divorce. Divorce rates are high among people of all ages, economic levels, and religions.

Adjusting to Divorce

Divorce creates many changes for many people. The two former spouses have to break their emotional ties to each other. They have to go through the legal process of ending their marriage. They have to set up two separate households. This means changing their budgets and usually leading simpler, less costly lifestyles.

Analyze and Solve

If your first marriage ended in divorce over financial matters, what would you do to help avoid divorce in your second marriage?

Divorced persons have to learn to think of themselves as individuals again. They have to adjust to independence. They have to learn to make decisions by themselves and lead their own lives.

Divorce affects not only the couple, but also the people they know. Friends, neighbors, and colleagues of the couple may choose sides and become either "his" or "her" friends. Some people who have a negative view of divorce may not want to remain friendly with either member of the divorce. Other people may remain supportive and help the divorced persons make new social contacts.

Children of a divorced couple face many changes, too. They have to adjust to living with one parent and visiting the other parent. They may have to move to a new home. They may have to go to a new school and meet new friends. In addition, they have to adjust to the changes in their parents' social lives.

Life Skills

Successful Marriages

With the divorce rate in the United States hovering between 40% and 50%, it is good to remember this means between 50% and 60% of marriages are successful.

Many young people assume that once you find a marriage partner, the relationship works because your partner will always simply "know" what you need and how to provide it. See 6-7. They think that getting married will make them happy. Nothing could be further from the truth. Your happiness as a person and as a partner comes from within you. While marriage may increase your happiness, it will never be the primary reason for it.

Every marriage is different because the people are different, as are their values, standards, and priorities. Numerous studies of healthy, long-lasting unions, however, indicate some qualities and characteristics are common to nearly all of them. Love and open, honest, and respectful communication are often given as the primary reasons for a marriage's success. While this may sound easy, there are times that individuals cannot (or choose not to) be openly communicative. What happens to love then? It is during difficult and trying times that marriages are tested.

The following tips from successful married couples are always good advice:
- Enjoy each other and laugh together.
- Be supportive and compliment each other often.
- Respect each other's need for privacy and space.
- Make decisions and parent together.
- Forgive one another.
- Keep the romance alive.

Remarriage

Remarriage is another event that causes family structures to change. Many single-parent families become stepfamilies when divorced people remarry.

Second marriages have just as many challenges as first marriages. When children from previous marriages are involved, second marriages may have even more challenges. Cooperation and communication can help spouses successfully handle these challenges. Spouses in second marriages may be more willing to cooperate with each other. They may try harder to keep communication lines open. This helps them keep in touch with each other's thoughts and feelings. Communication also prevents minor problems from growing and becoming major problems. With good cooperation and communication, any marriage can be successful.

6-7

Developing your marriage beyond the initial romantic stage takes dedication to each other and open communication, especially during challenging times.

Reading
Review

1. What are the six stages of the family life cycle?
2. True or false. When a couple divorces, their friends, neighbors, and colleagues are affected.
3. What qualities can help increase the success of second marriages?

Chapter 6 Review

Summary

The family is the most important social unit in cultures throughout the world. Each person fulfills various inherited and assigned roles as a family member. The family provides the functions of procreation, physical care, socialization, and emotional support for its members.

Families take the form of different family structures. A nuclear family includes a husband, wife, and their children. A single-parent family has one parent and one or more children. A stepfamily contains stepparents and stepchildren. Extended family includes relatives such as an aunt or a grandmother. An adoptive family forms when a couple or single person legally adopts a child from another family. A foster family forms when a couple temporarily provides care for a child because his or her parents cannot. A childless family consists of a couple without children. Single people do not live in any of these family structures. They meet their needs for the functions provided by a family in other ways.

Various outside forces may affect the roles and responsibilities of family members. Culture, society, and technology are strong influences. Some demographic factors that affect families include more women working outside the home, the longer lives of older family members, and more families moving more often. Economic forces and world events can also affect families.

Throughout their lives, the structures of families change. Some of these changes occur as a family goes through the stages of the family life cycle. Other changes in family structure are the result of divorce or remarriage.

 ## Critical Thinking

1. **Draw conclusions.** Which of the family structures discussed in this chapter do you feel is best equipped to provide the functions of the family? Explain your answer.

2. **Analyze decisions.** If you were going to choose a family-related career, which one would you choose? Why?

3. **Form a hypothesis.** Which stage in the family life cycle do you think would be the most exciting stage for parents? Explain your answer.

4. **Analyze effects.** List two consequences a divorce would have for each of the following: a husband, a wife, and children.

 ## 21st Century Applications

5. **Creativity and innovation.** Write a story about a family in the year 2050. Describe how roles of family members and functions provided by the family might change in the future.

6. **Global awareness.** Research the emphasis on family in different cultures. Then compare and contrast two cultures of your choice.

7. **Media literacy.** Develop a list of new technologies that influence families. For each item on your list, identify the positive and negative influences on families.

Core
Skills

8. **Social studies, reading.** Research how families in various countries perform the function of socialization. How are they similar or different than socialization customs with which you are familiar?

9. **Writing.** Research the current trends regarding the launching stage. Statistically, how many "launched" children return home to live with their parents again? Write a report including references of your findings.

10. **Speaking.** Research the current statistics on divorce and remarriage. Share your findings in an oral report.

11. **Social studies.** Discuss how the family unit has remained a constant in the evolution of the human race.

12. **Reading.** Use the Internet to research statistics on single adults. What percentage of the population stays single today as compared to 50 years ago? a hundred years ago? Why do you think this is the case?

13. **Math.** Use the Internet to find statistics on the percentage of women working away from home. Find statistics from the last 50 years, then use graphing software to make a graph illustrating the trend.

Leadership
Development

As a part of working on the Family Ties unit of the Power of One National Program, set goals for increasing your role in providing some of the functions of the family for family members. After carrying out a plan of action to achieve those goals, write a two-page report explaining how this project has made a difference in your life.

Portfolio
Builder

Perform volunteer work with a family service organization in your community. Possible organizations might include Big Brothers, Big Sisters, Habitat for Humanity, homeless shelters, and food banks. Document your experience for your portfolio, including:
- name and description of the organization
- dates of your participation
- description of what you did
- any photos showing your participation

Journal
Writing

Your family believes your older sister has been successfully launched. She has chosen a career, achieved the required education, completed training, and accepted a job within driving distance of her apartment. To your parents' surprise, she announces that she will be moving back home with them…and you.

Write About It: *How will this affect you? What rules and expectations might apply to your sister that do not apply to you? Which rules and expectations might apply to you that do not apply to your sister?*

Chapter 7
Strengthening Families

Reading Prep

Before reading this chapter, flip through the pages and make notes of the major headings. Compare these headings to the objectives. What did you discover? How will this help you prepare to read new material?

Concept Organizer

Create a spider map listing ways to make and keep families strong. For each way, add details of how you can help achieve this goal in your family.

G-WLEARNING.com

Click on the activity icon to visit www.g-wlearning.com/comprehensive/8062 to access online vocabulary activities using key terms from the chapter.

ESB_Basic/Shutterstock.com

Building Functional Families

Objectives

After studying this section, you will be able to

- **describe** characteristics of functional families.
- **list** techniques family members can use to build a functional family.
- **explain** how functional families fulfill their family rights and responsibilities.

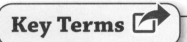
Key Terms

functional family   dysfunctional family   codependency

In today's complex world, people face the challenge of keeping the family unit strong. This challenge is not always easy to meet. However, many families face the challenge by making family life a top priority. Family members know and accept the responsibility they have for one another. They are committed to working together and making special sacrifices to help one another.

Making and Keeping Families Strong

A strong, healthy family is also called a **functional family**. A functional family provides a positive environment. Each family member is encouraged to grow and to reach his or her fullest potential, **7-1**. A functional family tries to stay balanced. The family works together to meet the needs of each member. In turn, each family member carries out his or her roles and responsibilities. Together, the family works to keep their unit strong, healthy, and happy.

Functional families have certain qualities in common. They communicate effectively. When problems arise, they try to solve them. Spending time together is important to them. Family members appreciate and support one another. Each member tries to understand the roles of other family members. Above all, they value family life.

Functional families also realize they are not perfect. Their lives do not always run smoothly. However, they have a sense of purpose. They work hard to overcome obstacles and stay strong. They feel the rewards are worth the effort they put into the relationship.

monkeybusinessimages/iStock/Getty Images Plus

7-1

Functional families provide for the physical, social, emotional, and spiritual needs of their members. They put the family first.

Communication. Addison supervises a large staff. Her employees always know what is expected of them because Addison gives clear, precise directions. When she gives criticism, it is constructive and helps her employees learn.

Have you thought about what you can do to strengthen your family and help keep it that way? Some helpful techniques you and your family can use to achieve this goal are described below.

Communicate Effectively

You can find ways to communicate more effectively with your family. Make a point to talk with other family members. Listen carefully to make sure you understand the other person's viewpoint. Plan to have mealtimes together to talk about daily events, or set up a regular family meeting. When schedules are hard to coordinate, try using notes, e-mail messages, and telephone calls as a pleasant surprise. This method may also help your family stay in touch with members who are away from home. Communicate positive feelings by planning special events the family can enjoy together. Communicate your understanding of others' feelings. Sincere words like "I love you" accompanied by a hug or a kiss can lift spirits or mend hurt feelings. Good communication promotes growth for all family members.

Solve Problems

Functional families try to resolve problems and conflicts in positive ways. When all family members tackle problems together, they develop a feeling of joint ownership. Jointly owned problems are usually easier to solve. There are more people to identify possible solutions.

Get Help When Needed

Functional families admit they have as many problems as less-healthy, or dysfunctional families. A **dysfunctional family** provides a negative environment that discourages the growth and development of family members. The difference between a functional family and dysfunctional family is the way they look at problems and solve them. For example, some dysfunctional families try too hard to help their members. They may assume responsibility for family members who have serious problems by covering for them. This is called **codependency**. A pattern of unhealthy behaviors is used by family members to cover up the problem. Codependency adversely affects the emotional health of everyone in the family and does not help the family member who has the problem.

Functional families look for positive outcomes in all types of situations—even problem situations. They deal with the problems instead of being destroyed by them. When they cannot solve a problem themselves, they seek outside help.

Life Skills

Facing Family Challenges

When your family faces what you consider a real problem, try using the problem-solving process. Openly discuss the problem; don't let it build up inside. State your feelings using I-messages. Avoid name-calling or blaming someone else for your problem. Try for an I win/you win situation by compromising or negotiating for a satisfactory solution. If a serious problem arises that cannot be resolved within the family, suggest seeking help outside the family.

Spend Time Together

Functional families spend time together whenever possible. They bring a sense of play and humor into their leisure time. Family interactions are balanced, so all members feel involved. Some families go to the movies, work on hobbies together, or have a family game night. What is most important is they do something together as a family.

You can find ways to spend time with your family, too. Look for special activities you and your family can share, like biking or preparing evening meals. Help plan a family vacation or outing. Share family celebrations like birthdays and anniversaries. Celebrate religious and patriotic holidays together. Start a new family tradition that will help create happy memories, such as visiting a museum or planting trees. Plan ahead with your family so everyone can get involved.

Show Appreciation

Functional families find ways to show appreciation. This form of emotional support encourages a secure and loving environment. Showing appreciation through words or actions contributes to each member's well-being and self-esteem.

Mental Health Awareness

Codependency and Self-Concept

Codependent family members often struggle with self-concept issues. Their sense of identity is often linked to pleasing and caring for other people. They look to others for approval and feel guilty if they do not meet others' expectations. This behavior can lead to other dysfunctional relationships outside the family.

You can show family members appreciation in your everyday actions. Offer to help out without being asked. Thank others when they help you. Give sincere compliments about a job well done or when someone looks nice. Create your own special event for a family member. Let others know they are special in your life by the things you say and do.

Show Respect

No two members of a family are exactly alike. To keep families strong, members need to show respect for one another. This can be done in a number of ways. They can respect one another's ideas and opinions, recognizing that not everyone will agree on every matter. Listening to what everyone has to say, no matter how old they are, is important. Each individual will have likes and dislikes. These, too, should be respected.

Family members can respect one another's privacy, as well as their personal belongings. Asking if you can borrow an item that belongs to a brother or sister rather than taking the item without a word shows respect. Showing respect for older members of the family is important in most cultures. When you show respect for family members, they feel valued and loved. Respect is an important part of emotional support and leads to feelings of trust.

Understand One Another

Functional families try to understand the changing roles of each family member. They recognize that family tensions may increase during the period of adolescence. The adolescent is learning independence, while parents are beginning to give up some controls. It is a period of uncertainty and adjustment for both adolescents and parents. Both parties must try harder to understand and accept the changes that occur during this period. All must make an extra effort to show respect for one another and trust one another.

Understanding your changing role may help you understand your parents' point of view. Your parents are watching you grow from a child to an adult. During this time, you and your parents will not always agree. Being patient and understanding may be helpful. Try speaking and acting in ways that help make this transition smoother for both sides.

Living Green

Family projects bring family members closer together. Spend time as a family by planting and caring for a garden. Flower gardens will add beauty to your home, and vegetables from your garden will add nutrition to family meals.

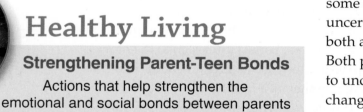

Healthy Living

Strengthening Parent-Teen Bonds

Actions that help strengthen the emotional and social bonds between parents and teens are important to family health. Try the following tips to strengthen these bonds:

- Conduct family meetings so everyone has a chance to bring up issues for discussion.
- Recognize potential problems and be willing to talk about them.
- Encourage open dialogue by listening and trying to understand the views of others.
- Communicate honestly and truthfully.
- Negotiate fairly.
- Use a normal tone of voice.
- Maintain self-control. When tempers flare, communication shuts down.
- Communicate without manipulating one another. Avoid trying to get your point across by making others feel guilty.
- Seek clarification when you lack understanding.

Fulfilling Family Rights and Responsibilities

In most families, family rights and responsibilities are closely linked. For each right a family member has, a responsibility comes with it. Functional families are committed to fulfilling these rights and responsibilities. They do so by sharing values and goals, responsibility for decisions, resources, and a commitment to one another.

Sharing Values and Goals

Family members have a right to expect support and guidance as they establish values and goals. Family members also have a responsibility to provide this support and guidance for one another.

Functional families share what is important to them both directly and indirectly. Parents directly teach their children *morals*—a sense of what is right or wrong. Children also learn what is important to their parents indirectly by watching what goes on around them. When family members live with certain values, these become important to all members. As a result, family members share many values even if they are not actually discussed.

Functional families help members develop values by being supportive. When a family member says "I think…" or "I believe…" others listen with respect and understanding. As a family, they are able to discuss issues openly. Open discussions also help family members develop good communication skills, self-respect, self-confidence, and self-esteem.

When family members share what they feel is important, they are likely to share goals, too. Families set goals that reflect their values. These goals give direction to their lives. When they share certain goals, it is easier for family members to work together with enthusiasm. Each person may try a little harder if the family is planning a vacation or saving for a new house.

Functional families encourage people to share goals. Family members can offer one another companionship as they work toward their goals. They can also celebrate together when their goals are reached.

Sharing Responsibility for Decisions

Family members have a right to learn and practice decision-making skills within the warm and supportive setting of the family unit. They also have a responsibility to provide input for family decisions that need to be made. Together, members of functional families can discuss ideas and explore alternatives. They can make wise decisions that are best for the entire family.

Sharing Resources

Functional families work together for the well-being of all members. Each member has a responsibility to contribute the special resources he or she has to offer. Each member also has a right to share in the resources contributed by others. Family members enjoy a sense of fulfillment in giving and receiving. See **7-2**.

The time, energy, interest, knowledge, and skills contributed by family members have economic value. When family members exchange these resources, they also help one another grow emotionally, intellectually, and socially. They all become better people. They help ensure economic security for their members.

Functional families use their resources for home management. They establish realistic expectations and set priorities.

Preparing work schedules and assigning responsibilities to all family members helps establish a balanced workload. Working together to manage the home gives members a sense of belonging. It also teaches job skills that will be useful when family members become wage earners.

Sharing a Lasting Commitment

Sharing commitment to one another is a right and a responsibility of family members. In functional families, a lasting commitment is the tie that binds family members. Commitment is an expression of love. It provides individualized attention to the needs of each person. This lasting commitment adds to a person's sense of security. At the end of a hard day, a worker needs to know that emotional support can be found at home. After surgery, a patient needs to know that family members will help make the recovery easier. People need to know they are not alone—their family will always be there for them.

The commitment among family members provides opportunities for giving as well as receiving. Cooking a special meal or mowing the lawn without being asked are thoughtful gestures that make everyone feel good. Just being there to listen is also important.

7-2

Children who learn about sharing family resources are more likely to contribute to the family group when they get older.

Reading
Review

1. Identify five qualities functional families have in common.
2. Explain the difference between a functional family and a dysfunctional family.
3. What is codependency? Give an example.
4. Explain how functional families fulfill their family rights and responsibilities.

Section 7-2

Balancing Work and Family

Objectives

After studying this section, you will be able to

- **explain** the relationship between family and work.

- **recognize** ways working families can manage multiple roles.

- **identify** ways employers can help dual-career families manage work and family roles.

Key Terms

dual-career family	**priority**	**flextime**
multiple roles	**job sharing**	**flexible workweek**

Families face challenges every day. One of the biggest challenges they face today is balancing the roles and responsibilities of family life and work. Not only do working parents provide economic support for family members, they must also fulfill parental roles. Work should be an enjoyable part of a well-rounded life. Work rewards and responsibilities should be balanced with those of personal and family life.

As employers face changing trends in the economy, they are trying to support harmony between work and family life. Family-oriented employers are adapting new programs and benefits to meet the needs of working parents. By allowing more choices, employers are helping working parents balance their family and work responsibilities.

The Relationship of Work and Family Life

The relationship between family life and work is complex. Each affects the other in both positive and negative ways. Work affects the quality of family life; in turn, the quality of family life affects work performance.

The Effects of Work on Family Life

Work has both positive and negative effects on family life. Many workers find satisfaction in developing their professional roles as well as contributing to the family's income. Job satisfaction is one positive effect that carries over to family life. People who find jobs for which they are well-suited receive more satisfaction from working. This helps them focus more positively on family responsibilities when they are at home. Work satisfaction gives them more confidence in managing everyday tasks and problems.

Parents who enjoy their work can convey this attitude to their children. They can encourage children to perform work tasks at home and praise them for well-done jobs. This helps children develop positive attitudes about work. Positive attitudes and skills that family members learn at home can be carried over into the workplace.

Work can have a positive effect on family relationships. Managing work and family time effectively becomes a shared effort among family members. Family relationships are often strengthened if members strive to be more supportive of one another in meeting responsibilities. Children often become more self-reliant and independent when both parents work.

Work can have negative effects on a worker's personal and family life, too. Time management and role overload are two common challenges faced by families with working members. Workers' job demands may leave them little time for themselves, family members, socializing, recreation, and household chores. Job demands may leave them too busy or too tired to devote enough time to family responsibilities.

Trying to fulfill too many roles can lead to role overload. Role overload can cause physical and emotional strain, which can lead to fatigue and irritability. Households with two working parents, single parents, and mothers with young children often experience the most difficulty with role overload, 7-3. These households have fewer family members with time available to handle child care, household, and job tasks.

When both spouses work outside the home, meeting family needs becomes even more challenging. Families in which both spouses are employed are called **dual-career families**. Spouses in these families must try to balance their work and marriage roles. If they have children, they also must manage their parenting roles. Dual-career families often need to make special efforts to keep communication open. Since family members may be away from home often, they must make the most of their time together.

The Effects of Family Life on Work

Just as work affects family life, family life affects work in positive and negative ways. Strong family relationships have a positive effect on work performance. A supportive family gives workers added energy to meet job demands.

Some aspects of family life can have negative effects on work performance. Having overly demanding family responsibilities is one example. Responsibilities such as caring for small children, older family members, or family members with disabilities place added role strain on workers. Work performance may suffer as the worker may be more tired, absent more often, and more focused on family matters.

7-3
Because a working mother with young children has many responsibilities to fulfill, she is more likely to experience role overload.

Managing Multiple Roles

People who combine family roles with their career roles have **multiple roles**. Balancing multiple roles is not easy since work roles often conflict with family roles. Fulfilling each of these roles places demands on all family members. Careful planning is needed for these families to meet their responsibilities. Managing family resources, such as time and energy, also becomes important.

Working parents face many decisions about how to manage their responsibilities at home and at work. Good managerial skills and relationship skills are the keys to balancing their busy lives. Setting priorities and making choices about household tasks, child care, and family schedules can help them make wiser decisions.

Set Priorities

To manage multiple roles, families have to learn to manage their time. This means the family must set priorities and then make choices accordingly. **Priorities** are important tasks ranked in order of importance. To set priorities, they must decide which tasks are most important to the family and then rank them in order of importance. Successful families need priorities to help them keep their focus and complete tasks. They must ask "What is of greatest importance to this family?" The answers

Self-direction. Cameron is considered to be proactive. He prioritizes tasks and works on important projects first. Cameron does not waste time because when he finishes a task, he finds additional tasks to do or asks his supervisor for more work.

will vary for different families. Decisions will be based on many factors, including family responsibilities. Some families may decide spending more time together is important. Others may choose to focus on meeting other basic needs. See **7-4**.

In making career-related decisions, parents must consider their children's needs, their own personal needs, and their career needs. Will their jobs provide enough financial resources? Will a job change interfere with the time they can spend with their children? Can they take on new job responsibilities and still devote quality time to family members?

Make Choices

Setting priorities is bound to create some priority conflicts that will need to be resolved. For instance, working late at the office might help a parent get a promotion and earn more money. However, this would mean spending less time with the children. This creates a conflict between the priorities of money and family interaction. Family members will have to pull together to make a choice.

Basic relationship skills help families work through situations when choices need to be made. Support, open communication, negotiation, and compromise help families make choices and keep responsibilities in balance. Family members can support one another to avoid feelings of guilt or resentment about work responsibilities. Single parents may look to close friends and relatives for extra support. All family members

7-4

This intergenerational family values their time together and make this time a priority.

may have to accept responsibility for household tasks such as laundry, cleaning, and cooking. Parents may sometimes need to adjust work responsibilities so they can spend more time with the family. They might have to make choices about working less overtime, changing to a part-time job, or working from home.

Working families must realize they cannot have it all. That is, in balancing family and work, they must have realistic expectations. They must be prepared to face potential problems. There are trade-offs between family life and work. Combining both is not always easy. Family time will have to be carefully planned. Housekeeping standards may have to be lowered. Some family activities may have to be missed. Job and career advancement may be slower.

Find Child Care

Working parents may need to make child care arrangements for their children. They must choose child care arrangements that best fit their needs and their children's needs. Some of the options available are discussed later in the text.

The Role of the Employer

In today's economy, employers are finding it more beneficial to help employees balance work and family roles. One way they do this is by offering flexible work arrangements that help employees handle family responsibilities. Offering family-related employee benefits is another option many are taking.

Such programs and benefits help both businesses and employees. Businesses are looking for new ways to increase productivity and cut costs. Hiring and training new, less-skilled workers can be costly for them. Not only do employers want to keep skilled employees, they want to increase employee morale. If employees are satisfied with their jobs, they are often more productive and committed to their employer.

Flexible Work Arrangements

Employers are more willing to accommodate working parents by offering flexible work options. Such options provide more opportunities for working parents to be available to their children and other family members as needed.

Telecommuting is one option. In this type of arrangement, an employee works from an office set up at home, **7-5**. The employee is connected with the office using a phone and the Internet. Companies are finding telecommuting makes good business sense. Work-at-home employees tend to work more hours, have better morale, and take fewer sick days.

Job sharing is another option growing in popularity. In **job sharing**, two people divide the work responsibilities of one job. Each person works

7-5

For employees seeking a flexible work schedule, telecommuting is a popular choice.

on a part-time basis rather than full time. This enables working mothers to remain in the workforce and still spend time with their children.

Flextime plans mean employees can set their own work schedule within certain terms. Some may choose to start later in the day to avoid heavy morning and evening traffic. Parents with school-age children can benefit from this plan, too. One parent can start work earlier and arrive home by the end of the school day. The other parent can start work later and be home to see the children off to school in the morning. Core hours are observed by companies that allow flextime. The total workday may run from 7:00 A.M. through 7:00 P.M. All employees must be on hand during core hours. Core hours may be from 10:00 to 11:30 A.M. and from 1:30 to 3:30 P.M. Employees are free to schedule the remaining hours to their convenience. This plan allows flexibility for parents to arrange their work schedules around their children. Medical appointments, school visits, and even parent volunteer hours at school can be easily arranged around core hours.

Flexible workweeks are in use at some companies. Some employees are now moving to four-day, 40-hour workweeks. They work a 10-hour workday rather than a traditional eight-hour workday.

Employee Benefits That Help Families

Employee benefits provided by the employer are known as fringe benefits. Fringe benefits are regarded as hidden pay. Life and health insurance, profit-sharing plans, and paid vacations are traditional fringe benefits offered by employers. On-site child care and parent education seminars are popular, family-oriented fringe benefits. Some companies provide college scholarships for children of their employees. Fringe benefits may even include family discounts for club memberships or amusement park tickets.

Reading
Review

1. Describe one effect of work on family life.
2. When both parents are employed outside the home, the family is called a _____-_____ family.
3. List four flexible work options offered by some employers that help employees balance work and family.

Section 7-3

Handling Family Crises

Objectives

After studying this section, you will be able to

- **describe** the types of events that can lead to a crisis.
- **describe** skills and resources for handling family crises.
- **summarize** the effects of various types of crises on families.

Key Terms 🔗

crisis	emotional abuse	alcoholism
support system	sexual abuse	alcoholic
physical neglect	substance abuse	enabler
emotional neglect	addiction	support group
physical abuse	drug abuse	

As you have read, a family's life is filled with challenges. Some of these challenges are fairly routine and easily managed. Others are much more serious, affecting the whole family system.

Difficult challenges can occur at any time in your life. Facing difficult challenges is not easy. That is why learning about these challenges and the changes that can result is important. This can help you prepare for and manage these events in your own life. Knowing what resources are available to help you deal with challenges is also worthwhile.

What Is a Crisis?

At some point in their lives, most people face some type of crisis. A **crisis** is an event or experience that greatly influences people's lives. These events cause people to make difficult changes in their lifestyles. The greatest challenge of a crisis is knowing how to handle these changes.

A crisis affects families in different ways. That is, a crisis to one family may not be a crisis to another. How the family views the situation and adjusts to it determines the impact it will have. For example, an unexpected baby may be a crisis in one family, but a welcome addition for another.

Characteristics of Crises

What types of events can lead to a family crisis? Crisis-producing events have certain traits that make it difficult for families to adjust to change. Four of these traits are described below.

- *A devastating event that causes a great loss for the entire family.* Property loss from a fire, a tornado, or an earthquake is an example. An automobile accident resulting in the disability or death of a family member or friend would be another example, **7-6**.

- *A stressful event that affects the entire family.* For example, moving and adjusting to a new home would be stressful for the entire family. A long period of unemployment would have serious effects on all family members.

- *An event that requires major adjustments by family members.* A major change in the family structure, such as separation, divorce, or remarriage would affect the way a family functions.

- *An event that occurs suddenly or unexpectedly.* A sudden loss of income, sudden illness, or the death of a loved one can be difficult for family members to face.

Sometimes a crisis is not triggered by a single event. It may be caused by a series of stressful events that build up over a period of time. The family may not realize a crisis is building until it actually happens. For instance, the combination of ending a relationship, moving to a new home, and starting a new job could lead to a crisis. How does a crisis event affect the family? The entire family system is affected. This is because the whole family's ability to function normally is changed. Family members are unable to carry out their roles and responsibilities. They need to use coping skills to adjust to the changes that have taken place. These skills help return balance to their lives as quickly as possible.

7-6

A serious accident can be the devastating event that causes a family crisis.

Skills for Coping with Crises

Why do some families seem to cope well during a crisis, while others let it destroy their lives? Functional families face a variety of crisis situations; they cope well because they communicate and cooperate. They have the confidence to meet any challenge. They deal with a crisis in three ways. First, they join together as a family to face the crisis head-on. Second, they focus on a positive aspect of a problem situation. They react positively and try to make the best of the situation. Third, they make use of their support system.

A **support system** is a network of people and organizations that family members can turn to during a crisis. The primary support comes from relatives, friends, neighbors, teachers, coworkers, and members of religious groups. These are individuals a family can contact in an emergency. For instance, a neighbor might look after a child on a moment's notice if the parents are suddenly called away. A support system also includes public and private agencies that help families. These agencies may provide health care, child care, financial aid, or legal assistance. Professionals at these organizations are trained to provide assistance to families during a crisis.

Dysfunctional families are unable to deal with crises in healthy ways. Many are poor problem solvers. They become locked into one way of responding to family problems. Anger, violence, and alcohol abuse are common responses. Some of these responses create new crisis situations. Dysfunctional families often depend on other people to rescue them from crises.

A crisis event cannot be ignored—it requires some type of response. A family who uses coping skills learns to handle these challenges. Learning how to handle change and unexpected events when they occur is the key to surviving any crisis. Families can use various resources to help them pull through difficult situations.

One resource is developing effective coping skills. A number of techniques may be helpful.

- *Plan how to handle a crisis before it happens.* To be prepared for change, families need to anticipate how to handle crises. As a family, they can plan how they would handle certain crisis situations. This helps the family in two ways. First, they can plan strategies that might help when the unexpected happens. Second, it prompts them to do as much as possible to prevent the problems from occurring.

- *Have clearly defined family goals.* This technique helps the family remain focused when emergencies arise. For example, the Browns have four family goals. They are to communicate openly, respect and support one another, deal fairly with problems, and get the best education possible. Having a child flunk out of college might be a major upset for them. How would they handle this crisis? They would discuss it, respect and support the child, and perhaps encourage the child to find other educational opportunities.

- *Maintain family unity.* In a crisis situation, family members need to band together, get involved, and help out. Family members that are supportive of one another have stronger emotional ties. They are better able to survive difficult times. Once they begin working together to solve a problem, they are likely to stay unified.

Mental Health Awareness

Coping and Self-Esteem

Having positive self-esteem helps people cope with crises. People with positive self-esteem have a strong sense of self-worth and are less prone to self-criticism and unreasonable guilt. They are confident about their ability to accept new responsibilities. They are also likely to acknowledge how they have grown by meeting new challenges.

- *Build on previous successes.* Families should use whatever techniques worked best for them in the past to help them through a crisis. For instance, if relatives or friends offered emotional support in the past, families should seek their help again. See **7-7**.

- *Maintain feelings of affection.* Feelings of affection among family members are especially important during difficult times. Although each family has its own way of expressing affection, an extra effort by each member can be helpful.

- *Place family needs before personal needs.* During a crisis, some family members may want to put their personal plans on hold. This is especially important if those plans would place additional stress on the family. For instance, a family member might delay moving out or buying a car until the crisis has passed.

- *Find ways to get help with family responsibilities.* Working together to share decision making and other family responsibilities is important. However, if extra help is needed, let others who have offered to help do so. Call on people in your support system.

- *Seek help for problems.* Some problems cannot be resolved within the family or seem too large to handle. In these cases, a family should not be afraid to seek outside help. Families should also know that many resources are available to help them. Knowing what help is available, where to find it, and how to ask for it are important coping skills.

7-7

Emotional support from friends can help teens work through a crisis.

Where can a family seek help? Friends, relatives, and neighbors can provide emotional support or emergency assistance. Many families seek guidance through their religious faith. Professional help can be found through local community services and government agencies. It is important to develop a support system of groups and individuals to whom you can turn for help.

Types of Crises

All families face different types of crises. Some of these—family violence, substance abuse, and death—are more difficult to face and manage than others. Learning more about each type can help families cope if one occurs.

Unemployment

A family's financial situation can change suddenly if a main provider becomes unemployed. This can happen for a number of reasons, many of which the individual has little control over. For example, a company may have to downsize and eliminate jobs if the economy declines. Sometimes, a serious health problem can force an individual into unemployment. Whatever the reason, unemployment drastically changes the income level of the family, and that can lead to a crisis. If a new job cannot be found right away, bills may not be paid. The family may find it harder to buy essentials such as food.

While a new job is sought, communication and cooperation among family members can help. With communication, the family can decide which wants and needs they can forego. The unemployed person could provide services that the family might otherwise hire others to do, such as child care, laundry, or lawn care. Teens might find part-time jobs. Families who band together and support one another can usually find ways to work through the crisis.

Living Green

Instead of tossing your old cell phone in the trash, remove all personal information and donate the phone to a recycling program. Some organizations refurbish the phones and donate them to families in need. Recycling phones can also keep spent batteries out of landfills.

Family Violence

In some dysfunctional families, poor family relationships can lead to violence within the family. A family member may resort to violence as a way of expressing anger or resolving conflicts. Unfortunately, this behavior often becomes a pattern that is repeated over and over.

Types of Family Violence

Family violence may take several different forms. One form of family violence is *neglect*. Neglect is a less violent but still serious form of abuse. It threatens the physical and mental well-being of family members. Neglect occurs when the needs of family members are not met. Not providing proper food, clothing, shelter, medical care, and parental supervision are forms of **physical neglect**.

Wellness Awareness

Research instances where children who were neglected emotionally developed physical health problems. What is the link between mental/emotional health and physical health?

Mental Health Awareness

Teasing Others

Although teasing others may seem harmless and intended as a joke, it can be a form of verbal abuse. Teasing can undermine a person's sense of confidence and well-being. It can cause a person to feel isolated and foolish and ultimately damage a person's self-concept.

Another form of neglect is emotional neglect. **Emotional neglect** is the failure to provide loving care and attention. A neglected family member who receives no signs of affection may grow to feel unloved and unlovable.

Abuse is the most damaging form of family violence. There are different forms of abuse. **Physical abuse** happens when one family member physically injures another family member. Abusive behavior includes hitting, kicking, biting, or throwing objects. This form of abuse often causes serious injury or sometimes death.

Emotional abuse happens when one family member purposely damages another member's self-concept. It destroys the abused person's self-esteem and makes the person feel worthless. *Verbal abuse* is a form of emotional abuse. This happens when the abuser constantly yells, teases, or insults the abused. Emotional abuse can also occur in parent-child relationships when parents have unrealistic expectations of a child. They expect the child to perform tasks that the child cannot do. Then they blame and punish the child for failing.

Sexual abuse in families occurs when one family member forces another family member to engage in sexual activities. One type of sexual abuse is incest. This is sexual activity between people who are closely related, such as between a father and a daughter.

Acts of physical violence within a family can occur among all family members. Children and wives are the most frequent victims. Children may be physically or emotionally abused by one or both parents. Husbands may batter wives, causing serious physical injuries. Sometimes children are the abusers rather than the victims. Adolescent children may assault their parents when something they want is withheld from them. Siblings may attack each other to settle an issue.

Why Family Violence Occurs

Why does family violence happen? The reasons vary. Abusive family members often have low self-esteem. They may feel unloved by other family members. Some adults may have been abused as children, so they have not learned to express their emotions properly. The abuser cannot deal with his or her emotions through acceptable behavior, so he or she becomes aggressive.

In families where physical violence is common behavior, the children may adopt the same type of behavior. Unemployment, financial problems, marital problems, job pressures, substance abuse, or illness are also contributing factors.

Where to Get Help

With help, neglect and abuse can be prevented. Various programs, facilities, and support groups are available to help families break out of the cycle of family violence.

Many types of programs are available in local communities. Social service organizations and mental health associations often provide information about individual and group counseling. Government programs and services may also be available. Emergency shelters are located across the country for providing temporary housing to abused women and their children.

Parents Anonymous is a self-help group that helps abusive parents and abused children. Most cities have chapters of this national organization.

There may be times when you must protect abused children. This may mean reporting the abuse and neglect of parents to a social service agency. Most agencies have special counselors to help parents and their children when cases are reported. Reporting is the key to such service. Counselors cannot help a family unless the situation is brought to their attention by a report.

Substance Abuse

One of the most serious crises affecting families involves substance abuse. **Substance abuse** is the use of illegal drugs or the misuse of legal drugs such as alcohol. The misuse of a substance, such as alcohol, can lead to physical and psychological addiction. An **addiction** is a dependence of the body on a continuing supply of the drug. After an addiction has developed, taking the drug away will cause agonizing withdrawal symptoms. When one family member becomes addicted, the entire family is affected.

Drug abuse is the use of a legal or illegal drug for a purpose other than its intended use. Illegal drugs include heroin, cocaine, and methamphetamine. Legal drugs, such as over-the-counter medications and prescriptions, can be abused as well.

An addiction to alcohol is called **alcoholism**. Like diabetes or cancer, alcoholism is a type of disease. A person who suffers from this disease is an **alcoholic**.

People become addicted to alcohol and other drugs for many different reasons. In response to the drug or alcohol, some may feel more relaxed. Some use it to deal with or overcome problems, such as job-related stress or family problems. However, addiction can trigger other stressful problems, such as losing a job. This added stress can cause the addict to drink or abuse drugs even more, which may lead to another more serious crisis.

Substance abuse seriously affects all family members. The spouse and children of an addict may have a hard time accepting the problem. They may blame themselves for the problem. As a result, they may avoid seeking help because they are too ashamed or embarrassed. A spouse may deny that his or her mate is an alcoholic or drug user. Younger children may not understand an alcoholic parent's behavior. Teens may try to hide the problem from others or avoid spending time at home. Because of their problems at home, children's schoolwork may suffer, **7-8**.

Codependency often occurs in families of addicts as family members try to find ways to survive the crisis. A family member may become an **enabler**—someone who unknowingly acts in ways that contribute to an

7-8

Because of problems they are experiencing at home, some teens may find it hard to concentrate on schoolwork.

Wellness Awareness

Research and write a report on the effects of substance abuse on the body.

addict's drug use. The enabler wants to help the alcoholic or drug addict with his or her problem. In so doing, they make the problem worse by denying that a problem exists. Enablers cover up for the behavior of the addict, allowing the addict's behavior to manipulate their own. They may lie for the addict or give excuses for the addict's actions. They unknowingly perpetuate the addiction.

To help an alcoholic or drug addict, family members should seek assistance from outside sources. Learning about the disease, talking about it, and learning coping skills can help family members handle the crisis. They may need professional help to identify any codependency behaviors.

Overcoming alcoholism or drug addiction is not easy, but it can be done. However, the user must make the decision to stop. They must first admit they have a problem and need help before anyone can help them. During the recovery period, an alcoholic or drug addict needs strong family support combined with professional help to overcome the illness.

Where to Get Help

Professional help is available from many local sources. Treatment and prevention services are available through community hospitals and health centers, family service agencies, and the National Council on Alcoholism and Drug Dependence (NCADD).

A **support group** is a group of people who share a similar problem or concern. *Alcoholics Anonymous (AA)* is a nationwide support group for alcoholics. *Narcotics Anonymous (NA)* is a support group for drug addicts who want to recover from their addiction. The goal of AA and NA is to help alcoholics and drug addicts help themselves to recovery. Help for family and friends of alcoholics is available through *Al-Anon*. Teen children of alcoholic parents can seek support by joining *Alateen*. *Nar-Anon* is for family members and friends of drug addicts.

By seeking out a support group, people find other individuals who are experiencing a similar crisis. Members of the support group come together to discuss common concerns, problems, and issues. People benefit from support groups by learning they are not the only ones with certain problems. They are able to talk with others who truly understand their situations. They share helpful information and resources while they listen and learn from one another.

Serious Illness or Accidents

A serious illness or accident can be a crisis for a family. The emotional drain of watching a loved one suffer or the anxiety felt when awaiting the outcome of an operation can be stressful for family members. Caring for a family member with a serious illness or disability can take a huge toll on the care provider—both physically and emotionally. The high costs of medical care can be a significant drain on a family especially if the income provider is the one who is sick or injured.

Support groups may be a source of strength for the family during this type of crisis. Learning more about a certain illness from other people who have had family members with this illness can be very beneficial. Spiritual ties help some families. The support of friends and relatives becomes even more important.

Death

Death is another crisis that all families face. Although death is as much a part of the family life cycle as birth, dealing with the loss can be difficult. However, families must learn to accept death as a reality of life, 7-9.

7-9

Everyone must eventually face the crisis of death in his or her family.

When a loved one dies, family members often experience a variety of emotions. Feelings of sadness, anger, and guilt are common. Such feelings are normal responses to a loss and are part of the grieving process. Family members may feel sadness because they miss the person. Some may feel angry that the person died and left them behind. Others may feel guilty about unfinished business, such as owing an apology or saying "I love you." Caregivers might feel an emptiness because they are no longer needed.

Accepting the reality of the loss can be hard. However, acceptance is an important part of adjusting to the loss. Then family members can take action to handle those feelings and get on with their lives. Although time will help ease the pain, family members can take other steps to work through their grief. They can

- accept the support of friends, relatives, and other people around them.

- talk about their feelings of sadness. They should not be ashamed to cry if they feel sad.

- recall the happy memories they shared with the deceased person with other family members and friends.

Reading
Review

1. List four traits of crisis events.
2. List eight coping skills that can help families survive a crisis.
3. Explain how alcoholism affects all family members.
4. List three steps family members can take to work through grief.

Chapter 7 Review

Summary

Making and keeping the family strong and healthy is a challenge faced by all families. Functional families don't just happen—family members must work together to achieve this goal. They are committed to communicating with one another, solving problems, showing appreciation, understanding one another, and sharing with one another. Functional families fulfill family rights and responsibilities by sharing values and goals, sharing responsibility for decisions, sharing resources, and sharing a lasting commitment.

Families face many different types of challenges. Balancing family and work roles and responsibilities is a continuing challenge, especially for dual-career families and single parents. For these families, good management and relationship skills are the keys to balancing their busy lives. To accommodate working parents' needs, more employers are offering flexible work schedules and employee benefits.

Of all the challenges families face, crises are the most difficult. The key to surviving a crisis is learning coping skills. Coping skills help families handle the changes a crisis causes. However, some types of crises, such as family violence, substance abuse, and death, are much more difficult to handle. Families with members who are struggling with addiction should be careful not to engage in enabling behaviors, which only contribute to the problem. Knowing how to cope and where to get assistance can help families work through these situations.

 Critical Thinking

1. **Evaluate resources.** Make a chart showing the organization of your support systems. Indicate yourself in the middle of the chart with primary support close around you. Other means of support can be placed farther away from you.

2. **Analyze behavior.** Evaluate how your parents balance their work and family roles. What types of problems do they encounter in trying to balance these roles? Why do you think it is important for them to balance these roles? What steps can you take to help them manage family responsibilities?

3. **Form a hypothesis.** Functional families tend to cope better with crisis situations. Why do you think these families cope better with crises than others? What steps can a family take to prepare for a crisis?

4. **Evaluate decisions.** Suppose a friend confides in you that he suspects the children he babysits are being abused. What advice would you give to your friend about this situation?

5. **Draw conclusions.** Research a family crisis that you have heard or read about recently. Write a report about your findings. Include information about possible causes, the effect on family members, coping skills, and where to get help.

6. **Visually present data.** Select three types of family crises. Using computer software, create a flowchart that represents how to respond to each crisis. Include various responses to each scenario.

21st Century
Applications

7. **Communication and collaboration.**
Work with a partner to create a script
and role-play common parent-teen
conflicts. Perform your script in front
of the class or create videos of your
role-plays. Discuss each scenario as
a class. How might each conflict be
resolved?

8. **Health literacy.** Use online or
print resources to examine how
certain types of substances can
physically harm the body. Select
one substance to research. Create a
diagram that shows the human body
and areas that are affected by abuse
of that substance.

9. **Leadership and responsibility.**
Suppose you work in a
manufacturing facility that utilizes
heavy machinery. Safe actions
are important to prevent employee
injuries. In an effort to promote
employee safety and health, the
company strictly follows a random
drug testing policy. One of your
coworkers often brags to you about
his off-hours alcohol and drug
use—the effects of which caused a
near-accident recently. You question
whether his actions are responsible
especially in light of the type of work
and machinery he uses on the job.
What would you do in this situation?
What is the responsible way to
behave in this situation?

10. **Critical thinking and problem
solving.** Which types of natural
disasters are likely to occur where
you live? Work with family members to
review how to handle natural disasters
such as tornadoes, earthquakes, floods,
hurricanes, or blizzards. Prepare a plan
of action for how to prepare for and
respond to these disasters. You may
refer to government websites or the
American Red Cross in your research.

Core
Skills

11. **Speaking.** Discuss similarities
between family members who share
responsibilities for making family
decisions and members of Congress
who share responsibilities for making
national decisions.

12. **History.** Discuss how families balanced
family life with work in the past. Include
discussions on poor working conditions,
child labor, and the evolution of unions
in the United States.

13. **Speaking.** Survey several dual-career
families to determine how they manage
their work and family responsibilities.
Summarize your results in a report to
the class.

14. **Listening.** Active listening is fully
participating as you process what
others are saying. Practice active
listening skills while listening to a
family-related news report or feature
story on the radio, television, or a
podcast. Pick a single story about
families and prepare a report in which
you analyze the following aspects of
the story: the speaker's audience,
point of view, reasoning, stance, word
choice, tone, points of emphasis, and
organization.

15. **Reading.** Use the Internet to research companies that offer job sharing, flextime, and flexible workweeks. Prepare a report on five companies where you would like to work. Include information on flexible work arrangements.

16. **Writing.** Use reliable print or online resources to research stages of substance abuse. Then narrow your research and focus on a specific type of substance abuse, such as the abuse of prescription drugs, methamphetamine, inhalants, heroin, cocaine, LSD, or alcohol. Prepare an essay that describes the type of substance abuse, physical effects, mental effects, and effects on family and friends. Include a list of how to help people experiencing that type of substance abuse. Cite any sources of information you use.

17. **Reading.** Research the material available on the websites for Alcoholics Anonymous and Students Against Destructive Decisions. List the resources available in your state or community.

18. **Writing.** Research codependency using reliable online sources. You may use books, articles, informational videos, or podcasts. Compare the information you find to related information presented in this chapter. Write a brief summary of codependency based on your research findings. Remember to cite any sources of information you use.

Leadership
Development

As a part of working on the Interpersonal Communications STAR Event, consider developing a community project designed to build more functional families through strengthened family communication. For example, you might plan a family communications workshop to be offered through an adult education program in the community.

Portfolio
Builder

Research careers working with families in the Human Services career cluster. What type of education and training is needed in this career area? What would be most satisfying about these careers? What would be least satisfying about these careers? Do you think this career area would be a good fit with your interests, aptitudes, and abilities? Prepare a summary of your findings for your portfolio.

Journal
Writing

You know a friend has been taking drugs, and you fear that addiction may result. You have promised not to tell anyone about the drug use. You have become codependent by trying to cover for your friend, thinking this will benefit everyone involved. You know the truth will cause some full-blown crises for the family and a lot of trouble for your friend.

Write About It: *Whom are you helping? Whom are you hurting? Who is being manipulated? What should you do at this point?*

Chapter 8
Personal Relationships

Reading Prep

Write a brief description of a positive relationship and a negative relationship. As you study the chapter, draw parallels between your descriptions and text material. Find a cartoon related to dating or marriage. Discuss its meaning.

Concept Organizer

Create a tree diagram to show ways to deal with negative peer pressure. List different alternatives and possible consequences of each.

G-WLEARNING.com

Click on the activity icon to visit www.g-wlearning.com/comprehensive/8062 to access online vocabulary activities using key terms from the chapter.

Developing Positive Relationships

Objectives

After studying this section, you will be able to

- **discuss** types of relationships.
- **list** benefits of positive relationships.
- **describe** how to develop key elements that form the basis of positive relationships.

Key Terms

sibling   mutual respect

Think about your current relationships. Now imagine all the relationships you have yet to develop in the future. That adds up to *many* different relationships you will be involved in throughout your life! Most of them will be positive relationships. This means they are healthy and satisfying for you and the people with whom you relate.

Positive relationships do not happen automatically. You have to work to develop them. In order to build positive relationships, you must feel true concern for other people. This sense of concern increases during adolescence. During the teen years, people become less self-centered and more aware of the needs of others. See **8-1**.

Types of Relationships

Learning to get along with others begins at an early age. Most people learn to develop positive relationships at home with their parents and siblings. Later, they expand their relationships to include peers, romantic partners, coworkers, and others. Learning about these different types of relationships can help you form successful bonds with others.

Parents

Infants form their first relationships with their parents. Infants are totally dependent on their parents and other caregivers to fulfill all their needs. These include the physical needs of food and clothing, as well as emotional and social needs. Children need to feel secure and loved. Because of this, they tend to behave in ways that will assure their

8-1

Spending time with friends helps people become more aware of the needs of others during the teen years.

Mental Health Awareness

Birth Order and Personality

Birth order, or the order in which a child was born in comparison with siblings, can influence personality. For example, oldest children are often responsible, because they may be responsible for caring for younger siblings. Experts agree that several other factors also influence personality, including parental involvement, family size, and age difference between siblings.

parents' love. As they grow older, they become more and more capable of supplying some of these needs themselves.

In early adolescence, children begin to demonstrate a measure of independence. Parents are still responsible for their children. However, the weight of responsibility begins to shift away from parents and toward the child.

This change in the parent-child relationship often causes conflict between parents and children. Parents may relinquish too much or too little control. Children may want too much or too little responsibility. Communication is needed to maintain a positive relationship between parents and their children during this period.

Siblings

Young children also begin building relationships with their siblings at an early age. **Siblings** are brothers and sisters. Siblings relate to one another on more equal terms. This type of interaction often leads to competition. Sometimes jealousies emerge as siblings compete with one another.

Building positive relationships with siblings prepares children to build positive relationships with their peers. Learning to handle jealousy and competition with siblings helps children know how to handle these situations with friends. See **8-2**.

Peers

Relationships with peers become very important during the teen years. Positive peer relationships form a support system for teens. Having friends reassures teens that other people are facing the same changes and decisions they are.

Most people tend to choose friends who have characteristics similar to their own. Perhaps you look for friends who are dependable, honest, sincere, thoughtful, and willing to help others.

You must have realistic expectations of others if you want to build positive relationships with them. Do not expect your peers to be perfect or to fit your exact mold. You must learn to accept your friends as they are. You may not always agree with their opinions. However, they have rights just as you do. You grow by being exposed to their different attitudes and beliefs.

Not all of your peers will be your friends. You will not have enough in common with some of your peers to build friendships. However, even acquaintances can become an important part of your relationship network.

8-2
Sibling relationships prepare children to interact with peers.

Romantic Relationships

During the later teen and adult years, romantic relationships become important to many people. Romantic relationships are positive because caring for someone and knowing he or she cares for you adds meaning to life. Sharing the joys and sorrows of daily experiences helps couples grow closer. Partners encourage each other to develop to their full potential as human beings.

Some romantic relationships lead to marriage. Marriage relationships grow and change as the people in them grow and change. To keep marriage relationships positive, couples need to work on keeping lines of communication open.

Work Relationships

People form less intimate relationships with their coworkers. Coworkers can enjoy working together even if they do not have much in common outside of work. They can enjoy job-related successes together.

Positive work relationships are based on respect for the feelings of others. A good attitude will help you relate to those with whom you work. Accept your fair share of responsibilities. Do not expect others to

Analyze and Solve

Working in a small group, prepare a list of suggestions for improving relationships in the workplace. Consider employee relationships with managers, coworkers, and customers. Share the lists with the rest of the class.

do your work for you. On the other hand, do not assume that you can get along without your coworkers. Most jobs are a team effort. If you show consideration to coworkers, they will be likely to cooperate with you.

Benefits of Positive Relationships

Positive relationships produce many benefits. Research has shown that relationships can affect a person's physical and emotional well-being. People who maintain positive relationships have fewer physical illnesses. They are also less prone to diseases and tend to live longer. Their emotional well-being is enhanced because they know people care about them. They can share their problems and thereby reduce the stress of daily living.

Positive relationships also provide social benefits. You are more likely to go places and get involved in activities when someone can join you. Your present relationships can serve as bridges to future relationships. Your social circle will expand as you meet new people.

Economic well-being can be a benefit of positive work relationships. People who relate well on the job are likely to enjoy their work. This will encourage them to stay on the job. They will increase their chances of being promoted and getting more pay raises.

Qualities Needed for Positive Relationships

As you read earlier, positive relationships do not happen automatically. Both people involved must work to develop key qualities that form the basis for positive relationships. These qualities include a positive self-concept, mutual respect, trust, openness, and reliability.

Serving Your Community

Investigate local programs focused on encouraging and helping older adults who live alone to socialize with others. Research why these programs are so important. Ask about volunteer opportunities for teens.

Healthy Living

Friendships and Emotional Health

Everyone needs friends. Positive friendships are important to emotional health. Characteristics of true friends include people

- with whom you feel you can talk about anything
- who make you feel peaceful just by being with them
- with whom you can have fun—even when you are not doing anything special
- to whom you can tell a secret and know it won't get spread around
- who understand and support you whether you're feeling up or down

Positive Self-Concept

As you have read, a positive self-concept means that you see yourself as worthwhile. Confident people who care for others may anticipate that others will care for them in return. In addition, when others see that you think highly of yourself, they are likely to think highly of you as well. They may realize that they would enjoy forming a friendship with you.

A positive self-concept usually results from positive feedback. Therefore, an important part of friendship is providing positive feedback to your friend. This will continue to help build your friend's self-concept. At the same time, a true friend will do the same for you.

Mutual Respect

Mutual respect means each person regards the other with honor and esteem. People in positive relationships do not expect each other to agree on everything. Neither person tries to force an opinion or idea on the other. They respect each other's right to differ. They respect each other for who they are.

Building mutual respect between teens and adults is sometimes a challenge. Some teens feel threatened by the experience and maturity of adults. They think adults judge them unfairly. On the other hand, adults fear that teens believe adults are not in touch with current youth culture.

Teens and adults both need to feel they are valued by one another. Teens can benefit by seeking wisdom from adults. Likewise, adults can be inspired by the enthusiasm of youth. Such worthwhile exchanges can help teens and adults build mutual respect and develop positive relationships.

Trust

Trusting people means having confidence in them. In a positive relationship, you must trust the other person. However, you must also prove that you are trustworthy. You must be careful not to betray the confidence that is vested in you. You must be able to keep secrets. You must not laugh at friends who share serious concerns with you. You must not encourage others to participate in activities that are not in their best interests.

Trust in a relationship can be fragile. If you give advice that backfires, you may not be trusted in the future. When advice is sought, it may be better to help friends view situations from several different perspectives. Allow them to analyze the possible alternatives and choose their own plan of action.

Integrity. Monique works on confidential reports. She is careful not to share any of the information she knows with people outside of her company.

Openness

Openness in a relationship refers to an atmosphere in which people feel free to share their thoughts and feelings. You must create this atmosphere for people with whom you relate. You must make them feel comfortable about opening up to you.

You must also be willing to open up to others. No one can second-guess what you think or feel. People cannot meet your needs unless you tell them what your needs are.

Analyze and Solve

List people in the community with whom you have developed or can develop positive relationships. Explain benefits that might come from networking with these people.

Reliability

People in positive relationships must be reliable. If you say you will do something, people must be able to count on you to do it. If you say you will be somewhere, people must be able to depend on you to be there.

Reliability goes beyond keeping your word. It also refers to routine patterns of behavior. For instance, perhaps people can rely on you to take a leadership role in a group. Maybe they can count on you to remain calm, even in frantic situations. Reliability helps people know what to expect from others in relationships.

Reading Review

1. True or false. Relationships between parents and teens can affect teens' future relationships.
2. List two benefits of positive relationships.
3. What are the key qualities that form the basis for positive relationships?

Section 8-2

Friendships and Dating

Objectives

After studying this section, you will be able to

- **name** three types of friends.
- **describe** factors that lead people to form friendships.
- **explain** three types of dating.
- **explain** the difference between love and infatuation.
- **analyze** factors involved in a responsible relationship.

Key Terms

multicultural society	casual dating	infatuation
group dating	steady dating	abstinence

Friends are people who know, like, and trust each other. They are people who spend time together, sharing thoughts and feelings. Friends complement one another's positive traits. They also care enough to tactfully point out habits and attitudes that may need to be changed.

Friendship is the bond that forms between friends. This bond is built through a process of give and take as two people learn to appreciate each other. The best friendships develop between people who share experiences, interests, and values.

Friendships

The type of friendship two people share is determined by the strength of the bond between them. An *acquaintance* is someone you know, but who is not a close friend. You know your acquaintances by name, but you probably do not spend much social time with them.

You may think of many of your friends as *good friends*. These are people with whom you share common interests. You talk, have fun, and enjoy social activities together. Acquaintances may become good friends if you spend time with them.

One or two of your good friends might become your *best friends*. These are the friends with whom you share your deepest thoughts and feelings. They are the ones you ask for advice when you have a problem. Best friends often share a common background and lifestyle.

Meeting New People

The first step in making friends is meeting people. You are most likely to meet people in your classes, at club meetings, and at parties. These groups will be close to you in age. However, do not exclude older or younger people from your friendships. You may find you share interests and values with people who are not your age. These are the qualities on which friendships are built. Sometimes people of other ages can provide other viewpoints that you had not considered.

Most of the people you meet are likely to live close to you. Likewise, you will meet more people from your neighborhood than from the other side of town. If you do meet people from other neighborhoods, states, or countries, take advantage of the opportunity.

We live in a **multicultural society**. That means there are people from many different cultures living in the same communities. Be open to forming friendships with people from different backgrounds. Through these friendships, you can learn about other cultures, including different religions, beliefs, and customs. As you do so, you will probably discover there are more similarities than differences. You may not agree with all you learn, but be open to this wider view of the world. You will probably see that most cultural groups have much in common.

Forming Friendships

You do not form friendships with everyone you meet. Friendships are more likely to form between people who have similar personalities, common interests, and like values.

Living Green

You want to meet new people, but where do you start? Consider working on a gardening or recycling project in your school or community. While helping the environment, you can cultivate friendships as well.

Mental Health Awareness

Only Children and Friendship Skills

Some studies show that children raised without siblings may lag behind peers in the social-emotional development skills needed to form friendships. They may have trouble cooperating and taking turns. However, the gap typically closes before adolescence. Socializing children outside the family can help children develop their social skills.

Networking skills. Liza realizes that being able to network with her coworkers is a valuable human relations skill. She uses these skills as she communicates with her coworkers, creating a positive work atmosphere.

You are likely to form a friendship with someone who has a personality similar to yours. If you are quiet, you will probably prefer being with someone else who is quiet. If you are outgoing, you will probably enjoy being with someone who is outgoing. When people think and act alike, they usually enjoy being together.

Friendships are also likely to develop between people who have common interests. Friends generally share the same interests. You can meet new people with similar interests while doing those things you enjoy, 8-3. For example, if you volunteer for a cause that interests you, you will meet others with similar interests.

You will probably form friendships with those who share your outlook on life. They will think about issues in the same way as you. Your values are likely to be similar, as are your goals.

You want to develop friendships with those who have values similar to yours because your friends influence your behavior. You want to do things together, so you need to be with a friend who has behavior standards similar to yours. If you go to a party, will your friend act in the same manner as you? Peer influence is at its greatest during the teen years. Be alert to the influence your friends have on you. Do these influences help you grow to your fullest potential? Friends should not drag each other down. Friendships should be mutually beneficial.

How to Make Friends

Have you ever gone to an event where you did not know anyone? You were probably nervous and even a bit scared. However, this is the best way to meet new people. If you are afraid to go up to someone you do not know and start a conversation, make yourself approachable. People are more likely to approach you when you are alone than when you are in a group.

No one wants to be rejected or made to feel silly if they do make an effort to talk to you. They need to feel that they will be received warmly. People are more likely to strike up a conversation with you if you

- show you are interested in them
- focus on what they are saying
- ask questions
- provide feedback to keep the conversation moving
- are open-minded

Remember, you do not have to wait for someone to speak to you. You can make that important first move.

8-3

These two friends met through their common interest in soccer.

Introduce yourself and have a question or conversation topic ready when approaching others. What do you have to lose?

Dating

The factors that attract people to friends also attract them to dating partners. Spending time with dating partners can teach people lessons that help them prepare for marriage.

While people are dating and having fun, they are also learning about themselves. Through dating, people learn how to give and take in personal relationships. They become aware of why these relationships are important to them. They learn to recognize the impact their words and actions can have on the lives of other people.

Dating helps people learn about members of the opposite sex. Dating shows a man that all women are not like his mother and his sisters. It shows a woman that all men are not like her father and her brothers.

Group Dating

First dating experiences for young people often take the form of **group dating**. This is when a number of people of both sexes go out together. Each member of the group has fun without feeling especially close to any one person. Each person is free to get to know all the members of the group. Teens may refer to group dating as "hanging out."

Group dating is an easy way to begin dating. Young people can interact with members of the opposite sex without pressure. For instance, with a whole group to carry on conversations, no one feels on the spot to keep talking. After learning to feel comfortable in a group, most people become ready to date as couples.

Casual Dating

Casual dating, also called *random dating*, allows people to date more than one person at a time. For instance, suppose Jorge takes Sara to a dance on Friday night. Sara not only socializes with Jorge, she also meets and interacts with his friends. Jorge may go with Maria to a picnic on Saturday. Here he meets and interacts with Maria's friends. If Jorge continues casual dating, he will have the chance to socialize with many different people. If Sara and Maria continue casual dating, they too will meet more new people.

In casual dating, everyone grows socially, and no one feels disloyal or jealous. The dating objectives are fun and entertainment. Everyone is learning about getting along with other people, but no one is falling in love.

Steady Dating

Through casual dating, two people may meet and find that they like each other very much. They may agree to date only each other. This is called **steady dating**, but may be referred to as "going out." If someone

Financial Literacy

Dating on a Budget

How can you have memorable dates without spending lots of money? Think of some fun, low-cost dates that cannot only save money, but also help strengthen your relationship. Some ideas might include:

- hiking or biking
- baking cookies
- working on a community recycling project
- playing board games
- attending community events at a local park
- visiting local museums and art galleries
- going on picnics
- watching videos and making popcorn

is said to be going out with another person, they are probably in a steady dating relationship.

Steady dating provides several types of security. For instance, you know that someone likes you and cares about you. You know that someone understands you and enjoys being with you. You can relax and be yourself without fear of rejection.

Another type of security is not having to worry about spending the evening with someone you do not know. When you date someone for the first time, you take some risks. The person's idea of fun may be different from yours. You may spend the evening watching a baseball game when you really wanted to go to a movie. When you date someone steadily, there are fewer chances for problems. You have a good idea of what to expect from your date.

Some teens may feel that steady dating gives them the security of having a date when they "need" one. They will not have to go to dances or parties alone. However, this is not a good reason to date. First, you may lead your dating partner to believe you care for him or her more than you really do. Second, going places by yourself can build your self-esteem. You may even meet new people who recognize and admire your confidence!

Although steady dating provides some security, it does not guarantee perfect peace and unity. Conflict occurs in any relationship. When a conflict occurs in casual dating, the couple may just stop seeing each other. The commitment involved in steady dating encourages the couple to resolve their conflicts. By learning to handle conflicts in a positive manner, the couple's relationship can continue.

Sometimes even steady dating partners cannot resolve their conflicts. This is normal. When this happens, partners may decide to end their relationship—perhaps willingly, perhaps not so willingly. Either way, former partners must adjust to the change. They also need to seek new interests.

What Is Love?

The word *love* has many different meanings. It can mean the way you feel when your brother mows the lawn for you. It can mean the way you feel when your friend lets you borrow a new sweater. It can mean the way you feel when you are going steady with someone.

Love involves caring deeply about your mate and his or her well-being. You want your mate to be happy. You look for ways to express your affection. You may send flowers. You may cook a special dinner. You may just give your mate an unexpected hug and say "I love you."

Is It Love or Infatuation?

Infatuation is often confused with love. **Infatuation** is an intense feeling of admiration. Although both of these emotions are directed toward another person, they differ in many ways.

You can be infatuated with someone you have never met, such as a political leader or a famous singer. You can also be infatuated with a fantasized image of someone you know. For instance, you may know the star of your school's wrestling team. You could build a fantasized image around him. You could view him as an ideal blend of good looks, strength, and courage.

Infatuation in a relationship is often short-lived. It may begin quickly and focus on just one trait, such as a person's appearance or special skill. It may end just as quickly if one person becomes impatient, bored, or dissatisfied with the relationship.

People may fall into infatuation, but they rarely fall into love. People are more likely to grow into love slowly as they learn more about each other. The focus of love is on the other person as a whole. When you love someone, you know the person well. You have a realistic view of the person's strengths and weaknesses. Since time and care are needed to build a love relationship, people are likely to try to make it last longer.

Perhaps the surest sign of infatuation is that it is self-centered. A person who is infatuated is concerned about his or her own feelings and desires. Love, on the other hand, is unselfish. A person in love is considerate of the other person. He or she thinks of the other person's wants, needs, and feelings, **8-4.**

8-4

A couple who is in love focuses on meeting each other's needs.

Responsible Relationships

Steady dating usually means that two people spend a great deal of time together, often alone. As they do so, they may develop feelings of love for each other. When this happens, it is only natural that the two will want to express their affection in some way. Certain hormones become active during the teen years, and the body

changes as well. Sexual urges may become strong, especially between two people who are attracted to each other. In some relationships, there may be pressure for sexual relations.

It is normal to experience sexual desires, but it is important to think through how you feel about having a sexual relationship. You need to think about this in case you find yourself in a situation where you are being pressured to have sex. If you know where you stand, you will be able to make a decision quickly, if necessary. You should also have a plan of action that will help you out of any difficult situation.

Facing Sexual Decisions

Deciding to have a sexual relationship can affect the rest of your life. The lives and health of both partners may be jeopardized when they make a careless choice.

Some teens are pressured into a sexual relationship they are not ready for. They may feel pressure from their date or even pressure from their friends. They may feel they are being left out if they do not give in to sexual pressures. Messages from movies, television, and music seem to imply that "everyone is doing it," even though this is not the case.

Self-esteem impacts almost all the decisions you make. If you feel good about yourself, you trust yourself to make good decisions. Having positive self-esteem can help you make important decisions that are right for you. If you always need the approval of others, you may tend to let others make decisions for you. If you lack self-esteem, you may let others pressure you into doing what they want you to do. If you think you lack self-esteem, plan now to make changes in your life. You need to be able to make decisions for yourself and stick to them.

If young people give in to sexual pressures, their self-esteem may suffer if they compromised their values, standards, and morals. They may also experience many emotions, such as feelings of shame and guilt. They may feel used rather than loved.

In addition to emotional consequences, there are physical consequences. Sexually transmitted infections (STIs) can sometimes occur as a result of sexual activity. Some STIs are life threatening. Another possible consequence is pregnancy. A pregnancy can alter the future of both partners. Anyone involved in a sexual relationship must be aware of these possible consequences.

To avoid these potential consequences and others, some people choose abstinence. Sexual **abstinence** is a choice to refrain from sexual intercourse until marriage. There are many reasons young people choose abstinence. Many choose abstinence for moral reasons, believing that sexual relations belong only in marriage. Abstinence fits with their values and standards and frees them from guilt. Others choose abstinence for reasons of health and safety. They recognize that sexually transmitted infections and infertility can result. They do not want to risk their health nor their chances of having children later on. Many teens see abstinence as a matter of personal integrity and an expression of self-esteem. They have control of their lives. They have goals they want to reach. They do not want to risk a pregnancy until they are ready for this responsibility.

Because teens are aware of the negative impact that sexual activity can have on their lives, there is a growing movement for sexual abstinence. Some teens sign declarations stating they will abstain from sexual activity until marriage.

Dealing with Sexual Pressures

When you make the decision not to have sex, you need to be prepared to follow through with your decision. Others must respect your decision. Make sure your date knows what your limits are. Talk about how you both feel. Knowing your limits can help you both stop before you go too far.

Practice saying no. You can just say "No." It is your right. You do not need to give any explanations or reasons, but you need to be firm. Other suggestions for what to say are given in **8-5**. If you know what you will say and do, it will be easier for you.

Avoid situations that may be difficult to handle. Do not spend time alone together in either of your homes when no one else is there. Go out with other couples or groups. Also stay away from parties where alcohol and drugs are available. Their use can cloud judgment.

Showing Affection in Other Ways

How do you let your partner know that you really care for him or her without having sex? Talk about your lives, hopes, and dreams. Be there to listen when he or she is going through a difficult time. Put a note in his or her locker. Make special greeting cards. Be creative! There are many ways to say "You are truly special to me."

Reading
Review

1. Name and describe three types of friends.
2. List two ways dating helps people prepare for marriage.
3. True or false. Infatuation is based on reality, not fantasy.
4. State three reasons why young people are choosing sexual abstinence.

8-5

If someone is pressuring you to have sex, use one of these ways to say no.

Ways to Say No to Sexual Activity

"I'm not ready for sex."

"If you love me, you won't pressure me."

"You mean a lot to me, and I want to keep it that way."

"I don't want to lose respect for you."

"I respect myself too much."

"I believe in waiting for marriage."

"I'm more comfortable in a group of our friends. We're spending too much time alone."

Section 8-3

The Marriage Relationship

Objectives

After studying this section, you will be able to
- **identify** the role of love in a marriage relationship.
- **describe** factors that influence mate selection and marital success.
- **explain** the importance of the engagement period and the process of adjusting to married life.

Key Term

intermittency of love

Marriage can be the closest and most satisfying relationship between two people. Loving someone and being loved in return can make life more meaningful and enjoyable.

In marriage, you can share the experiences of daily life with someone you love. You can laugh together and cry together. You can share your thoughts and feelings. You are encouraged to do your best and to be your best—to develop your full potential as a human being. You, in turn, encourage your mate to develop to his or her full potential.

Getting married does not magically end all problems. Marriage does not guarantee you love, happiness, and security forever. It is a growing, changing relationship. It has to grow and change because people grow and change. The challenge of marriage is to grow closer together rather than farther apart. If a couple meets this challenge, the marriage will be strong and healthy. If the couple does not meet this challenge, the marriage may end in unhappiness or even divorce.

Marriage is a part of most people's lives. They prepare for marriage by dating. They learn to love, and they choose a mate. They announce their engagement and plan their wedding. Then they work together to build a successful marriage.

Learning to Love

Dating serves many important functions. It helps people learn more about interpersonal relationships. Besides encouraging positive peer relationships, it helps people evaluate the personality traits they like or dislike in others. People learn to recognize the give-and-take involved in getting along with members of the opposite sex. The entire dating experience helps people prepare for marriage and be more successful marriage partners.

After dating for a while, two people may decide they are in love. They may wonder if they really love each other enough to spend the rest of their lives together. The surest sign of love is that it is unselfish. If you are in love, you genuinely care for and consider the other person's wants, needs, feelings, and preferences. You care about the other person's happiness and the feeling is mutual.

Sharing is an important part of the kind of love that leads to marriage. When you are in love, you and your mate enjoy spending time together, **8-6**. You find that activities are more fun and chores are less boring when you share them.

Communicating is one way of sharing. By communicating, you and your mate can share each other's thoughts and feelings. When one is happy, the other can share in that happiness. When one is upset, sad, or confused, the other can help by listening with empathy.

Good communication helps you and your mate know each other better. By staying in touch with each other's thoughts, you and your mate can grow closer and closer together. Without good communication, each of you may become involved in your own thoughts and plans. You and your mate may drift apart. Eventually, you may find that you have little in common.

Factors That Influence Marital Success

Many factors will help determine whether your future marriage succeeds. Having several positive factors is not a guarantee that your marriage will be happy. Having several negative factors does not necessarily mean that you will have a bad marriage. However, a couple who have several positive factors working for them have a better chance to make their marriage last. The following factors are known to influence marital success.

8-6
Activities are more fun and chores are more bearable when you share them with someone you love.

Family Background

Similar family backgrounds can strengthen a marriage relationship. At first, you may think that your family is not that important. After all, your mate should be interested in you, not your family. However, your family background has left lasting marks on you.

Family Lifestyle

Where you have grown up affects you in many ways. People from different regions of the United States have slightly different lifestyles. They dress differently, talk differently, and eat different foods. They have different occupations. People from large cities, suburbs, small towns, and farms have slightly different lifestyles, too. They may have different views on subjects such as privacy, recreation, and politics.

Family Relationships

Another aspect of your family background is the relationships within your family, **8-7**. How do you get along with your siblings? Have you learned to compromise? If you are female, have you learned something about men from your brothers? If you are male, have you

8-7

Relationships among members of your present family may influence the relationships that will form within your future family.

learned something about women from your sisters? The lessons you learn from your siblings will help you adjust to living with your mate.

The relationship you have with your parents may form the pattern for your future relationship with your own children. Do you have a good relationship with your parents? Can you talk with them? Can you settle conflicts in positive ways? Have you proven to them that you are responsible? Do they trust and respect you?

The relationship between your parents may affect your relationship with your mate. Do your parents communicate well? Do they show affection to each other often? How do they settle conflicts? Do they compromise, or does one parent always win? People learn from their parents and often imitate them. If your parents have a good relationship, you have the advantage of seeing how a good relationship works. If your parents do not have a good relationship, you are not doomed. You can learn from their mistakes and make your marriage a good one.

Family Customs

Family customs are another part of your family background. How do you celebrate birthdays and holidays? What kinds of vacations do you take? Who handles the money matters in your family? Who does the cooking and cleaning? Who is in charge of disciplining the children? You may take your family customs for granted now. However, they will affect the customs you follow when you establish your own family.

Values and Standards

To live in peace and harmony, marriage partners need to have similar values and standards. You have to know a person well before you begin to learn about his or her standards and values. This is why the time you spend dating someone is so important.

Values

A person's values affect many day-to-day matters. Someone who considers career success important may put extra time and energy into college classes and part-time jobs. Someone who feels that close family ties are important may be involved in many family activities. Someone who values physical fitness may spend time and money playing golf, tennis, and basketball. The list could go on and on. People invest effort, time, money, and other resources in the activities that are important to them.

Standards

Couples should share similar standards. Standards can affect daily routines. For instance, some people have high standards for cleanliness. They may expect everyone to help keep the home clean and neat. Following rules is another kind of standard. Some people never break a rule or law. Other people do not mind bending rules as long as they do not hurt anyone and they do not get caught.

8-8

As individuals mature, they are usually better prepared to build a successful marriage.

As time passes, values and standards become more and more important in a relationship. Unless they are shared, resentment may grow. A marriage has a better chance for success when the partners have similar values and standards.

Emotional Maturity

Another factor relating to marital success is emotional maturity. The more emotionally mature couples are, the better their chances are for successful marriages, **8-8**.

Emotionally mature persons are in control of their own lives. They make their own decisions and accept responsibility for the consequences. They recognize their own needs, values, and goals. They have self-discipline.

Emotionally mature people have their share of frustrations, failures, and disappointments. They accept these problems as part of life. They bounce back quickly from their problems and move on.

Because emotionally mature people have their own lives under control, they can be more understanding of others. They recognize other people's needs and values in addition to their own. They can offer emotional support to their mate so the mate can fulfill needs and meet goals, too.

Emotionally mature individuals deal with reality rather than fantasy. They do not expect people to be perfect. They know that everyone has both strengths and weaknesses. They are willing to share, cooperate, and compromise to get along with others. They do not ignore or run away from problems. When a conflict arises in marriage, an emotionally mature couple deals with it. They talk about it and resolve it in a way that satisfies both of them.

Age for Marriage

Age is an important factor in marital success. It is often a sign of emotional maturity. The younger couples are when they marry, the less likely they are to have successful marriages. Because marriage requires maturity, older couples usually have greater chances of success in their marriages.

Teenage Marriages

A couple without emotional maturity will have trouble building and maintaining a strong, healthy relationship. Many teen couples lack this emotional maturity. As a result, few teens are able to handle the pressures and responsibilities of marriage.

Financial demands are another reason for the failure of teenage marriages. Money can be an especially important issue to teenage couples. Neither spouse may have received enough education or training to get a good job. If both spouses remain unskilled, their financial pressures will grow. If one works while the other goes to school, their financial situation will gradually improve. However, the mate without the education may resent working so hard for the education of the other. At the same time, the mate with the education may begin to feel superior to the uneducated mate. The emotional pressures may destroy their marriage.

Emotional maturity grows with age. This is why emotionally mature people are usually better prepared for married life. They have had more time to handle responsibilities and become independent. They have had more chances to interact with people and are more likely to choose compatible mates. They have had time to receive education or training. They may have even had time to establish careers.

Mental Health Awareness

Teen Marriage and Emotional Development

Teen marriages face the additional challenge of incomplete emotional development. Although teens can make informed decisions using critical thinking skills, they are still learning emotional control. They may also be learning about and defining their self-concept. For these reasons, teen marriages often result in many conflicts and disagreements.

Common Interests

Having fun is an important part of married life. You do not have to do everything together, but you should have some common interests. You might enjoy going to concerts, playing cards, riding bikes, or watching sports.

A healthy social life includes activities with other people, too. Both you and your mate will bring some friends into the marriage. These friendships are important and should be continued. After you are married, your friends and your mate's friends may socialize with both of you. In addition, you will make some new friends together. Developing these mutual friendships is one of the adjustments you will need to make early in marriage.

Parental Approval

Parental approval is a positive factor in a marriage. Studies show that most successful marriages have the consent of all parents.

Why is parental approval important? It shows that the parents realize their child is mature enough to be married. It shows they are willing to entrust their child's well-being to the care of the future mate. It also shows they are supportive of the relationship.

Why do parents sometimes disapprove? Parents want their children to live happy lives. They may recognize some weak traits in the person their child wants to marry. They feel that in time, the child will recognize the weak traits, too. Disapproval is often their way of saying you should wait a while and learn a little more about this person before you commit yourself to marriage.

In any marriage, the spouses will have many adjustments to make. They will have many conflicts to settle and many compromises to make. If the parents do not approve of the marriage, the spouses have less incentive to settle their differences. They may give up easily. They may think, *Our parents said this marriage would be a mistake, and it is. We might as well give up.*

On the other hand, spouses seem to compromise more readily if their parents approve of their marriage. They may think, *Our parents thought this marriage would work. We don't want to disappoint them by giving up so easily. What's wrong with our marriage? What can we do to make it better?* This positive viewpoint can save a marriage that might otherwise fail.

Attitude Toward Marriage

The attitude spouses have about marriage plays a major role in their marital success. Too often people think that marriage means living happily ever after. However, all marriages have conflicts and challenges. Marriage means bringing two different people together. The process of give-and-take is a part of daily life.

The Engagement Period

The engagement period helps couples prepare for marriage. It marks the end of dating and the start of a couple's plan for married life.

The engagement period has several functions. It is a time for a couple to discuss important issues such as the ones listed in **8-9**. It is important for couples to learn their future spouse's point of view on each issue. Disagreeing on one or more of these topics may present problems in the future. The couple can use the engagement period to identify and discuss potential issues.

The engagement period is also a time for a couple to establish good relationships with future in-laws. Couples will also make plans for their wedding and future home.

While an engagement is considered preparation for marriage, not all engagements end in marriage. Many couples who approach engagement seriously find that they are not ready to commit themselves to marriage. They may find their differences are too great to resolve. For a couple in this situation, a broken engagement is better than a broken marriage.

8-9

Open communication about important issues helps a couple prepare for marriage.

Issues to Discuss During Engagement

Your attitudes toward marriage

Your readiness, as a couple, for married life

Your expectations of your husband or wife

Educational goals

Career goals

Family goals

Friendships

Social activities

Differences in
  age
  nationality
  race
  religion
  social class

Marriage roles

Financial matters

Where you will live

What transportation you will need

Making Marriage Work

People continually grow and change. It makes sense that a marriage relationship would continually grow and change, too. The most obvious changes occur early in marriage. Throughout a marriage relationship, the greatest challenge for most couples is to grow closer together, not farther apart.

Early Marital Adjustments

Whenever two people start a new life together, adjustments have to be made. Since no two people are alike, this is to be expected. Most newlyweds will be faced with several adjustments as they adapt to their new lifestyle. Their success in making these adjustments will affect the quality of their relationship.

Adjusting to a new home is one change for newlyweds. If they had been living with their parents, their new dwelling may seem small. Their furnishings may seem simple and sparse. The couple will have to adjust to housing they can afford. With a good attitude, the couple can enjoy the challenge of gradually improving their home.

Newlyweds have to adjust to some new daily living habits and routines. Morning and evening schedules will have to be adjusted to fit the couple's needs. Meal patterns will have to be adjusted according to food preferences, cooking skills, and time schedules. Plans will have to be made so household chores such as doing laundry, dusting, and mowing the lawn are done. Good communication and cooperation will help the couple make these adjustments easily.

Social activities tend to change and become less expensive. Married people tend to set many long-range goals. These goals may include further education, home ownership, and parenthood. Such goals require financial commitments. To meet their long-range goals, a couple may spend less money for recreation.

Relationships with family members and friends may change, too. A spouse usually receives top priority in marriage. Wise parents, other family members, and friends realize this is an important adjustment for newlyweds. This does not mean that others are forgotten. Since newlyweds tend to spend more time together, they have less time for family and friends.

Nurturing a Marriage

Subtle changes occur continuously in marriage. As people grow older, they face new challenges and accept new responsibilities. Some of their interests and attitudes change. Good communication helps marriage partners keep in touch with each other's changing personality. Then they can change together. Their relationship can become closer and stronger.

Living Green

Encourage family members who are planning a wedding or anniversary trip to think about the environment as they plan. Ask them to consider getting around at their destination by renting bikes or taking public transportation.

Two people can grow closer together in marriage, but they cannot achieve perfection. No person is perfect. No marriage is perfect. A couple should not expect to feel total love for each other all the time. They should not be disappointed if love seems to fade and then reappear. This is called **intermittency of love** and is normal in a relationship.

Sometimes a couple's love will have periods of growth; other times it will level out. If they have a strong relationship and keep communication lines open, their love will return.

Just as love has its ups and downs, so does happiness. Trying to maintain constant happiness can drain a marriage relationship. Married people should stay in tune with each other's feelings, supporting each other through these ups and downs. They may find happiness together in special occasions, such as anniversaries and holidays. They may also find happiness in simple acts of kindness and thoughtfulness. Sometimes one spouse may feel unhappy or upset. This is a normal part of most relationships. By offering love and understanding during these times, a couple can work through these feelings.

Any marriage will have good times and bad times. A successful marriage is one in which both partners want success and are willing to work for it. They focus on their love for each other and the good times they share. They make an effort to communicate their thoughts and feelings to each other. When problems or differences arise, they work together to resolve them.

Reading
Review

1. Name three factors that influence a person's choice of a marriage partner.
2. True or false. The relationships among members of a person's family may influence the relationships that will form within his or her future family.
3. Name two reasons for the high rate of failure in teenage marriages.
4. True or false. In successful marriage relationships, couples continually grow and change.

Section 8-4

Negative Relationships

Objectives

After studying this section, you will be able to

- **describe** a negative relationship.
- **explain** how to end and recover from a negative relationship.
- **explain** how a code of behavior can help you manage negative peer pressure.
- **give** examples of sexual harassment.
- **explain** what rape is and how to avoid being a rape victim.

Key Terms

| peer pressure | rape | date rape |
| sexual harassment | acquaintance rape | |

Unfortunately, not all relationships are positive. Learning how to identify and end negative relationships can help you protect your social, emotional, and sometimes physical health.

What Is a Negative Relationship?

A *negative relationship* is one that is neither healthy, satisfying, nor successful for one or both of the people involved. A negative relationship goes beyond simply being annoyed with another person or being tired of the relationship. A negative relationship threatens a person's physical and/or emotional well-being.

Negative relationships often involve some level of abuse. This abuse can range from name-calling and put-downs to physical violence. Verbally humiliating someone can cause emotional scars. The person may begin to feel unworthy, or even deserving of the abuse. He or she may lose self-esteem. Physical violence can result in cuts and bruises, broken bones, or even death. To avoid these destructive forces, negative relationships must be ended.

Ending a Negative Relationship

You may think that anyone who is in a negative relationship would want to end the relationship immediately. A person can detach himself or herself from a peer or coworker who is causing a negative relationship. However, ending a relationship with a parent, sibling, or dating partner can be much more difficult.

Some people find it hard to end even the most harmful relationships. A child may feel trapped by financial dependence on his or her parents. A wife may fear further abuse from her husband. Dating partners may be ashamed to turn to family or friends for help.

The first step in ending a physically abusive relationship is to get away from the abuser. Children and youth may need help with this step. Teachers, doctors, police officers, and religious leaders can guide young people to sources of assistance.

A plan should be formed to get away from an abuser in advance to avoid panic in a moment of crisis. Some clothes and a few personal items might be left with a friend. Money, keys, and important papers should be safely stored. These items can then be retrieved quickly if an emergency escape becomes necessary. Following an abusive incident, a police report should be filed as soon as possible. Any needed medical care should be obtained. Victims can then move into a shelter. There they will be able to get counseling and legal advice.

Emotionally abusive relationships are not life threatening. However, they must still be ended to preserve the well-being of the people involved. Again, getting away from the abuser is the first step. This gives the abused person a chance to regain some of his or her self-esteem. It gives the abuser a chance to face his or her use of negative relationship patterns.

Not all negative relationships must end unhappily. Relationship patterns that lead to negative relationships can be stopped. Counseling can help people change negative patterns of interaction.

Recovering from a Negative Relationship

Recovering from a negative relationship takes time. Spending some of this time alone can help begin the recovery process. People can use time alone to think about what may have led to the negative relationship patterns. They can consider how these patterns might be avoided in future relationships. See **8-10**.

Taking time to look back on the relationship may be helpful. However, this time should not drag on too long. People recovering from negative relationships need to get on with their lives. Pushing themselves to get involved in group activities will help them avoid spending too much time alone.

Not all of a person's relationships will be negative. His or her positive relationships may become more important during the recovery period. The support of family and friends can provide comfort during this time of healing.

Some negative relationships leave lasting scars. Some people find it hard to build new relationships. Their self-esteem has been damaged. Counseling may be needed to help these people regain a sense of

self-worth. Only after learning to love themselves will these people be able to love and trust others again.

8-10
Spending some time alone can give a person the chance to reflect on the causes of a negative relationship.

Negative Peer Pressure

Negative relationships are sometimes the result of negative peer pressure. **Peer pressure** is the influence a person's peers have on him or her. Peer pressure is positive when it is used to encourage someone to adopt acceptable behavior. For instance, someone might use positive peer pressure to prompt a friend to study for a test. Peer pressure is negative when it is used to urge someone to adopt unethical behavior. For instance, someone might use negative peer pressure to persuade a friend to shoplift.

Managing Negative Peer Pressure

Managing negative peer pressure is a skill all people need to develop. The first step to managing negative peer pressure is to identify when it is being used. Some teens have trouble with this step. This is because they have not decided what types of behavior they think are unethical. In other words, they do not know what activities they consider to be right and wrong.

Developing a code for your behavior will give you a defense against negative peer pressure. You will not have to make quick decisions about whether or not something is right for you. You will simply follow your code.

Analyze and Solve

Write a paper on self-esteem as it relates to the following: standing up to negative peer pressure with assertiveness (such as saying "I'm not interested"); responding to the pressure with aggression (as in yelling or criticizing); and simply going along with negative peer pressure to "fit in."

Your code will be based on your values. It will define what unethical behavior means for you. For instance, you may decide it is okay to tease people about things they say. However, you might decide it is wrong to tease people about their appearance or their skills. Therefore, if your friends start booing a basketball player for missing a shot, you will not feel pressured to join them. Booing goes against your code of not teasing people about their skills.

Parents and other trusted adults can help you form a code of behavior that is right for you. Talking to these adults can also help reassure you when your code is tested.

You will probably adapt your behavior code and beliefs from time to time. However, it is best not to do so when you are under pressure. Try to choose friends who will not urge you to act irresponsibly. Also, learn to avoid situations that might pressure you to break your code of behavior. When you run into unexpected pressure, try using your sense of humor. You can jokingly resist peer pressure without sounding afraid or unsure.

Sexual Harassment

A very difficult negative relationship is one that involves sexual harassment. **Sexual harassment** is defined as unwanted or unwelcome sexual advances, requests for sexual favors, or other verbal or physical sexual conduct. Sexual harassment can be a leering stare. Comments with sexual overtones are considered sexual harassment. Body contact, such as brushing too close to another person or deliberately touching someone in a sexual manner, are other examples of harassment. Sometimes demands are made for sexual favors with the promise of certain benefits if the person complies. This, too, is sexual harassment. All types of sexual harassment are illegal.

8-11

Any of these behaviors can be considered sexual harassment if they are unwanted and unwelcome.

You probably hear more about sexual harassment in the workplace, but it can happen anywhere, between people of all ages. It can happen at school, home, and social functions.

Being a victim of sexual harassment can be very frightening. Some victims feel ashamed and think they somehow are responsible. They may also try to ignore it, hoping it will stop on its own. Sometimes people are unsure whether or not sexual harassment is actually happening. To help you recognize behaviors that are often considered sexual harassment, review the list in **8-11**.

Identifying Sexual Harassment

Behaviors that are often considered sexual harassment include unwanted and unwelcome

- sexual language
- sexual name-calling
- pressure to engage in sexual activity
- personal questions about someone's sexual behaviors
- sexist or sexual remarks about a person's clothing, body, or sexual activities
- demands for sexual favors
- staring at, touching, or grabbing a person in a sexual manner

If you think you are a victim of sexual harassment, speak up. Tell the harasser that you resent the behavior, and you will take action if it continues. The person may not realize that you feel sexually harassed. If you do not say anything, the person may think you welcome the behavior. If you say something, it might stop.

If the harassment does not stop, talk to a person in charge. At home, you can tell a parent; at school, you should speak to a counselor. If sexual harassment occurs at work, speak to your supervisor. If your supervisor is the harasser, talk to the person designated by your employer to handle sexual harassment complaints. The important thing is to speak up. Do not allow the harassment to continue. You have the right to expect others to respect you as a person.

Rape

Rape is one of the most serious types of personal attacks. **Rape** is the crime of forcing another person to submit to sexual relations. During recent years, rape has increased rapidly. Young people under the age of 18, especially women, are often the victims. The majority of rapes occur at night. Many occur in the victim's home, at or near a friend's home, or on the street. Persons who rape strangers are more interested in gaining power over their victims than in satisfying themselves sexually. The victim may be in danger of being killed by the attacker.

Date and Acquaintance Rape

Rape committed by someone the victim knows is far more common than rape by a stranger. In over half of all reported cases involving teens, the rapist was someone the victim knew. **Acquaintance rape** is rape committed by a person who the victim knows. This may be a friend, someone at school, a coworker, or someone the victim just met. **Date rape** is the rape of a dating partner. In most cases of date or acquaintance rape, victims thought they could trust their attackers because they knew them.

When a person says no, yet is forced to have sex, it is rape. What the victim chooses to do to get through the rape encounter does not change the charge. Even if the victim used poor judgment, it is still rape. Rape is illegal; poor judgment is not.

Life Skills

Preventing Date and Acquaintance Rape

- Take extra precaution to avoid situations where you could be attacked. Don't walk alone in unsafe areas or after dark.
- Learn to recognize situations that could get out of control.
- Leave a situation in which someone tries to take advantage of you or if another person makes you uncomfortable.
- Learn to say "no." Let the other person know you mean what you say.

Rape can be an extremely traumatic experience for the victim, with serious long-term effects. Many victims are afraid to report rape by strangers and are even less likely to report date rapes. They may be afraid of getting into trouble with their parents, or may blame themselves for the incident.

Reporting incidents, however, is important for preventing other rapes. Medical care and counseling are needed to help victims recover from the experience. *Rape crisis centers* are community agencies that provide for victims' needs. They can arrange for medical help as well as counseling. Counseling provides emotional support that helps victims regain their self-esteem and trust in others. See **8-12**.

Reading
Review

1. True or false. Being angry with a dating partner is an example of a negative relationship.
2. Give three reasons why some people find it difficult to end negative relationships.
3. What is the first step to managing negative peer pressure?
4. Give three examples of sexual harassment.
5. True or false. Rape is usually committed by a stranger.

8-12

Victims of sexual abuse always benefit from compassionate counselling.

Chapter 8 Review

Summary

Building positive relationships with parents, siblings, peers, romantic partners, and coworkers will help you throughout your life. These relationships will build your self-concept and bring you physical, emotional, social, and economic benefits. Mutual respect, trust, openness, and reliability will help you build relationships that are positive.

Many of your positive relationships will be with acquaintances, good friends, best friends, and dating partners. You will be attracted to these people partly because you meet each other's complementary needs. Through group dating and casual dating, you will find partners with whom you want to have steady relationships. As you learn the difference between love and infatuation and learn how to have a responsible relationship, you will build more mature, lasting relationships.

Marriage can be the closest and most satisfying relationship between a couple. However, it takes prior preparation and continual effort to maintain this relationship.

Several factors influence marital success, including having similar family backgrounds values, and standards. Sharing common interests, having emotional maturity, and having parental approval also help marriages succeed. The engagement period is a time to examine relationships, establish positive in-law relations, and plan for the wedding.

Unfortunately, many people experience negative relationships. If you recognize that a relationship is damaging for you or the other person involved, it should be ended. Some negative relationships are the result of negative peer pressure. Forming a code for your behavior will help you manage this peer pressure. You should know how to recognize sexual harassment and how to avoid being a victim of either sexual harassment or rape.

Critical Thinking

1. **Evaluate relationships.** Evaluate the relationships between you and your parents, siblings, peers, romantic partners, or coworkers. Give five suggestions for improving relationships with the group you choose.

2. **Interpersonal relationships.** Name a career that is of interest to you. Explain how the skills taught in this chapter could help you become successful in that field of employment.

3. **Analyze characteristics.** Select two couples from movies, TV shows, or books that have complementary needs. Discuss how their complementary needs affect their relationship.

4. **Evaluate decisions.** Evaluate a recent decision you made in responding to a conflict with family, friends, coworkers, or a dating partner. What was the conflict and how did you respond? Consider the following questions as you evaluate your response:
   - Was the decision I made in response to this conflict ethical?
   - Was the decision in my best interest and the best interest of others?
   - What would have happened if my circumstances changed? Would I have made the same decision?

   After asking yourself such questions, what lesson did you learn to help you improve future decision making?

21st Century
Applications

5. **Global awareness.** Research marriage rituals in other cultures. What customs and traditions are involved? Write a brief report that summarizes your findings. Remember to cite any sources of information you used during your research.

6. **Information literacy.** Using word processing software, create a survey of issues to discuss during the engagement period. Use the topics from Figure 8-9 and other topics you view as important to discuss. Survey married couples and ask if they considered these points before marrying. Tabulate the responses. Compare your results with those of other students.

7. **Civic literacy.** Study the laws pertaining to sexual harassment cases in the last 50 years. How have the laws changed over time?

Core
Skills

8. **Listening.** Practice your speaking and listening skills by talking with a peer you have not spoken to before. Develop your friendship skills by introducing yourself and asking the person about his or her interests. Actively listen to what that person is sharing. How do you think having a conversation with someone you do not normally speak with is different than speaking with a friend or family member every day?

9. **Writing.** Write a short essay describing your most significant positive relationship. Explain how you have benefited from this relationship and what elements helped you build it and keep it strong.

10. **Reading, writing.** Research famous couples in literature. Choose one story or novel involving a dating couple and write a paper exploring their relationship. Is the relationship portrayed realistically or is it romanticized?

11. **Writing.** Write a paper describing some of your family's (or a fictional family's) customs, such as holiday celebrations, money matters, and disciplining children. Indicate whether you would like to include these customs in your future family. How might differences in customs affect a marriage?

12. **Reading.** Read some of the most famous love poems. Identify any *similes* (phrases that suggest love is like or similar to another object or concept) and *metaphors* (phrases that equate love to another object or concept). Why have there been so many different definitions and comparisons for the concept of love?

13. **Writing.** Write a fictitious letter to an advice columnist. Ask for advice on how to end a negative relationship, recover from a negative relationship, or manage negative peer pressure. Exchange letters with a classmate. Write a detailed response to the letter using information you learned in this chapter.

14. **Reading.** Search the Internet for current statistics on teen marriages. What percentage of these marriages succeed? Write a brief summary of

your findings. Propose a theory that might explain the trends reflected in teen marriage statistics.

15. **Math.** Review the factors contributing to marital success discussed on pages 191–196. Use software to make a graph showing the rankings of the factors according to importance in your opinion. Share your graph and discuss your reasons for rankings.

16. **Speaking.** Prepare a video on ways to manage negative peer pressure. Use role-plays to demonstrate effective management skills. Show the presentations in class.

17. **Speaking.** Interview at least five peers about their experiences with peer pressure. Were their experiences positive or negative? How did the pressure affect them? Knowing the outcome, would they respond to peer pressure differently next time? Why or why not? Write a report to summarize your research.

Leadership
Development

As part of working on the Interpersonal Communications STAR Event, develop a project designed to achieve one of the following goals:
- Evaluate how strong communication impacts positive relationships with parents and siblings
- Help engaged couples discuss important issues before marriage
- Strengthen communication between people and their in-laws

Portfolio
Builder

Building positive relationships with teachers, employers, and religious leaders can help you as you apply to colleges as well as for career opportunities. Ask a teacher, employer, or religious leader who knows you well to write a letter of recommendation about you. Ask the person to document career-related skills that you possess. Keep a copy of this letter in your portfolio.

Journal
Writing

Nicole and Shauna have been friends since they met in seventh grade and spend as much time together as they can. They love being the center of attention and are the loudest in every group. They think poor grades are hilarious. Lately, they have begun trying to outdo each other's outrageous behavior. They started having shoplifting competitions. At school, their last prank ended with the injury of a classmate. Nicole's parents have announced that they will be starting counseling sessions with her.

Write About It: *In what ways can you identify Nicole and Shauna's behavior as negative peer influence? What actions should their parents take? How might the girls actually develop a mutually beneficial friendship?*

Parenting, Child Care, and Guidance

Unit Four

Human Services

The Early Childhood Development and Services Pathway within the Human Services career cluster includes careers that foster the growth and development of young children. Examples of careers in this pathway include child care center directors and preschool teachers.

Human Services Pathways

Early Childhood Development and Services
Counseling and Mental Health Services
Family and Community Services
Personal Care Services
Consumer Services

michaeljung/Shutterstock.com

Education and Training

The Professional Support Services Pathway within the Education and Training career cluster includes professions that support teaching roles. Examples of careers in this pathway include social workers, program advisers, and psychologists.

Education and Training Pathways

Administration and Administrative Support
Professional Support Services
Teaching and Training

Lisa F. Young/iStock/Thinkstock

Career Spotlight: Child Care Center Director

- **Description.** Child care center directors oversee and manage child care programs. They are responsible for planning and supervising daily activities, teaching classes, communicating with parents, and managing staff. They may monitor students' progress and meet with parents to discuss any behavioral or learning problems a student might be having. Child care center directors also handle administrative tasks, such as managing the budget, setting program fees, and ensuring the child care center's facilities comply with state standards.
- **Education and training.** Requirements vary, but most states require child care center directors to have a bachelor's degree and some experience in early childhood education. Some employers may also require a recognized credential, such as the Child Development Associate (CDA) credential.
- **Skills and personal qualities.** Child care center directors must enjoy working with children. They should also have strong management, interpersonal, communication, leadership, and organizational skills. Child care center directors must be patient and kind.
- **Job outlook.** Job growth through 2028 is projected to grow faster than average for all occupations. Visit the *Occupational Outlook Handbook* online to learn more about a career as a child care center director.

Human Services

Career Spotlight: Social Worker

- **Description.** Social workers listen to clients' concerns, evaluate their needs, and help them develop plans and strategies to improve their well-being. Some social workers work with specific groups of people, such as children, adolescents, older adults, or people coping with chronic illnesses. Social workers often work to address crisis situations, such as child neglect and abuse, poverty, illness, divorce, and unemployment. They also help people identify and apply for government benefits. Social workers maintain contact with their clients and check in with them to ensure the situation has improved.
- **Education and training.** Most social workers have a bachelor's degree in social work or a closely related field. To earn a bachelor's degree, social workers attend classes and must complete an internship or supervised fieldwork. Clinical social workers must be licensed, which requires a master's degree in social work and at least two years post-master's experience in a supervised setting.
- **Skills and personal qualities.** Social workers must be compassionate and have the desire to help others. Strong communication, interpersonal, listening, problem-solving, and organizational skills are required. Because social workers often have many clients, time management skills are also important.
- **Job outlook.** Job growth for social workers through 2028 is projected to grow faster than average for all occupations. Visit the Occupational Outlook Handbook online to learn more about a career as a social worker.

Education & Training

Sources: States' Career Clusters Initiative, Bureau of Labor Statistics Career Guide to Industries

Chapter 9
Parenting Roles and Responsibilities

Reading Prep

Before you begin reading this chapter, consider how the author developed and presented information. How does the information provide the foundation for the next chapter?

Concept Organizer

+	−	I

Make a PMI (Plus, Minus, and Implications) chart about parenting. In the first column, write what you consider to be positive aspects of parenting. In the second column, write negative aspects. In the third column, write interesting facts about parenting.

Click on the activity icon ↗ to visit www.g-wlearning. com/comprehensive/8062 to access online vocabulary activities using key terms from the chapter.

Parenting Choices

Objectives

After studying this section, you will be able to

- **state** the goal of parenthood.
- **describe** the challenges of parenthood.
- **recognize** the challenges faced in youth parenting.
- **analyze** the factors that influence parenthood decisions.

Key Term

parenting

Parenting is the name given to the process of raising a child. It includes all of the love, care, and guidance given by parents in this process. Parenting begins with the birth or adoption of a child and lasts a lifetime. Even if the marriage breaks apart, parents are still the parents of their child.

Before committing themselves to parenting, people should have a full understanding of the demands and rewards of this important role. Any goal started without knowledge and planning has little chance for success. Likewise, people who begin parenting without knowledge and planning may fall short of their parenting goals.

The Goal of Parenting

The primary goal of parenting is to help children grow and become mature, independent individuals who can make their own decisions and accept responsibility for their actions. In simpler words, it might be stated in this way: The goal of parenting is to help children grow up responsibly.

There is no step-by-step recipe you can follow to reach this goal of parenting. Each child is unique, and each situation is unique. The best way to prepare yourself for parenthood is to learn as much as possible about children. The more knowledge you have, the better able you will be to handle any situation that occurs.

Helping Children Grow Up Responsibly

Helping children grow up responsibly is not always easy. One of the most important—and most difficult—tasks for parents is to teach their children values and standards. Another difficult task is to allow children to learn through new experiences. Parents also need to help their children learn to interact with other people.

Teaching Values and Standards

To teach children how to evaluate the importance of something, parents first must have firmly established values and standards of their own. They must be living a lifestyle that reflects their beliefs. Then their children will be able to follow their examples and adopt similar values and standards. See **9-1**.

Letting Children Learn Through New Experiences

Parents have a strong urge to cushion the path for their children. They should realize, however, that their help may actually hinder their children's development. Whenever possible, a child who demands "Let me do it myself" should be allowed to try. The child may not do the job perfectly, but perfection is not always necessary. Having the child learn to do it may be more important than having it done perfectly.

9-1

These children are learning the importance of family mealtimes shared together.

Recognizing the Importance of Other People in Children's Lives

This is an important factor in helping children grow up responsibly. Babies are happy to be completely dependent on their parents. As children mature, however, they want and need to meet many different people. Parents with a healthy attitude about their children recognize this as a positive mark of growth. Parents with a less healthy attitude may feel jealous about the loss of their children's attention.

The Challenges of Parenting

Being a parent involves commitments of love, time, energy, patience, and money. Most people gladly accept these commitments in order to have the rewards of parenthood.

- *Parenting involves commitments of time and energy.* Babies have to be fed, bathed, and clothed. Their cries have to be answered, even in the middle of the night. Sometimes the tasks involved in caring for a child seem endless, and parents become discouraged.

- *Parenting requires patience.* One frustration of parenthood is the hundreds of questions that children ask. Parents must remind themselves that this type of behavior is normal for young children. They must try to avoid becoming impatient.

- *Parenting involves a major financial commitment.* The costs for clothing, furniture, and toys add up quickly. As children grow, housing, food, transportation, education, medical care, and recreation become major expenses. If one parent leaves work to care for a child, the family must adjust to a reduced income. If both parents continue to work, child care will be an expense.

Teen Parenting

Parenting in the teen years presents many challenges for young couples. Few teenage parents are aware of the time, energy, and money required to

Healthy Living

Preventable Health Risks for Children of Teens

A poor diet and certain other behaviors can cause a number of preventable health conditions for children of teen moms. Here are a few health risks and behaviors to prevent them.

- **Low birthweight.** Eating a well-balanced diet with a proper amount of calories before and during pregnancy can help prevent low-birthweight babies. Smoking during pregnancy can also cause low birthweight. If you smoke, quit.

- **Neural tube defects (NTDs).** In the embryo, the neural tube is a structure that becomes the brain and spinal cord. Folate is a vitamin that can help prevent NTDs. Without enough folate, the neural tube does not close completely, causing brain and spinal cord defects. Eating a folate-rich diet (including dry beans, leafy greens, and oranges) before and during pregnancy is helpful.

- **Fetal alcohol syndrome (FAS).** Fetal alcohol syndrome is caused by drinking alcohol during pregnancy. The effects in children include central nervous system problems, abnormal facial features, other physical problems, and problems with learning. Women who are thinking about becoming pregnant, or those who are, should stop drinking alcohol.

rear a child. Many are not prepared to face the physical, emotional, social, and financial challenges of parenthood.

Teenage mothers face several physical health risks during pregnancy. A lack of medical care or poor nutrition during pregnancy puts both mother and child at risk. Pregnancy-related illnesses, such as preeclampsia, and other complications are also more common for teen mothers. Preeclampsia, also called *toxemia*, is high blood pressure caused by the pregnancy. Because their own bodies may still be developing, teens have higher risks of having premature, low-birthweight babies. The infant death rate is also higher for teen mothers than for mothers in their twenties. As research shows, a mother's age does make a difference in pregnancy. The best childbearing years for women are from ages 20 through 32.

Emotional Challenges

Teen parenthood will affect the young parents emotionally. Many teenage marriages occur because the young woman becomes pregnant. Because of emotional and financial pressures, these marriages have a fairly high divorce rate. The addition of a child adds even more pressures. Young couples, who are still growing up themselves, are often unable to deal with all the pressures they face.

Teen parents must cope with sudden changes in their roles from adolescents to parents. This often causes more emotional stress. They are faced with the challenge of growing up overnight to assume adult roles as parents. Their own parent-child roles are often conflicting. They are parents to their babies while they remain children of their own parents.

Social Challenges

The arrival of a baby greatly hinders teen parents' social life. Working and child-care responsibilities mean they are less likely to experience a normal social life with friends their age. Their opportunities to socialize with their friends are limited. They see that their friends have more freedom and fewer responsibilities. This sometimes creates feelings of frustration and even anger.

Education and Career

While some teen parents who have strong support at home are able to finish their high school education, many drop out of school. This may severely limit their lifetime earning potential. Not only do teen parents suffer the economic consequences, but their children suffer also.

The Children of Teen Parents

Teens are still developing physically, intellectually, emotionally, and socially. They are usually not yet financially independent either. Because of such factors, their children are subject to more risks than children born to older parents.

- *Health risks.* A young mother may not be aware of certain prenatal behaviors that could put her unborn child at risk. For example, taking certain medications not prescribed by your doctor may harm a fetus.

- *Academic risks.* The first two years of life are critical because the child is building the mental foundation that will dictate behavior through adulthood. Young parents may lack the time to adequately guide the development of their child, especially if they must work, attend school, and also care for their child's other needs.

Financial Literacy

Financial Challenges of Youth Parenting

Teen parents face many financial difficulties as they enter the adult world. Many lack stable financial resources, such as secure jobs. In trying to meet expenses, they are more likely to drop out of school and have low-paying jobs. Many also lack the skills and training needed to advance in their jobs. With little formal education, most do not find jobs to support themselves and their children. The following are some of the challenges teen parents may face:
- resorting to government aid programs for financial support
- being financially dependent on family members or others
- living in poverty

- *Emotional risks.* Recent research has shown that emotional development is the foundation of intelligence. Young parents may again be unable to spend this quality time with their babies.

- *Social risks.* Studies show that children born to teen parents are more likely to become parents themselves when they are teenagers.

- *Economics.* Because teen parents may lack education and job skills, their children have a greater chance of living in poverty.

- *Child care.* The children of teen parents are likely to have caregivers other than their parents while parents are in school or working. Finding quality care for children may be difficult and expensive.

- *Neglect and abuse.* It is difficult to meet the needs of another when your own needs may be unmet. A lack of experience in child care may result in a teen parent neglecting his or her child. In addition, a teen parent may find the pressures of parenthood too much to handle. He or she may take out frustrations on the child in abusive ways.

Deciding Whether to Have Children

Analyze and Solve

Interview parents about their decision to have children. When did they make this decision? What factors helped make the decision? How did they prepare for parenthood? Analyze the parents' responses and prepare a written report of the interview.

One of the most important decisions a couple will make together is whether to have children. Many personal factors need to be considered, including reasons for having or not having children. To make a wise decision, each partner needs a clear understanding of each other's feelings and goals as they relate to parenthood.

Reasons for Having Children

Why do so many people choose to have children? For many parents, bringing a child into the world is an expression of love. Sharing the joys

9-2

Sharing experiences with his child fulfills the life of this parent.

and responsibilities of rearing a child brings many couples closer together. The desire to have a family lifestyle is another reason for having children. Many people want to enrich their lives and share their experiences with children. They do not want to miss the special experiences of life that children make possible, **9-2**. Fulfilling role expectations is also a reason for having children.

Reasons for Not Having Children

Most couples choose to have children. However, after careful evaluation of their feelings, others choose not to become parents. Some couples may prefer the freedom of a childless lifestyle. The demands of a career may make others unwilling to take time to rear a child. The expense of rearing a child may deter some. An unhappy childhood or fear of rearing a child may influence other couples' decisions.

Other Factors Affecting Parenthood Decisions

Couples making a decision about parenthood will consider many personal factors. Each factor can affect their final decision. One factor they should discuss is the short- and long-term goals they have set for their life together. How will children fit into these goals? Another factor a couple needs to evaluate is their own relationship. Is it strong and growing? Are they both ready to accept the roles of father and mother?

Besides determining if they want to have children, couples also need to decide if they are ready to have children. They should not feel obligated to have children just to satisfy their friends and relatives. They also should not feel selfish if they decide to remain childless. Couples who decide they are ready to have children begin the process of preparing for a family.

Reading
Review

1. State the primary goal of parenthood.
2. Name two typical challenges faced by teen parents.
3. List three reasons why many people choose to have children.
4. Identify two personal factors affecting a couple's decision about parenthood.

Section 9-2

Being a Responsible Caregiver

Objectives

After studying this section, you will be able to

- **name** possible caregivers for children.
- **list** characteristics of a responsible caregiver.
- **describe** the responsibilities of caregivers.
- **determine** helpful resources for caregivers.
- **identify** employment opportunities for caregivers.

Key Terms

caregiver	nanny	foster care
hotline	child care cooperatives	

A **caregiver** is a person who provides care for someone else. A caregiver may be responsible for an older person, a person with disabilities, or a young child.

A child may have many different caregivers, including parents, grandparents, babysitters, and teachers, **9-3**. You, too, may be a child's caregiver. You may have younger brothers and sisters. You may babysit for children in your neighborhood. You may even choose a career that involves working with children.

Who Are the Caregivers?

Many people may fill the role of caregiver for a child. The primary caregivers are the parents. They have the main responsibility for providing for their child's needs. There are times, however, when they cannot be with their child. Then other caregivers fulfill this important role.

Many of a child's caregivers are related to the child. Older brothers and sisters may occasionally be left in charge of their younger siblings. Grandparents may care for grandchildren on an as-needed basis. In the case of a single parent, the grandchild and his or her parent may even live with the grandparents. They may provide much of the child's care if the parent must finish school or work.

9-3

Many different people will provide for a child's care through the growing years. Even people without children can enjoy being part of children's lives.

Other caregivers may be employed by the family to care for the child in their absence. These include babysitters, child care providers, and preschool teachers.

Guardians and foster parents may be responsible for a child's care. These individuals are legally required to care for a child if the parents are unable to do so. Sometimes the role of caregiver is more informal. For example, a caring neighbor may invite a child to go on an outing to give the parents some much-needed free time together. The neighbor becomes a caregiver for the time they are out.

Characteristics of Responsible Caregivers

A caregiver is patient, flexible, likes children, and is in good health. Every person is not equally qualified to be a caregiver. There are many skills to learn to be able to meet the many needs and demands of children. The characteristics of responsible caregivers fall into four categories: personal qualities, personal skills, knowledge and experience, and health. Where do you fit in the picture?

Personal Qualities

A person who is responsible for the care of children should have certain personal qualities. Responsible caregivers

- *enjoy children.* They find each child to be unique and fascinating. Good caregivers have a sense of humor and have fun with children.

- *are patient.* They can read the same books aloud, tell favorite stories, and play the same game again and again. They know that children learn at different rates. They can patiently wait for children to learn to do things for themselves, like tie their shoelaces. See **9-4**.

- *are flexible.* Children can be unpredictable. Caregivers must be prepared for anything and be willing to adapt to changing circumstances.

- *are alert to children's needs.* Children must be supervised at all times. Caregivers are always watchful to foresee and prevent problems that may occur. In the event that a child's safety is endangered, they are there to immediately offer aid and comfort. Emotional and social needs are also met promptly.

- *exercise self-control.* Caregivers should exhibit a calm and gentle demeanor. Caring for children can be stressful and tiring at times. Good caregivers know when to take a personal time out and calm themselves down. Sometimes caregivers need to "count to ten" to keep their emotions under control.

- *are consistent.* A responsible caregiver establishes routines and rules that are followed regularly. This prevents children from becoming confused. For instance, if children follow a certain bedtime routine night after night, they are more likely to go to bed without a problem. Rules also must be enforced consistently. This gives children a sense of security. If not, children learn that rules are meaningless and can be ignored.

- *set good examples.* Children like to imitate the behavior of adults because it makes them feel grown up. They especially imitate those whom they admire. They learn what to do—right or wrong—from watching others. Good caregivers know this and are careful to set good examples.

Personal Skills

Certain personal skills are needed to give care to young children. The skills needed by responsible caregivers include communication skills, judgment skills, and management skills.

Caregivers must be able to communicate with both children and adults. When communicating with children, they need to speak clearly and use words the children can understand. Using simple language is important. Young children have limited vocabularies. Also using positive statements will help children know what is expected of them. In other words, they tell children what to do rather than what not to do. For example, instead of saying "Do not run," they say "Please walk."

Caregivers may also need to communicate with other adults. Babysitters and child-care professionals need to be able to communicate with the child's parents or guardians about the care and needs of the child. They also may need to communicate with other caregivers if they are in a group child-care facility.

Judgment skills are important for caregivers to have. Every day child caregivers are required to make decisions on how to handle situations involving the children in their care. For example, they must help children deal with conflicts. All children have differences from time to time. The caregiver must know how and when to get involved. Sometimes children can be allowed to work through conflicts on their own. At other times, a decision must be made quickly to avoid a dangerous situation.

Conflicts between adults and children are bound to occur as children enter their toddler years. Again, judgment skills are needed. Caregivers are expected to use mature judgment in handling these

9-4

Caregivers must be patient and allow children to learn skills for themselves.

Analyze and Solve

Interview parents and grandparents about how they dealt with child care when they were new parents. How did they determine who their children's caregivers would be? What are the differences between generations? How do they compare with choosing child care today? Present your findings in an oral report.

disagreements. They need to know effective guidance techniques and how to use them. To foresee and prevent is the best way to avoid problems. Making sure children have a healthful, safe environment is another preventive measure. If children have ample age-appropriate toys and materials to explore, it is less likely that problems will arise.

Certain management skills can benefit caregivers. It helps to plan ahead. There may be moments when everything seems to happen at once. A responsible caregiver should try to foresee possible needs and prepare for them. For instance, having a good supply of diapers on hand shows good planning. Having activities planned to keep children actively involved shows planning, **9-5**. Knowing where the first aid supplies are kept and making sure all supplies are available is another example. Then, when unexpected events happen, the caregiver is ready.

A responsible caregiver also knows how to manage time well. Caregivers can organize their time, set priorities, and distinguish between important and urgent matters. If caregivers are to be ready for their responsibilities, they will need to make choices that make good use of their time. They will need to use basic time management skills.

Knowledge and Experience

Some knowledge about child growth and development is important for caregivers no matter what their role. All child caregivers need to know what children are like. Knowledge is basic to knowing what to

9-5

Quality caregivers plan a variety of activities to keep children actively involved.

expect of children at different ages—their needs, abilities, and interests. This understanding helps caregivers plan appropriate activities to meet their developmental needs. It helps them understand children's behavior and how to respond. For instance, if caregivers know children start becoming afraid of leaving their parents at about eight months, they can plan ways to help children through this stage.

The more experience caregivers have in being with children, the more they will learn about caring for them. New parents who have not been around babies may be very nervous when they become parents for the first time. Soon parents become quite comfortable with their babies. After the second or third child, they are experienced caregivers and feel much more comfortable in their role as parents.

This is true for all caregivers. Experience is often the best teacher. The more caregivers are around children, the more they learn about how to care for them. They become more comfortable in their presence. When you babysit a child for the first time, you probably feel nervous. After a while, you feel much more at ease as you get to know the child. You know more of what to expect from the child and how best to guide him or her.

New caregivers can learn about children by reading books on child development. Many child care classes are also available. Your school probably offers a child development or parenting class that you could take. Classes are also available for adults.

Good Health

Health is an important factor for caregivers. Much energy is expended physically, mentally, and emotionally during a day spent with children. The physical movement involved is almost continuous. Staying mentally alert to a child's ongoing needs gives little time to relax. The responsibility of helping each child develop to his or her fullest potential can be challenging. A lot of energy is expended. Good health is vital in order for caregivers to function to the best of their ability.

Responsibilities of Caregivers

Parents and other caregivers have tremendous responsibilities in their roles as caregivers. It is not an easy task. Anyone taking

Healthy Living

Caregiver Health

Because caring for children is demanding, maintaining good health is important. Ways for caregivers to maintain good health include the following:

- **Focus on proper nutrition.** Eat well-balanced meals and snacks that provide essential nutrients and calories for energy and stamina.
- **Get enough rest.** Adults need at least seven hours of sleep per night.
- **Exercise regularly.** Choose a routine that includes cardiovascular exercise along with strength and flexibility training.
- **Maintain immunizations.** Even adults need to keep up with some immunizations. In addition, parents and caregivers should get a yearly influenza shot to prevent the flu. Talk with a physician about immunization needs.

on this role must be ready to fulfill some very important jobs. They are responsible for meeting children's many needs, including the following:

- *Physical needs.* These include providing the child's food, clothing, shelter, and medical care. Caregivers are responsible for the health and safety of the children in their care.

- *Social needs.* A child must learn to interact with other children and adults. Children need to learn valuable lessons in sharing, communicating, and compromising. Children also need to develop character. They have to learn to behave in ways that are acceptable to society. Children are not born knowing right from wrong. Caregivers have the responsibility to guide children in ways that will promote their moral development.

- *Emotional needs.* Children need to feel loved no matter what they do. They also need to learn how to express their emotions in acceptable ways. This sometimes requires caregivers to set limits. Through love and guidance, parents and other caregivers help children grow toward independence.

- *Intellectual needs.* Caregivers must provide children with opportunities that will help them grow and learn. They can help children develop their language and thinking skills by providing them with suitable learning opportunities.

Resources for Caregivers

How can you learn to be a responsible caregiver? Don't assume knowing how to care for a child is intuitive. Be prepared to learn as much as you can using the many resources available to you.

You might begin by checking your local library for books and magazines you think will be helpful. In addition, you can go online and check out various websites for information. You must be very cautious, however, in selecting websites. Some you can count on for reliable information; others you cannot.

Get acquainted with the various public and private agencies available in your community. There are services for child care and parent education, and even recreation. Most will also have educational literature to distribute. Many of these agencies provide services for families in times of need. Some agencies can diagnose and treat health problems. Others offer financial advice and assistance. City, county, and state government agencies can also refer you to volunteer organizations and support groups that provide various types of assistance.

If an emergency occurs with a child in your care, you may need to call 911 for medical assistance. In certain situations, you might want to call a hotline. A **hotline** is a number people can call for information or other assistance with a specific problem. Many hotlines operate 24 hours a day. Persons familiar with the particular crisis will answer the phone, offer guidance, and refer callers to local services.

A support group might also be a resource for a caregiver. As you have read, a *support group* is a group of people who share a similar problem or concern. Members join together regularly to discuss the concern they have in common. The group might be led by a professional counselor who has special knowledge of the problem.

Employment Opportunities for Caregivers

Many child care experts feel the ideal environment for child rearing is in the home with at least one parent present. However, this arrangement is not always possible, especially in dual-career or single-parent families. The need and demand for quality caregivers is growing.

To determine quality child care, parents evaluate many factors, **9-6**. Professional child care workers must meet state licensing requirements in order to work with young children. Most child care jobs require a person to have additional education beyond high school. A two-year associate's degree in child development or a related area is often a minimum requirement. In order for a child care facility to be licensed by the state, the child care workers must meet these educational requirements. Licensing requirements vary from state to state.

Child Care in the Parent's Home

In this setting, the caregiver comes to the parent's home. Often the caregiver is a relative, grandparent, or close friend. Many parents prefer this option, especially for their infants and toddlers. Children feel more secure in a familiar setting where they receive individualized attention. They receive more consistent care. Their physical, social, emotional, and intellectual needs can be met more easily.

Some families obtain the services of a nanny. A **nanny** is a trained caregiver who provides quality care for children in the parent's home. Live-in nannies receive room and board, plus a salary for their services. Although this type of care is expensive, it is consistent. Some nannies also do household chores, which lightens the parents' workload when they are home. This allows the parents more time to spend with their child when they are home.

Child Care in the Caregiver's Home

This has been the most common type of child care in the United States. Most parents like having their young children in a family-type setting. This encourages children to develop a close relationship with the caregiver. Other benefits include less structure that allows time for play and relaxation. The hours are usually more flexible and the care costs less. Children are less likely to be over-stimulated by the activities of a large group of children. Most states require these homes to be licensed, but this is difficult to enforce.

Living Green

At an early age children can be taught about the environment. Plan an activity to help children to learn how to protect the earth and its resources. Ask permission to present your activity at a child care center.

Evaluating Quality Child Care

The Facility

- Does the care facility meet state, county, and city licensing requirements? Is it checked regularly by authorities to see that certain standards are maintained?
- Does the care facility have a good reputation?
- Is the care facility in a convenient location?
- What is the cost for each child?
- Are alternative schedules available to meet various needs for hours per day and days per week?

The Setting

- Does the setting have a warm, homelike atmosphere?
- Are the rooms and play areas designed and decorated with children in mind?
- Is the care facility equipped with a variety of safe play equipment and arranged with safety in mind?
- What precautions are taken to prevent children from wandering away and to prevent strangers from entering the premises?
- Are the restrooms clean, easy for children to use, and in good repair?
- Do the children have a comfortable and quiet place for naps?
- Is there an isolated place for an ill child?
- Is good emergency care available for the children if the need arises?
- Is the food nutritious, well prepared, and suited to the age of the children?

The Programs

- Are the children grouped according to age? Are suitable activities planned for each age group?
- Are children allowed to choose some of their own activities? Are they allowed time for quiet individual play as well as active group play?
- Is each child respected as an individual?
- Are the needs of the parents recognized by the caregivers?

The Adult-Child Ratio

- What is the adult-child ratio?
- Are all areas of the care facility supervised at all times?
- If a child needs individual attention at times, would this be available?

The Caregivers

- Are the caregivers well trained and experienced?
- Are interactions between caregivers and children pleasant?
- Do the caregivers encourage the physical, intellectual, emotional, and social development of the children?
- Do the caregivers attend promptly to children's needs?
- Are the caregivers calm, gentle, and fair to the children? Do they have a good sense of humor?
- Do the caregivers use guidance techniques without the use of harsh punishment?
- Do the children seem happy?

9-6

Parents carefully evaluate each of these factors before selecting a caregiver or child care program.

Child Care Cooperatives

Child care cooperatives are formed by groups of parents who share in the care of the children. These programs allow parents more control over the child care program. They formulate policy, establish the budget, determine the instructional program, and provide care for the children. Parents also hire teachers or other personnel who may be needed. Cooperatives are often formed so parents can take turns caring for children.

They pay for the care of their children by working in the center. Instead of paying a fee for child care, many volunteer for a certain number of hours.

School- or University-Sponsored Child Care Programs

Some parents enroll their children in a school- or university-sponsored program where student teachers are being trained in child care. These programs offer high quality in both staff and curriculum, **9-7**. Availability is limited to university towns or school systems that provide the caregiver training.

Religious or Social Group Programs

Child care programs sponsored by religious or social groups usually cost less because the sponsor helps fund the costs. For example, religious-linked child care would likely be based in one of the worship buildings. Eliminating the cost of providing a facility cuts the operating expense greatly. The staff for these programs are not only responsible to the parents, but also to the sponsor. These are usually high-quality programs.

9-7.

College child care programs offer quality care for children and excellent training for future child care workers.

Government-Sponsored Child Care Programs

Programs such as Head Start are sponsored by the government. These programs are offered to lower-income working families who may need low-cost child care. Again, the sponsor underwrites the expense of operating the facility. However, the program must meet strict guidelines to be licensed. Fees charged for participation are very low or nonexistent.

Employer-Sponsored Child Care Services

Employers sponsor different types of child care facilities. On-site child care facilities are located on the company grounds, so parents are close at hand if their children need them. Some facilities are off-site, near the workplace. Others are existing child care facilities contracted by the company for their employees. In each of these options, employers may pay all or part of the child care costs.

Privately Owned or Franchised Child Care Centers

These child care facilities are profit motivated. Privately owned child care centers are operated as any other business except they provide child care. Most franchised child care centers started as privately-owned centers. Entrepreneurs saw an opportunity to meet a need, so they created a larger group of centers. These chains try to offer uniform facilities, equipment, and programs.

Serving Your Community

Identify needs of child care centers, particularly nonprofit ones. Identify projects you might do to improve facilities or assist as volunteers. Projects might include planting trees, painting playground equipment, reading stories to children, and assisting with physical care.

The Role of Society in Protecting Children's Rights

Children are a precious resource. They are the hope for the future. Parents and other adults care for them while they are young. Children are easily hurt because they are physically weaker than adults and cannot reason as adults. It is society's responsibility to protect them.

In the United States, parents have the rights of guardianship and determine their children's upbringing. They are responsible for their physical care and their financial support. They provide moral teachings, provide for their education, and make health care choices. If the parents do not provide for these needs of their children, the state can act on the child's behalf and provide protection. This might mean the state would require foster care in extreme situations. **Foster care** is care provided for a child who needs a home temporarily. Children may be placed in foster homes because they have been abandoned, abused, or neglected by their parents. In other situations, children's parents may be temporarily unable to care for them and ask the state for help.

Laws are also passed to protect children's rights. School attendance, for example, is required by law up to a certain age. There are child labor laws that protect children from unsafe working conditions or jobs that interfere with their education. States also provide child welfare services. These services offer food and assistance to families who are unable to make provisions on their own.

All caregivers are responsible for the well-being of the children in their care. It is society's responsibility to make sure all children receive that care. If the parents cannot provide it, other adults will. Legislative policies are made to protect children as they grow to adulthood.

Reading
Review

1. Name four types of caregivers for children.
2. List five characteristics of responsible caregivers.
3. Describe the four main responsibilities of caregivers.
4. State four helpful resources for caregivers.
5. List eight employment opportunities for caregivers.

Life Skills

Starting a Child Care Business

If you enjoy caring for children and can learn the necessary skills, starting a child care business in your home could be a great career option. One of the advantages of this entrepreneurial venture is the ability to care for your own children at home and save money. Plus, the income you earn can help support your family. You are your own boss and can create appealing learning programs and activities.

The community also benefits from a home-based child care business by providing parents with quality care for their children in a safe environment. You could create a business to help fill a community need for types of child care that are unavailable. For instance, you might offer flexible hours to appeal to parents working weekend hours or needing after-school care.

Like any small business, licensing requirements for home-based child care businesses vary by state. There are often specific standards that must be maintained. If this career sounds interesting, do some research on your state's licensing requirements. A good place to start is the Child Care Aware website, a program of the National Association of Child Care Resource & Referral Agencies (NACCRRA).

Chapter 9 Review

Summary

Examining attitudes toward parenthood is important. Like marriage, parenting involves many goals and challenges. Parenthood challenges are likely to be magnified among youth parents. Many personal factors affect a couple's decision about whether or not to have children.

Many people may fill the role of caregiver for a child. The primary caregivers are the parents. Responsible caregivers have certain personal qualities, skills, knowledge, and experience. The responsibilities of caregivers include meeting children's physical, social, emotional, and intellectual needs. Professional caregivers work in a variety of settings.

Critical Thinking

1. **Analyze decisions.** Why do you think deciding about parenthood may be more difficult than deciding about other major lifestyle factors, such as careers?

2. **Apply ratings.** Rank the characteristics of responsible caregivers from the most important to the least important in your view. What did you choose as the most important characteristic and the least important characteristic?

3. **Analyze options.** Would you ever consider becoming a foster parent? Why or why not? What factors would help you make this decision?

4. **Analyze pros and cons.** Think about the pros and cons of hiring a live-in nanny. Do you think this would be an option you would consider in the future? Why or why not?

21st Century Applications

5. **Media literacy.** Research the challenges of teen pregnancy using articles, videos, books, and programs. What financial, emotional, social, and educational challenges do pregnant teens face? Review three separate informational sources. What main message does each source present?

6. **Civic literacy.** Research state licensing requirements for child care centers. How recent are these regulations? How do they protect the children? the caregivers?

7. **Critical thinking and problem solving.** Many parents and caregivers use the Internet as a source for child care information. Visit several websites for parents and caregivers. Set up a check sheet for evaluating each website. Which website would you rate the highest for accuracy, objectivity, currency, and coverage?

8. **Information, communications, and technology literacy.** Create a website that explains each type of child care discussed in the chapter. You may list the names of community child care programs on the site after receiving permission from the programs.

Core Skills

9. **Listening, speaking.** Interview one adult who has chosen to parent and one adult who has decided not to become a parent. Create a list of interview questions about parenting decisions. Based on your

interview responses, discuss the following topics in small groups in class:
- advantages and disadvantages of having children
- reasons for not wanting children
- the best age for becoming parents
- consequences of unplanned pregnancies

10. **Writing.** Write a character sketch of an imaginary couple who are not yet ready to have children. What factors influence their readiness to parent? Share your sketch with your classmates.

11. **Writing.** Write a paper completing one of the following statements: I would like to be a caregiver because…I would not like to be a caregiver because…I would make a good caregiver because…I would not make a good caregiver because…

12. **Reading.** Research the state and local regulations for child care in a caregiver's home. Discuss the regulations in class. What is the reasoning for these regulations?

13. **Listening.** Interview parents about what they consider to be challenges of parenthood. In class, brainstorm questions you might ask and use word processing software to create an interview planning sheet.

14. **Reading.** Research the requirements for becoming a foster parent in your state. How do the foster care requirements compare to adoption requirements in your state?

Leadership
Development

As part of work on the Focus on Children STAR Event, compile an activity booklet for caregivers. Booklets could include suggestions or directions for books, fingerplays, games, and recipes for doughs, paste, and finger paints. Plan a parent-child get-together to demonstrate selected activities from the booklet.

Portfolio
Builder

Being a caregiver for children involves a lot of responsibility. Take a babysitting course from a local community group or Red Cross chapter. Upon completion of the course, you will likely receive a certificate of completion. Write a reflection paper about what you learned from the course and include it and your certificate of completion in your portfolio.

Journal
Writing

Nikiah resents all the time her husband, William, spends at work. She does not like staying home alone on weekends and thinks having a baby would help.

William is getting quite tired of his long hours at work. However, he thinks they need the income to pay their bills, especially if they are going to start a family soon.

Write About It: *What threats to marital and parenting success do you see in this relationship? What misconceptions do William and Nikiah seem to have? What are some possible options for them?*

Chapter 10
Development Across the Lifespan

Reading Prep

Think about two biologically related people. Make a list of three characteristics they share, such as eye color, height, or personality. List three characteristics they do not share. Which traits do you believe are inherited?

Concept Organizer

Use a star diagram to show all the ways your cultural heritage has affected your life. Place your cultural group(s) in the center circle.

G-WLEARNING.com

Click on the activity icon to visit www.g-wlearning.com/comprehensive/8062 to access online vocabulary activities using key terms from the chapter.

Section 10-1

Growth and Development

Objectives

After studying this section, you will be able to

- **identify** factors that influence growth.
- **distinguish** between different types of growth.
- **relate** developmental theories of growth and development.
- **apply** developmental theories to examples and real-life situations.

Key Terms

heredity
environment
cultural heritage
cultural group
character
maturation
chronological growth
physical growth

intellectual growth
cognition
social growth
emotional growth
sequential steps
individual rates of growth
interrelated developmental rates

developmental theories
behaviorism
classical conditioning
operant conditioning

The lifespan can be viewed as a path that extends from birth to death. Most individuals progress through the same stages on that path. You may think that development stops after the teen years, but growth and change continue throughout every stage.

Many people display the same qualities that are observed in others. However, when you carefully examine each person independently, he or she possesses a makeup that is distinctly unique. Even identical twins have differences.

People may be very similar in some respects, yet different in others. In the same way, the stages of development are similar for almost everyone, but each person progresses in an individual way.

Science Connection

Genes and Heredity

Your body is made up of millions of cells. Each cell contains genes that you inherited from your parents. Genes determine what you look like. They also carry instructions for making proteins, the building blocks for everything in your body.

Factors Influencing Growth

Two main factors influence a person's growth and development. The first is **heredity**, which is the sum of all traits passed on through genes from parents to children. The second major factor influencing growth and development is the person's **environment**. This includes all the conditions and situations that surround and affect an individual. The reasons for everyone's growth and development are related to heredity or environment, but often to both, **10-1**.

Your Heredity

All people are influenced by their heredity. Heredity causes people to be alike in many ways. Heredity also causes people to be different. Some are tall; others are short. Some have black hair; others have blond hair. Some are gifted with athletic ability; others are gifted with intellectual ability.

10-1

Even siblings who share heredity and grow up in the same environment will have obvious differences.

Your Environment

Your inherited traits are influenced by your environment. Infants have little control over their environment and gain more control as they grow older. Physical conditions, such as food and rest, are part of the environment. So are relationships with others and the presence or absence of affection. All these factors affect the way a child grows and develops.

Factors in the environment can affect physical traits, too. For example, studies show that babies' brains develop at a slower rate if no one holds or talks to them. When children receive attention and many chances to learn, their brains develop to their full potential.

Healthy Living

Two Different Environments

Two different types of environments influence your personal development: psychological and physical. Both affect the way you look, think, and act.

Your psychological environment is composed of attitudes expressed by people around you. It includes the feelings and beliefs of your family members, teachers, classmates, and friends. These people influence the attitudes you have.

Your physical environment is composed of objects around you. One main factor in your physical environment is the place where you live. You had little control of your physical environment as a young child, but as you grow older, you have more options.

Heredity and Environment Combined

For years, people argued about which affected growth and development more—heredity or environment. Now, experts agree they work together. In the developing brain, for example, they work together to produce effects that are unique for each individual.

Two factors influenced by heredity and environment are *personality* and *self-concept*, which you learned about earlier. Other unique factors influenced by heredity and environment are your cultural heritage and character.

Cultural Heritage

Your **cultural heritage** is made of learned behaviors, beliefs, and languages that are passed from generation to generation, **10-2**. Your family helps you learn about the culture of your society. Their guidelines and beliefs become part of your heritage. The foods you eat, the holidays you celebrate, and the traditions you observe are part of your culture. Through all these cultural experiences, you learn appropriate behavior for your environment.

A **cultural group** is a group of people who share common racial and/or cultural characteristics such as national origin, language, religion, beliefs, and traditions. Cultural groups are important because they encourage a culturally healthy society. Understanding this may help you appreciate your own cultural heritage as well as others.

Cross-cultural skills. Saba tries to share her cultural background with her coworkers so they can get to know her as a person. Her coworkers value the similarities and differences among her culture and their own.

10-2

Cultural diversity among people helps to maintain a healthy society.

Character

Some parts of your personality are described as *character traits*. Character refers to inner traits, such as conscience, moral strength, and social attitudes. It is the inner force that guides your conduct and behavior toward acceptable standards of right and wrong.

Character development, like other personality traits, begins in childhood, **10-3**. Children are taught that certain behaviors are acceptable and others are not acceptable. For example, young children may be told not to hit others. As they begin to internalize the message, they conform because an internal control tells them what is appropriate. As character continues to grow, children develop acceptable standards of behavior and use them voluntarily. They can face new situations knowing right from wrong even without someone guiding them.

Types of Growth

The change that occurs between childhood and adulthood is frequently described as **maturation**. As you mature, your physical, personal, and behavioral characteristics become more adult. Changes that occur as you grow and develop are chronological, physical, emotional, intellectual, and social.

Chronological growth refers to a person's age. This is the only type of growth that takes place at the same rate for all people. Each birthday automatically adds another year to your age. Chronological maturity is often used for legal purposes. People have to prove their age to obtain a driver's license, vote in government elections, or enlist for military service.

Physical growth refers to changes in body stature. This growth is influenced by heredity and health habits such as the type and amount of food eaten. Also, the presence or absence of physical activity and the way you care for your body will influence physical development.

Intellectual growth means developing the ability to reason and form complex thought patterns. It is influenced by your heredity, environment, and desire to learn. When your environment offers learning experiences, you are stimulated to think and look for new solutions to problems.

As connections between the brain's nerve cells develop and strengthen, intellectual abilities increase. The individual can comprehend and organize thoughts of ever-increasing complexity. The processes involving thought and knowledge are called **cognition**.

Social growth means developing the ability to get along with other people. This process begins in early childhood as children learn to take turns and share. Through years of playing and working together, individuals learn to get along with others and participate in society. They also learn that different people like different activities.

Emotional growth refers to development in the range of feelings and the ability to express these feelings.

Social and emotional development are closely intertwined. Often they are considered together and called *social-emotional* or *socio-emotional development*. As social and emotional capabilities develop, children learn self-control, gain confidence, and develop self-esteem. When facing more complex social situations such as forming an identity and dating, individuals develop new skills to cope.

Rusiana Iurchenko/Shutterstock.com

10-3

As children interact with parents and other adults, they develop acceptable standards of behavior.

Patterns of Growth and Development

Growth and development occur in a series of patterns called **sequential steps**. Each new response is based on existing capabilities and skills learned in prior steps. For example, to learn to shake a rattle, a baby must already know how to grasp it.

Growth and development rates vary from child to child. One baby may grasp and shake a rattle at an earlier rate than another baby of the same age. This displays **individual rates of growth** as each child is unique, **10-4**. Factors such as heredity, environment, and motivation influence individual rates of growth.

10-4

Infants of the same age may have distinct developmental differences.

Growth is also influenced by **interrelated development rates**. Physical, intellectual, emotional, and social growth occur together all the time. For example, imagine you are babysitting an infant who is crying. You try to console the baby by giving him a rattle. The rattle is recognized intellectually as his hand grasps it physically. Emotionally, the baby is appeased by the distraction of the rattle. Socially, the baby smiles at you, signaling his pleasure. Strong and complex interactions among physical, emotional, social, and intellectual aspects of growth are always at work.

Theories of Growth and Development

Scientists have studied human growth and development to learn how these processes work and affect individuals. Their explanations are called **developmental theories**. Theories are not facts, but they are useful in understanding the capabilities of individuals at various stages in life. Here is a brief summary of the leading theories and their contributions to knowledge.

Behaviorist Theories

Behaviorism is a theory based on the belief that behavior is the response to stimuli from the environment. This means that, according to behaviorists, experiences shape people's behaviors. Behaviorists believe that babies are not born with behaviors. Instead, they learn as they interact with their surroundings.

Pavlov's Classical Conditioning

The theory of **classical conditioning** asserts that behaviors can be associated with responses. A Russian researcher named Pavlov observed that a dog salivated at the sight of food. He experimented with ringing a bell at feeding time, and before long, the dog salivated merely at the sound of the bell. Behaviorists say that experiences—positive, negative, or neutral—can affect a person's emotions, attitudes, and behaviors.

Skinner's Operant Conditioning

The principle of operant conditioning was identified by the researcher B.F. Skinner. **Operant conditioning** is a theory that people repeat behaviors that are positively reinforced, or *rewarded*. Similarly, people will discontinue behaviors that are met with negative reinforcement, or *punishment*. Where classical conditioning is based on the stimulus, operant conditioning is based on consequences. Additionally, classical conditioning involves involuntary behavior, whereas operative conditioning is based on choices in behavior.

According to this theory, behavior is changed as the reinforcements (rewards or punishment) are gradually removed. This theory is popular in working with children. Grades received in school are just one example, **10-5**.

10-5
Children who are praised for receiving good grades may continue to strive for that reward.

Bandura's Social Cognitive Theory

In opposition to the conditioning theories, Albert Bandura created the *social cognitive theory*. This theory includes people's own thoughts and motivations for reactions to stimuli. It explains why not every person has the same reaction to the same stimuli.

Although Bandura believed people are affected somewhat by rewards and punishments, his theory focused more on people's imitation of others. He also emphasized the unique qualities of both the person and the way each person perceives a situation.

Piaget's Cognitive Theory

Jean Piaget's theory of development focuses on thinking at different stages of development. He identified four stages throughout life:

10-6

Children who recognize letters and words are in the preoperational stage.

- The *sensorimotor stage* takes place from birth to 2 years of age. In this stage, infants use their senses and reflexes to explore. As infants mature, their movements become intentional.

- The *preoperational stage* takes place from ages 2 to 7. Children begin to use language and symbols, **10-6**. They begin to understand some concepts, but they are not yet thinking logically.

- The *concrete operational stage* occurs from ages 7 to 11. Children begin to think logically, but it is at first based on only what they have experienced. As they age, children depend less on actual objects and activities.

- The *formal operational stage* begins at age 12 and continues through adulthood. As children become young adults, they have the ability to think logically and abstractly. They begin to predict future effects of their actions.

As you can see from the stages, Piaget believed that children build their knowledge by developing on skills learned in the previous stage. This theory explains how children learn as they grow.

Vygotsky's Sociocultural Theory

Lev Vygotsky believed that children learn through interactions with others instead of objects. He believed social interaction with both adults and peers help children learn. Through the social environment, children learn about their culture.

Vygotsky's theory includes the *zone of proximal development (ZPD)*. The zone describes a level at which a child is capable of learning. Outside the child's zone are concepts or tasks he or she cannot yet learn, even with adult help. The zone does include tasks a child *can* accomplish with help from others. This help is referred to as *scaffolding*.

Erikson's Psychosocial Theory

Erik Erikson's theory focused on the development of personality. He defined eight stages of development that take place in the lifespan. A crisis or conflict occurs at each stage. The outcome of each crisis influences personality development. The following are Erikson's eight stages:

- *Trust versus mistrust—infancy.* Babies learn trust as caregivers meet their basic needs. If needs are not met, babies will learn that the world is unpredictable and they cannot trust it.

- *Autonomy versus shame and doubt—toddlerhood.* Toddlers use their new skills to become more independent. If toddlers are not allowed autonomy, they will not become achievers. They will feel self-doubt and shame.

- *Initiative versus guilt—early childhood.* Children begin to learn that they can have an effect on the world around them. They feel a sense of accomplishment. Harsh criticism can make them feel guilty for incompetence.

- *Industry versus inferiority—middle childhood.* Children begin to make and carry out plans. This gives them confidence and a feeling of confidence. If they are discouraged or compared harshly with others, they can feel inferior and insecure.

- *Identity versus role confusion—adolescence.* Teens begin to realize they have many different roles. In spite of this, teens need to establish who they really are. If a sense of self is not recognized, role confusion will occur.

- *Intimacy versus isolation—young adulthood.* Young adults form close, intimate relationships. They share their emotions with others, **10-7**. Failing this task results in becoming lonely and isolated.

- *Generativity versus self-absorption—middle adulthood.* Adults of this stage begin thinking about the next generation. They may feel the need to help or nurture others. Adults who fail in this task may think only about themselves and have little to do with the world around them.

10-7

A marriage commitment is one type of intimate relationship.

- *Integrity versus despair—late adulthood.* Older adults will think back on their lives with a sense of satisfaction. They will feel fulfilled by the meaning their lives have held. Adults who do not feel fulfilled will instead feel regretful and hopeless.

Kohlberg's Theory of Moral Development

Lawrence Kohlberg researched how people come to believe what is right and wrong. Kohlberg's theory of moral development is divided by six stages, grouped into three main levels. Each stage is a higher level of moral reasoning than the previous stage. Kohlberg's research led him to classify moral decisions in the following ways:

- *Pre-conventional level:* At the first stage of this level, children understand right and wrong only in terms of whether they will be punished. In the second stage, children have a self-centered viewpoint. They ask how doing the right thing will benefit them.

- *Conventional level:* At stage three, people begin to understand that morality involves meeting social expectations. In stage four, they understand that obeying rules and laws helps society function in an orderly fashion.

- *Post-conventional level:* At stage five, individuals may form their own principles of right and wrong. These views may replace those of society in personal importance. In stage six, people believe in abstract rules such as human rights and justice. These are examples of *universal ethical principles.*

Reading
Review

1. Explain how heredity and environment affect growth.
2. What are the five types of growth? Give an example of each.
3. Explain how growth and development occur in sequential steps.
4. How would Bandura explain why two people respond to the same experiences differently? What is his theory called?
5. According to Piaget's cognitive theory, why do young children think differently from the way teens do?
6. Vygotsky believed that a child's learning is influenced by the people who interact with the child. Give an example of this type of learning.
7. According to Kohlberg, at which stage of moral development does a person ask, "How does doing the right thing benefit me?" At which stage does a person ask, "How does doing the right thing benefit all of society?"

Section 10-2

Infants, Toddlers, and Preschoolers

Objectives

After studying this section, you will be able to

- **describe** the characteristics and basic needs of newborns.
- **summarize** the physical, emotional, social, and intellectual development of infants.
- **give examples** of physical, emotional, social, and intellectual characteristics of toddlers and preschoolers.
- **describe** types of special needs children might have and how to meet those needs.

Key Terms

newborn	solitary play	cognitive disability
infant	parallel play	learning disability
pediatrician	preschooler	behavioral disorder
sudden infant death syndrome (SIDS)	gross-motor skills	gifted and talented
	cooperative play	inclusion
toddler	children with	
fine-motor skills	special needs	
object permanence	physical disability	

The first five years of life is an exciting time for children and their parents. Children have changing needs as they grow and develop. Parents can create a nurturing environment to help meet those needs.

Newborn Babies

For the first month of life, a baby is called a **newborn**. (Babies age 2 to 12 months are called **infants**.) Having a newborn in their home will be a big adjustment for parents and other family members. Parents must be prepared to care for this new little person.

Characteristics of Newborns

Newborns look different from older babies. The average newborn weighs about 7½ pounds and is about 20 to 21 inches long. The newborn's skin may appear red and wrinkled. The head may be misshapen. The

chin recedes, the nose is flattened, and the ears are pressed against the head. (Some of these characteristics are less apparent on babies delivered by cesarean section.) The eyebrows and eyelashes may be barely visible. Some newborns are nearly bald.

Newborns have large heads compared to their bodies. They often have bowed legs and bulging abdomens. Newborns also have very short necks, sloping shoulders, and narrow chests.

Care of Newborns

Newborns have relatively simple needs. They need to eat and sleep. They need to be kept clean, warm, and dry. Above all, they need to be loved, **10-8**.

Parents will have many questions about caring for their newborns. A **pediatrician** is a doctor specializing in the care and development of children. He or she can be a vital source of information for parents when problems arise.

10-8

Newborns' needs are very basic, but their main need is for love and affection from all family members. The family is also where they learn to trust.

Wellness Awareness

Research the latest information available on SIDS. Check out organization websites, such as the American Sudden Infant Death Syndrome Institute. What are the latest research findings on SIDS prevention?

Feeding

Babies are not able to digest solid foods until they are four to six months old. Therefore, parents must choose breast milk or formula to provide all the nutrients their newborn needs. Newborns need to be fed six to eight times a day. They generally wake up once or twice during the night to be fed.

Sleep

Newborns sleep about 18 to 20 hours a day. They tend to sleep about four to five hours at a time. Then they awaken for an hour or so to be changed and fed before going back to sleep.

Babies need a firm, flat mattress for support and posture development. The mattress should fit inside the crib very snugly. There should be no way for children to get their heads caught between the crib and the edge of the mattress.

Sudden infant death syndrome (SIDS) is one concern of parents. SIDS is the sudden death of an apparently healthy baby during sleep. Although the cause is still unknown, several factors may be involved. As a precautionary measure, caregivers should place babies on their backs rather than their stomachs when placing them in the crib to sleep.

This practice has reduced the rate of SIDS significantly. Also keep stuffed toys, pillows, and soft bedding out of the crib to prevent suffocation in bedding.

Bathing

For the first few weeks after birth, babies should be given sponge baths several times a week. Once a baby's navel has healed, he or she may be given tub baths.

Clothes

Clothing for newborns should be made of soft, flame-resistant fabrics. Garments should be loose fitting and easy to put on and take off. Clothing should be appropriate for the existing temperature. Infants can quickly become too hot or too cold. Use sweaters and blankets as needed.

Life Skills

Bathing Newborns

Planning ahead is key to making the bathing process efficient and enjoyable.

- Gather all bathing supplies and towels and place them near the bathing area.
- Clean the baby's eyes, ears, nose, and face first.
- Carefully lower the baby into a small tub containing a few inches of warm water. Wash the baby's body with a mild soap. Gently clean the diaper area and the folds of the baby's skin.
- After rinsing thoroughly, lift the baby out of the tub and gently pat dry with a soft towel.
- Apply baby oil or lotion to moisten the baby's skin.
- Put clothes on immediately to keep the baby warm.

Be sure to test the water before bathing to make sure it is warm, not hot. Also, never leave a baby unattended in a bathtub.

Diapers

Diapers are a basic clothing need of babies for two or more years. Parents may choose cloth or disposable diapers. Newborns need to be changed about 10 times a day. Changing diapers promptly and thoroughly cleansing the diaper area will help prevent diaper rash.

Infants

During the first year, babies change in many ways. When watching for signs of development, parents need to remember that each child is an individual. The signs of growth mentioned here are averages. Each child will develop at his or her own rate.

Physical Growth of Infants

In their first year of life, infants will triple in weight. They will grow to 1½ times their length at birth. Their gross- and fine-motor skills develop at an amazing rate. Parents can notice changes almost daily.

Infants progress from reflex actions to controlled muscle movement. Newborns are not able to hold up their heads. For this reason, their heads must be carefully supported when they are being held. By six months, infants can roll over. At seven months, many babies are beginning to crawl. (Once infants reach this stage, increased supervision will be needed to protect them from hazards.) Eight-month-old babies can sit alone for a period of time. By 10 months, infants may be able to stand up by themselves. Many children are able to start walking by their first birthdays.

Intellectual Growth of Infants

Newborns receive information and show intellectual development through their senses. They follow moving objects with their eyes and listen attentively to sounds with their ears. By two months, infants are able to discriminate between different voices. They also show preference for people over objects. At three months of age, infants begin to show signs of memory. As infants grow older, they remain alert for increasingly longer spans of time. By six months, infants show improved eye-hand coordination. At eight months, infants understand simple concepts, such as *in* and *out*. Ten-month-old infants will search for hidden objects. By their first birthdays, many children can put nesting toys together correctly. They may also show a preference for one hand over the other.

Toys provide infants with intellectual stimulation. Babies like toys that appeal to the senses. Bright colors, varied textures, and interesting sounds attract their attention. Since infants tend to put objects in their mouths, toys need to be kept clean. Children should not be allowed to play with small objects that could be swallowed.

Language development is a sign of intellectual growth. Newborns cry to express their needs. By three months, infants make vowel sounds, like *ooh* and *ah*. Consonant sounds begin to appear in the fourth month. Five-month-olds understand their own names. Infants begin to recognize some words at eight months. At nine months, infants may say *mama* and *dada*. They can also follow simple directions. By the end of the first year, most infants have a vocabulary of several words. They begin to use language to express themselves.

Speaking to infants will have a great impact on their language development. Newborns do not understand words, so the content of your message is unimportant. However, speaking to them allows them to enjoy human contact and helps them become familiar with specific voices. Newborns can perceive a parent's mood. Therefore, parents should speak in pleasant tones that reflect an interest in and love for the child.

The content of messages becomes increasingly important as infants grow older, **10-9**. Infants begin to understand the words being spoken to them at about eight months. They begin to repeat the words they hear by 11 or 12 months. Parents have a responsibility to use messages that provide guidance with love. They must also teach children to use appropriate terms.

Early Brain Development

Scientists have recently discovered that experiences soon after birth affect much of the brain's development. The first two years of life are

Wellness Awareness

Read current journal articles on early brain development. What affects early brain development? How can caregivers contribute to development?

10-9

Speaking to and interacting with infants is important to their intellectual growth.

critical in determining how the circuits of the brain are wired. How the brain grows is dependent on emotional interaction, which involves the parents and other caregivers. Babies whose parents and caregivers talk and read to them and play simple games with them have enhanced intellectual, physical, and emotional development.

The first few years of a baby's life are the most important ones for brain development. Some abilities are acquired more easily during certain time-sensitive periods. These are sometimes referred to as *windows of opportunity*. Time taken to interact with the baby then will have lifelong positive effects. Time lost can be difficult to make up later.

If physical and emotional needs are met in a predictable, responsive way in the first years of life, the foundation is set for healthy emotional development. Emotional health is necessary for the development of intelligence.

Emotional and Social Growth of Infants

Emotionally and socially, infants, like all people, need love and attention from others. From birth, infants respond to human contact and a warm, loving environment. Infants begin to show emotions at a very young age. Two-month-olds can show when they are distressed, excited, or happy. By five months, the range of emotions has expanded to include fear, disgust, and anger. Eight-month-old infants often demonstrate fear of strangers and may seek the comfort of parents in a stranger's

Wellness Awareness

Research neuromuscular diseases such as muscular dystrophy and Lou Gehrig's disease. How are toddlers' muscle skills affected by these diseases?

10-10

Books with large, easy-to-turn pages help toddlers develop small muscle skills.

presence. By the time infants are 10 months old, they begin to cry less frequently. At one year, babies begin to develop their own identities. They are also able to recognize emotions expressed by others.

Socially, newborns can recognize a parent's voice. As they grow older, infants respond to familiar faces. They also begin to show sensitivity around strangers. By five or six months, infants start to enjoy playing games like peek-a-boo. At nine months, they begin to show interest in play activities of others. At 12 months, infants socialize by practicing communication skills with adults.

Toddlers

One- and two-year-old children are called **toddlers**. This term comes from the unsteady way children move, or toddle, when they begin to walk. As children gain mobility, they have more opportunities to develop mentally and socially.

Physical Growth of Toddlers

During the toddler years, parents will see steady improvements in their child's motor skills. As leg muscles develop, toddlers become able to run, jump, kick, and climb as well as walk. Strengthening arm muscles enable 18-month-old toddlers to throw a ball and 36-month-old toddlers to catch one.

Fine-motor skills are the movements that involve smaller muscles, such as fingers and wrists. They improve as children grow. Toddlers become able to fill and empty containers, turn knobs, and build block towers. They like to scribble, paint, play with modeling clay, and string beads. By the time a toddler is 30 months old, he or she can turn the pages of a book. See **10-10**.

Toilet Learning

One important physical skill most children begin to learn during the toddler years is toilet learning. As children learn to control their muscles, toilet learning will come naturally. Children should not be pushed to learn how to use the toilet. At some point, children will begin showing signs of awareness of their bowel movements. At this time, caregivers can begin offering the "potty" about every two hours. This helps a child stay dry. The child may have frequent bathroom accidents, but caregivers should not show disappointment. It is best to praise desired behaviors and to let undesired ones pass with minimum attention. Success in toilet learning, like other successes, will come in time.

Intellectual Growth of Toddlers

Children have much to learn about themselves, other people, and the world. Children do not need to be pushed to learn. They absorb much of what they need to know from their environments. Thus, a rich environment offers rich learning experiences.

Caregivers need an understanding of what they might expect from children within a given age range. Knowing about patterns of growth and behavior is helpful. Caregivers should also remember that all individuals are unique. Sometimes a toddler will behave as a five-year-old. At other times, the same toddler may behave as an infant. Caregivers must always maintain a flexible attitude as they work with individual children.

Intellectually, toddlers have an increasing attention span. They begin to show signs of memory. Children learn that objects and people still exist even when they cannot see them, which is called **object permanence**. For example, imagine you are hiding a toy under a blanket, then bringing it back out and showing it to the child. A toddler understands that the toy is simply under the blanket; it has not disappeared forever.

This is also a time when children learn to identify shapes and familiar objects. Toddlers enjoy imitating others, and by 20 months of age, they begin to enjoy imaginative play. Concepts learned during the toddler years include the differences between *one* and *many* and between *before* and *after*. Toddlers display active curiosity. They use thought processes to solve simple problems, and they enjoy putting puzzles together.

Toddlers show rapid increases in their language skills. They understand more words than they can say. Between the ages of one and three, however, toddlers' vocabularies will grow from three or four words to over 500 words. Two-year-olds use language to show their understanding of simple concepts. They begin to speak in two- and three-word sentences.

Emotional and Social Growth of Toddlers

A toddler's emotions are difficult to predict. Many toddlers have strong reactions and react differently at different times. Their expanding range of emotions includes pride, affection, stubbornness, jealousy, and sympathy. Toddlers are quite self-centered and are often demanding, possessive, aggressive, and insecure. They seek approval and are easily hurt by criticism.

Some people refer to later toddlerhood as the "terrible twos." Behaviors displayed at this age may be caused by changing abilities and desires. Toddlers are dependent on their parents, but sometimes desire to be independent. They frequently respond by saying no, even when they plan to do what is asked. Also, toddlers can become frustrated when they find themselves limited in physical or intellectual abilities. Caregivers can respond to upset behavior by acknowledging a toddler's feelings. Temper tantrums may be prevented by allowing toddlers to make some safe decisions for themselves. Warning toddlers that an activity must soon end may also prevent tantrums.

Young toddlers like playing alone. This is called **solitary play**, 10-11. Toddlers also like to play beside other children rather than with them, which is called **parallel play**. Two children may be playing the same thing, but there is little to no interaction between them. This pattern of play may continue until preschool.

Toddlers prefer the company of family members to the company of others. Two-year-olds can be expected to be socially aggressive. They do not like to share and have not learned to say *please*. Instead, they snatch the toys they want.

Preschoolers

Three-, four-, and five-year-old children are called **preschoolers**. During the preschool years, children become increasingly independent as they acquire new skills.

Physical Growth of Preschoolers

Physically, preschoolers do not gain weight and height as fast as younger children. However, **gross-motor skills** (skills requiring the use of large muscles) continue to become more refined as children grow. Preschoolers have better balance and coordination. Gross-motor skills expand to include hopping, skipping, dancing, and jumping rope. Preschoolers have improved accuracy in throwing and catching. They are able to use tricycles and other pedal toys. They enjoy playing on playground equipment, such as swings, slides, and jungle gyms. They can also dress themselves with greater ease.

Improved fine-motor skills allow preschoolers to unbutton buttons and pull up large zippers. By age four or five, they can also lace their shoes and may be able to tie knots. They can brush their teeth and feed themselves with spoons and forks. Preschoolers can draw shapes and cut on lines with scissors. They can put puzzle pieces together and turn pages in a book.

Intellectual Growth of Preschoolers

Throughout the preschool years, attention span and concentration skills continue to improve. By age five, many children are eager to go to school. Intellectual growth at this age is shown by a child's ability to plan in advance. A five-year-old can tell you what he or she is going to draw before drawing it.

10-11

Young toddlers enjoy playing by themselves. because they have not yet learned to play with other children.

Preschoolers ask many questions in order to learn about their environments. Caregivers must show an interest in children and give honest but simple answers.

Caregivers can show an interest in preschoolers' intellectual growth by asking questions as well as answering them. Which is larger? Which is smaller? Which is taller? Which is shorter? Which is near? Which is far? What color is this? Which one is blue? Questions such as these are often called *reading readiness exercises*. They help prepare children for reading lessons that will come later.

Preschoolers learn how to count and begin to understand number concepts. Their vocabularies expand to over 2,000 words. They enjoy listening to rhymes and stories. They also enjoy games and puzzles that allow them to use their word and number skills.

With their larger vocabularies, preschoolers begin to speak in complete sentences. Their grammar reflects that used by people around them. Therefore, caregivers have a responsibility to use correct grammar since they are serving as role models for children.

Emotional and Social Growth of Preschoolers

Three-year-olds are generally cooperative and like to perform simple chores. Being a helper seems special at age three. Four-year-olds tend to be emotionally unpredictable. Four-year-olds are friendly one minute and quarrelsome the next. They like being independent and resist pressures placed on them by demonstrating stubbornness and temper. Five-year-olds generally try to please, so this is a pleasant age. They tend to be more patient and generous and less combative. They express their feelings through language rather than emotional outbursts.

Preschoolers are proud of their parents. They seek comfort, approval, and emotional support from parents. However, friends are important to preschoolers, **10-12**. Preschoolers make friends easily and begin to seek status among their peers. They play with their friends, which is called **cooperative play**. Two or more children play complementary roles and share play activities. They make rules, assign roles, and create new games and activities. Competitive games become popular.

To encourage social growth, preschoolers should be given opportunities to practice sharing. They need to learn to assume responsibilities and develop dependability.

Children with Special Needs

All children have needs. Some have greater needs than others. Children with disabilities and children who are gifted and talented are often called **children with special needs**. These children may need different or more care than average children, including extra support, instruction, or guidance.

Analyze and Solve

Investigate programs in your school district that are available to assist children with special needs. Identify additional programs and resources that might be beneficial. Report your findings in class.

10-12

Preschoolers enjoy playing with other children their age.

Some special needs are described below:

- A **physical disability** limits a person's body or its functions. Limitations include either leg or arm movements or both. Physical disabilities also include vision, hearing, or speech impairments.

- A **cognitive disability**, or *intellectual disability*, limits the way a person's brain functions. The child's intellectual abilities, when compared with the average, are a year or more delayed. These children have a limited learning capacity. Learning takes place slowly. Cognitive disabilities range from mild to severe.

- A **learning disability** is a limitation in the way a person's brain sorts and uses certain types of information. Dyslexia, for example, impairs the ability to read. A person with dyslexia sees certain letters and numbers either backwards or inverted. Learning disabilities may also affect math skills. Many learning disabilities can be treated. Others can be overcome with training in ways that compensate for the disability.

- A **behavioral disorder** affects the way a person functions emotionally and socially. A behavioral disorder may cause a child to be too insecure or fearful to play with other children. On the other hand, the child may be too aggressive. Behavioral disorders are often marked by extremes of behavior and can limit a child's ability to concentrate. Unfortunately, these disorders do not go away on their own. They require a diagnosis by a health care professional.

- A child who is **gifted and talented** shows outstanding ability in either a general sense or in a specific ability. A child who is gifted may have above-average intelligence overall or excel in a specific academic area. A child who is talented may possess extraordinary skill in an area such as art, music, or athletics.

Children with special needs require the same basic care as other children. They need love and support. They need encouragement to develop their skills. They may also need some extra attention in certain areas. For instance, a child with a cognitive disability may need directions to be given one step at a time. This child may also need to have directions repeated more often. However, caregivers should resist the urge to do a child's tasks for him or her. The child needs to do as much as possible on his or her own, **10-13**. This will help the child develop independence and a strong self-concept.

Inclusion

There was a time when educators thought it was best to teach children with special needs with others who had similar needs. There were separate classes for the gifted and for those with specific disabilities. Today, many children with special needs are placed in classes with children who are nondisabled for at least a part of each day. This practice is called **inclusion**—the placing of students of varying abilities in the same class. It is believed that all children benefit from being together.

Including all children in the same classrooms helps them all experience and value diversity. Children who are nondisabled learn valuable lessons in understanding, caring, and compassion. Children with disabilities benefit from the acceptance and assistance of their peers who are nondisabled. Children with special needs learn valuable social skills that prepare them for society at large.

Children with special needs create unique challenges for their caregivers. They even create hardships at times. Caregivers must treat each child according to his or her needs. Professionals can assist caregivers in meeting the unique needs of a child with special needs. Every child deserves an opportunity to be the best person he or she is capable of being.

10-13

Providing ways for children with physical disabilities to do things on their own helps their self-esteem.

Reading Review

1. Describe three characteristics of newborns.
2. How much will a baby's weight and length increase in the first year of life?
3. Explain briefly what has been learned about early brain development.
4. List four fine-motor skills that develop during the toddler years.
5. True or false. Five-year-olds tend to express their feelings through emotional outbursts.
6. Explain the difference between a cognitive disability and a learning disability.
7. What is inclusion?

Section 10-3

Children Age 6 Through 12

Objectives

After studying this section, you will be able to

- **describe** physical development of school-age children.
- **summarize** intellectual development of school-age children.
- **give examples** of social-emotional development of school-age children.

Key Terms ↗

middle childhood   growth spurt   gender roles
school-age children

Between the ages of 6 and 12 years, children are in **middle childhood**. Children of this age are called **school-age children**. Children develop very quickly—physically, intellectually, emotionally, and socially—during this time.

Physically, children will be developing more gross- and fine-motor skills. Intellectually, they develop greater language skills. Their vocabulary grows. They begin to think more logically. Emotionally and socially, they begin to evaluate themselves in relation to other people. They also form strong friendships with peers.

Physical Development

During middle childhood, growth continues steadily. Children may experience **growth spurts**, or periods of rapid growth. Growth spurts usually occur at the onset of adolescence. Height and weight will both increase. Arms and legs become longer. In general, body proportions become more adult. Boys will be taller and heavier than girls until girls enter a growth spurt. This usually happens around age 11.

Although muscles grow steadily during middle childhood, bones grow more quickly. As a result, children may experience growing pains.

Organs continue to grow and mature. The brain will be 95 percent of its adult weight. At this point, the brain will be almost completely developed. Any "rewiring" in brain development is difficult after this stage.

School-age children will begin losing baby teeth, or *deciduous teeth*, **10-14**. *Permanent teeth*, which will last the rest of a child's life, replace the deciduous teeth. Children will have all permanent teeth by about age 12.

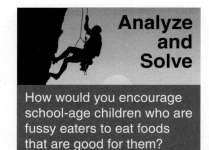

Analyze and Solve

How would you encourage school-age children who are fussy eaters to eat foods that are good for them?

Motor Development

During middle childhood, motor skills improve. Gross-motor skills develop as children play active games. Children become faster and stronger. Their flexibility, related to fine-motor skills, also improves. Boys are stronger and faster than girls until girls hit their growth spurt. Throughout middle childhood, girls are generally more flexible than boys.

Physical Development and Health

Factors such as nutrition affect physical development. As the child grows, the body needs more energy. This energy makes it possible for the body to continue growth as the child gets older.

A healthful diet is important for keeping children healthy. Being underweight or overweight can cause other health problems. Caregivers should make sure children have plenty of fresh fruits and vegetables for meals and snacks.

Children must also get plenty of physical activity. Exercise is important for managing weight and developing gross-motor skills. This is especially meaningful today, when so many activities involve computers or television. These are *sedentary* activities, which means they are done while sitting.

10-14
Throughout the school-age years, children lose their baby teeth and develop permanent teeth.

10-15

Taking time to help with school assignments is one way for caregivers to offer social and emotional support while they also foster learning.

School-age children also need plenty of sleep. Getting too little sleep can affect children's ability to learn. Lack of sleep can weaken their desire to participate in physical activities. It can also make them irritable.

Intellectual Development

Children's intellectual development occurs swiftly during middle childhood. Their thinking becomes more logical. They begin to reason more and depend less on their perceptions. They begin to recognize and understand others' points of view.

School-age children are able to see changes in objects, and they can perceive more than one change at a time. They understand relationships and differences among objects. They also understand more concepts, including space, distance, and cause and effect. Memory improves dramatically.

Language

Vocabulary continues to grow in middle childhood. Children are exposed to many more words through reading. They learn to write and spell. Articulation of sounds is mastered by about age eight.

By age nine, children have learned the rules of grammar they hear most often. If the grammar they hear is incorrect, that is what they will learn. Learning proper grammar rules after this stage will require relearning.

Caregivers' Role in Guiding Intellectual Development

Of course, many of school-age children's intellectual needs are met at school. However, caregivers must make sure children's intellectual needs are met outside of school, too. Adults should provide stimulating activities every day for children. Caregivers should encourage children to participate in as many activities as the children will enjoy. They should also encourage children to take pleasure in learning. By providing children with help for school activities, such as homework, caregivers reinforce the importance of learning, **10-15**.

Rido/Shutterstock.com

Social-Emotional Development

Social and emotional development become very important during this period. Children begin to make many more friends, and relationships become more complicated. The opinions of peers begin to become more important than those of family members. Children learn more about socialization from their peer groups.

Children are becoming more independent during this stage. They begin to develop a sense of work, which will lead to independent industry. This will help them as they learn to participate as team members in school projects. It will also help prepare them for the work they will do in their careers as adults.

Emotions

As children get older, they learn more emotional control. Some fears decline. Anxieties that do not disappear at this stage often continue into adulthood. Anger is not displayed physically, as with younger children. Anger is expressed verbally and indirectly. In this period, children learn to become angry on behalf of others as well as themselves.

Caregivers should be aware that building self-esteem is vital during middle childhood. Adults can boost children's self-confidence by encouraging and praising them. Love and support will communicate acceptance and approval to the child. These will all help reinforce the child's positive self-concept.

Modeling Behavior

School-age children are becoming more independent. They may not be as willing to follow the guidance of adults. However, they will still watch adults for behavior to model.

Parents and other adults model **gender roles**, which are the behaviors of males and females expected by society. Parents and other adults model behaviors for males and females, **10-16**. Children also learn ways of interacting with the opposite sex from their adult role models.

Caregivers model attitudes children will adapt as adults. Children will develop positive feelings about school and, later, their careers if they are encouraged by adults. Recognition of their successes will increase their self-esteem.

Mental Health Awareness

Conditional Love and Emotional Development

Children who believe a parent's love is based on "being good" may never develop a sense of trust and security. They may grow up with poor self-esteem and anxiety. During adulthood, they may be overly concerned with "earning" love and winning approval from others.

10-16

Children learn roles and behaviors by interacting with their parents and other adults.

Adults can promote good communication by listening to children's concerns. They can encourage school-age children to express their feelings. This will help establish a pattern of openness and trust that can continue into the teen years. It will also help strengthen the family unit. However, caregivers should understand how important peer friendships are in this period. Adults must make sure children have plenty of time to develop friendships.

Caregivers should be aware that they are modeling ways to control emotions. Children will see how adults handle strong feelings, such as anger and fear. Adults can also model acceptable ways to release frustrations through productive actions, such as physical activities or hobbies.

 **Reading**
Review

1. What are growth spurts?
2. List two ways caregivers can help guide intellectual development in school-age children.
3. How do adults model gender roles for school-age children?

Section 10-4

Teens

Objectives

After studying this section, you will be able to

- **identify** common signs of physical, intellectual, and social-emotional development during the teen years.
- **relate** the impact of physical growth to concern over body image.
- **explain** how character and values affect teens' social-emotional development.

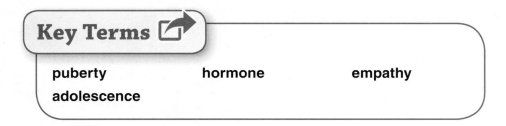

Key Terms

puberty	hormone	empathy
adolescence		

If growth and development during the teen years can be summarized in one word, that word is *change*. As teens mature, their physical, personal, and behavioral characteristics more closely resemble those of an adult. Teens of ages 13 through 18 are the focus of this section.

Physical Development

An important stage of physical growth is called **puberty**. In this stage of development, an individual becomes capable of sexual reproduction. This stage lasts two to five years and is characterized by growth spurts, **10-17**.

Girls generally mature before boys. Beyond that, the specific timing considered normal for the physical growth of teens varies widely. Puberty generally begins between the ages of 8 and 13 for girls, with the onset of menstrual cycles. For boys, puberty begins between the ages of 10 and 15. Puberty ends when sexual reproduction becomes possible, but growth continues. Everyone develops at their own individual pace.

Adolescence is a term used to describe the period from puberty until growth ceases and adulthood is reached. This period usually lasts from ages 11 through 19. During these years, the body changes from a child's body to an adult's body. The heart doubles in size and lung capacity greatly increases. These physical changes give both females and males greater strength and endurance.

The physical changes that take place during adolescence are caused, in part, by hormones. A **hormone** is a chemical substance in the body that triggers a certain type of physical growth. Growth does not proceed uniformly across the body, however. Hands and feet increase in size before the legs and arms do, causing teens to look and act uncoordinated.

Changes in Appearance

During adolescence, visible signs of adult characteristics and sexual development appear. Members of both sexes experience an increase in their muscle tissue that results in a weight gain.

10-17
Young teens experience growth spurts at the onset of puberty.

Science Connection

Hormonal Changes That Trigger Puberty

Puberty is a time of change for teen females and males as their bodies become physically and sexually mature. Did you know that puberty starts in the brain? The hypothalamus, a part of the brain, begins releasing the hormone *gonadotropin releasing hormone (GnRH)*. GnRH signals the pituitary gland to release two more hormones. These hormones—*lutenizing hormone (LH)* and *follicle-stimulating hormone (FSH)*—start sexual development. When teens start noticing physical changes in their bodies, the brain has already started its work.

Skeletal development causes increased height and wider shoulders among males. Other physical changes in males include the enlargement of the genitals, the appearance of pubic hair, and a deepening of the voice. Facial and underarm hair appear later.

Females grow taller. They also have an increase in fat, or *adipose tissue*. Breasts enlarge, and pubic and underarm hair appear.

Body Image

As their bodies change, teens focus to the point of obsession on their physical development. Are they attractive? Is their size and shape normal? How can they change certain body parts to make them look more like the ideal?

A great deal of time is spent on grooming, experimenting with new hairstyles, and trying new clothes. Disappointment with their appearance may last through adolescence into adulthood. Good exercise habits and food choices are steps teens can take to improve their body image.

Intellectual Development

Young teens in middle school begin to develop abstract thinking skills. They are generally curious and anxious to use their new intellectual abilities.

As they move into high school and face new intellectual challenges, most teens become more skilled at complex thinking such as problem solving and decision making. They enjoy trying new ideas and possibilities.

The teen years present a window of opportunity for increasing cognitive ability for life. By performing activities that continually stimulate the brain, the brain's ability to function quickly and effectively increases. Opportunities that offer such stimulation include challenging classes and group activities such as sports, band, and debate.

By the time teens reach older adolescence, they are better able to handle abstract thinking. They think more about their self-identity and the type of person they would like to become. They develop a more in-depth self-concept and examine the different roles they may play in society.

Some high school teens, unfortunately, are attracted to experimenting with alcohol. This presents a serious risk—permanent injury to the brain—because the brain is still developing.

Healthy Living

Personal Hygiene

You may have noticed certain changes that occurred in your body during adolescence. Due to changes in hormones, your skin may produce more oil. You may perspire more often, and bacteria feeding on this perspiration can cause unpleasant odors.

Personal hygiene is important for everyone of any age, but it becomes especially important during the teen years. You need to take a bath or shower every day. Soap and warm water will remove dirt, oils, and dead skin cells. This will help you feel and smell fresh. Deodorants and antiperspirants will help control body odor throughout the day.

Social-Emotional Development

The hormones that stimulate changes in physical development during puberty and adolescence stimulate changes in the emotional state as well. It is common during adolescence to have significant mood swings. Perhaps a teen will feel up one minute, but down the next. Teens may want independence from their family. A little later, however, they long for the security their family offers.

As a teen, there are times you will want to express your own identity. You may want trendy clothes or a new haircut. At other times you will want to be just like everyone else. You may feel you are on an emotional roller coaster.

Sensitive is a key word to describe teens' emotions. Adolescents crave acceptance and are sensitive to criticism, especially about their appearance. Sometimes they are disappointed with who they are, which intensifies their already-low self-concept.

The teen years are a time of ever-more-complex social relationships. School activities provide opportunities for individuals to meet new people. Some of these become new friends, but perhaps many do not. Friendships tend to develop among teens with common interests, **10-18**. Becoming popular is a goal of many, but being accepted by peers is a much deeper need.

10-18
Best friends often share many common interests.

Teens' relationships with adults change. Teens no longer wish to be treated as a child by parents, teachers, and other adults. They want more control over social situations and more time with their peers.

With added control comes added responsibilities. You will be expected to learn to interact with adults on a more mature level and show respect for their wisdom and authority. Also, authority figures will count on you to relate to your peers in ways that foster your positive development and theirs.

Romantic Relationships

When teens feel a romantic attraction, often shyness and anxiety follow. Rather than pairing off, some prefer group activities with friends of both sexes. They may choose a partner for a special event such as a school dance, but the relationship rarely lasts long.

Some teens may rely on a one-on-one relationship for a sense of self-worth. Others may do so to seek acceptance. These are not the goals of teens having positive self-esteem and a strong sense of self-worth. For them, dating is an opportunity to learn about a special someone's personality and interests, especially if his or her background differs.

Character Development

Character refers to inner traits, such as conscience, moral strength, and social attitudes. It is the inner force that guides your conduct and behavior toward acceptable standards of right and wrong.

Character development, like other personality traits, begins in childhood. As an individual's character develops, beliefs about right and wrong and what is fair and just evolve. Younger teens tend to view moral issues in all-or-nothing terms. For example, they may say that stealing is always wrong.

More-mature teens recognize that such issues require consideration of all the facts, not snap judgments. They know that wrongs have different levels of seriousness and, therefore, deserve different degrees of punishment. For example, they would carefully examine what and why something was stolen. Did a toddler take a neighbor's toy? Did a widow take bread for her hungry family? Did a police officer knowingly take someone's car? Older teens understand that justice calls for matching the punishment to the seriousness of the misdeed. They recognize that rules of conscience may differ from rules of society.

Personal Values

Your character is shaped in part by your *values*. These are the beliefs, feelings, and experiences you consider important and desirable. One of the most important tasks of adolescence is developing personal values and a related code of conduct.

Mental Health Awareness

Environment and Moral Behavior

Certain elements in a situation may trigger varying degrees of moral responses. For example, someone who believes in honesty might choose to fail a test through an honest effort, even if it were possible to cheat without getting caught. However, that same person might cheat at sports. This person ranks school and studying with higher moral regard than athletics. This is an example of the post-conventional stage in Kohlberg's theory of moral development.

As the ability to analyze and reason increases, teens reexamine their parents' beliefs and society's rules and laws. Teens want and need to understand their underlying reasons. The "think of yourself first" lifestyle portrayed by media seems personally rewarding. Yet, teens find real satisfaction in helping others and showing empathy, **10-19**. **Empathy** means understanding how others feel even when personal feelings may differ.

Ultimately, teens must consider what kind of adult they want to be. What are their personal goals? Many look to role models to identify the characteristics they would like to possess. Even their role models change with more maturity. For a 13-year-old, it may be the latest movie star. For a 17-year old, it is more likely to be someone with true character.

Reading
Review

1. At what stage of development does an individual become capable of reproduction?
2. Why are mood swings common during adolescence?
3. What is empathy?

10-19

Teens show empathy to their friends by helping them through difficult times.

Section 10-5

Adults

Objectives

After studying this section, you will be able to

- **name** the three main challenges adults face during young adulthood.
- **summarize** the common causes of stress in middle adults.
- **identify** the challenges of late adulthood and factors that promote successful aging.

Key Terms ↗

menopause	midlife crisis	hospice
climacteric	empty nest syndrome	stages of dying
sandwich generation	Alzheimer's disease	grieve

The term *adulthood* often refers to the years from the beginning of maturity, around age 18, until the end of life. Since average life expectancy is 75+ years for males and 80+ years for females, adulthood spans over 50 years. Within this timeframe, three general age groups are studied: young, middle, and older adults.

Young Adults

There is no clear way to decide when a person stops being an adolescent and becomes an adult. Defining this transition requires knowing what the adult roles and responsibilities are. These include

- forming an independent household
- forming meaningful relationships, which usually include marriage and parenting
- establishing oneself in a satisfying career

These are not simple tasks. In fact, they are quite challenging. They form the basis for the direction of the remainder of a person's life. These tasks are usually accomplished during the ages of 20 to 39, when a person is considered a *young adult*.

The young adult years are interesting and exciting. Although personal relationships and jobs may not always succeed, there is time to learn from mistakes and explore new directions.

Physical Development

The body of a young adult in good health is usually at its peak of physical functioning during the 20s, **10-20**. The skeleton is mature, and muscles are strong. All aspects of the sensory system—vision, hearing, taste, smell, and touch—function well.

Physically, a person matures in about 25 years. At this time, the body's framework reaches its maximum size and strength. Full brain weight is achieved in healthy individuals by age 30.

Intellectual Development

By age 20, the individual has developed a distinct personality and sense of identity. Mental functions are sufficiently developed to form enduring relationships and use time productively. Although learning occurs throughout life, one type of learning peaks in young adulthood— the ability to process novel information.

Socio-Emotional Development

Many young adults are still immature emotionally. They may "fall in love" too quickly and commit to an unwise relationship. On the other hand, they may find it difficult to commit at all.

Before making decisions about marriage and parenthood, they must settle questions about how and where to live. When will they leave home? Do they want single or shared living? Can they afford to live independently?

Firm decisions about living arrangements and marriage cannot be made without the guarantee of a steady paycheck. Ideally, young adults have prepared well for a career and are ready to step into their chosen fields. However, those who are unprepared may move from job to job until settling for work that "feels right."

Besides dealing with everyday challenges, young adults may still feel troubled about issues left over from adolescence. The issues may involve substance abuse problems, conflicts with parents, or lingering doubts about self-worth. These concerns need to be addressed before a person can heal emotionally and move on.

Middle Adults

Middle age includes ages 40 to 65. These are busy years involving a wide variety of activities. During this period, many people reach a top level in their careers.

Wellness Awareness

Married life isn't for everyone. Some prefer single living for these reasons: more independence, fewer living expenses, and greater mobility, especially to make a career change and move to another city.

10-20

Healthy young adults have physically developed to their peak size and strength.

Financial Literacy

Social Security

Social Security tax is deducted from paychecks under a *FICA* heading. This refers to the tax imposed on employees and their employers by the Federal Insurance Contributions Act. This tax funds the Social Security and Medicare programs. Money deducted from your paycheck pays for the benefits of others, such as your grandparents. When you are retired, your monthly Social Security payments will be funded by the taxes collected from people still employed. To learn more about Social Security, visit the U.S. Social Security Administration website.

Some, however, realize they are unsatisfied and transition to entirely different work.

Middle-aged parents may send their children to college and see them marry. They may also care for older family members, their grandchildren, or both. Additionally, middle-aged adults may begin to experience signs of aging and recognize their mortality. They may feel regret over missteps or failings in life.

Physical Development

After the body's physical development peaks in the 20s, it slowly begins to deteriorate. Some parts of the body age more quickly than others. Hair loss and the need for eyeglasses or other corrective lenses are examples. Loss of their youthful appearance is very upsetting to some.

Overall, the rate of aging differs for each person. Those who take care of their health, stay active, and keep a positive attitude are less likely to feel the negative effects of aging. Weight gain is a common problem that most middle-agers continuously battle.

Both women and men experience a decrease in certain hormones in middle age. This change can affect both sexes emotionally and women physically. The period during this change is known as *menopause* in women and *climacteric* in men.

Menopause and Climacteric

Menopause is the normal stoppage of menstrual cycles, possibly resulting in changes in moods and emotions. Decreased production of the female hormones estrogen and progesterone are part of the cause. Menopause lasts for a few years beginning around age 50. Women may have *hot flashes*, sudden feelings of heat that may include sweating and a red, flushed face. Some women may also feel chills or rapid heart rate. These are normal signs of aging in females, but they may reach uncomfortable levels for some. Hot flashes are especially bothersome when trying to sleep.

Irregularity in hormone production can be emotionally disturbing to a woman. Mood swings, nervousness, irritability, and increased fatigue may result. However, women who adjust well to various situations in life usually experience no overwhelming problems during menopause.

During the **climacteric**, a reduced supply of testosterone production in a man results in changes in moods and emotions. The climacteric in men is a much-less-pronounced change than menopause in women. Production of the male hormone peaks at about age 20. That level of production usually continues until a man is in his 50s. Then testosterone decreases steadily until age 80, when very little is produced.

Intellectual Development

The ability to apply knowledge gained over time increases in middle age. This ability uses judgment and experience to decide responses to new situations.

Some aspects of memory decline very gradually as the brain ages. For example, newly acquired data can be forgotten more quickly than data learned earlier. Also, some details about facts and figures may become difficult to recall.

Socio-Emotional Development

Middle age is often a stressful time for adults, **10-21**. They must handle the responsibilities of the many family, work, and community roles they hold. Sociologists label middle-age parents the **sandwich generation**. These adults are "sandwiched" between caring for their children and caring for their parents. Finding time to spend quietly as a couple or alone is rare for middle adults.

When an older parent's health declines, caregiver responsibilities increase. Many middle adults suffer from guilt if they feel they are not providing enough help. They may have the older parents move in with them, which can cause greater stress.

At the same time, young children need parental care, too. However, adult children are increasingly seeking help from their middle-age parents. Reasons include difficulty in affording the cost of living away from home or in finding and keeping a job. Divorce and separation are other reasons for adult children to seek temporary living space. Sometimes the adult children have children who also need help.

Midlife Crisis

The increased responsibilities of the sandwich generation are a big reason for the event called **midlife crisis**. It is the difficulty in adjusting to the changes that occur during middle age. Signs of midlife crisis are withdrawal from family members, high rates of alcoholism, and decreased self-esteem.

10-21

Middle-age parents may have to deal emotionally with their children becoming adults.

Research shows that people who claim to have a midlife crisis are really experiencing common stressful events. Because demands have intensified to overwhelming levels, they feel their life is in crisis.

Generally, middle adults show good ability to cope with these stressful situations and find help and support they need from others. Those who have no help can get overwhelmed and fall victim to poor health habits. These include chain smoking, overeating, and excess alcohol and drug use.

Empty Nest Syndrome

Some middle-agers see their homes get very quiet when grown children move away. The quiet is a sign of loss to some parents. They have difficulty in redefining their roles when they stop actively parenting. They may display **empty nest syndrome**, a feeling of loneliness and depression caused by children leaving home.

Experts recommend finding and using opportunities for growth and renewal rather than dwelling on negative feelings, **10-22**. Middle-aged parents can begin new recreational and leisure activities. They can finish projects started earlier, but never finished. They can enjoy visiting their adult children, who will seem more like friends and less like dependents.

10-22

Middle-age adults may choose to sell a large family house and move into a smaller dwelling once the children have left home.

Older Adults

People's attitudes about aging vary. Some dread late adulthood, which includes ages 65 and older. They view this period as a time of life they want to avoid.

Others view aging with the same zest for living they always had. They are glad to have the chance to experience a new phase of life. They accept the changes that aging brings and take advantage of new opportunities presented.

Physical Development

All people, if they live long enough, will show signs of aging. One of the earliest visible signs is noticed in the skin. Loss of elasticity results in wrinkling.

Another sign is slower reaction time for muscles to respond to brain impulses. Movement of the body's large muscles is slower and less coordinated. The ability to manipulate small objects decreases, too.

Bones change little in size, but they do change in chemical composition. Bones become weaker and more fragile. Many older people suffer from *osteoporosis*—a bone disease caused by insufficient calcium in the diet.

The heart muscles may become less efficient, and blood vessels may narrow. As a result, circulation problems can develop. The supply of blood to the legs and the brain may also decline.

Sensory problems often begin with a hearing loss. Adding to an older adult's frustrations, loss of vision and the ability to read may follow, **10-23**. When the senses of taste and smell diminish, there is less interest in eating. If an older adult's diet improves, overall psychological and physical health can improve, too.

Aging also includes greater risk of diseases typically associated with old age. These include arthritis; macular degeneration, which leads to vision difficulties; and **Alzheimer's disease**, a degenerative brain condition. When something is *degenerative*, it causes a weakening or reduced functioning as time passes. Such illnesses can pose special challenges for older people and their families.

Intellectual Development

In late adulthood, the ability to apply knowledge gained over time increases. This ability, also called wisdom, uses judgment and experience to decide responses to new situations.

People can continue learning at all ages, but some mental abilities decline in late adulthood. For example, understanding new methods or situations and staying highly focused for long periods become more challenging. Also, memory loss is greater when the person is pressured to quickly learn or recall messages sent to the brain.

Memory decline during aging has been extensively studied, concluding that other factors may be involved. Some complaints of memory loss are due to the person experiencing depression, not actual memory loss. Other false claims of memory loss have been linked to sensory loss instead. If a person has impaired hearing or vision, the brain receives incomplete sensory input. Therefore, the brain cannot remember information it never received.

10-23

Older adults may need bifocal glasses for reading. They may also prefer large-type books.

10-24

Grandparents often enjoy participating in activities with their grandchildren, while also teaching many life skills in a subtle way.

Memory loss should always be checked carefully. Such a claim could signal Alzheimer's disease or another type of brain impairment.

Socio-Emotional Development

Aging people may lose some strength or physical vigor. However, they can gain new leisure interests and more meaningful relationships with family members and friends. Older adults who focus on enjoying life cultivate new friendships and maintain close family ties.

Those who are grandparents are freer to be friends with their grandchildren, **10-24**. They can share social events with them as well as experiences from the past. They may act as babysitters, or they may help raise the grandchildren in times of crisis.

Research has shown that avoiding disease and disability while staying involved in social and productive activities are the ingredients for successful aging. Nevertheless, people must go through certain events in old age that all would avoid if possible.

Retirement

Retirement can be a pleasant stage of life, or it can produce frustration and loneliness. It is more pleasant for those who make positive plans and goals. People should start planning for retirement years before they actually reach this stage. Retirement presents opportunities for outside interests and leisure-time activities. Some people even turn a hobby into a second career.

Retirement causes many changes in a couple's daily schedule. These changes may be difficult for the husband and wife to suddenly accept. Married couples should develop common areas of interest and maintain close relationships with friends. They should consider helping meet human needs in their community or beyond. Many organizations eagerly accept the volunteer help of older people. These organizations can be identified by contacting local hospitals, religious groups, community centers, or by researching volunteer opportunities online.

New Living Arrangements

Where people live is a major factor in their lives. Many older adults want to continue living where they have lived for years. That is the best plan if the housing is convenient, safe, comfortable, and easy to maintain. Moving older people from familiar surroundings can be a devastating blow to their feelings of security.

Sometimes a move must be made. If older adults move in with their children, they may need to accept a secondary role. The adult children should clearly define their own roles without offending their parents. Older adults should be able to feel they are a useful and active part of the family even though the adult children make the major family decisions.

If low-cost housing is needed, public housing facilities may provide special units for older adults. Housing facilities for low or moderate incomes are sometimes sponsored by churches and other nonprofit groups with federal aid. Some have private units, and some offer services such as meals and recreation.

There are many retirement communities for older adults. Most are designed exclusively for older residents and do not allow children or younger people, except as visitors. Social activities, complete health care, and shopping facilities are often provided. Retirement communities should be carefully examined before making a commitment. Many people still prefer a typical neighborhood rather than a secluded community of older adults.

Death and Dying

When a family member or friend is dying, people often turn to hospice programs for help. The term **hospice** refers to a way of caring for people who are living with a serious illness that cannot be cured. Hospices provide a more-homelike atmosphere, with emphasis on eliminating pain and offering a peaceful, supportive environment. Hospice-type care can be provided in the home by family members and friends or in a medical facility. This is done with the assistance of hospice health professionals and volunteers.

Hospice care or hospice-type home care appeals to those who prefer to die in a peaceful environment with their family present. If an illness will lead to certain death, some people prefer this alternative.

On the other hand, some terminally ill people wish to remain hospitalized. A *terminal* illness is one that cannot be cured. In spite of this, the patient prefers to fight the illness with whatever medical resources are available.

Death can come at any time to people of any age. Those who are dying pass through distinct stages in accepting their death. These stages, called the **stages of dying**, are described in **10-25**.

Not everyone goes through each of the stages in exactly the same way. However, knowledge of the stages can help family members and friends understand what the dying person feels. You should not let a dying person feel forgotten or disregarded, and never offer false hope. Being caring and honest is the best response.

Analyze and Solve

What are some ways that adult children can help aging parents who can no longer climb stairs continue to live in their two-story home?

Mental Health Awareness

Denial of Aging

The physical and mental decline of old age can be frightening, both to the aging adults and their family members. Children of older adults may deny that an older adult needs help with daily activities, which can endanger an older adult's health and safety. Family members may delay or refuse to make needed arrangements concerning care, housing, and end-of-life decisions. Honestly assessing the situation is important for providing optimal care for everyone's physical and mental well-being.

Stages of Dying	
Stage One—Denial	When a patient learns about the terminal illness, the typical reaction is denial: "This can't be happening to me."
Stage Two—Anger	The patient resents the fact that others will continue living while he or she will die.
Stage Three—Bargaining	The anger stops and the patient accepts the coming of death, but tries to postpone it. A pledge to live a better life in exchange for another week or month or year of life may be offered.
Stage Four—Depression	The person mourns past wrongs and things that should have been done. He or she wants to be quiet and may reject visitors, signs of readiness to die.
Stage Five—Acceptance	The patient knows that death is near and displays a calm acknowledgment of that reality.

10-25

Many people with terminal illnesses pass through these stages.

Those Left Behind

The death of a loved one is painful to survivors. Thoughts of what might have been stays on that person's mind. Eventually survivors adjust to the loss. How survivors **grieve** generally follows a series of stages similar to the stages of dying. Eventually, the passage of time will help ease their pain.

Some marriages end with the death of one spouse. The widow is the usual survivor. (A *widow* is a female survivor, while a *widower* is a male survivor.) With the death of a spouse, widows and widowers must adjust to a single lifestyle and learn how to deal with their loneliness. They must accept total responsibility for the home, the finances, and other activities that once were shared.

Reading
Review

1. What are the three key challenges of young adulthood?
2. The equivalent of climacteric in men is _____ in women.
3. True or false. *Sandwich generation* is the term that best describes adults who care for their parents as well as their children, sometimes in the same house.
4. What are the ingredients for successful aging?

Chapter 10 Review

Summary

People grow and change all throughout the lifespan. Heredity, environment, cultural heritage, and character are factors that help make each person unique. People grow and develop at different rates physically, emotionally, intellectually, and socially. Developmental theories help people understand how development takes place.

Parents must quickly learn how to care for their newborns during the first year of life. Then as infants grow, parents enjoy watching for signs of development. Although growth is fastest in the first year, children from ages one to five continue to develop with amazing speed. Caregivers must provide an atmosphere that will foster growth in all areas.

Children from age 6 to 12 are in middle childhood. Growth and development continue quickly at this stage. Caregivers must be aware that they are modeling behavior for children.

Puberty marks the onset of adolescence. Teens go through many physical, intellectual, social, and emotional changes during this time. Hormones trigger changes in the body. Many teens begin feeling empathy with others.

Adults pass through young adulthood, middle adulthood, and late adulthood. Young adults are at the peak of physical development. They also have developed mental functions and distinct personalities, but may be emotionally immature. Middle-age adults must begin to deal with the physical effects of aging. Memory begins to decline. Social and emotional challenges of middle-age adults include adult children, aging parents, midlife crises, and empty-nest syndrome. People in late adulthood face sensory problems and increased risk of disease. Mental abilities may deteriorate.

Older adults may enjoy retirement and grandparenting. However, they may also have to deal with the death of a spouse and certainty of their own approaching death.

Critical Thinking

1. **Summarize details.** Summarize ways you are influenced by each of the following:
   A. heredity
   B. environment
   C. cultural heritage
   D. character

2. **Draw conclusions.** Taking Erikson's theory into consideration, how might a child who has not successfully developed trust have a more difficult time starting kindergarten than a child who had developed trust?

3. **Compare and contrast.** What do you think would be the greatest challenge of caring for a newborn? What do you think would be the most joyful part of caring for a newborn?

4. **Predict outcomes.** What types of activities and behaviors would you expect if you were babysitting a toddler? What activities and behaviors would you expect if you were babysitting a preschooler?

5. **Recognize alternatives.** What types of games and play activities would you use to encourage physical development in school-age children?

6. **Assess options.** What are some ways you could help a school-age child develop a positive self-concept?

7. **Analyze behavior.** Can you think of any specific examples that effect your social-emotional growth since you entered adolescence? Do you believe you have developed a sense of empathy?

8. **Apply concepts.** Using family photos or records, work with other family members to map the growth and development of three individuals for the first 15 years of their lives. Use spreadsheet software to prepare a time line documenting specific details and important milestones for each person. Compare your growth pattern to those of other family members and summarize similarities and differences.

21st Century
Applications

9. **Information literacy.** Research the connection between the environment and the physical and mental well-being of individuals. Use information from the chapter as well as information from local, state, or government health agencies to research this connection. How does one element influence the other? Create a graphic illustration to demonstrate the connection.

10. **Critical thinking and problem solving.** Research and plan activities designed to teach children independence and responsibility. How would these activities encourage independence and responsibility? If possible, volunteer to work in a preschool program or day care center and conduct the activities. Write a report about the results.

11. **Civic literacy.** Write a brief reaction to this statement: All assisted living facilities and services should be paid for by government funding.

Core
Skills

12. **Science.** Research the science of genetics and inherited traits. Explain how genes determine physical traits.

13. **Social studies.** Select a character from a movie, book, or TV program. Explain how this character's environment influenced his or her intellectual growth.

14. **Science.** Investigate human growth hormone. What is the result of either a deficiency or an excess of human growth hormone? When might a physician recommend administering this hormone to a child? What is the controversy about using this hormone on children? Summarize your findings in a written report.

15. **Reading.** Select one of the behavioral, cognitive, social cognitive, sociocultural, psychosocial, or moral development theories discussed in the text. Research one theory in depth. Which researcher developed the theory? How did the theory develop? Describe the theory and how it applies to human development. Create a presentation with visuals to display your findings to the class.

16. **Science, writing.** Research the details of the roles played by the hypothalamus, gonadotropin releasing hormone, lutenizing hormone, and follicle-stimulating hormone in sexual development. Write a brief report on your findings.

17. **Speaking.** Research local hospice programs in your community. Interview a member of a hospice team, such as a home health aide. If possible, interview someone you know who has had experience with using a hospice program. Present your findings to the class in an oral report.

18. **Speaking.** Prepare an electronic presentation on an activity children enjoy. Explain the developmental reasons why children enjoy the activity. Include digital pictures or scanned images to illustrate your topic. Share your presentation with the class.

19. **Reading, writing.** Using reliable print or online resources, research psychologist James Cattell. How did Cattell impact the field of psychology? Write an informative essay describing his biography and include a time line outlining his achievements.

Leadership
Development

As part of work on the Focus on Children STAR Event, compile an activity booklet for children from age three to 12. Booklets could include suggestions or directions for books, fingerplays, games, and recipes for doughs, paste, and finger paints. Use principles of child development to guide your activity choices. Identify the appropriate age ranges for each activity.

Portfolio
Builder

Being a caregiver for children involves a lot of responsibility. Take a babysitting course from a local community group or Red Cross chapter. Upon completion of the course, you will likely receive a certificate of completion. Write a reflection paper about what you learned from the course and include it and your certificate of completion in your portfolio.

Journal
Writing

You are planning a baby shower for Melanie and her husband Manchester. The shower theme is "Books for the Baby." Melanie and Manchester have already started in utero reading to their unborn child. You are trying to decide what types of books are most appropriate for small children.

Write About It: *Which types of books seem appropriate for in utero and newborn reading? What types of books would be more suitable when the child is a toddler? Why? What type of book do you think Melanie and Manchester would most enjoy reading to their child?*

Chapter 11
Caring for Children

Sections

11-1 Meeting Children's Needs
11-2 Guidance

Reading Prep

- Recall meaningful or important events from your childhood. Relate the events to the topics to be studied in this chapter.
- What experiences have you had with children? Based on these experiences, do you feel you know how to raise a child?

Concept Organizer

K	W	L

Create a KWL chart about the role of play in children's development. In the first column (K), write what you already know. In the second column (W), write what you want to learn. In the third column (L), write what you learn as you are reading.

G-WLEARNING.com

Click on the activity icon to visit www.g-wlearning. com/comprehensive/8062 to access online vocabulary activities using key terms from the chapter.

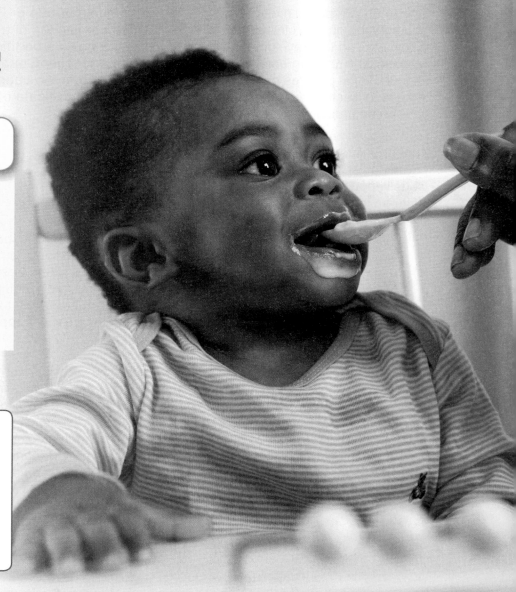

Rayes/DigitalVision/Getty Images

Section 11-1

Meeting Children's Needs

Objectives

After studying this section, you will be able to

- **describe** how a child's likes can be used to encourage good eating habits.
- **explain** factors to consider when selecting clothes for children.
- **list** guidelines to help parents maintain a healthy and safe environment.
- **describe** various activities that stimulate children's development.

Key Terms

self-help features
immunizations
communicable
  diseases
first aid
active-physical play
manipulative-
  constructive play
imitative-
  imaginative play
dramatic play
socio-dramatic play

Parents and caregivers have a responsibility to provide for children's physical needs. They must supply adequate food, clothing, shelter, and medical care. Parents and caregivers must also teach children how to eat, dress, and care for their bodies. This will help children develop independence and assume responsibility for their own physical care.

Caregivers need to provide children with stimulating activities. However, they should be careful not to challenge children to do too many difficult tasks. Children need to value themselves and feel good about what they do. This helps them develop self-esteem.

Serving Food

Food is one of a child's primary physical needs. Caregivers need to provide nutritious meals for their children. However, children have small stomach capacities. Therefore, they may not be able to eat all the foods they need at meals. Thus, snacks become an important part of a child's food plan each day, **11-1**.

DenKuvaiev/iStock/Getty Images Plus

11-1

Healthy snacks help meet a child's nutrient needs.

Mealtime Psychology

Children sometimes need to be persuaded to eat foods that are good for them. Caregivers can use a bit of mealtime psychology to accomplish this goal.

Adults should try to avoid making an issue over food habits. When a fuss is made over behavior—even bad behavior—children enjoy the attention. Children will repeat the behavior to get more attention. Children eat best when parents praise their good habits and ignore undesirable ones.

Children like small servings of food. Many children are discouraged from eating by the sight of a large plate of food. Providing children with small portions allows them to ask for second helpings when they enjoy a food.

Children like bright colors. Foods like bright yellow peaches or bright green broccoli often appeal to them. Children are also likely to enjoy eating from a table set with brightly colored plates and glasses. They may even prefer one special plate and always want to be served from it.

Involving Children in Meal Preparation

Children like to choose their own food. Adults can encourage small children to eat by allowing them to help with the menu plan. They can provide children with a variety of healthy food options. Then the children can choose which foods they want to eat.

Children are more likely to eat foods they help to prepare. Children can spread peanut butter on crackers. They can prepare vegetables for a raw salad or beat eggs that are to be scrambled. These tasks teach children food preparation skills as well as encouraging them to eat.

Healthy Living

Nutritious Snacks for Children

Snacks supplement the foods children eat at meals. To avoid interfering with meals, snacks should be served at least an hour before meals. Snacks should be nutritious and help meet the body's requirements for a balanced diet. Here are some possible snack ideas.

- fresh fruits cut in bite-size pieces
- whole-grain crackers and low-fat cheese
- low-fat or nonfat yogurt with cut-up fruit
- vegetable sticks with low-fat yogurt dip
- pretzels, unbuttered popcorn, or raisins
- whole-grain toast with peanut butter
- celery sticks with peanut butter and raisins
- fruit smoothies or low-fat pudding

Choosing Clothes

Clothes are another basic need for children. However, clothes provide more than just physical protection. Clothes can help children develop decision-making skills. As with foods, children like to choose the clothes they wear. Caregivers can offer two options and allow children to select the outfit they wish to wear.

Clothes can also help stimulate intellectual development. Children can be asked to identify the colors of their clothes. They can name items pictured in fabric prints.

Following a few guidelines can help parents select clothes that their children will enjoy wearing.

- *Fit.* Children need clothes that allow freedom of movement as they play. Clothes that are too tight can bind and restrict them. Clothes that are too loose may cause children to trip and fall.

- *Fabric and construction.* Children prefer soft fabrics that feel good against their skin. Firm weaves and close knits help clothes resist wear, tear, and frequent laundering. Double-stitched seams, well-made buttonholes, and securely attached fasteners are signs of durable construction. Avoid drawstring tops and hoods for young children to prevent choking hazards.

- *Self-help features.* **Self-help features** are clothing design details that make clothes easier for children to put on and take off. They include elasticized waistbands, large buttons or snaps, and large neck and arm openings.

- *Size of wardrobe.* Because children grow rapidly, new clothes must be purchased often. A few sturdy garments can be washed and worn repeatedly before children outgrow them.

Living Green

Organize a toy and clothing swap party for parents of young children. Ask them to bring clean, gently-used items to swap with other parents. Donate leftover items to a local shelter.

Creating a Healthy and Safe Environment

Physical needs include the need for proper health care and a safe environment. Failure to meet these needs can result in illnesses, accidents, or even death.

Health Care

Providing nutritious food, adequate clothing, and a warm home will help keep children healthy. However, children are still likely to become ill from time to time. When this happens, parents have a duty to see that their children receive proper medical care. Children should be taught not to fear doctors, dentists, and other health professionals who might provide this care.

Children can be taught to be responsible for their own health. Parents can teach children proper eating and sleeping habits and

Living Green

When caring for babies, try to use reusable washcloths instead of baby wipes. If you must use baby wipes, tear off half of a wipe for small clean-ups.

Science Connection

The Need for Immunizations

What do diphtheria, pertussis (whooping cough), polio, and smallpox have in common? These are all diseases that caused death or disability before vaccines were available to prevent them. Due to immunization of children, teens, and adults during the 20th century, most of these diseases and many others are now rare. What would happen if people stopped having immunizations? Diseases that are now rare or unknown would begin to be seen in epidemic proportions. More people would get sick, and more would die. Visit the CDC website for more information regarding immunizations for children, teens, adults, and older adults.

dressing skills. Parents can also set a positive example by practicing good health care themselves. The following guidelines will help parents establish a healthy routine for their children:

- Maintain a clean environment.
- Teach children the importance of body cleanliness.
- Take children for regular medical checkups.
- Keep children's immunizations up to date. **Immunizations** are injections or drops given to a person to provide protection against certain diseases.

- Keep children away from people who have **communicable diseases**. These are illnesses that can be passed on to other people, such as colds and sore throats. Also, discourage habits that might spread communicable diseases, such as sharing drinking cups.

- Have a knowledge of common childhood illnesses and diseases. Be familiar with their symptoms and how to treat them.

- Treat wounds, bites, and stings promptly.

- Avoid foodborne illnesses by carefully selecting, preparing, and storing foods.

Safety

Caregivers have two responsibilities regarding children's safety. They must make the environment safe for children. Also, they must teach children to recognize and avoid safety hazards.

Caregivers need to look for safety hazards from a child's low vantage point, **11-2**. They should look for possible hazards to a child who is learning to sit, creep, stand, or walk. Caregivers must remove all items that could be dangerous to young children. They must teach older children to avoid dangerous items and to stay out of harmful areas.

The following guidelines will help maintain a safe environment for children:

- Supervise children at all times. Their mobility, desire for independence, and curiosity prompts them to explore items that could be hazardous.

- Place gates at the top and bottom of stairs to prevent falls.

- Keep sharp and breakable objects out of the reach of children.

- Keep hot water, hot food, and other hot objects out of children's reach to prevent burns.

11-2

Playing with the child at floor level allows the caregiver to stay mindful of items that need to be moved.

- Keep medicines and cleaning agents in a locked cabinet. Do not remove product labels.

- Place fencing around swimming pools, garden ponds, and other bodies of water to prevent accidental drownings. Supervise them constantly when they play near water.

- Provide safe, sturdy places for children to climb. Watch them closely when climbing is allowed.

- Keep plastic bags and large sheets of plastic away from children to prevent suffocation.

- Protect children from electrical hazards. Unused outlets should be capped with a safety device. Keep appliance cords out of a child's path to prevent tripping. Do not allow cords to hang where children could grab them. If an appliance has a retractable cord, leave only the length that is needed outstretched. Keep electrical appliances at the back of the counter where children cannot reach them.

- Check fire extinguishers regularly and know how to use them.

- Plan and practice evacuation procedures for the home in case of fire.

- Secure children in a car seat for even short distances. Older children should always use safety belts.

Healthy Living

Selecting Safe Toys for Children

Toys should be chosen to stimulate—but not overstimulate—a child's total development. Select toys that are appropriate for the child's age and skill level. Look for age suggestions from toy manufacturers on labels and packaging.

Avoid the following:

- toys with small parts that can be swallowed
- sharp points and rough edges
- long cords or strings (for infants and young children)
- flammable materials
- nonwashable dolls and stuffed toys
- toxic paints

All toys are hazardous when they are left on floors, stairways, and driveways. Providing adequate and safe storage space will help children take responsibility for putting away toys.

Protecting Children from Strangers and Abductions

Unfortunately, there is a fine line between teaching children to love and accept all people while also teaching them to act with caution. While children are young, caregivers are charged with protecting them from strangers who might abuse or abduct them. Caregivers must keep an eye on children at all times.

As children grow and are allowed to accept some independence, there are times when an adult is not there to protect them. Teach children not to open the door to strangers. Explain why they should not get into a car or go anywhere with people without first getting approval from a caregiver. Teach children how to politely hang up the phone without saying their parents are not home. They also need to know how to speak to strangers without getting into a conversation that reveals personal information. Children should not accept gifts unless one of their caregivers is present. Teach them that it is appropriate to respond to such offers by smiling and politely saying "No thank you."

First Aid in Emergencies

No matter what you do as a caregiver to prevent injuries to children, accidents are bound to happen. When they do, you need to know how to react. **First aid** is emergency care or treatment given to people right after an accident. It relieves pain and prevents further injury. Caregivers need to know basic first aid procedures so they can treat minor injuries promptly. The following are some basic first aid techniques:

- *Small cuts and abrasions:* Wash area with clean water. Apply antibiotic ointment and a bandage.
- *Deep cuts or puncture wounds:* Place a clean cloth or bandage over the wound. Press the wound with the palm of your hand to stop the bleeding. Then get medical help.
- *Minor burns:* Run cool water over the burned area for a few minutes until the pain subsides. Do not apply ointment.
- *Severe burns:* Do not put anything on the burn or try to remove any material stuck to the skin. Get medical help right away.

Wellness Awareness

Research the availability of pediatric first aid training in your area. Courses are usually offered by the American Heart Association or the American Red Cross. Consider enrolling in a course if you are a caregiver.

- *Broken bones:* If you think the child broke a leg or something more serious, get medical help immediately. Do not try to move the child yourself. For a broken arm, use a makeshift sling to reduce movement. Then promptly get medical help.

- *Splinters:* Wash the area with soap and water. Using a pair of sterilized tweezers, remove the splinter at the same angle it entered the skin. Clean the wound and cover with a bandage.

- *Insect stings:* If the child is stung by a wasp, bee, hornet, or yellow jacket, watch for a severe allergic reaction, such as difficulty breathing, dizziness, or abdominal pain. If these or other unusual symptoms occur, get prompt medical help.

- *Electrical shock:* Do not touch the child with your bare hands until the electrical connection is broken or you, too, will be shocked. Turn off the electricity, pull the plug, or use a long towel or a rope to pull the child away from the source. If the child is not breathing, give cardiopulmonary resuscitation (CPR) or hands-only CPR. Get medical help immediately even if the child appears fine because there may be damage to internal organs.

- *Poisoning:* Have the phone number for the poison control center posted near the phone. If a child swallows something that could be poisonous, you will need to call this number immediately. Be prepared to report what the child swallowed. Then follow the directions given.

- *Choking:* If a child cannot speak or breathe, he or she may have swallowed something that is blocking the airway. Get medical help immediately. The American Red Cross and the American Heart Association recommend different techniques to relieve choking in conscious victims. The American Red Cross teaches delivering five back blows between the shoulder blades, followed by five abdominal thrusts. For simplicity in instruction, the American Heart Association teaches use of only the abdominal thrust. Both organizations recommend these procedures only for children one year of age or older. Slightly different procedures are recommended for infants under one year of age. If a choking child becomes unconscious, begin CPR or hands-only CPR.

If serious illness or injury occurs, you may need to call for an ambulance. For less-serious emergencies, you may want to drive the child to a hospital emergency room or clinic for treatment. The severity of the injury will determine which action you should take.

Providing Stimulating Activities

Meeting children's needs includes providing them with opportunities to play. Social, emotional, intellectual, and physical development are all interrelated. Therefore, play activities that stimulate physical growth will stimulate growth in other areas as well. Offering children a variety of activities gives them the opportunity to use a range of skills.

Life Skills

Selecting Enrichment Activities for Children

Books. The content of books should be chosen with a child's age in mind. Look for books that show both men and women in various careers. Also select multicultural books that involve characters from a variety of racial and ethnic groups.

Stories. Caregivers can show regard for children by preparing stories that meet the children's interests. Good storytellers put a lot of action into stories. They change the tone of their voices to fit the moods of the story. They use their hands to create sounds as needed.

Art Activities. Caregivers can give children some basic guidelines about how art materials should be used. However, adults should not control art activities too carefully. Caregivers should not criticize children's artwork or guess what children have made. A good alternative is saying, "This is interesting. Tell me about it."

Music Activities. Children like songs they understand. Children especially like action songs so they can use their bodies. Children also enjoy making rhythm sounds with sandpaper blocks, rhythm sticks, finger cymbals, shakers, and bells.

Watching TV and Videos. Watching a limited amount of TV and videos may offer educational enrichment for children age 2 and older. Caregivers should be actively involved in helping children select appropriate programs. Select programs that teach children such basic concepts as numbers and letters. Other programs may present examples of accepted social behavior, like sharing and telling the truth. Some programs also inform children about current issues, such as the environment.

Enriching Physical Development

Active-physical play helps children develop their large-muscle skills for movements like walking, running, and jumping. *Gross-motor skills* are the abilities required to control large muscles such as the trunk, arms, and legs. Movement helps them gain an understanding of space and the position of the body in space. They learn to understand concepts such as *front, back, side, up, down, high, low, through,* and *between.* Children learn to react quickly. They also gain more control over their body movements. As children get older, this control allows them to master more refined physical skills, such as skiing, skating, and dancing.

Manipulative-constructive play helps children develop small-muscle skills. *Fine-motor skills* are the abilities required to use small muscles that control the wrists, hands, thumbs, fingers, and ankles. As smaller, finer muscles develop, you will see children picking up blocks with their fingers. As their skills develop, they begin to stack the blocks. By manipulating objects, children learn about the world around them.

Fine-motor development encourages eye-hand coordination. For instance, children learn to pick up shaped objects and drop them into containers with matching shapes for openings. Other small-muscle tasks include writing, drawing, stacking, stringing beads, and fitting puzzles and building pieces together. Caregivers need to provide children with play materials that will help them develop these fine-motor skills.

Physical skills improve as a child grows and develops. For example, an infant will crawl after a rolling ball. A preschooler might run after a ball. An older, more surefooted child might kick a ball. Each child has demonstrated a higher level of physical development.

Wellness Awareness

How will participation in physical play activities help children set life habits? Develop lists of physical play activities for toddlers, preschoolers, and school-age children.

Games and play activities can be chosen to help build physical skills. Children enjoy walking, running, jumping, balancing, and swinging their arms. They like to throw, catch, roll, and bounce balls. Riding tricycles and playing with outdoor equipment are also fun physical activities.

Enriching Social-Emotional Development

As children play, they interact with the world of people and objects. As they do so, they develop socially and emotionally. For instance, a game that babies enjoy playing is peek-a-boo. They will play this game with their caregivers. It helps them develop a sense of trust. The face of the caregiver reappears after it disappears. This is an important learning for infants.

Caregivers can promote social-emotional development by initiating play activities appropriate for the age of the child. Peek-a-boo games with infants can be followed with games such as pat-a-cake. The actual game is not as important as the social interactions and the trust that forms between caregiver and child.

As children get older, they play more with other children, **11-3**. This group play promotes skills such as cooperation, sharing, and property rights. Playing with others helps children learn to give and receive. Self-esteem develops when there is a balance between giving and receiving. The goal is to help children learn to make and maintain relationships where they also develop healthy self-concepts.

Serving Your Community

Obtain permission to give a presentation on "Teaching Children to Live in a Multicultural Society" at your public library. Make a display of multicultural books from the children's section of the library. Prepare a discussion of the various aspects of diverse cultures that are illustrated in the books. Invite people from different ethnic groups in your community to participate in the presentation. Ask them to share examples of children's stories, art, and music that are typical of their heritage.

11-3

A group of neighborhood children may work together to set up a lemonade stand.

Enriching Intellectual Development

Children learn through their play activities. They experiment to see how things work. They use their imaginations and try new ideas. Play allows children to experience different sights, sounds, textures, smells, and tastes. Children are introduced to their environment and objects in their environment. They learn to use these resources. Through play they learn number concepts such as more and less and large and small. Puzzles and nesting toys help them see size and shape relationships. Many activities encourage creative thinking. Some activities can also be chosen to help children build reasoning skills. All these activities lead to learning, but without any pressure to succeed.

In **imitative-imaginative play**, children use their imaginations as they pretend to be other people or objects. This form of play begins at about two years of age. At this age, children are capable of having an object stand for something else. For instance, a cardboard box might represent a car or a plane. By three or four years of age, children begin **dramatic play**. This form of play involves role playing. A child imitates another person or acts out a situation, but does so alone. **Socio-dramatic play** involves several children imitating others and acting out situations together. They mimic such adult roles as mommy, daddy, doctor, or astronaut. They make decisions and learn problem-solving skills. Language concepts also develop as they generate plots and story lines. Creativity and imagination are fostered.

Reading Review

1. True or false. Caregivers should repeatedly scold children who refuse to eat foods that are good for them.
2. List four factors to consider when selecting clothes for children.
3. List five health and five safety guidelines caregivers should follow to protect children.
4. Explain the difference between active-physical play and manipulative-constructive play.

Section 11-2

Guidance

Objectives

After studying this section, you will be able to

- **summarize** techniques for communicating with children.
- **give suggestions** for guiding children's behavior.
- **explain** how to help children develop independence and responsibility.
- **describe** ways to help children overcome their fears.

Key Terms

guidance	setting limits	redirection
developmentally appropriate practices	consistency	prompting
	positive reinforcement	consequences
modeling		time-out

Very early in life, children begin to interact with their parents and siblings. As they get older, they interact more with people outside their family, including caregivers, teachers, playmates, and school friends. Meeting children's needs includes helping them learn behavior that others will find acceptable. Children need guidance to help them handle life's experiences. **Guidance** includes everything caregivers do and say to promote socially acceptable behavior.

Factors in a child's environment that guide his or her behavior are called *extrinsic guidance*. This is the type of guidance caregivers provide. A caregiver's goal is to encourage children to begin guiding their own behavior. When children adopt a socially acceptable behavior pattern, they are practicing *intrinsic guidance*. Intrinsic guidance is also known as self-control or *self-discipline*.

Communicating with Children

Caregivers communicate with children in order to guide them. Children can be guided by both verbal and nonverbal messages. The following techniques can help make communication with children more effective:

21st Century Skills

Communication. Eric just received the top sales award. Eric is a great communicator. He establishes a relationship with his customers. Once he does that, he listens to what they need and lets customers know how his company can help them to achieve their goals.

- *Maintain eye contact during conversations.* Eye contact makes listening easier for a child. It also helps you, the speaker. By looking into a child's eyes, you can usually tell when the child understands. You may need to kneel down to a child's level in order to do this.

- *Keep messages simple and brief.* When talking with a young child, use small words and short sentences. Give children only one or two simple instructions at a time. Children become confused when too many difficult words are used or too many directions are given at one time.

- *Speak in a relaxed voice.* Use a calm, quiet, relaxed tone of voice with children. They are more likely to listen to this type of voice. Then when you must raise your voice in an emergency, they will be more likely to pay attention to you.

- *Reinforce words with actions when necessary.* Remember that actions speak loudly. For instance, suppose Tommy is busy playing when you call him to dinner. He ignores your call. You may need to go to him, take him by the hand and say, "Let's eat now." By walking the child to the table, your message is made clear.

- *Use positive statements.* Emphasize what children should do rather than what they should not do, **11-4**. For instance, suppose two children were throwing sand in the sandbox. You could say, "Don't throw the sand." Since throwing was fun, however, the children are likely to begin throwing something else. A more effective approach might be to say, "Instead of throwing the sand, try using it to build a sand castle." Another positive approach might be, "I see you want to throw something. Here is a ball. See if you can throw it instead." Children are easy to distract—especially if the tone of your voice makes your idea sound like fun.

11-4

Positive statements clearly tell children what they should do.

Using Positive Statements	
Negative	Positive
"Don't spill your milk."	"Hold your glass steady."
"Don't talk with your mouth full."	"Wait until you have swallowed your food before you begin talking."
"Don't put your feet on the chair."	"Keep your feet on the floor."
"Don't yell."	"Please talk softly."
"Don't push and shove."	"Keep your hands by your side."
"Don't interrupt when others are talking."	"Wait for your turn to talk."
"Don't throw blocks."	"Keep the blocks on the table, please."
"Don't pull the kitten's tail."	"Pet the kitten gently."
"Don't leave the toys on the floor."	"Put the toys on the shelf."

- *Answer children's questions briefly and truthfully.* No matter what children ask, a simple answer is likely to satisfy their curiosity. Answer any question in a manner appropriate for the child's level of understanding.

Developmentally Appropriate Guidance

Caregivers need to use different guidance techniques for children of different ages. A technique that is effective with four-year-olds may not work with toddlers. **Developmentally appropriate practices** are those that are suited to the developmental characteristics and needs of the individual child.

By the time children reach the toddler stage, they are old enough to understand simple words. Caregivers can use brief statements, such as "Pet the bunny gently." Toddlers should be able to follow such simple directions.

Caregivers need patience when they are with toddlers. Children of this age have a very short attention span. Caregivers may need to repeat a suggestion many times before a toddler adopts the desired behavior.

By the age of four, children are beginning to be able to reason. Briefly explaining why a certain behavior is or is not appropriate will help children use acceptable behaviors.

Guidance Techniques

Caregivers can use a number of techniques to guide children's behavior. Caregivers must first act as positive role models. Children learn by imitating others. Whenever you speak, you are **modeling** behavior. At an early age, children are aware of the actions of the adults around them. They copy the behavior of the adults they see every day. If you want their behavior to be positive, you must model that behavior yourself and set a good example. Also remember that children are probably listening and watching you when you do not realize it. For example, if the rule is to chew with your mouth closed, all caregivers should also be sure to chew with closed mouths.

Children need to know what they may and may not do. This is called **setting limits**. These may also be called *rules*. They are made to keep children safe. For example, a young child may be allowed to play only in the fenced backyard away from the street. This is a limit set to protect the child. Limits should be reasonable and appropriate for the child's age. An older child may be allowed to play anywhere within the caregiver's view. With permission, an older child may even play at another child's home.

If rules are made, they must be enforced with **consistency**. This means the same behavior is expected at all times. Children feel secure when limits are enforced consistently. If they are not, the child becomes confused. Using the above example, a young child may play in the front yard one day instead of the backyard. If the rule is not enforced, the child will play in the front yard on other days. The child broke the rule and nothing happened. When limits are consistent, children are more likely to respect them. When they are not consistent, children will ignore them.

Children's behavior can often be molded by rewarding positive behavior. This is called **positive reinforcement**. Caregivers should try to reward good behavior with attention and praise. Undesirable behavior should be ignored if possible. Gestures as well as words can be used to guide behavior. A smile, a nod, or a gentle hug will reinforce positive actions.

Even babies realize that if an action brings a desired response, repeating the action will bring a repeated response. For instance, a baby sitting in a high chair may throw a spoon on the floor. If you give the spoon back to the baby, he or she may throw it on the floor again. If you give the spoon back a second time, the baby is likely to think you are playing a game. The baby is too young to understand if you say "Keep your spoon on the tray." The best way to handle this situation is to simply stop giving the spoon back to the baby.

Another guidance technique is **redirection**, or focusing the child's attention on something else. For instance, suppose a child wants a toy another child has. Offering the child a different toy is a way of turning his or her attention in a different direction. The key to redirection is providing an appealing substitute.

Caregivers can use a technique called **prompting**. Questions can prompt children to exhibit desired behavior. A caregiver might ask "Where does the ball belong?" A child may respond by putting the ball on the proper shelf. Asking "What are you supposed to do when you are finished painting?" may encourage children to wash their hands.

Caregivers need to give children time to make a transition from one activity to another. Play is important to children, and they do not like to be suddenly interrupted. If possible, a warning should be given five or ten minutes before a change of activities. This gives children time to finish what they are doing.

Children tire of activities quickly due to their short attention spans. A caregiver may need to provide new activities for children to encourage positive behavior, **11-5**. Positive reinforcement should be used as much as possible to guide children's behavior. When misbehavior occurs, however, consequences may become part of the guidance process.

Using Consequences

Consequences are results that follow an action or behavior. When using consequences, the negative results of the child's own actions influence future behaviors. If a child's health or safety is at risk, a caregiver

11-5

Providing children with interesting activities reduces behavior problems.

must step in at once. However, if a child's well-being is not at risk, consequences can act as a deterrent to inappropriate behavior. For instance, playing with food is inappropriate behavior at the dinner table. Suppose a child plays with his or her food until it becomes cold. He or she then asks to have the food reheated in the microwave oven. The request is not honored. The child learns that the consequence for not eating promptly is to eat cold food.

Caregivers can set up consequences that relate to misbehaviors. These are called *logical consequences*. For instance, a child who throws blocks may not be allowed to play with the blocks for a period of time. Once consequences are imposed, they must be enforced. Otherwise, children will not learn from the consequences of their behavior.

Another logical consequence might be a time-out. A **time-out** involves moving a child away from others for a short period of time. It should be used only when a child's disruptive behavior cannot be ignored. The child needs time to calm down and gain self-control. A time-out is not appropriate for children younger than the age of four. Younger children are not able to understand their behavior can have negative consequences. The time-out should be limited to a few minutes.

A caregiver should be careful never to threaten to withdraw love. A child needs to feel loved regardless of his or her behavior. Love should not be used as a reward that has to be earned by a child. It should be given freely.

Parenting Styles

Parents tend to develop a parenting style they use to guide their children's behavior. Parenting styles can be grouped into three categories:

- *Authoritarian parents* tend to rule single-handedly. They maintain control and expect conformity. The children are not encouraged to negotiate or present different views.

- *Permissive parents* allow children to set their own rules. Children are allowed to make most of their decisions. Without boundaries, these children may feel insecure. They sometimes fear the natural consequences of decisions they are not prepared to make.

- *Authoritative* or *democratic parents* allow freedom within structure. Rules are established and explained. Children are allowed to ask questions and present their views. Children feel secure because they know what to do and why they are doing it.

Helping Children Develop Independence and Responsibility

Young children want to become independent. This is evidenced by two-year-olds who insist "I can do it myself." Caregivers can help children build independence by giving help only when children need it. Caregivers often perform chores for children even though the children could do the chores themselves. In many cases, a better approach would be to wait for the children while they do the chores. Then the caregiver can praise the children for their efforts. Children want the praise and approval of their caregivers.

Decision-making skills are needed for independent living. Caregivers can help children learn these skills by allowing them to make as many choices as possible. The choices do not have to be major ones. For instance, children can help choose the foods they eat, the clothes they wear, and the activities they do. See **11-6**. By being involved in the decision-making process, they gain self-confidence.

Children can help make many decisions every day. However, you should offer a choice only when you plan to abide by the decision. It is unfair to ask children to make decisions and then disagree with their choices. This harms children's self-concepts. It leads them to believe that you do not care what they think. It makes them feel their decisions are invalid.

One way to avoid this situation is to offer a child two equally acceptable alternatives. For instance, do not ask a child what he or she wants to eat for dinner. The child might say "Candy," which you are unlikely to consider a worthwhile entree. Instead, ask if the child would rather have turkey or chicken.

Another way caregivers can help children build independence is by allowing them to solve their own problems when possible. When given a chance, many children are able to find satisfactory solutions.

11-6
Children learn decision-making skills when they are allowed to choose their own toys.

For example, a father and his two children were ready to drive to school when the two children began quarreling about who would sit in the front seat of the car. The father decided to let them try to work it out. The children decided one child would always sit in the front seat when leaving home, and the other would always sit in the front seat for return trips. The children's own solution worked out well.

A goal of child care is helping children prepare to become responsible adults. An important part of being responsible is accepting the consequences of decisions. Children need to learn that they will have to live with the results of their decisions—good or bad.

Another way children develop responsibility is when adults encourage care for children's belongings. This can be done by providing storage within their reach. Low closet rods and dresser drawers help children to keep their clothes in place. Easy-to-reach shelves allow children to store their own toys.

21st Century Skills

Responsibility. Rita is a good worker, however, sometimes she makes mistakes. Rita always accepts responsibility for her work and does not blame others.

Helping Children Overcome Fears

Children between the ages of two and six are quite likely to develop a number of fears. A caregiver needs to respect a child's fears. A caregiver can try to find out the reason for a child's feelings. This may suggest ideas for helping the child overcome his or her fright. For instance, a boy

Mental Health Awareness

Stress and Anxiety in Children

Just like adults, children also experience stress and anxiety. Caregivers can teach children techniques to help reduce anxiety. For example, caregivers can show children how to take deep, steady breaths when feeling overwhelmed. Saying reaffirming statements, such as "I can do it," can also help. These techniques teach children that they can manage stress.

had a fear of swimming. His parents asked why he was afraid. The boy said he would not be able to breathe if his head went under the water. The parents used this information to gradually introduce the boy to shallow water. Soon the boy felt safe enough to get his head wet.

A caregiver can encourage a child to overcome a fear. However, the caregiver should avoid forcing the child into a situation that he or she finds frightening. Children will try new experiences when they feel ready. Forcing them only prolongs their apprehension.

The majority of children's fears are fears of unfamiliar objects and situations. As children gain experience with something, they typically lose their fear of it. Caregivers need to clearly explain new circumstances before children have a chance to become fearful. For example, children are often afraid of doctors. A caregiver can use a toy medical kit to show a child tools similar to those used by doctors. This will help the child feel more relaxed when he or she sees these tools in a doctor's office.

A caregiver may be able to distract a child's attention away from his or her fears. For example, a four-year-old cried when riding over a bridge on the route to her home. Her caregiver asked her why she was afraid of the bridge. The child said, "It goes hmmm." The caregiver said, "Since the bridge hums to us, maybe we can hum to it next time." They rehearsed their humming sound several times. On the next trip, the child looked forward to humming so much that she did not cry. Through distraction, the child's attention was diverted from her fear of the bridge to humming.

Reading Review

1. Everything caregivers do and say to promote socially acceptable behavior is called _____ .
2. Describe three guidance techniques you can use to guide children's behavior.
3. Identify the three parenting styles and briefly describe each type.
4. Describe three ways caregivers can help children develop independence.
5. True or false. Most fears among children are caused by bad experiences they have had.

Chapter 11 Review

Summary

Parents and caregivers must make sure children's needs are met. They need to offer children a variety of nutritious and appealing foods for meals and snacks. They must consider the fit, features, fabric, and construction of the clothes they select for their children. They also need to create a healthy and safe environment for their children.

Adults also need to provide stimulating activities for children. They should encourage children to be physically active. They can read to them and tell them stories. Art and music activities can be intellectually stimulating. When choosing toys that promote intellectual growth, caregivers must consider age appropriateness and safety.

Parents and caregivers need to communicate with children and teach them independence and responsibility. They need to provide guidance to direct children's behavior. Caregivers also need to help children learn to overcome fears.

Critical Thinking

1. **Analyze effects.** Observe a children's story hour at your local library. Give a brief oral report describing how the librarians stimulate interest as they read.

2. **Assess options.** Visit a toy department and compile a list of five toys that would be appropriate for preschoolers. Briefly describe how each toy will foster the development of a child.

3. **Predict outcomes.** Describe common issues that arise with small children, or problems you have had when working with small children. How might good guidance techniques have simplified the situations?

4. **Recognize alternatives.** Why is positive reinforcement so important? Are there any times, even in adulthood, when negative reinforcement is an acceptable alternative?

5. **Analyze behavior.** In a small group, discuss fears that you had as a young child. Talk about what you think motivated the fears. Describe the role older individuals played as you overcame the fears.

6. **Analyze multiple sources of information.** Look up the term *parenting styles* online. Browse through some of the websites returned as matches. Discuss in class the range of information offered on the Internet on the topic of parenting. Do you think most of these sites provide useful information? Why or why not?

21st Century Applications

7. **Creativity and innovation.** Write and illustrate a children's storybook that focuses on children around the world. Share the book with classmates, friends, and young children.

8. **Health literacy.** Review the information on children's nutrition at the United States Department of Agriculture's (USDA) MyPlate website. Develop a list of tips for caregivers and parents.

9. **Leadership and responsibility.** Research currently popular children's toys. Evaluate the toys on age appropriateness and safety. Use presentation software to share your findings with the class.

10. **Information, communications, and technology literacy.** Obtain permission to visit a child care center and videotape children at play. View the videos in class to identify which types of play children prefer. Identify the approximate age of each child.

11. **Critical thinking and problem solving.** The ability to read and interpret information is an important workplace skill. Presume you work for a day care center in your community. The day care center is considering adding a new playground to the premises. They have asked you to evaluate and interpret some research on different types of playgrounds and their benefits to children. You will need to locate three reliable sources of the latest information on playgrounds. Read and interpret the information and write a brief report summarizing your findings. Assume you have an unlimited budget.

12. **Initiative and self-direction.** There will be instances in which you will need to use critical thinking skills to solve a problem. One way to approach a problem is to create a pros and cons chart. Imagine that you have been offered a job as a summer camp counselor. Place all of the positive things about working as a camp counselor under the pro side and all the negative things on the con side. Circle the items on your list that you consider the most important. Did the pros and cons chart help you make a decision? Why or why not?

 **Core Skills**

13. **Math.** Use online retailers to select clothes for a child to wear for one week. Make sure you include sleepwear, shoes, and outerwear. Print pictures of the outfits and mount them on paper with the price of each outfit listed. Add up the total cost. Are you surprised at what it costs to clothe a child?

14. **Social studies, history.** Discuss "guidance techniques" directed at whole nations, such as Wilson's Fourteen Points following WWI. Discuss whether these methods are examples of positive reinforcement.

15. **Reading.** Select one parenting style discussed in this chapter to research in depth. Describe the style of parenting, give examples, and discuss the possible effects of the parenting style on children.

16. **Speaking, history.** Discuss the famous quote by Franklin D. Roosevelt: "The only thing we have to fear is fear itself." In what context was this speech given? How can this quote relate to childhood fears?

17. **Writing.** Successful employees model integrity and ethical decision making. What roles do you think ethics and integrity have in working with children? Write a brief response relating the importance of integrity and ethics to providing care for children.

18. **Listening.** Informative listening is the process of listening to gain specific information from the speaker. Interview a person who works with children, such as a teacher, camp counselor, day care provider, or nanny. Ask that person to explain their challenges and struggles of working with children. Take notes during the interview. Evaluate the speaker's point of view and reasoning.

Leadership
Development

As part of work on the Focus on Children STAR Event, obtain permission to facilitate enrichment activities at a local child care center or after-school program. Plan and organize age-appropriate activities to stimulate physical, intellectual, and social-emotional development.

Portfolio
Builder

Knowing the characteristics and basic needs of children can help you if you are interested in pursuing a career that involves working with children. You can learn a lot by observing children.

Obtain permission to observe children of various ages at a day care center, elementary school, or a summer camp. As you observe the children, take careful notes regarding the following:

- ages of children
- date
- time
- setting
- account of what you saw

Record your observations, and based on what you have learned in this chapter, describe how this information could help you if you pursue a career working with children.

Journal
Writing

Charise babysits four-year-old Ana on a regular basis. Charise tries to help Ana develop independence and responsibility by giving her choices. Today, Charise offered Ana a choice of an apple or a banana at snack time, and she chose the apple. After taking a few bites, Ana said, "I don't want this apple. May I have chocolate instead?"

Write About It: *How can Charise teach Ana about making decisions and the consequences of her decisions? What suggestions would you offer to Charise in this situation?*

Wellness and Nutrition

Unit Five

Human Services

The Family and Community Services Pathway within the Human Services career cluster includes careers that help individuals promote their physical and social-emotional well-being. Dietitians, social services workers, and religious leaders are examples of careers in this pathway.

Human Services Pathways

Early Childhood Development and
  Services
Counseling and Mental Health Services
Family and Community Services
Personal Care Services
Consumer Services

Liquidlibrary/liquidlibrary/Thinkstock

Education and Training

The Teaching and Training Pathway within the Education and Training career cluster includes helping individuals, families, or groups learn new strategies for improving their health and well-being. Examples of careers in this pathway include fitness trainers, nannies, and special education teachers.

Education and Training Pathways

Administration and Administrative
  Support
Professional Support Services
Teaching and Training

arek_malang/Shutterstock.com

Career Spotlight: Dietitian

- **Description.** Dietitians use their expertise in food and nutrition to help people make healthful food-related decisions. They may work with individuals, groups, or organizations to create and evaluate diets and meal plans. Dietitians teach clients about nutrition and food preparation and help them develop healthy eating habits. They may help clients meet certain health or weight goals, lead healthy lifestyles, or manage dietary restrictions. Some dietitians conduct dietary and nutritional research and publish their findings for other professionals in the field.
- **Education and training.** Dietitians typically have a bachelor's degree in dietetics, foods and nutrition, clinical nutrition, food systems management, or another related field. These programs include courses in nutrition, chemistry, biology, and psychology. Most dietitians must also complete an internship in the field. Many positions require advanced degrees, such as a master's degree or Ph.D., in a related field. Most states also require dietitians to be licensed. The requirements for licensure vary by state.
- **Skills and personal qualities.** Dietitians must have excellent analytical and problem-solving skills. They should be good listeners and compassionate. They should also have strong organizational, speaking, and critical-thinking skills.
- **Job outlook.** Job growth for dietitians is projected to grow much faster than average for all occupations through 2028. Visit the *Occupational Outlook Handbook* online to learn more about a career as a dietitian.

Human Services

Career Spotlight: Fitness Trainer

- **Description.** Fitness trainers instruct, motivate, and lead others in physical exercise. They help clients improve their skills and progress toward their physical goals. Fitness trainers lead one-on-one sessions with individuals, teach classes, and coach groups. They demonstrate proper techniques and forms of various physical activities, such as aerobics, yoga, and weight training. Fitness trainers work with people of all ages and fitness levels. They also make sure clients safely complete activities and do not overexert themselves.
- **Education and training.** Requirements vary, but most fitness trainers must have at least a high school diploma. Some employers require an associate's or bachelor's degree in a health science field such as kinesiology or exercise science. Some employers require fitness trainers to be certified, which includes taking classes and working with an experienced trainer.
- **Skills and personal qualities.** Fitness trainers must be physically fit and enjoy exercising and teaching fitness activities. Because this job is customer oriented, fitness trainers should have strong customer service, motivational, speaking, and listening skills. They should also have good instructing and time-management skills.
- **Job outlook.** Job growth for fitness trainers is projected to grow much faster than average for all occupations through 2028. Visit the *Occupational Outlook Handbook* online to learn more about a career as a fitness trainer.

Education & Training

Sources: States' Career Clusters Initiative, Bureau of Labor Statistics Career Guide to Industries

Chapter 12
Health and Fitness

Reading Prep

Think of some of your life goals. How are these goals affected by your health choices? As you read the chapter, focus on how your health and physical activity choices affect your future goals.

Concept Organizer

Create a sequence chain that starts with a risky behavior. What consequences can you see for the behavior?

G-WLEARNING.COM

Click on the activity icon to visit www.g-wlearning.com/comprehensive/8062 to access online vocabulary activities using key terms from the chapter.

andresr/E+/Getty Images

Section 12-1

Your Health and Wellness

Objectives

After studying this section, you will be able to

- **explain** why good health is important.
- **describe** the benefits of physical activity.
- **use** suggestions for getting adequate sleep.

Key Terms

physical wellness   physical fitness   insomnia

While some people are not born with good health, everyone wants to be healthy. Most people know good health means more than merely being free from disease. A concept known as *wellness* describes a desired state of health. **Physical wellness** means the body is able to fight illness and infection and repair damage. This state of health makes you feel and look better. It gives you energy to do your daily tasks and helps you enjoy life more fully. Only a small percentage of people currently enjoy this level of good health. However, attaining physical wellness is a worthy goal that all people should try to achieve.

Two key factors can help you achieve physical wellness. First, you need professional medical care. This includes preventive health care with regular checkups and any needed emergency treatment. Second, you need self-care. This means meeting your body's needs through good nutrition and weight management. It also means getting enough physical activity and rest as well as learning to manage stress. Finally, self-care includes grooming and personal hygiene.

Physical fitness refers to the condition of your body. When you are physically fit, your muscles are toned, your heart is strong, and your lungs are clear. You are able to perform a variety of tasks.

Fitness and wellness go hand in hand. You cannot be healthy if your body is not strong. Likewise, you cannot keep your body strong if you are not healthy.

Many factors play a role in determining your state of physical wellness and physical fitness. However, the care you give yourself has the greatest impact on both areas of your well-being. You need to assume responsibility for your health and fitness.

The Importance of Good Health

Your health can affect you in a number of ways. Your ability to succeed at school depends on your health. When you are physically fit, you are better able to stay alert and learn. Poor health can prevent you from attending classes regularly. Your grades may suffer if you are not able to attend lectures and participate in labs. This can affect any plans you may have to go to college or technical school.

Good health is important to career achievement. Some careers require excellent health and physical fitness. You need to be in your workplace daily. If poor health causes you to miss work, you may have trouble keeping your job. If you stay healthy, you will be more likely to advance in your career.

Your personal and family life will also be more satisfying if you have good health. You will be able to more fully enjoy interacting with people and taking part in activities. You will feel better as you do your daily tasks. Good health will help you get more enjoyment from daily living.

Being Physically Active

Getting daily physical activity is a key part of building and maintaining physical fitness. Regular physical activity can enhance your posture. It can improve your blood circulation and increase your lung capacity. Building more movement into your day can help relieve stress, boredom, and depression. Physical activity can help you build strength and flexibility. It can also help you manage your weight. Besides all that, physical activity can be fun, especially if you do it with friends.

Physical activity does not have to be a strenuous exercise program. Many of the tasks that are part of your daily routine are forms of moderate physical activity. For instance, walking, bicycling, raking leaves, and cleaning the house will all help you develop fitness. If you enjoy activities that are more vigorous, you might try dancing, swimming, or playing tennis.

Mental Health Awareness

Physical Activity and Mental Health

Physical activity is a healthy form of stress management. While you exercise, you give yourself a mental break from a stressor. This can give you time to reevaluate the situation and see new solutions. Physical activity is also a mood booster. During physical activity, your body releases *endorphins*, or hormones that improve your mood.

Math Connection

Calculating Distances

Sarah has read that walking is a great way to stay physically fit. She walks 3 miles 6 days per week. How many feet does Sarah walk in a week?

First, she calculates how many total miles she walks.

$3 \times 6 = 18$

Then she multiplies the total number of miles by the number of feet in a mile (5,280 feet).

$18 \times 5,280 = 95,040$ feet

The Importance of Leisure Activities

Leisure is freedom from chores, homework, jobs, and other responsibilities. It is the time you have to do something just because you want to do it. Leisure is not only fun—it is also good for you. The greatest benefit derived from leisure is the reduction of stress. Leisure activities help keep the body, mind, and spirit ready to fight any challenging forces you might face.

Many busy people fail to plan for leisure. Some think it is selfish to claim time for themselves when they could be doing something more important. This is a mistake. The ability to be productive requires you to first care for yourself.

Leisure can be used to do anything you like as long as it is not a responsibility. Some teens may choose to watch a favorite TV show or read. Others might use their leisure time for skateboarding or bicycling. You may spend your leisure time alone or with others. Many families use their leisure time to enjoy recreational activities together. See **12-1**.

The Importance of Sleep

Teenagers and adults often fall into the trap of not getting enough sleep. You need to find time to sleep, even if it means cutting down on your activities. People who lack sleep may become irritable or show a decline in muscle coordination. The quality of their work usually suffers, too.

The amount of sleep a person needs is an individual matter. Some people get by with six hours a night. Others need nine or ten hours. Most people feel best when they sleep seven to eight hours a night.

Insomnia is the inability to get the amount of sleep you need when you need it. Taking sleeping pills is a poor solution to the problem. Most sleeping pills become ineffective after a few weeks of use, and they can be addictive. If you have trouble sleeping, try the following suggestions listed.

- Make physical activity a part of your daily routine. It can help you sleep deeper and longer.

- Establish regular times for going to bed and waking up. You can program yourself into a sleeping schedule.

- Form a habit of doing a relaxing activity just before bedtime. Read, listen to soft music, or take a hot bath.

Healthy Living

Physical Activity Guidelines for Americans

The Department of Health and Human Services provides guidance on the types and amounts of physical activity that provide health benefits. Consider the following guidelines when planning for physical activity:

- Children and adolescents (ages 6–17) should do 1 hour or more of physical activity every day. Most of the 1 hour or more a day should be either moderate- or vigorous-intensity aerobic physical activity.
- Children and adolescents should do vigorous-intensity activity at least 3 days per week. They should also do muscle-strengthening and bone-strengthening activity at least 3 days per week.
- Adults should do 2 hours and 30 minutes a week of moderate-intensity or 1 hour and 15 minutes a week of vigorous-intensity aerobic physical activity. Additional health benefits are provided by increasing to 5 hours a week of moderate-intensity aerobic physical activity or 2 hours and 30 minutes a week of vigorous-intensity physical activity.
- Adults should also do muscle-strengthening activities involving all major muscle groups on 2 or more days per week.

Living Green

If you enjoy being outdoors, gardening is a good way to spend leisure time. Try planting fruits, vegetables, or herbs. Use a rain barrel to collect water for your plants.

12-1

Strengthening family relationships can be one effect of enjoying leisure time together.

- Use your bed strictly for sleep. This will help program your body to know that getting into bed means "it is now time to sleep." If you want to read or watch TV, do so before getting into bed.
- Stay away from coffee, tea, or cola in the evening. The caffeine in these beverages may keep you awake.
- Sleep on a mattress that is neither too soft nor too firm.
- Keep the temperature in the bedroom at a moderate setting—not too cold and not too warm.

The Importance of Personal Hygiene

Other people's impressions of you are influenced by the way you look. Your appearance can also have a great impact on your self-image. However, you do not need beautiful features to be attractive. Your appearance is largely determined by the way you care for yourself.

Basic *hygiene*, or cleansing practices that promote good health, includes your whole body. Taking a bath or shower every day and caring for your skin, teeth, and hair play an important role in presenting an attractive appearance.

Reading
Review

1. True or false. A person's health can affect his or her ability to get and keep a job.
2. Name five benefits of daily physical activity.
3. How many hours of sleep do most people need each night in order to feel their best?

Section 12-2

Your Mental Health

Objectives

After studying this section, you will be able to

- **describe** a healthy mental state.
- **demonstrate** ways to cope with stress and depression.
- **identify** warning signs of depression that indicate a need for help.

Key Terms

defense mechanism   stress   depression

Your health involves more than being fit physically. Your well-being also includes mental health. Many factors, such as stress and personal or family crises, can affect your mental health. Serious mental conditions, such as depression and bipolar disorder, require psychiatric help.

Maintaining a Healthy Mental State

People who are mentally healthy look for, and find, the best in their surroundings. They understand themselves and what makes them think and act as they do. They can accept their weaknesses and recognize their strengths. People with a healthy mental state are self-confident. They are more likely to follow their principles than to respond to peer pressure. They also have a sense of humor and seem to enjoy life.

Mental Health Awareness

Defining Mental Health

According to the World Health Organization, *mental health* is defined as "a state of well-being in which every individual realizes his or her own potential, can cope with the normal stresses of life, can work productively and fruitfully, and is able to make a contribution to her or his community." Aspects of positive mental health include emotional, psychological, and social well-being.

Serving Your Community

Read an article on the health benefits of volunteering. Then, as a class, participate in a volunteer activity in your community. Possible activities include volunteering at a soup kitchen or recycling center or visiting residents of a nursing home.

Mentally healthy people are able to deal with change. When they have difficulties, they are able to analyze the causes of the problems. They find solutions and put them into action. Once they solve problems, they can look back on the problems as learning experiences. This approach allows them to avoid similar problems in the future.

Maintaining a healthy mental state is an important aspect of self-care. Mentally healthy people know how to relieve frustration. They try not to think self-defeating thoughts. They are able to peaceably resolve conflicts with others to avoid negative feelings.

Using Defense Mechanisms

Sometimes situations occur that can challenge your healthy mental outlook. Wanting to guard yourself against pain, stress, and frustration in these situations is only natural. Using defense mechanisms is one way you care for your mental health. **Defense mechanisms** are behavior patterns people use to protect their self-esteem. See **12-2**.

Defense mechanisms can be positive or negative solutions to problems. It depends entirely on how they are used. When people are aware they are using defense mechanisms, they are in control of their actions. They are using the defense mechanisms in an attempt to maintain a healthy mental state. However, some people fail to realize they are relying on defense mechanisms. In these cases, defense mechanisms can cause people to lose touch with reality.

Stress and Your Health

Stress is your body's reaction to the events of your life. When something bad happens, such as forgetting your homework or losing your job, you feel stress. You also feel stress when good things happen, like winning a race or meeting someone special. In either case, your body responds. Your heart beats faster. Your face flushes. You perspire more. Perhaps your stomach tightens.

Change is frequently a cause of stress. Graduating from high school, taking a new job, getting married, and moving into a new apartment are all major changes. Doing all these at the same time would be likely to cause a lot of stress.

You need stress in your life to add excitement, but too much can affect your physical and mental well-being. Excessive amounts that are not managed can result in physical and emotional problems. Someone under stress may experience headaches, stomachaches, high blood pressure, or changes in sleep patterns. Emotional signs of stress include tension, anger, and an inability to concentrate.

Defense Mechanisms

compensation. Using a substitute method to achieve a desired goal.

Example: This year, you did not make the basketball team despite much practicing. Instead, you try out for track and make the cut.

conversion. Transferring an emotion into a physical symptom or complaint.

Example: You fear you do not know the material to be covered on the test and you get a headache.

daydreaming. Accomplishing through the imagination something you have not accomplished in reality. Daydreaming can provide both positive and negative solutions. When daydreams are used to find creative solutions to problems, this is positive. When they are used frequently to escape reality through fantasy, they are negative.

Positive example: Sue was daydreaming about having the "latest look" for her party outfit. She suddenly thought of how she could combine some of her old clothes to get just the look she wanted.

Negative example: Maggie turned down Sam's invitation to the school party. Sam went with another girl and daydreamed he was with Maggie.

direct attack. Overcoming obstacles or problems through realistic efforts to find solutions.

Example: You are overweight because you eat mostly high-calorie foods. You decide to replace high-calorie foods with nutritious foods and eat low-calorie foods between meals.

displacement. Transferring an emotion connected with one person or thing to another person or thing.

Example: You get upset with a friend and take it out on your sister.

giving up. Allowing discouragement to get you down.

Example: You try to lose weight. After two weeks, you have not lost an ounce. You just give up the idea of losing weight and go back to your old eating habits.

idealization. Placing a value on something or someone that is beyond its worth.

Example: You lose a favorite piece of jewelry and lie in bed and cry for two days.

projection. Placing the blame for your failures on other people or things.

Example: You blame the teacher when you fail a test because he did not tell you what would be covered on the test.

rationalization. Explaining your weaknesses or failures by giving socially acceptable excuses.

Example: You tell your parents you went to a movie they had forbidden you to see because all your friends were going.

regression. Reverting back to a less mature stage of development.

Example: You get angry with someone and slam the door as you leave.

12-2

These defense mechanisms are sometimes used to hide or counterbalance feelings or behaviors.

Coping with Stress

Learning to manage the stress in your life can help you become more mentally fit. When physical or emotional problems result from stress, look at your lifestyle. Ask yourself the following questions:

- Am I following good health practices? Am I eating regular meals and getting plenty of physical activity? Do I get an adequate amount of sleep?

- Am I realistic about the goals I have set for myself?

Life Skills

Techniques to Reduce Stress

- Be physically active each day to help relieve the pressures of stress. Go for a brisk walk or play a game of basketball or tennis.
- Be your own person. Do not let others put too much pressure on you. Learn to say no.
- Talk to someone about your concerns.
- Take time for leisure activities to escape from your everyday worries.
- Manage your time. Set realistic goals for the tasks you need to accomplish, including paid employment if you work. Prioritize the tasks. Then work toward your goals—do not procrastinate!
- Take care of your health. Eat right and get plenty of sleep and physical activity. Stress is easier to handle when you are rested and in good health.

12-3

Prolonged symptoms of depression indicate a need for professional help.

Symptoms of Depression

- continual sadness, anxiety, or empty moods
- feelings of hopelessness and helplessness
- lack of interest in pleasurable activities
- sleeplessness or oversleeping
- decreased appetite or overeating
- difficulty concentrating, remembering, or making decisions
- headaches, digestive disturbances, nausea, or chronic pain
- feelings of isolation from family members and friends
- excessive crying

- Am I managing my time and energy efficiently in order to meet my commitments?
- Are there many changes occurring in my life at one time?

Answering these questions will help you identify the events in your life that cause stress. Once you have recognized these situations, you can work to resolve them. This will help you reduce any symptoms that have resulted from too much stress in your life.

Depression

Depression is an emotional state that ranges from mild, short-lived feelings of sadness to a deep, despairing sense of dejection. Becoming depressed after a failure or loss is normal. However, a lingering depression whose onset does not seem to be triggered by a particular event is not normal.

Clinical depression has a number of symptoms, **12-3**. Clinical depression may have several causes and requires professional treatment. A psychiatrist can determine appropriate therapies based on the needs of the patient. The psychiatrist may prescribe antidepressant drugs. He or she may also advise the patient to check into a psychiatric ward or hospital.

It may take months or even years for a patient to recover from clinical depression. During the recovery period, he or she will need patience and support from friends and family members.

Suicide

Sometimes depression goes beyond a person's capacity to cope. The person may think everything will go wrong and nothing will help. The individual feels hopeless and powerless. Thus, he or she settles for failing and stops trying. Intense emotions impair the ability to see that everyone gets depressed at times. When a person always feels depressed, he or she may have thoughts of suicide.

Suicide attempts are often cries for help. Victims are asking someone to understand and care. People who attempt suicide rarely wish to die. They just wish to end life as they know it.

Teen Suicides

Some teen suicides correspond to the following factors:

- *A breakdown of the family support system.* When the family structure is not intact, teens have fewer chances to communicate with parents.

- *Intense competition.* Teens undergo intense pressure competing for leadership roles, athletic teams, part-time jobs, college admissions, and scholarships.

- *Peer rejection.* Feelings of rejection can lead to depression. Teens can also be easily hurt in relationships with members of the opposite sex.

Some teens express feelings of anger, depression, and anxiety through harmful behavior. They may feel that life itself no longer matters. A sense of failure at life can breed thoughts of suicide.

Suicide Prevention

Talk of suicide should not be taken lightly. If you suspect someone is suicidal, immediately seek the help of a teacher, school counselor, religious leader, or medical professional. Suicide prevention hotlines are also available to help people deal with thoughts of suicide.

When People Need Help

People may need to seek help when they are not in top mental health. First, they should try talking with family members or trusted friends. If this does not resolve the feelings, a visit to a family physician may be in order. The physician can rule out the possibility of a physical illness that could cause depression. He or she will be helpful in locating a mental health counselor if one is needed.

Maintaining mental health may not always be easy. However, people should not feel there is nowhere to turn. Many mental health specialists are available for counsel. Most school systems also have psychologists and psychiatrists for students who need specialized care.

Life Skills

Handling Bullying and Cyberbullying

Bullying is intentionally hurting or scaring another person. People may be bullied verbally, physically, or emotionally. *Cyberbullying* is the use of text messages, e-mail, social media, or other digital mediums to threaten, intimidate, harass, or otherwise cause harm to another person.

Bullying and cyberbullying can negatively impact mental health. Victims of bullying often have low self-esteem, are depressed, feel lonely, and may consider suicide. Use the following tips to handle bullying and cyberbullying:

- Don't be a bully. Bullying includes name-calling, sending mean messages, excluding others, and attacking others.
- If you are bullied, or if you witness bullying, tell an adult. Report cyberbullying to the service provider and other adults. If your life is being threatened, call the police.
- Be kind to students who are bullied. Ask them to join your group of friends.

Reading
Review

1. Describe what is meant by a healthy mental state.
2. True or false. Stress is your body's reaction to both good and bad events in your life.
3. List five symptoms of depression that should not be ignored.

Section 12-3

Health Risks

Objectives

After studying this section, you will be able to

- **list** health risks associated with tobacco, alcohol, and other drugs, and sexually transmitted infections.

- **explain** how routine decisions can affect your health.

Key Terms

secondhand smoke

vaping

smokeless tobacco

opiates

sexually transmitted infection (STI)

acquired immune deficiency syndrome (AIDS)

human immuno-deficiency virus (HIV)

Practicing health habits to promote wellness involves avoiding certain health risks. These risks include tobacco as well as alcohol and other drugs. They also include sexually transmitted infections.

Tobacco

Cigarette smoking is the largest preventable cause of illness and premature death in the United States. Many thousands of deaths each year are linked to cigarette smoking. People who smoke are more likely to suffer from heart disease, respiratory infections, and lung cancer.

Smoking during pregnancy can be harmful to the unborn child. Pregnant women who smoke have a higher risk of miscarriage and premature delivery. Babies born to women who smoke often weigh less, and their future growth and development may be impaired.

Even if you are not smoking, inhaling the smoke of others is still a health concern. **Secondhand smoke** is the smoke caused by smoke-producing substances, such as cigarettes, cigars, and pipes. For people with lung and heart problems, breathing secondhand smoke can be very irritating. Children are also highly affected by secondhand smoke. Studies show that children of smokers are more likely to suffer from respiratory ailments than children of nonsmokers.

The use of e-cigarettes to inhale vapor through the mouth, most of which contain nicotine, is known as **vaping**. Such exposure can harm the adolescent brain, which continues to develop until about the age of 25. In addition to nicotine, the aerosol that users inhale and exhale may increase the risk for future addiction to other drugs and can expose innocent bystanders to the harmful substances. Moreover, some of the chemicals used to provide the desired flavors used for e-cigarettes may also have health risks.

The use of **smokeless tobacco** products involves health risks as well. These are products such as chewing tobacco and snuff, which are chewed or placed against the gums. Their use has been linked to gum cancer and irritations of the gums and lips.

For people who have never used tobacco products, continuing to avoid these products is the most health-conscious choice. For people who have used tobacco products, quitting is one of the best steps they can take for their health. People who quit smoking enjoy almost immediate health benefits. Within 24 hours, the risk of heart attack decreases. After three days, breathing becomes easier and lung capacity increases. Within weeks, the body's energy level increases.

Alcohol

Alcohol is a depressant drug that is a serious health risk. Health care for alcohol-related illnesses and accidents costs millions of dollars every year. Alcohol can damage the brain, liver, stomach, and other organs. It also interferes with judgment, vision, muscle coordination, and reaction time. This is why it poses such great danger to people who drive under its influence. See **12-4**.

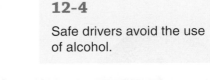

12-4

Safe drivers avoid the use of alcohol.

Another health problem related to alcohol is alcoholism—an addiction to alcohol. It is a disease that affects teenagers as well as adults. Alcoholics lose control of their drinking. They become dependent on alcohol. Alcoholism interferes with health, personal relationships, and ability to function.

Once alcohol has entered the body, it will continue to circulate until it is processed in the liver. This occurs at the rate of about 0.25 to 0.50 ounces every hour.

Alcohol has legal risks as well as health risks. It is illegal for teens to buy alcohol. It is illegal for *anyone* to drive under the influence of alcohol.

You can protect your health and your legal status by avoiding alcohol. You can also protect yourself by refusing to ride in a car with a driver who has been drinking.

Other Drugs

Alcohol is not the only drug that poses a health risk to teens. A variety of other drugs—both legal and illegal—can be hazardous to health.

Drug abuse is the use of a drug for a purpose other than it was intended. Even legal drugs purchased over the counter or with a prescription, including **opiates**—drugs derived from opium, such as codeine—can be abused. These drugs should be used only according to package directions or as directed by a doctor. Also, never use someone else's prescription drugs.

Drug abuse can damage your health, interfere with your ability to function, and affect your mind. Some drugs cause *addiction*, which is a dependence of the body on a continuing supply of the drug. After an addiction has developed, taking the drug away will cause agonizing withdrawal symptoms.

Even experimenting with drugs can be dangerous. Experimenting often leads to more frequent drug use. If an addiction develops, serious health and legal problems may result.

Sexually Transmitted Infections

As a health risk, **sexually transmitted infections (STIs)** are a major concern in the United States. This concern is especially great for young adults. STIs are spread mainly through sexual contact. They can also be passed

Healthy Living

Long-Term Health Risks of Drugs

Caffeine: headaches, nervousness, stomach disorders

Depressants such as PCP, tranquilizers, and barbiturates: fatigue, confusion, paranoia, addiction

Hallucinogens such as LSD: hallucinations

Inhalants: damage to the nervous system, kidneys, and blood

Marijuana: learning difficulties, lung damage, possible damage to reproductive organs, psychological addiction, possible link to use of other illegal drugs

Narcotics such as heroin and other opiates: addiction, malnutrition, risk of overdose and hepatitis, severe withdrawal symptoms

Steroids: acne, stunted growth, sterility

Stimulants such as cocaine and amphetamines (speed): nervousness, severe depression, nose damage, hallucinations, damage to the heart and brain

from pregnant women to their infants. They are not spread through casual contact, such as hugging or shaking hands.

The main STIs that are of concern are AIDS, gonorrhea, syphilis, chlamydia, human papillomavirus, and herpes. The symptoms and side effects of these diseases range from an outbreak of blisters to blindness to death.

You have a responsibility to prevent the spread of STIs. You can do this by becoming educated about STIs. If you know of someone who has an STI, encourage him or her to get prompt, effective treatment. Also encourage this person to behave responsibly and avoid spreading the STI to others. The only sure way to prevent STIs is to abstain from sex. The risk of contracting STIs becomes higher as a person has more sexual partners. You owe it to yourself to stay healthy and avoid contracting STIs.

AIDS

The most deadly STI is **acquired immune deficiency syndrome (AIDS)**. This disease is caused by the **human immunodeficiency virus (HIV)**, which breaks down the body's immune system. This leaves the body vulnerable to diseases a healthy body could resist. Most people with AIDS eventually die from one or more of these diseases.

HIV is transmitted through such body fluids as blood and semen. HIV can be contracted through sharing contaminated intravenous needles as well as through sexual contact. Infants can contract HIV during the birth process or through breast-feeding.

In the past, some people contracted HIV from blood transfusions. However, this risk is now very small since all blood is screened for HIV. There is no risk of contracting HIV from donating blood because fresh needles are used for each donation.

Decisions That Affect Your Health

You make many routine decisions every day. You decide what to eat, where to go, and what to wear. Take a minute when making these decisions to think about how they might affect your health. For instance, keep in mind that limiting high-fat foods can reduce your risk of heart disease. Wearing your seat belt will help protect you in the event of a car accident. Keeping your health in mind will help you make decisions that will promote wellness.

Not all health-related decisions are routine. You might decide you want to go skydiving or bungee jumping. If you are intrigued by a certain degree of risk, take precautions. You do not have to avoid all potentially dangerous activities to protect your health. However, you have a responsibility to be fully aware of the risks you are taking. Then you need to do whatever is necessary to make the activity as safe as possible. Take lessons from trained professionals to learn how to do activities properly. Wear protective clothing. Plan what you will do if problems arise.

Avoid risks when you can. When you must take risks, address them sensibly. This will help you protect your health and make your life more fulfilling.

Reading
Review

1. The use of e-cigarettes, most of which contain nicotine, is called _____.
2. List three long-term health risks of each of the following: marijuana, stimulants, inhalants, steroids, and caffeine.
3. What is HIV and how is it transmitted?
4. Give an example of a routine decision and explain how it can affect your health.

Section 12-4

Strategies for Healthful Personal Development

Objectives

After studying this section, you will be able to

- **summarize** factors that contribute to a quality of life.
- **identify** roadblocks to personal development.
- **explain** the consequences of risk-taking behavior.
- **relate** the importance of supportive relationships.

Key Term

quality of life

Quality of life is a phrase used to describe many factors that work together to foster personal well-being. How would you describe a good life? What do you want out of life? What is most important to you and your family? These are questions you might ask yourself in forming your view of a quality life.

What Contributes to Quality of Life?

The following are some of the factors people mention when describing a quality of life:

- *Good health.* Your health and the health of the other members of your family is very important. Remember the last time you were ill. Did you tell yourself "if I can just get better, everything will be okay"? People often do not realize how important their health is until they lose it.

Life Skills

Setting Personal Health Goals

Setting goals can help you achieve and maintain good health. For example, you need to include at least 60 minutes of activity in your daily schedule. (Urge adults in your family to include at least 30 minutes of activity in their schedules.) You do not have to spend 60 minutes all at once. To achieve this goal, you can accumulate a number of 10 to 20-minute segments of activity throughout the day. Talk to your doctor about your personal health goals before making any drastic changes.

- *Environmental factors.* Clean air and water, a safe neighborhood, and access to recreational facilities are just some of the environmental factors that can impact the quality of your life.

- *Emotional closeness.* To feel you are loved and to feel love for others is important to most people. Without this emotional tie to at least one other person, life may not be as satisfying as it could be. People who feel loved are usually happier, more enthusiastic, healthier, less prone to illness, and generally live longer.

- *Social ties.* Having friends and feeling like a member of a community is part of a fulfilling life. Those who feel isolated and alone are usually less likely to be satisfied with their lives.

- *Educational opportunities.* Everyone has the right to a good education in a safe school environment. Qualified teachers and up-to-date classroom materials allow you to reach any educational goals you set for yourself. A variety of educational opportunities are available after high school. If you choose to pursue these, they can greatly impact the quality of your life in the years to come.

- *Satisfying work.* Wages bring buying power and essential needs, such as nutritious food and health care. A work environment that is free of hazards to your physical and emotional health is also important. Being a productive member of a work group can give you personal satisfaction.

Living Green

Reading is a good way to enhance your personal development. The next time you have the impulse to buy a new book to read, borrow it from the library or a friend instead of buying a new copy. Sharing books is a great way to reduce waste and reuse materials.

You cannot always change the circumstances under which you live. However, you can look for ways you can change your life to bring it closer to the quality you desire. A positive attitude helps. Those who think of their glass as half full will enjoy a better quality of life than those who feel their glass is half empty.

What Roadblocks Might Lie Ahead?

As you strive to achieve the quality of life you desire, there will be roadblocks along the way. These may interfere with the quality of your life. There may be temporary setbacks that can be overcome with hard work. Some people will be challenged to do so, whereas others may give up altogether.

Some roadblocks may be permanent obstacles. If such a roadblock occurs, you must find a way to cope with the situation. No matter what the obstacle, you can find a way to bring quality and meaning to your life.

The roadblocks typically encountered are usually the opposite of those factors that make for a quality life. For example, poor health can present special challenges. If you or someone close to you is injured or develops a major health problem, it will significantly impact your life. You may be challenged in new ways to live a normal life.

The abuse of alcohol or other drugs can be a roadblock. Such abuse can interfere with personal relationships, educational goals, and employability. Drug addictions, which lead to physical dependence on a drug, can seriously interfere with people's lives. Other types of addictions can also occur, such as addictions to gambling. These can be as difficult to overcome and as destructive of people's lives as physical addictions.

Emotional closeness may be difficult to attain if you lack self-esteem. If you have not learned to love yourself, it may be difficult for you to love someone else. Your challenge will be to find ways to improve your self-esteem in order to overcome this roadblock. Emotional dependencies can also leave people feeling unable to control their destinies. These feelings of inadequacy can lead to severe depression.

Stress in the workplace can be a debilitating factor for some people, **12-5**. Such stress can be caused by work that is too demanding, keeping people away from family and friends. Working extremely long hours and spending days and even weeks away from home can make it difficult to have a normal family life. A threatening psychological environment or sexual harassment can also create an intolerable work situation. Another work situation that can create roadblocks is a low-paying job that makes it difficult to meet living expenses. The stress of living from paycheck to paycheck can impact many aspects of a person's life. The prospect of unemployment is also a possibility.

Violence or the threat of violence is another potential roadblock. Anyone who lives in fear for his or her health and safety cannot live a satisfying life. Violence can occur on the street or within the home. It can be gang violence or violence within the family, such as spouse or child abuse. Just the threat of violence can create an intolerable situation. Those who live with such threats cannot move forward with their lives until the threats to their safety are removed.

21st Century Skills

Flexibility. Fiona is in a stressful career. She finds that being flexible and having a balanced life can help to relieve some of the stress.

Prostock-Studio/iStock/Getty Images

12-5
A stressful period at work may interfere with the quality of your life.

These are just some of the potential roadblocks that you may be facing now, or may face in the years ahead. Others may also lie in your path as you move toward adulthood.

What Tactics Can Aid Personal Development?

Learning some tactics that can aid in your personal development may be helpful to you in overcoming these roadblocks, should any occur. Avoiding risks along the way is one of the keys to avoiding roadblocks. Building relationships with people is another skill that will help you in your personal development.

Avoid High-Risk Behavior

Risks involve uncertainty, and they often have an element of danger. There may even be the possibility of harm or loss. Risk-taking behaviors are common among teens. It is a normal part of their desire for independence. Some teens get a natural high from taking risks. They feel alert, excited, and alive. Others like to take risks to prove they can stretch the limits and succeed.

Not all risks are bad. For example, you might risk being turned down when inviting someone new to a school dance. Many risks, however, are quite serious due to their consequences. They can result in physical or mental harm to a person, cause injury or death, and even affect the lives of innocent people. These consequences are severe.

Carefully analyze the risks you take and consider the possible outcomes. Some risks, such as having sex, using illegal drugs, drinking alcohol, smoking cigarettes, and driving while intoxicated, can have lifetime consequences. Some risks can endanger the health and well-being of others. No one has the right to take risks that might cause harm to others.

For example, riding in a car is a routine risk, but doing so without fastening your seat belt raises the risk factor for physical injury. Riding with someone who has been drinking raises your risk factor and the driver's risk factor for serious injury or death. Going to a party and using drugs increases your risk factor for physical and social-emotional consequences. The use of illegal drugs can lead to serious health consequences and even death. There is also the risk of possible arrest for possession of drugs. When people are under the influence of drugs or alcohol, they are also less able to make good decisions involving their behavior. None of these consequences can lead to positive outcomes concerning the quality of your life.

Some teens think they are immune to danger, but no one really is. Consider any risk seriously. Then, if you choose to proceed with an activity, plan ahead to reduce the gravest consequences. For instance, if you want to raft a dangerous river, train for it and go with a team of rafters who are also well trained. Before you take off, secure your helmet and life vest, know how to avoid falling off, and know how to get back on if you do.

Build Supportive Relationships

You will come in contact with many people throughout your life. Some of these people will be very close to you. They are the people who will love you, encourage you, support you, and make you feel worthwhile. These are likely to be your parents, your close friends, a dating partner, and may eventually include a marriage partner. Even in the workplace, you may find a mentor who will help you along in your career.

The relationships you share with these people have a great effect on the quality of your life. You are healthier, both physically and mentally, when you have these supportive relationships in your life. Your happiness and success in life are closely related to your ability to form meaningful relationships with others.

The caring people in your life will support you in times of stress, **12-6**. They will help you solve problems and find direction. Supportive relationships go both ways. That means both people in the relationship meet needs and contribute to the personal development of the other.

Wellness Awareness

Compile a list of activities that help promote wellness and can be done by an entire family. Examples include walking, riding bicycles, swimming, and preparing healthy recipes. Try one of the activities with your family and share the experiences in small groups or with the entire class.

12-6
For many young people, close friends can provide support in both good times and bad.

Relationships involve sharing feelings, experiences, problems, interests, and activities. People share and work toward common goals. They respect each other. They also trust each other, knowing that each is honest and reliable. Openness is also important to any relationship. Sharing thoughts, opinions, and feelings is key to a successful relationship.

Unfortunately, some people lack this supportive network of people. They are unable to form meaningful and positive relationships with others. What happens when people lack these relationships? Self-esteem suffers. They feel unworthy of anyone's love.

People lacking close relationships may attempt to fill this void in various ways. For instance, a young woman may feel if she gets pregnant and has a baby, she will have someone to love her. She thinks her baby will always be there for her. This is the wrong reason for having a baby. She is choosing to have a baby for selfish reasons and is not considering the welfare of her child. Some young people join gangs to fill their need to be a part of a group. Once they are in the gang, they get trapped into participating in unhealthy or illegal activities that may include violence. Many times it is difficult to get out of a gang safely.

Analyze and Solve

Consider a dysfunctional family, perhaps due to alcoholism, drug abuse, or family violence. Identify ways that teens in those families could cope with a lack of supportive relationships at home. How might they form such relationships with other caring adults and thus develop resiliency in their lives?

Life Skills

How to Develop a Social Support Network

Because supportive family, friends, and coworkers are such an important part of your life, it's never too soon to cultivate these important relationships. A social support network is different than a support group, which exists to help a group of people with the same problem cope with it. You can create your own social support network any way you choose.

A good place to start is by thinking about the activities you enjoy and values that are most important to you. For instance, if you love to ski, take the local weekend ski bus to your nearest ski area, start a ski club at school, or join a competitive ski team. If your spiritual life is a priority, join or start a youth group based on your faith. You will meet other people who enjoy the same things you do, which is a great basis for building and maintaining an ongoing, supportive network of friends.

Some other ideas of groups to join—or start, if there are none in your community—can include

- a book club or creative writing group
- a hiking, kayaking, basketball (or other sport) group/team
- a movie or video group
- a group based on a hobby, such as building model planes or making quilts
- a rotating cooking or dinner group
- a science or inventor's club

As you can see, it is important to surround yourself with people who will support you in a positive manner. Some young people feel they are lacking such a support group. If you feel this way, try to connect with some caring adults. Remember that adults other than parents can help you. An older sibling, a grandparent, a favorite teacher, a religious leader, a neighbor, or your employer are all possible candidates. Close friends should also be an important part of your support group.

Reading Review

1. List three factors that can contribute to a quality life and give an example of each.
2. Identify three roadblocks to personal development.
3. Give an example of a positive risk and an example of a risk that can have negative consequences. Explain your answers.
4. Give three characteristics of a supportive relationship.

Chapter 12 Review

Summary

You need to take an active role in keeping yourself physically fit. Maintaining good health can have a positive effect on your school, work, and family life. Getting daily physical activity will help you stay in shape. Enjoying leisure activities and getting adequate sleep will also help you perform at your highest level. Caring for your body will affect your appearance as well as your health.

Your mental health as well as your physical health can affect your overall well-being. Occasionally using defense mechanisms and learning to cope with stress can help you protect your mental health. Clinical depression is one type of mental illness. Counseling and other sources of help are available to people who are having trouble maintaining a healthy mental state.

Some people knowingly take health risks. Using tobacco products can cause heart disease and various types of cancer. Drinking alcohol can impair muscle coordination and cause organ damage. Abusing other legal and illegal drugs can lead to a range of long-term health risks. Behavior that causes the spread of sexually transmitted infections is also an extreme health risk. When faced with decisions regarding risky substances or behaviors, carefully consider how your health might be affected.

Your health and fitness include deciding what makes a quality of life for you. You need to be aware of possible roadblocks that may lie ahead. Developing tactics that can aid your personal development will help you along the way. You need to be aware of certain high-risk behaviors that can have negative consequences. It is best to avoid these risks. Finally, building supportive relationships can have a positive effect on the quality of your life.

Critical Thinking

1. **Make inferences.** Give examples of defense mechanisms used by literary characters. What was the situation in which the defense mechanism was used? Why was that particular situation stressful to the character? How did the use of the defense mechanism affect the character's relationships with others?

2. **Analyze trends.** Interview an older adult and a young professional in the same occupation. Ask about the factors that cause stress in their jobs and how they manage that stress. Compare the older adult's entrance to the career field to the young professional's experience. Has the occupation become more or less stressful? Share your findings with the class.

3. **Analyze risks.** The health risks associated with tobacco, alcohol and other drugs, and sexually transmitted infections are widely known. However, people still take these risks. How do you think people could be encouraged to show more consideration for their health regarding these risks?

4. **Make predictions.** List some quality of life factors that are important to you right now. Create another list of quality of life factors that will be important to you in ten years.

5. **Analyze behavior.** Choose a song, story, book, or movie that illustrates a supportive relationship. Write a paper describing the relationship and the role the relationship played in each person's development.

21st Century Applications

6. **Environmental literacy.** Research an environmental problem that affected the quality of life for a community. How were people affected? What was done to correct the environmental problem?

7. **Information literacy.** Research biofeedback on the Internet. You may want to investigate the website of the Association for Applied Psychophysiology and Biofeedback. Write a brief summary of your findings.

8. **Health literacy.** Many roadblocks are also considered crises and cause stress to individuals and family members. Using the National Institute of Mental Health website and other reliable resources, research the effects of stress on the body. Then create a graphic representation of the body and highlight areas of the body affected by stress. Also include possible sources of stress, management strategies or coping methods, and resources people can use for stress management.

9. **Communication and collaboration.** Work in teams to select one health risk and plan an ad campaign to reduce its appeal to teenagers. Design posters, bumper stickers, T-shirts, bulletin boards, or commercials using scanners, drawing software, color printers, or video cameras.

10. **Health literacy.** Research the ten most common sexually transmitted infections in the United States. Prepare a chart listing the STIs and symptoms and causes of each one.

Core Skills

11. **Science.** Visit the National Sleep Foundation website to obtain information for a brief oral report. Focus on the following topics: key changes in sleep needs and sleeping patterns associated with puberty, signs of sleep loss, and the consequences of sleep deprivation.

12. **Speaking, listening.** Select one type of defense mechanism mentioned in the chapter. Work with a partner to role-play a scenario that demonstrates a positive and negative use of each type of defense mechanism. Have peers identify which defense mechanism you have chosen.

13. **Writing.** Select one major family crisis that afflicts many families. Examples include unemployment, death of a loved one, addiction, abuse, and learning of a disorder or chronic illness. Using reliable sources of information, write an informative essay for how a teen within that family might cope with this crisis. Include sources of help specific to the crisis.

14. **Reading, writing.** Using reliable online sources, research the effects of bullying and cyberbullying on teens. How does bullying affect a person mentally, physically, and socially-emotionally? Use your research to write an essay describing effects of bullying and cyberbullying.

15. **Speaking.** Research a famous successful person who appeared to take great risks. Prepare a

presentation explaining the history of this person, risks he or she made, and the outcome of the risks.

16. **Research, writing.** Survey nonsmokers in your school to determine how they feel when they are forced to inhale cigarette smoke produced by smokers.

17. **Reading.** Research the average life expectancy for males and females in three countries of your choice. Of these countries, which country has the highest life expectancy? the lowest? What factors contribute to these life expectancies? Write a brief report comparing your findings for each country. Include a graph to organize the life expectancy data.

Leadership
Development

Sponsor a community health fair as a Community Service project. Make plans for speakers and displays to educate community members about the resources that are available locally.

Portfolio
Builder

Each job has a certain level of stress. Interview someone who has a career you would like to have someday. Prepare questions prior to the interview to find out about the role stress plays on the job and how this person deals with it. Take accurate notes. If possible, and with the person's permission, record the interview. Write a summary of the interview, including a section with what you learned and your personal thoughts about how you would deal with stress in this career. Add the document to your portfolio.

Journal
Writing

After a summer where you had a job working on computers all day, you decide to try out for an athletic team. The coach welcomes you but restricts you to short, simple workouts and limited practice. You know you will not make the beginning lineup at this level. You mention this to the coach, state that you are disappointed, and hint that you might drop out if things don't change.

Write About It: *Why would the coach limit the activity of a player who has been fairly inactive all summer? How can you use the situation to still become the best player you can be? How can you use this outcome to help with future goals?*

Chapter 13
Nutrition

Reading Prep

- Have your family's eating habits changed in the last few years? If so, describe how.
- Create a list of foods that you know are good sources of a specific nutrient. For example, milk is a good source of calcium. As you read the chapter, check the accuracy of your list.

Concept Organizer

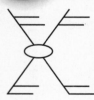

Use a spider map to organize the different types of fat-soluble vitamins and their sources.

G-WLEARNING.COM

Click on the activity icon to visit www.g-wlearning.com/comprehensive/8062 to access online vocabulary activities using key terms from the chapter.

Nutrients at Work for You

Objectives

After studying this section, you will be able to

- **explain** the importance of choosing nutritious foods.

- **identify** good food sources of various nutrients and describe how your body uses them.

Key Terms ↗

nutrient	fats	vitamin
nutrition	saturated fats	fortified
carbohydrate	unsaturated fats	enriched
protein	cholesterol	Dietary Reference
amino acid	mineral	Intakes (DRIs)

Pizza, milk, apples, and popcorn—these foods, and all the other foods you eat, provide nutrients for your body. **Nutrients** are chemical substances from food, which the body uses to function properly. After your body digests food, your bloodstream absorbs nutrients from the digestive tract and carries them to body cells. In the cells, nutrients help maintain and regulate body processes and promote growth.

Nutrition is the science of how nutrients support the body. The nutrients that keep your body working properly are divided into six major classes:

- carbohydrates
- proteins
- fats
- minerals
- vitamins
- water

Each of the nutrients performs special functions in the body. You get different nutrients from different foods. Therefore, you need to eat a variety of foods to get all the nutrients you need. By knowing the functions and sources of the nutrients, you will be able to make nutritious food choices.

Serving Your Community

Plan a schoolwide activity for collecting foods for a local food pantry. Before conducting the drive, research the concept of nutrient density and develop a list of nonperishable foods that are nutrient dense. Focus your drive on these types of foods.

Carbohydrates

Carbohydrates are the major sources of energy in your diet. There are three kinds of carbohydrates: sugars, starches, and fiber. Your body can change both sugars and starches into energy.

Sugars are *simple carbohydrates*, **13-1**. Your body can use some sugars right away for energy. Other sugars must first be broken down into simpler sugars.

Starches are often called *complex carbohydrates*. Before your body can use starches for energy, it must convert the starches into simple sugars during digestion. Nutrition experts recommend most people get more than half of all their daily calories from complex carbohydrates. (People who are diabetic must monitor their carbohydrate intake and follow a prescribed diet.)

Like starch, fiber is a complex carbohydrate. Although your body cannot digest fiber, you need fiber in your diet. This is because fiber provides roughage that stimulates the normal activity of your intestines. Fiber moves food through your body and helps your body get rid of solid wastes.

When you eat more carbohydrates than your body can use, some of them are changed to glycogen. Glycogen is stored in your body for times when you need quick energy, such as when you run to catch a bus. Your body maintains only a small amount of glycogen. Excess carbohydrates that are not stored as glycogen are changed to fat for storage in the body.

13-1

Milk and cookies are both sources of simple carbohydrates.

Proteins

Proteins are a nutrient found in every cell in your body. They are needed for growth, maintenance, and repair of body tissues. Proteins are made up of **amino acids**, which are building blocks for your cells.

Not all protein sources are the same. There are two classes of proteins—complete proteins and incomplete proteins. *Complete proteins* supply all the amino acids your body needs. Foods that come from animals are sources of complete proteins. *Incomplete protein* sources contain some, but not all, of the amino acids your body needs. Few plant sources provide complete proteins.

People whose diets are low in protein experience poor muscle tone, lack of energy, and reduced resistance to disease. Severe protein shortages may result in a disease called *kwashiorkor*. Protein consumed beyond the body's needs is stored in the body as fat.

Fats

Fats are concentrated sources of food energy. They provide slightly more than twice as much energy per unit of weight as carbohydrates and proteins. Fats supply essential fatty acids, which are needed for normal growth.

Fats are divided into two classes. **Saturated fats** are solid at room temperature and are often referred to as *solid fats*. **Unsaturated fats** are usually liquid at room temperature and often referred to as *oils*. Foods from animal sources tend to be higher in saturated fats. Foods from plant sources tend to be higher in unsaturated fats, **13-2**.

Sometimes manufacturers process unsaturated fats to make them solid. This process is called *hydrogenation* and the solid fat that is created is called *trans fat*. Although some are naturally present in food, most trans fats in the diet are man-made. Man-made trans fats are often found in foods such as solid vegetable shortening, microwave popcorn, and frozen pizza.

Cholesterol is a fatty substance found in every body cell. The body uses cholesterol to make a number of important materials, including sex hormones and vitamin D. Your body manufactures all the cholesterol you need. However, you also get cholesterol from your diet when you consume foods from animal sources.

Saturated fats, trans fats, and dietary cholesterol tend to raise blood cholesterol levels. Excessive cholesterol in the blood can form deposits on the inside of blood vessels. This causes the flow of blood to be restricted or blocked completely. A heart attack can result. Therefore, health experts advise people to limit their intake of saturated fats and cholesterol, and avoid man-made trans fats.

When the diet is deficient in fat during infancy and childhood, growth can be stunted. A diet too low in fat can cause skin problems and the

13-2

Sources of unsaturated fats include avocados, fish, and many nuts and seeds.

poor utilization of some vitamins. Of the fats needed in the diet, fish, nuts, and seeds are good sources. However, excessive amounts of any fat can cause weight problems. People who eat such amounts tend to eat less of other needed foods. This should be avoided because a well-balanced diet is important for good health.

Minerals

Minerals are inorganic substances needed for building tissues and regulating body functions. They are an essential part of bones, teeth, and red blood cells. Minerals also aid in the proper functioning of muscles and nerves and in the clotting of blood. Like proteins, minerals are needed for growth and repair of body tissues. Unlike the nutrients already discussed, minerals do not provide the body with energy. They do not need to be broken down by digestion for the body's use. Your body can absorb minerals directly from the foods you have eaten.

Calcium and Phosphorus

Calcium and *phosphorus* are the most abundant minerals in the body. Reserves are stored in the bones. Calcium and phosphorus are also found in teeth, soft tissues, and body fluids.

If a person's diet is low in calcium, his or her bones will serve as a reserve to fill immediate calcium needs. However, a low calcium intake over a long period could lead to osteoporosis. This is a disease characterized by weak, brittle bones, which are more likely to fracture. As osteoporosis progresses, bones become too weak to support the body's weight. They are unable to withstand force from routine chores like lifting and bending. See **13-3**.

Fluoride

Fluoride is needed for the proper development of bones and teeth. When added to the diets of children, it helps reduce tooth decay. Fluoride is not readily available in foods. Therefore, many cities add fluoride to the supply of drinking water.

Iodine

Iodine is present in very small amounts in the body, but it is essential for good health. Iodine is used to make thyroxine. *Thyroxine* is a hormone produced by the thyroid gland, which is located at the base of the neck. Thyroxine controls the rate at which the body uses nutrients. When the diet is low in iodine, the thyroid gland enlarges. This condition is called a *goiter*.

13-3

Osteoporosis weakens bones and can cause an increased risk of fractures and curving of the spine.

50 Years
60 Years
70 Years

Calcium: A Summary of Current Research for the Health Professional

Iron

Iron is another essential mineral. Iron combines with protein to make *hemoglobin*. Hemoglobin is a substance in the blood that carries oxygen from the lungs to cells throughout the body.

Women generally require more iron than men. To meet their needs, some women may need to take iron supplements prescribed by a doctor. A diet that is constantly low in iron results in a condition known as *iron-deficiency anemia*. Symptoms of this condition include extreme fatigue, pale skin, and poor appetite.

Sodium

Sodium works with other minerals to help maintain the balance of fluids in the body. It also plays a role in transmitting nerve impulses to the brain. Few people get too little sodium in their diets. In fact, many people get too much. Diets high in sodium are linked with high blood pressure.

Zinc

Zinc is important for normal growth and development. It helps the immune system work properly. Zinc also helps wounds heal. Too little zinc in children's diets can stunt their growth. An excess of zinc can be toxic.

Other Minerals

The body needs a number of other minerals to maintain good health. These include copper, potassium, chloride, magnesium, and selenium. Each of these minerals performs specific functions. Eating a variety of foods is the best way to make sure you get all the minerals you need.

Vitamins

Vitamins are organic substances needed in small amounts for normal growth and the maintenance of good health. Vitamins are regulators of body processes. Like minerals, they do not directly supply energy. Vitamins are necessary to enable the other nutrients to do their work. Most vitamin needs can be met by eating a variety of foods.

Fat-Soluble Vitamins

Vitamins can be divided into two groups. One group is *fat-soluble vitamins*. These are vitamins that can be stored in your body in fatty tissues and in the liver. The fat-soluble vitamins are A, D, E, and K.

Vitamin A

A deficiency of vitamin A can cause night blindness and drying of the eyes and skin. *Night blindness* occurs when the eyes cannot adjust from bright to dim light.

Wellness Awareness

Find out how much a woman's need for iron increases during pregnancy. How can she meet this greater need? Why do these needs increase during pregnancy?

Mental Health Awareness

Superfoods Myth

Many food trends today concern "superfoods," or foods rich in certain nutrients. Some superfoods are claimed to improve mental health, alertness, and mood. It's more accurate to say, however, that healthful foods of all types improve health, including brain function. A healthy brain, in turn, promotes a healthy mind.

Science Connection

An Increasing Need for Vitamin D

Recent research indicates that many children, teens, and adults are deficient in vitamin D. Extreme shortages of this vitamin may result in conditions called rickets in children and osteomalacia in older adults, both of which involve softening and weakening of the bones. The best way to find out if you are vitamin D deficient is to see your doctor. Treatment may include consuming dairy products and foods rich in vitamin D, taking supplements, and getting adequate sun exposure. (Note: Because sun exposure is linked to skin cancer, consult your doctor about the best way to make sure you get enough vitamin D.)

An excess of vitamin A from food is not common. However, an excessive intake of vitamin pills containing vitamin A can be dangerous. People who get too much vitamin A over a long period may experience fatigue, headaches, and vomiting.

Vitamin D

Vitamin D is often called the "sunshine vitamin." This is because your body can manufacture vitamin D when your skin is exposed to sunlight. However, foods such as eggs and fortified milk are more reliable sources. (**Fortified** means nutrients have been added to a food to improve its nutritional value.)

Vitamin D that is not used is stored in the body. Excessive amounts of vitamin D may cause diarrhea, nausea, and headaches.

Vitamin E

The main function of vitamin E in the human body is to act as an *antioxidant*. This is a substance that protects compounds from the damaging effects of oxygen. Vitamin E protects blood cells and cells in the lungs from oxygen damage. It also protects vitamin A and fats in the body.

Vitamin E is so widely distributed in foods that developing a deficiency is rare. Because excess vitamin E is stored in the body, large doses from supplements may be harmful.

Vitamin K

A vitamin K deficiency is rare because vitamin K is widely available in most diets. If a severe deficiency occurs, however, it could cause bleeding. Although a vitamin K excess is also rare, it can be toxic. Bacteria in the human digestive tract make about half of the body's needed vitamin K. The remaining need must be met by food sources.

Water-Soluble Vitamins

The B vitamins and vitamin C make up the second group of vitamins—the *water-soluble vitamins*. Excess amounts of water-soluble vitamins are excreted in the urine rather than stored in the body. Therefore, you need to eat good sources of these vitamins every day.

Because these vitamins dissolve in water, it is best to cook most foods quickly in as little water as possible. After cooking, do not throw away cooking liquid. Instead, save it for use in a sauce or soup.

B Vitamins

The B vitamins are a group of similar vitamins, but each plays its own role in helping the body function properly. *Thiamin*, *riboflavin*, and *niacin* may be the most well-known B vitamins. They help you obtain energy from the foods you eat. *Folic acid* and *vitamin B₁₂* are also members of this vitamin group. See **13-4**.

Good sources of thiamin include whole-grain and enriched grain products. (**Enriched** means nutrients that were lost during processing have been added back to a product.) A deficiency of thiamin can result in nausea, depression, loss of appetite, and fatigue. A severe deficiency can lead to a disease called *beriberi*. This disease causes numbness in the ankles and legs and leads to paralysis and heart failure.

13-4
Breads made with enriched or whole-grain flour are good sources of the B-vitamins thiamin, riboflavin, niacin, and folic acid.

Riboflavin and niacin play an important role in the health of your skin and digestive system. A deficiency of riboflavin can cause cracked lips, a skin rash, and extremely sensitive eyes. A deficiency of niacin can cause *pellagra*, which affects the skin and digestive system.

The body uses folic acid to make all new cells. All women of childbearing age are urged to be sure they are meeting their folic acid needs. The spine and brain of a baby growing in its mother's womb may not develop properly if the mother's diet lacks folic acid.

Vitamin B₁₂ naturally occurs only in foods of animal origin. People who do not eat these foods may obtain the vitamin from supplements or fortified soy milk. A vitamin B₁₂ deficiency can result in anemia and nerve damage.

Vitamin C

To prevent a deficiency of vitamin C, be sure to eat at least one serving of a food high in this vitamin each day. A lack of vitamin C over time may result in bleeding gums, loose teeth, bruising, and sore joints. A severe deficiency of vitamin C can lead to a disease called *scurvy*.

Water

Perhaps you do not think of water as a nutrient, but it is one of the most important nutrients. Over half the body's weight is water. A general recommendation is to drink nine to twelve cups of water each day, although most people can let thirst determine their intake. You get additional water from the foods you eat. Water is also a product of chemical reactions that take place in your body.

Living Green

Drinking bottled water may be convenient, but it takes a lot of resources to produce. Many empty plastic bottles end up in the trash. Save money and help the environment by filling up your own reusable drinking bottle instead.

Healthy Living

What Do the DRIs Tell You?

The estimated average requirement (EAR) is a level of nutrient estimated to meet the requirements of half the healthy population. RDAs are based on EARs. Adequate intake (AI) levels are set for the nutrients for which no RDA has yet been determined. The tolerable upper intake level (UL) is the highest amount of a nutrient a person can consume daily without health risks. All of these DRI values are based on consumption by a healthy person.

You can get the water your body needs from drinking other beverages in addition to water. However, limit your intake of soft drinks and fruit punches. These beverages are high in added sugars. Sugars promote tooth decay and may be a source of excess calories in the diet.

You should also avoid drinking large amounts of caffeinated beverages, such as coffee, tea, and cola. Excessive intake of caffeine has been linked to such symptoms as anxiety, restlessness, and headaches. Read labels and choose caffeine-free beverages.

Figure 13-5 provides a summary of the basic functions and important sources of nutrients discussed in this text. Review this chart to help make sure your diet includes the variety of foods you need for good health.

13-5

All the nutrients work together to build, maintain, and repair the body and provide it with strength and energy.

Nutrient	Function	Sources
Carbohydrates	Supply energy. Help the body digest fats efficiently. Spare proteins so they can be used for growth and maintenance. Provide bulk in the form of cellulose (needed for digestion).	Sugar: Honey, jam, jelly, sugar, molasses Starch: Breads, cereals, corn, peas, beans, potatoes, pasta Fiber: Fresh fruits and vegetables, whole-grain breads and cereals
Proteins	Promote tissue growth and repair. Help make antibodies, enzymes, hormones, and some vitamins. Regulate many body processes. Regulate fluid balance in cells. Supply energy when needed. Helps wounds heal.	Complete proteins: Meat, poultry, fish, eggs, milk and other dairy products Incomplete proteins: Cereals, grains, nuts, dried beans and peas
Fats	Supply energy (most concentrated energy in food). Carry fat-soluble vitamins. Insulate the body from shock and temperature changes. Protect vital organs. Add flavor to foods. Serve as a source of essential fatty acids.	Butter, margarine, cream, whole milk, cheese, marbling in meat, bacon, egg yolks, nuts, chocolate, olives, salad oils and dressings

(continued)

Nutrient	Function	Sources
Minerals Calcium	Helps build bones and teeth. Helps blood clot. Helps muscles and nerves to work. Helps regulate the use of other minerals in the body.	Milk, cheese, other dairy products, leafy green vegetables, fish eaten with the bones
Fluoride	Helps in proper development of bones and teeth. Helps reduce tooth decay.	Fluoridated drinking water
Iodine	Enables normal functioning of the thyroid gland.	Iodized table salt, saltwater fish and shellfish
Iron	Combines with protein to make hemoglobin. Helps cells use oxygen.	Liver, lean meats, egg yolk, dried beans and peas, leafy green vegetables, dried fruits, enriched and whole-grain breads and cereals
Phosphorus	Helps build strong bones and teeth. Helps regulate many internal bodily activities.	Protein and calcium food sources
Sodium	Helps maintain the balance of body fluids. Helps transmit nerve impulses.	Table salt, processed foods
Zinc	Promotes normal growth and development. Helps the immune system work properly. Helps wounds heal.	Meat, fish, poultry, whole grains
Vitamins Vitamin A	Helps keep skin clear and smooth and mucous membranes healthy. Helps prevent night blindness. Helps promote growth.	Liver, egg yolk, dark green and yellow fruits and vegetables, butter, whole milk, cream, fortified margarine, ricotta cheese, Cheddar-type cheese
Vitamin D	Helps build strong bones and teeth in children. Helps maintain bones in adults.	Fortified milk and margarine, butter, fish liver oils, liver, sardines, tuna, egg yolk, the sun
Vitamin E	Acts as an antioxidant.	Liver and other variety meats, eggs, leafy green vegetables, whole-grain cereals, salad oils, shortenings and other fats and oils
Vitamin K	Helps blood clot.	Organ meats, leafy green vegetables, other vegetables, egg yolk

(continued)

Nutrient	Function	Sources
Thiamin	Helps promote normal appetite and digestion. Forms parts of the coenzymes needed for the breakdown of carbohydrates. Helps keep nervous system healthy and prevents irritability. Helps body release energy from food.	Pork, other meats, poultry, fish, eggs, enriched or whole-grain breads and cereals, dried beans, brewer's yeast
Riboflavin	Helps cells use oxygen. Helps keep skin, tongue, and lips normal. Helps prevent scaly, greasy areas around the mouth and nose. Forms part of the coenzymes needed for the breakdown of carbohydrates.	Milk, all kinds of cheese, yogurt, liver, other meats, fish, poultry, eggs, dark green leafy vegetables
Niacin	Helps keep nervous system healthy. Helps keep skin, mouth, tongue, and digestive tract healthy. Helps cells use other nutrients.	Meat, fish, poultry, milk, enriched or whole-grain breads and cereals, peanuts, peanut butter, dried beans and peas
Folic Acid	Helps the body make all new cells. Protects unborn babies from damage to the brain and spinal cord.	Fresh fruits and vegetables, enriched and whole-grain breads and cereals
Vitamin B$_{12}$	Helps the body make red blood cells. Protects nerves.	Meat, fish, poultry, eggs, dairy products, fortified soy milk
Vitamin C	Is needed for healthy gums and tissues. Helps heal wounds and broken bones. Helps body fight infection. Helps hold body cells together.	Citrus fruits, strawberries, cantaloupe, broccoli, green peppers, raw cabbage, tomatoes, green leafy vegetables, potatoes, sweet potatoes
Water	Is a basic part of blood and tissue fluid. Helps carry nutrients to cells. Helps carry waste products from cells. Helps control body temperature.	Water, beverages, soups, most foods

Dietary Reference Intakes

To help you determine your daily nutrient needs, the *Recommended Dietary Allowances (RDAs)* were established in 1941. The Food and Nutrition Board of the National Academy of Sciences issues the RDAs. From time to time, the RDAs are revised to reflect the latest nutrition findings.

The RDAs are one of the five references called **Dietary Reference Intakes (DRIs)**. The other four references in the DRIs are the *estimated average requirements (EARs), chronic disease risk reduction intake (CDRR),* *adequate intakes (AIs)*, and *tolerable upper intake levels (ULs)*. These four references are used by professionals to plan and assess diets.

The DRIs outline nutrient requirements for both sexes and for several age groups. Allowances include needs for energy, protein, and many vitamins and minerals. Another goal of the DRIs is to help reduce the risk of some diseases. Allowances given in the DRIs are designed to meet the needs of healthy people. The DRIs are not useful guides for people who have special dietary needs.

Reading
Review

1. What are the three kinds of carbohydrates?
2. What is the difference between a complete protein and an incomplete protein?
3. Which nutrient serves as a concentrated source of food energy?
4. Which type of vitamins cannot be stored in the body to a great extent and need to be consumed daily?
5. What are two main functions of water in the body?

Section 13-2

Making Daily Food Choices

Objectives

After studying this section, you will be able to

- **describe** how food choices are influenced by physical, emotional, social, and cultural factors.

- **identify** a well-balanced eating plan based on the MyPlate food guidance system.

- **list** the foods to increase in the healthy eating plan, as recommended by the *Dietary Guidelines for Americans.*

Key Terms

MyPlate	***Dietary Guidelines***	**nutrient dense**
refined grain	***for Americans***	

13-6

The MyPlate symbol illustrates five main food groups that are the foundation of a nourishing diet.

Eating right requires more than knowing the names of the nutrients. You also need to know how to choose a variety of foods that will supply those nutrients.

Influences on Food Choices

Food choices vary because of the different influences that affect individual food preferences. Some of these influences are physical, emotional, social, or cultural factors.

Physical factors include a person's age, level of activity, and state of health. Someone with diabetes must choose foods more carefully than someone who does not have diabetes. An athlete can eat many foods without gaining weight, but a less-active person will likely gain weight. Wise people choose foods that are best for their physical health.

Emotional needs may influence food choices. For instance, some people may eat more when they are happy or sad. Others may have no appetite when they are excited or upset.

Social influences impact food choices because people tend to eat the foods others around them are eating. You may avoid high-fat foods at lunch if your friends are weight-conscious. On the other hand, you may overeat at a party where everyone is eating appetizers and snacks all night.

Cultural factors will also affect the foods you eat. For example, a Jewish family might eat traditional potato latkes, but avoid eating shrimp because of dietary law. A family living close to the coast might eat lobster regularly because it is affordable. A family in the Midwest might order lobster only on special occasions because of the expense.

Every person makes personal food choices. Think of the influences that help direct your choices. Every food has the potential to make a dietary contribution. Be sure you choose foods that will keep you healthy.

MyPlate

An easy way to plan a nutritious diet is to choose foods using the MyPlate food guidance system developed by the U.S. Department of Agriculture. **MyPlate** permits a personalized approach to healthful eating, **13-6**. It groups foods based on their similarity in nutrient content. The food groups are fruits, grains, vegetables, protein, and dairy. Oils are not a food group, but are essential for good health.

The MyPlate symbol is a simple visual reminder of how consumers

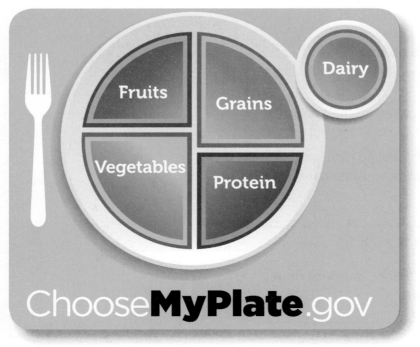

can prepare a healthy plate at mealtime. The plate in the MyPlate visual contains four food groups. A circle next to the plate represents the fifth group, dairy. One of the primary messages of MyPlate is to make half your plate fruits and vegetables.

The MyPlate food guidance system emphasizes eating a variety of foods from each of the food groups.

Fruits

Fruits may be fresh, canned, frozen, dried, or 100% fruit juice. Whole or cut-up fruits are excellent sources of fiber and should be chosen more often than juice, which lacks fiber. The richest sources of vitamin C are citrus fruits, such as oranges and grapefruit. Cantaloupe, strawberries, and kiwifruit are also good sources of vitamin C. Bananas are a good source of potassium. See **13-7**.

Vegetables

The vegetable group includes all forms of vegetables: raw, cooked, canned, frozen, dried, and juices. Fresh vegetables provide good amounts of nutrients and fiber, but cooking causes the loss of some nutrients. MyPlate recommends selecting vegetables daily from these five subgroups:

- *dark green vegetables* such as spinach and broccoli
- *red and orange vegetables* such as carrots, red peppers, and sweet potatoes
- *beans and peas* such as kidney and soy beans and lentils
- *starchy vegetables* such as potatoes, peas, and corn
- *other vegetables* such as cucumber, zucchini, and celery

Many Americans need to significantly increase the quantity and variety of vegetables they consume daily and weekly.

Grains

The grains group includes food made from wheat, rice, oats, cornmeal, barley, or other cereal grains. Common food sources include bread, cereal, and pasta. This food group provides carbohydrates for energy. Products from whole or refined grain are important sources of thiamin, niacin, folic acid, and iron. **Refined grain** has parts of the kernel removed during the milling process. Whole-grain foods are also high in fiber. When choosing grains, MyPlate advises selecting whole-grain foods for at least half of your grains intake.

Protein

This group includes meat, poultry, fish, and eggs, as well as nuts, seeds, and beans and peas. Beans and peas are also found in the vegetable group. The vegetable sources of protein are called *meat alternates*.

Cross-cultural skills.
Manny appreciates the cultural diversity in his workplace. He is a member of the diversity committee and helps plan an annual potluck lunch. Employees are encouraged to bring in a dish reflecting their cultural heritage.

13-7

Choose whole fruit more often than fruit juice. When you choose a fruit juice, make sure it is 100% juice, not a juice drink with added sweeteners.

When choosing meats and poultry, MyPlate recommends selecting lean or low-fat cuts to avoid saturated fats and cholesterol. An increased intake of seafood is also recommended—at least 8 ounces of cooked seafood per week.

Dairy Foods

Milk, yogurt, and cheese are the primary foods in this group, but it also includes calcium-fortified soymilk. Calcium-fortified foods and beverages provide calcium, but may lack other nutrients supplied by dairy foods.

Dairy foods are high in protein and calcium for bone health and also provide vitamin D, riboflavin, phosphorus, and many other nutrients. Dairy foods are also high in fat, so choose fat-free and low-fat varieties whenever possible.

MyPlate Plan for a Healthy Eating Style

The MyPlate website, ChooseMyPlate.gov, provides tools and resources to help people build a healthy eating style throughout life. One of these tools, "MyPlate Plan," uses data on a person's age, sex, height, weight, and activity level to identify a personalized healthy eating plan. Many teens require an eating plan based on 2,200 calories daily, **13-8**. Notice that total daily amounts of food needed from each food group are listed, along with limits for sodium, saturated fat, and added sugars. This information makes it easier to choose healthy foods from each food group to serve at each meal.

The *Dietary Guidelines for Americans*

The basis of MyPlate's advice on nutrition and good health is the **Dietary Guidelines for Americans**. These recommendations from the U.S. Department of Agriculture and Health and Human Services are for individuals two years and older to help promote health through improved nutrition and physical activity. Evidence-based research shapes these guidelines, which are updated every five years.

The *2015–2020 Dietary Guidelines* emphasize several key factors that most people need to follow to improve their eating patterns, **13-9**. Part of developing healthy eating patterns is choosing foods and beverages that are *nutrient dense*. **Nutrient dense** foods and beverages supply vitamins, minerals, and other nutrients that provide positive health with little or no solid fats and added sugars, refined starches, and sodium.

United States Department of Agriculture

MyPlate Plan
ChooseMyPlate.gov
Find your Healthy Eating Style

Everything you eat and drink matters. Find your healthy eating style that reflects your preferences, culture, traditions, and budget—and maintain it for a lifetime! The right mix can help you be healthier now and into the future. The key is choosing a variety of foods and beverages from each food group—*and making sure that each choice is limited in saturated fat, sodium, and added sugars*. Start with small changes—**"MyWins"**—to make healthier choices you can enjoy.

Food Group Amounts for 2,200 Calories a Day

Fruits	Vegetables	Grains	Protein	Dairy
2 cups	3 cups	7 ounces	6 ounces	3 cups
Focus on whole fruits	**Vary your veggies**	**Make half your grains whole grains**	**Vary your protein routine**	**Move to low-fat or fat-free milk or yogurt**
Focus on whole fruits that are fresh, frozen, canned, or dried.	Choose a variety of colorful fresh, frozen, and canned vegetables—make sure to include dark green, red, and orange choices.	Find whole-grain foods by reading the Nutrition Facts label and ingredients list.	Mix up your protein foods to include seafood, beans and peas, unsalted nuts and seeds, soy products, eggs, and lean meats and poultry.	Choose fat-free milk, yogurt, and soy beverages (soy milk) to cut back on your saturated fat.

Limit — **Drink and eat less sodium, saturated fat, and added sugars. Limit:**
- Sodium to **2,300 milligrams** a day.
- Saturated fat to **24 grams** a day.
- Added sugars to **55 grams** a day.

Be active your way: Children 6 to 17 years old should move **60 minutes** every day. Adults should be physically active at least **2 1/2 hours** per week.

In addition to a healthy eating pattern, regular physical activity helps promote health and a healthy body weight. It also builds and maintains strong bones and muscles and reduces the risk of chronic disease. The *Guidelines* encourage everyone to meet the latest *Physical Activity Guidelines for Americans*. These identify the amounts and types of physical activity recommended for individuals at different life stages to achieve health benefits.

To maintain body weight in a healthy range, balance the calories eaten with the calories expended. When people are overweight or underweight, they are more likely to develop health problems. Overweight is linked to high blood pressure, heart disease, stroke, certain cancers, and other illnesses. People who are underweight have little to lose in the event of a wasting illness.

13-8

This MyPlate Plan is suitable for a person needing 2,200 calories daily.

Dietary Guidelines for Americans

1. **Follow a healthy eating pattern across the lifespan.** Choose a healthy eating pattern at an appropriate calorie level to help achieve and maintain a healthy body weight, obtain adequate nutrients, and reduce risk for chronic disease.
2. **Focus on variety, nutrient density, and amount.** Choose a variety of nutrient-dense foods from all food groups in recommended amounts to meet nutrient needs within calorie limits.
3. **Limit calories from added sugars and saturated fats and reduce sodium intake.** Cut back on foods and beverages higher in these components to amounts that fit a healthy eating pattern.
4. **Shift to healthier food and beverage choices.** Choose nutrient-dense foods and beverages from all food groups, considering cultural and personal preferences.
5. **Support healthy eating patterns for all.** Help to create and support healthy eating patterns from home to school to work and to communities.

13-9

The *Dietary Guidelines for Americans* encourage habits that promote good health.

Analyze and Solve

Work with your family to analyze your eating habits and identify one that needs improvement. Examples include too many high-fat meals, frequent eating on the run, lack of planning for food intake, or frequent snacking. Make use of your knowledge about nutrition and eating habits to help family members brainstorm possible solutions and make a plan to carry out the changes.

No single food can supply all the nutrients in the amounts you need. For example, milk supplies calcium but little iron. Meat supplies protein but little calcium. To have a nutritious diet, you must eat a variety of foods. This is the best way to get the range of nutrients you need.

Grains are rich in complex carbohydrates—your body's best source of energy. Whole-grain foods, such as oatmeal and whole-wheat bread, supply fiber to help your digestive system work properly.

Fruits and vegetables also supply fiber as well as vitamins, minerals, and complex carbohydrates. A diet high in produce is generally low in fat.

To find nutrient-dense foods and beverages, look for those without added sugar. Many foods that are high in sugar have low nutritional value. Such foods include soft drinks, cookies, ice cream, and candy. Limiting these foods may help you avoid unwanted pounds and cut down on tooth decay. Watch for ingredient labels that list brown sugar, honey, corn syrup, molasses, sucrose, dextrose, glucose, and fructose. These are all forms of sugar.

To find nutrient-dense foods and beverages, also look for those without solid fats. Diets high in saturated fat increase the risk for heart disease. High-fat diets are also linked to obesity and certain types of cancer. Many protein and dairy foods contain high amounts of saturated fats that should be avoided. Solid fats are not necesssary for good health and are considered *empty calories*, or calories with few or no nutrients.

The body needs certain oils that come from vegetables and some fish, but only in small quantities. Common sources of the healthy oils are nuts, olives, avocado, cooking oils, margarine, and certain salad dressings. You need to be aware of all sources of fats to determine which contribute to a healthful diet.

Following these guidelines cannot guarantee people they will never get sick. However, eating and activity habits do have an effect on health. Forming good habits can keep healthy people feeling well.

Reading
Review

1. List the five main food groups in MyPlate.
2. What determines which foods belong in each of MyPlate's food groups?
3. What are the *Dietary Guidelines for Americans*?

Section 13-3

Nutrition Across the Lifespan

Objectives

After studying this section, you will be able to

- **identify** dietary needs of people in different stages of life.
- **describe** special nutrient needs of athletes.
- **explain** how some diseases can be related to diet.

Key Terms 📲

vegetarian diet	**food allergies**	**lactose intolerance**
dehydration	**food intolerance**	

All people need the same nutrients. However, the amounts needed vary from person to person. For instance, women need more iron than men. Someone who has a large body build needs more food than someone who has a small build. People who perform hard physical work need more nutrients than those who lead less-active lives, **13-10**. A person who has a disease or is recovering from illness needs more nutrients than one who is in good health.

Nutritional needs vary with age as well as with gender, body size, activity level, and health. Needs change across the lifespan. Meal managers need to know how to meet the needs of people at different ages.

13-10

People who do work that is physically demanding need more calories to fuel their high level of activity.

Needs of Pregnant Women and Infants

Nutritional needs begin before birth. Pregnant women must eat foods that will supply nutrients for their babies as well as for themselves. Once babies are born, they have significant nutrient needs that support their rapid growth.

Nutrition Before Birth

An unborn child has no way to get nutrients except through the mother's diet. Thus, the mother's body needs to be well nourished prior to and during pregnancy. Pregnant teenagers have more difficulty meeting the needs of their developing babies than pregnant adults. This is because teenagers must fulfill their own nutrient needs for growth as well as the needs of the growing baby.

Women who have good eating habits will not need to make drastic dietary changes before or during pregnancy. Consuming two to three daily servings from the dairy group will provide the calcium needed during pregnancy. Two added servings from the grains group will help meet increased calorie needs. An extra serving from both the fruit and vegetable groups will provide needed vitamins, minerals, and fiber. Doctors may also prescribe prenatal supplements to help meet increased needs for folic acid and iron during pregnancy.

Nutrition in Infancy

Every part of a child's body grows and develops most rapidly during the first year of life. Good nutrition is most important during this year to build a strong foundation for a healthy lifetime.

Breast milk or formula is a baby's first food. Breast milk is perfectly designed to meet most of a baby's nutrient needs. Formula also provides needed nutrients, but health professionals agree that breast milk is the best choice for infant nutrition. To protect her health while breast-feeding, a mother needs to maintain a healthy eating plan. See **13-11**.

Babies need vitamin C early in life. Breast milk and formula contain adequate vitamin C. The *American Academy of Pediatrics (AAP)* suggests delaying the introduction of fruit juice until babies are about 12 months of age. Juice should be served in a cup (not a bottle) and no more than four ounces per day. Doctors may also recommend vitamin supplements for babies.

According to the AAP, it is best to wait until a baby is about six months of age to introduce solid foods unless otherwise directed by the doctor. Cereals are generally introduced first. Other foods, such as fruits and vegetables, are then introduced gradually. Babies can soon begin eating a variety of foods from all the food groups.

13-11

By eating well, a nursing mother gets the extra nutrients her body needs to make milk for her baby.

Tomsickova Tatyana/Shutterstock.com

As children grow teeth and learn to control chewing and swallowing, table foods can replace strained baby foods. Foods should be cut into small pieces and offered in small servings. As energy needs increase, larger servings can be offered.

Needs of Children and Teens

As children grow, their nutritional needs continue to change. Their food preferences also change. Caregivers must help children sample and select a variety of foods from each of the food groups.

Nutrition During the Preschool Years

Adults and children need the same nutrients. However, preschool children need larger proportions of nutrients to support their rapid growth. Caregivers need to make a special effort to include vitamins A and C in the diets of preschoolers. Raw fruits and vegetables, which are good sources of these vitamins, can be offered as snacks.

Most preschoolers cannot eat enough at mealtimes to meet all their nutrient needs. Thus, snacks are needed to supplement nutrients provided by meals. In addition to fruits and vegetables, nutritious snacks include cheese cubes, cereals, and crackers spread with peanut butter.

Adults play a key role in teaching preschoolers good eating habits. Children are great imitators. If an adult refuses a certain food, a preschool child is likely to refuse it, too. Adults can encourage good nutrition by offering children a variety of nutritious food choices. Adults also need to set an example by eating nourishing foods with their children.

Nutrition During the Early School Years

Starting school changes a child's daily routine and eating schedule. A nutritious, energy-packed breakfast is needed to help children stay alert in class.

While at school, children are exposed to the eating habits of others. They may refuse a food simply because their peers do not eat it. Children may sometimes need to be encouraged to eat well-balanced lunches at school. They need the energy and nutrients provided by fruits, vegetables, grains, protein, and dairy foods. See **13-12**.

Healthy Living

Carbonated Soft Drinks Versus Milk

Recent studies show that the majority of teens do not get enough calcium in their diets to promote strong bones and healthy teeth. Part of the reason for this problem is that teens tend to choose carbonated soft drinks over milk. These soft drinks do not contain calcium or other nutrients, but do contain phosphates that can actually leach calcium from bones and teeth. Some studies show that teens who drink carbonated soft drinks are more likely to have bone fractures, dental problems, and problems with obesity. Choosing milk not only strengthens bones and teeth, but also promotes good health.

Monkey Business Images/Shutterstock.com

13-12
Balanced meals provided by the school lunch program are designed to meet the nutrient and energy needs of young children.

Nutrition During the Teen Years

Like infancy, adolescence is a period of rapid growth. Teens are growing taller and gaining weight. Their bones are increasing in density. Their muscles are developing in size and strength. Proper development requires good nutrition.

Busy schedules, however, often cause teens to skip meals. Many teens also select snack foods that are high in fats and sugars and low in other nutrients. Therefore, nutrient needs do not always get met.

Meals and snacks for teens must provide the nutrients needed for growth and maintenance of strong, healthy bodies. Foods must also supply enough energy to meet a teen's high level of activity.

Special Needs of Vegetarians

During the teen years, many young people try new eating patterns. One type of pattern followed by a number of teens is a **vegetarian diet**. This diet largely or entirely provides foods from plant sources. People choose vegetarian diets for various reasons. These reasons include health, economy, religious beliefs, animal rights, and availability.

People who follow vegetarian diets are called *vegetarians*. The four groups of vegetarians are described by the types of animal foods they consume.

- *Vegans* consume no foods of animal origin.
- *Lacto vegetarians* include dairy products, but exclude meat, poultry, fish, and eggs.

- *Ovo vegetarians* include eggs, but do not eat meat, poultry, fish, and dairy products.
- *Lacto-ovo vegetarians* include eggs and dairy products, but omit meat, poultry, and fish.

The key to good nutrition is a variety of foods from many sources. Thus, total exclusion of animal food sources may lead to some deficiencies. Vegetarian diets can be healthful, but they require planning.

As you have read, animal foods serve as main sources of complete protein. By combining incomplete proteins, vegetarians can get all the amino acids they need. Vegetarians who consume eggs and/or dairy products can usually meet their needs for other nutrients, too. Those who omit dairy products from their diets may have difficulty getting enough calcium and vitamin D. Vegans may also have trouble meeting their needs for iron, zinc, and vitamin B_{12}. Some vegetarians may need fortified foods or supplements to meet all their nutrient needs. Refer again to Figure 13-5. It will help you review some rich sources of protein, calcium, iron, zinc, vitamin B_{12}, and vitamin D.

Sports Nutrition

Many people take part in athletic activities and need to know how more physical activity affects nutritional needs. In most cases, athletes do not need dietary supplements. Eating a nutritious diet each day is the best way to meet nutrient needs. Athletes need to follow the *Dietary Guidelines*, but pay special attention to four particular needs, **13-13**.

Increase Daily Calorie Intake

Athletes need extra calories to fuel high levels of activity. For optimum performance, 60 to 65 percent of calories should come from carbohydrates, including breads, cereals, and pasta. Protein should supply 10 to 35 percent of calories. Between 20 to 25 percent of total calories should come from unsaturated fats, with saturated fats no more than 10 percent of total calories.

Eating a small meal three to four hours before a workout or competition will provide needed energy. This meal should be high in carbohydrates, which are stored in the body as glycogen. Excess fats and proteins are stored as body fat. During activity, the body releases energy from glycogen at first, then from body fat.

Drink Plenty of Fluids

Drinking fluids during activity helps prevent **dehydration**, or an abnormal loss of body fluids. Athletes lose a lot of water through sweating and need to drink enough to replace those losses. Thirst does not always indicate fluid needs. Fluid intake should begin two hours before exercise and continue at fifteen-minute intervals throughout exercise. Liquids should also be consumed after exercising.

Wellness Awareness

Interview school sports coaches about what they tell athletes regarding their diets. For instance, interview a wrestling coach about the use of weight supplements and weight loss for wrestlers.

Water is a good fluid choice for athletes. It is easily absorbed and rarely causes cramping. Beverages containing caffeine should be avoided because they can cause dehydration.

Eat Plenty of Iron-Rich Foods

Iron helps the blood carry needed oxygen to muscles during physical activity. Good sources of iron are lean meats, enriched and whole-grain breads, and leafy, dark green vegetables.

Meet Daily Calcium Needs

Meeting the daily requirement for calcium is especially important for female athletes. Calcium helps build strong bones that are more resistant to stress fractures. Dairy products and leafy, dark green vegetables are good calcium sources.

Supplements

Athletes should avoid depending on supplements to replace a well-balanced diet. Supplements such as vitamins, high-energy bars, and sports drinks are not dangerous. However, they should not be consumed instead of healthful foods and water.

Anabolic steroids are powerful, dangerous drugs that some people take to boost athletic performance. Such drugs mimic the natural male hormone testosterone. This helps build muscle tissue and body mass. However, steroids do not improve agility or skill. They may also cause many serious health problems, such as high blood pressure, heart disease, and liver damage. Steroid use may cause adolescents to stop growing. Males may begin producing less of their own testosterone, and females may show the effects of increased male hormone. For these reasons, steroids should not be used to attempt to boost athletic ability.

Needs of Adults

By the time people reach their early twenties, their bodies are generally considered to be physically mature. Gradually, metabolism begins to slow, causing adults to need fewer calories. If adults do not decrease their food intake, they are likely to put on weight.

The need for nutrients during adulthood does not diminish because body tissues must be maintained. The diet needs to supply adequate amounts of protein, vitamins, and minerals to help keep the body healthy.

13-13

Making a few small adjustments to a healthful diet can help teen athletes meet their nutrient needs.

Analyze and Solve

Research the disadvantages of using steroids to try to enhance athletic performance. Summarize your findings in two lists: the negative effects of short-term use and of long-term use. Prepare recommendations for a school coach or nurse about addressing this topic in school sports.

13-14

Because older adults are often less active than younger adults, they need fewer calories from foods.

Nutrition for Older Adults

Many older adults are less active than younger adults so they need fewer calories. For most other nutrients, however, older adults still need about the same amounts as when they were younger. The need for calcium actually increases for adults over age 50. See **13-14**.

Physical changes caused by the aging process can affect the eating habits of older adults. Such obstacles need to be kept in mind when planning meals. For instance, people who have trouble chewing may find it easier to eat softer foods, such as pudding and applesauce. People who have sensitive stomachs may prefer milder versions of spicy foods like chili.

While some changes in the diet are needed, it is important that foods remain appealing. Older adults must be willing to eat the foods they are served so that nutrient needs are met.

Special Diets and Nutrition Needs

People who are sick usually have additional nutrient needs. Fevers, vomiting, or diarrhea create the need for more water than usual to replace lost fluids. People recovering from some illnesses, as well as surgery, need additional protein. The need for some vitamins and minerals, such as vitamin C and zinc, also increases.

Those with diseases such as diabetes mellitus, cancer, and HIV/AIDS require a medical diet. These diets are prescribed by doctors and registered dietitians.

Food Allergies

Food allergies are abnormal reactions of a body's immune system to certain proteins in food. Symptoms usually come on quickly, often in only a few minutes. They can range from nausea to rashes, shortness of breath, or even sudden death. Allergies usually develop in stages. When you first encounter a food to which you are allergic, there may be mild or no symptoms. With later exposures, symptoms will likely appear and then recur whenever you eat the food. Over time, the severity of symptoms may increase or decrease. Ninety percent of food allergies are caused by eight food allergens: milk, eggs, tree nuts, peanuts, wheat, soybean, fish, and crustacean shellfish. People with food allergies must modify their diets to avoid foods that contain allergens.

Food Intolerances

Food intolerance is an adverse reaction to the consumption of certain foods. Usually symptoms appear more slowly than in the case of food allergies and are milder. Symptoms include upset stomach, minor headaches, and loss of sleep. Food intolerance is caused by deficiencies or reactions in the digestive tract.

Lactose intolerance is a form of food intolerance in which the body is unable to digest dairy products that contain lactose. *Lactose* is a sugar that is broken down into glucose by the enzyme *lactase*. Some people's bodies produce insufficient amounts of lactase. Instead of being broken down, lactose ferments in the intestines. This causes symptoms ranging from bloating and nausea to diarrhea. Lactose intolerance is controlled by limiting lactose intake or omitting dairy products from the diet.

High Blood Pressure

Blood pressure is the force of blood pushing against the walls of the arteries. High blood pressure usually has no symptoms until it leads to problems with the heart, brain, or kidneys. High blood pressure can cause arteries to harden, leading to a heart attack or stroke. Once high blood pressure develops, it usually lasts a lifetime. However, it can often be controlled.

Many times, the cause of high blood pressure is not known. Weight loss, physical activity, and a healthful diet are usually recommended to help prevent and control high blood pressure. A healthful diet includes foods low in sodium, fat, and cholesterol, and rich in potassium.

Diabetes

In a healthy body, the hormone insulin helps move the glucose used for energy throughout the body. In the body of a person with diabetes, the production of insulin is limited, or the body cells do not respond properly to insulin. Glucose stays in the blood where it can cause serious damage to body organs. Complications include the destruction of small blood vessels in the eyes, the slow deterioration of the kidneys, cardiovascular complications, and nerve damage.

Some of the symptoms of diabetes include increased thirst and urination, unusual weight loss, frequent infections, and slow-healing wounds. People with diabetes must monitor their blood glucose level. They must learn to carefully control their sugar intakes while still eating a diet high in complex carbohydrates. Weight control and regular exercise are also important. Some people with diabetes must receive insulin to replace the natural supply.

Wellness Awareness

Ask your school nurse to demonstrate how to measure a person's blood pressure with a sphygmomanometer. This instrument includes an inflatable cuff that is wrapped around the upper arm and tightened, while a read out displays the person's blood pressure in the arteries.

Osteoporosis

Osteoporosis is a disease that weakens bones, often causing severe fractures. It occurs primarily in people over 50 years of age. Osteoporosis is caused from a depletion of calcium in the body. This results in porous and brittle bones that break easily. Osteoporosis is more common in women than in men.

Almost all cells of the body require calcium. The body absorbs calcium directly from the food consumed. However, if there is insufficient calcium in food, the body will withdraw calcium from the bones. When supplies are insufficient, the body will also slow the loss of calcium through the urine. Gradual loss of calcium in bones is a normal part of aging. A diet rich in calcium and vitamin D promotes healthy bones, **13-15**. This can slow bone loss and lessen the risk of fracture.

Cancer

Cancer refers to a disease in which abnormal cells divide uncontrollably and invade other body tissues. The abnormal cells may also spread to other parts of the body. The development of abnormal cell masses are called tumors. In some cases, no tumors develop. Instead, uncontrolled cell growth occurs in the blood and blood system.

In most cases it is not known what causes cancer, but there are risk factors that are often associated with an increased prevalence. One such risk is a diet high in fat. The American Cancer Society recommends that you eat an abundance of fruits and vegetables each day, as well as whole grains and beans. Limit fat intake, especially animal fat. Use alcohol in moderation or not at all. It is also recommended that you stay active and maintain a healthy weight.

13-15

Milk and other dairy products provide calcium needed to fight osteoporosis.

Reading
Review

1. Why do pregnant teenagers have more difficulty meeting the needs of their developing babies than pregnant adults?
2. Of the four types of vegetarianism, what distinguishes one type from another?
3. What are the four particular needs that an athlete's diet must address?
4. True or false. Adults need more calories than teenagers.

Section 13-4

Balancing Calories and Energy Needs

Objectives

After studying this section, you will be able to

- **identify** factors that affect energy needs for metabolic and physical activity.
- **outline** guidelines for healthy weight loss and healthy weight gain.
- **describe** three common eating disorders.

Key Terms

calorie	overweight	bulimia nervosa
basal metabolism	obese	binge-eating disorder
body mass index (BMI)	underweight	orthorexia nervosa
	anorexia nervosa	

Energy is needed to support every activity of your body. From sleeping to running a marathon race, your body constantly requires energy. You obtain needed energy from the foods you eat. This food energy is measured in units called **calories**. Learning to limit your calorie intake to your calorie needs will help you maintain a healthy weight.

You already know that some foods produce more energy per serving than others. Foods high in fats, such as fried foods and ice cream, are higher in calories than other foods. Foods with high water content, such as watermelon, tomatoes, and lettuce, are lower in calories per serving. See **13-16**.

Meeting Energy Needs

People have different calorie needs. Needs are based on a person's age, sex, body size, and level of physical activity. The body needs energy to support both metabolic and physical activity.

Metabolic Energy Needs

Even when you sleep, your body is working. Your heart keeps pumping blood. Your lungs keep drawing oxygen. Your tissues are being built and repaired. These life-sustaining activities are collectively called **basal metabolism**. Basal metabolism accounts for the energy required when your body is at physical, emotional, and digestive rest.

13-16

Tomatoes, lettuce, and the other ingredients in this salad are high in water content and thus low in calories.

Mental Health Awareness

Childhood Obesity

Obesity rates among young children are rising. Children who are obese are more prone to problems in emotional and social development. They may show disruptive behavior or have trouble making friends.

The *basal metabolic rate (BMR)* varies greatly from person to person. The BMR is higher while a person is growing. Thus, the BMR of children and teenagers is greater than that of adults. This is why people need to decrease the amount of food they eat when they get older. Older people do not need as many calories to sustain their body processes as younger people.

Other factors, such as glandular secretions and body temperature, can affect your metabolic energy needs. For instance, when there is an undersecretion by the thyroid gland, basal metabolism is lower. When there is an oversecretion, basal metabolism is higher. The higher your body temperature is, the greater your metabolic needs are. Therefore, when you have a fever, your basal metabolism will be higher.

Energy for Physical Activities

Physical activity raises energy needs above basal requirements. Whenever you use your muscles, you use energy. The amount of energy you need is related to the amount of work you do. For instance, you need more energy to walk than to sit and rest. You need more energy to run than to walk. If your level of physical activity is light, you will need fewer calories to fulfill your energy needs. If you are very active, you will need more calories to meet your energy needs.

Controlling Your Weight

Weight management involves eating and physical activity. The foods you eat give your body energy, which is measured in calories. When you are active, you burn these calories. To control your weight, you need to compare the total calories eaten to the total calories used.

How Much Should You Weigh?

To set goals for weight management, you need to know what weight range is considered healthy for you. Health professionals determine this by using a calculation called **body mass index (BMI)**. The BMI is very useful for measuring body fat.

For adults age 21 and older, the BMI is a number that simply relates weight to height. As shown in Figure **13-17**, an adult BMI of 18.5 to 25 refers to a healthy weight. A BMI of 25 to 30 is viewed as **overweight**. A BMI over 30 is considered **obese**.

For people age 2 to 20, healthy weight is interpreted differently. The reason is children and teens have different body-fatness levels as they grow and mature. Their BMI, called "BMI for Age" or "BMI for Children and Teens," is plotted on age- and gender-specific growth charts. These charts are far more complex than the simple chart used for adults. Four weight classes exist for 2-to-20-year-olds: *underweight*, *healthy weight*, *overweight*, and *obese*.

13-17

Balancing calories and energy needs allows people to stay within a healthy weight range for their height.

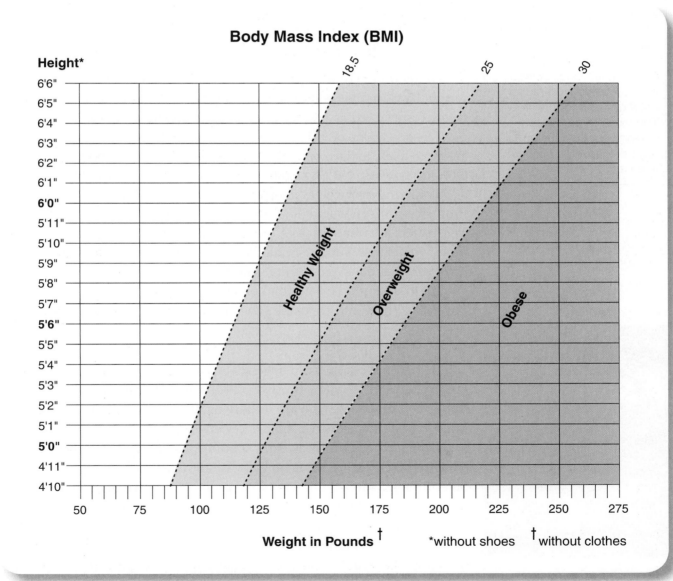

Overweight adults are encouraged to lose weight, but overweight children and adolescents are not. This is because young people can "grow into" leaner bodies by slowing their weight gain as they grow and develop. Weight loss could negatively affect normal growth. Overweight adults, however, are advised to lose weight and stabilize their weight at a healthy level.

In addition to fat, the body's bone and muscle also contribute to its weight. These two body components actually weigh more than fat tissue. An athlete's BMI, therefore, may fall in the overweight range due to a large muscle mass. For nonathletes, however, a high BMI usually indicates excess body fat.

Overweight and obesity are common at all age levels, but not everyone needs to lose weight. People at a healthy or normal weight should try to maintain it. Those who are underweight should focus on gaining weight.

Healthy Weight Loss

Many people have a goal to lose unwanted pounds. Most people gain weight because they consume more calories than they burn. The excess calories are stored as fat. As fat stores accumulate, weight gain occurs.

Obesity is one of today's major health problems. Obese individuals are more likely to develop high blood pressure, diabetes, and heart disease. Obesity may also have a negative impact on a person's self-concept.

For many overweight people, reaching a healthy weight is difficult. Promises of quick weight loss from diets and diet aids may be tempting. These diets are often *fad diets*, or popularized diets that usually promise rapid weight loss. People should beware of quick weight-loss promises, however. Dietitians agree there is no fast and easy way to lose weight. Weight loss should be a gradual process. It is best achieved by increasing physical activity and choosing sensible portions of healthful foods.

Healthy Weight Gain

Being underweight can have adverse effects on health just as being overweight can. Adults who have a BMI below 18.5 are considered **underweight**. People who are underweight may suffer from more infections. They also tend to have low energy levels and may chill easily.

People who are underweight should consult a physician before adjusting their eating habits to gain weight. This will help them determine if a physical or emotional problem is preventing them from gaining weight. To gain weight, choose nutritious foods that provide more calories per serving. Increasing portion sizes and adding nutritious snacks will add calories to the diet. Eating five or six small meals rather than three large meals each day will also foster weight gain.

Eating Disorders

Many people have poor eating habits. They may not eat a wide variety of foods, or they may eat too many high-fat foods. However, *eating disorders* are recognized as life-threatening physical and mental health conditions that include extreme emotions, attitudes, and behaviors surrounding weight and food issues. Ninety percent of those likely to develop eating disorders are teen girls and young women. Such disorders have been found in elementary school children and middle-age women, as well.

Two common eating disorders are anorexia nervosa and bulimia nervosa. Both are serious and life-threatening. The causes of eating disorders are still largely unknown. There is evidence in some cases that eating disorders are hereditary, as well as being related to depression, stress, and low self-esteem. **Anorexia nervosa** is an eating disorder in which a person avoids eating, sometimes to the point of starvation. A person with anorexia typically weighs herself or himself repeatedly and eats very small quantities of only certain foods. Overexercising to avoid weight gain is also a symptom.

The effects of anorexia nervosa on health can be devastating. Body temperature drops, and females may stop menstruating. Skin becomes dry; hair becomes dull and falls out. Often a growth of fine hair develops on the body to compensate for the loss of healthy fat. Failure to meet nutrient needs can cause heart damage and loss of bone and muscle tissue. Severe cases can result in death. Even those who recover may have permanent physical damage.

People who have **bulimia nervosa** eating disorder go on eating binges and consume excessive amounts of calories. They then take steps to avoid weight gain. Some bulimics purge themselves of the food by vomiting or taking laxatives or diuretics. Others with this disorder fast or exercise intensely to avoid weight gain. This binge-purge pattern is repeated at least twice a week.

Healthy Living

Healthy Weight Loss Tips

- Avoid eating more calories than you burn. Try to maintain a balance between food intake and physical activity.
- Spend at least 60 minutes each day in moderate physical activity. Plan to walk briskly, bike, swim, or jog. The more active you are, the more calories you burn. Schedule your physical activity about an hour before dinner. Vigorous activity helps suppress the appetite.
- Base your diet on grains, vegetables, and fruits. Then select moderate portions of low-fat dairy products and lean meats, poultry, and fish. Limit foods that are high in fat and/or sugar. Read labels to determine the fat and sugar content of foods you eat.
- Avoid omitting any group of foods from your diet. You can reduce portion sizes, but continue eating a variety of nutritious foods.
- Avoid making drastic changes in your food intake without the advice of your doctor. A high percentage of people who lose weight by radically changing their diet habits regain the weight.
- Beware of fad diets that focus on one or two foods. A variety of foods are needed for overall health and well-being.

Bulimia nervosa can take quite a toll on health. Frequent vomiting can erode the teeth and irritate the esophagus. Imbalances of body fluids can damage the heart and kidneys.

Binge-eating disorder is a third type of eating disorder. Similar to bulimia nervosa, people with binge-eating disorder often consume large amounts of food in one sitting, sometimes to the point of discomfort. Binge-eating disorder differs from bulimia nervosa, however, because no action is taken to purge the food or avoid weight gain.

Binge-eating disorder impacts people physically and socially-emotionally. Physical effects of binge-eating disorder include increased risk factors for obesity, diabetes mellitus, heart disease, and high cholesterol and blood pressure. Social-emotional effects include depression and feelings of guilt and lack of control over eating patterns. People with binge-eating disorder may also seclude themselves from friends and family to hide their eating behaviors.

Orthorexia nervosa is similar to anorexia nervosa and shows similar symptoms. This eating disorder, however, is characterized by an unhealthy obsession with "healthful eating" that results in severely limiting *food choices*. A person with orthorexia will eventually experience health problems due to the lack of nutrients that would be present in a variety of foods.

People with eating disorders often do not recognize or admit they are ill. As a result, they may strongly resist getting and staying in treatment. The earlier that eating disorders are detected, the better are the chances of recovery without long-lasting medical problems.

Treatment of an eating disorder involves a team of health professionals. Physician treatment in a hospital is needed for severe malnutrition, irregular heartbeats, or other serious medical conditions resulting from the severe weight loss. Individual, group, and family counseling is necessary to help understand the problems and learn to cope in healthy ways. Eating disorders are treatable, but success often takes years.

Reading
Review

1. A _____ is the unit used to measure food energy.
2. Describe basal metabolism.
3. What type of weight-loss advice should be avoided?
4. True or false. There are no health risks for people who are underweight.
5. Identify four types of eating disorders and briefly describe each type.

Chapter 13 Review

Summary

Carbohydrates, proteins, fats, minerals, vitamins, and water serve different functions in the body. Each nutrient can be obtained from a number of food sources. Knowing your nutrient needs will help you meet them through the foods you eat each day.

Many factors influence a person's food intake, and the goal of achieving good health is one. MyPlate is a food guidance system that helps you meet your nutrient needs. It divides foods that have similar nutrient content into five groups: fruits, grains, vegetables, protein, and dairy. MyPlate is based on the *Dietary Guidelines for Americans*, which can help you form healthful eating and activity habits.

Dietary needs vary at different stages of life. During childhood and the teen years, people have increased needs for some nutrients to support rapid growth. As people reach adulthood, their needs for many nutrients remain high, but their calorie needs decrease. As dietary needs change, be prepared to adjust your eating habits.

Your body needs energy for both metabolic and physical activities. Balancing these needs with the calories you get from foods will allow you to control your weight. Being either overweight or underweight can cause health problems. People who need to lose or gain weight need to take steps to do so in a healthful manner. Dramatic, unhealthy weight loss or gain can be the result of an eating disorder. Four types of eating disorders are anorexia nervosa, bulimia nervosa, binge-eating disorder, and orthorexia nervosa.

Critical Thinking

1. **Analyze decisions.** Why do you think some people do not eat the proper nutrients? What could be done to change this?

2. **Analyze effects.** Research cultural influences on food choices. Explain how the MyPlate system could be used to meet dietary needs in another culture.

3. **Compare and contrast.** Work in a small group to discuss the nutritional needs of people at a specific stage of life. Compare and contrast your group's findings with the nutritional needs of people at different stages identified by your classmates in other groups.

4. **Predict outcomes.** How would following a daily program of physical activity affect your calorie needs and your weight? Identify the specific results expected.

5. **Analyze trends.** Research and write a report on obesity in the United States. What trends did you find? What steps are being taken to address these trends?

21st Century Applications

6. **Global awareness.** Clean, pure drinking water is not available to many people in various parts of the world. Identify key areas where this is a problem. What are some cost effective ways to provide clean, pure drinking water? What are the social and economic impacts of countries failing to provide basic water purification for its citizens? Write a report of your findings to share with the class.

7. **Health literacy.** Use the Internet to research the roles of copper, potassium, chloride, magnesium, and selenium in the diet. What are the functions of each mineral in the diet? What can happen if

you have an excessive amount of each in the diet? an insufficient amount? Also investigate good food sources of these minerals.

8. **Health literacy.** Choose one vitamin or mineral and investigate the amounts present in same-size portions of three fruits and three vegetables. Use charting software to make a graph illustrating the amounts present.

9. **Leadership and responsibility.** As a member of the fitness club at your school, you have been nominated and put in charge of organizing a voluntary exercise program for club members after school. The fitness club meets for one hour after school one day each week. Research information using the *Physical Activity Guidelines for Americans.* Organize fitness activities centering on aerobic, muscle-strengthening, and bone-strengthening activities. Be sure to allow time for adequate warm-up, workout, and cooldown periods. Include ideas for keeping peers motivated to participate. Share your plan with the class.

10. **Critical thinking and problem solving.** A friend from school and work confides in you about her struggle with an eating disorder and makes you promise not to tell anyone about it. You've noticed over a period of time that your friend's productivity at work is declining. You have concern about her health and life. You wonder if you should talk with your friend's parents or the school counselor about your observations about her apparent symptoms of this condition. What should you do? What is the best way to practice integrity in this situation? What decision is best for your friend? Write a

response for how you would respond in this situation.

 Core Skills

11. **Science.** Research the different types of amino acids, including chemical structure. Research the function of DNA as a protein template. Report your findings in class.

12. **Writing.** Research Doris Calloway and Carl Pfeiffer and their contributions to the nutrition and dietetics fields. How were their approaches to nutrition similar? different? Write a report on your findings.

13. **History, writing.** Write a paper about the history of nutrition that addresses the following questions: When was the first nutrient discovered? Were the nutrients discovered by scientists focused on understanding human nutrition? How old is the actual science of human nutrition?

14. **Reading.** Research current articles about spine and brain development in fetuses. Find an article in which folic acid is mentioned. Summarize your findings in a written report.

15. **Research, writing.** Choose one tropical fruit and prepare a research report on it. Identify the regions and climate in which it grows, and the cost of transporting it to the continental United States.

16. **Math.** Find out how to determine the amount of fat and saturated fat in your diet so you can follow the percentage guidelines. Report your findings to the class.

17. **Math, writing.** Conduct a survey to find out if males and females are equally concerned about weight. Develop

a survey form and give it to an equal number of teen boys and teen girls. Tally the results and write an article for the school paper summarizing the findings.

18. **Speaking.** Compare the varieties of yogurt for serving size and calorie content. Make sure to include some artificially sweetened brands. Prepare an electronic presentation to illustrate your findings.

19. **Reading.** Search the Internet for a reputable website offering advice to women during pregnancy. Find out how many extra calories a pregnant woman is advised to eat daily during the nine months. What kind and how much physical activity is recommended? What weight gain is recommended for a woman with a healthy normal weight? Share your findings and the name of the website with the class.

20. **Writing.** Select one type of eating disorder and research it in depth. What are the signs of this eating disorder? What are the physical and social-emotional effects? What are possible causes of the eating disorder? How can a person with this type of eating disorder receive help? Write an informative essay outlining this particular eating disorder. Include a list of any sources you used in your report.

21. **Listening.** Interview a dietitian to find out more about his or her job. Why did he or she become a dietitian? What education and training is needed? What challenges and rewards are involved with the job? Prepare a list of questions prior to the interview, including any questions of your own. Summarize the interview and share your responses with the class.

Portfolio
Builder

Visit the MyPlate website and click on *MyPlate Plan*. Enter your age, gender, weight, height, and physical activity to generate your own personal food plan. Determine the recommended amounts you should eat from each food group daily. Describe how following the plan would be beneficial to you. Include your plan and description in your portfolio.

Leadership
Development

Plan a dinner for a group of older adults. The older adults may be friends or relatives of the chapter members, or members of a senior care center, retirement community, or religious organization. Include foods from all the food groups and consider the nutritional needs of this population.

Journal
Writing

It seems that everywhere you look, a different weight management plan appears. You wonder how to evaluate each one in terms of healthy living. You refer to the MyPlate website and study its suggestions.

Write About It: *In what ways do government research and recommendations help you make wise food choices? How does knowledge of the MyPlate recommendations affect your perception of other weight management plans? According to MyPlate, how can you make food intake and physical activity work together to achieve a healthy lifestyle?*

Chapter 14
Selecting Foods

Reading Prep

Before reading this chapter, review the objectives in each section. Based on this information, analyze the author's purpose for this chapter.

Concept Organizer

Use a star diagram to record suggestions on how to stretch your food budget.

G-WLEARNING.com

Click on the activity icon to visit www.g-wlearning.com/comprehensive/8062 to access online vocabulary activities using key terms from the chapter.

Menu Planning

Objectives

After studying this section, you will be able to

- **write** a menu displaying variety in color, flavor, texture, shape, size, and temperature.

- **evaluate** your cooking skills, food budget, and preparation time as they apply to meal management.

Key Terms ↗

meal management   convenience food

Imagine this situation: You arrive home at six o'clock to prepare dinner. Then you must rush to meet a seven o'clock appointment. Unfortunately, today's hurried lifestyles often result in this type of schedule. A nutritious, economical meal may be a small concern when you are in a hurry.

To guard against the pitfalls of busy days, meal management is a must. **Meal management** involves using the resources of skills, money, and time to put together nutritious meals. A meal manager must plan well-balanced menus, shop for healthful foods, and prepare meals according to the time and budget available.

How do you begin to plan great meals? Cookbooks, magazines, and websites often have many good menu suggestions, **14-1**. You might also keep a collection of your family's favorite recipes and add to it as you discover new favorites.

Finding tasty menus and recipes is just the beginning of meal planning. You will want your meals to be nutritious, as the previous chapter explained. You will also want meals that look appetizing, but also suit your cooking skills, food budget, and available preparation time. Planning is the key to preparing and serving good meals.

Special Food Needs

When planning meals, consider the special needs of family members or guests. For a person trying to lose weight, you might select foods that are lower in calories. People with food allergies, diabetes, or heart disease may require special diets. People who are ill or recovering from surgery may also have particular food needs.

Mental Health Awareness

Meal Time and Socialization

Meal time can be a great time for catching up with friends and family members. Preparing foods, eating, and cleaning after a meal can be ideal quality time spent with others. Strengthening friendships and family relationships can help relieve stress and, in turn, benefit mental health.

14-1

Great meals begin with advance planning. Websites, cookbooks, and magazines are good places to look for menu ideas.

Wellness Awareness

Search the Internet for examples of diet plans for people with diabetes or heart disease. Evaluate how these diets differ from MyPlate recommendations.

Whenever you invite guests to dinner, politely ask if certain foods should be avoided. Your guests will appreciate your thoughtfulness.

Variety in Meals

Color, flavor, texture, shape, size, and temperature are important points to consider in planning meals with variety. Choosing foods that appeal to the senses (sight, smell, and taste) will make meals enjoyable. Foods that complement each other also add interest to mealtime.

- *Color.* Color adds eye appeal to meals, so plan meals with a variety of colors. *Garnishes*, items used to decorate foods, can add color and interest.

- *Flavor.* The flavors of foods should complement each other. A sweet flavor blends well with a sour flavor. A mild flavor offsets a strong flavor. Vary the flavors of food items to avoid repeating one flavor.

- *Texture.* Textures of foods should offer variety. *Crisp, tender, soft, creamy, smooth, crunchy,* and *chewy* describe common food textures. Try to serve at least three textures in each meal.

- *Shape and Size.* Use your creative flair to combine a variety of shapes and sizes in your meals. Avoid serving several foods at the same meal that are the same shape and size.

- *Temperature.* Plan to include foods that differ in temperature as part of the meal plan. Cold foods, such as crisp vegetable salads, contrast well with hot foods, such as sliced meat and a baked potato.

Cultural and Societal Influences

Variety in colors, flavors, textures, and shapes plays a role in foods of all cultures. However, the specific foods and seasonings that make up this variety differ from one culture to another.

Different cultural preferences have influenced people's food choices since the earliest times. These societies did not have access to foods from all over the world. They had to eat whatever was available. Those who lived in coastal areas ate seafood. Those who lived in woodlands might have eaten deer, caribou, and other wild game. As time passed, people moved to different regions where new foods were available. However, the regional foods that were familiar to people remained their cultural preferences.

You can still see regional and cultural food influences today. Cheese soup is more common on restaurant menus in Wisconsin than in Oklahoma. You are likely to see lobster on most menus in Maine, but much less often in Utah, **14-2**. You will find few Asian markets in an area with a large Latin population, and the opposite is just as true.

If you are like most people, you tend to choose foods that reflect your culture. You also select foods that are typical of the society in which you live. As a meal manager, you can add variety to your family's meals by occasionally serving foods from other cultures.

When You Are the Meal Manager

Healthy Living

Veggie Values—Fresh, Canned, or Frozen

Everyone knows that vegetables are an important part of daily food intake. However, many wonder which is best—fresh, canned, or frozen. Fresh, just-picked vegetables from the farm or garden are the most nutritious. Because most frozen and canned vegetables are processed immediately after harvest, they also have good nutritional levels. The key to retaining nutrients with fresh, frozen, or canned vegetables is the cooking method. Lightly steaming, microwaving, or stir-frying vegetables retains the most color, texture, and nutritional value.

As a meal manager, you need to consider more than the nutrition and appearance of the food. You also need to consider your skills, your budget, and the amount of time you have available.

Your Cooking Skills

The meals you plan are often determined by the preparation skills you possess. People who have little cooking experience tend to plan meals that require little preparation. As experience increases, they become more confident and try more complex recipes.

14-2

Grilled lobster is a more typical entrée in New England than in the Southwest.

If you are a beginner, trying to prepare three new recipes for one meal could be frustrating and confusing. One new recipe at a time is enough for adventure. After you master a new main dish recipe, you may wish to try a new salad recipe to accompany it.

Have patience with yourself as you learn to cook. If you can manage to cook only one dish, plan to serve it with other foods that require no cooking. With practice, your cooking skills will develop. In time, you will be able to cook anything you wish.

Energy Costs

When planning meals, do not forget about energy costs. Energy not only costs money, it uses limited natural resources. The longer foods cook, the more energy is used. Therefore, consider the cooking times of foods when choosing a menu.

How food is prepared can affect cooking time. For instance, you can steam rice on top of the range in 15 minutes. If you bake rice in the oven, it will take about an hour. However, if you were already baking a dish, it would be more economical to bake the rice at the same time.

Foods that can be cooked together can save energy. Try preparing one-dish meals, such as vegetable and meat dishes, stews, or casseroles.

Your Preparation Time

With careful planning, you can control the use of time to prepare meals. Here are some ways to save preparation and cooking time by planning ahead.

Consider using some convenience foods to save time. **Convenience foods** are food products that have some preparation steps already finished. The manufacturer has done most of the measuring and combining. With only a few steps, you can prepare the food successfully. For instance, a frozen dinner requires only reheating. Canned and frozen vegetables have already been cleaned, pared, and chopped. They are usually ready to heat and serve, which greatly reduces preparation time. Mixes for muffins, cakes, cookies, breads, soups, and puddings are other examples. These foods still require some preparation, but they require less time than made-from-scratch foods. Although convenience foods save time and energy, they are often more costly than foods prepared from scratch.

Plan foods that require no cooking. A cottage cheese and fruit salad served with wheat crackers and a beverage makes a complete, timesaving meal. A nutritious breakfast featuring ready-to-eat cereal is also quick and easy to prepare.

When you have extra time, prepare large portions of food that can be used for more than one meal. For instance, leftover ham, turkey, or beef can be used later in sandwiches, casseroles, and soups.

Plan meals that suit the time you have available for preparation, **14-3**. If you have only enough time to heat a plate of leftovers, do not try to prepare an entire meal.

DragonImages/iStock/Thinkstock

Different Eating Schedules

Everyone in your family may not be able to eat meals at the same time. In many families, all adults may be employed outside the home, and their work schedules may vary. Some adults may work nights or evenings. Children may be involved in activities that take them away from home during normal mealtimes.

In these busy households, traditional eating patterns may be difficult to follow. Meals should be planned to meet these various schedules. Keep in mind that young children and older family members often prefer to eat on a regular schedule. Teenagers and most adults are usually more flexible.

When planning meals for a variety of eating schedules, select foods that taste good when reheated. Family members who are unavailable to eat when meals are served can reheat foods in the microwave oven later. For instance, many one-dish meals can be refrigerated and reheated. Some one-dish meals, such as chili or beef stew, can also cook all day in a slow cooker. Family members can serve themselves as their schedules allow. Prepare menu items on weekends and freeze them for use during the week. Make recipes in large quantities and freeze individual portions for later use.

Plan to have food items on hand for family members to make their own meals. You can keep sandwich and salad items in the refrigerator. Fresh fruits, cheeses, and canned or dry soups can also form the basis of quick meals.

14-3

Weekends usually offer teens the most time for preparing complete meals.

Reading Review

1. Name five points to consider in planning meals with variety.
2. Besides nutrition and food appearance, what should a meal manager consider when menu planning?

Section 14-2

Shopping Decisions

Objectives

After studying this section, you will be able to

- **plan** and organize a shopping list.
- **describe** different types of food stores.
- **use** unit pricing to compare the cost of food products.
- **describe** four types of open dating used to indicate the freshness of food products.
- **identify** the types of information found on food product labels and its usefulness in making wise purchase decisions.

Key Terms

unit pricing	pull date	food additive
open dating	freshness date	universal product code (UPC)
pack date	expiration date	

Shopping for food is an important part of meal planning. Whether you shop in a supermarket or neighborhood store, grocery shopping involves many decisions. You must decide what to buy and where to shop. Many resources are available to help you get the most for your food dollars. These resources include unit pricing, open dating, and package labeling.

Preparing a Shopping List

A *shopping list* is a detailed list of the kinds and amounts of food you want to buy. You can save three valuable resources—time, energy, and money—by planning your shopping list carefully.

You should write your shopping list before you go grocery shopping, **14-4**. As you make out your list, review all the recipes you are planning to prepare. List all the items you need for your weekly menus and snacks. Add any staple items you have used during the week, such as bread, milk, and eggs.

As you prepare your list, use weekly food ads to compare food items and prices. You may want to stock up on items that are on sale. However, read carefully to find out if you are really saving money. Some foods featured in ads are not on sale. Also, note special promotions and clip coupons you want to use. A coupon can save you money, providing you need the item and plan to buy it.

Save time and energy by organizing your shopping list according to the grocery store's layout. List the items you will need in each aisle or department of the store. For instance, keep all fresh fruits and vegetables in one group on your list and all frozen foods in another. This step will help you avoid going back and forth to find items. It will also help you avoid overlooking needed items on your list.

SDI Productions/E+/Getty Images

14-4
A grocery list helps you focus on your needs and avoid tempting items.

Deciding Where to Shop

Once you have prepared your shopping list, you must decide the best place to shop. Different types of stores offer different product selections, prices, and customer services.

Types of Food Stores

Five of the most common types of food stores are supermarkets, discount supermarkets, specialty stores, warehouse clubs, and convenience stores. Comparing them will help you decide which type will best meet your shopping needs.

Large *supermarkets* sell a wide range of food and household products. They often charge lower prices because they do a high volume of business. Many supermarkets offer customer services, such as check cashing or carrying groceries to your car.

Discount supermarkets are sometimes known as warehouse supermarkets. These stores sell foods and household items at discounted prices. To keep

21st Century Skills

Adaptability. Jamal never knows what he will be doing each day when he arrives to work at the local grocery store. One day, his supervisor asks him to stock shelves. The next day, he works as a cashier. On another day, he serves as the store greeter. He enjoys the variety in his job, and his supervisor appreciates Jamal's flexibility.

prices low, many offer less variety and fewer customer services. For instance, shoppers may have to bag their own groceries.

Specialty stores specialize in carrying one type of food item. A seafood store or a bakery are examples of specialty stores. Prices are often higher, but shoppers may prefer the quality and personalized service.

Warehouse clubs sell a variety of products in fixed quantities. The products are often sold in bulk at lower prices. Customers usually must purchase a membership to the warehouse club that allows them to shop there. Services are minimal.

Convenience stores offer convenient locations, longer hours, and fast service. However, product selection is limited, and prices are higher than in supermarkets. Shoppers must decide if the added conveniences are worth the cost.

Using Unit Pricing

Comparison shopping is made easier with unit pricing. **Unit pricing** shows the cost per standard unit of weight or measure. You can use unit pricing to compare prices among brands, package sizes, and product forms (fresh, frozen, canned). Unit pricing labels are usually posted on the shelves beneath food items. See **14-5**.

Open Dating

You can judge the freshness of *perishable foods*, or foods that spoil easily, through **open dating**. It appears in four forms.

- Canned foods are often stamped with a **pack date**. This tells you when the food was processed.

  - A **pull date** is often used on dairy products and packaged cold cuts. This is the last day a store should sell the product. The pull date allows for some storage time at home.

  - Bread and baked goods usually have a **freshness date**. It indicates the end of the product's peak quality, but the product can be used beyond this date.

  - **Expiration dates** appear on products such as yeast and baby formula. An expiration date is the last day a product should be used or eaten. When shopping, avoid buying outdated foods.

14-5

Unit pricing allows you to compare prices of various products.

Understanding Food Labeling

You cannot examine the contents of a box or can of food before you buy it by opening it. However, you can learn a great deal about the foods you buy by reading their labels.

Food Label Information

According to government regulations, certain information must appear on food labels, **14-6**. Every food label must include

- the common name of the product and its form, such as whole, sliced, or diced
- the net contents or net weight
- the name and address of the manufacturer, packer, or distributor
- a list of ingredients
- any required allergy labeling

Ingredients must be listed on the label in descending order by weight. For example, *peas, carrots, water,* and *salt* may be printed on a can label. This means the can contains more peas than carrots, more carrots than water, and more water than salt. Manufacturers must also identify any ingredients that are a major food allergen (milk, eggs, tree nuts, peanuts, wheat, soybean, fish, or crustacean shellfish). The allergen can either be noted in parentheses following the ingredient or in a separate *Contains:* statement.

Descriptive terms are often used on food labels. The Food and Drug Administration (FDA) set uniform definitions for descriptive terms such as *light, reduced,* and *free.* This assures consumers that terms appearing on food products are accurate.

Math Connection

Using Unit Pricing to Compare Prices

Nathan often uses unit pricing to compare products. Today, unit price labels are not posted in the yogurt case. Cahill Farm's one 8-ounce container is $0.89 while Emerson Dairy's 6-ounce container is $0.79. Nathan can determine which is a better buy by calculating the price per ounce of each product.

Nathan divides the price by the number of ounces per container to find the cost per ounce. The lowest price per ounce is the Cahill Farm's brand.

$0.89 \div 8 = $0.11

$0.79 \div 6 = $0.13

14-6

This example of a food label shows the information required by government regulations.

Parts of a Food Label

Description: The FDA has set specific definitions for descriptive terms, assuring shoppers that they can believe what they read on the package:
- free
- high
- light
- low
- more
- reduced
- good source
- less

For fish, meat, and poultry:
- lean
- extra lean

Ingredients, listed in descending order by weight, are required on almost all foods.

FROZEN MIXED VEGETABLES
IN SAUCE

Low Fat
Cholesterol Free
Good Source of Fiber

[See back panel for message on saturated fat and cholesterol and heart disease.]

NET WT. 8.9 oz. (252 g)

Ingredients: Broccoli, carrots, green beans, water chestnuts, whey (**milk**), modified cornstarch, salt, spices

Health Claims: Food labels are allowed to carry information about the link between certain nutrients and specific diseases. For such a "health claim" to be made on a package, the FDA must first determine that the diet-disease link is supported by scientific evidence.

Major **food allergens** must be labeled.

Health claim message referred to on the front panel is shown here.

"While many factors affect heart disease, diets low in fat and cholesterol may reduce the risk of this disease."

Some foods are labeled *organically grown*. This means they were grown without the use of manufactured fertilizers or pesticides. Natural versions were used instead of chemicals. The USDA Organic label may be used only on foods that are certified at least 95 percent organic.

Organic foods are often more expensive than non-organic foods. However, they taste the same and have similar nutritional value.

Food Additives

Food additives may be among the items found in a food product ingredient list. **Food additives** are substances that are added to food for a specific purpose. For instance, some food additives help keep foods from spoiling. Other food additives are used to enhance flavor, color, or texture; add nutrients; or aid processing.

Food additives may be added during any phase of producing, processing, storing, or packaging. Many familiar substances, such as salt, sugar, and vinegar, are common food additives.

Food additives are a subject of concern to some people. However, laws require substances to be carefully tested before they can be used as food additives. Additives must be proved safe for their intended uses. Certain additives must be identified on ingredient lists, as some people may be allergic to them.

Nutrition Facts Label

By law, most foods are required to include nutrition labeling. In July of 2016, the new FDA regulation for the Nutrition Facts label became effective with a manufacturer-compliance date of January 1, 2020. Based on current nutrition research, the updated label is designed to help consumers make healthful food choices. See **14-7**.

The Nutrition Facts label includes the following:

- Servings per container
- Serving size
- Calorie amount per serving
- Percent Daily Values (%DV) that reflect total fat, saturated fat, cholesterol, sodium, total carbohydrate, dietary fiber, added sugars, vitamin D, calcium, iron, and potassium
- A footnote to better explain Percent Daily Values (%DV)

Life Skills

Understanding Food Product Terms

Descriptive terms used on food labels often create confusion for consumers. As a result, the Food and Drug Administration (FDA) provides definitions for descriptive terms such as *free*, *light*, *reduced*, and *high*. This assures consumers that terms appearing on food products are accurate and easy to compare.

A label describing a product as *sugar free* or *fat free* means the food has less than 0.5 gram of the component per serving. Either the component is missing or it is present only as a trace amount. The terms *zero*, *no*, or *without* may be used in place of *free*.

The label term *light* means the product has one-third fewer calories or half the fat of the regular product.

A product labeled *reduced calories* has 25% fewer calories than the same amount of the regular product. Another term to describe this reduction is *fewer*.

Use of the term *high* means the food offers 20% or more of the Daily Value for a given nutrient per serving.

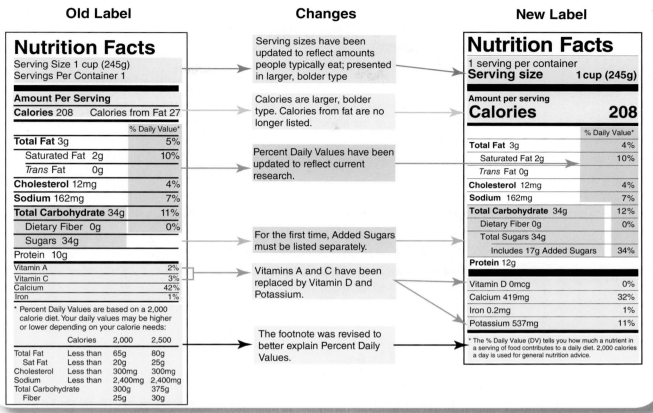

Old Label

Nutrition Facts

Serving Size 1 cup (245g)
Servings Per Container 1

Amount Per Serving

Calories 208   Calories from Fat 27

	% Daily Value*
Total Fat 3g	5%
Saturated Fat 2g	10%
Trans Fat 0g	
Cholesterol 12mg	4%
Sodium 162mg	7%
Total Carbohydrate 34g	11%
Dietary Fiber 0g	0%
Sugars 34g	
Protein 10g	

Vitamin A	2%
Vitamin C	3%
Calcium	42%
Iron	1%

* Percent Daily Values are based on a 2,000 calorie diet. Your daily values may be higher or lower depending on your calorie needs:

	Calories	2,000	2,500
Total Fat	Less than	65g	80g
Sat Fat	Less than	20g	25g
Cholesterol	Less than	300mg	300mg
Sodium	Less than	2,400mg	2,400mg
Total Carbohydrate		300g	375g
Fiber		25g	30g

Changes

Serving sizes have been updated to reflect amounts people typically eat; presented in larger, bolder type

Calories are larger, bolder type. Calories from fat are no longer listed.

Percent Daily Values have been updated to reflect current research.

For the first time, Added Sugars must be listed separately.

Vitamins A and C have been replaced by Vitamin D and Potassium.

The footnote was revised to better explain Percent Daily Values.

New Label

Nutrition Facts

1 serving per container
Serving size   1 cup (245g)

Amount per serving

Calories   208

	% Daily Value*
Total Fat 3g	4%
Saturated Fat 2g	10%
Trans Fat 0g	
Cholesterol 12mg	4%
Sodium 162mg	7%
Total Carbohydrate 34g	12%
Dietary Fiber 0g	0%
Total Sugars 34g	
Includes 17g Added Sugars	34%
Protein 12g	

Vitamin D 0mcg	0%
Calcium 419mg	32%
Iron 0.2mg	1%
Potassium 537mg	11%

* The % Daily Value (DV) tells you how much a nutrient in a serving of food contributes to a daily diet. 2,000 calories a day is used for general nutrition advice.

U.S. Food and Drug Administration (FDA)

To get a quick idea of how a food product rates for certain nutrients, look at the %DV. A food that contains 5 percent or less of a nutrient per serving is considered low in that nutrient. A food that provides 20 percent or more of a nutrient per serving is considered a good source of that nutrient. Use this information on food labels to help you limit total fat, saturated fat, cholesterol, sodium, and added sugars. Also, use it to ensure you are getting enough fiber, vitamin D, calcium, iron, and potassium in your eating plan.

By using nutrition labeling, you can compare the nutritive values of various foods. This will enable you to get the most nutrition for your food dollar.

Universal Product Code

Another item found on most product labels is the **universal product code (UPC)**. This is a group of bars and numbers that contains price and product information, **14-8**. In stores using a computerized checkout system, the grocery checker passes each UPC over a scanner. The computer reads the bar code and automatically records the information. The customer's receipt lists the items purchased and their prices, along with the total.

14-7

The revised Nutrition Facts label is based on current scientific research. Use this information to compare the nutrient values of various foods.

14-8

The universal product code (UPC) appears on various products as a group of lines, bars, and numbers.

Reading Review

1. List the five basic types of grocery stores available to consumers.
2. A consumer aid that shows the cost per standard unit of weight or measure for a food product is known as _____ .
3. List the four forms of open dating.
4. List the information required to appear on a food label.

Section 14-3

Buying Foods

Objectives

After studying this section, you will be able to

- **list** factors to consider when buying meat, poultry, fish, and alternates.
- **identify** signs of quality in fruits and vegetables.
- **describe** types of grain products.
- **explain** how to select milk products.

Key Terms ↗

meat	meat analog	pasteurization
poultry	produce	homogenized
finfish	cereal	natural cheese
shellfish	pasta	process cheese
legume		

Knowing how to buy and store foods are basic skills. When buying foods, choose the products that best meet your needs. Learn to select nutritious foods at the lowest possible prices. By carefully choosing and storing foods, you will get the most for your money.

Meat, Poultry, Fish, and Alternates

Meat, poultry, and fish are the most costly protein foods, so select them carefully for the best value. Less costly but equally nutritious protein alternatives are also available. Eggs, dry beans, and nuts are good sources of protein, vitamins, and minerals. To stretch your food dollar, plan some menus around these alternates.

Meat

Meat is the edible portion of animals, including muscles and organs. Beef, veal, pork, and lamb are the most common forms of meat. Mature cattle provide beef, while young cattle provide veal. Pork comes from swine. Lamb comes from young sheep.

You should consider two major factors when buying meat. One is the quality of the meat; the other is the cut of the meat.

Meat Inspection and Grading

In the United States, all meat shipped across state lines must be inspected. This is done by the United States Department of Agriculture (USDA) to certify that the meat is wholesome. An inspection also indicates the plant and processing conditions were sanitary.

In addition to an inspection stamp, beef, veal, and lamb may be stamped with a grade shield, **14-9**. (Pork is considered tender, so it is not graded for retail sale.) This shield indicates the meat was voluntarily graded for quality. Grades help consumers determine the tenderness and juiciness of the meat. Meat from a young animal is usually tender; meat from an older animal is usually tougher.

The grade of a food does not affect its wholesomeness or nutritive value. For instance, a tough cut of beef may be just as wholesome and nutritious as a tender cut. However, its grade will not be as high.

The three top grades for beef established by the USDA are prime, choice, and select.

- *Prime* beef has the best quality and flavor. It is the most tender because it has the most *marbling* (fat that is mingled throughout the lean). This grade is mainly sold to restaurants.

Math Connection

Determining How Much Meat to Buy

Kyle is planning to make hamburgers on the grill. He needs to buy enough ground beef for eight people. He plans to shape patties that are four ounces each. How much ground beef will he need to buy?

Kyle multiplies the number of people by the number of ounces per patty.

$8 \times 4 = 32$

Kyle knows that there are 16 ounces in a pound. So he divides 16 into 32 to find out how many pounds of ground beef he will need.

$32 \div 16 = 2$

The price of high-quality ground beef that will yield little shrinkage is $4.99 per pound. To find out how much the ground beef will total in cost, Kyle multiplies the cost per pound by the number of pounds he needs.

$4.99 \times 2 = 9.98

14-9

The USDA stamp on the top certifies that meat is wholesome. The grade shield below is an indication of quality.

- *Choice* beef has excellent quality, but has less fat and flavor than prime. It is the highest quality found in grocery stores and meat markets.

- *Select* beef has less flavor and marbling than prime and choice. However, it has less fat and a somewhat lower cost, so it is a good buy in terms of your health and budget.

Meat Selection

In selecting meat, you can be sure the quality is good if the lean has good color and is marbled with fat. Meats are generally pink to red in color. Quality meat also has firm fat that is creamy white in color. Meat with yellow fat is of poorer quality.

Regardless of the grade, some cuts of meat are more tender than others. The location of the meat in the animal determines tenderness. Cuts from the less-used muscles along the back are more tender. These include rib and loin cuts. Cuts from the muscles that are frequently used are less tender. These include leg and shoulder cuts.

You can also determine whether a meat cut comes from the tender part of an animal by looking at bone shape. T-shaped bones, flat bones, and wedge bones indicate tender cuts. Round bones (from the arm and leg area) and blade bones (from the shoulder area) indicate less-tender cuts of meat.

Buy the cut of meat best suited to your needs by reading meat labels. See **14-10**. Meat labels make meat identification easy. By reading the meat identification label, you can find out the

- type of meat

- wholesale cut (location of the meat in the animal)

- retail name of the cut

The most tender cuts of meat make up a very small portion of the animal. They are in greatest demand, which is why these cuts are so expensive. When buying meat, consider the cost per serving rather than the cost per pound. If two cuts of meat cost the same, the cut with less fat and less bone will yield more servings.

14-10

A meat package label shows the names of the wholesale and retail cuts, the weight, and the price.

MEAT DEPARTMENT

WEIGHT Lb. Net	PAY	PRICE Per Lb.
2.45	$13.45	5.49

BEEF CHUCK
BLADE ROAST

Poultry

Poultry describes any domesticated bird raised for meat and/or eggs. Chicken, turkey, duck, and goose are the most popular types of poultry in the United States. Like meats, poultry must be federally inspected for wholesomeness. It may also be voluntarily graded for quality. Only U.S. Grade A poultry is sold at the retail level. However, "ungraded" poultry is usually equal in quality to Grade A poultry.

Ready-to-cook poultry is sold fresh-chilled or frozen. Poultry should look moist and plump and have clean, blemish-free skin. Choose birds with meaty breasts and legs. Avoid buying frozen birds that show signs of thawing or freezer burn (brownish spots).

Fish

Finfish and shellfish are two forms of fish that are eaten as food. **Finfish** have fins and backbones. **Shellfish** have shells instead of backbones. Both are available in many forms, depending on where you live. Be alert to the visible signs of freshness and quality when selecting fish and shellfish. Inspection and grade seals can help you determine quality. You should also consider appearance and form when making a purchase decision.

Finfish

The most popular finfish are cod, flounder, halibut, salmon, sole, snapper, and trout. When buying fish, look for regional specialties. They will usually cost less than varieties that must be shipped in from other areas. When buying fresh finfish, you will want to watch for the following signs of quality:

- Eyes should be bright and clear.
- Gills should be reddish in color.
- Scales should be tight to the body and shiny.
- Flesh should be firm enough to spring back when gently pressed.
- Odor should be fresh.

Fish are marketed in a variety of forms. The most popular choices are drawn, dressed, fillets, and steaks. *Drawn fish* have the entrails (guts) removed. *Dressed fish* have been cleaned. In addition to the entrails, they have had the head, tail, fins, and scales removed. *Fillets* are sides of the fish, which are cut away from the bone lengthwise from head to tail. Fillets are popular because they are usually boneless and ready to cook. *Steaks* are cross-sectional slices of larger fish with one large, central bone. Steaks are also ready to cook.

Fish is available frozen, canned, or dried as well as fresh. Fish sticks are a common form of frozen fish. Canned tuna, salmon, sardines, and mackerel are economical buys. In some areas, dried, salted, and smoked fish are popular menu items.

Financial Literacy

Your Food Budget

Planning well-balanced meals on a budget is a challenge, but it can be done. Here are some helpful tips to get you started.

- Check newspapers, magazines, and websites to find coupons for items you need and use regularly.
- Check newspaper and online advertisements for weekly specials. Look for sale prices on foods your family enjoys. Then plan your menus around these advertised specials.
- Use seasonal foods as much as possible when planning menus. Fresh fruits and vegetables are plentiful, tasty, and less expensive in season.
- Stretch your food budget by planning menus that include less-expensive cuts of meat. Stretch the number of meat servings in main dishes by using bread crumbs, cereals, rice, or pasta as meat extenders.
- Make some meals meatless by using protein alternates such as eggs or beans and peas.

Shellfish

Clams, crabs, lobsters, mussels, oysters, shrimp, and scallops are all varieties of shellfish. If oysters, clams, scallops, and mussels are purchased fresh, the shells should be tightly closed. Fresh shellfish such as crabs, lobsters, and shrimp should retain their natural color. You can also buy shellfish in canned or frozen form.

Eggs

When buying eggs, size and condition are important factors to consider. Choose the size that best meets your needs. Open the carton to be sure eggs have clean, uncracked shells.

Size and Color

Eggs are classified by size according to weight per dozen. Medium, large, and extra large are the sizes most commonly sold in grocery stores. Recipes are usually based on using large eggs.

Eggshells may be either white or brown. The color of the shell has nothing to do with the quality or nutritive value of the egg. (The breed of chicken determines the egg color.) See **14-11**.

14-11

White eggs and brown eggs have the same quality, nutritive value, and taste.

Grades

The USDA has set standards of quality for grading eggs. The grade of an egg is based on interior quality and the condition and appearance of the shell. Most eggs sold in grocery stores are Grade AA or A and are suitable for all uses.

Plant-Based Meat Alternates

Some plant-based foods provide low cost, high-protein alternatives to meat, poultry, fish, and eggs. They help consumers make the most of their protein food buys. These popular choices include legumes and meat analogs.

Legumes

High in essential amino acids, **legumes** are seeds that grow in the pods of some vegetable plants. Legumes include beans, lentils, peas, and peanuts. Served alone, they are nutritious; however, they provide incomplete protein. Team them up with a grain or animal food and you have a complete source of protein.

Legumes are often purchased dried. When buying dried legumes, look for uniform color and size to ensure freshness and even cooking. High-quality legumes are free from debris (stones, sticks, and dirt) and visible defects (cracks, insect holes).

Meat Analogs

Meat analogs are plant-based protein products made to resemble various kinds of meat. These products are made from soybeans, wheat, yeast, and other vegetable sources of protein. Bacon bits and soyburgers are common meat analogs.

When you buy these products, read the nutrition labels carefully. The food values vary depending on the foods used to make the analogs.

Fruits and Vegetables

Fruits and vegetables are available in fresh, frozen, canned, and dried forms. With so many choices, how do you decide what to buy? Learning how each form differs and following some basic selection tips can help you make smarter choices.

Healthy Living

Quality Grades for Fresh Fruits and Vegetables

The U.S. Department of Agriculture (USDA) has established voluntary grade guidelines for fresh fruits and vegetables. These grade designations refer to the appearance of fruits and vegetables, not their nutritional quality. Quality grades are most often seen on potatoes, onions, apples, and pears. The following lists the grades and a description:

- U.S. Fancy identifies premium quality. These fruits and vegetables have a uniform shape and few defects.
- U.S. No. 1 is the most common grade. It indicates fruits and vegetables of good quality, fresh appearance, good color, and relatively free of bruises and decay.
- U.S. No. 2 and U.S. No. 3 are lower in quality. These fruits and vegetables are less uniform in shape and have more defects.

Fresh Fruits and Vegetables

Fresh fruits and vegetables, which are called **produce**, are available year-round. Buy produce *in season*, or during the time of the year when it is harvested. In-season produce is fresher, higher in quality, and lower in price.

When shopping for produce, always look for the highest quality. Learn to judge produce by its appearance. All fresh produce should feel firm and have bright colors. Mature, ripe produce has the best flavor. Bruised, wilted, or decayed produce is a sign of poor quality. See **14-12**.

When selecting produce, handle it carefully to avoid bruising it. Buy only amounts of produce that you can store and eat before it spoils.

Frozen Fruits and Vegetables

Frozen fruits and vegetables retain much of the same appearance, flavor, and quality as fresh produce. However, the texture of thawed or cooked fruits and vegetables may be less crisp. Frozen fruits and vegetables are available in plastic bags or paper cartons.

You should select frozen fruits and vegetables with care. Buy packages that are undamaged and frozen solid. A soft package is an indication of thawing. Thawing affects quality, taste, and storage time.

14-12

Use this selection guide for choosing these popular fruits and vegetables.

Buying Fruits and Vegetables		
Fruits		
Type of Produce	**Look For:**	**Avoid:**
Apples	Bright color, firm texture	Bruised spots, shriveled skin
Bananas	Bright color, firm texture	Bruised skin
Berries	Bright color, plump fruit	Soft, moldy, or leaky fruit
Cantaloupe	Yellowish rind, pleasant aroma	Soft spots
Citrus fruits	Bright color, heavy for size	Dull or shriveled skin, soft spots, lightweight for size
Grapes	Bright color, plump fruit	Soft, shriveled, or leaky fruit
Peaches	Slightly firm flesh	Bruised spots; hard, immature fruit; greenish skin
Pears	Firm flesh, good color	Bruised spots; hard, immature fruit
Watermelon	Smooth outer surface, firm texture, juicy fruit	Pale color, dry flesh

(continued)

Vegetables		
Type of Produce	**Look For:**	**Avoid:**
Asparagus	Closed, compact tips; rich green color; tender stalk	Open tips, moldy spots
Beans (snap)	Bright color	Limp, dry pods; blemishes; thick, tough pods
Broccoli	Tight flower clusters, uniform green color	Yellow or brownish color, wilted stalks
Cabbage	Firm head, heavy for size, bright color	Wilted, decayed, or blemished leaves
Carrots	Bright orange color, smooth skin, firm texture	Limp texture, discolored skin
Cauliflower	Tight flower clusters, white color	Discolored appearance
Celery	Crisp stalks, bright color	Discolored or limp stalks
Corn	Plump kernels	Wilted husks, small kernels
Cucumbers	Bright green color, firm texture	Yellow color, limp texture
Lettuce	Bright color, heavy for size, crisp leaves	Blemished or wilted poor color
Onions	Smooth skin, firm texture	Soft spots
Potatoes	Smooth skin, firm texture, appropriate shape	Bruised spots, shriveled skin, signs of sprouting
Tomatoes	Bright red color, firm texture, smooth skin	Soft spots, cracked surfaces, bruised skin

Canned Fruits and Vegetables

Canned fruits and vegetables come in many convenient forms, such as whole, sliced, and pieces. Fruits may be packed in heavy syrup, light syrup, or fruit juices. Fruits packed in juice are lower in calories than those packed in syrup. Vegetables are usually packed in water. Look for those packed without added salt to help avoid excess sodium in your diet.

How do you get the best buys in canned fruits and vegetables? Several factors affect cost, including brand, can size, and packing liquid. House brands and generic products are often priced lower than national brands. Large cans often cost less per serving than small cans. Plain canned fruits and vegetables are usually a better buy than those packed in flavored sauces.

Dried Fruits and Vegetables

Dried fruits and vegetables are light in weight because the water has been removed. The flavors and textures are slightly different from

Analyze and Solve

Make arrangements to visit a local food pantry to learn how foods are obtained, stored, and distributed. With the staff, find sources of fresh produce and ways to distribute it before it spoils.

fresh, frozen, and canned forms. However, they can be *rehydrated* (have the water content restored) for a softer texture. Both dried fruits and vegetables are packaged in sealed bags or boxes. Look for well-sealed packages that are free of moisture. Dried fruits should feel soft and pliable in the package. Dried vegetables are brittle and hard.

Grain Products

Grain products, especially whole-grain products, are good sources of nutrients, energy, and fiber. In addition, they are economical, easy to store, and easy to prepare. Knowing what is available will help you choose the products that meet your needs and food budget.

Cereals are starchy grains, including wheat, corn, rice, and oats, that are used as food. These grains can be used in their natural form. They can also be used to make products such as flour, pasta, breakfast cereals, and breads.

Flour

Flour is made by grinding grains into powder. Removing parts of the kernel also removes nutrients contained in those parts. Flour can be *enriched* to add back B vitamins and iron lost during milling.

In the United States, wheat flour is the most common type. However, flour can be made from any grain. At the supermarket, you can choose among several types of flour. These include all-purpose flour, self-rising flour, cake flour, and whole-wheat flour.

All-purpose flour is used for general cooking and baking purposes. When a recipe merely calls for flour, all-purpose flour is usually intended.

Self-rising flour has a leavening agent (a substance that makes baked goods rise) and salt added. This flour is often used to make quick breads.

Cake flour is made of softer wheat and may be milled more finely than the other flours. This flour is used for delicately textured cakes and other baked products.

Whole-wheat flour has a coarser texture than other flours. It is made from the entire grain kernel. Whole-wheat flour is often used in breads. It gives them a coarser texture and nuttier flavor. For best results, use this flour in recipes calling for whole wheat flour.

Pasta

Pasta is the family name for a group of products that includes spaghetti, macaroni, and noodles. These products add interest to meals because they offer such a wide variety of shapes, **14-13**. Whatever the shape, however, all pastas are made of the same ingredients: flour and water. Noodle products also contain eggs. Most pastas are enriched by the addition of thiamin, niacin, riboflavin, folic acid, and iron.

Pasta products are made from *semolina*, which comes from durum wheat. Durum wheat is specially grown for use in pasta products. This hard wheat yields pasta that holds its shape when cooked.

Rice

The two major types of rice are white rice and brown rice. *White rice* is produced when the bran layer of the rice kernel is removed. When shopping for white rice, look for the word *enriched*. *Brown rice* is whole-grain rice. Because the whole-grain is used, brown rice is higher in fiber than white rice.

Precooked or *instant rice* is an expensive form of rice, but it is popular with many people. It is white rice that has been fully cooked and dried. It can be prepared very quickly to restore the moisture.

Rice grains come in various sizes. Short and medium grains tend to cling together when cooked. Long grain rice cooks to a fluffy texture, and the grains are more likely to stay separate.

In spite of its name, *wild rice* is not rice at all. It is the seed of a wild grass that grows in marshes. Wild rice is much more expensive than rice. To lower the cost, wild rice is often mixed with brown rice.

Breakfast Cereals

Both ready-to-eat and cooked cereals come in a variety of flavors, textures, and forms. Use nutrition labeling to compare different cereals for nutritive value. Many are high in sugar or may contain fat. Some are low in fiber. In general, however, whole-grain, enriched, and fortified cereals are nutritious and filling. Served with milk and fruit, cereal can be a nourishing meal.

Some types of cereal are more expensive than others. Ready-to-eat cereal is more expensive than cereals that require cooking. Cereals with dried fruits or nuts added and presweetened cereals are more costly than plain cereals. Although convenient to serve, quick-cooking and instant cereals are also more costly than regular cereal.

When evaluating cereal cost, it is best to compare cost per serving. Cereals differ greatly in weight. Packages of the same size may not contain the same number of servings. Also, compare the size of the serving before you decide which cereal to choose.

14-13
These are only a few of the shapes available when selecting pasta.

Serving Your Community

Explore the possibility of establishing an area for a community garden and work to make this become a reality. Also, investigate the options for composting food waste into free fertilizer for the community garden.

Breads

A wide variety of breads are available, **14-14**. White, whole-wheat, raisin, and rye bread are just a few examples. Rolls, muffins, and bagels are other types of bread products you can find at your local supermarket or bakery. For the best flavor and texture, look for freshness dates on the products.

You can choose from commercially prepared bread products or in-store bakery products. Commercial breads are prepared in large quantities, so they are reasonably priced. They are prepackaged and then sold on grocery store shelves. Supermarket bakeries sell freshly baked bread products directly to you. These products may be more costly, but they offer a fresh-baked taste and texture.

Convenience bread products also come in many forms. *Brown-and-serve products* are partially baked; you finish baking them at home. *Refrigerated doughs* need only to be baked at home. *Frozen doughs* must be thawed and then baked.

Dairy Products

Many types of dairy products are available to consumers. Milk, cheese, yogurt, frozen milk products, cream, and butter are included in this group of foods. The two most common dairy products—milk and cheese—are covered in this chapter.

14-14

Breads can come in different shapes, sizes, and flavors.

Forms of Milk
Fresh Fluid Milk
• Whole milk contains at least 3.5% milk fat.
• Reduced-fat milk contains 2% milk fat.
• Low-fat milk contains 1% milk fat.
• Fat-free milk, also called skim or nonfat milk, contains less than 0.5% milk fat.
• Chocolate milk is usually made by adding chocolate flavoring to whole milk.
Canned Milk
• Evaporated milk is obtained by removing about 60% of the water from whole milk.
• Evaporated fat-free milk is obtained by removing about 50% of the water from fat-free milk.
• Sweetened condensed milk is made by partially removing water from whole milk and adding 45% sugar.
Dry Milk
• Nonfat dry milk is produced by removing the water and fat from fluid whole milk.
• Dry whole milk is made by removing the water from fluid whole milk.
Cultured Milk
• Buttermilk is produced by adding special bacterial cultures to fluid milk.

14-15

Milk is available in various forms. Buy the form that best suits your needs.

All dairy products shipped across state lines for retail sale in the United States are pasteurized. **Pasteurization** is a heating process that destroys harmful bacteria in dairy products. This process prevents illness and helps milk products stay fresh.

Milk

You can purchase milk in several forms at the grocery store. See **14-15**. The form you choose usually depends on the following factors:
- whether the milk is intended for drinking or cooking
- your budget
- your storage facilities

The price of milk is partly determined by its fat content. The higher the proportion of fat, the more the milk costs. Fluid milk must be refrigerated unless it is aseptically packaged. Dry milk and canned milk can be stored on a shelf before being reconstituted for use.

Besides being pasteurized, most milk and milk products are homogenized, and many are fortified. **Homogenized** refers to a process by which milk fat is broken into tiny particles that stay evenly suspended in the milk. Without homogenization, the fat (also known as cream) would rise to the top. *Fortified* means nutrients, such as vitamins A and D, have been added to the milk.

Cheese

Most cheese is made from milk. In simple terms, cheese is made by *coagulating* milk, which concentrates the protein. The *curd* (solid portion of the milk) is separated from the *whey* (liquid portion).

Food values vary in different cheeses. Cheddar cheese, for example, contains milk fat, protein, minerals, and vitamins. Cottage cheese is not as rich in fat, minerals, and vitamins, but it is a good source of protein. Cream cheese has a high fat content, but it is not a good source of protein.

Hundreds of varieties of cheeses are available. They differ in aroma, body, flavor, color, and texture. Cheeses also vary in cost. All cheeses, however, have some common characteristics. They can be divided into two classes: natural and process.

Natural Cheese

Natural cheeses are made from milk, whey, or cream. The type of cheese produced depends on the

- source of the milk (cow, sheep, or goat)
- seasonings used
- method of preparation
- ripening or curing process

Unripened cheeses, such as cream cheese and cottage cheese, have soft textures and mild flavors. As soon as the whey is removed from them, they are shipped to the grocery store.

Ripened cheeses are stored for certain lengths of time at specific temperatures to develop their flavors and textures. Cheddar and Swiss are typical examples of ripened cheeses.

Process Cheese

Blending and melting two or more natural cheeses results in **process cheeses**. The natural cheeses are grated and shredded. The cheeses are then combined and heated.

There are two types of process cheese. *Process cheese food* has slightly higher moisture content than natural cheese. However, the fat content for process cheese food is lower than natural cheese. *Process cheese spread* has a higher moisture content and lower fat content than process cheese food. Process cheese products may contain meats, fruits, or vegetables. They are sold as slices, in blocks, or in jars.

Consumers often choose process cheeses for their convenience. These mild-flavored cheeses melt easily when heated, making them popular for sauces and casseroles. Spreadable forms are popular for serving on crackers, raw vegetables, and sandwich breads.

Reading
Review

1. Describe the appearance of high-quality poultry.
2. How can legumes be served as a complete source of protein?
3. What is the value of buying produce that is in season?
4. List factors to consider when selecting canned fruits and vegetables.
5. Give four examples of grain products made from wheat.
6. Explain the difference between pasteurized and homogenized milk.
7. A process cheese _____ has more moisture and a lower fat content than a process cheese _____ .

Section 14-4

Storing Foods

Objectives

After studying this section, you will be able to

- **describe** proper storage methods for foods.
- **identify** two examples of technology in food packaging.

Key Terms

| food rotation | aseptic packaging | retort packaging |

Storing food properly is just as important as selecting it. In general, the foods you buy should be stored at home as they were stored at the grocery store. Fresh food in particular needs to be used relatively quickly or a loss of flavor occurs. For this reason, make **food rotation** a part of your storage routine. Store the freshest food at the back of the shelf and older foods up front.

Meat, Poultry, Fish, and Alternates

Prepackaged meats and poultry can be stored in the original wrapping. Store them in the coldest part of the refrigerator. Meat should be used within three to four days. Use poultry within one to two days. Never store stuffed poultry (cooked or uncooked) in the refrigerator. For food safety, stuffing should be refrigerated and heated or cooked separately.

14-16

Airtight storage keeps legumes fresh and pest-free.

Fresh fish is more perishable than meat or poultry. When stored in the refrigerator, fish must be tightly wrapped in foil or plastic wrap. Otherwise, the odor of the fish will penetrate other foods stored in the refrigerator. Fresh fish should be eaten within one or two days.

For longer storage, meat, poultry, and fish can be frozen. Use airtight bags or containers to store food items in the freezer.

Properly stored fresh eggs will keep up to four weeks in the refrigerator. The best way to store eggs in the refrigerator is in the original carton. Store them with the large end up to keep the yolk centered. Keep the carton away from foods with strong odors, which eggs can absorb. Eggs should not be washed.

Store unopened packages of dried legumes in a cool, dry place. After opening packages, transfer the legumes to an airtight container. This will keep the unused portion fresh and free from insects. See **14-16**.

Because of their high oil content, nuts may become *rancid* (develop a bad flavor). Storing nuts in the refrigerator is best if you plan to keep them for a few months. For longer storage, freeze them.

Fruits and Vegetables

Proper storage protects the nutrients, flavors, and freshness of perishable produce. The quality of most fruits and vegetables is maintained by storing them in the crisper section of the refrigerator. Do not wash fruits and vegetables before storing them as this may hasten spoilage.

Some vegetables with high water content, such as lettuce and celery, need to be kept moist. Wrap lettuce with damp paper towels. Sprinkle celery with water. Store both of these vegetables in perforated plastic bags to retain moisture without trapping it.

Some fruits and vegetables are stored at room temperature, such as bananas. Stored on the countertop, they will continue to ripen. Banana skins turn dark quickly when refrigerated. This makes them less attractive, but the flavor remains good for a few days.

Store vegetables that do not require refrigeration in a cool, dry place. Onions, potatoes, sweet potatoes, tomatoes, and hard-rind squash are examples of vegetables that do not need to be refrigerated.

Frozen fruits and vegetables should be stored in the coldest part of the freezer. Store canned products on a shelf in a cool, dry place.

After opening canned goods, store any leftovers in an airtight container in the refrigerator. Store dried products in a cool, dry place. After opening packages, reseal them tightly. Then check package directions for proper storage.

Grain Products

Grain products, including flour and pasta, should be stored in tightly covered containers in a cool, dry place. For short-term storage, store breads, cakes, and cookies in airtight bags, bread boxes, or a covered container.

Storage times vary depending on the product. Breads stored in a cool, dry place will last about one week. Ready-to-eat cereals keep well for two to three months. Wild rice and brown rice will keep for six months. Refined flour, pasta, and white rice will keep for one year.

Some grain products may require refrigeration. Whole-grain products, which contain some fat, stay fresher in the refrigerator. Cakes and cookies with perishable fillings and frostings will need refrigeration. Bread may be stored in the refrigerator to prevent mold growth.

Baked products can be frozen for several months. Wrap tightly to keep out excess moisture. Frozen bread defrosts quickly, so you can use slices as you need them. Stored properly, most baked goods will taste as fresh as when you purchased them.

Dairy Products

Dairy products are perishable, so they need refrigeration to stay fresh and wholesome. Before you buy, look for the date stamped on the product. Choose the latest date possible. Take them directly home, especially in hot weather, and be sure to store them promptly.

Store milk, yogurt, sour cream, and butter in the coldest part of the refrigerator. Because these foods may develop off-flavors by absorbing odors from other foods, keep them tightly covered.

The dates stamped on milk products are called *pull dates*, **14-17**. Dairy products will remain fresh and wholesome in your refrigerator for a few days after the pull date.

Keep all cheese—whether natural or process—tightly wrapped and refrigerated. After opening, cheese tends to dry out quickly and may pick up strong odors from other foods. Re-cover or tightly wrap any unused portions.

14-17

A pull date on milk indicates the last day the product should be *sold*. After purchase, signs that milk is no longer safe to drink include a sour smell, change in color, and a lumpy texture.

Science Connection

BPA and Food Packaging

Used since the 1960s, BPA (bisphenol A) has been used at very low levels in hard plastic bottles and metal-based food and beverage cans. It suppresses bacterial growth and prevents cans from rusting. In recent years, however, the safety of this packaging component has been questioned. While some reputable groups believe it poses almost no risk to human health, other such groups disagree.

To learn the latest on this controversy, visit the website of the Food and Drug Administration (FDA). What does this agency recommend? Determine what FDA's recommendations mean to you and share your findings with the class.

Leftovers

Store leftovers within two hours after the time they were served. Bacterial growth can contaminate hot foods that have cooled or cold foods that have warmed to room temperature. Most breads can be stored on a shelf in a tight container.

Technology in Food Packaging

Food technologists and packaging specialists have developed a number of new packaging technologies in recent years. By using these methods, some perishable foods can be stored at room temperature with no loss of flavor or nutrition.

One type of modern packaging technology is **aseptic packaging**. In this type of packaging, foods and containers are sterilized separately. Then the food is packed in the container in a sterile chamber. The foil-lined boxes commonly used for juices and milk are examples of aseptic containers. Many other products, such as soups and tofu, are also packaged aseptically.

A second type of packaging technology is **retort packaging**. With this method, foods are sealed in foil pouches and sterilized. This type of packaging is used for some shelf-stable entrees. Food items sold in these types of packages can be stored on shelves for up to six months.

Reading
Review

1. Explain the meaning of the term *food rotation*.
2. True or false. The best way to store eggs is in the carton with the small end up.
3. Describe how most grain products should be stored.
4. How should milk, cheese, and butter be stored?

Chapter 14 Review

Summary

Basic meal management skills are an important part of meal planning. Meal management skills can also help you plan varied meals that suit your food budget and available preparation time.

Following a carefully planned shopping list will save you time and energy when you shop. Listing what you need and avoiding impulse buying will save you money. Understanding unit pricing, open dating, food labeling, and UPCs will also help you save money as you shop.

Consider factors such as grade, age, quality, appearance, form, and preparation time when buying foods. Identify the grade on foods such as eggs, meat, fish, and poultry. Inspect these products for texture, spots, odor, and appropriate color. Inspect fresh fruits and vegetables for freshness, bruises, spots, and ripeness prior to buying. Note the date given on dairy products for product freshness.

Proper storage helps maintain the quality of foods you buy. An easy guide is to store food at home as it is stored in the supermarket. Consider food rotation as you organize your refrigerator. For best quality, use the products within the suggested storage times.

Critical Thinking

1. **Draw conclusions.** Why do you think meal management skills are an important part of meal planning?

2. **Analyze trends.** Why do you think meat alternates, such as legumes, are becoming more popular as main dish choices?

3. **Analyze options.** Perform a market survey comparing the cost of various egg sizes available. Determine the best buy. Report your findings to the class.

4. **Recognize value.** Create a checklist for evaluating fresh produce.

5. **Compare and contrast.** Compare various types of milk, such as whole, low-fat, fat-free, nonfat dry (reconstituted), evaporated, and buttermilk. Which would you buy for drinking? Which would you buy for cooking purposes? Compare the cost per serving of these products.

21st Century Applications

6. **Leadership and responsibility.** Presume you are part of the management team for a small restaurant. You are in charge of creating one dish that features vegetables. First, plan a nutritious vegetable dish. Consider the types of produce available and whether they are in season. As you are creating your vegetable dish, create a shopping list for how much of each ingredient you will need to buy for the restaurant's inventory. Assume you will serve your vegetable dish five times in one week. Also include a plan for how you will inspect each type of vegetable before purchase. Share your dishes, shopping lists, and shopping tips with the class.

7. **Global awareness.** Research the many types of meatless dishes that are served as main dishes in various cultures around the world. What types of protein sources are used? Are the protein sources complete or incomplete? Report your findings to the class.

8. **Financial literacy.** Visit a supermarket, specialty store, warehouse club, or convenience store. Determine the unit price for five items your family regularly purchases. Then compare your answers to the unit price listed on the shelf label, if given.

9. **Health literacy.** Use the MyPlate website to create a plan for incorporating the recommended number of fruit and vegetable servings into meals for one week. Work with a 2,000-calorie diet. Use charting software to show your recommendations for each day of the week.

10. **Entrepreneurial literacy.** Making small improvements in the way things are usually done or made can bring about great benefits. Conduct an Internet search for entrepreneurs in the food industry. Choose three individuals and explain how they used innovation to start a new business based on a food product. Write an essay describing the product, challenges, and rewards of each entrepreneur's business.

Core
Skills

11. **Math.** Keep a food log for one week of all the foods you eat for each meal and during snack times. At the end of the week, compile your data into a graph or pie chart that represents the percentages of your diet that are fruits, vegetables, protein foods, grains, dairy, or other. Analyze your graph to see how you can improve your diet.

12. **Math.** Work in small groups to check advertised prices at two or more grocery stores. Compare prices for poultry pieces as well as whole birds. As a class, determine what, according to the ads, would be the best poultry purchase of the week.

13. **Research, writing.** Conduct research on finfish hatcheries. Where are they located? What are their goals? What procedures are followed in the hatcheries? Write a summary of your findings.

14. **Science.** Research the process of making natural cheese. Find out what types of cheeses result from using different milks and coagulating agents.

15. **Science.** Investigate the concepts of osmosis and semipermeable cell membranes. How do these concepts relate to the storage of produce with high-water content?

16. **Reading, history.** Research the role played by retort packaging in bringing a wider variety of foods to remote locations, such as to soldiers in war zones and to astronauts on space missions.

17. **Speaking.** Working in small groups, create an informational video explaining tips for selecting foods at the grocery store. Select one of the following foods or food categories to be the topic of your video:
    - meat, poultry, or fish
    - fruits

- vegetables
- dairy products
- grain products

In your video, include qualities of the product to inspect and important information listed in the product's food label, Nutrition Facts panel, or product packaging, if given. Share your video with the class.

18. **Listening.** Conduct a consumer survey to determine why people shop where they do. Use word processing software to design the survey questionnaire and use spreadsheet software to tabulate results.

 ## Leadership
Development

As a part of working on the Culinary Arts STAR Event or Food Innovations STAR Event, demonstrate restaurant menu planning, quantity food purchasing, and preparation techniques. Relate these real world skills to meal management skills discussed in the chapter.

 ## Portfolio
Builder

Being familiar with foods from other cultures is an advantage whether you work in the food industry or with people of other cultures. List at least six cultures different from your own. Next to each culture, describe common foods, giving examples of typical menu items. Include this document in your portfolio.

Journal
Writing

A family needs to spend less on food while still preparing healthful, satisfying meals. You analyze the family's typical shopping list. It includes such items as tender cuts of meat, instant rice, no vegetables, several boxes of cake mix, and out-of-season fruit.

Write About It: *What do you think is contributing to this family's high food costs? What changes can you make without sacrificing nutrients? without sacrificing convenience?*

A family discovers that they, like many families, are throwing away 40% of the food they buy from the supermarket. They are sometimes confused by the many different types of dates found on food packaging, such as the open date, pack date, pull date, freshness date, and expiration date.

Write About It: *Assume the weekly food purchases for this family are $100. What is the cost of the food being thrown away? What strategies and techniques can you suggest to help this family use more of the food they buy?*

Chapter 15
Food Safety

Reading Prep

Find several recipes you would like to try. Read through each recipe and highlight terms and abbreviations unfamiliar to you. Then, as you read the chapter, write definitions of these terms as they appear in the text. Use the dictionary to look up any remaining words not discussed.

Concept Organizer

Create a cluster diagram for kitchen safety. Place *kitchen safety* in the middle circle. Make four sublevel circles for *clean*, *separate*, *cook*, and *chill*. Add third-level ideas to each of these sublevel circles.

G-WLEARNING.com

Click on the activity icon  to visit www.g-wlearning. com/comprehensive/8062 to access online vocabulary activities using key terms from the chapter.

Dustin Dennis/Shutterstock.com

Know Your Equipment

Objectives

After studying this section, you will be able to

- **explain** how to use and care for major kitchen appliances.
- **use** portable appliances in the foods lab.
- **identify** various types of kitchen utensils and explain their uses.

Key Terms ⬀

convection cooking	kitchen utensil	bakeware
portable appliance	cookware	

Meal preparation can be made easier by using the right tools for food preparation tasks. With the help of various kitchen appliances and utensils, you can save time. Knowing how to use and care for your kitchen tools can make meal preparation run smoothly.

Major Appliances

Major appliances are the most costly kitchen tools. They are used for storing and cooking foods and for kitchen cleanup tasks. Refrigerators, ranges, and microwave ovens are found in most kitchens. Dishwashers, food waste disposers, and trash compactors are also widely used major appliances.

The Refrigerator

The refrigerator is the main food storage appliance. Its primary job is to keep food cold and retard food spoilage. It does this by using a system of circulating cold air. The temperature inside the refrigerator should be maintained at 35°F to 40°F.

To keep foods safe, keep the refrigerator clean. Wash and dry inside and outside surfaces often. If the refrigerator has coils, vacuum them at least twice a year. (Coils are usually located on the back of the refrigerator.)

You can take two key steps to maintain the proper temperature inside the refrigerator. First, do not open the door unnecessarily. This wastes energy by causing the refrigerator to work too hard. Second, try not to overcrowd the refrigerator. This may interfere with air circulation.

Life Skills

Selecting Appliances

Before you begin cooking, you need to know how to choose the cooking equipment that will best meet your needs.

Refrigerators

Refrigerators are available in single-door, refrigerator-freezer (two-door), and compact-portable styles. Compare energy costs and decide whether you need special features, such as an automatic icemaker. Make sure the refrigerator will fit the space available in your kitchen.

Ranges

Ranges are available in gas or electric options. Your cooking and baking needs and available fuel hookup will determine which fuel and features you need. The most common types of ranges have ovens below the cooktop:

- *freestanding ranges* may have second oven above the cooktop
- *drop-in ranges* sit on a cabinet base
- *slide-in ranges* sit on the floor

Cooking appliances are also available as separate built-in cooktops and ovens. Cooktops are built into a countertop. Ovens are built into a wall.

Microwaves

Countertop ovens are the most popular style with the best feature choices. Some models can be mounted under a cabinet to save counter space. *Over-the-range* microwave ovens hang over the range or are the upper oven on a two-oven range. *Microwave drawers* mount into lower cabinetry, saving valuable counter space.

The Range

The range is a basic meal preparation appliance. Most ranges have four surface units, an oven, and a broiler. The range may use either electricity or gas for fuel.

Follow the manufacturer's instruction manual for proper use and care of your range. Wipe up spills on cooktop surfaces immediately. Clean the oven surfaces as recommended or set the self-cleaning cycle.

Practice energy-saving habits when cooking or baking. Match the cooking utensil size to the surface unit size. When baking, keep the oven door closed. Opening the door to peek inside lets heat escape, and this wastes energy.

When using a *convection oven*, be sure to adjust cooking times and temperatures. **Convection cooking** involves circulating hot air over all food surfaces. This allows the convection oven to cook more quickly and evenly than a conventional oven. The convection oven uses lower temperatures to cook food than a conventional oven. This type of oven is available in gas and electric models.

Practicing safety habits when using a range is important. If the controls on a gas range are turned off and you smell gas, leave the house immediately and call the gas company from another location.

The Microwave Oven

A microwave oven cooks food using microwaves. Microwaves are high-frequency energy waves that cause food molecules to vibrate rapidly. The friction produced by these molecules creates heat that cooks the food.

Cooking with a microwave oven saves time and energy. You can defrost, reheat, and cook food in much less time than in a conventional oven. Because heat is created inside the food, the oven stays cool.

Use and Care

Follow the manufacturer's cooking guidelines. Because microwave ovens cook foods quickly, you must time foods carefully to guard against overcooking.

Do not turn on a microwave oven when it is empty. This could damage the oven. Also avoid using metal utensils in the microwave oven. Metal reflects microwaves and could damage the oven. Use microwave-safe paper, glass, and plastic cooking utensils. These materials allow the microwaves to reach the food being cooked.

Wipe up spills with a damp cloth. Keeping the oven interior clean is important because food spills may damage the door seal.

Science Connection

How Microwave Ovens Work

Microwave ovens operate like a small radio system. The energy that these ovens produce is a form of electromagnetic energy similar to radio waves. However, the waves of microwave energy are much shorter.

The oven cavity is a strong steel box. Located near the top of the oven cavity and above the control panel is a magnetron tube. When the oven is turned on, the *magnetron tube* produces high-frequency waves of energy. These energy waves travel through a wave-guide tunnel to the *stirrer blade* in the top of the oven cavity. The stirrer blade distributes the microwaves which bounce off the sides of the oven and into the food.

Because microwaves cannot go through the metal oven cavity, they stay inside the oven and agitate the food molecules. This agitation, or friction, produces heat and cooks the food. When the timer stops or the door is opened, the oven stops producing microwaves.

The Cleanup Appliances

The cleanup appliances include dishwashers, food waste disposers, and trash compactors. These appliances aid in making cleanup quick and easy. Follow the manufacturer's use and care instructions when using these appliances.

Dishwashers

Dishwashers offer many benefits. They save time and energy. Hot water and strong detergent help sanitize dishes.

For best cleaning results, load the dishwasher properly and use the recommended type of dishwasher detergent. Avoid overcrowding dishes so water and detergent can circulate freely.

To save energy, operate the dishwasher only when you have a full load. To save more energy, turn off the dry cycle. The heat created in the dishwasher by the hot water is used to dry the dishes.

Food Waste Disposers

Food waste disposers are used to dispose of soft food waste. Two types of food waste disposers are available. A switch turns on a *continuous feed* disposer. Then food is pushed into the disposer in a continuous manner. When operating a *batch feed disposer*, food is added in small amounts. The disposer is then turned on when the lid is placed over the opening.

Operate food waste disposers carefully. Before using a disposer, check to be sure there are no foreign items in it. When operating a disposer, use cold running water. Use a rubber spatula to push foods into the disposer. Never use your fingers or metal objects to place food in the disposer. Do not put grease or oil in a food waste disposer.

Trash Compactors

Trash compactors are used to compress disposable wastes into a neat bundle. Compacted trash uses about one-fourth the space of waste that has not been compacted. Nonrecyclable containers and some food scraps can go in a trash compactor. However, do not place aerosol cans or flammable materials in this appliance.

Portable Appliances

A number of portable appliances are found in most kitchens. **Portable appliances** can be easily moved from one place to another. These appliances are designed to help people save time and energy when preparing foods.

Some portable appliances, such as popcorn poppers, are designed to do special jobs. Others, such as mixers and food processors, can perform a variety of tasks. See **15-1**. Other common portable appliances include electric skillets, toasters, toaster ovens, blenders, food processors, coffeemakers, and electric mixers.

Kitchen Utensils

A **kitchen utensil** is a handheld kitchen tool used for measuring, cutting, mixing, cooking, or baking tasks. Specialized utensils are available to perform almost any food preparation task. To get the most satisfaction from your cooking utensils, read and follow the manufacturers' use and care instructions.

To make utensils convenient to use, store them near where you will be using them. For instance, store a soup ladle near the range. Store measuring cups near your electric mixer. Be sure to store utensils safely, too. Keep knife blades covered and sharp edges pointing down.

15-1

Small appliances can perform many tasks or one specific task. The food processor can shred, slice, mix, chop, puree, or knead foods.

Measuring Utensils

Measuring utensils will help you correctly measure recipe ingredients. Each type of utensil has a specific measuring function. See **15-2**.

Dry measuring cups are used for measuring dry ingredients, such as flour and sugar. They are also used for measuring shortenings and chopped foods.

Liquid measuring cups are used to measure liquid ingredients, such as water, milk, oil, and syrup. They are clearly marked with levels to allow accurate measurement of various amounts of ingredients. Liquid measuring cups should have a lip and a handle to make pouring easy.

Measuring spoons are used to measure small amounts of liquid, dry, and solid ingredients. These spoons are made of metal or plastic.

Although spatulas are not measuring utensils, they can assist you with measuring tasks. Use a *straight-edged spatula* for leveling dry and solid ingredients in measuring cups or spoons. A *rubber spatula*, or rubber scraper, can help you scrape wet or solid ingredients from measuring utensils.

Cutting Utensils

In meal preparation, cutting utensils are used to peel, pare, chop, slice, shred, carve, and debone foods. One type of cutting utensil that can do all these tasks is the knife. However, there are many types of knives, and each one is designed to handle particular cutting tasks. Some knives are long; others are short. Some have straight blades; others have *serrated*, or toothed, blades. The style of each knife depends on the preparation tasks for which it is used. The most popular types of knives are described in **15-3**.

You can use a *paring knife* to pare (cut the skin off) vegetables and fruits, such as cucumbers and apples. It will also help you with small slicing and trimming jobs.

15-2

Use of standard measuring utensils helps assure the success of a recipe. The most common ones are shown here. Spatulas are used to level off or scrape out measured ingredients.

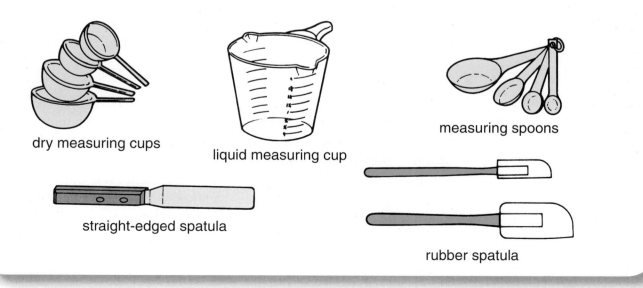

dry measuring cups

liquid measuring cup

measuring spoons

straight-edged spatula

rubber spatula

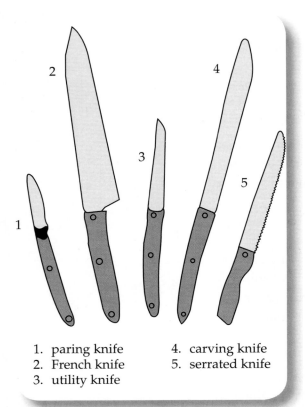

15-3

A variety of cutting tools are used for food preparation tasks.

1. paring knife
2. French knife
3. utility knife
4. carving knife
5. serrated knife

A French or *chef's knife* can chop, dice, and mince such foods as fruits, vegetables, nuts, and garlic. It is one of the most versatile knives you can own.

A *utility knife* is also versatile. It is a good choice for slicing foods, such as tender vegetables and cheeses.

A *carving knife* is used mostly for meats and poultry. Choose this type of knife when slicing ham, turkey, roasts, and other large food items for serving.

You need at least one *serrated knife* in your kitchen. Use this type of knife for slicing bread, sponge-type cakes, and soft vegetables like tomatoes.

Keeping the cutting edges of knives sharp is important. Sharp knives produce smoother, cleaner cuts with an easy hand motion. Exerting pressure to cut with a dull knife may cause an accident.

A *cutting board* should be used when cutting food with a knife. It protects your hand, the countertop, and the cutting edge of the knife. Cutting boards are made of wood, acrylic, and glass-ceramic. The only wooden boards to consider are hardwoods such as oak or maple. Softwoods such as pine are too porous. Bacteria can collect in porous wooden boards as well as deeply worn or grooved hardwood or acrylic boards. A glass-ceramic board resists the buildup of bacteria, but it dulls knives. All cutting boards should be washed and sanitized after each use.

Another type of cutting tool is *kitchen shears*. Use them for cutting dried fruits. They are also useful for snipping herbs, cutting meat or pizza, and opening food packages.

A *peeler* with a floating blade is used to remove the skin of fruits and vegetables. Because it removes a very thin layer, the nutrients near the surface are preserved. Peelers are also used to make garnishes such as carrot curls.

A *shredder-grater* is a four-sided utensil used for shredding, grating, and slicing tasks. Use it to grate lemon rind, shred cheese or cabbage, and slice potatoes.

Mixing Utensils

Mixing utensils are used for tasks such as mixing, combining, stirring, beating, blending, and whipping. Basic mixing utensils include bowls, spoons, scrapers, and beaters.

Use a *mixing bowl* to hold the recipe ingredients you want to mix. These bowls come in various sizes. A large *mixing spoon* makes it easy to mix, stir, or blend ingredients. *Rubber scrapers* are versatile tools. They are useful for folding ingredients and cleaning the sides of your mixing bowl. *Rotary beaters* have a crank, which you turn to make the beaters rotate. Use a beater to blend, beat, and whip ingredients in a mixing bowl. Another utensil that can do these mixing tasks is a *whisk*.

Cookware and Bakeware

Special equipment is needed for cooking food. **Cookware**, which includes saucepans and skillets, is used for cooking on top of the range. **Bakeware** is used for baking foods in the oven. Figure **15-4** gives some general tips for selecting cookware and bakeware.

Cookware

Saucepans and pots with tight-fitting lids serve many uses. Both are used for cooking foods over direct surface heat. Saucepans usually have one handle while pots have two handles. Several sizes are commonly used in most kitchens.

A *double boiler* is a small pan that fits inside a larger pan—usually a saucepan. Food is placed in the top pan. Water is placed in the bottom pan. The steam produced when the water is heated cooks the food in the top pan. This gentle heat is less likely to burn delicate foods, such as milk and cream-based dishes.

Skillets, or frying pans, are used for shallow fat frying, panbroiling, searing, and braising foods. Heavy materials that distribute heat evenly, such as cast iron or cast aluminum, are desirable for skillets.

Griddles are skillets without sides. They are used for grilling sandwiches and cooking pancakes and French toast.

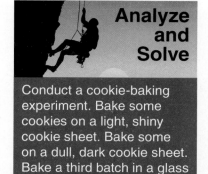

Analyze and Solve

Conduct a cookie-baking experiment. Bake some cookies on a light, shiny cookie sheet. Bake some on a dull, dark cookie sheet. Bake a third batch in a glass dish. Compare the results and offer explanations.

15-4

Follow these helpful tips when selecting cookware and bakeware.

Selecting Cookware and Bakeware

When you select cookware, look for these features:

- durable materials that distribute heat evenly
- sturdy designs with flat bottoms and smooth edges
- heat-resistant handles that are securely attached
- tight-fitting lids with easy-to-grip knobs
- durable pieces that are light enough to handle comfortably
- easy-to-clean design

When you select bakeware, look for these features:

- appropriate materials (glass, metal, glass-ceramic) that suit your specific baking needs
- the correct size for the intended use
- easy-to-clean design

Large kettles are used when cooking foods in quantity, such as soups and pastas. Some of these pots come with a basket that is useful for steaming foods.

Bakeware

Several baking utensils are customized for specific tasks. Bakeware includes loaf, muffin, tube, pie, springform, pizza, and round and square cake pans.

When selecting bakeware, consider the surface of the utensil. If the surface is light and shiny, part of the heat will be reflected away from the food. Foods baked in shiny pans will have light, soft crusts. Dull, dark surfaces absorb heat and cook faster. Foods baked in dark pans will have crisper crusts. Glass also absorbs heat and cooks faster. Most recipe baking times are based on using light and shiny cooking surfaces.

Cookie sheets have a low rim on one or more sides of the baking sheet for strength. They are used for baking cookies, rolls, and biscuits and for heating frozen foods such as pizza.

Most *roasting pans* have high domed lids to cover meats. They also have removable racks to hold meat out of the drippings that form during cooking. Roasting pans may be oval or rectangular in shape and can be purchased in various sizes.

Casseroles are baking dishes with high sides. You can use them for both baking and serving foods. Some casseroles are designed for freezer-to-oven use. They may be made of glass, glass-ceramic, or earthenware. Sizes range from single servings to several quarts.

A *cooling rack* is an important accessory for baking. A cooling rack allows air to circulate around food so it can cool evenly.

Cookware and Bakeware Materials

Learning about the materials used to make cookware and bakeware can help you make wiser choices. Well-constructed, high-quality materials will likely last many years. Read and follow the use and care instructions that come with the products.

All materials are not suited for every use. For instance, plastic bakeware is often used for microwave cooking. It is easy to clean, sturdy, and dishwasher safe. However, most plastic bakeware cannot be used in a conventional oven at high temperatures. When choosing cookware and bakeware, look for materials that are versatile.

Reading
Review

1. List four major appliances commonly found in a kitchen.
2. How does a portable appliance differ from a major appliance?
3. List and state the specific use of four cutting tools.
4. Explain the difference between cookware and bakeware.

Section 15-2

Safety and Sanitation

Objectives

After studying this section, you will be able to

- **follow** safety practices in the kitchen when preparing foods.
- **list** specific guidelines that fall under the steps *clean*, *separate*, *cook*, and *chill* for keeping foods safe to eat.

Key Terms

sanitation   foodborne illnesses   cross-contamination

In addition to preparing tasty, nutritious meals, a successful kitchen follows safety and sanitation practices. A safe kitchen is one that is as free as possible from risks of injury. Taking precautions can help you keep your kitchen work area safe and free from accidents. Handling food properly and keeping food safe to eat are important sanitation practices. **Sanitation** is the process of maintaining a clean and healthful environment. Following sanitary food preparation measures assures that food is safe to eat.

Make It Safe

Following safety practices will help you prevent accidents in the kitchen. The most common types of accidents in the kitchen are electrical shocks, fires, burns, falls, cuts, and poisonings. Remember to practice safety habits when using appliances and utensils.

Using Appliances and Utensils Safely

Many accidents in the kitchen are caused by the misuse of equipment. Accident prevention depends on your knowing how to safely use each appliance. You must follow all manufacturers' use and care instructions carefully. You also need to know how to use all utensils, cookware, and bakeware correctly. Knowing how to use and care for equipment is only the first step. Follow up by practicing safety procedures. Some important kitchen safety guidelines are listed in **15-5**.

Analyze and Solve

Work with your family to analyze sanitation and safety practices in your home. Develop checklists based on Figure 15-5 plus other information in this section. Work together with your family to make any changes needed.

Kitchen Safety

Preventing Cuts and Minor Injuries

- Hold the tip of a knife down when carrying it.
- If you drop a knife, step back and let it fall. Do not try to catch it.
- Keep knife blades sharp.
- Store knives in a rack or drawer with the cutting edges down.
- Chop, dice, and slice foods on a cutting board.
- Use knives for cutting only. If a can opener or screwdriver is needed, find the appropriate tool.
- Cut down and away from yourself when using a knife.
- Wash sharp knives separately.
- Wrap broken glass in heavy paper before putting it into the trash.
- Do not leave drawers and cupboard doors standing open.
- Turn off appliances such as electric mixers, blenders, and food processors before cleaning the sides of the container with a rubber scraper.

Preventing Burns

- Use a pot holder, not a dishcloth or towel, to handle hot utensils.
- Keep a fire extinguisher near the kitchen entrance.
- Lift pot lids away from your body to avoid steam burns.
- Dry foods before putting them into hot fat to avoid spatters.
- Do not put water on a grease fire. Turn off the source of heat. Cover the fire with the lid of a pan or smother it with baking soda.
- Do not carry a container of hot food across the room without first giving a loud warning to others.
- When draining hot food from a pan, use the lid as a shield from the steam.
- Open the oven door flat and pull out the oven rack when removing foods from a hot oven.
- Keep pan handles turned away from the front of the range when cooking.

Preventing Fires

- Roll up long sleeves when cooking and avoid wearing loose clothing.
- Tie back long hair.
- Dip a burned match in water before putting it into a trash can.
- Never leave food cooking on the range unattended.
- Keep aerosol cans away from heat.
- Clean grease from the range top and exhaust fan to prevent grease fires.

Preventing Electrical Shocks

- Read and follow manufacturer's directions before using any electrical appliance. Disconnect appliances by pulling on the plug rather than the cord.
- Avoid overloading electrical outlets. Unplug an electrical appliance before cleaning it.
- Handle electrical appliances only when your hands are dry.

Preventing Falls

- Wipe up spills immediately.
- Keep a sturdy step stool handy for reaching high places.

Preventing Poisonings

- Keep all chemicals, such as medicines, household cleaners, and pesticides, away from food storage areas.
- Keep food out of range when spraying chemicals. Wipe counters thoroughly when spraying.

15-5

Following safety guidelines while preparing and serving foods can help protect you and others from injury.

Keep It Sanitary

Many cases of foodborne illness occur each year. **Foodborne illnesses** are sicknesses caused by eating contaminated food. The contaminants that cause illness are often bacteria. If you suspect any food is spoiled, do not taste it. Throw it out immediately.

Pregnant women, young children, older adults, and people with weakened immune systems are at greater risk of foodborne illness. These groups of people need to take extra precautions to handle food safely.

Food safety involves four basic steps—clean, separate, cook, and chill. If you remember these steps and observe the following tips, you can help prevent foodborne illness.

Clean Hands, Utensils, and Surfaces

Cleanliness is essential. Keep utensils and work areas clean. Pay attention to personal cleanliness. Wash your hands before handling food. Make sure your fingernails are clean, too. Some other important principles of sanitation include the following:

- Tie back hair or wear a chef's hat or hairnet to keep hair from falling into food.

- Wear a clean apron to avoid transferring bacteria from your clothes to the food. Use clean equipment.

- Do not use a hand towel to dry dishes.

- Do not touch food with your hands if you could use tongs, a fork, or a knife. Rewash hands after handling raw meats, poultry, fish, or eggs.

- Wear plastic gloves when working with food if you have an open sore on your hand.

- Do not lick fingers or cooking utensils. Use one spoon for stirring and another spoon for tasting.

- Replace cutting boards when they become worn and hard to clean.

- Wash dishes thoroughly with hot soapy water and sanitize eating utensils with scalding water or sanitizer.

Science Connection

Bacteria and Foodborne Illnesses

Symptoms of foodborne illness can occur within 30 minutes of eating contaminated food. However, sometimes symptoms take a few weeks to appear. Most foodborne illnesses usually last no more than a couple days, but some can have lasting effects.

The USDA identifies several types of bacteria that contribute to common foodborne illnesses. Here are a few:

- *Campylobacter* causes headaches, fevers, diarrhea, and stomach cramps. It is usually transmitted through contaminated water, raw milk, and raw or undercooked meat, poultry, and shellfish.

- *Escherichia coli (E. coli)* causes severe, bloody diarrhea and stomach cramps. It may be found in contaminated water, raw milk, raw or undercooked ground beef, unpasteurized apple juice, and raw fruits and vegetables.

- *Clostridium botulinum* produces a toxin that affects the central nervous system. It is usually transmitted through improperly canned foods, jarred foods, and vacuum-packed foods.

- *Salmonella* causes stomach pain, fever, and diarrhea. It may be found in raw milk, raw or undercooked eggs, poultry, seafood, and meat, or dairy products.

Living Green

Fresh fruits and vegetables should be washed. However, you can minimize the use of running water when cleaning produce. For example, do not leave the water running when peeling potatoes—only turn it on when rinsing.

Healthy Living

Handwashing Savvy

According to the *Centers for Disease Control (CDC)*, the best way to stay healthy is by keeping your hands clean. Always wash your hands before eating, after using the restroom, after changing diapers, blowing your nose, coughing, handling garbage and pet waste, and before and after treating a wound. Here are simple steps for good hand hygiene:

- Wet hands with warm, clean running water and apply soap.
- Create a lather by rubbing hands together. Wash hand fronts and backs, between the fingers, and under fingernails.
- Continue rubbing hands for 20 seconds.
- Rinse hands well under running water.
- Use a paper towel or air dryer to dry hands.

- Keep kitchen counters clean.
- Wash tops of cans before opening them to keep dust and bacteria out of food.
- Wash fresh fruits and vegetables under running water to flush away dirt and pesticides before preparation.

Pest Control

Pests can transfer disease-causing bacteria to food during storage. Therefore, you need to take steps to keep mice, rats, ants, flies, and cockroaches out of your home. You must prevent these pests from contaminating surfaces, utensils, or food supplies.

Methods for pest control vary. You can use a variety of traps or sprays. However, you must exercise great caution because chemicals can also contaminate surfaces, utensils, and food. If pest problems persist, contact your local health department for their suggestions. You may need to call a professional exterminator to keep pests away.

Separate Raw and Cooked Foods

You must handle all foods properly to prevent contamination. However, you must handle perishable protein foods (meat, poultry, fish, and eggs) with extra care as they are easily contaminated. When these foods are raw, you must also keep them separate from other foods. If these foods happen to be contaminated, keeping them separate will help you prevent cross-contamination. **Cross-contamination** is the spread of bacteria from a contaminated food to other food, equipment, or surfaces.

- Place fresh meats, poultry, and fish in individual plastic bags at the grocery store. This will keep juices from getting on other foods in your shopping cart. Place these foods in sealed plastic containers and store them on a lower shelf in the refrigerator. This will prevent them from dripping on other foods.

- Wash cutting boards and other equipment immediately after using them to prepare raw meats, poultry, fish, or eggs. This will help you avoid transferring bacteria from uncooked foods to other foods.

- Never serve cooked meat, poultry, or fish on the same plate that held these foods before cooking.

Initiative. Laura works in the accounting department. Although it is not part of her job, she makes sure the lunchroom is clean without being asked.

Cook Foods Thoroughly

Raw and undercooked meat, poultry, fish, and eggs may contain disease-causing bacteria. Thoroughly cook these foods and all dishes that contain them. Also, be sure food you order in restaurants is completely cooked. The temperatures used for cooking can kill many harmful bacteria.

- Use a food thermometer to be sure meat, poultry, fish, and egg products are cooked to the recommended internal temperatures. Color is not an accurate indicator of doneness. See **15-6**.

- Do not partially cook meats, poultry, or fish. Cook them thoroughly and serve immediately.

- Stuff meats, poultry, and fish just before baking. Remove stuffing promptly after baking; refrigerate leftovers separately.

- Never set the oven lower than 325°F when cooking meats.

- Keep hot foods hot—above 140°F. Bacteria grow fast in warm foods at lower temperatures.

- If you are heating leftovers, be sure to heat them to at least 165°F before serving. Heat sauces, soups, marinades, and gravies to this temperature as well.

Chill Foods Promptly

Refrigerator temperatures slow the growth of harmful bacteria. This is why it is important to keep perishable foods chilled until you are ready to prepare or eat them. It is also important to chill leftover foods as soon as you are done eating.

- Put frozen and refrigerated foods in your shopping cart last.

- Get foods home as quickly as possible. In warm weather, carry a cooler in your car to keep foods cool until you get home.

- Promptly store foods that should be chilled and frozen.

- Wrap foods properly for freezer and refrigerator storage.

- Use thermometers to monitor storage temperatures. Be sure your freezer is kept at 0°F or lower and your refrigerator is kept at 40°F or lower.

- Thaw perishable foods overnight in the refrigerator or in the microwave oven just before cooking. Never thaw on the counter or in the sink.

- Marinate meat, fish, and poultry in the refrigerator.

- Never leave perishable foods out over two hours. This includes takeout foods and foods on a buffet table.

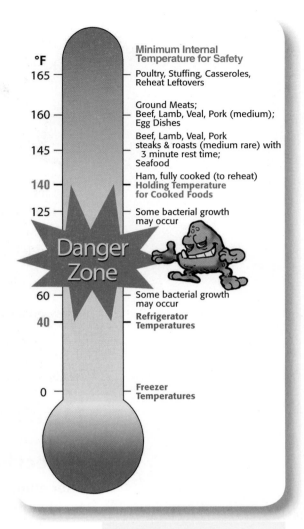

15-6

Thoroughly cooking food to the proper temperature kills harmful bacteria.

- Place leftovers in shallow containers to promote rapid cooling. Then refrigerate or freeze leftovers promptly.

- Keep cold foods cold—below 40°F. Bacteria grow fast in cool foods at higher temperatures.

Reading
Review

1. List three safety practices that help prevent kitchen accidents.
2. Explain how foodborne illnesses occur.
3. List the four basic steps to food safety and give two specific guidelines for each step.

Section 15-3

Using a Recipe

Objectives

After studying this section, you will be able to

- **identify** the information found in a recipe and follow it successfully.

- **demonstrate** proper measuring techniques for different types of ingredients.

- **define** cooking terms used in recipes.

- **describe** two categories of cooking methods.

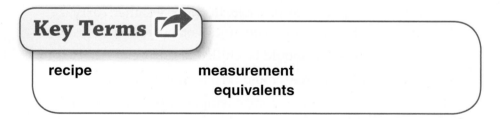

Key Terms

recipe   measurement
                            equivalents

Cooking, like other skills, is learned through practice. Before you begin to cook, you need to know certain information about the food product you want to make. What ingredients do you need, and in what amounts? What utensils do you need to use? What steps should you follow? All this information is included in a recipe. A **recipe** is a list of ingredients with a complete set of instructions for preparing a food product.

Learning to use a recipe correctly is the key to good meals. If you can read and follow recipe instructions, you can prepare almost any food product. With experience, you can even develop your own recipes.

Understanding How to Use Recipes

All recipes include certain information, **15-7**. The *ingredient list* tells you what food items you need. It also lists the exact amount of each ingredient you need to make the product. Preparation directions for combining the ingredients are next. Utensil sizes for cookware or bakeware are given, as are oven temperatures and cooking times. The recipe *yield* tells you how many servings the recipe makes.

Steps for Using Recipes

Many factors—measurements, preparation methods, cooking utensils, temperatures, and cooking times—can affect the outcome of a recipe. That is why it is important to follow all instructions. Following the guidelines below can help you get great results from the recipes you prepare. Here are some steps to help you get started.

- Read the entire recipe carefully *before* you start to cook. Make sure you have all the ingredients and utensils listed on hand. Check the preparation and cooking times in the recipe to make sure you have enough time to prepare it.

- Note any abbreviations used in the ingredient list. Be sure you understand what each one means. Abbreviations often used in recipes are given in **15-8**.

- Before you start measuring and mixing, gather all the ingredients and cooking utensils you will need.

- If your recipe tells you to *preheat* the oven, turn the oven on before you begin to cook. Set the temperature given in the recipe. The oven will then be hot when you are ready to put the food in it.

- For successful results, follow recipe directions exactly. Measure the exact amounts of each ingredient. Mix ingredients in the order listed, using the method given. Use the correct utensil sizes.

- For best flavor and appearance, accurate timing is important. Follow cooking or baking times as stated in the recipe. If your range has a timer, use it to remind you when cooking times end.

Living Green

Fresh herbs add flavor to many dishes. You can have a small herb garden in your kitchen. Just snip off what you need for your recipe.

15-7

A recipe includes all the information you need to successfully prepare a food product.

Taco Frittata
(2 servings)

1 tablespoon butter
4 eggs
2 tablespoons chopped green chiles
2 tablespoons water
½ teaspoon Worcestershire sauce
¼ teaspoon salt
¼ teaspoon ground cumin
   dash pepper
⅓ cup chunky taco sauce

Melt butter over medium heat in a 6- to 8-inch omelet pan or skillet with ovenproof handle. Beat together remaining ingredients, except taco sauce, until blended. Pour into pan. Cover and cook over low to medium heat until eggs are almost set, about 6 to 8 minutes. Pour taco sauce over top. Remove pan from heat. Cover and let stand 5 minutes or broil about 6 inches from heat until eggs are completely set, about 2 to 4 minutes.

Abbreviations Used in Recipes	
tsp. or t.	teaspoon
tbsp. or T.	tablespoon
c. or C.	cup
pt.	pint
qt.	quart
gal.	gallon
oz.	ounce
lb. or #	pound

15-8

Recognizing the abbreviations used in recipes will assist you in measuring ingredients accurately. The most common abbreviations are listed here.

In the early stages of learning to cook, using simple recipes is smart. Simple recipes have few ingredients and easy preparation steps. As you develop your cooking skills, you can try more difficult recipes and experiment with some of your own ideas.

Using Ingredient Substitutions

As you assemble your recipe ingredients, you may find you do not have a certain item on hand. In some recipes, you may be able to substitute one ingredient for another. In some cases, a substitution may affect the results of the finished product. If you are in a pinch, however, the substitution may be necessary.

Measuring Techniques

Learning to measure ingredients accurately is important for successful results, especially in baked products. Dry, liquid, and solid ingredients each require special measuring techniques. Figure **15-9** lists the right technique to use for each type of ingredient.

For measuring dry ingredients, such as flour and sugar, use dry measuring cups. Use measuring spoons for measuring leavening agents, spices, and small amounts of dry ingredients. The general technique for measuring dry ingredients is to overfill the cup or spoon. Then level it off with a straight-edged spatula or knife.

Measure liquid ingredients in glass or clear plastic liquid measuring cups. Place the measure on a flat surface and then carefully fill it to the correct measurement line. Check the accuracy of your measurement at eye level. Use a measuring spoon for measuring small amounts of liquids.

Science Connection

What Can You Substitute?

Have you ever started to prepare a recipe and discovered you were missing an ingredient? Many times, you can make a substitution that will save a trip to the supermarket.

- Use 1 whole egg in place of 2 egg yolks
- Use 1 cup of milk with 1 tablespoon of vinegar to replace a cup of buttermilk
- Use 2 tablespoons of flour in place of 1 tablespoon of cornstarch
- Use ⅞ cup all-purpose flour in place of 1 cup of cake flour
- Replace 1 cup of heavy cream with ¾ cup milk plus ½ cup butter

Although some substitutions will not significantly change the end product, others do—especially for baked goods. Changing a leavening agent, substituting oil for solid fat, or changing the amount of sugar can alter the chemical balance of ingredients in a recipe, and thus affect color, flavor, and texture.

Measuring Techniques	
Brown sugar	Pack firmly into a dry measuring cup and level off top with straight edge of spatula or knife.
Granulated sugar	Spoon sugar into a dry measuring cup until it is overfilled. Level off the top of the measure with a metal spatula or knife.
Flour, powdered sugar, fine meal, or crumbs	Stir lightly with a fork or spoon. Spoon lightly into a dry measuring cup until it is overflowing. Do not shake or tap measure. Level off top with straight edge of spatula or knife.
Baking powder, cornstarch, spices	Dip small measuring spoon into container and bring it up heaping full. Level off top with straight edge of metal spatula or knife.
Solid fats	Pack fat firmly into a dry measuring cup and level off top with straight edge of metal spatula or knife. Remove fat with a rubber spatula. Butter and margarine usually come in sticks with measurements marked on the wrapper.
Liquids	Place liquid measuring cup on a flat surface. Pour liquid into the measuring cup until it reaches the desired level. View at eye level.

15-9

Proper measuring of ingredients will help ensure good results when cooking.

Shortenings and other solid foods, such as peanut butter, are measured with dry measuring cups. Measuring spoons work well for small amounts. Press the ingredient into the cup or spoon so no air space remains. Level it off with a straight-edged spatula or knife. For sticks of butter or margarine, cut through the wrapper at the correct measurement line.

Understanding Recipe Terms

As a beginning cook, you may come across recipe terms or directions you do not understand. Understanding these terms will help you use the right method for preparing the recipe correctly. Some common terms used in recipe directions are defined in **15-10**.

Changing the Yield

What do you do if you need more or fewer servings than your recipe makes? You can double or halve the ingredient amounts to change the recipe yield if you understand measurement equivalents. **Measurement equivalents** are amounts that are equal to other amounts, **15-11**. For instance, one-fourth cup equals four tablespoons. To halve one-fourth cup, you would use two tablespoons.

When doubling or halving a recipe, write down the amounts of ingredients you will be using. This will help you avoid confusion while you are preparing the food.

Recipe Terms to Know

baste. To keep food moist during cooking by spooning or pouring melted fat, meat drippings, fruit juice, or sauce over it.

beat. To make a mixture smooth by adding air using a brisk stirring or whipping motion with a spoon or an electric mixer.

blend. To combine two or more ingredients until smooth and of uniform consistency.

bread. To dip food into a mixture, such as beaten eggs and milk, and then roll it in crumbs.

brown. To cook food quickly at a high temperature so the surface becomes brown.

chop. To cut into pieces with a knife, scissors, or food chopper.

cream. To stir or beat solid fat, such as shortening or butter, with sugar until the mixture is soft, smooth, and creamy.

cut in. To mix dry ingredients into shortening by using a pastry blender, two knives, or a fork.

dice. To cut into small even pieces, smaller than ½ inch.

dredge. To dip into or sprinkle with flour.

fold. To combine ingredients into a light, airy mixture using a down, across, up, and over motion with a rubber spatula.

knead. To use a fold-push-turn motion when working with doughs.

marinate. To let a food, such as meat, stand in a liquid to increase the flavor and/or tenderness of the food.

mash. To crush food until it has a smooth texture.

mince. To cut with a sharp knife or scissors into very small pieces.

mix. To combine ingredients until evenly distributed or blended.

reconstitute. To restore foods to their normal state by adding water.

scald. To heat milk just below the boiling point.

sear. To brown the surface of meat quickly with intense heat.

sift. To pass dry ingredients through a mesh or screen to add air or to combine dry ingredients.

slice. To cut or divide into flat pieces.

stir. To mix foods with a circular motion.

whip. To beat rapidly to incorporate air and to increase volume.

15-10

As you learn to cook, it is helpful to know the meaning of these terms.

Learning Cooking Methods

When preparing food, you want it to be both appetizing and nutritious. Some foods can be served raw. Others require cooking. Cooking is a science as well as an art. When heat is applied to food, certain changes take place. When different foods are combined, physical or chemical changes may also take place. Knowing various cooking methods will help you create tasty, nutritious meals.

Basic Cooking Methods

Foods can be prepared in a variety of ways. The method you use depends on the food you are preparing.

The basic methods of cooking food can be grouped in two general categories. The first category is *moist heat cooking methods*. In these methods, food is cooked in a humid environment. Moisture may be due to water or a water-based liquid being added to the food. Moisture may also result when steam released from the food is trapped in the cooking utensil or appliance. Boiling or stewing, braising, simmering, and steaming are all moist heat cooking methods. Basic microwave cooking is also considered a moist heat cooking method. This is because steam is enclosed in the sealed microwave oven cavity during cooking.

The second category of cooking methods is *dry heat cooking methods*. In these methods, food is cooked in hot air or on a hot surface without added moisture. Baking or roasting, broiling, deep-frying, grilling, panbroiling, panfrying, and stir-frying are all dry heat cooking methods. These methods allow food products to become brown and develop crisp crusts, which cannot form in a moist atmosphere.

Moist and dry heat cooking methods are described in Figure **15-12**.

General Cooking Guidelines

A general rule to follow when cooking food is to avoid overcooking it. Overcooking makes protein foods, such as meat and eggs, tough and causes milk to curdle. Baked products become dry. Fruits and vegetables become mushy and discolored when overcooked. Overcooking also causes foods to lose water-soluble vitamins.

Try to conserve nutrients when preparing food. If foods are simmered, use as little water as possible. When foods are boiled, plan a way to use the liquid in which they were cooked. Valuable vitamins and minerals are often discarded when cooking liquids are poured down the drain. Use these liquids in soups, sauces, and gravies.

Common Measurement Equivalents	
1 tablespoon	= 3 teaspoons
⅛ cup	= 2 tablespoons
¼ cup	= 4 tablespoons
⅓ cup	= 5 tablespoons + 1 teaspoon
½ cup	= 8 tablespoons
⅔ cup	= 10 tablespoons + 2 teaspoons
¾ cup	= 12 tablespoons
1 cup, ½ pint	= 16 tablespoons
1 pint	= 2 cups
1 quart	= 2 pints or 4 cups

15-11

Knowing equivalent measures can help you change recipe yields.

Math Connection

Changing Recipe Yields

Kayla is making punch for her sister's graduation party. Her friend gave her a recipe that serves 15 people. However, 30 people will be at the party. Kayla will need to double all of the ingredients in the recipe to have enough servings. She will do this by multiplying the amount of each ingredient in the original recipe by 2 to arrive at the new recipe yield.

Original Recipe Yield (15 servings)
½ (64 fluid ounce) bottle fruit punch
1 (15 ounce) can pineapple chunks
¾ cup strawberries, hulled and sliced
2½ cups fruit flavored sherbet
½ (2 liter) bottle lemon-lime flavored carbonated beverage

New Recipe Yield (30 servings)
1 (64 fluid ounce) bottle fruit punch
2 (15 ounce) cans pineapple chunks
1½ cups strawberries, hulled and sliced
5 cups fruit flavored sherbet
1 (2 liter) bottle lemon-lime flavored carbonated beverage

Cooking Methods		
Moist Heat		
Method	**Procedure**	**Foods**
Boil/Stew	To cook in water or liquid in which rolling bubbles have formed	Vegetables, meats, pasta
Braise	To cook in a small amount of liquid in a tightly covered pan over low heat	Meats, vegetables
Microwave	To cook in a microwave oven	Vegetables, meats, fruits, casseroles
Simmer	To cook in liquid just below the boiling point	Eggs, meats, soups
Steam	To cook in steam, with or without pressure	Vegetables, meats, fish
Dry Heat		
Method	**Procedure**	**Foods**
Bake/Roast	To cook in an oven in a covered or uncovered container	Cakes, cookies, breads, eggs, some vegetables, meats
Broil	To cook uncovered by direct heat	Meats, seafood, fruits, and vegetables
Deep-fry	To cook in a large amount of hot fat	Meats, seafood, vegetables, doughnuts, fritters
Grill	To roast slowly over coals or another intense heat source	Meats, vegetables
Panbroil	To cook uncovered in a fry pan, pouring fat off as it accumulates	Bacon, sausage, and similar meats containing a large amount of fat
Panfry	To cook in a small amount of fat	Meats, seafood, vegetables, eggs
Stir-fry	To cook foods quickly in a small amount of fat at a high temperature	Thinly cut meats, fish, vegetables, rice

15-12

Choose the cooking method best suited to the food you are preparing.

Microwave Cooking

Most foods cook much faster in a microwave oven than they do in a conventional oven. Therefore, you need to use some special cooking techniques when preparing foods in a microwave oven to achieve best results.

The defrost cycle is a popular feature on most microwave ovens because you can defrost foods at the last minute. *Defrosting time* is determined by the size and density of the food you wish to defrost. You will need more time to defrost a four-pound roast than four pounds of individually wrapped steaks. This is because the roast is larger and denser than the steaks.

Many microwave ovens have an automatic defrost cycle. A sensor measures the steam generated as a food product defrosts. This sensor automatically stops the defrost cycle at the right time. Most microwave ovens have a chart in the use-and-care manual to help you determine correct defrost times. Many food packages also give directions on how to defrost the products in a microwave oven.

Foods such as eggs, apples, potatoes, and many prepackaged foods are covered with a tight skin or wrapper. Moisture in foods turns into steam during the cooking process. If this steam is trapped inside the skin or wrapper covering a food, the encased food can explode. Exploding food items can be dangerous as well as messy and unattractive. *Piercing* the skin or wrapper of such foods before microwaving allows the steam to escape slowly as the food cooks.

Covering foods in a microwave oven prevents them from drying out due to loss of moisture. There are several popular coverings. You might simply cover foods in a microwavable dish with the lid to the dish. Microwave-safe plastic wraps may be used to cover foods. Leave about one inch of space between the plastic wrap and the food. Plastic wraps can form tight seals, so you will need to leave a loose corner to allow steam to escape. This is called *venting*. Paper towels are used for covering foods that produce fats, such as bacon, or breads that produce moisture. The paper towel absorbs the fat or moisture so the food does not become soggy. Wax paper can be placed atop a casserole in a microwave oven for efficient cooking.

Microwaves cook the outer edges of foods first. Microwave ovens also tend to cook faster in the center of the oven. You can promote even cooking by stirring, rearranging, or rotating the food. *Stirring* will bring food from the center of a dish to the outer edges for faster cooking. You cannot stir some foods, such as chicken pieces. *Rearranging* these foods halfway through the cooking cycle will help them cook more evenly. What about a pineapple upside down cake, which cannot be stirred or rearranged? *Rotating* such foods a quarter or half turn several times during the cooking cycle will help distribute microwaves more evenly. Most microwave ovens come with a turntable to rotate foods for you.

Science Connection

Safety of Plastics for Cooking Food

To reduce the risk that plastic chemicals will leach into food during heating, avoid cooking in plastic containers, even if the label says they are microwave- or oven-safe. There is a growing evidence that indicates using plastic containers, especially those made with *phthalates* or *bisphenol A (BPA)*, to store and cook foods in the microwave may be harmful to health. Small particles of plastics may leach from the plastic into food especially when heated. To avoid this consequence:

- Use glass containers when microwaving foods.
- Avoid leaving foods and drinks in plastics in the sun, such as in a hot vehicle.

Research suggests that people should avoid heating foods in plastic containers in the microwave and opt against buying products that are stored in plastics. Also, remember that many plastics that are designed for single use should be used only once.

15-13

Today's powerful microwave ovens cook foods faster than ever.

Hot foods continue to cook as long as they are hot. Therefore, many microwave recipes recommend *standing time* to allow the food to finish cooking. Standing time should begin just before a food has finished cooking. Failing to allow for standing time can result in overcooked foods.

Many of today's microwave ovens cook even faster than models sold a few years ago, **15-13**. You may need to alter the cooking times of your favorite microwave recipes if you get a new microwave oven. You should always read the recipe you are using and the directions that come with a new oven.

Reading
Review

1. What is the first step to follow in using a recipe?
2. Describe the technique used for measuring flour.
3. Briefly explain each of the following recipe terms: blend, mix, and stir.
4. What are the two general categories into which cooking methods can be grouped?

Section 15-4

Cooking Smart

Objectives

After studying this section, you will be able to

- **plan** a meal management time plan at home.
- **demonstrate** how to work as an effective team member in the foods lab.

Key Term

work plan

Cooking smart means getting foods prepared with a minimum of time and a maximum of efficiency. Some tricks that will help you master these skills can be used both at home and at school.

There is one major difference between meal preparations at home and at school. At home, you may prepare foods your way. At school, you are a part of a team. Besides learning cooking skills, you learn the importance of teamwork. See **15-14**.

At Home

The key to successful meal preparation at home lies in planning. Timing is one of the most difficult skills in meal preparation. This means having all the food ready and at the right temperature at serving time. You can achieve this goal, but it takes careful scheduling.

Using a Time Plan

As a beginning cook, you will want to write out a time plan. A time plan helps you coordinate your cooking schedule. You will know exactly when you must complete certain preparation tasks to serve the meal on time. You will also avoid the confusion and frustration of having several tasks to complete at the same time.

Try to pace your cooking activities according to the clock. You can do this by establishing the time the meal is to be served. Then count back in time to decide when you should start each part of the meal.

Suppose you want to prepare this meal: baked chicken, hot rolls, a salad, and chocolate pudding. Here is how your time plan would work. Because the chicken will take the longest to cook, prepare it first and place it in the oven. Then prepare the pudding. You can prepare the salad next. Chill both the salad and the pudding in the refrigerator until serving time. About 15 minutes before you plan to eat, heat the rolls in the oven. During this time, you can set the table and prepare the beverage. At mealtime, the chicken and rolls should be hot, the salad crisp, and the pudding

15-14

Teamwork in the home kitchen, and in the foods lab, requires cooperation in working together.

Aldomurillo/E+/Getty Images

chilled. When serving many foods that are to be cooked in the oven, choose foods that have compatible oven temperatures. For instance, stuffed pork chops, green bean casserole, and a quick bread can all be baked at 350°F.

As you gain experience, you will find it easier to prepare simple meals without a time plan. However, good cooks with years of experience still use time plans when they prepare food for special occasions.

Making Meal Preparations

Making meal preparations means doing meal-related tasks ahead of time. It could mean baking a large ham, roast, or turkey on the weekend to eat during the week. It could mean preparing a salad or casserole the night before you plan to serve it. It might also mean setting the table in the morning before you go to work or school. Use any time available to prepare for meals. You will be glad you did when it is mealtime.

Many foods lend themselves to being prepared and stored ahead of time. By preparing large amounts of foods such as soups and casseroles, you can freeze leftovers for other days, **15-15**. This is a real time-saver. Most cooking time is spent assembling ingredients and utensils and then cleaning up afterwards. By preparing several dishes at once, you save much time and effort. On a busy day, all you have to do is allow time to heat the dish in the oven or microwave.

Using Technology

Time planning is crucial for people with busy lifestyles. As a result, many people are using the convenience of technology to save time in the kitchen. Both large and small appliances and personal computers are used to perform daily kitchen tasks.

Many modern appliances use microprocessors to make meal preparation easier. A *microprocessor* is a tiny computer control. Both large and small appliances use these computer controls to simplify many cooking tasks. For instance, you can program a range or microwave oven to operate at certain times and temperatures. You can set a coffeemaker to turn on in the morning or evening.

Computers and other digital devices offer many time-saving uses in the kitchen, too. Instead of using cookbooks, you might use a software program to store recipes and menu plans on your device. When you are ready to cook, you can call up the recipe file. The program

15-15

The effort required to make one large pot of stew can provide several meals for a family.

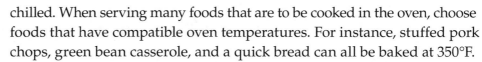

can calculate the amount of each ingredient needed and even prepare a shopping list. You can also look up recipes and meal preparation tips on the Internet.

At School

When you prepare food at school, you learn two important skills: cooking and teamwork. Thorough planning and good cooperation are needed for a successful foods lab experience.

Working with Others

Learning to work well with others in your foods lab is an important skill. Because your class time is limited, lab time must be carefully scheduled. In the foods lab, you are likely to be working with a larger group than you work with at home. You may not be familiar with your classmates' work habits, so planning lab time eliminates confusion. You need to know what is expected of you as part of the team. You also need to know when to complete your tasks.

Make the most of this opportunity to be part of a team. Such an opportunity improves your ability to get along with others, now and in the future as in **15-16**. Be cooperative and keep a positive attitude. If you have a concern about an assigned task, talk with your group.

Planning the Lab

To have a successful lab experience, you need a work plan. A **work plan** is a detailed list of all the duties that must be completed during the lab. The list also includes who will perform each task as well as the ingredients and utensils needed. Your teacher will probably ask you to complete the plan at least a day before you will be cooking.

Making Out the Shopping List

The first task in your work plan is determining what foods you will prepare. Most likely your teacher will plan this portion of the lab. Locate the necessary recipes and make an accurate list of all the ingredients needed. Your teacher may inform you that some staple ingredients are already on hand. You may be asked not to write those ingredients on your list.

Making a Time Schedule

Next, make a time schedule that includes all the tasks to be done. Prioritize the tasks in order of importance. List first those tasks that require the greatest amount of time. Allow enough time for preparation, serving, and cleanup. As a group, decide who will perform each task. For each lab planned, rotate job tasks. This way each member has the experience of performing each task. Once your schedule is complete, your lab group will be ready to prepare your planned food.

Analyze and Solve

To gain experience in preparing meals during periods too busy for careful planning, plan a menu around food products and ingredients already on hand. Review the menus according to principles of good meal planning.

Wellness Awareness

Ask permission to observe your school foodservice staff preparing a meal. Be prepared to ask questions as you observe the specialized equipment, utensils, and procedures used in preparing quantity recipes. If possible, obtain copies of the recipes so you can evaluate the nutritional value of the meal. Identify ways to increase the nutritional content.

15-16

Learning to work with others in the foods lab is good training for the teamwork needed in the professional kitchen.

Evaluating the Lab Experience

Evaluation is an important individual and group process. It gives you an opportunity to identify your strengths and weaknesses. This process also reinforces the positive aspects of the lab experience.

Evaluate yourself first; ask yourself what you did well. Did you use utensils, appliances, and food preparation techniques correctly? Identify areas in which you can improve. Second, evaluate the performance of your group as a whole. Be sure to discuss how, as a group, you can improve on the weak areas. Do not hesitate to admit your strengths and weaknesses. This is how members of your group can learn from one another.

Reading
Review

1. True or false. A time plan helps people determine what preparation tasks must be completed so their meals are prepared on time.
2. Name two ways in which technology can assist with meal management.
3. List three steps to follow for planning a successful foods lab.

Summary

Kitchen appliances include major and portable appliances. Utensils are used for measuring, cutting, and mixing tasks. Cookware and bakeware are used for cooking and baking foods. With proper use and care, all these kitchen tools will provide many years of service. The more you know about cooking equipment, the greater your chances are for a successful cooking experience.

Good safety and sanitation habits must also be a high priority when you cook. Following the steps of clean, separate, cook, and chill when handling food will help you avoid foodborne illnesses. Your health and the health of others depend on the way you practice these habits.

Knowing how to read and use recipe information is another basic cooking skill. Learning to measure accurately is essential for preparing a recipe properly. Understanding cooking terms, making substitutions, and adjusting yields are other important techniques for cooking success.

Techniques for cooking smart can be used at home or at school. At home, it means using a time plan and making preparations. At school, it means practicing teamwork and preparing a work plan.

Critical Thinking

1. **Evaluate options.** If you could only have one oven in your kitchen, which type would you choose: a conventional oven, microwave oven, or convection oven? Explain your choice.

2. **Predict outcomes.** Figure 15-5 lists guidelines for preventing fires. List the three guides you think are most frequently ignored. What happens as a result of ignoring fire prevention principles?

3. **Analyze information.** In what careers do you see the information in this chapter being helpful? Share these insights with your classmates.

4. **Assess safety and sanitation.** Conduct a safety and sanitation check of your foods laboratory at school and your kitchen at home. What can you do to improve the safety and sanitation standards at school and at home?

5. **Make adaptations.** Choose any recipe and adapt it by
   A. doubling the ingredients
   B. cutting the ingredients in half

6. **Summarize details.** Write a menu for a family meal to be served at 6:30 p.m. Prepare a time plan. (You will need to refer to the recipes for the required cooking times.) As you prepare the time plan, ask yourself these questions: When will you complete certain tasks? Which tasks can be done ahead of time?

21st Century Applications

7. **Financial literacy.** Search online for range manufacturers. Save photos of ranges along with information on their styles, options, and prices. Based on your research, which range do you think is the best purchase option? Why?

8. **Financial, economic, business, and entrepreneurial literacy.** Assume you plan to open your own restaurant, café, or bakery. What types of appliances and kitchen utensils will you need to successfully run your kitchen? How many of each item? Create an inventory wish list, listing the type of equipment you will need, how many of each, and the cost of each item. Research prices online to find realistic pricing. Then tally the total cost of buying supplies for your foodservice establishment. Share grand totals with the class.

9. **Information, communications, and technology literacy.** Research state-of-the-art computerized kitchen appliances on the Internet. One suggestion is the website for LG Appliances. Prepare a report describing the technology used in such appliances.

Core
Skills

10. **Reading, speaking.** Research methods of cooking and storing food before modern appliances were invented. Include such subjects as outdoor brick ovens, wood-burning stoves, and ice boxes. Share your findings in an oral report.

11. **Speaking.** In small groups, study the use-and-care instructions for a classroom appliance. Create an informational video for how to properly use and care for this appliance. Share your videos with the class.

12. **Science.** Conduct an experiment in which you place a mixture of beef broth and unflavored gelatin in two petri dishes. Let the mixture gel. Then place one of the dishes in a refrigerator and leave one in the classroom at room temperature. Check the dishes daily for a week and record any changes. How does this experiment illustrate the importance of keeping foods at safe temperatures?

13. **Science.** Make a dessert following the recipe, and make the same dessert using substitutions listed in "Science Connection" in Section 15-3. Sample both versions and compare appearance, flavor, and texture. How is the product affected by the substitutions? Discuss the cooking principles illustrated in the preparation of the product.

14. **Research, science.** Prepare a research report on microwave ovens. Include in the report the discovery of microwaves as well as the operation of a microwave oven and principles of microwave cooking.

15. **Listening.** Use word processing software to develop a survey form and conduct a survey on the use of microwave ovens. Ask how many people have microwave ovens in their homes. Can they relate any interesting experiences they have had while using a microwave oven? How much do they depend on the microwave oven? For what food items do they use it most often? Compile the survey results in a report.

16. **Reading.** Search the Internet to find recipes that use the terms in Figure 15-12. Enter the terms in the first column of a chart and the names of recipes that use the term in the

second column. Use charting software to create the two-column chart.

17. **Speaking.** The director of the food pantry at which you volunteer overheard you explaining the directions for cooking a low-cost chicken dish to a client. The director asks you to demonstrate your dish to a group of clients at the monthly nutrition and cooking class. The food pantry will supply your ingredients. You will need to supply the recipe and demonstrate how to safely prepare the dish. Your chicken dish is a one-dish meal that uses chicken, broccoli, whole-grain noodles, and a grated cheese topping. Assume your recipe yields 10 portions, but you will be responsible for feeding 50 clients. In small groups, prepare an instructional video demonstrating your recipe. Include the following information in your video:
    - how to modify the recipe to feed 50 people
    - ways to save time during food preparation
    - safety and sanitation practices to follow

Leadership
Development

In the Baking and Pastry or Culinary Arts STAR Events, you will showcase various techniques of measuring, cutting, mixing, and cooking food. Then produce an instructional video. This can be used in food labs at school or loaned to other groups (such as Girl/Boy Scouts, 4-H, and Boys' or Girls' Clubs) as the basis for culinary classes or badge work.

Portfolio
Builder

Safety and sanitation are a part of cooking smart whether at home or on the job. Demonstrate safety and sanitation techniques to follow when working in the kitchen. If possible, create a video of your demonstration and include it and a written summary in your portfolio.

Journal
Writing

You have watched movies and news reports featuring other cultures and countries. You have noticed that some people use food preservation, cooking, and storage techniques that differ from the concepts most familiar to you. For example, some cultures do not use refrigerators.

Write About It: *What ways can you think of to preserve other food without refrigeration? How might this apply to you if your home lost electricity due to a natural disaster? What other cultural differences related to food can you name?*

Chapter 16
Food Preparation

Reading Prep

As you read this chapter, stop at the Reading Review questions and take time to answer the questions. Are you able to answer these questions without referring to the chapter content?

Concept Organizer

Create a spider/web map with *Meal Service* in the middle circle. Make arms for each type of meal service. Then add characteristics of the types of meal service to each arm.

G-WLEARNING.com

Click on the activity icon 📲 to visit www.g-wlearning.com/comprehensive/8062 to access online vocabulary activities using key terms from the chapter.

Cooking Methods

Objectives

After studying this section, you will be able to

- **describe** cooking methods used to prepare meat, poultry, fish, and alternates.
- **identify** preparation and cooking methods for fruits and vegetables.
- **list** methods used to prepare grain products.
- **explain** how to prepare milk and cheese.

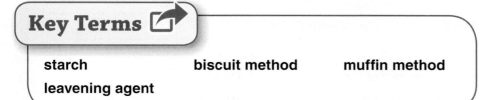

Key Terms

starch   biscuit method   muffin method
leavening agent

Choosing the right cooking method for the type of food is the key to successful preparation. In this section, you will learn how to prepare protein foods, fruits and vegetables, grain products, cakes, cookies, and dairy products. Learning cooking methods will help you make the most of your food budget while serving delicious, nutritious meals.

Meat, Poultry, Fish, and Alternates

Meat, poultry, fish, and eggs are high in protein. Therefore, these foods require low to moderate cooking temperatures. Such temperatures will prevent protein foods from becoming tough and dry.

The two main cooking methods for preparing protein foods are dry heat and moist heat. *Dry heat methods* include roasting or baking, grilling, broiling, pan-broiling, and frying. *Moist heat methods* include braising, steaming, and poaching.

Meat

When you prepare meat, you want it to be tender, juicy, and flavorful. Meat that is cooked at high temperatures becomes dry and tough. High cooking temperatures also cause meat to shrink and lose some B vitamins. When you cook meat at low temperatures, there is less shrinkage.

Choosing a Cooking Method

The type of cut will determine the cooking method you will use to prepare meat, **16-1**. Tender cuts of meat are often prepared using a dry heat cooking method. Less tender cuts are usually cooked using a moist heat cooking method. The addition of water or other liquid in these methods helps reduce toughness in less tender meats.

Less tender cuts of meat are tough due to *connective tissue*. They can be tenderized by marinating them, which also adds extra flavor.

Judging Doneness

Using a *meat thermometer* is the best way to judge when meat has reached the desired degree of doneness. Color is not an accurate

16-1

The method you use to prepare meat often depends on the cut of the meat.

Cooking by Cut		
Tender Cuts—Cook with Dry Heat		
Beef	Lamb	Pork
Chuck top blade steak	Center-cut leg steaks	Chops
Ground beef patties	Ground lamb patties	Cutlets
Porterhouse steak	Kabobs	Ground pork patties
Rib roast	Loin chops	Ham
Rib steak	Rib chops	Ham slices
Sirloin steak	Shoulder chops	Kabobs
T-bone steak	Sirloin chops	Leg roasts
Tenderloin roast		Loin roasts
Tenderloin steak		Shoulder roasts
Top loin roast		Tenderloin medallions
Less-Tender Cuts—Cook with Moist Heat		
Beef	Lamb	Pork
Beef for stew	Breasts	Loin chops
Chuck pot roast	Neck slices	Shoulder cubes
Chuck short ribs	Riblets	
Corned beef brisket	Shanks	
Cubed steak	Shoulder cuts	
Flank steak		
Round steak		
Round tip roast		
Shank cross cuts		
Skirt steak		

indicator of doneness. When using a meat thermometer, insert it into the thickest part of the meat. The bulb of the thermometer should not rest in fat or touch the bone. Meats are done when they have reached the recommended internal temperatures. See **16-2**.

Poultry

Properly prepared poultry is tender and juicy. Virtually all poultry sold in grocery stores is young and tender. Dry heat cooking methods, such as frying and roasting, are popular ways to prepare poultry. However, moist heat cooking methods, such as stewing and braising, are desirable for many poultry dishes. Regardless of the method you choose, do not overcook poultry as it will become dry and flavorless.

If you plan to roast poultry with stuffing, stuff the poultry just before roasting. (If you buy frozen commercially stuffed poultry, do not thaw it before cooking.)

Judging Doneness

A food thermometer is the only reliable guide for judging doneness of poultry. The thermometer should be centered in the thickest part of the breast or thigh. Whole poultry is done when it reaches an internal temperature of 165°F. When poultry is properly cooked, the meat should be fork tender and the juices should run clear.

Fish

Properly prepared fish is moist, tender, and flavorful. Both moist heat and dry heat methods can be used when preparing fish. Avoid overcooking fish to keep it from becoming dry and tough. Finfish is done when the flesh is firm and flakes easily when pressed with a fork. Shellfish should be cooked for a short time at moderate temperatures.

16-2

Using a meat thermometer correctly can help you determine when meat has reached the proper degree of doneness.

Meat Doneness Temperatures	
Meat	**Temperature (°F)**
Beef, pork, and lamb	
ground	160
medium rare	145
medium	160
well done	170
ham, fresh	145
ham, precooked	140

Eggs

The secret to cooking eggs properly is to use low to moderate heat for just the right amount of time. Undercooked eggs may contain bacteria that can cause foodborne illness. Therefore, it is important to cook eggs and egg dishes thoroughly. When properly cooked, egg whites are set and egg yolks are thickened. Egg dishes should reach an internal temperature of 160°F as measured on a food thermometer. If cooked too long or if the cooking temperature is too high, eggs become tough and rubbery.

Eggs are a versatile food. They can be scrambled, fried, poached, baked, hard cooked, or soft-cooked. They can be used alone or as ingredients in other foods. Omelets, custards, and soufflés are examples of foods made with eggs. Eggs are also used as a

- thickening agent to help thicken mixtures such as custards, sauces, and puddings
- leavening agent to make products such as cakes, soufflés, and quick breads rise
- glaze on breads or pastries
- coating on foods for frying (Foods can be dipped into a beaten egg mixture and then dredged in flour, cornmeal, or bread crumbs. The egg holds the coating in place and makes a crispy crust for fried foods.)
- binder to hold ingredients together, such as in a meat loaf
- garnish to make other foods more attractive and nutritious

Legumes

Properly prepared legumes are tender, but not mushy. Wash dried legumes and remove any foreign matter, such as sticks and stones. Dried beans need to be soaked before cooking. Read package directions to determine how much water to use. You do not need to soak dried peas and lentils.

To soak dried beans, quickly boil them for two minutes. Then remove them from the heat and let them stand for one hour. You can also soak dried beans overnight. After cooking, you may simply season and eat them. You may also combine cooked beans with other ingredients to make dishes such as baked beans.

Fresh Fruits and Vegetables

Fruits and vegetables are versatile. They are easy to prepare, and you can serve them in a variety of ways. You can eat them raw or cooked. You can also use fruits and vegetables for salads and snacks or mix them with other foods.

The cooking process changes the flavor, color, and texture of fresh fruits and vegetables. Choose the method that best suits your planned use.

Wellness Awareness

With your family, plan, prepare, and eat a meal consisting of foods that your family does not usually eat. For example, consider preparing a fish dish if your family does not usually eat fish. Discuss with your family individual reactions to the meal, including taste, preparation compared with another meal they might have had, cost, and nutritive value.

Before eating or cooking fresh fruits and vegetables, wash them thoroughly. Use cool running water to remove dirt, pesticides, and bacteria. You should even wash produce with inedible rinds and skins, such as citrus fruits. Avoid soaking vegetables while cleaning or storing them as this causes nutrient loss.

Some fruits, such as apples and bananas, may become discolored when cut and exposed to air. Dipping them in an acid, such as orange, lemon, or pineapple juice, can prevent this.

Crisp, crunchy raw fruits and vegetables taste best when they are served cold. Prepare them and then store them in the refrigerator until serving time.

Serve fruits and vegetables soon after you cut, peel, or cook them. Vitamins are lost when these foods are allowed to stand.

Cooking Methods

Although most fruits and vegetables are tasty and more nutritious when eaten raw, some require cooking. Cooked fruits may be served as desserts or side dishes at any meal. Cooked vegetables are often served as side dishes, in soups, or in casseroles.

Both moist heat and dry heat cooking methods can be used to cook fruits and vegetables. They can be simmered, steamed, microwaved, baked, or broiled. Two common cooking methods—simmering and microwaving—are described here.

When *simmering* fruits and vegetables, use a small amount of water or liquid and a short cooking time. Heat the liquid to boiling before adding fruits or vegetables. (Adding a small amount of sugar adds flavor and helps fruit hold its shape.) You can reduce cooking time and nutrient loss by covering the pan. However, you should leave the lid off strongly flavored vegetables, such as turnips and onions. You should also cover these vegetables with water. These steps will help some of the strong flavors to escape. Cook fruits and vegetables until they are tender, but slightly crisp.

The liquid in which fruits and vegetables are cooked contains nutrients. Save it and use it later in gravies, sauces, soups, and stews.

Microwaving fruits and vegetables is a popular cooking method. This method helps retain the colors, flavors, and nutrients because produce cooks quickly using little or no water. Pierce whole fruits or vegetables before cooking to allow steam to escape.

Healthy Living

Choose Healthful Cooking Methods

Making careful choices about the foods you eat and how you cook them can help you maintain good health for a lifetime. Here are some healthful cooking methods:
- Steaming
- Stir-frying
- Grilling
- Roasting

Remember, cooking foods in large amounts of water for extended times tends to destroy nutrients. High-fat cooking methods, such as deep-fat frying, add unnecessary fat to healthful foods.

When cutting up fruits or vegetables, cut them into same-sized pieces for more even cooking. Cover and cook until crisp-tender, stirring once or twice during the cooking time. Whether whole or cut up, let fruits and vegetables stand a few minutes before serving to complete the cooking process.

Other Forms of Fruits and Vegetables

Canned fruits are ready to serve right from the can. You can drain them or serve them in the fruit juice or syrup in which they were packed. If you are heating canned fruits, heat them in their juice or syrup. Drain canned fruits before using them in baked products.

Canned vegetables are precooked, so you can simply heat them through before serving. Avoid overcooking as this makes canned vegetables mushy.

You may use frozen fruits in many of the same ways as fresh or canned. Serve them slightly frozen with some ice crystals remaining. Fully thawed fruit will have a softer, mushier texture. To retain the fruit's shape, do not thaw it before cooking.

Cook frozen vegetables from the frozen state using the same methods you use for fresh vegetables. However, use slightly shorter cooking times.

You may serve dried fruits right from the package or use them as is in baked products. To rehydrate dried fruits, soak them in hot water for about an hour and then cook as directed.

Cooking times for dried vegetables are much longer than for fresh or frozen vegetables. Simmer or bake dried vegetables in liquid until they are tender.

Grain Products

The preparation methods used for grain products depend on the product you are preparing. Products prepared from the grains group include sauces, gravies, and puddings thickened with flour or cornstarch. Pasta, rice, cooked cereals, and breads also have special preparation methods.

Cooking with Thickeners

Starch is the complex carbohydrate part of plants. It makes up the major portion of grain products. When starch and water are heated, the starch granules swell. This is because the granules absorb the water, which makes them soft and thick. As a result, grain products increase in volume as they cook.

The key to smooth, lump-free mixtures is proper temperature and gentle stirring. Low heat slows the absorption of water by the starch granules. High heat causes granules to lump together. Gentle stirring prevents lumps; overstirring causes the granules to break down.

Flour, cornstarch, and other starches are grain products often used to thicken sauces, gravies, and puddings. When preparing these foods, lumps may form if starch is added directly to hot liquid. Separating the starch granules before adding them to the hot liquid can prevent this.

Mental Health Awareness

Cooking as Stress Management

Some people prefer to prepare recipes by hand when possible. For example, they may knead dough by hand instead of using a bread machine. They feel more personally involved in the process, which adds to the sense of creativity, relaxation, and satisfaction. Preparing food can also be a form of stress management.

You can use three methods to keep starch granules separated. The first is to coat the starch granules with melted fat to make a paste. Then add the liquid slowly, stirring constantly. This method is used for sauces and gravies, **16-3**. The second method is to combine the starch with sugar, then stir in the liquid slowly. This method is used when making puddings. Mixing the starch with a cold liquid to form a paste is the third method. The paste is slowly stirred into the hot mixture. Mixtures thickened with flour or cornstarch should be stirred constantly during cooking to achieve a smooth texture.

Pasta

"Tender but firm" describes properly prepared pasta. You must cook pasta in a large amount of rapidly boiling water to keep it from becoming sticky. To test for doneness, remove a piece of pasta from the water and bite into it.

Rice

Properly cooked rice is tender and fluffy. Combine the rice with water or other liquid in the proper size pan. Bring it to a boil and then stir. Lower the heat and cover the pan. As the rice cooks, it absorbs the liquid and swells. Rice may also be baked in the oven.

16-3

To achieve the smooth texture, this gravy was stirred constantly during cooking.

Cooked Cereals

Cooked cereals, such as oatmeal and grits, should be smooth and free of lumps. Like all starch products, when cereals are cooked, they absorb liquid and increase in volume.

There are some general rules to follow when preparing cooked cereals. Add cereal slowly to boiling water, stirring constantly. (This will help prevent lumps.) While the cereal is cooking, keep stirring it constantly. Cook the cereal for as long as directed on the package. Be sure to use the recommended pan or bowl size.

Cereals cooked in a microwave oven can be prepared and served in the same dish. Use a dish large enough to allow for boiling and swelling. Microwave cereals according to package directions, stirring as directed. Let stand a few minutes before serving to complete the cooking process.

Breads

The two main groups of breads are yeast breads and quick breads. Breads need air, steam, and leavening agents to rise. Air is added as ingredients are mixed. Steam is produced when liquid ingredients are heated during baking. **Leavening agents** are ingredients used to produce carbon dioxide, which causes breads to rise. Yeast breads and quick breads are prepared with different leavening agents and mixing methods.

Yeast Breads

Yeast is a tiny plant used as a leavening agent in yeast breads. When mixed with the right ingredients, yeast produces carbon dioxide. Yeast breads must be mixed, kneaded, and allowed to rise before they are ready for baking. The basic steps in preparing yeast breads are shown in **16-4**.

Quick Breads

As their name implies, quick breads are faster to make than yeast breads. You can mix and bake quick breads in a short period.

Quick bread mixtures can be divided into three classes of batters and doughs. *Pour batters* are thin. Typical pour batters are used for pancakes, waffles, tortillas, and some coffee cakes. *Drop batters* are thick. Typical drop batters are used for muffins, drop biscuits, and coffee cakes. *Soft dough* is sticky but can be handled. Soft doughs are used for rolled biscuits, dumplings, and some coffee cakes.

You prepare some quick breads using the biscuit method and others using the muffin method. With the **biscuit method**, you mix the dry ingredients together, and then cut fat into the mixture. Next, you add the liquid ingredients. Then you knead the dough before cutting or shaping it. Biscuits and doughnuts are among the quick breads produced by the biscuit method.

A—Combine ingredients and beat until smooth. Stir in enough additional flour to make a moderately stiff dough.

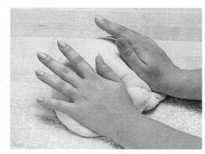

B—On a lightly floured pastry board or cloth, knead dough until smooth and elastic.

C—Place dough in a lightly greased bowl; turn once to grease top.

D—Let dough rise in a warm place until double in bulk. Test dough for lightness with two fingers.

E—When dough is light, punch down.

F—Shape dough into loaves or rolls and bake as directed. Use of these preparation techniques can produce successful yeast breads.

16-4

These are the basic preparation steps you would follow to prepare yeast breads from scratch.

In the **muffin method**, you mix the dry ingredients. Mix the liquid ingredients together in a separate bowl. Make a well in the center of the dry ingredients and then pour in the liquid. Stir the batter until all the dry ingredients are just moistened. Then spoon the batter into a loaf pan or muffin pan and bake it. (Fill muffin cups about two-thirds full with batter.)

Cakes and Cookies

Cakes and cookies are popular baked products served as desserts. You can prepare all types of cakes from scratch or from convenience cake mixes sold at the grocery store. Homemade cookies are just about everyone's favorite. Many varieties are available at the grocery store, too.

Success in cake and cookie baking depends on a number of factors. You need to measure accurately and use quality ingredients. You must have an understanding of the mixing method and follow the baking directions correctly.

Preparing Cakes

Cakes are divided into two main groups: shortened and unshortened. *Shortened cakes* contain fat, such as butter, margarine, or vegetable shortening. Baking powder or baking soda plus buttermilk are used to make them rise. Layer cakes and pound cakes are shortened cakes.

Unshortened cakes contain no fat. Beaten egg whites and steam formed during baking makes them rise. Angel food and sponge cakes are unshortened cakes.

Chiffon cakes are a combination of the two types described previously. They contain fat and beaten egg whites to make them rise.

Baking Guidelines

Shortened and unshortened cakes have different ingredients and different mixing procedures. The finished products look and taste different. Whichever type you make, follow recipe directions carefully and use the right size pans. The following tips will help you prepare cakes successfully.

- Prepare the pans. For shortened cakes, grease cake pans with solid shortening. Then coat the pans lightly with flour to allow the layers to turn out easily. Fill the pans half full with batter. Unshortened cakes are baked in ungreased tube pans. This allows the batter to cling to the sides of the pan. Fill the pan almost full of batter.
- Preheat the oven to the correct temperature.
- Allow at least one inch between pans and the sides of the oven when baking. This will allow heat to circulate freely.
- Check cakes for doneness at the end of the shortest recommended baking time. The cake should slightly pull away from the sides of the pan when done. Check the recipe for the proper doneness test.
- Follow the recipe directions for cooling and removing the cake from the baking pan. Some cakes should be removed from the baking pan immediately. Some should be cooled on a rack about ten minutes before removing. Unshortened cake pans are turned upside down over a bottle for cooling.

Preparing Cookies

Many varieties of cookies are easy to make at home. Among them are dropped, refrigerator, bar, rolled, molded, and pressed cookies. These types differ in the ingredients used, the consistency of the dough, and the way the dough is handled.

Dropped cookies are made from soft dough that is pushed from a spoon onto a baking sheet. Space the dough on the baking sheet to allow for spreading while baking. Chocolate chip cookies are one of the most popular dropped cookies.

Refrigerator cookies are made by shaping stiff dough into a long, smooth roll. Wrap the roll in waxed paper or plastic wrap and place in the refrigerator. Chill the dough until it is firm enough to slice easily. Then cut with a thin, sharp knife to ensure even slices. Bake according to recipe directions.

Bar cookies are made from soft dough that is spread in a greased baking pan. The cookies are baked, cooled, and cut into squares. Carefully

Analyze and Solve

Working in small groups, try to identify different spices used in foods from the grains group. Place a small amount of each spice in a paper cup. Place a number on each cup. Number your papers to correspond with the number of samples and write down the name of the spice by number. Compete to see which group identifies the most spices.

remove bars from the baking pan with a spatula. Brownies are a favorite bar cookie.

Rolled cookies are made from stiff dough that is chilled, rolled, cut into desired shapes, and then baked. Many decorative cookie shapes, such as gingerbread people, can be made using this method. Sugar cookies are another popular type of rolled cookie.

Molded cookies are formed from stiff dough that is broken off and shaped by hand, **16-5**. For some types of molded cookies, the dough is shaped into crescents or tied into knot shapes. Some types, such as peanut butter cookies, are flattened before being baked. Others are filled with jelly or candied fruits.

Pressed cookies are made of rich dough. The dough is forced through a cookie press onto an ungreased baking sheet. The cookie dough can be pressed into a variety of shapes by changing the tip on the cookie press. Spritz cookies are one common type of pressed cookie.

16-5
For best results, follow the recommended method for shaping molded cookies.

Baking Guidelines

As with cakes, the best cookies result from following the recipe directions. Here are some baking tips.

- Preheat the oven to the correct temperature.

- Use the correct pan size. Heavy aluminum cookie sheets or pans work best for many types of cookies.

- Follow specified baking times. For chewy cookies, bake long enough to set the dough (the shortest recommended baking time). For crisp cookies, bake a little longer (the longest recommended baking time).

- Follow recipe directions for removing cookies from the cookie sheet. Some cookies must be cooled slightly on the baking sheet before removing them to the cooling rack. Others must be removed immediately.

- Store cooled cookies to maintain top quality. Keep crisp, thin cookies in a can or jar with a loose cover. Keep soft cookies in an airtight container.

16-6

Low cooking temperatures help keep foods prepared with milk, such as this soup, smooth and creamy.

Dairy Products

Many recipes for puddings, cream soups, casseroles, and sauces call for milk or milk products. As you know, milk products contain protein. This is important to remember because protein foods are sensitive to heat. For best results when cooking with milk products, always use low cooking temperatures, **16-6**.

Cooking with Milk

Milk and milk products are often used as ingredients in heated mixtures, such as sauces and puddings. The proteins in milk will *scorch* (burn) if they are cooked over high heat. Scorching causes milk to develop a bitter taste. Cooking milk slowly over low heat will prevent scorching. Using a double boiler when preparing heated mixtures also helps.

High cooking temperatures can cause milk proteins to *curdle* (form clumps). High acid foods, such as fruits and vegetables; salt cured meats; and certain enzymes can also cause curdling. Using low cooking temperatures and fresh milk prevents curdling.

Sometimes a film will form on the surface of milk as it is being heated. This is called *scum*. Scum can cause the milk to boil over. Beating milk to produce a foam layer on top of the milk will keep scum from forming. Covering the milk during heating will also prevent scum formation. If scum does form, you should remove it because it will cause lumps in the milk or milk mixture.

Cooking with Cheese

Cheese can become tough and rubbery when it is cooked at a high temperature. To prevent overcooking, add cubed or shredded cheese to sauces and casseroles at the end of the cooking time. Sprinkle cheese on casseroles after they are baked.

To melt cheese in a microwave oven, use a medium to medium-high power setting. Using high power will cause cheese to become rubbery.

Reading
Review

1. Why does the cooking temperature matter when preparing meat, poultry, fish, and eggs?
2. What factor should be used to determine the cooking method for preparing meat?
3. True or false. Most fruits and vegetables should be cooked in a covered pan to reduce cooking time and nutrient loss.
4. What is the key to smooth, lump-free sauces, gravies, and puddings?
5. Identify the six types of cookies.
6. True or false. For best results, when cooking with milk and cheese, use high cooking temperatures.

Section 16-2

Food Presentation

Objectives

After studying this section, you will be able to

- **state** how family mealtime can affect family relationships.
- **describe** four types of meal service.
- **identify** tableware included in a place setting.
- **demonstrate** how to set a table properly.

Key Terms

meal service	place setting	cover
tableware		

Thought should go into serving foods just as it goes into planning and preparing them. After taking time to prepare delicious meals or refreshments, take care to serve them properly. A casual setting is suitable for an informal meal, but an elegant meal deserves an elegant setting. There are no rigid rules for how you should serve meals or refreshments. However, by following some general guidelines, you can help make your meal a success. Whether you are serving family members, friends, or honored guests, you can make the people who eat with you feel special.

Healthy Living

Health Benefits of Family Meals

Studies confirm a concept that people have known for generations—eating together as a family is important to healthy living. How does eating together benefit families and health? Families that eat meals together

- eat healthier meals, including more fruits and vegetables and less fat
- are less likely to be overweight
- grow stronger family bonds due to increased quality time and conversation at the dinner table
- are less likely to abuse alcohol and other drugs

Planning meals in advance, keeping ingredients on hand, and having family members help with preparation are key to eating together and having less stress over making meals.

Mental Health Awareness

Social-Emotional Benefits of Family Dining

The social-emotional benefits of family meals begin in childhood and extend through adulthood. Eating as a family improves children's language skills. It encourages community involvement in teens. Family meals also become more important to older adults as busy schedules, illness, or mature age become concerns. Maintaining close family relationships is important for mental well-being throughout the lifespan.

Family Mealtime

Families are busily involved in numerous activities. In many homes, the evening meal is one of the few opportunities family members have to get together during the day. This makes family mealtime more than just a chance to satisfy hunger. It becomes a time of important social interaction. Family members can use this time to discuss what is going on in their lives. Together they can make plans and share hopes for the future. This type of communication helps build family strength and unity. Members learn to develop tolerance and respect for individual differences.

Family mealtime provides a chance for parents to teach children. One area on which parents often focus is table manners. As children practice good manners, parents can provide positive reinforcement. This will help children remember to use these social skills as they grow up and begin interacting with people outside the family.

Many parents use family mealtime to help children develop a healthful appreciation for food. Parents can teach children family customs and food traditions. They can encourage children to try a variety of new tastes. Parents can help children select nutritious diets by offering them choices from each of the groups in MyPlate. Parents can also teach children to eat slowly and chew food thoroughly. Learning to approach food this way aids digestion and helps children avoid overeating.

You can play a role in making mealtime a positive experience in your home. You might set the table attractively and put on some soft music. Giving a little extra attention to details will show that you respect and care for family members.

You can also make meals enjoyable by keeping conversation pleasant. Save upsetting issues to discuss at another time. Treat your family members as you would treat your best friends. Show genuine interest as they share stories and ideas.

Types of Meal Service

Meal service is the way a meal is served. There are several types of meal service. The type you use will depend partly on the menu and the number of people you are serving. The formality of the occasion will also affect your choice of meal service.

Family Service

Family service, also known as *American service*, begins with a table that has been set with plates and flatware. The beverage is also on the table. All foods are placed in serving dishes and placed on the table. Family members pass the food from one person to another. Everything should be passed in one direction. People serve themselves as the foods come to them. This style of meal service is popular. However, it is inconvenient when serving dishes are hot or heavy. It may also be difficult if children at the table are too young to handle dishes of food.

Plate Service

Plate service is often used in restaurants. Individual portions are placed on each person's plate in the kitchen. The plates are then brought to the table and placed in front of each diner. Breads and condiments are usually passed at the table where family members may help themselves. This style of service is convenient when there are small children. It is also a good choice when some family members have special diets.

Buffet Service

Buffet service allows both large and small groups to be served with ease. Food is placed in serving dishes on a buffet table, with special care taken to keep everything at the proper temperature. Guests walk around the buffet and help themselves. Serving dishes are refilled as needed.

When serving a buffet, arrange items on the table in the order in which guests will pick them up. Plates are first. Flatware and beverages are often placed last. Gravies and sauces should come after the foods they accompany. Place serving utensils to the right of each dish. Leave space between serving dishes for people to rest their plates while serving themselves. See **16-7**.

Analyze and Solve

Analyze mealtime at your home. Does your family all eat together or does each person have his or her own schedule? Discuss why people often act differently with family from the way they act in situations outside the home. If you discover areas for improvement, work with other family members to plan a meal in which everyone can participate, or work to develop guidelines on which everyone can agree for behavior while eating.

16-7

This diagram of a buffet table shows the arrangement of the items in the order they will be picked up. Guests can take a plate, serve themselves the entree, and then move to the side dishes.

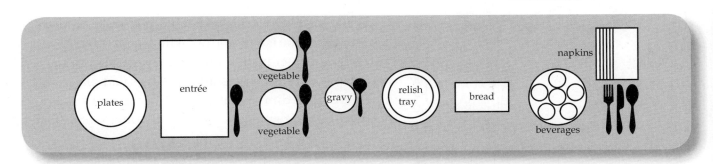

plates · entrée · vegetable · vegetable · gravy · relish tray · bread · beverages · napkins

You may not have enough table space to seat a large group of guests. In this case, you may invite guests to sit in any available space and hold their plates in their laps. However, be sure the menu includes foods that can be cut with a fork or eaten with the fingers.

English Service

Some families use *English* or *head-of-table service* for special occasion meals, such as Thanksgiving dinner. This formal type of service requires the table to be set with flatware in advance. Salads may be set at each person's place. All plates are stacked at the head of the table. The server sits at the head of the table. He or she fills each plate and passes it to a diner seated at the table. Bread and condiments are passed so individuals can serve themselves. Eating begins after everyone has been served.

There are no hard and fast rules for meal service. You can vary and combine different styles of service to meet your needs.

Tableware

Regardless of the type of meal service being used, tableware can enhance the dining atmosphere. **Tableware** refers to dinnerware, flatware, and glassware.

You can buy tableware in sets, as place settings, or as open stock. A set includes all the tableware needed to serve a group of people. Most sets include four or eight place settings. A **place setting** is the dinnerware or flatware that one person would need. A place setting of dinnerware might include a dinner plate, salad plate, cup, and saucer. A place setting of flatware might include a knife, dinner fork, salad fork, teaspoon, and soup spoon.

When selecting tableware, consider its care requirements. For instance, you might want to be sure your tableware is dishwasher-safe.

16-8

This diagram of an individual cover shows the proper placement of dinnerware, flatware, and glassware.

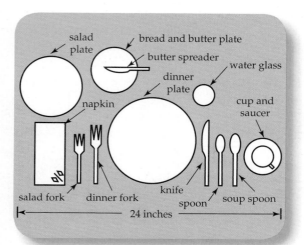

Setting the Table

An attractive table setting can enhance any meal. There is no prescribed formula for setting a table. The primary goals in table setting are convenience and comfort. A pretty table helps diners feel special and enjoy meals more.

When setting a table, you should place tableware to look similar to the **cover** (individual place setting) shown in **16-8**. The dinner plate should mark the center of the space allowed for each person. Place the salad plate to the upper left of the dinner plate. Place the cup and saucer to the lower right. Position the bread and butter plate above and slightly to the left of the dinner plate.

Flatware should be placed in the order in which it will be used. Place the knife to the right of the plate with the blade toward the plate. Place the spoons to the right of the knife. Lay the butter knife on the bread and butter plate. You will usually place forks to the left of the plate. However, if a fork is the only utensil needed for a meal, you should place it on the right. Place cocktail forks to the right of the spoons.

Set the water glass above the knife. Place other glasses to the right of the water glass. You may want to place only those pieces of tableware needed for the meal being served.

For most settings, you can simply fold napkins into rectangles. You can also fold and pleat napkins in a variety of ways to add a creative touch. Place napkins on the dinner plates, to the left of the forks, or be creative with your placement.

Try to achieve a balanced, organized look when setting the table. Items need not match, but they should harmonize with one another. What is important is the way the table looks when it is complete.

Clearing the Table

At the end of a course, you should remove everything that will not be needed for the next course. Remove serving dishes first. Then remove dinnerware, beginning with the guest of honor. Clear each person's cover, moving around the table in sequence. Be careful not to reach in front of another person when clearing the table.

When clearing a cover, remove the dinner plate first. Pick it up with your left hand and transfer it to your right hand. Next, remove the salad plate and place it on top of the dinner plate. Then remove the bread and butter plate and place it on top of the salad plate.

Reading
Review

1. True or false. Family mealtime provides a chance for parents to teach children table manners.
2. In what type of meal service are serving dishes passed from one person to another, allowing people to serve themselves?
3. What is the difference between plate service and English service?
4. Approximately how wide should each cover be?
5. True or false. When setting a table, flatware should be placed in the order in which it will be used.
6. When clearing a cover, which type of dish should you remove first?

Section 16-3

Dining Etiquette

Objectives

After studying this section, you will be able to
- **list** responsibilities of someone hosting a meal.
- **describe** appropriate manners to use when dining.
- **explain** guidelines to follow when dining in a restaurant.
- **explain** the process of paying and tipping in a restaurant.

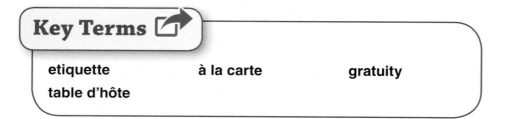

Key Terms

etiquette	à la carte	gratuity
table d'hôte		

Using a formal style of meal service and setting an attractive table can make any meal a special occasion. However, the easiest way to make dining truly enjoyable is to use proper etiquette. **Etiquette** refers to approved social conduct, or good manners. At the table, using proper etiquette is an essential social skill. See **16-9**. Rules of etiquette apply to those who serve meals as well as to those who eat meals. Etiquette rules also apply when dining in a restaurant.

Hosting a Meal

Offering food to guests is a common gesture of hospitality. When you host a meal, you can make it a pleasant experience for diners by practicing good manners. This includes being willing to accept a guest's offer of assistance.

As host, you should invite guests to the table when a meal is ready to be served. You need to inform guests where they are to sit at the table. After all guests are seated, serving may begin.

You should see that all guests are served before serving yourself. (Family style service can be an exception to this guideline. If someone else begins passing a dish, you may take a serving as the dish comes to you.) Guests generally wait for the host to begin eating. Therefore, if you are busy serving, invite those who have been served to begin eating. This allows guests to enjoy their food while it is still hot. During the meal, you should offer second helpings of food if they are available.

Mealtime Manners

- Sit up straight and avoid placing your elbows on the table during a meal.
- At the beginning of a meal, lay your napkin across your lap. A luncheon napkin may be unfolded completely. However, leave a dinner napkin folded in half. Never tuck a napkin in your collar.
- Use the serving utensils offered with each dish of food. Never put a utensil from which you have eaten into a serving dish.
- Try a small portion of all foods that are offered to you. Do not discuss foods that you do not like or those that you are unable to eat for dietary reasons.
- Flatware is usually placed on the table in the order of use. Use the outermost pieces first.
- If you drop your flatware on the floor, leave it there. The host will offer you another piece. Unless the host invites you to begin eating, you should wait for him or her to start the meal. (At very large gatherings, you may begin eating when those seated near you have been served.)
- Never chew with your lips open so others can see the food in your mouth.
- Never talk when your mouth is full.
- Eat and drink quietly. Smacking your lips, slurping, gulping, and making other noises is inappropriate at the table.
- When in doubt about how to eat a food, follow the lead of your host. In a restaurant, you may quietly ask your waiter for advice.
- Never spit food out of your mouth at the table. If it tastes spoiled, quietly leave the table and go to the bathroom. If it is too hot, quickly take a swallow of a cold beverage. (This is the only time it is appropriate to consume a beverage when your mouth has food in it.) Inconspicuously remove fish bones or fruit pits from your mouth with your thumb and forefinger.
- Use fingers to eat only those foods that can be eaten without leaving traces of the food on your fingers. For instance, carrot sticks and cookies are finger foods. Barbecued chicken and cakes with sticky frosting are fork foods.
- Cut food one or two bites at a time as you are ready to eat it.
- Do not gesture with flatware in your hand.
- Cut sandwiches in halves or quarters before eating them.
- Break off small pieces of bread rather than biting into a whole slice. Break rolls in the same way. Butter one small portion of bread at a time.
- Place used flatware on the edge of a plate or saucer, not on the table.
- Never use toothpicks or dental floss while at the table.
- If you spill something at the table, be as inconspicuous as possible. If cleanup is necessary, offer to help. Apologize briefly, but do not allow the incident to spoil your meal or that of others.
- When you have finished your meal, lay your knife and fork together across the center of your plate. Before you leave the table, lay your napkin beside your plate.
- After the meal, avoid leaving the table until the host rises. If you must leave, ask the host if you may be excused.

16-9

Following these guidelines will help you appear polite and feel comfortable at any meal.

You should be able to enjoy a meal with your guests. Proper planning and preparation will keep you from leaving the table repeatedly to attend to kitchen tasks. As a host, you have a responsibility to guide conversation during the meal. You may suggest topics of interest and encourage all guests to become involved in the conversation. Controversial or unappetizing topics are best saved for another time. Continue eating until all guests have finished. At the end of the meal, you may invite guests to move to another room. You may need to do some after-dinner cleanup. For health and safety, store leftover foods promptly after the meal. You may also want to remove dirty dishes from the view of your guests. However, save detailed cleanup for later so you can return to your guests as quickly as possible.

Being a Dinner Guest

Everyone should assume a role in making dining an enjoyable experience. As a dinner guest, plan to arrive on time. Come to the table in a pleasant frame of mind. Be prepared to help those dining with you to relax and enjoy themselves.

Knowing proper etiquette can enhance your self-esteem. You will feel good about yourself when you know how to behave in social situations. Using appropriate behavior will help you feel comfortable in almost any setting. Using good manners will also help others feel comfortable in your presence.

Many employers consider the ability to use proper etiquette an important employability skill. If you are invited to lunch when you are on a job interview, be sure to use your best table manners. The employer may be evaluating how you will behave when dining with future clients and customers.

You do not need a special occasion to practice good table manners. You should use proper etiquette whenever you eat. Using good manners should become a habit. Table manners are influenced by culture. Rules of table etiquette vary in different countries. However, following some basic guidelines will help you feel comfortable no matter where you are.

Dining in Restaurants

The same good table manners you use daily will make you comfortable in any restaurant. You should also keep a few special pointers in mind when in restaurants.

Before going to a restaurant, call to see if you will need reservations. If you make reservations, be sure to arrive on time.

Upon arrival, tell the host the name in which your reservation is made and the number in your party. If you are asked where you would like to sit, respond promptly. When your table is ready, the host will seat you. (In more casual restaurants, a sign may indicate that you should seat yourself.)

If you are unfamiliar with a restaurant, ask to see a copy of the menu before being seated. Evaluating the menu in advance allows you to decide if the foods and prices suit your tastes and budget. Many restaurants post menus outside their doors for this reason.

21st Century Skills

Integrity. Frank goes out to lunch with his coworkers. When the coworkers begin criticizing their supervisor, Frank changes the subject to talk about sports.

While in a restaurant, talk in a low but comfortable tone of voice. Others in the restaurant will not want to hear your conversation.

Types of Restaurants

When you are in a restaurant, you should be as polite as if you were a guest in someone's home, no matter what type of setting you choose. Sometimes you will choose a restaurant where you can eat quickly because you are hungry. At other times, you will choose a restaurant with fine food and a nice atmosphere because you want to be pampered, **16-10**.

People who do not want to spend much time eating like the quick service fast-food restaurants deliver. For extra fast service, customers often prefer using the drive-up window offered at many fast-food restaurants.

Cafeterias and buffets have a variety of foods placed along a serving line. You choose the items you wish to eat. Cafeterias price each food item separately. At the end of the line, you pay for the specific items you chose. You can control the cost of your meal by choosing foods that fit your budget.

Buffets are offered at a fixed price. Most food items are self-serve. Customers can take as much or as little of each food as they like. They may also return to the buffet for additional servings.

Living Green

The variety of foods at a buffet is tempting. However, when dining at a buffet, take only the amount of food you know you will eat. Food waste depletes natural resources, adds to landfills, and increases food costs to consumers.

16-10

Outdoor dining is popular in warm weather, offering people to enjoy a casual meal with friends and family.

rblfmr/Shutterstock.com

The atmosphere is casual in most family restaurants. Menus list a variety of foods that appeal to all age groups. Prices are reasonable to make dining affordable for the entire family.

Formal restaurants offer customers an elegant dining atmosphere. Customers enjoy attractive surroundings, dine on excellent food, and receive superb service. Prices in formal restaurants tend to be high due to these features.

Specialty restaurants serve specific types of food. Pizza parlors, steak and seafood houses, and ethnic restaurants are examples.

Ordering from a Restaurant Menu

Fast-food and some casual restaurants post their menus on the wall. After reading your choices, you place your order at a counter. Most other restaurants provide printed menus listing the foods available. A waiter will come to your table to take your order. He or she may mention other food specials that you can select.

When you are given a menu, you can quickly determine if you will order table d'hôte or à la carte. **Table d'hôte** means the entire meal has one price. Usually the meal will include a salad or soup, a main course, a side dish, and bread. Sometimes table d'hôte meals also include a beverage, appetizer, and dessert. **À la carte** menus feature items that are priced individually. A separate charge will be made for the soup, salad, and main dish.

Some menus use French terms to describe the way food has been prepared. See **16-11**. Do not hesitate to ask questions when you do not understand the menu. Your waiter should be happy to assist you. Also, do not be afraid to ask the price of specials described by the waiter. These items may be the most expensive dishes the restaurant serves.

16-11

Becoming familiar with these terms will help you read restaurant menus.

Menu Terms

à la Kiev. Containing butter, garlic, and chives.

à la king. Served with a white cream sauce that contains mushrooms, green peppers, and pimentos.

à la mode. Served with ice cream.

almondine. Made or garnished with almonds.

au gratin. Served with cheese.

au jus. Served with natural juices.

du jour. Of the day. For instance, *soup du jour* means *soup of the day.*

en brochette. Cooked or served in small pieces on a skewer.

en coquille. Served in a shell.

en croquette. Breaded and deep-fried.

en papillote. Cooked in parchment paper to seal in juices.

Florentine. Prepared with spinach.

julienne. Cut into long, thin slices.

Marengo. Sautéed with mushrooms, tomatoes, and olives.

piccata. Prepared with lemon.

Provençale. Prepared with garlic, onion, mushrooms, tomato, herbs, and olive oil.

Making Healthful Food Choices

You need to consider the impact of meals eaten away from home on your overall health. When you select foods from a menu, keep MyPlate in mind. Consider how your food choices will contribute to your daily needs.

Your goal should be to meet your needs throughout the day. You can balance food choices made at one meal with food choices made at the next. For example, if you consume a meal that mainly consists of protein and grains, such as a hamburger and pasta salad for lunch, balance other meals with fruits, vegetables, and dairy. In this case, you might consider preparing a dinner that features vegetables as the main course, with a fruit salad and a glass of milk on the side. However, aim to have each meal balanced with fruits, vegetables, grains, dairy, and protein foods.

If you eat out often, learn to choose foods carefully. This may require you to choose restaurants carefully as well. Plan to eat in those restaurants that offer nutritious options.

Paying the Check

At the end of a meal in a restaurant, the waiter will bring your check. Sometimes the waiter will place the check in a folder or on a small tray. The waiter will usually tell you if he or she will return for the payment when you are ready. In some restaurants, you may be asked to pay the cashier on your way out the door.

When paying at the table, place cash or a credit card in the folder or on the tray with the check. The waiter will return your change if you pay cash. He or she will return with a receipt for you to sign if you pay with a credit card. Be sure your bill is accurate before you sign the receipt.

You may leave your *gratuity* for the waiter on the tray or in the folder with the check. A **gratuity**, or tip, is a measure of your gratitude for good service. A gratuity usually ranges from 10 to 20 percent. You may want your tip to be toward the higher end of the range if you receive excellent service.

The type of restaurant also influences the amount of your tip. Take the following factors into consideration when deciding what to leave for a tip:

- Since no meal service is provided, fast-food customers are not expected to leave a tip.
- Ten percent is an appropriate tip for services offered at cafeterias and buffets.

Wellness Awareness

What can you do to make healthful choices in restaurants? For starters, select baked, broiled, roasted, or grilled foods rather than fried. Choose vegetables that are steamed, not buttered or creamed. Select whole grain breads and rolls. Ask to have salad dressings, sour cream, cheese and barbecue sauces, and butter served on the side. Choose water instead of soda. To practice, view a restaurant menu online and use these principles to select what you would order.

Math Connection

Calculating Tips

The waiter brought the check. The total before tax was $40.00. Liza wants to leave a 15% tip. There are two ways she could do this:

She could calculate 15% of $40.00.

$0.15 \times 40.00 = \$6.00$

Another way to figure the tip would be to determine 10% of the cost of the meal ($4.00). Find half of that amount ($2.00). Then add the two together.

$\$4.00 + \$2.00 = \$6.00$

Science Connection

Kitchen Chemistry

Cooking is really a common form of chemistry with a set of predictable chemical reactions. For instance, baked goods rise due to the heat and other ingredients reacting with the leavening agent to form bubbles. There are many interesting experiments that can be done in any kitchen. Try this one, which is a simple way of detecting whether different foods contain starch.

Supplies:
Waxed paper
Tincture of iodine (check a first aid kit or the local pharmacy)
Different kinds of foods, such as:
  cut potatoes
  apples slices
  orange segments
  bread slice
  crackers
  cheese
  string beans
  peanuts

Directions:
1. Place each food on a separate piece of waxed paper.
2. Predict which foods will indicate starch before you add the iodine.
3. Place a drop of the tincture of iodine onto each food.
4. The foods containing starch will turn purple or blue where the iodine touches them.

How many did you guess correctly?

- A tip of 15 percent is considered appropriate in family restaurants. However, when servers have to clean up after messy children, a larger tip is in order.

- A tip in a formal restaurant may be as much as 20 percent of the cost of your food.

- No tip is expected for carryout service. However, customers are expected to tip delivery people.

- If you are paying with a credit card, you may add the tip to the receipt before writing the total. If there is no folder or tray provided, you may leave your tip inconspicuously on the table.

Reading Review

1. Approved social conduct is known as ____ .
2. Why might a host invite guests who have already been served to begin eating?
3. Briefly describe what would be served if a diner ordered roast beef au jus with green beans almondine and julienne potatoes.
4. Give three tips for making healthful food choices in restaurants.
5. What would be an appropriate tip when the check total is $27.96 in a cafeteria? at a family restaurant? in a formal restaurant?

Chapter 16 Review

Summary

Learn to prepare foods successfully by following the recommended preparation techniques. Choose the techniques best suited to the type of food you are preparing.

After preparing your meals, you will want to serve the food attractively. Such attention to detail can even make family meal time a more pleasant experience. Choose a style of meal service that suits your menu and the people you are serving. Select tableware that harmonizes and complements the dining area. Set the table with both convenience and appearance in mind.

To make dining enjoyable, be considerate of every person at the table, especially guests. Know and practice good table manners so they become second nature to you.

Dining out can be just as enjoyable as eating at home. There are several types of restaurants from which to choose. Becoming familiar with menu terms will help you order your meal. Learning to make wise food choices will allow you to fit restaurant meals into a healthful diet. Being aware of restaurant etiquette will enable you to feel more comfortable when dining out. Knowing about methods of payment and tipping will also help you feel more at ease when eating away from home.

Critical Thinking

1. **Analyze effects.** Describe some cultural differences among people that would affect preparation of foods.

2. **Analyze pros and cons.** Evaluate the pros and cons of making your own breads, cakes, or cookies from scratch versus buying them from the store.

3. **Evaluate decisions.** Suppose you were in another country and noticed that your table manners were different from those of your host. What would you do? If you were the host and your international guest used different table manners, what would you do?

4. **Analyze priorities.** What would you consider to be the three most important table manners?

5. **Predict outcomes.** What negative consequences might arise when dining with family members or coworkers if you did not know proper restaurant etiquette?

6. **Analyze behavior.** Role-play various dining situations showing a lack of table manners. Discuss the situations. Then repeat the role-plays using appropriate manners.

21st Century Applications

7. **Information, communications, and technology literacy.** Use spreadsheet software to make colorful bar graphs showing the temperature to which different types of meat, poultry, fish, and eggs should be cooked.

8. **Civic literacy.** Responsible citizens consider the environmental, social, and economic impacts of decisions that are made. Research what restaurant establishments do with their extra food. Is extra food donated, thrown away, or repurposed? What impact do these decisions have on the community? Write a report discussing your findings.

9. **Leadership and responsibility.** Successful managers model integrity and

use effective management techniques. Research tips and advice from successful managers. Make a list of management techniques that would provide guidance for a new restaurant manager. Rank the information according to your opinion of which tips are most important.

10. **Health literacy.** Create an electronic presentation comparing and contrasting healthful menu choices at fast-food restaurants with less-healthful choices. Check fast-food websites to find nutrition facts. Include in your presentation the amounts of calories and fat grams found in the foods.

11. **Communication and collaboration.** With a partner, create a flowchart based on Figure 16-9. Identify potential dining mishaps that could occur in a restaurant setting or dining situation. Place each brief scenario in separate boxes. In linked boxes, identify different responses to the situation that demonstrate proper etiquette.

12. **Initiative and self-direction.** Most employers value employees that can set and achieve reasonable, attainable goals. Here are a few things you need to know about goals. Goals should
   - be specific and positive
   - be measurable
   - have a target deadline (either short-term—several months, or long-term—several years)

Think about your knowledge of etiquette and manners, and how it relates to you as an employee. Then, set a goal for improving your interpersonal and communication skills. Determine how you will measure achievement of this goal, and identify a deadline for meeting it.

Core
Skills

13. **Science.** Calibrate traditional meat thermometers and thermometer forks by taking the temperature of boiling water, which is 212°F. Note which thermometer is most accurate.

14. **Science.** Work in three groups to cook the same type of pasta, but for different lengths of time. One group should undercook the pasta, one group should cook the pasta for the recommended length of time for al dente pasta, and one group should overcook it. As a class, compare the overcooked and undercooked groups with the al dente pasta and describe the differences detected.

15. **Reading.** Research the origins of your favorite foods and identify the geographical area where the food was first prepared. Also mention places in which the food is most popular today.

16. **Speaking.** With a partner, select one of the food preparation methods discussed in the chapter. Work together to create a video that demonstrates how to use that food preparation technique. Describe how to carry out the method in step-by-step instructions and include any safety and sanitation precautions needed to successfully prepare the food. Share your videos with the class.

17. **Reading, history.** Research types of meal service typically used by the nobility or upper classes throughout history. For example, what was used in a Medieval castle versus a Victorian mansion?

18. **Math.** Search the Internet for an online restaurant menu guide with pricing.

Review a menu and consider what you might select for a meal. Total your selections and calculate the tip.

19. **Speaking.** With a partner, prepare regular oatmeal, quick-cooking oatmeal, and instant oatmeal. Taste and compare the flavor, texture, and appearance of each product and discuss the differences. Which method of cooking oatmeal does each person prefer? Why? Practice active listening skills when you partner expresses his or her opinion.

20. **Writing.** With a partner, identify careers relating to the chapter. Then work together to select one career and write a description of the job requirements, education and training needed, salary, and outlook for that career. Revise, edit, and proofread your report before finalizing the assignment.

21. **Listening.** Interview a person who works within the foodservice industry about his or her experiences in the field. What is his or her role within the foodservice industry? What type of service is used at his or her workplace? Has this person experienced situations in which etiquette was not used? What were the effects on staff and other diners? Prepare a list of questions prior to the interview, including other questions you may have. Share your responses with the class.

FCCLA Leadership Development

Using the Families First National Program, you can develop basic lessons on good manners that can be taught to young children. These activities will need to be action-based and contain visual reminders of appropriate behavior. (Role-playing is a good example.) Then eat lunch with the children to help them practice what they have been taught.

Portfolio Builder

Knowing proper etiquette can help you feel comfortable in social situations now and in future business situations. Make a list of situations that might arise during mealtimes. Using information in this chapter, describe proper ways of handling these situations. Write a reflection paper describing how this information may be useful to you in your future career. Add the list and reflection paper to your portfolio.

Journal Writing

You are volunteering for a community service project, and you want to learn more about serving food. You know about an opportunity to help at a local food kitchen. You are not yet sure about working there and want to think over this decision.

Write About It: *What can you learn about foodservice from working in a food kitchen? What might be the advantages and disadvantages? What could you learn about yourself from this exercise?*

Human Services

The Consumer Services Pathway within the Human Services career cluster includes careers that help people make consumer-related decisions, such as purchasing, investing, and selling. Examples of careers within this pathway include personal financial advisers, sales consultants, and real estate agents.

Human Services Pathways

Early Childhood Development and Services
Counseling and Mental Health Services
Family and Community Services
Personal Care Services
Consumer Services

stockyimages/Shutterstock.com

Education and Training

In addition to teaching academic subjects, the Teaching and Training Pathway within the Education and Training career cluster includes training others in career development. Careers in this area include career and technical education teachers, human resources trainers, and corporate trainers.

Education and Training Pathways

Administration and Administrative Support
Professional Support Services
Teaching and Training

Goodluz/Shutterstock.com

Career Spotlight: Personal Financial Adviser

- **Description.** Personal financial advisers help clients reach both short-term and long-term financial goals. They may help people with education financing, investments, taxes, real estate, insurance, and pensions. Personal financial advisers assess each client's assets, liabilities, cash flow, and other financial factors before developing a plan. They help clients implement financial strategies and reassess plans as needed.
- **Education and training.** Most personal financial advisers need a bachelor's degree. Although a specific degree is not usually required, a degree in finance, accounting, mathematics, economics, business, or law would be good preparation for this job. Some personal financial advisers pursue a master's degree in finance or business administration to increase their chances of advancing in the field or gaining more clients.
- **Skills and personal qualities.** Personal financial advisers need good critical-thinking, analytical, math, and complex problem-solving skills. They should also have good listening, speaking, and interpersonal skills. Successful personal financial advisers are service oriented and have the sales skills to expand their clientele.
- **Job outlook.** Job growth for personal financial advisers is projected to grow faster than average for all occupations through 2028. Visit the *Occupational Outlook Handbook* online to learn more about a career as a personal financial adviser.

Human Services

Career Spotlight: Career and Technical Education Teacher

- **Description.** Career and technical education (CTE) teachers instruct students and help them prepare for a particular field, such as automotive repair, culinary arts, health care, or agriculture. CTE teachers often blend classroom experience with hands-on experience, which involves applying knowledge and skills in a realistic setting. They may work at the middle school, high school, or postsecondary level. In some programs, CTE teachers may help students prepare for a particular certificate, degree, or license.
- **Education and training.** Requirements vary by state, but most CTE teachers have a bachelor's degree related to the subject they will be teaching. They must also have years of experience in that field. Some teachers have an associate's degree in addition to years of experience. Teachers in public schools are usually required to be licensed or certified.
- **Skills and personal qualities.** CTE teachers must have the desire to help others learn necessary skills and training for employment within a particular field. They must also have excellent communication, interpersonal, analytical, and critical-thinking skills. Patience and creativity are also needed.
- **Job outlook.** In the next ten years, job prospects for career and technical education teachers are expected to have little change through 2028. Visit the *Occupational Outlook Handbook* online to learn more about a career as a CTE teacher.

Education & Training

Sources: States' Career Clusters Initiative, Bureau of Labor Statistics Career Guide to Industries

Chapter 17
Managing Personal Finances

Reading Prep

- What challenges have you faced concerning money?
- Identify three goals that require saving money. Estimate the amount of money needed to reach each goal. How long will it take to save each?

Concept Organizer

Make a Y-chart with each segment labeled for one of the three Cs of credit: *Character*, *Capital*, and *Capacity*. Write the traits of each item in its segment.

G-WLEARNING.com

Click on the activity icon to visit www.g-wlearning. com/comprehensive/8062 to access online vocabulary activities using key terms from the chapter.

Using Financial Services

Objectives

After studying this section, you will be able to

- **describe** various services offered by financial institutions.
- **write** and endorse checks correctly.
- **balance** a checkbook.

Key Terms

money transfer app	endorse	reconciling
direct deposit	account statement	overdraft

As a child, you may have kept pennies in a piggy bank. When you start earning money, however, you should start dealing with financial institutions. Piggy banks lack the safety and earnings potential found at financial institutions.

Financial Services

Saving money, making payments, and obtaining loans are the most common financial services used. These services and their features differ from one financial institution to another. You must decide which financial services are important to you. Then you should look for an institution that offers the services that meet your needs.

Savings Accounts

Savings accounts are a key service available through financial institutions. These accounts pay various amounts of *interest*, or a percentage of money added to the account by the financial institution over time. Some accounts have restrictions regarding the length of time money must stay on deposit.

Checking Accounts

One of the main financial services people want is a checking account. You can withdraw a sum of money from a checking account simply by writing a check or using a debit card. Several types of checking accounts are available.

Debit Cards and Money Transfer Apps

A *debit card* shows that you have an established checking account with the financial institution identified on the card. It looks like a credit card and is swiped through a point-of-sale terminal in much the same way. However, swiping the card immediately transfers payment from your checking account. You may have to key in a security code called a *PIN* (personal identification number).

A **money transfer app** is a person-to-person payment *app* that allows individuals to send and receive money to and from friends and family using a mobile device. Examples include *Venmo*, *Cash App*, and *Paypal*. A working bank account tied to your money transfer app account is necessary to transfer money. You must be very careful when transferring money as there is no proper recourse to getting your money back if transferred to the wrong party.

You will need to record each transaction immediately in your checkbook, just as you do when writing checks. Debit purchases are itemized on your monthly checking account statement.

Electronic Banking

Electronic banking, or *e-banking*, is banking through a digital device, such as a phone, tablet, or computer. Through e-banking, you can retrieve information about your accounts, move money between accounts, or make check deposits or payments.

One of the greatest advantages of e-banking is that you can do your banking at any time of day. You can pay bills without mailing checks and worrying about the time it takes for them to be delivered. E-banking also allows you to more easily manage your accounts. See **17-1**.

One disadvantage is that you will not be able to e-bank when your computer or the bank's computer system is down. There are also concerns about the security of e-banking. However, banks are working hard to make the systems secure. You can also take precautions. Always make sure you are at a secure website before transmitting any personal or financial information. Never transmit usernames or passwords through e-mail.

17-1

Once you have set up an online banking account and money transfer app, you can easily pay bills or transfer money to friends and family.

Automated Teller Machines (ATMs)

Automated teller machines offer people the flexibility of banking at any time. ATMs are available locally in a variety of convenient locations, including shopping malls and convenience stores and most banks. To use an ATM, you need a special banking card with a PIN. The card and PIN number allow a customer to access his or her accounts, withdraw cash, and make deposits.

Some ATM cards can also be used as debit cards. When making a debit purchase or using the ATM card to withdraw cash, always record the transaction immediately in your checkbook.

fizkes/iStock/Getty Images Plus

Loans

Loans are another service many people seek from financial institutions. People apply for both short- and long-term loans. They may borrow money to pay existing bills or make purchases, such as major appliances, cars, and houses.

Different types of financial institutions make loans for different types of purchases. For instance, some institutions loan money for a home purchase, but not a car purchase. Check to be sure your financial institution makes the type of loan you are seeking.

Other Financial Services

Financial institutions may offer a number of other services for customer convenience. These include credit cards, drive-up windows, estate management, brokerage accounts, and financial counseling. Special services like these are worth considering when you select financial institutions.

21st Century Skills

Ethics. Eli looked at his paycheck and realized that he had been paid for a day he did not work. Eli alerted his boss to the situation. Eli's boss appreciated his honesty.

Types of Institutions

Before choosing a financial institution, do some comparison shopping. Interest rates vary among different institutions. This applies to interest earned on savings accounts as well as interest charged on loans.

- *Commercial banks* are owned by stockholders and are run for a profit. Commercial banks offer a great variety of services to both businesses and individuals.
- *Savings and loan associations* typically focus on savings accounts and home loans.
- *Credit unions* are nonprofit financial institutions owned and operated by members. A credit union is usually sponsored by a company or professional association. Membership is open only to people associated with the sponsoring organization.

You should always choose an insured financial institution. The Federal Deposit Insurance Corporation (FDIC) insures most banks. The National Credit Union Administration (NCUA) insures most credit unions. Your deposits are protected up to a certain amount if an insured bank fails.

Using a Checking Account

A checking account is convenient for making purchases and paying bills. Money needed for these expenses can be held in a checking account. Anytime payment needs to be made, you can simply use a debit card or write a check.

Math Connection

Making a Bank Deposit

Addison is going to the bank to make a deposit. She has a check for $75.33 from her part-time job and another check of $20.00 she received from her Aunt Joan for her birthday. She has $8.56 in coins that were on her dresser and in her purse. She would like to receive $25.00 back. How much would her total deposit be?

First, add the amounts to be deposited.

$75.33 + $20.00 + $8.56 = $103.89

Next, subtract the amount she will receive back to find what the total deposit will be.

$103.89 − $25.00 = $78.89

Types of Accounts

With some checking accounts, you need a minimum amount to open the account. Interest earned by the bank on this balance pays for the costs of handling the account. You usually do not pay service charges, except for purchasing personal checks. If the account balance falls below the minimum required, however, you must pay a service charge.

Some checking accounts do not require a minimum balance. For such an account, you usually pay a service charge. This covers the financial institution's cost of handling the account. This charge may be a monthly fee, a set fee for each check written, or both.

Some checking accounts pay interest if you maintain a balance over a certain amount. This is an advantage for people who keep a large amount of money in their checking accounts.

When deciding which type of account to open, determine how much money you can afford to keep in the account. Think about how much you are willing to pay for service fees. Consider how important it is for you to earn interest.

Opening an Account and Making a Deposit

When you open a checking account, you will be asked to sign a *signature card*. The financial institution keeps this card on file to compare with signatures made during transactions. This helps to eliminate forgeries.

If you are the only person who will use the account, you will open an individual account. If someone else, such as a spouse, will also use the account, you will open a joint account.

You may add money to your checking account by **direct deposit**. This is a method of transferring money into an account through electronic means. Many employers distribute wages to employees by direct deposit. Using e-banking to transfer money from a savings account into a checking account is also direct deposit. Filling out a deposit slip is another way to add money to your account. See **17-2**.

17-2

A deposit slip must accompany cash or checks being deposited in a checking account.

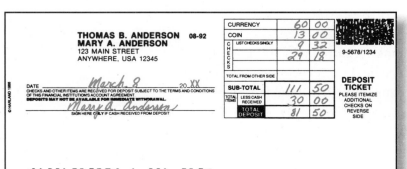

Writing a Check

A check instructs your financial institution to pay a certain sum of money to a person or company. Checks should be clearly written in ink. Be sure to fill in all the required information in the appropriate spaces, as shown in **17-3**.

Complete a check stub or fill in a register at the time that you use your debit card or write a check. Record the number of the check, date, payee, and amount. Subtract the amount from your balance so you always know how much money is in your account. This will keep you from writing checks when you do not have sufficient funds. See **17-4**.

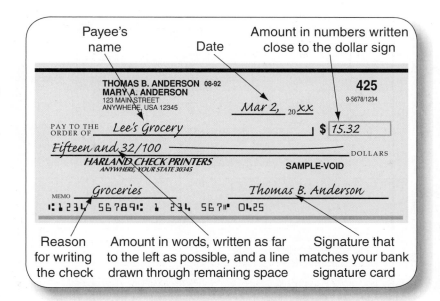

17-3

This check is correctly written.

Endorsing a Check

Before you can cash or deposit a check that has been written to you, you must **endorse** it. This means you must sign your name on the back, at the left end of the check. The signature on the back must match the name on the face of the check.

Balancing Your Checkbook

Your financial institution will send you a monthly, bimonthly, or quarterly summary of your checking account. This summary is called an **account statement**. This statement lists checks, deposits, withdrawals, charges, and interest earnings on the account. Many financial institutions also send digital statements.

When you receive an account statement, you will begin a process called **reconciling**. You will compare the account statement to your check stubs or register. The institution's record should match yours. This is known as *balancing your checkbook*.

Your account statement will list each check by amount and check number. In this way, you will be able to tell which checks were cashed. These checks are called *canceled checks*. The checks you wrote that were not yet cashed when the statement was made are called *outstanding checks*. Debit card and ATM card withdrawals will also be listed on your account statement.

In your check register or on the check stubs, mark off the canceled checks. Also mark off any deposits and other withdrawals shown on the statement. If the financial institution has made any service charges, subtract them from the balance in your checkbook. Likewise, if you have earned interest on your account, add that amount to your checkbook balance.

RECORD ALL CHARGES OR CREDITS THAT AFFECT YOUR ACCOUNT										
NUMBER	DATE	CODE	DESCRIPTION OF TRANSACTION	PAYMENT/DEBIT (−)		✓ T	FEE (IF ANY) (−)	PAYMENT/ CREDIT (+)		BALANCE $
	3/1		Opening balance		00			100	00	100 00
										100 00
101	3/2		Lee's Grocery	15	32					15 32
			Groceries							84 68
	3/3		Cash withdrawal	20	00					20 00
										64 68
102	3/4		The Book Shelf	11	75					11 75
			Calendar							52 93
	3/6	DC	No Limits	35	13					35 13
			Jeans							17 80
	3/8	D	Deposit					130	00	130 00
										147 80
103	3/9		Lee's Grocery	18	35					18 35
			Groceries							129 45
	3/11	AP	Unified Utilities	23	07					23 07
			Electric bill							106 38
	3/14	DC	Mary's Dept. Store	34	60					34 60
			Navy skirt							71 78
104	3/16		Richard's Records	21	20					21 20
			CD							50 58
	3/22	D	Deposit					130	00	130 00
										180 58
105	3/26		Lee's Grocery	47	58					47 58
			Groceries							133 00
	3/29		Cash withdrawal	30	00					30 00
										103 00
106	3/30		Dr. Harvey	65	00					65 00
			Dental checkup							38 00
	4/1	D	Deposit					130	00	130 00
										168 00
			Service charge	5	00					5 00
										163 00

17-4

A check register keeps track of how much money is in a checking account.

At this point, a little math will help you see if your checkbook has balanced. Most account statements have a worksheet printed on the back to help you with the math. See **17-5**. Complete the following steps in the spaces provided on the worksheet:

1. Write the closing balance shown on the bank statement.
2. List the deposits you have made that are not shown on the statement.
3. Add the amounts from steps 1 and 2 and record the total.
4. List by number and amount all outstanding checks and withdrawals. Find the total and record it.
5. Subtract the total in step 4 from that in step 3. The difference should match the balance shown in your checkbook. What should you do if the balance on the statement does not match yours? Begin by double-checking your math. Be sure you have made no errors before you question the financial institution about its statement.

Balancing your checkbook promptly is always wise. Financial institutions can make errors. You should not depend completely on them to keep your account in order. The sooner you notice an error, the sooner it can be corrected.

There is another good reason for balancing your checkbook promptly. People who neglect this task are more likely to have **overdrafts**. These are withdrawals made when there is not enough money in the account to cover them.

Most financial institutions fine account holders for overdrafts. Many businesses also fine customers for purchases resulting in overdrafts. The total fines for an overdraft can easily exceed $40.

Financial Literacy

Special-Use Checks

A *certified check* is a personal check for which the financial institution guarantees payment. When the institution certifies your check, the amount of the check is immediately deducted from your account to reserve it for the payee.

A *cashier's check* is a check drawn on the institution's own funds and signed by an officer of the institution. You present the money to the institution along with the name of the payee. The institution then issues a check made out to that person or business.

Reading Review

1. List six financial services offered by financial institutions.
2. How does a debit card work?
3. Describe *e-banking*.
4. What is the purpose of a signature card?
5. Give two reasons for balancing a checkbook promptly.
6. Why might your checkbook balance and the balance on a bank statement differ?

BALANCING WORKSHEET

MONTH ___March --___ , 20 _XX_

BANK BALANCE
shown on this statement $ ___48.73___

ADD+
$ ___125.00___

DEPOSITS made but not shown on statement because made or received after date of this statement.

TOTAL $ ___173.73___

SUBTRACT–

CHECKS OUTSTANDING ....$ ___68.40___

BALANCE...............$ ___105.33___

The above balance should be same as the up-to-date balance in your checkbook.

CHECKS AND DEBITS OUTSTANDING
(Written but not shown on statement because not yet received by Bank.)

NO.		
498	28	40
499	15	00
ATM	25	00
TOTAL	68	40

17-5

A form such as this is often printed on the back of a bank account statement to help customers balance their checkbooks.

Section 17-2

Saving for the Future

Objectives

After studying this section, you will be able to

- **explain** why it is important to save money.
- **list** five factors to consider when deciding how to save.
- **describe** various types of savings accounts.
- **determine** why people need to plan their estates.

Key Terms ↗

liquidity	stock	portfolio
certificate of deposit	dividend	diversified
securities	bond	estate
	mutual fund	will

Putting money in savings before making other purchases is a wise decision. Later, if you need money, it will be available. You also earn additional money on savings in the form of interest.

Why Save?

Why should I save? When should I use the money in my savings? The answers to these two common questions vary for different people. A few facts about savings might help reveal the right answers for you.

- Money in a savings account will be available to spend for future wants and needs.
- Savings can be the most direct path to your long-term goals. By saving, you can make purchases that would otherwise be beyond your reach.
- Money in a savings account can be considered an emergency fund. As a rule, a person should have at least three-months' income saved to cover any emergencies that might arise.
- Savings can ensure that retirement will not put a strain on your standard of living. The sooner you begin to plan and save for retirement, the more money you will have when you retire. See **17-6**.

Factors in Deciding How to Save

You should consider five factors in deciding how to save.

- *Safety.* Savings should be protected against loss, theft, fire, and other risks. Most financial institutions insure savings accounts up to $250,000.
- *Rate of return.* Savings institutions offer different interest rates on accounts. They also calculate interest in a variety of ways. You should investigate each savings option to find the highest rate of return available to you.

17-6

People can enjoy financial freedom during their retirement if they budget well and save money while employed.

- *Liquidity.* **Liquidity** is the degree to which you will be able to get cash quickly. A high degree of liquidity is important for savings that is used for emergencies. Some savings accounts pay very high interest, but withdrawal of funds is restricted. Plan your savings so that some cash will be immediately available without loss of interest. Stocks, bonds, and real estate are not liquid.

- *Purchasing power.* Your savings should be protected against inflation. Savings in stocks, bonds, and real estate usually have better protection against inflation than savings accounts. These investments usually increase in value in step with inflation. They do not offer liquidity, however. Once money is invested, you may eventually increase your purchasing power, but you may not be able to get it back for several years.

- *Convenience.* A financial institution near your home or along your route to work is very convenient for routine services. E-banking can be done from home.

Ways to Save

Regular savings accounts allow deposits and withdrawals to be made in any amount at any time. This savings account pays the lowest interest rates, but provides the greatest liquidity.

Another type of savings account is a **certificate of deposit (CD)**. CDs pay a set rate of interest on money that is deposited for a set period of time. A higher interest rate is paid on CDs than on regular savings accounts. Interest rates on such accounts vary according to the length of time the money must be left on deposit.

A minimum deposit is required for most CDs. All CDs can be cashed before maturity, but doing so results in a loss of interest income and a penalty fee.

Investing

Investing involves purchasing a financial product or item with the expectation that its value will increase over time. Investments generally offer greater profits than savings accounts, but they can also lose value.

Unlike putting money into an insured savings account, putting money into investments involves risk. You may not get

Financial Literacy

Investing Vs. Saving

People choose investments because of the following advantages over savings accounts:

- Prices of investments usually increase over time. Their average annual increase in value is often greater than interest rates on savings accounts.
- Inflation is an economic factor commonly at work in the economy. It causes money to decrease in value. Due to the higher long-term returns on investments, however, they usually offset the effects of inflation better than savings accounts do.
- Investments usually increase in value during times of economic prosperity and growth. Investing provides a way to participate in this economic growth, which is not offered by savings accounts.

Mental Health Awareness

Money and Mental Health

Do you know that money and mental health issues can go hand-in-hand? Mental health issues make it more difficult to earn and manage money. Financial stress, in turn, creates mental issues that decrease productivity or joy in living. Life stress can be treated with the help of a mental health counselor, while a financial counselor can help with all areas of your finances including developing a budget.

all your money back. Investments are not insured. Carefully choosing investments and holding them for long periods of time reduces risk.

When people talk about investments, they often are referring to securities. **Securities** are proof of debt or ownership of a company or government. This proof is often in the form of stocks and bonds.

Stocks

Stocks are certificates that represent ownership of a small portion of a company. When people buy shares of stock in a company, they are actually buying part of that company. Stockholders take part in the business by electing the board of directors. The directors run the company for the benefit of all the owners.

A stockholder shares in the profits and losses of the company. Some of the company's profits are distributed to stockholders as **dividends**. Some of the profits are reinvested in the company to help it grow. If the company makes no profit, the value of its stock usually goes down. If the company fails, the investment will be completely lost.

Bonds

Bonds are certificates that represent a promise by a *company* or *government* to repay a loan on a given date. Companies sell corporate bonds. In effect, the companies are borrowing money from the people who buy the bonds. Companies promise to pay a certain amount of interest on these loans. The loans are repaid in full when the bonds reach maturity.

Governments also sell bonds. One type of savings bond offered by the federal government is the Series EE savings bond. Series EE bonds can be bought at their face value. If the bond is held until its maturity date, it can be cashed for the original amount invested plus the interest earned. Bonds can also be cashed before maturity at a reduced interest rate. Interest earned from the bond is usually taxed. See **17-7**.

Local governments sell bonds, too. These are called *municipal bonds*. Voters are often asked to approve bond sales in local elections. Funds from municipal bonds may be used for such projects as building schools or improving streets.

Mutual Funds

A **mutual fund** is a group of many investments purchased by a company representing many investors. These funds are classified according to the types of investments purchased and called a **portfolio**. When you buy a share of a mutual fund, you become part owner of everything in that portfolio. There are stock funds, bond funds, and balanced funds that include stocks and bonds.

Many people prefer to invest in mutual funds rather than directly in stocks or bonds. A mutual fund offers three advantages to the casual investor.

- A professional fund manager does the buying and selling. Individual investors rely on that person's expertise to manage the fund.

- The investment is **diversified**. This means money is invested in many different stocks and bonds, so decreases in some are offset by increases in others. Overall, the investor is likely to make good returns on the total investment.

- Mutual funds have good liquidity. They are much easier and quicker to buy and sell than individual stocks and bonds.

Exchange-Traded Funds (ETFs)

An *exchange-traded fund (ETF)* is a type of investment fund that offers investors a way to pool their money in stocks, bonds, commodities, and futures, which are divided into shares that are traded on stock exchanges. U.S. Securities and Exchange Commission (SEC)-registered investment companies offer these funds. Although most of these funds are professionally managed, the investor can also buy and sell their ETFs with the same decision-making control as a stock investor. This investment form is gaining popularity as it is a lower-cost way for the new investor to gain exposure to a broad view of investing. As with other investment forms, however, it is important to learn about the strategies, risks, and historical performance of an ETF fund before investing.

401(k) Retirement Plans

A *401(k) retirement plan* is offered by some employers. The employer sets up a trust, a legal entity that holds assets benefiting more than one person. Full-time employees are allowed to contribute money from their paychecks before it is taxed. This savings builds retirement funds. It also delays and perhaps reduces taxes. You will pay taxes when you withdraw the funds. If you wait to withdraw the funds until after you have retired, you may be in a lower tax bracket.

Individual Retirement Accounts (IRA)

An IRA is another tool for investing. The investor typically contributes money on a regular basis from their paycheck. (This is one way to pay yourself first while you prepare for retirement.) There are two types of IRAs: (1) *tax-sheltered IRAs* and (2) *Roth IRAs*. Either fund will invest your money in savings products, stocks, or bonds to generate a profit. A major difference between the two is when you pay taxes on the

John Clark/Shutterstock.com

17-7

Series EE bonds can be purchased through the U.S. Department of Treasury's website. Federal government bonds are considered safe investments.

money you invest. The money an investor chooses to tax shelter is taxed at the time the money is withdrawn. The money an investor chooses to pay into a Roth account is taxed before it is invested. Contributions to either IRA have annual limits. Choosing an IRA depends on your tax rate now, what you expect it to be in the future, and the rate of return you expect on your investment. Conservative investors will likely choose a specific rate of return on their investment. Those who are comfortable with risk may choose to go with the fluctuating market in hopes of earning a higher rate of return. Like stocks, board of directors manages IRAs.

Planning an Estate

An **estate** is what a person leaves behind when he or she dies. People who have saved and invested throughout their lives generally have plans for their estates. They want their property to be distributed in a certain way. Perhaps they want to be sure to provide support for their survivors. Maybe they want to donate funds to a favorite charity. In order for their wishes to be fulfilled, they must take appropriate legal steps. Otherwise, their estates will be distributed according to state laws.

A **will** is a legal document describing how a person wants his or her property to be distributed after death. It specifies who will be in charge of carrying out the deceased person's wishes.

One main reason parents need to prepare wills is to name legal guardians for their children. If they do not do this, the court will become responsible for the children. The court can then name any legal guardian. This guardian may or may not be the person whom the parents would have chosen.

Wills may be written or oral. However, a written will prepared by an attorney is the most legally binding. This type of will provides the greatest protection against disputes by unhappy heirs.

People have many options as they plan their estates. The size of the estate and the goals of the individual affect those options. Lawyers, bankers, investment counselors, insurance agents, and accountants can assist with estate planning.

 **Reading**
Review

1. Give two reasons for saving money.
2. What are the five factors that should be considered when deciding how to save?
3. Which type of savings account allows deposits and withdrawals to be made at any time?
4. A portfolio of diversified investments purchased by a company representing many investors is called a _____ _____.
5. List four professionals who can assist people with estate planning.

Section 17-3

Using Credit

Objectives

After studying this section, you will be able to

- **identify** different types of credit.
- **analyze** the pros and cons of using credit.
- **describe** how to establish a credit rating.

Key Terms

credit

creditors

collateral

credit report

credit score

finance charges

interest

annual percentage rate (APR)

credit contract

Consumer credit is widely used in the United States. **Credit** is an arrangement that allows consumers to buy goods or services now and pay for them later. Credit has been called savings in reverse because it involves the present use of future income.

Credit can be a successful buying tool, but if misused, it can cause many problems. As a consumer, you have choices to make in determining whether or not to use credit. Use it wisely and it may help you enjoy a more comfortable lifestyle. Take it for granted and it can lead to serious financial difficulties.

Types of Credit

Consumer credit can be classified as either sales credit or cash credit. Those who have goods or services to sell offer *sales credit*. Department stores, car dealers, repair services, and professional services offer sales credit. Those who have money to loan offer *cash credit*. Lending and financial institutions offer cash credit.

Sales and cash credit can then be divided into one of two categories based on how they are repaid. Credit to be repaid in full at the end of the month is called *noninstallment credit*. Dentist bills, utility bills, and repair bills are examples of noninstallment credit.

Installment credit is repaid in a series of regular, equal payments. Such payments may be made at regular intervals over several weeks, months, or years. The period of time depends on the contract between you and the creditor. Installment credit is used primarily for major purchases—homes, cars, household furnishings, and large cash loans. See **17-8**.

Sales Credit

Sales credit is widely used because it is convenient. The cost of using sales credit varies. Three types of sales credit are commonly used.

Regular charge accounts are forms of noninstallment credit. They are used as a shopping convenience and as a way for customers to avoid carrying large amounts of cash. The customer can charge as much as is needed as long as the account is paid in full at the end of the billing period. These accounts are a form of open-end credit. This means that any number of items can be charged. Finance charges are not usually added to regular charge accounts if bills are paid promptly.

Installment charge accounts are forms of installment credit, as the name suggests. The buyer signs a contract and agrees to make a fixed number of payments at certain intervals over a set period of time. This contract is known as a *closed-end credit contract*. This means that no further items may be purchased on the contract. If other purchases are made, other contracts must be signed. This type of credit is usually used for major purchases, such as furniture.

Revolving charge accounts combine the features of noninstallment and installment credit plans. They are a form of open-end credit. Consumers are allowed to make purchases up to a credit limit established in the

17-8

An expensive item such as this car might be bought using installment credit.

credit contract. Consumers may pay their bills in full each month. When this is done, no finance charge is applied to the account. Consumers also can pay in installments over a longer period. Then a finance charge is applied to the unpaid balance. Department stores often offer this type of account.

Credit Cards

A credit card shows that the company or bank that issued the card honors your credit. Most credit cards are revolving charge accounts. You are billed at the end of each billing period. There is no charge for use of credit if the bill is paid in full each month. If payment is spread over a period of several months, a finance charge is made on the unpaid balance.

What happens if you lose a credit card? If you report a stolen credit card within two days, you are responsible for no more than $50 worth of charges made by someone else. If you report the card before any unapproved charges are made, you are responsible for no charges. You are still responsible, however, for the charges you have made. It is important to report the loss immediately.

Loans

A loan is a financial transaction in which the lender agrees to give the borrower a certain amount of money. Total repayment is expected by a specified time. Sometimes payment is due in a lump sum on a certain date. More commonly, regular payments are spread over a period of time agreed to by lender and borrower. Usually interest is paid in addition to the principal.

A promissory note or contract spells out the details of the transaction. Financial penalties are often incurred for missed or late payments. Loans are often used in the purchase of major items such as a new car or house.

The Pros and Cons of Using Credit

The use of credit has advantages, but it has several dangers, too. The main advantage of credit is convenience. You do not need to carry large amounts of cash when shopping or vacationing. In an emergency, credit can provide temporary help for an unexpected expense. Credit allows you to use expensive goods and services, such as a car or a home, as you pay for them. See **17-9**.

One great danger of credit is that it makes spending too easy. It can encourage impulse spending. Also, merchandise bought on credit does not really belong to you until the debt has been paid.

If payments are not made on schedule, you may lose the merchandise. Some **creditors** (people who give credit and to whom debts are owed) ask for collateral. **Collateral** is something of value that you own and that you pledge to a creditor as security for a loan. If you fail to make credit payments, you may lose more than the money you have already paid and the merchandise. You may also lose the items that were pledged as collateral.

Mental Health Awareness

Compulsive Shopping

Compulsive shopping is making frequent purchases to achieve brief feelings of happiness. Some people use shopping to cope with negative emotions. However, frequent spending can lead to feelings of guilt and shame as well as credit problems. Similar to other types of addictions, compulsive shopping can be treated with the help of a mental health counselor.

alice-photo/Shutterstock.com

Using credit is expensive. The more you use and the longer you take to repay, the higher the cost. By using credit now, you are reducing future income. That means you will have less money to spend in the future. Misusing credit can have serious long-term effects. It can lead to a bad credit rating, repossession of goods, or bankruptcy.

Applying for Credit

How do creditors determine if you are a good credit risk? When you apply for credit, prospective creditors will evaluate you. The creditors will determine if they think you can handle credit.

17-9

Credit can be a useful buying tool only if it is used sensibly and carefully.

Establishing a Credit History

Your credit history affects your ability to get credit. The basis for your credit history is your *credit report*. A **credit report** is a statement that includes your bill-paying history, loans, current debts, banking, and other financial information. It also includes your name, address, birth date, phone number, credit accounts, and your social security number. Credit-reporting agencies, such as *Experian*, *Equifax*, or *TransUnion*, collect this information. Each agency may have slightly different information on your credit report.

Lenders and other companies use information from your credit report to calculate your *credit score*. Your **credit score** is a three-digit number that rates your credit risk. It is usually a number ranging from 300 to 850. Depending on which credit-reporting agency information is used, a credit score ranging from 670 to 749 is considered *good*. A good credit score can help you get a better interest rate on a loan.

You may be thinking, "How will I be able to get credit if I need a good credit report and credit score to do so?" Young people are at a disadvantage when first applying for credit. Proving ability to handle credit is not easy. Typically, you must be 18 years of age to get credit. Here are some tips you might use to establish your credit history and credit score.

- Open a checking account and a savings account. A good banking record can serve as a reference to show you have been responsible in handling your accounts.

- Buy an item on a layaway plan. Some stores will give credit accounts to customers who successfully handle layaway purchases.

- Apply for a credit account at a local department store. If offered, accept even a small amount of credit. Buy small items and make your payments promptly.

- Plan to make a big down payment on your first attempt to get credit for a bigger purchase, such as a car. Most lenders are more willing to extend credit if you are able to make a sizeable investment in the purchase.

- Ask a relative to cosign (guarantee repayment of) a loan for you. This method gives you credit on your cosigner's record. Once the debt is paid, you will have established your own credit history.

Maintaining a Good Credit Report

Credit is a privilege that you should not take lightly. Once you establish a good credit report, you need to protect it. Whenever you apply for credit, be truthful. Use credit in amounts you can afford to repay. By meeting all the terms of your credit agreement and paying on time, you will maintain a good credit report. Late payments or failure to pay will lead to a poor credit report and credit score. A poor credit report or score will make it difficult to get credit in the future.

Checking Your Credit Report

As you have learned, credit-reporting agencies gather information about your credit activities. In turn, these agencies sell your information to potential creditors, employers, and other businesses to use to evaluate your applications for credit. It is important to check your credit reports regularly to ensure the information is accurate and to catch any signs of identity theft.

You are entitled to a free credit report every 12 months from each of the three agencies (Experian, Equifax, and TransUnion). These three agencies have set up a central website (annualcreditreport.com) through which you can order your *free* annual report. You can also download an *Annual Credit Report Request Form* from the Federal Trade Commission (FTC) website. Simply complete the form and mail it to the address on the form. You can request all three reports at one time, or request them one at a time.

Additionally, check your credit report before applying for any major loan to make sure there are no errors on your report. If you find errors, immediately contact the credit-reporting agency and request a correction of the errors.

The Three Cs of Credit

The three Cs of credit will be used to evaluate you. They are character, capital, and capacity. See **17-10**.

Character is an important consideration to creditors. Personal attributes, such as your honesty and reliability, will be studied. Creditors will also review your established record of financial responsibility. For instance, they will see if you consistently paid your bills on time.

Your *capital* is important. This refers to your income. Your occupation and years you have held your job will be considered. The length of time you expect to remain at your job will also be considered. In addition,

Ethics. Joseph's customers and coworkers know that they can always count on Joseph to tell the truth. He has a reputation for being honest and fair.

BELK CREDIT APPLICATION

EMPLOYEE NO.	DATE

Type of Account Requested:
☐ INDIVIDUAL   ☐ JOINT

PLEASE TELL US ABOUT YOURSELF

FIRST NAME (TITLES OPTIONAL)	MIDDLE INITIAL	LAST NAME		AGE

STREET ADDRESS (IF P.O. BOX — PLEASE GIVE STREET ADDRESS)	CITY	STATE	ZIP

| ☐ OWN   ☐ LIVE WITH RELATIVE | MONTHLY PAYMENT | YEARS AT PRESENT ADDRESS | HOME PHONE NO. | NO. OF |
☐ RENT ☐ OTHER	$		( )	DEPENDENTS

PREVIOUS ADDRESS	CITY	STATE	ZIP	HOW LONG

NAME OF NEAREST RELATIVE NOT LIVING WITH YOU	RELATIONSHIP	PHONE NO. ( )

ADDRESS	CITY	STATE

NOW TELL US ABOUT YOUR JOB

EMPLOYER OR INCOME SOURCE	POSITION/TITLE	HOW LONG EMPLOYED YRS. MOS.	MONTHLY INCOME $

EMPLOYER'S ADDRESS	CITY	STATE	TYPE OF BUSINESS	BUSINESS PHONE ( )

MILITARY RANK (IF NOW IN SERVICE)	SEPARATION DATE	UNIT AND DUTY STATION	SOCIAL SECURITY NO.

SOURCE OF OTHER INCOME (Alimony, child support, or separate maintenance need not be revealed if you do not wish to have it considered as a basis for repaying this obligation)	SOURCE	INCOME $	☐ MONTHLY ☐ ANNUALLY

AND YOUR CREDIT REFERENCES ARE

NAME AND ADDRESS OF BANK/SAVINGS AND LOAN	☐ CHECKING ☐ SAVINGS ☐ LOAN	PREVIOUS BELK OR LEGGETT ACCOUNT? ACCOUNT NO. HOW IS ACCOUNT LISTED?	☐ YES ☐ NO

List Bank cards, Dept. Stores, Finance Co.'s, and other accounts:

NAME	ACCOUNT NO.	BALANCE	PAYMENT
		$	$
		$	$
		$	$
		$	$

INFORMATION REGARDING JOINT APPLICANT

COMPLETE THIS AREA IF   ☐ JOINT ACCOUNT IS REQUESTED   ☐ YOU ARE RELYING ON SPOUSE'S INCOME OR CREDIT HISTORY TO OBTAIN CREDIT

FIRST NAME	MIDDLE INITIAL	LAST NAME	AGE	RELATIONSHIP	SOCIAL SECURITY NO.

JOINT APPLICANT'S ADDRESS IF DIFFERENT FROM APPLICANT ADDRESS	CITY	STATE	ZIP

JOINT APPLICANT'S PRESENT EMPLOYER	ADDRESS	HOW LONG EMPLOYED YRS. MOS.

BUSINESS PHONE ( )	POSITION/TITLE	MONTHLY INCOME $

YOUR SIGNATURE PLEASE   Store Stamp Below

I have read and agree to the Terms and Conditions of the Belk Retail Charge Agreement as set forth on attached. Belk is authorized to investigate my credit record and exchange credit experience with other creditors and Credit Reporting Agencies. This information is given to obtain credit, and is true and complete.

FOR OFFICE USE ONLY

Letter _____

CB. RPT. _____

EMP. VER _____

_____
Applicant's Signature   Date

_____
Joint Applicant's signature
(required if joint applicant section completed)   Date

DATE	EMP.	#CARDS	T/C	CR/LN.	APPROVED

17-10

When applying for credit, you will fill out an application such as this one. The information you provide helps creditors determine if you are a good credit risk.

your other financial resources will be examined. Do you have savings or insurance? Do you own an automobile or a home?

Your *capacity* to repay will also be examined. Other debts that you have and your general living expenses will be reviewed. Creditors must know that you have the capacity to repay before they can extend credit to you.

The first time you use credit, you establish a record at your local credit reporting agency. Your file will grow as you use credit throughout your life. Maintaining a good credit record is important. Then you can prove your character, capital, and capacity when you need to use credit.

Why Credit Costs

Providing credit for consumers is costly for businesses. Businesses often have to borrow money to cover operating costs until debtors begin to pay. These businesses have to pay interest on the money they borrow. In addition, they have to pay the costs involved in running a credit department. Employees must be hired to interview credit applicants and to check over the information on completed credit applications. Bookkeepers are needed to keep credit accounts up-to-date. Bills must be sent and payments accepted and recorded. Because all people do not pay on schedule, businesses have to pay for additional help to collect bad debts. They must compensate for losses on unpaid bills.

How can businesses afford to extend credit? They make up part of their expenses by slightly raising the prices of their goods and services. They collect a credit charge from their credit customers. The credit charge is related to the cost of providing credit. The more money a business spends to provide credit, the more it must charge its credit customers.

Shopping for Credit

Wise consumers shop for credit as they shop for other goods and services. As with any form of purchase, they shop for the best value. They compare the total costs of using credit at several different places. They also compare terms of credit agreements. Since credit charges vary from source to source, comparison shopping is smart.

When shopping for credit, compare sources. A car dealer may offer credit for the purchase of a car or truck. A store may offer credit for major purchases. Credit unions, savings and loan associations, and banks are other sources. Finance companies specialize in offering credit, but their interest rates are usually high.

Find out the exact cost of using credit. This helps you compare finance charges and determine how much credit you can afford. **Finance charges** are the total amounts a borrower must pay the creditor for the use of credit. These charges include interest, service charges, and any other fees. Creditors are bound by law to tell borrowers the dollar amount of all finance charges.

The Cost of Credit

Three factors determine the total cost of using credit. These factors are the size of the loan or amount of credit used, the annual percentage rate, and the repayment time. By comparing these factors, you can shop for the best deal.

The Amount of Credit Used

As you borrow or charge greater amounts, you will pay more in interest. Interest is the price you pay the creditor for the use of money over a period of time. Interest is a rate, expressed as a percentage. For example, the interest rate paid on a credit card account may be 1.5 percent a month.

The Annual Percentage Rate

To compare credit costs fairly, be sure to consider the annual percentage rate (APR). This is the actual percentage rate of interest paid per year. A monthly 1.5-percent rate equals an APR of 18 percent.

Comparing APRs from different sources is an easy way to choose the lowest interest rate. The higher the APR is, the more you will pay in interest. For instance, an 18-percent APR would mean higher interest payments than a 15.5-percent APR.

The Repayment Time

The longer you take to repay your credit debt, the larger the amount you will pay in interest. For instance, the interest on a $100 loan at 18-percent APR repaid in two years would cost $36. If the same loan is repaid in one year, the interest would be $18.

Credit Contracts

A credit contract is a legally binding agreement between creditor and borrower. It details the terms of repayment. A contract provides protection for both creditor and borrower, 17-11. It tells what is expected of each party. If either party fails to carry out the terms of the contract, the other may take legal steps to enforce the terms.

Read all contracts carefully before signing. Make sure you understand every term and the meaning of each statement. Question any point that you do not understand. Be sure that all blank spaces on the contract have been filled. Look for dates, total finance charges, and the annual percentage rate. This information is required on the contract by law.

A credit contract is a serious commitment. Before you sign, ask the creditor these important questions:

1. What action can be taken if I skip a payment or make it late?
2. Can I repay the debt in advance? For example, if the contract states I have a total of 24 monthly payments, can I repay in 12 months instead?
3. If I pay in advance, will part of the finance charges be refunded to me?

When a contract that involves a large sum of money is being considered, you may need legal advice. Do not hesitate to hire a lawyer. The fee you pay an attorney may save you a lot of money later. People who have either a weak credit report or no credit report may need a cosigner or guarantor on a contract. The cosigner may be a parent, older sibling, or family friend. Anyone who cosigns a contract agrees to pay the debt if the debtor fails to pay.

KEEP THIS NOTICE FOR FUTURE USE
BELK RETAIL CHARGE AGREEMENT

1. Each time I receive the monthly statement (at about the same time each month) I will decide whether to pay the New Balance of the account in full or in part. If full payment of the New Balance shown on the statement is received, by BELK, by the Payment Due Date, No FINANCE CHARGE will be added to the account. Any month I choose not to pay the New Balance in full, I will make at least the minimum partial payment listed on the statement as Minimum Payment Now Due. Each month the Minimum Payment Due will be calculated according to the following schedule:

If New Balance Is	Less Than $10	$10-100	$101-150	$151-200	$201-250	$251-300	Over $300
Minimum Monthly Payment Is	Balance	$10	$15	$20	$25	$30	1/10 of account balance rounded to next highest $5 increment

2. If payment in full is not received by the Payment Due Date, I agree to pay a FINANCE CHARGE at the rate described below for my State of residence.

Annual Percentage Rate for Purchases	10% to 21% (see table below)		
State of Residence	Periodic Rate	Annual Percentage Rate	Portion of Average Daily Balance To Which Applied
DE., KY., VA., MS., GA., OK., MD.	1.75%	21%	ENTIRE
NC., PA., TN., FL., TX and all other states	1.50%	18%	ENTIRE
AL.	1.75%	21%	$750 or less
	1.5%	18%	over $750
WV.	1.5%	18%	$750 or less
	1.0%	12%	over $750
SC.	1.75%	21%	$650 or less
	1.5%	18%	over $650
MO.	1.5%	18%	$1,000 or less
	1.0%	12%	over $1,000
AR.	.083%	10%	ENTIRE
Grace Period:	You have until the next billing date which on average is 23 days if the balance is paid in full, before a finance charge will be imposed.		
Method of Computing the Average Daily Balance.	Average Daily Balance Method: We figure a portion of the finance charge on your account by applying the periodic rate to the "average daily balance" of your account (including current transactions). To get the "average daily balance", we take the beginning balance of your account each day, add any new purchases and subtract any payments or credits, and unpaid finance charges. This gives us the daily balance. Then, we add up all the daily balances for the billing cycle and divide the total by the number of days in the billing cycle. This gives us the "average daily balance".		

3. Credit for returned merchandise will not substitute for a payment.

4. BELK has the right to amend the terms and conditions of this agreement by advising me of its intentions to do so in a manner and to the extent required by law.

5. If any payment is not received by BELK by the Payment Due Date, the full unpaid balance of the account may, at the option of Belk, become due and payable. If the account is referred for collection by Belk to any outside agency and/or attorney, who is not a salaried employee of BELK, I will, to the extent permitted by law, pay all costs including attorney fees.

6. BELK reserves the right to charge a handling fee, not to exceed the amount permitted by law, on any check used for payment on the account that is returned by the bank for insufficient funds or otherwise unpaid.

7. If this is a joint account, both of us agree to be bound by the terms of this agreement and each of us agrees to be jointly and severally liable for payment of all purchases made under this agreement.

8. The credit card issued to me in connection with this account remains the property of BELK and I will surrender it upon request. I understand that BELK is not obligated to extend to me any credit and, without prior notice, may refuse to allow me to make any purchase or incur any other charge on my account. Such refusal will not affect my obligation to pay the balance existing on my account at the time.

9. If any provision of this agreement is found to be invalid or unenforceable, the remainder of this agreement shall not be affected thereby, and the rest of this agreement shall be valid and enforced to the fullest extent permitted by law. No delay, omission, or waiver in the enforcement of any provision of this agreement by BELK will be deemed to be a waiver of any subsequent breach of such provision or of any other provision of this agreement.

10. I hereby authorize BELK, or any credit bureau employed by BELK, to investigate references, statements, and other data contained on my application or obtained from me or any other source pertaining to my credit worthiness. I will furnish further information if requested. I authorize BELK to furnish information concerning its credit experience with me to credit reporting agencies and others who may lawfully receive such information.

11. Except as provided in paragraph 2 above, this agreement will be governed by the laws of the State of North Carolina.

Handling Credit Problems

Credit problems can result when difficult situations arise. Sometimes an unexpected illness, job loss, emergency, or accident can lead to financial problems. If this happens, do not ignore your credit bills. Notify your creditor and be honest about your situation. You may be able to work out a different payment plan.

Credit problems can also result from misusing credit. Some people spend more than they can afford. Financial problems may also result from lack of

17-11

This is an example of a typical credit contract. When you are issued a credit card, you agree to abide by rules such as these.

Financial Literacy

Using Credit Wisely

Managing credit wisely is an important consumer skill. You can learn to manage your credit wisely by using the following guidelines:

- Stay within your credit limits. Use credit sparingly and only after much thought.
- Shop around for the best credit terms before you borrow or charge.
- Deal only with reputable creditors.
- Read credit agreements before signing. Make sure you understand all the credit terms and can fulfill your obligation.
- Keep records of all credit transactions. Include receipts, payments, contracts, and correspondence. Keep records neatly organized in a file.
- Maintain a good credit report and credit score by paying promptly. Pay off balances on revolving charge accounts each month to avoid interest charges.
- Correct billing errors immediately.
- Notify creditors promptly if your credit card is lost or stolen.
- If you have trouble making credit payments, contact your creditors right away.
- If you decide to use credit, shop for the best terms to meet your needs.

management skills, loss of income, illness, or an emergency. Learning to use credit wisely can help people avoid some of these problems.

Once a financial problem becomes serious for any reason, notify your creditors promptly. If they are aware of the facts and your sincere intention to repay, they may defer payments for a while. They may allow you to return merchandise for credit. They may offer to extend the payment period, thus decreasing the size of your monthly payments.

When creditors will not offer a more lenient plan for paying, you may need to *consolidate* your debts. To do this, you must find a financial institution that will loan you enough money to pay all other debts. This institution will then arrange a monthly payment plan that you can afford. Monthly payments may be smaller, but the repayment schedule may be longer.

Credit Counseling

When credit problems get out of control, people can seek help from nonprofit credit counseling services. Credit counseling services can help debtors in two ways. First, an effort is made to work out a reasonable budget based on available income. This budget must allow a certain amount of income to be applied to paying debts. Sometimes the difference between income and living expenses is not enough to pay debts. Then the credit counselors will try to help the debtor to arrange new payment schedules.

The second kind of help is training in money management. Counselors teach people management skills so future problems can be avoided.

Court Protection

People who cannot resolve serious long-term credit problems on their own may seek legal protection through the court system. Two choices are available: a Wage Earner Plan or bankruptcy.

The *Wage Earner Plan* (or Chapter 13 bankruptcy) is a legal arrangement by the courts that schedules debt repayment. With this plan, the debtor's income, property, and other assets are protected while the debtor repays all debts. This plan may be very costly.

When a person files *bankruptcy* (Chapter 7, or "straight" bankruptcy), the court declares that the person is unable to pay debts. The debtor's possessions are sold. The cash from the sales, with the exception of a small amount, is distributed to creditors. Filing bankruptcy will probably prevent you from obtaining credit for at least 10 years.

Reading
Review

1. Explain the difference between sales credit and cash credit.
2. List three advantages and three disadvantages of using credit.
3. List four ways to establish a credit report and credit score.
4. What three factors do creditors use to evaluate people who are applying for credit?
5. True or false. The three factors affecting the cost of credit are size of the loan, annual percentage rate, and the repayment schedule.
6. A _____ _____ is a legally binding agreement between the creditor and borrower that details the terms of repayment.
7. List two ways in which credit counseling services help debtors handle credit problems.

Section 17-4

Meeting Insurance Needs

Objectives

After studying this section, you will be able to

- **describe** different kinds of insurance protection.
- **evaluate** the types of insurance that you will need.

Key Terms

policy	loan value	health maintenance organization (HMO)
policyholder	deductible	
premium	coinsurance	preferred provider organization (PPO)
beneficiary	copayment	
cash value		

Nobody likes to think about getting sick, injured, or killed. However, these events are realities of life. Preparing for them can make them less devastating. One way to prepare is to purchase insurance. Insurance can protect your investments, provide for your loved ones, and cover costs of damage repairs and medical treatments.

Insurance Basics

Insurance is a risk-sharing plan. Insurance companies offer a way in which many people can unite to protect each other from income losses. These losses may be due to death, disability, natural disasters, thefts, accidents, or other misfortunes.

Insurance contracts are called **policies**. A person who has a policy is called a policyholder. A **policyholder** agrees to regularly pay a certain amount of money, called a **premium**, to the insurance company. In return, the insurance company provides financial protection for the policyholder in the event of a misfortune covered in the policy.

When an insurance company collects premiums from policyholders, the money is promptly invested. In this way, the premiums earn money for the insurance company. The insurance company uses part of the earnings to pay the claims made by policyholders. Some earnings are also used to cover the company's operating expenses.

A good insurance agent will help you determine the types of insurance you need. The agent will also help you find a plan you can afford to provide the amount of coverage you need.

The information that follows describes several types of insurance that you are likely to buy.

Life Insurance

Life insurance is protection against financial loss due to death. This type of protection is especially important for people who have dependents. A *dependent* is someone, such as a spouse, child, or elderly parent, who relies on another person for financial support. See **17-12**. Life insurance should be bought when a person begins to have financial responsibility.

Most families carry life insurance on the parent who is the chief wage earner. However, some insurance should be carried on both parents. Should either parent die, survivors need protection against the loss of that parent's income and services.

When a life insurance policyholder dies, the insurance company pays the *death benefit* of the policy, called *face value*. The person who receives the death benefit is called the **beneficiary**.

Two basic types of life insurance are available—term and whole life. Many variations of each type are available. You should know the difference between the basic types, then obtain the advice of a reliable agent to help determine your needs.

Analyze and Solve

Interview family members about life insurance. Find out why family members have or do not have life insurance. If they have life insurance, what type do they have? Write a report detailing what sort of additional life insurance you believe your family members need.

Mental Health Awareness

Emotional Buying

Emotions can influence purchasing decisions. For example, fear is often a factor concerning insurance options. Although planes are one of the safest forms of transportation, some people buy life insurance before flying because air travel makes them feel anxious. Recognizing when an emotion is the true motive behind a purchase may help you have better control over your finances.

17-12
Life insurance protects dependents from a loss of income due to a wage earner's death.

Term Insurance

Term insurance covers the owner of a policy for a specific number of years. The most common term policies available are annually renewable, 5-year renewable, 10-year renewable, 20-year renewable, and term to age 65. At the end of the term, coverage stops. Benefits are payable only if the policyholder dies within the term.

If you buy term insurance, look for a policy with a *renewal privilege*. This allows the policyholder to renew the policy without having a physical examination. Without a renewal privilege, you might not be able to obtain more insurance when the term expires. A term policy may also carry a *convertible clause*. Under this clause, the owner may later exchange the term policy for a whole life policy without a physical examination.

Whole Life Insurance

Whole life insurance covers the policyholder for a lifetime rather than for a specific number of years. Whole life policies acquire cash value and loan value after premiums have been paid for at least two years. **Cash value** is the amount the policyholder can collect if he or she decides to give up the policy. **Loan value** is the amount the policyholder can borrow from the insurance company using the cash value as collateral. The cash value and the loan value are usually equal.

When choosing whole life policies, you have two basic options. One option is called a *straight life policy*. Fixed premiums based on your age at the time you buy the policy are paid throughout your lifetime. The second option is a policy that can be purchased outright over a shorter period of time. These policies are called *limited payment life policies*.

Universal Life Insurance

A relatively new form of life insurance is universal life insurance. It is similar to to whole life insurance in that it includes cash value; however, the premiums for universal life are *flexible*, not fixed. The cash value accumulated on the policy is invested to earn interest. The return will vary from year to year as a result of the insurer's investment success.

Health Insurance

Under the Affordable Care Act, almost everyone is required to have health insurance. Health care is expensive. The costs of medical checkups, medicine, and hospital care can add up quickly. Health insurance helps cover these costs.

Many people are able to get health insurance coverage through a group plan. Companies, unions, and professional organizations often offer group plans. With these plans, all members of the group can buy the insurance at reduced rates. Employers may pay all or part of the cost of premiums as an employee benefit.

People who do not have group plans available to them may purchase health insurance individually or through the government. See **17-13**.

Health insurance policies differ in terms of what they cover. Evaluate a policy carefully before making a purchasing decision. Find out whether certain illnesses are excluded from coverage. See if there are any limits on the amount of costs that will be covered.

Most insurance policies do not pay 100 percent of a policyholder's medical expenses, even for items that are covered. Some policies have provisions for deductibles, coinsurance, and copayments. A **deductible** is an amount that a policyholder must pay before the insurance company will pay anything. If you have a $250 deductible, you would pay the first $250 of medical expenses covered by the insurance. The insurance company would pay the remaining expenses covered. **Coinsurance** requires the policyholder to pay a certain percentage of medical costs. Many coinsurance policies cover 80 percent,

17-13

For many people, a key factor in selecting health insurance is being able to see the doctor of their choice.

requiring policyholders to pay the remaining 20 percent. **Copayments** are fixed fees for certain items or services. For instance, you may have a $40 copayment for each doctor visit. These provisions help defray the costs of settling insurance claims and therefore reduce premiums.

Types of Health Coverage

Like health care, health insurance is expensive. The cost of insurance premiums may seem high. However, medical expenses can lead to financial ruin if you do not have insurance.

Three main types of health insurance coverage are available. These are basic medical coverage, major medical coverage, and disability insurance.

Basic medical coverage pays standard hospital costs. These costs include room, meals, nursing care, drugs, X rays, and laboratory tests. Some policies also pay for doctor visits and simple medical procedures.

Major medical coverage pays the bulk of expenses resulting from major illness or serious injury. It covers surgery and other expenses not covered by a basic medical policy.

Disability insurance provides payments for people who are unable to work because of illness or injury. It generally pays two thirds of a person's gross salary.

Workers' Compensation

Workers' compensation is a type of health insurance required by state law. It is carried by employers to provide benefits for employees who suffer illness or injuries due to their work environment. Private insurance companies handle the policies. Medical expenses, hospitalization, lost wages, and a disability pension are included in the coverage.

Health Maintenance Organizations

A **health maintenance organization (HMO)** is a group of medical professionals and facilities that provides health care services to members. HMO members pay a flat fee regularly. When medical service is needed, members go to a doctor associated with their HMO. They receive care at little or no added cost.

It is less costly to prevent an illness than to cure one. Therefore, HMOs focus on preventative health care. Because the charge, if any, for office visits is minimal, members are encouraged to get regular checkups. This eliminates the need for more costly health procedures that result from a lack of routine care.

Preferred Provider Organizations

A **preferred provider organization (PPO)** is a group of doctors and medical facilities that contract to provide services at reduced rates. PPOs make agreements with employers or insurance companies. They designate fixed fees and terms for the health care services to be provided.

PPOs benefit all involved. The employer or insurance company can better control medical care costs. The doctors and hospitals have more clients. Patients pay less for health care when they use the preferred provider.

Before you choose a PPO, know who the preferred providers are. Find out what services are provided. Be aware of the costs. All doctors do not participate in PPOs; neither do all hospitals. You may see a doctor who is not a member of the PPO, but it will cost you more. Be sure you have access to the health services you will need before you join.

Automobile Insurance

Because automobile insurance premiums are high, many people are tempted to drive without insurance. This is not a wise decision. The losses from a single accident could destroy a family's financial security. In addition, states require drivers to be responsible for accidents in which they are at fault. Having insurance is one way to prove responsibility. See **17-14**.

Types of Auto Coverage

An automobile insurance policy usually includes several kinds of coverage. The six basic types of coverage are: bodily injury liability,

17-14

Everyone who drives a car should be protected by automobile insurance.

property damage liability, medical payments, uninsured motorists, comprehensive physical damage, and collision.

Bodily injury liability covers you if you are legally liable for the death or injury of others. Bodily injury pays for any loss of earning ability as well as medical expenses of the injured. It pays the legal fees and the damages assessed against you, up to the limits of the policy. Liability insurance covers the car's owner. It may also cover anyone else who drives the car with the owner's permission. The amount of coverage is usually stated in two amounts. For instance, $100,000-$300,000 coverage means the insurance company will pay up to $100,000 for any single injury and up to $300,000 for any single accident.

Property damage liability pays for damages that your car causes to the property of others. Like bodily injury liability, it will also pay legal fees. It does not pay for damages to your property—your car.

Medical payments coverage pays medical costs resulting from an accident regardless of who was at fault. It covers anyone in your car if your car is involved in an accident. It also covers you and your family if you are injured while riding in another car or while walking.

Uninsured motorist coverage pays for bodily injuries for which an uninsured motorist or hit-and-run driver is responsible. You and your family are covered as drivers, passengers, and pedestrians. Guests in your car are also covered.

Comprehensive physical damage coverage protects your car from damage by something other than another vehicle. Such damage may be caused by fire, theft, water, hail, and vandalism.

Collison insurance pays for damages to your car caused by collision with a vehicle or other object. Damages are paid regardless of who was at fault. Collision coverage usually has a deductible option. With a $100 deductible option, if damages to your car amount to $250, you will pay the first $100. The insurance company will pay the $150 balance. You can get coverage with different deductible options.

Automobile Insurance Premiums

Premiums for auto insurance vary greatly and depend on a number of factors. Your age, your driving record, and the year and model of your car affect your insurance premium. Where you live and the distance you drive in a year are factors as well.

Some companies offer discounts on premium costs. Have you completed a driver education course? Are you a good student? Does your family own more than one car? If you can answer yes to any of these questions, you may be eligible for a discount.

When buying auto insurance, shop carefully. Check several companies to get the best price for the coverage you need. Research the company's long-term ratings before you make a final decision.

Housing-Related Insurance

If you own or rent your home, insurance can provide financial protection in the event of loss or damage. The cost of this insurance will depend on the type and amount of coverage and the insurance rates in your area.

Homeowner's insurance provides two basic types of coverage: property protection and liability protection. Property coverage insures you against such dangers as fire, lightning, vandalism, burglary, theft, and explosions. It covers the damage or loss of the dwelling and your personal possessions, such as clothes and furnishings. It also pays for your living expenses if you must move out of your home because of damages to the property.

Liability coverage protects you against financial loss if others are injured on or by your property. It also offers protection if you or your property accidentally damages the property of others. It pays for legal costs if you are sued because of injuries to others or damages to their property. It pays for damages assessed against you if you are held legally liable for injuries or property damage.

Renter's insurance is similar to homeowner's insurance. It covers a renter's personal possessions and liability.

Insurance coverage should be kept in line with the value of your home and belongings. Make an inventory of your possessions and estimate their values. This will help you decide how much coverage you need. Periodically update your coverage as you make major purchases.

Some policies pay *actual cash value*, which equals today's costs less depreciation for the use of the item. Thus, an old item may have depreciated to the point where it is no longer considered to have value. Such an item may not be covered in the case of loss. Other policies pay *replacement costs*, which equal today's costs without considering any depreciation. Replacement cost protection generally is somewhat more expensive. However, the expense may be worthwhile in the event of a major loss.

 **Reading**
Review

1. Regular payments made by a policyholder to an insurance company are called _____ .
2. What is the difference between term and whole life insurance policies?
3. True or false. Coinsurance is an amount of money that a policyholder must pay before the insurance company will pay.
4. What kind of automobile insurance coverage pays for damages that your car causes to the property of others?
5. What factors affect the cost of homeowner's and renter's insurance?

Chapter 17 Review

Summary

Several types of financial institutions can help you manage your money. Your choice of institutions will be based partly on the services you need. One of these services is sure to be a checking account. Learning how to correctly write and endorse checks and balance your checkbook will give you convenience and flexibility in managing your money.

The unexpected can happen to even the best of money managers. Having some money in savings can help you prepare for the unexpected. Your savings options range from regular savings accounts and CDs to stocks, bonds, and mutual funds. When deciding how to save, you will want to consider safety, rate of return, liquidity, purchasing power, and convenience. Your savings will become part of your estate when you die. Preparing a will enables your wishes to be observed regarding the distribution of your estate.

Deciding whether or not to use credit is an important financial decision. It involves knowing how each type of credit works and the pros and cons of credit use. Shopping for the best credit terms helps consumers compare finance charges and get the best deal. Misusing credit can lead to serious financial problems. Those consumers who cannot handle serious credit problems should seek help from credit counseling services or through legal protection.

Insurance can protect you against huge losses. You may need life insurance to provide for dependents in the event of your death. You are likely to need health insurance to help cover the high costs of medical treatments, drugs, and hospitalization. If you drive a car, you need to be protected by automobile insurance. If you own or rent a home, insurance will cover your property and protect you against liability.

Critical Thinking

1. **Evaluate options.** Which of the different financial services do you see yourself using in the next five years? Which type of financial institution do you think would be best able to provide you with the services you will need?

2. **Analyze risks.** In which type of security would you most prefer to invest? Explain your answer.

3. **Recognize value.** How might the information you learned in this chapter help you in your career?

4. **Analyze options.** Suppose you lost your job and had no means of paying your creditor. How do you think you would handle your problem?

5. **Assess details.** Gather credit applications for different stores. Study the applications in class. What information do all the applications request? Do some of the applications ask for different information? Which information should you be hesitant to disclose?

6. **Analyze priorities.** Imagine you are 25 years old. You are married, and both you and your spouse work. You do not have any children. What specific types of insurance would you choose to purchase? Explain your choices.

21st Century Applications

7. **Financial literacy.** Research different types of checking accounts offered by local banks. Then write a report discussing the differences between the accounts and explaining which checking account would be most appropriate for your needs.

8. **Economics literacy.** Investigate CDs at various banks. Find information on the minimum deposit required, current interest rates, and how interest rates vary with length of time. Determine which type of CD would yield the most interest.

9. **Critical thinking and problem solving.** Research different auto insurance options for teens. Find average prices for males and females between the ages of 16 to 18. Who is more expensive to insure? Why? What discounts are available to help lower auto insurance costs?

Core Skills

10. **Reading.** Read a magazine, newspaper, or article about online or mobile banking. Determine the central ideas of the article and review the conclusions made by the author. Provide an accurate summary of your reading. Remember to cite the source of your article.

11. **Speaking.** Research current trends in the stock market. Which stocks are most profitable? If you were to invest in a company's stock, which would you choose and why? Create an electronic presentation analyzing stock market trends. Recommend at least one stock in which to invest.

12. **Listening.** As your classmates make their presentations on the current trends in the stock market, evaluate each presenter. Review the presenter's point of view and use of digital media. Was the presentation effective? Why or why not?

13. **Reading.** Check out the websites for the National Credit Union Administration or the Credit Union National Association. What kinds of information are available at these sites?

14. **Math.** Do research on current car prices and loan and lease incentives. Add the cost of the loan or lease into the price of the car to assess the total amount. Which vehicle would be the best buy?

15. **Math.** Obtain a variety of credit contracts and bring them to class. Study the terms of the contracts. Do any of the credit agencies charge an annual fee? What is the interest rate in each of the contracts? Are there service charges or any other fees? Calculate interest rates on a large purchase, such as a new television, using interest rates from each contract. How much would you pay in total for your purchase in each instance?

16. **Reading.** Research the bankruptcy process. Find out if there are different kinds of bankruptcy that can be filed and what laws govern these procedures.

Find out what possessions can be kept and how long it takes before credit can be granted again.

17. **Reading, writing.** Research James Lind and his contributions to the health care field. Write an informative essay about his accomplishments and include a time line summarizing his biography.

18. **Writing.** Select two financial-related careers to research on O*NET. Read the summary reports for these careers, especially the knowledge, skills, abilities, and interests required to do the work. Analyze whether your personal interests, skills, and abilities are a logical fit with one or both careers. Write a summary explaining why you think you are well-suited for either career.

Leadership
Development

As a part of the Financial Fitness National Program, develop a project applying concepts from this chapter. Suggested projects include: assembling this information into a resource booklet for teens seeking new sources of income; interviewing students about how they spend money for a school newspaper article; investigate the types of credit that are available to teens and the conditions for receiving each type of credit.

Portfolio
Builder

Achieving financial strength takes planning. Write a reflection paper regarding how you see your financial future. Set financial goals for yourself and describe how you plan to meet them. Add this document to your portfolio for future reference. Topics to address in your paper should include the following:

- checking accounts
- savings accounts
- investments
- insurance

Journal
Writing

Tameka has taken her first job and is excited about her forthcoming paycheck. Her grandfather says, "You have a lifetime of earning power ahead of you. Pay yourself first. Start with an amount you know you can afford and increase the amount periodically. You will have it when you need it most."

Write About It: *What does Tameka's grandfather mean by "pay yourself first"? Assuming she is earning minimum wage, what percentage of Tameka's income would you suggest she save? If she pays herself first, how can she manage to pay her other bills? How can she ensure the greatest financial gain on her savings?*

Chapter 18
Consumer Decisions

Reading Prep

Before you begin reading each section, skim the Reading Review questions at the end of each section. Use these questions to help you focus on the most important concepts as you read the chapter.

Concept Organizer

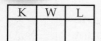

K	W	L

Create a KWL chart about consumer laws. In the first column (K), write what you already know about each consumer law. In the second column (W), write what you want to learn. In the third column (L), write what you learn as you are reading.

G-WLEARNING.COM

Click on the activity icon to visit www.g-wlearning.com/comprehensive/8062 to access online vocabulary activities using key terms from the chapter.

Making Shopping Decisions

Objectives

After studying this section, you will be able to

- **evaluate** options available when deciding where to shop.
- **analyze** the factors affecting consumer buying decisions.
- **utilize** comparison shopping techniques when making shopping decisions.

Key Terms

impulse buying   sale   comparison shopping

Informed consumers are smart shoppers. They use the decision-making process in many ways as they make choices in the marketplace. They learn as much as they can about goods and services before making buying decisions. They plan their shopping in advance by deciding where to shop and when to buy. In deciding what to buy, they consider factors such as price, quality, suitability, and use and care. They know how to compare goods and services, and what to look for in warranties.

Being an informed consumer can help you get the most for your money. With practice, you can learn to recognize the best buys among your choices and to shop wisely. Improving your buying habits will also help you become a better consumer.

Deciding Where to Shop

As a consumer, you will have many choices to make when you shop. One of your first choices will be to decide where to shop for the items you want. Retail stores, catalogs, and electronic shopping are some of the more popular choices you may consider.

Retail Shopping

In deciding where to shop, you consider many factors. Which types of stores carry the item you want to buy? Store location, product price and quality, and product selection will also influence where you choose to shop.

Department stores are large retail firms that offer a wide variety of consumer goods and services, all under one roof. Departments within the stores offer many lines of merchandise including clothing, cosmetics, jewelry, household goods, and home furnishings. Department stores also offer customers extra services such as personal shopping, gift registries, gift wrapping, delivery, and charge accounts. Because of higher operating costs to provide these services, department store prices are often higher.

Discount stores sell a wide assortment of goods at lower prices. Unlike department stores, they may not offer services such as providing delivery and accepting all credit cards. Discount stores save money by offering fewer customer services and having smaller sales staffs. They pass their cost savings on to consumers.

Specialty stores specialize in selling one line of goods such as shoes or books. These stores are often found in shopping centers or malls. Since they carry one type of product, their salespeople know the merchandise well. For consumers who want to select from one complete product line, these stores often carry a wider selection. The prices in these stores vary depending on how unique their products are and how high their sales volume is. See **18-1**.

Off-price retail stores buy designer label products or brand name products at low prices from manufacturers. Then they pass the cost savings on to consumers. However, because they often purchase excess merchandise from manufacturers, the types of products they offer frequently change. Prices are lower than retail department stores and fewer customer services are offered.

18-1

This specialty store features a wide selection of denim clothing.

Factory outlet stores are one type of off-price retail store. These stores, owned by the manufacturer, sell directly to the consumer. Sometimes the goods are irregulars or closeouts on discontinued lines. Merchandise that is not bought by retailers is sold to consumers as overruns. Because the manufacturer sells directly to the consumer, the merchandise is sold for less. Many of these stores are located in outlet malls, which are shopping centers consisting of off-price retail stores.

Online Shopping

Two types of online shopping methods exist: television and online retailing. Online retailing includes mobile commerce (*m-commerce*), or purchases made through handheld digital devices, such as tablets and smartphones. Instead of fighting crowded stores and heavy traffic, shoppers can order merchandise from their homes or other locations at any hour. Then orders are delivered to the shipping address of their choice.

Television retailing involves showing merchandise on certain television channels. TV channels devoted to 24-hour home shopping focus on clothing, accessories, and beauty care products. Viewers order by phone and pay by credit card.

Online shopping is another in-home option. Retailer websites show items in sharp detail and include extensive product information. The ability to locate difficult-to-find items is a key reason for shopping online. Some websites have a search agent that tracks down rare items or items that meet certain criteria. Many sites offer free standard shipping or upgrades to express shipping.

Before giving credit card information online, always make sure you are at a secured site. A special icon, such as a padlock, is an indication sign that a retailer's website is secure.

Some of the advantages of online shopping are as follows:

- It saves time. You can quickly visit hundreds of merchants offering almost limitless choice.

- Prices are comparable to or slightly lower than in-store prices. The lower operating costs of online retailers make this possible, **18-2**.

- You can choose to have an item shipped more quickly if you need it.

- Ordered items are delivered to the address of your choice.

- Policies on returning merchandise are usually generous.

18-2

Online shoppers save time and money by shopping at home.

There are also drawbacks to online shopping. These include the following:

- You do not have the personal assistance of a salesperson.

- Some manufacturers will not allow their products to be sold through online channels, thus eliminating those options.

- You cannot check or test a product before purchasing it. However, you can usually return or exchange it later.

- You will have to wait at least a day for an item to be shipped.

- Shipping costs may add to the cost of the purchase, however, some offer free shipping.

- Unless you buy from a local vendor, you are not contributing to your local economy. When you shop locally, your purchases help to keep area stores in business. That, in turn, provides jobs for people in the community. With their salaries, they buy local products and services. This cycle contributes to making your town a better place to live.

- You need to be sure the vendor from whom you are buying is legitimate and not someone who will cheat you, or abuse your personal information.

Catalog Shopping

Almost any product imaginable is available through a catalog. This type of shopping offers many advantages, although catalog shopping has some drawbacks, too. Convenience and saving time are the main advantages of catalog shopping. Busy people can shop at home from a catalog, and then order items online or by phone or mail. Although consumers pay charges for shipping and handling, they save time, energy, and driving expenses by shopping at home.

Selection and price savings are other advantages. Some catalogs offer a wide variety of goods. Others specialize in one type of item, such as shoes or clothing. Prices are often lower than in department stores.

Catalog shopping has some disadvantages, too. You cannot see the item before you buy it. The color, size, or material may not be exactly as it appears in the catalog. You may have to wait for the item to be shipped. If you are not satisfied with the item after you receive it, you are responsible for returning it and paying for the shipping.

Shopping Guidelines

The following guidelines can help you make wise purchasing decisions when catalog shopping:

- Read the catalog before you place an order. Find out the company's policy for returning items in case you are not satisfied.

- Fill out the order form accurately and completely before sending in your order.

- Avoid sending cash through the mail to pay for your order. Pay by check, money order, or credit card.

- Keep a record of your order until you receive the goods. Keep a copy of the company's name, address, and telephone number in case you need to contact the company.

- When the order arrives, check it over carefully. If something is wrong or not completely satisfactory, return the item to the company.

Other Shopping Options

Thrift stores, consignment shops, garage or yard sales, and *flea markets* are other popular shopping options. These businesses sell new and used merchandise at greatly reduced prices. Shoppers with limited budgets who know quality may find true bargains. Impulse shoppers may be enchanted by amazingly low prices and buy items they really do not need. **Impulse buying** is making an unplanned or quick purchase without giving it much thought. To buy wisely, consumers must analyze their shopping goals and buy only what they need. Also, they must realize that purchases are usually final. These vendors rarely accept returns.

Deciding When to Buy

Knowing when to buy is as important as knowing where to shop. Smart shoppers plan their purchases ahead of time and watch for sales. Those who can anticipate their needs save money by shopping at sales. They are also aware of factors that can affect their shopping decisions.

Shopping at Sales

Wise shoppers try to get the most value for their shopping dollars. Shopping at store sales is one way they can save money. A **sale** is a special selling of goods at reduced prices. Smart shoppers buy items because they need them, not because the sale price is low. Shoppers carefully plan their purchases to match the timing of sales.

Many stores offer *preseason sales* when new merchandise arrives. For example, winter coats may be on sale in August to encourage people to shop early. For consumers who need new coats and want the best selections, preseason sales usually offer good savings.

End-of-season sales, or *clearance sales*, take place when retailers are making room for new merchandise for the next season. For instance,

Math Connection

Calculating Sale Prices

Jackson is happy to see that a $125.00 jacket he likes is on sale for 30% off. How can Jackson determine the sale price?

First, determine the dollar value of the discount. To do this, multiply the original price of the jacket ($125.00) by the rate of discount (30%). Be sure to change 30% to decimal form.

$125.00 × 0.30 = $37.50

Next, find the sale price by subtracting the discount from the original price.

$125.00 − $37.50 = $87.50

snow blowers may be on sale in March so retailers can make room for lawn furniture. Consumers who are able to wait until the end of the season often receive large discounts on merchandise. However, disadvantages of an end-of-season sale are that selection may be limited and return policies may be strict.

Seasonal sales take place throughout the year. This type of sale often offers consumers the best sale price. Knowing when to expect these sales helps consumers plan their purchases. Winter clothing, for example, is usually on sale in January. Sports equipment is a good buy in August. Holiday sales take place throughout the year. These are good times to buy needed items at reduced prices.

Coupons and Rebates

Coupons are small discounts on products offered by a store or manufacturer. They are often found in newspaper advertisements and direct mailings. Coupons usually offer a direct reduction in price when the proper coupon is presented at the time of a purchase.

Rebates are sometimes instant reductions in price offered at the time of purchase. However, they more commonly require initial payment of full price. Then, after submission of proof of purchase, a rebate check is mailed to the purchaser. It may take several weeks for the rebate check to arrive.

Other Factors Affecting Buying Decisions

Certain factors can affect consumer-buying decisions. Being alert to these factors can help consumers decide when to buy. Two major factors are the shopper's mood and the time available for shopping. How people feel when they shop affects their buying decisions. People who feel down when they shop tend to buy items they do not need to make themselves feel better. People who are hungry, tired, or rushed tend to buy impulsively. If they shop when they are tired or not feeling well, they will not be as alert to details. They may make hurried decisions because they are too tired to evaluate the merchandise properly.

Time is another factor that affects consumer-buying decisions. It is a resource that should be used wisely. Not allowing enough time to shop, shopping when the store is crowded, or shopping late in the day encourages impulsive shopping. Smart shoppers plan their shopping to allow plenty of time for making buying decisions.

Deciding What to Buy

When you decide to make a purchase, do you buy the first item you see? Probably not. Most likely you shop around to find the right product at the right price. There are other factors to consider in your buying decisions. The ability to judge quality, suitability, use and care, and product warranties is also an important part of your decision.

Comparison Shopping

Comparison shopping means comparing products and prices in different stores before buying. Comparison shopping helps you get the best value for your money. Look at features, price, quality, use and care, and other characteristics that are important to you. It takes time to make such comparisons. However, you will get better quality and find the product that best suits your needs for the money you invest. Comparison shopping helps you avoid impulse buying. Impulse buying may seem like fun at the time of the purchase. Later, though, you may regret spending money for the item. You may pay too much for an item or buy something you really do not need. A sale item may be hard to resist, but it is no bargain if you do not use it.

You save time, energy, and money by comparison shopping. This is because you plan your shopping in advance. You first consider what features are important to you. Then make a list of the features you want and the price you want to pay. At this point, you are ready to shop for what you need.

Financial Literacy

Understanding Warranties

A *warranty* is a written promise that a product will meet specified standards of performance and states the procedures the manufacturer or vendor will follow if the product fails to perform as stated.

Two basic types of warranties may be found on products.

- A *full warranty* is required by law to provide broad coverage on a product. It includes free repair or replacement of defective parts or products within a reasonable time frame and replacement if attempts to repair the product are unsuccessful. No unreasonable demands are placed on the consumer as a condition for receiving repair or replacement service.
- A *limited warranty* provides less coverage. It always specifies the degree to which it is limited.

When you comparison shop, carefully read product warranties. Knowing the following warranty-related information can help you make a more informed choice:

- What protection do the warranties guarantee and for how long?
- Are they full or limited warranties?
- What must you do if the product does not comply with its warranty?
- If you have a problem with a product, who is responsible for honoring the warranty?

Judging Quality

Price is not always the most important factor to consider in your buying decision. Shopping for value also means judging the quality of a product.

Product price is not always a guide to a product's quality. Although better-quality products usually cost more, a lower-cost product sometimes offers the same quality. When you shop, compare nationally advertised name brands with lesser-known brands. If the lesser-known brand is the same quality as the more expensive brand and costs less, it is a better buy. As a smart shopper, you will learn that a store's own brand is often worth considering.

Learn to inspect products as you shop so you can recognize different quality levels. Checking the quality is important if you plan to use the product often or for a long time. Higher-quality products are made to higher standards, so they usually last longer. This makes them a better value, too. Consumer research publications also offer helpful information to help you judge quality.

Sometimes a lower-priced, good-quality item may best meet your needs. For instance, if you are learning to play tennis, a less expensive racket may suit your needs until you improve your skills.

Suitability

Before you go shopping, find out as much as you can about a product. When you are ready to shop, you will be prepared to make a wise selection from all the choices. You will be able to find the most suitable product to meet your needs.

Use and Care

Read labels and care instructions on the product to be sure it is what you want. Suppose you are shopping for a casual shirt that you plan to wear often. You find one you like that must be dry-cleaned. You must then decide if you want the added expense of dry cleaning, or if you want to look for a machine washable shirt instead. Your shopping decision will be affected by the use and care information.

Reading
Review

1. A _____ store sells a certain type of product such as athletic shoes, toys, or jewelry.
2. List four advantages and four disadvantages of catalog shopping.
3. Explain the difference between a preseason sale and an end-of-season sale.
4. What is the purpose of comparison shopping?
5. Name the two types of warranties found on consumer products.

Section 18-2

The Impact of Technology on Consumers

Objectives

After studying this section, you will be able to

- **analyze** the impact of information technology on the lives of consumers.
- **summarize** ways to manage technology.

Key Terms

computer-aided design (CAD)	simulation software	obsolescence

Technology provides ways to perform complicated tasks more quickly and easily. What is learned with new technology translates into applications in other areas. Technological advances can help people manage resources, solve problems, and achieve goals.

Technology Options Available

Some definitions of technology are complex. Very simply, technology is the practical application of knowledge. Reviewing everything that technology has achieved would be a huge task. The task would be never-ending because as each second passes, more new processes and inventions are created.

Of the many inventions created by applying scientific principles, the computer is perhaps the most influential. It is responsible for the current era known as the *Information Age*. Laptops, tablets, and smartphones are types of computers. At home, computers help control the car, heating and cooling equipment, and home appliances. Computers also control the television and practically all other types of electronic equipment.

The Functions and Benefits of Technology

Technology helps perform many everyday functions faster. People can process information, manage money, and keep records better by using technology. Also, high-tech equipment can help people gather information, learn, enjoy entertainment, and communicate with others.

Healthy Living

Computer Use—Protecting Eye Health

Since computer use is a great part of every-day life for children and adults, many people have an increased risk factor for developing *computer vision syndrome*. According to the *American Optometric Association (AOA)*, symptoms of this syndrome include eyestrain, headaches, blurry vision, dry or red eyes, double vision, and sensitivity to light. The following tips can help you protect your eyes while using a computer:

- Take an eye break. For every two hours of computer use, rest your eyes for at least 15 minutes.
- Make sure the workstation is set up correctly for your body. Use good posture.
- Reduce glare.
- Increase font size so you can read in a comfortable position.
- Wear glasses instead of contacts (if needed) when working on the computer. Contact wearers blink less when using a computer, therefore increasing the likelihood of symptoms.

Information Processing

Software programs and applications can quickly process words, numbers, images, and sound. Technology is helpful for doing reports, writing letters, making presentations, and creating charts and graphs. Businesses, students, and individuals can benefit from information processing.

Landscapes or interiors for homes can be created with the use of special design software. This is called **computer-aided design (CAD)**, which is graphics software that assists in creating a design. CAD software lets you electronically change the color, size, shape, and arrangement of various elements. This prevents costly mistakes and allows last-minute changes to occur on screen or paper before implementing the final design.

Money Management

Creating budgets is easy with the help of technology. Systems software, apps, and websites devoted to money management help you prepare worksheets of various savings and spending plans. You can also write checks and balance a checkbook with special software. With online and mobile banking, you can bank from home.

Information Gathering and Learning

Perhaps the greatest value of technology today is accessing the wealth of information available online. Any given subject can be explored on numerous websites. You can search online libraries of major universities and government agencies. Encyclopedias, databases, magazines, and newspapers are also available. In addition, major television news organizations provide current events information online.

Besides finding factual information, discussion groups and review websites provide opinions about various products, services, and issues. You can read comments and join the discussion by posting a message.

Entertainment

Sometimes software programs and websites present information in such an entertaining way that the line between information and entertainment is blurred. Consider the purpose of certain products.

Mental Health Awareness

Gaming Addiction

Using technology for entertainment can be a form of stress relief and enjoyment. Too much time spent playing video games, however, can cause feelings of isolation. People can become addicted to gaming and neglect relationships with friends and family. Face-to-face relationships are important for healthy social-emotional growth and development.

Some products are designed specifically to entertain, such as video games, **18-3**. Also, **simulation software** imitates an actual experience. For example, you can sense some of the fun of piloting a hot-air balloon, surfing the Pacific, and investigating other adventures while staying at home.

Communication

As families and friends are separated by distance, the desire to stay in touch is strong. This is the main reason for the popularity of e-mail, text messaging, video calling, and social networking sites.

Managing Technology

Just as pencil and paper are neither good nor bad, the same is true for technology. How digital devices are used is what really matters. To get full value from information technology, you must make good buying decisions and use the items to enhance your life. You should also be aware of some cautions in the use of technology.

Drawbacks to Using Technology

Technology can impact lives in a negative way as well as a positive one. Sometimes the use of technology leads to undesirable or harmful effects. You will want to recognize that these possibilities exist so you can avoid them in your life. These are some of the possible drawbacks of using technology.

18-3
Colorful graphics and a speedy response to commands are the key reasons for the popularity of computer games.

Innovation. Kayla is ambitious. She regularly takes continuing education courses in technology. She often uses the technology skills she learns to develop new techniques that improve work procedures.

Financial Literacy

Making Technology Purchases

Acquaint yourself with the high-tech market and the basic types of items available before buying anything. Talk with friends about the products and services they recommend. Also talk with knowledgeable people who can offer good advice. The following are some of the questions to answer before buying high-tech equipment:

- *What equipment features do you need?* It is best to buy equipment that satisfies your current and short-term needs. Determining what features to shop for will help you determine what you need.
- *What new products will be introduced soon?* Every 12 to 18 months, technological advances create new products with more speed, convenience, and feature options. Read magazines from the technology industry to see what new features to expect in the coming months.
- *What nonproduct factors should you consider before buying?* Besides examining equipment features, consider other important questions. For example, is the dealer reputable? What must you do to get service? Is a training program offered?
- *What is the total cost?* Sometimes a great deal includes signing up for a multiyear service contract or buying other extras. If costs for competing services should drop in the future, you could be stuck with an expensive obligation to pay off. To make a wise decision, research the average costs and fees involved in getting everything you will need to use your equipment. Then you can judge whether the item purchased with the advertised extras represents a good buy for you.

- *Personal privacy may be threatened.* Many fear the invasion of their privacy as a result of data collecting through technology. Because computers can compile and access data quickly, it is possible to combine all the existing information on each person. Purchases made with a credit card, data provided in a loan application, facts in your medical records—all can be combined to develop a profile of you.

Some people worry that a personal profile created by computer can include wrong information that is never corrected. They also worry that a personal profile would give marketers and others special insight. It could reveal who you are, how you think, and what you are likely to do. Consequently, many experts recommend giving only as much information as needed. For example, when filling out a product warranty form, it is not necessary to answer the unrelated questions about educational status and annual income. Also, it is appropriate to ask data collectors to explain all the uses of any personal information you may provide.

- *Information may be unreliable.* There are many sources of information online, but some are unreliable. Carefully analyze each source. Not all websites are current, accurate, and trustworthy. Note the date the website was last updated. Identify the author or sponsor of a website to ensure objectivity and reliability. For example, was the website created by an educational institution, a company, or a blogger? Different individuals and organizations have different motives for creating websites. Educational and governmental websites are considered credible sources.

- *Health and development can be adversely affected.* Too much time spent alone with technology can lead to loneliness and isolation. By interacting with people, you develop social skills that cannot be gained by communicating solely through technology. Physical inactivity is another factor often associated with frequent technology use. While sitting for hours at the computer can promote intellectual growth, it does not help—and can actually harm—your physical, emotional, and social growth.

- *The natural environment could be endangered.* The pace of high-tech advances is fast, resulting in rapid **obsolescence**. This is the state of uselessness. When items that were high-tech just a few years ago are not powerful enough for today's uses, they are quickly discarded. Often they end up in landfills, which are filling up fast. Citizens concerned about the environment can find ways to recycle their equipment or discard it in a responsible way. Contacting the local waste collection authority and the product manufacturer should provide alternatives.

- *Spending can occur too easily.* With instant access to cash and credit, online purchases can be made in seconds. When purchases are not planned or budgeted, people can quickly find themselves in a serious financial crisis.

- *Too much pressure can be exerted on other family resources.* Money and time are the resources most often affected. A student's desire to keep up with peers and have the very latest equipment can test the family budget. The burden is even greater when a family has several children, all wanting their own equipment. If items must be shared, prepare a schedule showing who gets them and when.

- *Family life may be threatened.* Digital equipment may not encourage family interaction. Relationships are threatened if members skip family activities for solitary entertainment. Having face-to-face interactions with family members and others is important for the health of the relationship.

Living Green

Some manufacturers of electronic equipment accept obsolete items for recycling or refurbishing. Contact manufacturers of items you own to find out how they suggest you dispose of obsolete equipment. Many manufacturers have websites and describe environmentally-responsible ways of disposing of their products.

Reading
Review

1. List five functions in which technology can help people perform everyday activities.
2. What four questions should be asked before buying high-tech equipment?
3. List five ways in which technology can negatively impact your life.

Section 18-3

The Role of Advertising

Objectives

After studying this section, you will be able to

- **explain** the role of advertising in promoting goods and services.
- **identify** how advertising influences consumer spending.
- **evaluate** various types of advertising.

Key Terms ↗

advertisement   bait and switch

As a consumer, are you aware of the methods businesses use to promote their goods and services? Through advertising, businesses inform you about their goods and services. They use various media such as radio, television, magazines, direct mail, the Internet, and billboards to convey their messages. Businesses are interested in increasing sales and profits. Their ads are designed to attract your attention and get you to buy.

Before you buy any goods or services, you need to understand the role of advertising. If you understand that the main purpose of advertising is to sell, you can make advertising work for you. You can use the information to buy what you need.

Advertising plays an important role in the economy. It benefits both consumers and businesses. Through ads, consumers are informed about the many goods and services available to them. Businesses are able to market their goods and services more efficiently. Advertising helps businesses introduce new or improved products to the marketplace. As a result, the economy grows as consumers make more purchases.

How Advertising Affects Consumer Spending

An **advertisement** is a paid public message communicated through various media that promotes the sale of goods and services. You see and hear many different types of advertisements every day. However, you may not be aware of the effects these ads have on your buying behavior. See **18-4**.

Do you look for a certain brand of shoes or jeans when you shop? When you go out to eat, do you meet your friends at a certain restaurant? Do you watch the latest movies when they arrive at your local theater? In some way, advertising likely influenced your decisions about all these issues.

As a wise consumer, keep in mind that the main goal of all ads is to convince you to buy something. Ads are designed to show products in the best possible ways, so only persuasive information appears. If you realize this, you can benefit from it. Carefully evaluate the information presented in ads. Look for factual information, such as features and price, to help you make buying decisions. Do not be sold on a product just because of the ad. Beware of ads that try to persuade you to buy unneeded, unwanted, or unaffordable items. This cautious approach can help you improve your buying decisions.

Types of Advertising

Advertisers use certain types of ads to influence consumer choices. Effective ads gain your attention and hold your interest. Six of the most common types of ads are described here. As you read about these ads, think how each type may influence your buying decisions.

Factual ads provide useful consumer information. They describe a product's features, benefits, and cost, and tell where the product is sold. Some factual ads are used to introduce a new product to the market so consumers become aware of it.

Mental Health Awareness

Consumer Psychology

Emotions can be useful in buying decisions if they are based on reasoning and not on advertisement bias. For example, having positive feelings about a product because it works well is useful for future purchasing decisions. In contrast, positive feelings based on a celebrity endorsement or emotional appeal do not help you make informed decisions.

Comparison ads make comparisons with competing products. They stress the advertised product's beneficial features over the other choices. Some may also spotlight new or improved product features.

Testimonial ads use celebrities, sports professionals, or experts to endorse products. This makes the products' claims seem more believable. Some consumers may be persuaded to buy a product if they think a well-known person likes it. However, keep in mind that these people are usually paid to endorse the products. In some of these ads, average people who use the product tell how they like using it.

Attention-getter ads are designed to be entertaining. These ads use creative techniques, such as humor or visual images, to gain and hold consumers' attention.

Bandwagon ads try to be persuasive. These ads imply that many people use and enjoy the product and you should, too. You are encouraged to become part of the crowd by using the product.

Sex-appeal ads have strong emotional appeal. These ads make consumers feel they will be more attractive and popular if they use the product.

In addition to these six types, *infomercials* are extended-length television advertisements that blend product information and commercials. Most are shown at off-hours. An infomercial may appear to be a talk show or news program with product demonstrations. Household, cooking, and fitness products are often sold via infomercials.

Direct mail is the process of mass mailings. A variety of information is sent to people selected as the most likely to respond positively. Direct mailings are often used by charities and political organizations as well as companies selling products to consumers. See **18-5**.

Advertising Online

A great deal of advertising takes place through websites and apps. Most websites include advertisement banners or pop-up ads. Some apps also include advertisements that link to sponsoring websites or add-on purchases. If portions of an app or the pages of a website try to persuade you to make a purchase, they are advertisements.

Some retail websites may appear to be authoritative sources of information. Before accepting any advice from a website at face value, determine who sponsors the website or app. If the sponsor is a manufacturer or retailer, recognize the information provided by the site reflects just one viewpoint. If the sponsor of the site cannot be determined, it is best to remain skeptical of any information provided.

Evaluating Advertisements

Remember, no matter what method advertisers use, their final purpose is to get you to buy. As a consumer, you have the responsibility of evaluating advertisements. By using helpful information and ignoring the rest, you will improve your buying decisions. Use these evaluation questions to help you sort through the information presented in ads.

18-5

Direct mail from retailers usually offers incentives for you to buy additional products.

- Can you determine the purpose of the ad?
- Is it designed to inform you or persuade you to buy a product or service?
- Is the information in the ad useful to you?
- Is it factual and easy to understand?
- Does it tell what you want to know about the features, quality, and price?

As part of your evaluation, you also need to determine whether the ad is using a persuasive or deceptive advertising method.

Persuasive Advertising

Remember, persuasive advertising offers little or no useful information about a product or service. Be aware of this type of advertising so you can avoid being influenced by it. When you are gathering information about products or services, focus on the facts conveyed by advertising. Then you can make choices based on the quality of the product or service.

Deceptive Advertising

Some types of advertising are misleading. Although the illegal methods used in the past have been stopped, some deceptive advertising still occurs.

Bait and switch is one deceptive advertising method used to lure shoppers who are looking for bargains. The advertiser offers a low-priced item as bait to get shoppers in the store. Once shoppers are there, the advertiser tries to switch them to a more expensive item. They may do this by telling shoppers the advertised item is sold out. Another approach advertisers use is convincing shoppers the advertised item is poor quality and will not meet their needs.

In another type of deceptive advertising, consumers are informed by mail or by phone that they have won a free gift. They may be required to come to a store to receive the gift. Once there, they may have to answer questions, listen to a sales presentation, or fill out a coupon to earn their gift. The advertiser may give the consumers a catalog of merchandise as well. More gifts are offered to the consumers for ordering additional merchandise from the store's catalog. The "free" gift may turn into an expensive purchase.

Offering free items or services to consumers who buy their product is another common sales strategy for some advertisers. For instance, a book club may offer free books if you agree to buy a certain number of monthly selections. However, the cost of the free books is actually figured into the cost of the books you buy. This practice is legal because all terms are advertised. Taking the time to figure the costs involved may help you understand the books are not really free.

Consumer Protection Against Deceptive Advertising

To help protect consumers, advertising is regulated by federal government agencies. The *Federal Trade Commission (FTC)* is responsible for preventing false advertising and deceptive advertising practices. The *Federal Communications Commission (FCC)* regulates ads aired on television or radio. These agencies can impose steep fines on advertisers who violate advertising laws. They can also challenge advertisers to prove claims made in ads.

If you observe false or deceptive advertising practices, what can you do? It is your responsibility to bring them to the attention of the advertiser immediately. If they are not corrected, report them to a consumer protection agency promptly.

Reading
Review

1. Explain how advertising can affect consumer spending.
2. Name six types of advertisements.
3. True or false. Being aware of deceptive or persuasive advertising helps consumers make wiser buying decisions.

Section 18-4

Consumers and the Law

Objectives

After studying this section, you will be able to
- **identify** consumer protection laws.
- **practice** techniques for protecting your privacy.
- **describe** your consumer rights and responsibilities.

Key Terms ↗

identity theft

Food and Drug
Administration
(FDA)

Consumer
Product Safety
Commission
(CPSC)

redress

Businesses and consumers are active participants in the United States economy. In the free enterprise system, businesses produce goods and services. Consumers then buy and use these goods and services. This puts money back into businesses so they can continue producing. Keeping this economic cycle strong depends on businesses and consumers treating each other fairly. Laws that prohibit unfair business practices protect consumers' rights. To protect these rights, consumers must act responsibly.

Understanding your consumer rights and responsibilities can help you become a better consumer. As you use your rights and take on your responsibilities, you help keep the economy strong. See **18-6**.

Consumer Protection Laws

The federal government passes laws aimed at protecting consumers' rights. How do such laws aid consumers? They help consumers understand and compare credit costs. They also provide guidelines for consumers if they are denied credit, find a billing error, or receive an inaccurate credit rating. A few of the many consumer protection laws are summarized as follows.

The *Credit Card Accountability, Responsibility, and Disclosure Act* includes a variety of protections for consumers related to credit cards. For example, the act places limits on the amount of fees that creditors may charge for late payments. It also requires creditors to show the amount of time and interest it will take to pay off a balance when making the minimum payment.

18-6

The economy is stimulated by consumers making purchases.

The *Truth in Lending Law* requires creditors to provide a complete account of credit costs and terms. Ask for this information before you sign any credit contracts. This law also requires creditors to send debtors regular statements. These statements must show the unpaid balances of the accounts and any finance charges that have been made.

The *Equal Credit Opportunity Act* protects people from discrimination because of sex, marital status, race, religion, or age. In other words, credit can be denied only for financial reasons. People who have been denied credit can demand to receive written explanations of why credit was denied.

The *Fair Credit Billing Act* states the rules by which consumers and creditors must settle disputes about billing. If a debtor thinks there is a mistake in a bill, the creditor is required by law to pay attention to the complaint. If an error is found, it must be corrected without charge to the debtor.

Consumers who wish to complain must follow certain rules. They must send the complaint *in writing* to the creditor within 60 days after the bill was mailed. The consumer's name and account number plus the amount and description of the error must be clearly stated.

The *Fair Credit Reporting Act* protects you against an inaccurate credit record. Your credit rating is based on information in your credit file. Under this act, you have a right to see the contents of your file. In addition, you can file a letter to explain any information in the file that you feel is not correct.

Protecting Your Privacy

You have the right to decide who has access to your personal information. This includes such information as your social security number, credit card numbers, and e-mail address.

How do you make sure your personal information is kept private? There are several steps you can take to protect yourself. First, do not share personal information with others who do not have the right to know. Be wary about sharing your social security number or credit card numbers. Only do so if you are confident about the reliability of the person or company with whom you are dealing. Ask your bank to notify you in writing when someone wants to check your records. Check your bank records carefully to make sure that no one is tapping into your account electronically.

Be cautious when giving information over the phone or Internet. Online privacy is especially difficult. Take care when providing information to websites you browse. If you are placing an order online, make sure you are at a secure website.

Identity Theft

One of the dangers of not controlling your personal information is identity theft. **Identity theft** is the unauthorized use of someone's personal data or documents (usually social security number or credit cards) to obtain merchandise, services, or credit. It occurs when someone wrongfully obtains and uses another's personal information in a way that involves fraud.

Some scam artists send bogus e-mails that appear to come from a legitimate source. The e-mails may request credit card or other personal information. If you receive a request for personal information or passwords, make sure the e-mail is genuine before complying. Most Internet providers, online stores, and banks will *not* request such information, especially in an e-mail. Such a request could be an attempt to steal your identity.

If someone uses your personal information to pretend they are you, they can make purchases that will be charged to you. In some cases, unauthorized people take funds from their victims' bank accounts and run up huge credit debts. Some even commit crimes while using the names and private information of others.

While laws protect you from such losses, it is still a long, difficult task to clear up the confusion. You may lose some money. If your credit rating is damaged, you will have to reestablish it and your reputation. The thief may use your insurance or set up new credit accounts in your name. If this happens, working through the red tape to set things right can take years.

To prevent identity theft, memorize your social security number and keep your card in a safe place—not in your wallet. Carry only those credit cards you use regularly. Cut up old cards before you throw them away, **18-7**. Make sure the number and your signature are unreadable.

When choosing PIN numbers, do not use obvious numbers such as those from your address, phone number, or birthday. Memorize your PIN. Do not write it down on your card. Be constantly aware of the need to protect your personal information.

21st Century Skills

In this growing digital world, identity protection is essential. It is important to make sure you install some sort of security software on your devices to protect your personal information from hackers. Many companies refer to their services as *identity theft protection*, but no service can protect you from identity theft if you are not very careful with your personal information. What these companies offer are monitoring and recovery services that help you deal with the effects of identity theft after it happens.

18-7

Expired credit cards should be cut before they are thrown out so all personal information is destroyed.

Fraud

Fraud is a deliberate misrepresentation that causes another person to suffer damages, usually the loss of money. Fraud can take many forms.

Telemarketing schemes involve using the phone to take money from victims. Telemarketers will call victims and promise goods or services for a fee. Some may offer prizes in exchange for personal information. Then the promised goods, services, or prizes are never provided.

Pyramid schemes and *chain letters* depend on a continuing supply of people investing in the system. They depend on people recruiting more and more people to join in the scheme. The problem is that eventually, they always wind down. The people who come in late lose their money. To protect yourself from these schemes, always be wary of the following:

- an investment that promises quick profit with no risk
- an investment that does not indicate how and where your money will be invested
- an offer to sell an item at much less than the known value

Internet fraud may involve the same kinds of schemes already discussed. One reason Internet fraud is easy is because the thief has the ability to carry it out quickly. In addition, many potential victims can be reached anywhere in the world.

Consumer Rights and Responsibilities

Fairness to both buyer and seller is the basis of the free enterprise system. Unfair business practices hurt both consumers and producers. For this reason, monopolies, price fixing, and deceptive business practices are illegal. When consumer rights are protected, the whole economic system benefits. In accepting these rights, consumers must meet certain responsibilities as well.

The Right to Be Informed

As a consumer, you have a right to accurate information about products and services. Such information can help you make good buying decisions and use products wisely after purchase.

You have the right to be informed through reliable sources. Information should be available on product cost, features, benefits, and uses. An honest, knowledgeable salesperson can answer questions about product quality and performance. See **18-8**. Consumer publications provide comparison shopping advice and product test results. They also inform consumers on many other related issues. *Consumer Reports* is one such publication. Product labels include information about use and care, features, and warranties.

The Responsibility to Seek and Use Information

You have a responsibility to seek and use reliable information about products and services. Advertising simply informs; it is not intended to provide all the information you need to make good buying decisions. Read consumer articles in reputable newspapers and magazines. Read product labels and service agreements. Ask reliable, experienced sources to share their opinions. Carefully compare competing products and services before you buy.

The Right to Selection

Consumers have a right to choose the products they want. However, this presupposes that a variety is available. Suppose that only the Make-Believe Company supplies a certain product. Also, suppose this company has used unfair business practices to drive competing products out of the market. Then the Make-Believe Company would have a monopoly on the product since it would be offered nowhere else. Without competing products, you would have to buy from the Make-Believe Company at whatever price it charged.

18-8

When you order merchandise from a catalog, the salesperson should be able to answer any questions you have.

Laws prohibit monopolies to ensure that competing products and services remain available to consumers. Sellers then compete for consumers' money with products of different price and quality levels. The result of competition is the creation of more selection at better prices.

The Responsibility to Select Wisely

When variety is available, you are responsible for wise choices. Select the product or service that best meets your needs. Shop carefully for the right quality. This does not mean that you should always look for the very best quality or lowest prices. Make a wise selection by purchasing the best quality to meet your needs at a price you can afford.

The Right to Performance

As a consumer, you have the right to expect that the product you buy will perform as it should. Suppose an ad claims that a certain cleaning fluid will not damage the finish of your furniture. Then you have the right to expect that it will not remove varnish from your dining room table. What if you buy a laundry detergent that claims it is safe to use with all fabrics? Then your best shirt should not fall apart after being washed with it.

The Responsibility to Read and Follow Instructions

To get good performance from a product, you must use it as it is meant to be used. Suppose the label on a bottle of cleaning fluid reads *Use on tile only; may be harmful to wood finishes.* If you used it on your dining room table and ruined the finish, you would have only yourself to blame.

Clothing manufacturers are required to put care labels on the garments they make. Read and follow the manufacturer's directions carefully. What if the label on your new sweater reads *dry-clean only* and you wash it? Then you cannot complain if it shrinks.

Most manufacturers provide use-and-care booklets with the products they sell. These booklets give detailed instructions for using and maintaining products. You are responsible for reading and following these instructions. If you do not operate products properly, you could damage them or cause an injury. The products you buy will give you the performance you expect only if you do your part.

The Right to Safety

Consumers have a right to protection against harmful products. They have the right to know the products and services they buy will be safe if used properly. Several government agencies were developed to protect this right. These agencies provide consumer protection by screening products for safety and taking steps to prevent unsafe products in the market.

The **Food and Drug Administration (FDA)** watches over sales of food, drugs, and cosmetics. The FDA may prohibit the sale of or require safety warnings on products that may harm people.

The **Consumer Product Safety Commission (CPSC)** handles complaints about unsafe products such as household appliances, toys, and tools. It protects consumers from unsafe products and encourages safe product use at all times. This agency investigates reports of dangerous products and bans hazardous products.

Each year the CPSC receives thousands of complaints from unhappy consumers. When a pattern becomes evident, the agency studies the product and reviews news reports about it. If a product is considered hazardous, the CPSC takes steps to ban it. For example, one study resulted in the recall of several million coffeemakers. Defective wiring made the coffeemakers a fire hazard.

The Responsibility to Use Products Safely

As a consumer, you have a responsibility to use products safely. Read product labels to find out if products may be dangerous if used in a certain way. Some products that are perfectly safe when new may become unsafe after lengthy storage. Ingredients may deteriorate or become unstable.

Always review guidelines, operating instructions, and other product materials provided by the manufacturer. One of the greatest mistakes is dismissing instructions for products that you do not regard as potentially dangerous. Always follow all guidelines. Use products for the purposes for which they were designed.

One of the greatest consumer responsibilities in the area of safety is that of making hazards known. Return a dangerous product to the store where you bought it. Notify its manufacturer of your action. You can also report hazards to appropriate government agencies.

The Right to Redress

If you buy a product and it does not perform as expected, you have the right to redress. **Redress** means to solve a problem. In other words, you have the right to have your complaint heard and to have action taken on it as in **18-9**. You have the right to complain if

- a product you bought is defective

- services or product repairs are not satisfactory

- merchandise you ordered was not received

- a warranty or guarantee is not honored

- a refundable deposit is not refunded

When problems are beyond the help of consumer agencies, legislation may be needed. State legislators can be contacted for problems confined to one state. Federal legislators can be contacted for nationwide problems. If enough people appeal to their state or federal government representatives, legislation may be considered to handle the problem.

A sampling of private and government agencies to contact for help with consumer problems are described here.

Chambers of commerce usually have divisions that accept and act on consumer complaints. Your chamber of commerce may keep a file on local businesses, including complaints that consumers have filed against them.

18-9

When services you paid for are unsatisfactory, ask for the problem to be fixed or resolved first before filing a formal complaint.

Conflict resolution. Mia deals with customers on a daily basis at the retail store where she works. When customers have complaints, she listens to what they have to say and then tries to come to an acceptable solution to the complaint.

Better Business Bureaus (BBB) perform services similar to those of a chamber of commerce. Their information usually covers more than just local businesses. The BBBs are nonprofit organizations sponsored by private businesses. They try to settle complaints against local businesses.

Media complaint desks of newspapers, radio stations, and television stations provide outlets for consumer complaints. Complaints reported by the media reach the greatest number of people in the quickest possible way.

Licensing boards have been set up by state governments to issue licenses to persons who are qualified to perform certain services. These boards set standards that must be met before a license to perform a service is granted. Boards may also cancel a license. For example, suppose someone who is licensed to perform a service has acted unethically. The board may suspend or cancel the person's license to practice in that state. Licensing boards cover many areas of service. If you have a complaint, report it to the appropriate board in your state.

State government consumer protection divisions are under the direction of the state's attorney general. These agencies aim to protect consumers from unfair and deceptive business practices.

Small claims courts handle claims that involve relatively small amounts of money. Consumers represent themselves instead of hiring attorneys. Booklets that describe such courts can be obtained from your local government, from consumer agencies, or from your state's attorney general.

Private or public legal services may be needed to settle larger claims. Persons who can afford legal services must pay for them. Persons who cannot afford private legal aid may ask for public legal aid.

The Responsibility to Let Dissatisfactions Be Known

When you pay for a product or service and are dissatisfied, you have a responsibility to voice your dissatisfaction. By complaining, you bring problems to the only people who can do something about correcting them—the providers of goods and services.

When you complain to a company, do so in an organized way. Whether you call or make a personal visit, state your name, address, and account number. Describe the nature of your complaint (for example, poor service or faulty merchandise). Tell when and where the incident happened. Tell what goods or services you purchased and how much you paid. Briefly explain what happened. Finally, tell what action you want the company to take.

For a more serious problem, you may decide to write a complaint letter to the manufacturer. Address your letter to the consumer affairs department of the company. If you feel top management should know about the problem, write to the president of the company. In either case, include a clear, concise explanation of the problem. Give the date and place of purchase, model number, and purchase price. Enclose a photocopy of the receipt or bill in question. At the close of the letter, suggest the action you want taken, such as a refund or replacement. A sample complaint letter appears in **18-10**.

18-10

When writing a complaint letter, clearly explain the problem and suggest a solution.

Complaint Letter

> 2201 Mountain Drive
> Tucson, Arizona 85719
> March 21, 20XX
>
> Hillary Willis
> Consumer Relations Manager
> Great Time Watch Company
> 12 North Hunter Trail
> Carol Stream, IL 60188
>
> Dear Ms. Willis:
>
> I purchased a Great Time watch for $35.99 on March 10, 20XX, from the Discount Center in Tucson. The model number is 923. A photocopy of my receipt and the warranty is enclosed.
>
> After one week of use, the watch stopped working. I changed the battery, but it still doesn't work. I carefully followed your directions for use, so I think the watch was defective. I am concerned that other consumers who buy this watch may have the same problem.
>
> The warranty states that I should receive a replacement if the product is defective. Even after explaining my problem to the manager at the Discount Center, he said he could not help me. Since I am not satisfied with this product, I would like my watch replaced within the next month.
>
> If you need more information about this problem, please call me at (602) 555-1700. I appreciate your help and look forward to receiving a replacement watch.
>
> Sincerely,
>
> *Alex Reiko*
>
> Alex Reiko
> Enclosures

Life Skills

Writing Letters to Legislators

Use the following tips to write effective letters to your legislators:

- Be clear! State the issue and how you want your legislator to handle it in the first few sentences.
- If you are writing about a specific bill that has already been introduced, identify the bill by name and number. (If you do not know the name and number, give some description of its contents.)
- Write about only one issue in each letter.
- Be persuasive. Tell why you feel the way you do.
- Be brief. Write legibly or type. Legislators do not have time to read long, scribbled letters.
- Be courteous. Anger and threats may work against you.
- Do not pretend to have vast influence.
- Be constructive. Do not just say what is wrong. Go further and say what is right.
- Write only to legislators who represent you.
- Send notes of appreciation when your legislators do something you like.

Do not let your temper interfere with your complaint. If you are angry, cool off before you call or write. This will make your complaint easier to understand. Remember that the person who reads your letter or answers your call is not personally responsible for your problem. He or she is just trying to help settle it.

Resolving Consumer Problems

Knowing and practicing both your consumer rights and responsibilities is the key to resolving consumer problems. There are consumer laws that protect you, but you certainly will not want to go to court to resolve every problem.

Sometimes people are responsible for creating their own consumer problems. This happens when they ignore their consumer responsibilities. Not using information available, buying unwisely, ignoring instructions provided, and ignoring safety precautions means they lose their right to complain.

How to Resolve a Consumer Problem

When you have a legitimate complaint, follow a step-by-step procedure to resolve it. Begin by contacting the place where you bought the product or service. If that fails, write a letter to the manufacturer. As a final step, contact a consumer protection agency, such as the BBB. Government agencies at the local, state, and federal levels can also assist you with your complaint.

Reading
Review

1. What is identity theft?
2. Name the consumer protection law that requires creditors to provide a complete account of credit costs and terms.
3. List the five basic consumer rights and their corresponding responsibilities.
4. Outline the step-by-step procedure for resolving a consumer complaint.

Chapter 18 Review

Summary

Consumers must choose from a variety of goods and services in the marketplace every day. It pays to be an informed consumer and shop wisely to get more value for the money. Knowing where to shop, when to buy, what to buy, and how to use the decision-making process keeps smart shoppers on target.

In today's Information Age, almost everyone uses technology regularly. When used well, technology provides many useful functions including information processing, money management, information gathering, and communicating. When not managed well, technology does not improve the quality of life and even creates drawbacks.

One of the strongest influences on consumer spending is advertising. Advertising affects consumer attitudes, tastes, and preferences. It can be informative as well as persuasive. Understanding the types of advertising and how to evaluate them can help consumers make informed choices.

To help keep the economy strong and productive, consumers must understand their rights and be prepared to exercise them. Consumers have the right to information, selection, performance, safety, and redress. In turn, consumers must recognize that every right carries a basic responsibility that must also be followed.

Critical Thinking

1. **Analyze information.** Determine an item that would be of interest to members of your class. Go through the process of comparison shopping. Consider quality, suitability, use and care, warranty, and cost. Choose the best buy.

2. **Compare and contrast.** What are some possible advantages and disadvantages associated with using technology?

3. **Summarize details.** Give three examples of how you have been influenced by advertising to buy goods and services. For each example, describe the type of advertising used. How did each ad make you feel about technology?

4. **Analyze decisions.** Explain how the following factors influence your consumer decisions:
   A. culture
   B. economics
   C. society
   D. environment

5. **Draw conclusions.** Choose to agree or disagree with one of the following statements. Explain your response.
   A. Consumer rights are more important than consumer responsibilities because…
   B. Consumer responsibilities are more important than consumer rights because…
   C. Consumer rights and responsibilities are equally important because…

21st Century Applications

6. **Economic literacy.** Shop for one item at several different online stores. How is comparison shopping online easier than comparison shopping in actual stores?

7. **Media literacy.** Compare a currently popular video game to an early version of Pac Man. How do the games compare in price, entertainment value, and ease of use?

8. **Environmental literacy.** Research what happens to obsolete technology. Is the equipment recycled, reused, or thrown away? Give a brief oral presentation discussing your findings. Include examples and graphics in your presentation.

9. **Health literacy.** As you find information online for school or work, it is important to determine the reliability and validity of each source. Find three websites that discuss health topics. Identify the author, date the material was written and last updated, and sponsoring organization (if available). Also determine if the information given is of good quality. For example, do the key points support a main idea? Is the information biased? Does the text use good grammar and correct spelling and punctuation? Which of the three websites would you consider reliable? Present your analysis to the class.

10. **Global awareness.** Research consumer rights in different countries. Are the consumer rights in other countries similar to those in the U.S.? What are some differences? List countries that have a consumer rights website.

Core Skills

11. **Math.** Many online stores offer discounts to offset the cost of shipping. Compare the cost of an item you can get at a nearby store with the price you would pay, including shipping, from an online store.

12. **Math.** Visit a local mall or department store and make note of current sales. What types of items are on sale? What are the terms of the sales? Will people really save money on the items? (For example, you can buy one $25 sweater or two for $40. If you only need one sweater, are you really saving money if you purchase two?)

13. **Listening.** Listen to three commercials or radio advertisements about any product. Is it a factual ad, comparison ad, testimonial ad, attention-getter ad, bandwagon ad, or sex-appeal ad? How can you tell? Do the advertisements seem to be persuasive or deceptive? Why?

14. **Reading.** Find an article discussing a case in which a product was considered unsafe. How did the manufacturer respond? Was the item recalled? Did the manufacturer have to pay a fee? Write a brief summary of your article.

15. **Speaking.** Form small groups to design a television ad for toothpaste. You may perform or read your advertisements for the class, or create a video demonstration of your advertisement to present to the class. Present your ad as if you work for an advertising agency and are trying to sell your ad ideas to the toothpaste manufacturer. Which type of ad will you choose to create?

16. **Writing.** Practice writing a letter, citing an error in a credit card statement. You may also practice writing letters to correct inaccurate information filed in a credit report. Exchange letters and critique them on grammar, spelling, and punctuation.

17. **Speaking.** Search the Internet for tips on identity protection. Refer to the Federal Trade Commission's website for Identity Theft. Prepare an electronic presentation to educate students about identity theft.

18. **Reading, writing.** Research careers within the Consumer Services Pathway of the Human Services career cluster. Which careers relate to this chapter? Select two careers and write a brief summary of each, including a job description, education and training needed, skills and qualities needed for job success, and job outlook. Would you be interested in pursuing either career? Why or why not?

Leadership
Development

As a part of working on the Financial Fitness National Program, develop a project applying concepts from this chapter. The following are some suggested projects: conduct a comparison shopping workshop to teach this consumer skill to other teens; conduct a six-month study on price competition for teen products; conduct a study on the influence of advertising on teen shopping.

Portfolio
Builder

As a consumer, you have rights and responsibilities. You have both a right and a responsibility to resolve consumer issues. Think of a consumer problem you are having or have had. Document the issue and describe how you will handle the situation or how you handled the situation. Place this information in your portfolio for future reference. Try using the following steps to resolve your issue:

- Contact the place where you bought the product or service.
  If that fails,
- Write a letter to the manufacturer.
  If that fails,
- Contact a consumer protection agency.

Journal
Writing

Marjon recently went to the mall with some friends. While shopping, she noticed a cute sweater on clearance. When she tried it on, her friends were very enthusiastic and encouraged her to buy the sweater. Marjon liked the sweater, too, so she decided to make the purchase.

When she got home, Marjon realized the sweater did not match any of her pants or skirts. Also, one of the buttons was loose. She tried to return the sweater a few days later. However, she had not noticed the store's return policy—all sales are final on clearance items.

Analyze It: *What are Marjon's consumer rights and responsibilities in this situation? What recommendations do you have for Marjon? How could this situation have been avoided?*

Career Discovery

Human Services

The Consumer Services Pathway within the Human Services career cluster includes careers that focus on expanding and maintaining business' customer base. Event planners, market researchers, and buyers are examples of careers in this area.

Human Services Pathways

Early Childhood Development and Services

Counseling and Mental Health Services

Family and Community Services

Personal Care Services

Consumer Services

szefei/Shutterstock.com

Education and Training

The Administration and Administrative Support Pathway within the Education and Training career cluster includes careers that help support teaching roles. Examples of careers within this area include postsecondary education administrators, principals, and educational researchers.

Education and Training Pathways

Administration and Administrative Support

Professional Support Services

Teaching and Training

M. Thatcher/Shutterstock.com

Career Spotlight: Event Planner

- **Description.** Event planners coordinate the details of different kinds of events. They may plan events such as conventions, business meetings, fashion shows, weddings, or conferences. They meet with clients to discuss the event and any details or specifications they need met. Event planners then look for possible locations and venues. They plan agendas or programs and arrange for speakers, entertainment, and other activities at the event. They also coordinate services for events such as transportation, catering, and security. Event planners ensure their clients' needs are met and that costs are within the budget.

- **Education and training.** Requirements vary, but most employers require event planners to have a bachelor's degree. Previous experience in event planning and hospitality management may also be required or preferred.

- **Skills and personal qualities.** Event planners need excellent communication, interpersonal, and customer-service skills. They should also be able to keep their composure in a fast-paced environment and have good time-management and problem-solving skills. Event planners should be good at negotiating to get the best prices for their clients.

- **Job outlook.** Job growth for event planners through 2028 is projected to grow faster than average for all occupations. Visit the *Occupational Outlook Handbook* online to learn more about a career as an event planner.

Human Services

Career Spotlight: Postsecondary Education Administrator

- **Description.** Postsecondary education administrators may work in student affairs, admissions, or the registrar's office at a college or university. Administrators in student affairs work with college students to address issues such as housing problems and student disputes. Administrators who work in admissions create materials and events to attract potential students to campus and review numerous student applications. Administrators who work in the registrar's office work with students to select classes, create a schedule, and enroll them into the classes. Some postsecondary education administrators also help manage university finances.

- **Education and training.** Requirements for this position vary. A master's degree is typically needed, but there are some opportunities for those with a bachelor's degree. Common areas of study include higher education administration, social work, or marketing. Experience in a related field is often preferred.

- **Skills and personal qualities.** Postsecondary education administrators must have excellent interpersonal, communication, and problem-solving skills. They must also have great reading and writing skills.

- **Job outlook.** Through 2028, job prospects for postsecondary education administrators are expected to grow faster than the average for all occupations. Visit the *Occupational Outlook Handbook* online to learn more about a career as a postsecondary education administrator.

Education & Training

Sources: States' Career Clusters Initiative, Bureau of Labor Statistics Career Guide to Industries

Chapter 19
Choosing and Caring for Your Clothes

Sections

Reading Prep

Before reading the chapter, skim the photos and their captions. As you read, determine how these concepts contribute to the ideas presented in the text.

Concept Organizer

Create a fishbone map, making *Design Elements* the label for the body. Create scales labeled with each design element: *Color*, *Line*, *Texture*, and *Form*. Write details for each design element on lines connected to each scale.

G-WLEARNING.com

Click on the activity icon to visit www.g-wlearning. com/comprehensive/8062 to access online vocabulary activities using key terms from the chapter.

Clothing Needs

Objectives

After studying this section, you will be able to

- **list** ways in which clothing meets physical needs.
- **explain** how clothing satisfies psychological and social needs.
- **choose** clothing that would be appropriate for specific occasions.

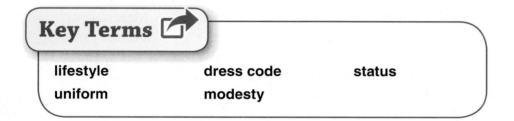

Key Terms

lifestyle	dress code	status
uniform	modesty	

Buying clothes can be expensive. Deciding what to wear can take time out of your day. Clothing choices are important decisions. Thinking about your choices helps you choose clothes that will meet your needs.

Factors That Influence Clothing Decisions

A number of factors influence your clothing decisions. Besides your basic needs, you are likely to consider your peers' opinions when you are choosing clothes. You may think about what your clothes say about you. You will undoubtedly think about what activities you will be doing when you wear the clothes. Your physical, psychological, and social needs are factors that influence your clothing decisions.

Physical Needs

Clothes help meet your basic *physical needs* to protect your body. Your body requires protection from the weather, environmental dangers, and occupational hazards.

Weather can be a threat to the body. People need to be protected from cold and heat and such elements as sun, rain, and snow. Jackets, gloves, scarves, hats, heavy socks, and boots keep people warm and dry on cold days. In warm weather, lightweight clothes in light colors help keep people cool. Garments that repel water provide protection from rain.

The environment also poses certain physical dangers that can be moderated through clothing. Life jackets provide safety for those who work and play near water. In areas where insects are bothersome, some people wear special jackets and hoods to protect their skin from bites. Hiking boots help prevent skids and falls and protect feet from the impact of harsh, rocky terrains.

Clothes protect many people from hazards in their workplaces. Road workers wear brightly colored, reflective clothing so they will be visible to drivers. Firefighters wear heat- and fire-resistant garments. Health care workers often wear masks and gloves when working with patients. These items protect patients as well as workers from the possible transfer of germs.

Lifestyle

Many of your physical needs for clothing are determined by your **lifestyle**. This is your way of life or your style of living. You may own a few garments to wear for special occasions such as school dances. However, you probably do not wear these clothes often. Most of your clothing choices are dictated by your daily activities. If you enjoy playing sports, you probably own several pieces of activewear. If you spend much time outside, you are likely to own more outerwear than someone who prefers being indoors.

Psychological Needs

Any garment might meet a physical need. However, clothes must have certain characteristics to meet psychological needs. Certain colors, fabrics, and styles of clothing can affect how you feel. For instance, bright colors might make you feel happy. Perhaps you feel relaxed in soft fabrics and confident in formal styles.

Choosing clothes you find appealing gives you a sense of well-being by helping to meet your psychological need for attractiveness. Wearing clothes that enhance your appearance can boost your self-esteem.

Social Needs

The social need for acceptance plays a big role in the clothing choices most people make. This is especially true during the school years when children and teens are seeking the approval of their peers. Teens often wear clothes that identify them with a specific group. They may use clothing to exhibit a desired level of status. Teens also tend to choose clothing that conforms to styles worn by their friends.

Group Identification

People who identify with a group often use clothing as a sign of belonging. Members of certain groups wear uniforms as marks of identification. Other groups choose less rigid attire.

Uniforms are distinctive outfits that identify those who wear them with a specific group. See **19-1**. You can look at athletes in their uniforms and immediately identify their sports and their teams. Military personnel on duty always wear uniforms.

Mental Health Awareness

Clothing and Self-Image

People often choose clothes that reflect their self-image. People can also use clothing to change their self-image. For example, a person who wants to see himself as bold and confident may dress in a unique style that does not follow popular trends.

Jetta Productions/Photodisc/Getty Images

19-1
These uniforms are worn by students at a high school in the state of Washington.

Many schools, especially private schools, require students to wear uniforms. The uniforms of exclusive schools often serve as symbols of prestige. Some public school systems require students to wear uniforms as an antiviolence measure. Wearing uniforms sends a message that all students belong to the same "team." This results in less competition and more cooperation among "team members." Uniforms keep fashion from being an issue so students can focus more on learning.

Some groups do not have specific uniforms. However, they use certain colors or symbols to identify their members. For instance, members of sororities and fraternities often own garments with Greek letters representing the names of their organizations.

Many people show group identity simply by yielding to the influence of their peers. Your peers form an informal group. By wearing the kinds of clothes your friends wear, you are showing you are a member of that group. Jeans and T-shirts are typical attire of many teen peer groups.

Life Skills

Clothing for Special Needs

Some people, such as older adults or people with disabilities, have special clothing needs. Older people may choose more casual, comfortable clothes for their daily activities. Easy care is another important factor. People with disabilities may want clothes that are stylish, yet easy to get on and off. Elastic waists and knit fabrics allow both comfort and ease of movement. People with physical limitations or low vision also need simple fasteners and larger openings.

Dress Codes

Dress codes are standards of dress that are enforced in a social setting. Formal dress codes are based on the belief that how people dress tends to affect their behavior. For instance, many businesses have formal dress codes for their employees. Employers believe requiring employees to wear professional clothing encourages them to act professionally. Likewise, most school systems have written dress codes. These policies are designed to keep both teachers and students from wearing clothes that detract from teaching and learning.

Informal dress codes also exist in society. People within a culture commonly accept these unwritten standards of dress. Societal dress codes reflect popular beliefs about **modesty**, or dressing in a manner in which the body is covered in an appropriate way according to a setting. For instance, one social dress code may regard swimsuits as suitable for wearing at a beach, but not at the office. There, swimsuits are viewed as immodest attire because they do not cover enough of the body.

Some religious and ethnic groups have informal dress codes that are stricter than the society in which they live. These stricter codes are based on standards of modesty that are more conservative.

Status

Status is a person's rank within a group. People often use clothing as signs of their status. Certain garments, styles, and brands carry a higher status than others. In many high schools, varsity jackets are signs of status. They indicate the wearers rank high among their classmates in athletic or academic skills.

People who want a certain status often desire clothes that reflect that status. In some groups, this means clothes that display names and logos of specific brands. Wearing these clothes can cause some people to feel they have a higher status just because they are fashion conscious.

21st Century Skills

Communication. Caesar's job involves public speaking. He realizes that his hand gestures, facial expressions, posture, tone of voice, and speed of speaking all play a big role in how he communicates ideas. He takes care with his appearance and dresses professionally to present a positive image.

Choosing Clothes for Specific Occasions

You need different types of clothes for different occasions. For instance, you would probably wear formal attire to a wedding or prom. You will need clothing that reflects your career choice when you go to a job interview. You will want your clothes looking their best when you go on a date.

Choosing the right clothes for the occasion can greatly influence your personal effectiveness. For instance, at a job interview, you need to emphasize your qualifications. A potential employer will have an easier time assessing your qualifications when your clothing is not distracting.

If you are uncertain about what to wear for an occasion such as a party, check with your host. You could also ask others planning to attend the event. For an occasion such as a job interview, consider the type of job you are applying for and research the work environment. If possible, contact someone you know at the company and ask what type of attire is appropriate.

Reading
Review

1. What are three factors from which clothing provides physical protection?
2. A distinctive outfit that identifies someone who wears it with a specific group is a _____ .
3. True or false. Choosing the right clothes for a specific occasion can greatly influence a person's effectiveness.

Section 19-2

Clothing Design Basics

Objectives

After studying this section, you will be able to

- **identify** the colors that look best on you.
- **explain** how line, texture, and form can affect the way clothes look on you.
- **apply** the elements and principles of design to clothing selection.

Key Terms ↗

elements of design	secondary colors	principles of design
hue	intermediate colors	
value	neutrals	balance
intensity	line	proportion
color wheel	texture	rhythm
primary colors	form	emphasis
		harmony

Earlier you learned that good grooming and health habits can improve your appearance. Now you will see how the clothes you choose can enhance your appearance, too. Clothes can highlight your best features. At the same time, they can draw attention away from problem areas.

Which of your clothes are most flattering to you? Do those clothes have anything in common? Are most of them the same color? Do they have distinct lines? Are the textures mostly rough or mostly smooth? Do the forms of the garments enhance your body shape?

Color, line, texture, and form are the **elements of design**. These are factors that affect the appearance of a garment. Each element influences the way you look in your clothes. Whether you buy or make garments, you can consider these elements. Using the elements effectively can help you dress to look your best.

Color

Of all the design elements, color is the most exciting in clothing selection. Color is an expression of you. It reveals something about your looks, feelings, and moods. Knowing how to use color will help you achieve a pleasing appearance by enhancing your best features.

Color Characteristics

The color used in clothing is *pigment*, which is a substance that gives color to other materials. Color has three distinct characteristics. First, color can be defined in terms of hue. **Hue** is the name given to a color. Red, blue, violet, and orange are hues. Hue is what distinguishes one color from another. It makes red different from green or blue. If you make red lighter or darker, you will not change the hue—the changed color is still red.

A second characteristic of color is **value**. Value refers to the lightness or darkness of a color, such as light green and dark green. The value of a color changes when either black or white is added to it. Adding black to a color creates a *shade*. For instance, burgundy is a shade of red. A *tint* results when white is added to a color. Pink is a tint of red.

Intensity is the third characteristic of color. **Intensity** is the brightness or dullness of a color. Bright colors such as red or yellow have a high intensity. Pale colors such as pink or violet have a softer, less intense appearance.

Science Connection

Color Vision

Special cells in the retina of the human eye, called *cones*, allow us to see in color. The three types of cones (red, green, and blue) are named for the colors of light they receive. Cones send signals to the brain that cause us to perceive color. When more than one type of cone cell is stimulated, the brain perceives colors made by combining red, green, or blue.

The Color Wheel

How do colors relate to one another? The **color wheel** is a tool that shows this relationship, **19-2**. The color wheel is very helpful for choosing and studying color in design. It shows the primary, secondary, and intermediate colors.

Yellow, blue, and red are known as **primary colors** because they cannot be created from other colors. The primary colors are equally spaced from one another on the color wheel. By mixing, darkening, or lightening the primary colors, you can fill in the rest of the color wheel.

Mixing equal amounts of two primary colors produces a **secondary color**. Green, violet, and orange are the three secondary colors. You get green by mixing yellow and blue. Mixing blue and red produces violet. Mixing red and yellow results in orange. On the color wheel, each secondary color lies halfway between the two primary colors used to make it.

Intermediate colors are produced from equal amounts of one primary color and one secondary color. These colors lie between the colors used to make them. Intermediate colors take their names from the colors that produce them. The primary color is always listed first. Yellow-green, blue-green, blue-violet, red-violet, red-orange, and yellow-orange are the names of the intermediate colors.

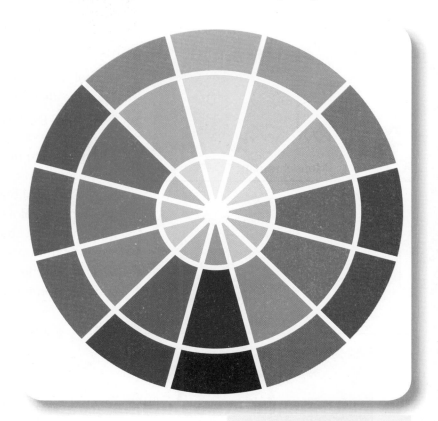

19-2

Study the color wheel to understand color relationships.

Color Schemes

When you select clothing, you can use the color wheel to create a color scheme. Three common color schemes are monochromatic, analogous, and complementary. See **19-3**.

Using different values of the same hue creates a *monochromatic color scheme*. A maroon skirt and a pink blouse or brown pants and a beige shirt are examples of this color scheme.

Combining adjacent colors on the color wheel creates an *analogous color scheme*. Wearing an outfit with blue and green, or orange and yellow, are examples of this color scheme.

Combining two colors that are directly across from each other on the color wheel creates a *complementary color scheme*. Because these colors are contrasting, they make each other look intense. Wearing an orange T-shirt with blue jeans is an example of this color scheme.

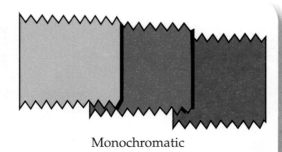

Monochromatic

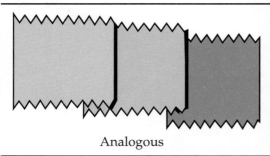

Analogous

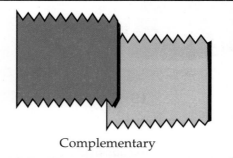

Complementary

19-3

As you select clothes for an outfit, try these common color schemes.

Warm and Cool Colors

Colors on the color wheel are considered either warm or cool. *Warm colors* are related to red, orange, and yellow. They are also described as *advancing colors*. Clothes in warm, advancing colors seem to make the body appear larger.

Cool colors are related to blue, green, and violet. These colors seem to move away, so they are called *receding colors*. Receding colors make the body appear smaller.

White and black are considered **neutrals**. Neutrals are not true colors. White is the absence of color; it reflects all light. Black absorbs all color and light. Combining varying amounts of white and black creates another range of neutrals, the grays. Neutrals can be used alone or in combination with colors.

The Other Design Elements

Color may seem like the most interesting element of design. However, it is not the only one. Line, texture, and form also affect how your clothes will look on you.

Line

Line is the design element that gives direction to a design. Vertical, horizontal, curved, and diagonal lines are the most common types of lines used in clothing design. Vertical lines move the eye up and down. Horizontal lines carry the eye from side to side. Gently curved lines add softness to clothing designs. Diagonal lines, which slant or slope, give a feeling of motion.

Clothing has both structural and decorative lines. *Structural lines* are seams. They are created as the various pieces of the garment are sewn together. An example of a structural line can be seen when two different colors of fabric are sewn together in a garment. *Decorative lines* are those added to the fabric or garment to make it visually appealing. Striped fabric, for example, has decorative lines. Braids, buttons, another trims are sometimes used to add decorative lines to garments.

Structural and decorative lines can be used to create optical illusions. Vertical lines in clothes tend to make the body look taller and thinner. Horizontal lines have the opposite effect; they tend to make the body look shorter and wider. Diagonal lines add a feeling of movement to any design. They may add visual height or width to the body, depending on their angle.

Texture

The **texture** of fabric refers to the way the fabric looks and feels. Fabric textures can be rough or smooth, shiny or dull, crisp or soft, bulky or silky.

Each texture gives garments a different overall appearance. Garments made from soft and silky fabrics slenderize a figure, but they also reveal the silhouette. In contrast, some fabrics are crisp and stiff. They are great for either making a body appear larger or concealing areas of the body. Rough and bulky textures also make a body look larger.

Fabrics with dull textures absorb light. They have a slenderizing effect. Shiny textures reflect light and increase the apparent size of the body.

Stripes, checks, plaids, geometric shapes, flowers, and other patterns add *visual texture* to fabrics. Bold color, large plaids, and wide stripes will make a person look shorter and wider. Small patterns with little contrasting color tend to make the body look smaller. The most suitable patterns are those that harmonize with a person's body size. Very large patterns overpower a small body frame, while a tiny pattern seems lost on a large frame.

Form

The shape of a three-dimensional object is its **form**. Your body outline and the clothes you wear create your form. Clothes that produce a *full form*, such as a full skirt or wide-legged pants, may make you appear larger and heavier. A *tubular form*, such as a one-color suit or straight-legged pants, may make you appear taller. The *bell-shaped form*, which flatters most people, is created by flared designs.

Consider the Principles of Design

The **principles of design** are the guides for combining the elements of design. The principles of design are balance, proportion, rhythm, and emphasis. Using each principle correctly creates a feeling of harmony in the design. That is, all parts of the design appear to belong together.

Balance

A garment with equal visual weight on both sides of a central point has **balance**. This means the garment is equally interesting when examined from side to side, or above and below the waist. No one part of the design overpowers the other.

Balance can be formal (symmetrical) or informal (asymmetrical). *Formal balance* creates a centered balance, meaning both sides are the same. A solid-colored shirt is a garment with formal balance. This is the most common type of balance. *Informal balance* means the two sides are different, but have the same visual impact. A child's blue shirt with one red sleeve and one yellow sleeve has informal balance. This type of balance is more visually appealing than formal balance.

Proportion

Proportion is the spatial relationship of the parts of a design to each other and to the whole design. In other words, the size of one part should balance the size of another part. Picture a man's suit with a knee-length jacket. The jacket would not be proportional to the pants. In a well-proportioned outfit, all parts are in scale with one another.

Rhythm

Rhythm creates a feeling of movement. Your eye moves from one part of the design to another. All parts of the design seem related. Rhythm is achieved through repetition, gradation, and radiation of colors, lines, shapes, or textures. Imagine a white knit shirt with a navy collar worn with navy shorts and sport socks with navy stripes. The repeated use of navy in this outfit gives it rhythm. An outfit of dark green pants, a light green shirt, and a medium green vest would have rhythm through gradation of color.

Emphasis

What do you first see when you look at an outfit? You see the center of interest in the design, which is called **emphasis**. You can use emphasis to draw attention to or away from an area. For instance, a colorful belt draws attention to the waist. A bright tie draws the eye upward, away from the waistline.

Strive for Harmony

Harmony is the pleasing effect created when all the elements of design work together. Harmony creates a sense of relatedness between all the design principles. The total effect is more important than any of the parts. An outfit composed of colors and textures that work well together will give a harmonious appearance.

Reading
Review

1. What are the elements of design?
2. Identify the three characteristics of color.
3. Name the principles of design.

Section 19-3

Shopping for Clothes

Objectives

After studying this section, you will be able to

- **develop** a wardrobe inventory.
- **give guidelines** to follow when shopping for clothes.
- **recognize** common fashion terms.
- **assess** how the fashion cycle impacts clothing decisions.
- **evaluate** the quality of garments by considering their durability and fit.
- **use** the information on labels and hangtags to make wiser clothing selections.

Key Terms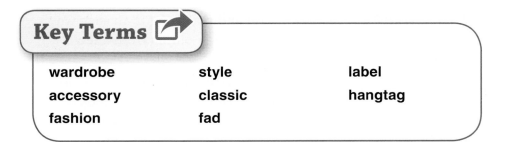

wardrobe	style	label
accessory	classic	hangtag
fashion	fad	

By shopping wisely, you will find the right clothes to complete your wardrobe at the right price. Your **wardrobe** is all the clothes and accessories you have to wear. **Accessories** are items that accent your clothes, such as shoes, hats, belts, jewelry, neckties, and scarves. A well-planned wardrobe will include appropriate clothing and accessories for all your activities.

Planning Your Wardrobe

As you plan your wardrobe, consider four factors.

1. *Separate your needs from your wants.* Wants can persuade you to fill a closet with garments you seldom wear.
2. *Select appropriate clothes for your lifestyle.* For example, a student needs casual clothing while a working professional needs business clothing.
3. *Consider your climate—warm or cold.* Select clothes that will suit both your activities and the climate in which you live.
4. *Determine what kinds of clothes meet your approval and the approval of others.* You know what kinds of clothes make you feel best. You also know what your friends and employers consider acceptable.

Living Green

Instead of going shopping, host a swap party. Invite your friends to bring clean, good-quality clothing or accessories they no longer wear to swap for others' clothing items. Arrange to bring leftover goods to a local donation center.

Mental Health Awareness

Clothing Psychology

The state of a wardrobe can be a reflection of a person's mental state. For example, a wardrobe organized by bright colors may reveal a sunny, confident personality. A wardrobe that is disorganized and cluttered, however, may reflect a person who is depressed or struggling with stressful issues.

Taking an Inventory

Wardrobe planning begins by taking an inventory of what you already have. This will help you decide what garments you need to add.

Begin your inventory by making a detailed list of every wearable garment you own. Do not forget accessories—they are part of your wardrobe, too. Once you know what you have, you can set specific goals. Make a list of new clothes you need to buy to replace any basic items that have worn out. Also consider what garments or accessories would help update your existing wardrobe.

Extending Your Wardrobe

After completing your wardrobe inventory, you may decide to extend your wardrobe. You can do this by choosing multipurpose clothing and mixing and matching garments. You can also use accessories to extend your wardrobe.

- *Choose multipurpose clothing.* As the name implies, *multipurpose clothing* can be worn several ways to satisfy different needs.
- *Mix and match garments.* Mixing and matching is an easy way to stretch your wardrobe and make many outfits from a few clothing items.
- *Use accessories.* Accessories can give a finished look to your outfits and let you express your personality. They also add variety to the clothes you wear.

Shopping Guidelines

Based on your wardrobe inventory, make a list of the clothes and accessories you need. Then decide how much money you have to spend. Next, prioritize your list so you know which wardrobe additions to buy first. You may want to give the highest priority to items you will wear most often, such as a coat or shoes.

Financial Literacy

Consider the Cost

Cost is a key factor affecting clothing purchases. When shopping for clothes, consider the following:

- Can you afford the garment? Does it fit into your price range? (Consider clothing "finds" that show up in thrift stores, garage sales, and resale clothing shops.)
- Would you be willing to wait for a sale price? (However, this might mean losing the garment to another buyer while you wait.)
- How many times will you wear the garment? (This will determine the cost per wear.)
- How long will you be able to wear a garment? (If you are still growing, the garment may not fit you very long. If the item is not well made, it may wear out quickly. If it is a fad style, it may go out of fashion.)
- How much will it cost to maintain the garment? (For instance, a silk shirt may seem like a bargain at $15. However, spending $5 each time it is dry-cleaned will soon exceed the cost of the shirt.)

Get the most for your money by following these shopping tips:

- *Refer to the shopping list you made when completing your wardrobe inventory.* This will show you exactly what you need to buy.

- *Comparison shop at several different retail sites before making a buying decision.* Check for sales or end-of-season clearances.

- *Buy only what you really need.* Avoid impulse buying and expensive trendy styles.

Technology Brings New Ways to Shop

When you cannot make purchases locally, shopping online is another option. Although the sensory experience of seeing and feeling merchandise is missing, online shopping offers many advantages over in-store shopping. For example, comparison shopping is much easier. You can compare products and prices from the convenience of your own home at any hour. Customer service is generally very reliable. Delivery of items to your home is quick, and you can return them if dissatisfied.

Stores cannot always carry a wide assortment because their limited space must be devoted to merchandise that appeals to everyone. Online retailers are not bound by this restriction. They offer a wider array of items that appeal to smaller segments of consumers, **19-4**. The ability to locate difficult-to-find items is a key reason for shopping online.

The main drawback to online shopping is not being able to try on garments before ordering. However, this is being addressed in several ways. Some websites display garments on various body frames so you can judge how it might look on you.

To be a wise online shopper, always follow the shopping guidelines. These apply equally to in-store and online purchasing.

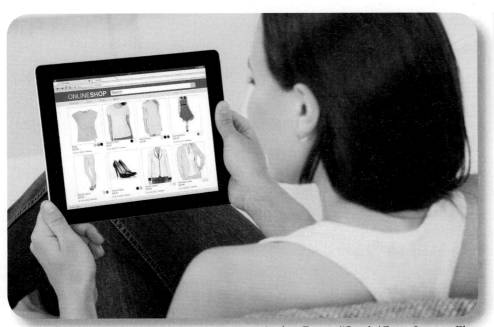

19-4

Online retailers usually have more in-stock clothing styles, colors, and sizes than available in many stores.

AndreyPopov/iStock/Getty Images Plus

Understanding Fashion Terms

Do you have an awareness of what it takes to achieve a well-dressed look? This is called *fashion sense*. Learning about fashion terms will help you build your wardrobe-planning fashion sense.

- In wardrobe planning, the term **fashion** refers to the current mode of dress. Fashion looks can change from year to year, and even from season to season.

- The term **style** refers to specific construction details that make one garment differ from another garment of the same type. Straight legs, flared bottoms, and cropped length are examples of pant styles.

- A **classic** style is one that is in fashion year after year. Business suits, jeans, and crew-neck sweaters are examples of classic styles.

- A **fad** is a style that is popular for a short time and then disappears. People who invest in fad items often discard them as soon as they go out of fashion.

Being Aware of Fashion Cycles

To keep people buying new clothes, the fashion industry must constantly produce new designs. After a new clothing style is introduced, it goes through a period when it gains popularity. Then the style reaches its height of acceptance before consumers begin to tire of it. The time from the introduction of a new fashion idea to its eventual decline in popularity is called a *fashion cycle*.

As you assemble your wardrobe, identify garments that are classic styles and fads. As a general rule, you will get the most wear from classic garments that last for many seasons. For variety, add a few inexpensive fad items you will be able to reuse in a different way when fashions change.

Judging Quality

When you consider buying a garment, inspect it for quality. Quality is an important factor in clothing. It affects a garment's look, durability, and fit.

Durability

Durability refers to how a garment will hold up under use. A garment's construction and the fabric from which it is made affect durability.

Before buying, examine a garment carefully. Signs of poor construction are most noticeable inside the garment, but also show on the outside. Check for quality construction features, such as secure buttons, neatly stitched buttonholes, smooth seams, and matched patterns. A well-constructed garment will provide many seasons of use. A poorly constructed garment will show wear and tear after using and cleaning it a few times.

21st Century Skills

Innovation. Alexis works as a fashion designer. She researches fashion trends and attends industry events to stay up-to-date on the latest styles. Alexis is very effective in applying fashion trends to designs that appeal to the mass market.

Evaluate the type of fabric used for the garment. Some fabrics wear better than others. Fabrics that snag and bag easily will not wear as well as sturdier fabrics that will hold their shape.

Crushing a corner of the garment tightly between two fingers will show you how easily the fabric wrinkles. If creases or wrinkles remain, the garment will crease or wrinkle when you wear it. Figure **19-5** describes features you would find in quality-made clothing.

Fit

An important point to consider when buying clothes is fit. The *fit* of a garment refers to how it conforms to the size and shape of the body of the wearer. The three categories of a garment's fit are fitted, semifitted, and loose. A fitted garment is shaped to conform closely to the lines of your body. If a fitted garment does not fit properly, it will not lie smoothly. Semifitted and loose garments do not conform to the body as closely as fitted garments. However, they must still fit properly to look neat and move freely as you move.

You must try on a garment to determine whether it fits. The best time to do this is before you buy the garment. Doing this will prevent the needless step of returning items that fit poorly. If possible, try the garment on with the accessories you plan to wear with it. That way, you can see if the new garment matches the accessories you already have.

When you try on a garment, you should move normally. Try sitting, bending, and raising and crossing your arms and legs. Note how comfortable the garment feels with each movement. Also notice how the garment looks. Does it pull or wrinkle anywhere? If the garment feels or looks too tight or too loose in a given body posture, it does not fit right.

Reading Labels and Hangtags

Is this garment the right size? What kind of fabric is it? Can it be machine-washed? Does it need ironing? If you have questions about a garment, carefully read the label and hangtags attached to it. Labels and hangtags on clothing provide useful information for the shopper.

Look for Quality Clothing
• **Garment construction**—Are designs matched at the seams? Do linings lie flat?
• **Fabric**—Is it easy to clean and maintain? Is it loosely or tightly constructed? The tighter the construction, the better the fabric will hold its shape.
• **Trim**—Do decorative features appear as durable as the rest of the garment? Are they securely attached?
• **Fasteners**—Are buttons, snaps, hooks and eyes firmly attached? Are extra buttons included for replacements? Are zippers inserted neatly and working smoothly?
• **Hem**—Are the stitches invisible on the outside of the garment? Is the hem wide enough for future adjustments? Is the edge finished to prevent raveling?
• **Seams**—Are all stitches straight, even, and free of puckers? Are they secured so they will not pull apart? Are edges finished to prevent raveling?
• **Reinforcements**—Are points of strain, such as armholes and crotches, reinforced with extra stitching? Wherever fasteners and pockets are sewn to a single thickness of fabric, are they reinforced?

19-5

Check for quality before you buy. As you examine garments, keep these questions in mind.

Math Connection

Cost Per Wear

Maggie bought a blouse for $45. She wore the blouse five times before she grew tired of it and gave it away. Maggie also bought a pair of nice jeans that fit her well for $68.50. She wore the jeans once a week for a year (52 times). How much did it cost Maggie to wear each garment?

To determine the cost per wear, Maggie takes the cost of each item and divides it by the times she wore it.

Blouse:
$45 ÷ 5 = $9

Jeans:
$68.50 ÷ 52 = $1.32

Labels are informative cloth tags permanently attached to garments. They provide important facts to the consumer, many of which are established by laws. These include the following:

- *The Textile Fiber Products Identification Act* requires all products to identify fiber content, the name of the manufacturer, and country of origin.

- *The Care Labeling Rule* mandates the listing of specific instructions for a garment's care. Look for whether the garment needs machine washing or dry cleaning. Dry cleaning can significantly add to the upkeep cost of a garment over time.

- *The Wool Products Labeling Act* calls for the type of wool, the percentage of wool, and its country of origin to be listed.

- *The Fur Products Labeling Act* requires the identification of a fur's animal source and its country of origin.

- *The Flammable Fabrics Act* prohibits the sale of very hazardous materials for use in clothing. It also requires fabrics used in children's sleepwear to stop a flame.

In addition to the required information, labels may also list the brand name, size, special finishes, and construction features.

Hangtags are larger tags attached to new garments. Before wearing a garment, you would remove these tags. Unlike labels, hangtags are not required by law. They include useful information, such as trademarks, guarantees, style numbers, sizes, and prices.

Reading
Review

1. What factors should you consider in wardrobe planning?
2. What is the purpose of a wardrobe inventory?
3. Give three guidelines to follow when shopping for clothes.
4. Explain the difference between fashion and style.
5. How is clothing quality judged?
6. List the information found on a label versus a hangtag.

Section 19-4

Caring for Clothes

Objectives

After studying this section, you will be able to

- **explain** daily clothing care.
- **care** for your clothes by using proper laundering, drying, ironing, and storing techniques.

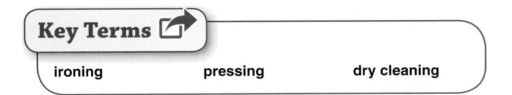

Key Terms

| ironing | pressing | dry cleaning |

After spending your time and money to get the right clothes, you will want to take good care of them. Proper care of clothes helps to ensure a neat personal appearance. Your clothes will look better and last longer if you care for them properly.

Daily Clothing Care

Setting a daily routine will help you keep your clothes in good condition. You will always have clean clothes ready to wear.

When you dress and undress, try not to damage or soil your clothes. Open fasteners so garments will slip easily over your head, arms, and hips. Avoid placing undue strain on any part of the garment. Strain can result in rips, broken zippers, and missing buttons. Taking the extra seconds to open fasteners can save hours in repairing damages.

As you pull garments over your head, try to protect the clothing. Avoid letting the garment touch your head or face to prevent stains from hair products, makeup, skin lotions, or sunscreens.

Allow an extra minute or two to care for your clothes when you undress. Inspect garments closely for stains, rips, hanging threads, and missing buttons. Put clothes with any of these problems in a special place. This will remind you to take care of the problems before wearing or cleaning the garments. Items that need dry cleaning should be set aside and taken to the dry cleaner promptly.

Laundering Steps

Washable garments will look their best and last longer when you launder them properly. Laundering not only cleans garments, but also removes wrinkles and perspiration odors. To care for clothes properly, you need to know some basic laundry principles.

Read Care Labels

The Care Labeling Rule, issued by the Federal Trade Commission, requires care labels to clearly identify the correct procedures for each garment's upkeep. The label must also warn against care procedures that are likely to damage the item. The label must remain readable for the life of the garment.

Symbols, as shown in Figure **19-6**, indicate the various care methods used. If the clothing is to be washed, the following information must be included on the label:

- washing method
- water temperature
- drying method
- drying temperature
- type of bleach that can be used safely
- use of iron
- ironing temperatures

Always follow care labels to keep clothes looking neat and colors staying bright.

Sort Clothes Properly

The purpose of sorting is to separate items that could cause damage to others. One key way to sort clothes is by color. Separate whites from colors, and light colors from bright or dark colors. Different wash water temperatures are needed to keep some colors from either fading or bleeding onto other garments. When fabrics *bleed*, they emit color to adjacent clothing. *Colorfast* means the color will withstand washing, dry cleaning, perspiration, sunlight, and rubbing.

Sorting clothes by fabric will help you determine what wash cycle to use. White cottons and linens require hot water and a regular wash cycle for cleaning. Permanent press fabrics require warm wash water and a cold rinse. Other fabrics require cold water and a short, gentle wash cycle to prevent fading and shrinking.

Sort clothes by their surface texture to separate lint-catchers from lint-producers. Corduroy, velveteen, and fabrics of manufactured fibers catch lint. On the other hand, chenille and terry cloth produce lint.

Another factor you should consider when sorting clothes is the degree of soil. Heavily soiled clothes require different laundry procedures than lightly soiled items.

19-6

This chart explains the clothing-care symbols and instructions printed on garment labels.

Prepare Clothes for Laundering

Visually inspect your clothes before laundering. Remove surface soil by shaking or brushing it away. Be sure all zippers and hooks are closed. They may get damaged or may cause damage to other items when left open. Repair snags and mend rips and tears to prevent greater damage from occurring during washing or drying.

Check pockets carefully before putting garments in the washing machine. A pen, tissue, or other object left in a pocket can produce stains or lint. This could damage every item in a wash load.

Pretreat Stains and Heavy Soil

Treat and wash stains promptly, when they are easiest to remove. Heavily soiled items should be pretreated by soaking, or by applying a liquid detergent or a prewash product.

One way to promote a healthy relationship between people and their environment is with the use of *high efficiency (HE)* laundry detergents that can help in diverse ways. For green living,

- Buy powdered detergent, which weighs less and has a lower shipping cost than a liquid detergent.
- Use cold-water detergents to save on the energy needed to heat water.
- Look for detergents that have harmful chemicals, such as phosphates and dioxanes, removed.
- Use high-efficiency (HE) detergents that can be used in cold water, require less detergent, and use less water per load.

Both consumers and the environment reap the benefits. You can also strengthen the impact of HE movement by using a top-loading or front-loading HE washer that also requires less water.

Read the package labels on all soil and stain removers before using them. Always test the product first to see if it discolors the fabric. Use an unseen part of the garment, such as the back of a hem. Test the product by waiting 5 to 10 minutes after applying it and rinsing the area thoroughly.

Understand Laundry Products

Many types of laundry products are available. For best laundry results, you need to use the right types of products and follow package directions carefully.

Soaps and Detergents

Soaps and detergent remove soil from fabrics. *Soaps* work best in soft water. *Detergents* work well in hard or soft water. Detergents come in both liquid and powder forms. Detergent should always be mixed into wash water before clothes are added to allow it to dilute or dissolve completely. See 19-7. Use the amount of detergent indicated in the package directions.

Bleach

Bleach helps remove stains and whitens, disinfects, and deodorizes clothes. *Chlorine bleach* can weaken fabric fibers if it is used too often or is too concentrated. It should not be used on wool, silk, spandex, noncolorfast fabrics, or on some fabric finishes.

If your washer has a built-in bleach dispenser, read the use and care instructions for exact directions. If your washer does not have a bleach dispenser, the bleach must be diluted and added after agitation begins.

Oxygen bleach helps remove stains and whiten clothes. It is milder than chlorine bleach and safe for all washable fibers.

Science Connection

How Softeners Work

Water softeners replace calcium and magnesium ions in hard water with sodium ions. Calcium and magnesium reacts with water pipes, leaving a filmy residue in sinks and bathtubs. Calcium and magnesium also react with soap to leave a dulling residue on laundered clothing. By replacing the calcium and magnesium with sodium, water softeners reduce the negative effects of hard water.

Fabric softeners are made of *surfactants*, chemicals that coat the surface of fabrics with a thin film. Surfactants are made up of positively charged ions that reduce static electricity. Surfactants also make fabrics soft and fluffy and reduce wrinkling.

Using the Washing Machine

For good cleaning action, distribute items evenly in the washer. This balances the wash load. Do not overload the washer. Too many garments in the wash prevent good circulation of water and cleaning agents.

Select a wash cycle suitable for the wash load. Delicate items need a *gentle* or *delicate cycle* with warm or cold water. Permanent press garments will need a *permanent press cycle* with a cold-water rinse if they are to remain free of wrinkles.

The *regular cycle* handles all other laundry items. Select wash temperature according to fiber content and care labels. A cold-water rinse is suitable for all fabrics and saves energy, too.

Drying Clothes

Clothes can be dried in an automatic dryer, on a clothesline, or on a flat surface. Check garment care labels for drying directions.

Tumble-drying clothes in an automatic dryer is convenient, especially for large loads. Most clothes are softer and more comfortable when tumble dried.

Never overload the dryer. If clothes are too crowded to tumble freely, they will probably wrinkle. Larger loads take longer to dry. You should remove clothes as soon as the tumbling stops to prevent wrinkles. Remember to clean the lint filter after each use.

Different brands and models of dryers have different cycles, but three are common. The *regular cycle* is used for items that are not heat sensitive. The *permanent press cycle* provides moderate heat at the start and no heat for the last 10 minutes. The *air-dry cycle* provides unheated air to freshen or fluff items. Follow the use and care instructions that come with the dryer for best results.

Line drying is recommended for some fabrics and is often done indoors. Garments are hung above a bathtub or in a shower stall to drip-dry. In areas not affected by smog or high humidity, line drying can be done outdoors. Line drying gives clothes a fresh smell, while saving the cost of using an electric or gas dryer.

The flat-drying method is used for garments such as sweaters to avoid shrinking or stretching them out of shape. Remove excess moisture first by rolling the garment in a towel. Then unroll and shape the garment by hand on a clean, absorbent surface, such as a towel. Keep the garment away from direct heat.

19-7

Cleaning aides should be blended into the water before adding clothes.

Ironing and Pressing

The terms ironing and pressing are often used interchangeably, but they have slightly different meanings. **Ironing** is a process of moving an iron across fabric to smooth wrinkles, usually after laundering.

Pressing is a process of lifting the iron up and down to apply pressure in one area at a time. **Pressing** is done on seams and curves as garments are sewn or to touch up wrinkles after laundering.

Always use a heat setting that is safe for the fabric and any attached trim. A too-hot iron will scorch some fabrics, melt others, or create permanent wrinkles.

Dry Cleaning

Some care labels indicate that garments require dry cleaning instead of laundering. **Dry cleaning** is a process that cleans clothes using organic chemical solvents. Water is not used in this process. Because dry cleaning is a delicate cleaning process, clothes should be cleaned before they become heavily soiled.

Professional dry cleaners know how to treat various fabrics and most spots and stains. You can assist them, however, by pointing out stains when you take garments to be cleaned. Explain the cause of the stain and how old it is. You may also want to request the addition of sizing to make a limp garment look fresh again. Likewise, you can have a water-repellent finish restored to a garment after cleaning. To air out any cleaning fumes, hang dry-cleaned garments in an open area awhile before storing.

Another choice for garments marked "dry-clean only" is a home in-dryer kit. Home dry-cleaning kits can remove odors, wrinkles, and light stains in most linen, silk, wool, and rayon clothing. The kits also work well on garments with beads, sequins, and other trims. It is an economical way to freshen a special-care garment when you cannot get to a dry cleaner. However, the kit may not remove all stains and will not give the "pressed" look of a professional dry cleaner.

Environmental Awareness in Clothing Care

Modern technology has developed laundry appliances that use energy and water very efficiently. Laundry products are continually improved, too, with formulas and packaging that are environmentally sound. As a consumer, you can also play a part in protecting the environment by following the recommendations in Figure **19-8**.

Living Green

After bringing clothes home from the dry cleaners and transferring clothes to their original hangers, return the wire hangers to the dry cleaners. Many dry cleaners gladly accept returned hangers.

Analyze and Solve

Research the cost of dry cleaning an all-weather coat in your area. Assume you will be wearing the coat for three years. Determine how much you would need to spend to keep it clean.

The Environmental Laundry List

- Do laundry at times other than peak energy-use hours.
- Use high-efficiency (HE) detergents when possible.
- Buy laundry products in concentrated form and recycle containers.
- Pretreat heavily soiled spots and stubborn stains to avoid the need for additional washings.
- Sort and wash full loads of compatible garments.
- Adjust the water level to the size of the load.
- Use cooler wash water whenever possible. Hot water may be needed for heavily soiled clothes, but warm water handles light soil, and cold water is fine for everything else.
- Save energy by line drying whenever possible.
- Clean the lint filter before each load.
- Avoid overloading the dryer.
- Remove clothes from the dryer promptly to prevent wrinkling and unnecessary ironing.
- Iron as many items as possible at one time to prevent the repeated heating of the iron for individual uses.

Storing Clothes

19-8

These simple steps show how to handle laundry tasks and demonstrate ways to save water, save energy, and reduce waste.

If your clothes are clean and in good condition, store them properly. Always store knit garments in drawers to prevent the stretching and sagging that occurs when they are hung.

Store similar garments together. For instance, put all your T-shirts in the same drawer and hang all pants together in the same corner of the closet. When you need the items later, you will do less searching to find them. Mixing and matching garments to create outfits will be easier, too.

Clothes stored in the closet should be neatly hung on hangers. Close top buttons, zippers, and other fasteners so clothes will retain their shape and not slip off hangers. Have a clothes brush handy to remove any lint or dust. Allow enough space in the closet for clothes to hang loosely without becoming wrinkled as in **19-9**.

Specialty hangers can help you store certain garments more easily. Hangers designed for blazers, jackets, and coats are curved to simulate the curve of the shoulders. This helps the garments retain the best shape. Hangers covered with a thin layer of foam keep garments made from slippery fabrics from falling. Hangers with clips conveniently hang skirts and pants from the waistline.

Many accessories are available to increase the clothing storage space in your home. With some ingenuity, you can create other storage containers. Large boxes that slide under beds are one storage option that works well for clothes. This frees up closet and drawer space for the garments you use most often.

19-9

When clothes are stored properly, they are always easier to find and keep wrinkle free.

When storing out-of-season clothes, be sure to consider the possibility of insect damage. Moths and crickets can eat holes in your clothes, especially woolens. To protect wool garments, store them in cedar-lined closets or chests. If these are not available, place mothballs or crystals into their drawers or containers.

Reading Review

1. List five steps to take daily to keep your clothes in great shape.
2. List four factors to consider when sorting clothes for laundering.
3. Which drying method is preferred for garments that might stretch or shrink?
4. What are five steps you can take to conserve energy as you care for your clothes?

Chapter 19 Review

Summary

A number of factors affect your clothing decisions. Clothes meet a basic physical need by protecting your body from weather and various safety hazards. How a garment makes you feel is a result of clothing's effect on your psychological needs. Clothes also meet some of your social needs by helping you identify with groups and serving as status symbols. The occasion for which you will wear clothes is another factor that sways your clothing decisions.

Use the elements and principles of design in choosing clothes that reflect your personal tastes and style. Choose colors that flatter your skin tone and hair and eye color. Use line, texture, and form in clothing design to complement your body shape.

Planning your wardrobe takes skill. A wardrobe inventory helps you identify what clothing you own and what you need to add. Wearing multipurpose clothing as well as mixing and matching garments extends your wardrobe options.

Understanding fashion terms can help you shop for a basic wardrobe to suit your activities and lifestyle. Try to get the best quality you can afford. As you shop, watch for sales. Use the information on labels and hangtags to make informed decisions. Also, consider the cost of garments and their care as you shop for clothes to fit your budget.

Proper care of clothing always means longer wear. Establish a daily routine for clothing care. Read clothing labels for care instructions. Follow proper steps for laundering, drying, ironing, or dry-cleaning clothes. Take steps to care for the environment as you care for your clothes, too. When storing clothes, handle them properly so they will look their best on you.

Critical Thinking

1. **Evaluate needs.** Evaluate the garments you already have. What garments and accessories do you need to add to your wardrobe in the future?

2. **Choosing clothing.** Illustrate what clothes you would choose to wear to a prom. Also illustrate what you would wear to a job interview as a salesperson in an apparel department. You may draw sketches or clip pictures from catalogs or magazines.

3. **Analyze decisions.** Assess your clothing-selection habits. What changes would you make to improve your shopping skills?

4. **Evaluate quality.** Use Figure 19-5 to evaluate the quality of several pieces of clothing.

5. **Analyze choices.** Use spreadsheet software to make pie charts showing the factors that influence your wardrobe planning. Assign percentages to each factor based on how important each factor seems to you. For instance, someone who bases most clothing choices on comfort might assign a value of 60% to comfort. Another person may assign a value of 60% to latest fashion trends.

21st Century Applications

6. **Social and cross-cultural skills.** Research clothing customs in other

countries, cultures, and religions. What message can an item of clothing communicate to others about the wearer's religion, marital status, or other cultural aspect? List three examples of clothing items that carry a specific meaning. Share your findings with the class.

7. **Information, communications, and technology literacy.** Use drawing software to make color wheels beginning with the three primary colors. Add shades and tints using the drawing program's color palette.

8. **Creativity and innovation.** Create one outfit for any occasion that demonstrates the elements and principles of design in use. Identify how you are using each element or principle. Share your designs with the class.

9. **Productivity and accountability.** Use a word processing program to create a clothing inventory chart. Print one copy to take an inventory of the clothes you own. Save the file and reuse it for future clothing inventories as needed.

Core
Skills

10. **Science.** Discuss how the body is cooled or warmed by various types of fibers and fabric construction. Name some fabrics that are worn primarily in hotter weather and fabrics that are preferred for cold weather.

11. **History.** Identify the types of clothing worn by people of different social classes during an important historical period. Name fabrics, colors, or styles that were characteristic of a particular class or status.

12. **Reading.** Research the history of women's clothing. Why did women wear only skirts and dresses until the twentieth century? What historical occurrences brought about the acceptance of women wearing pants? How revolutionary was this concept at the time? Why?

13. **Writing.** Using reliable print and online sources, research clothing psychology. How can clothing affect a person's self-concept? How do psychological needs impact clothing decisions? Write a report outlining your findings. Include examples from your research and cite any sources you used.

14. **Speaking.** Create a digital presentation demonstrating color as a design element. Find pictures of garments and outfits that demonstrate different hues, values, and intensities of a color. Also include outfits demonstrating the monochromatic color scheme, analogous color scheme, and complementary color scheme. As an alternative to this activity, work in small groups to create and record a fashion show to display different color options and schemes. Show your presentations or videos to the class.

15. **Listening.** Interview a clothing designer or interior designer in your area. Find out how the elements and principles of design impact his or her work. How does the designer use each aspect of design to complete a job? Report your findings to the class.

16. **Math.** Go to stores and compare the prices of different brands of laundry products. Make note of your findings and share them with the class. Which products do you think are the best buys and why?

17. **Speaking.** Learn about other uses of 3D body scanning and body shape analysis by searching these terms online. How are these tools used in the fashion industry? Prepare a report about your findings and the websites you explored.

18. **Writing.** Locate the website for a clothing retailer and find an item that interests you. Consider the style, durability, fit, care instructions, and cost of the garment. Which factors can you easily evaluate online and which are more difficult? Write a brief summary of your analysis and findings.

19. **Writing.** Research careers related to this chapter. Then select one career and write an outline about the job description, education and training needed, personal qualities and skills needed, and job outlook. Would you be interested in pursuing this career? Why or why not?

Leadership
Development

Organize a career fashion show as a Career Connection project. Ask students to volunteer as models dressed for success in the workplace. Feature clothing appropriate for interviews and in a variety of workplace settings. Offer tips for shopping for career clothing on a budget.

Portfolio
Builder

Think about your future career. What type of wardrobe would it require? Put together a wardrobe appropriate for your future career. Cut pictures from catalogs or obtain them online. Write brief descriptions next to each picture describing why these garments would be good choices for your career wardrobe. Add your wardrobe choices to your portfolio.

Journal
Writing

You are almost late for a special date. You grab your favorite black shirt from the closet. There is a grease stain on the front and imprints made by the hanger on both shoulders. Lint is scattered all over it. About four inches of the hem is ripped and hanging down. There is a fold across the front where the shirt was wedged too tightly between other garments.

Write About It: *Would you really wear this shirt on a date? Could you do anything quickly to make the shirt wearable? What steps might have prevented this situation? What storage advice would you be likely to follow in the future?*

Chapter 20
Textiles, Patterns, and Equipment

Sections

20-1 Understanding Fabrics and Patterns

20-2 Sewing Equipment

Reading Prep

Before reading, preview the illustrations. As you read the chapter, cite specific textual evidence to support the information in the illustrations.

Concept Organizer

Create a cluster diagram with two main topics: Natural Fibers and Manufactured Fibers.

G-WLEARNING.com

Click on the activity icon to visit www.g-wlearning.com/comprehensive/8062 to access online vocabulary activities using key terms from the chapter.

Understanding Fabrics and Patterns

Objectives

After studying this section, you will be able to

- **explain** how fibers, yarns, and fabrics are produced and manufactured.
- **distinguish** various fabric finishes.
- **identify** a suitable pattern and interpret the information on its envelope.
- **select** appropriate fabric and notions for your garment.

Key Terms

fiber	manufactured fibers	knitting
yarn		nonwoven fabrics
fabric	microfibers	notions
natural fibers	weaving	

The freedom to choose design, color, and fabric is yours when you learn how to sew. You can make wise fabric selections when you know how fabrics are made. Then, pairing the right fabric with the right pattern will lead to sewing success. By using your imagination, you can create original garments that reflect your fashion taste and style. Understanding today's fabrics is the first step in the sewing process.

Fibers

The **fiber** is the basic unit of all fabrics. Fibers are combined to form a continuous strand called a **yarn**. The weaving and knitting of yarns make **fabrics**.

Fibers have certain characteristics that determine the texture, strength, warmth, absorbency, and durability of fabrics. The characteristics of a fiber depend on its source, either natural or chemical. Thus, the two major groups of fibers are natural fibers and manufactured fibers.

Natural Fibers

Natural fibers are those that exist in nature. Their composition does not change during processing. Plants such as cotton and flax are sources of natural fibers. The wool of sheep, specialty hair fibers such as mohair and cashmere, and silk are also natural fibers. See **20-1**.

The Natural Fibers

Cotton

Advantages	Disadvantages
Absorbent; soaks up water easily	Wrinkles easily unless treated with special finish
Comfortable and cool to wear in warm weather	Shrinks in hot water if not treated
Dyes and prints well	Mildews if left damp or stored in damp area
Does not build up static electricity	Weakened by wrinkle-resistant finishes and by prolonged exposure to sunlight
Withstands high temperatures; can be boiled to sterilize	Highly flammable unless treated with flame-retardant finish
Combines with other fibers easily	
Wide variety of uses	

Linen (Flax)

Advantages	Disadvantages
Strongest of natural fibers	Wrinkles and creases easily unless treated
Cool to wear; absorbs moisture from skin and dries quickly	Shines if ironed
Looks smooth and lustrous	Expensive if of good quality
Withstands high temperatures; will not scorch easily when ironed	Poor resistance to mildew and perspiration
Durable; withstands frequent laundering	
Lint-free; used for dish towels and for cloths in medical profession	

Wool

Advantages	Disadvantages
Warmest of natural fibers	Expensive
Highly absorbent; absorbs moisture without feeling wet	Will shrink and mat when moisture and heat are applied
Resists wrinkles	Usually requires dry cleaning
Holds and regains shape	Burns easily
Creases well	Attracts moths and carpet beetles
Durable	
Combines well with other fibers	

Silk

Advantages	Disadvantages
Looks and feels smooth and luxurious	Usually requires dry cleaning
Very absorbent	Yellows with age
Strong but lightweight	Weakened by detergents, perspiration, and long exposure to sunlight
Resists wrinkling	Attacked by insects such as silverfish
Resists soil	Spotted by water unless specially treated
Combines well with other fibers	Expensive

20-1

The natural fibers have advantages and disadvantages.

Cotton

Cotton fibers come from the seedpod of the cotton plant. The fibers are versatile, absorbent, and durable, qualities that make cotton the most widely used natural fiber. Although cotton wrinkles and shrinks easily, finishes can be applied to fabrics to prevent these undesirable qualities.

Linen

Flax, the fiber used to make linen, comes from the woody stalk of the flax plant. Flax is the oldest known fiber used for fabrics. Remnants of linen have been found in Egyptian tombs as old as 5000 B.C. Linen was the fabric used to wrap bodies for burial.

Linen is best known for its strength, durability, absorbency, and luster. Like cotton fabric, linen wrinkles and creases easily unless treated with a special finish. Ironing makes the fiber shiny.

Wool

Wool, a protein fiber, comes from the fleece of sheep. Wool is an absorbent, resilient (springy), and elastic fiber. Even though wool fabric is warm, it can also feel cool in lightweight fabrics. Wool fibers let heat out and air in to keep the body dry and cool. These and other qualities make wool a very comfortable and durable fabric.

Consumers cannot know the type and quality of wool simply by looking at wool fabric. To inform and protect consumers, Congress passed the Wool Products Labeling Act in 1939. This legislation requires that wool in any garment or fabric must be labeled as *new* or *recycled*. Wool, as defined by the act, means fibers from the coat of a living animal that are being used for the first time. This wool is often called *virgin wool*.

Recycled wool refers to fibers from previously made wool fabrics that were never used. This wool often comes from cutting scraps, mill ends, or garments. Fabrics made from recycled wool are often used as interlinings in heavy coats.

Silk

Silk was first produced in China where the process of *sericulture* (silkworm cultivation) was kept a secret for more than 2,000 years. Silk production is still mainly in China, Japan, and other Asian countries. Silk, characterized by long, lustrous filaments, is often called the luxury fiber.

Silk is a fiber excreted from the silkworm when it builds its cocoon. The cocoons are then soaked in warm water and unwound (either by hand or machine) as one strong continuous filament about 1,000 feet long. Most silk garments should be dry-cleaned, but washable silk fabrics are now more common.

Ramie

Ramie fibers are obtained from the stalks of China grass, which is grown in Southeast Asia. Ramie is a linenlike fiber that is strong, durable, washable, and lustrous. Ramie absorbs body moisture, dries quickly, absorbs dyes readily, and is often blended with other fibers.

Manufactured Fibers

Manufactured fibers are produced through chemical and technical means from natural cellulose or crude oil products. For centuries, clothing consisted of animal pelts and fabric made from natural fibers. In 1924, the first manufactured fiber, *rayon*, was produced. *Acetate* was developed a few years later, and more manufactured fibers followed. See **20-2** for manufactured fibers that are commonly used in fabrics and apparel.

Rayon, acetate, triacetate, and lyocell are made from *cellulose*, the fibrous substance from plants. Wood pulp is used most often. The other manufactured fibers are called *noncellulosic fibers* because they are completely chemical based.

As with all fibers, manufactured fibers have both advantages and disadvantages. Noncellulosic fibers are generally *thermoplastic*, which means they soften at high temperatures. Fabrics made of these fibers can be heat-treated to form pleats, shape fabrics, or emboss fabric designs.

Rayon and lyocell are somewhat absorbent, while acrylic moves moisture away from the skin. Other manufactured fibers are less comfortable to wear in hot, humid weather. Because they do not absorb or move moisture, they can generate static electricity. Fiber blends and special finishes can overcome some of these limitations.

Microfibers

A relatively recent development in textile technology is the creation of microfibers. A **microfiber** is an extremely thin filament of a manufactured fiber. *Filaments* are continuous strands of fibers. The resulting fabric has all the qualities characteristic of the fiber plus a luxurious look and feel.

Polyester microfiber, for example, often looks like fine silk. Yet it has the strength, durability, and easy-care qualities associated with polyester. In addition, the fabric has a natural resistance to water since the thin fibers pack together so closely that a water molecule cannot penetrate. However, body heat can escape so the wearer remains comfortable. Acrylic, rayon, nylon, and polyester are available as microfibers.

Yarns

A yarn is a continuous strand made by combining staple fibers or filaments. *Staple fibers* are short fibers. All natural fibers except silk are staple fibers. Manufactured fibers are made in filament form, but can be cut to form staple fibers.

The Manufactured Fibers

	Acetate	Acrylic	Aramid	Lyocell	Metallic	Modacrylic	Nylon	Olefin	Polyester	Rayon	Saran	Spandex
Absorbent				●						●		
Colorfast		●			●	●	●	●	●	●	●	
Easy to dye	●		●	●		●			●			
Easy to launder		●	●	●	●	●	●	●				●
Easy to iron			●			●		●	●			
Elastic						●						●
Exceptional durability			●	●	●		●	●	●		●	
Flame resistant			●			●				●		
Good drapability	●		●	●		●				●		
Good shape retention		●				●	●		●			●
Quick drying		●	●			●	●	●	●			●
Resilient		●	●	●		●			●			
Resistant to: ■ abrasion		●					●	●	●			
■ chemicals		●	●			●	●	●	●	●		
■ moths	●	●	●		●	●	●	●	●	●	●	●
■ mildew	●	●	●		●	●	●	●	●		●	●
■ oil/grease		●	●			●						●
■ pilling	●								●			
■ stretching		●						●				
■ soil		●						●				
■ shrinking		●	●	●	●		●		●	●		
■ weather		●			●	●		●	●	●	●	
Soft	●	●		●		●				●		
Strong			●	●			●	●	●	●		
Warm		●				●	●		●			
Wide color range	●	●		●		●	●		●	●		
Wrinkle resistant		●							●			●

20-2

This chart lists the most important properties of common manufactured fibers.

Many yarns on today's market are either blends or combinations of different fibers. Blends and combinations are often used to make fabrics with better performance. In the case of a polyester/cotton shirt, the polyester is wrinkle-resistant, and the cotton is absorbent. By blending the fibers, the shirt has the best characteristics of both fibers. Sometimes blends and combinations are used to make more-affordable fabrics.

Fabric Construction

Two common methods of fabric construction are weaving and knitting. Other methods are felting, fusing, braiding, knotting, and quilting.

Woven Fabrics

A woven fabric is composed of two sets of yarns crossing at right angles. The process of interlacing these two sets of yarns to produce a fabric is known as **weaving**. Weaving is done on machines called *looms*.

Passing crosswise yarns over and under different numbers of lengthwise yarns creates different weaving effects. The plain, twill, and satin weaves are the three basic weaves.

Plain Weave

The plain weave is the simplest form of weaving. It is made by passing a crosswise yarn alternately over and under the lengthwise yarns. The plain weave produces strong, durable fabrics such as muslin, percale, dress linen, gingham, and broadcloth.

Twill Weave

The twill weave is formed when a crosswise yarn passes, or floats, over two or three lengthwise yarns. The twill weave leaves the surface appearance of a diagonal line or wale. Twill weaves are often used to produce

20-3

Denim is a popular twill weave because it is strong and durable.

Africa Studio/Shutterstock.com

strong, durable fabrics such as denim and gabardine, **20-3**. Twill-weave fabrics resist wrinkles and hide soil.

Satin Weave

A satin weave is made when a crosswise yarn floats over four or more yarns and under one. Satin-weave fabrics are characterized by their lustrous shine, the result of long floats reflecting light.

Since the floats tend to snag easily, the satin weave does not produce durable fabrics. Satin weave fabrics are often used as lining fabrics because they are smooth and slippery.

Knit Fabrics

The process of looping yarns together to form a fabric is called **knitting**. The loops are varied to create numerous patterns and textures. One yarn can form the entire fabric.

Knit fabrics are best known for their stretch, which allows the fabric to move with and fit the body. They also resist wrinkles well. When threads are broken, however, a *run* can form, as in nylon stockings. Knits also can snag or ravel if a yarn is pulled.

Other Fabric Constructions

Not all fabrics are knitted or woven. Some are made by locking fibers together or by braiding, knotting, or quilting yarns.

Nonwoven fabrics are made by pressing, bonding, or interlocking fibers together without using yarns. This can be done with mechanical action, chemicals, and/or heat. Nonwoven fabrics have many industrial and medical uses. They are also used as interfacings in garments. *Interfacings* give support to collars, waistbands, and cuffs. Batting, a lightweight layer of insulation used inside quilts, is also a nonwoven fabric.

Applying heat, moisture, agitation, and pressure to wool fibers results in *felt*. Due to the nature of wool fibers, the *felting* process causes fibers to permanently interlock. Felt is easy to mold and is often used to make hats and craft items. It has many industrial uses, too.

Braiding is the process of interlacing three or more yarns lengthwise and diagonally to make fabrics. Braided fabrics are usually narrow. They are used to make decorative trims, shoelaces, and rugs.

Knotting or twisting yarns produces *laces* and *nets*. These fabrics can be constructed by hand or machine. Lace and net fabrics can be fine and sheer, or coarse and open.

Quilting is the process of stitching a layer of insulating material between two layers of fabric. Often the stitching is regular and consistent to produce an all-over pattern. Sometimes decorative stitching is used, especially to emphasize a unique design. Quilting is used to make warm articles such as jackets, coats, and bed coverings. When quilting for crafts and home-decorating items, hot glue is sometimes used to seal the fabric layers.

Fabric Finishes

20-4

Fabric finishes are applications and processes that affect how a cloth looks, feels, and functions.

All fabrics go through some type of finishing process before they are ready for use. Most finishes add certain characteristics to the fabrics. Common fabric finishes are listed in **20-4**. They improve the appearance, feel, or performance of fabrics.

Common Fabric Finishes	
Type of Finish	**Description**
Antistatic	Prevents garments from clinging to the body.
Bleaching	Whitens fabrics and removes impurities. Is usually used on cotton and linen fabrics.
Brushing	Uses circular brushes to remove short, loose fibers from the surface and produce an even, soft pile.
Calendering	Is the process of pressing fabric between heated rollers to make it smooth and glossy.
Dyeing	Adds color to fabric. Colorfast means the color will withstand washing, dry cleaning, perspiration, sunlight, and rubbing.
Flame Retardant	Prevents the fabric from supporting a flame by cutting off the oxygen supply. Is used on children's sleepwear, general wearing apparel, carpets, rugs, and mattresses according to flammability standards set by the Flammable Fabrics Act.
Mercerization	Is most often used on cotton, linen, and rayon fabrics to increase luster, strength, and affinity (attraction) for dyes.
Permanent Press	Helps fabric retain its original shape and resist wrinkling after washing and drying. Is also called durable press.
Preshrinking	Shrinks fabrics in a heat-and-moisture process. Garments labeled preshrunk will not shrink more than three percent. Sanforized™ is a trademark name, guaranteeing less than one percent shrinkage in length or width.
Sizing	Is a solution of starch, glue, or resin applied to fabric to increase weight, body, and luster. May be temporary or durable.
Soil Release	Helps water-resistant fibers become more absorbent so detergents can release soil. Makes possible the removal of oily stains from durable-press fabrics.
Stain Resistance	Makes fabrics less absorbent to resist water and oil stains so spills can be lifted or sponged off easily. Scotchguard™ is a trademark for a stain-resistant fabric.
Water Repellent	Makes a fabric resistant to liquids, but must be renewed after several launderings. Does not waterproof the fabric against heavy rain.

Choosing a Pattern

Successful sewing begins with choosing the right pattern. Since pattern sizes vary slightly from ready-to-wear sizes, you will need to first take your measurements. These measurements will help you identify the best size to choose.

You will also want to select a style that suits you. Try to visualize how the finished garment will look on you. Apply what you have learned about design lines that flatter your figure.

In making your decision, consider your sewing skill. Using an easy pattern will help assure your success. A clue to a pattern's sewing ease is its number of pieces. Fewer pattern pieces usually mean the garment's construction will be easier.

Figure Type and Size

Body-measurement charts for all body types appear in pattern catalogs at fabric stores. The charts usually appear near the last page. Choosing a pattern of the correct figure type will result in a garment that fits well.

If you are a female, two measurements are used to determine your figure type—your height and back waist length. The *back waist length* is the distance from the most prominent bone at the center back of the neck to the waistline. Females must also analyze body proportions and shape to determine figure type. For males, choosing the right pattern size is simpler.

Taking Measurements

To ensure accuracy, ask someone to help you take your measurements. Measure over the undergarments you normally wear. Do not try to take measurements over bulky clothing. When taking measurements, put the tape measure snugly around the body, but not too tight. Be sure the tape measure is always parallel to the floor.

The Pattern Envelope

After selecting the pattern, read the information on the front and the back of the pattern envelope. The front of the envelope usually has drawings or photos of more than one image, or *pattern view*. Each pattern view shows a variation of the basic pattern. See **20-5**.

The back of the pattern envelope usually includes the following information:

- the number of pattern pieces included
- written description of the garment

Living Green

If your friends are similar in size to you, trade or borrow patterns. You can save money and paper, while still having one-of-a-kind fashions by varying fabrics and trims.

Life Skills

Taking Measurements

Learning to take your measurements accurately will help you choose the best pattern sizes. To measure the head for a hat or cap, bring the tape measure around the head at the fullest part of the forehead. Hips should be measured around the fullest part of the hip section. This is about seven or eight inches below the waistline. The waist should be measured at the smallest part of the midsection on females. For males, it may be where the waistband of pants usually falls. The bust or chest is measured with the tape straight across the back and around the fullest part of the bust or chest while holding your arms at your sides.

20-5

The front of a pattern envelope usually shows the different ways to vary the pattern.

- fabric recommendations
- supplies needed to complete the garment
- drawing of the back of each garment view
- measurement chart
- how much fabric to buy
- any interfacing or lining fabrics needed

Choosing a Fabric

The pattern envelope identifies fabrics appropriate for the pattern, **20-6**. Beginning sewers will want to follow these recommendations closely. This section also alerts you to fabrics that should not be used, such as pile fabrics or diagonal patterns.

Also consider your sewing skills when choosing fabric. A medium-weight fabric is easiest to sew. Very heavy or light fabrics are more challenging. The same is true for fabrics that ravel easily, are slippery, or have a design that must be matched at the seams. You should also consider the care requirements of a fabric before making a purchase.

How Much Is Needed?

A chart on the back of the pattern envelope shows the amount of fabric to buy for various fabric widths and pattern sizes. To find out what you need, use the chart. First locate the section for the pattern view you will make. Then find the column for the size of your pattern. Go down the column until you come to the width of the fabric you have chosen. Circle this figure. This is the number of yards of fabric you should buy. The envelope will also tell you how much interfacing is needed.

Choosing Notions

The notions needed to complete the garment are listed on the back of the pattern envelope. **Notions** are small items needed to construct a garment. They include thread, buttons, trims, fasteners, seam binding, and bias tape. Purchase these items when you buy your fabric to make sure the colors match your fabric.

Math Connection

Determining Project Cost

Joe is making pull-on jogging pants with side pockets. The pattern calls for 2¼ yards of 60-inch wide fabric. The fabric sells for $4.98 per yard. The sale price of the pattern is $1.99. One-inch-wide elastic for the leg bottoms and waist costs $1.59. Joe was able to use thread left from an earlier project. How much will the jogging pants cost?

First Joe determines how much the fabric will cost. He multiplies 2.25 (2¼) yards by $4.98 to find the cost of the fabric.

$2.25 \times \$4.98 = \$11.21$

Then Joe adds the cost of the fabric to the cost of the pattern and elastic to determine his project's total cost.

$\$11.21 + \$1.99 + \$1.59 = \$14.79$

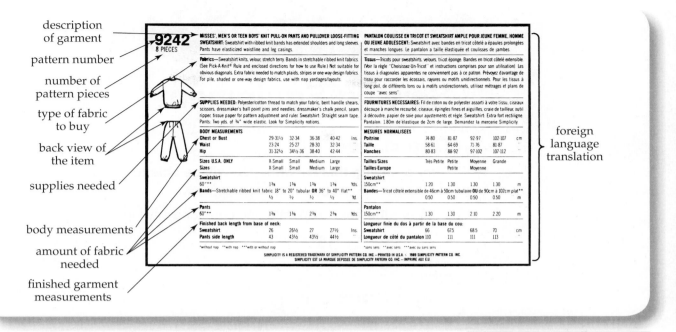

Labels pointing to the diagram (left side):
- description of garment
- pattern number
- number of pattern pieces
- type of fabric to buy
- back view of the item
- supplies needed
- body measurements
- amount of fabric needed
- finished garment measurements

Label (right side):
- foreign language translation

20-6

The back of the pattern envelope includes information you will need when purchasing your supplies.

If you cannot match the exact color, choose a slightly darker color. Thread will appear lighter when sewn. Polyester or cotton-covered polyester thread is good for working with most fabrics on a standard sewing machine.

Reading
Review

1. Name the five most commonly used natural fibers and list two characteristics of each.
2. Name five common manufactured fibers and list two characteristics of each.
3. Explain the basic difference between weaving and knitting.
4. Why are finishes applied to fabrics?
5. What should you look for when choosing a pattern that will be easy to sew?
6. List three factors to consider before choosing a fabric.
7. What three factors will help you locate the number of yards of fabric to buy on a yardage chart?
8. What should you do when you cannot find thread that is an exact match for your fabric?

Instead of discarding unwanted notions, trade them for items needed in sewing projects you are planning. Get together with other sewers to swap notions, patterns, and even fabrics.

Section 20-2

Sewing Equipment

Objectives

After studying this section, you will be able to

- **determine** the basic sewing supplies.
- **describe** how to operate and care for a sewing machine.
- **list** the uses of a serger.

Key Terms

lockstitch

bobbin

presser foot

feed dogs

thread-tension regulator

serger

looper

Having the proper equipment and knowing how to use it will help you become a successful sewer. There are certain supplies every sewer needs. Begin by purchasing the basics, **20-7**. As you progress, you may want to add equipment that will simplify construction and reduce sewing time.

Small Equipment

One of the first things you will need is a sewing box to keep sewing items in one place. Use dividers or small containers to keep small equipment organized.

You will need measuring tools, cutting tools, marking tools, pins and needles, and pressing equipment. All of these items can be bought in fabric stores.

Measuring Tools

A *tape measure* is essential for taking body measurements. Most tape measures are 60 inches long. Make sure the tape is made from a material that will not stretch. Choose one that has protectors on the ends to give the tape durability. Also check to be sure the numbers are clearly visible and printed on both sides of the tape.

A *sewing gauge* is a 6-inch metal or plastic ruler with a sliding marker. It is used to measure small areas, such as hems, cuffs, and the space between buttons.

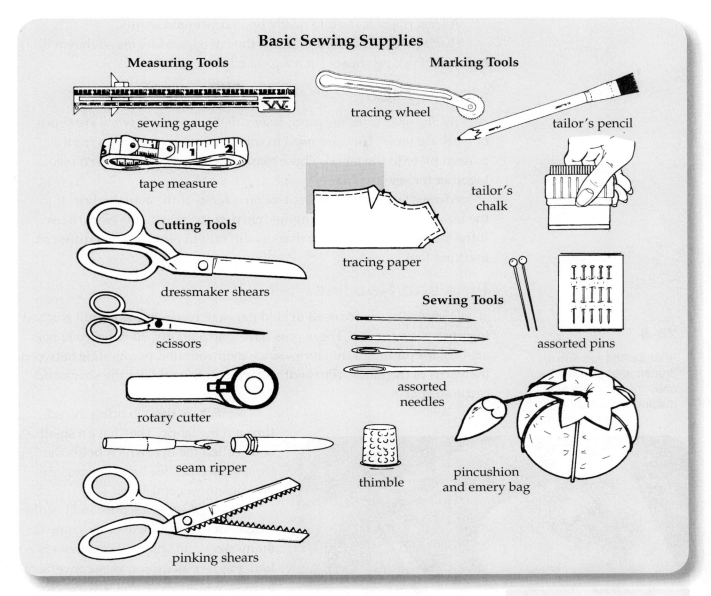

Basic Sewing Supplies

Measuring Tools

sewing gauge

tape measure

Cutting Tools

dressmaker shears

scissors

rotary cutter

seam ripper

pinking shears

Marking Tools

tracing wheel

tailor's pencil

tailor's chalk

tracing paper

Sewing Tools

assorted needles

assorted pins

thimble

pincushion and emery bag

20-7

These are the basic sewing supplies you will need.

Cutting Tools

Having sharp, quality shears and scissors is very important in sewing. Before buying cutting tools, always test them to be sure they cut cleanly. Shears and scissors come in various sizes and have many different uses. Make your selections based on what you will be cutting.

Dressmaker shears are used to cut pattern pieces from the fabric. A bent handle allows the fabric to lie flat on the worktable while cutting. This makes it easier to cut smooth, accurate edges. Shears are available in right- and left-handed versions.

Scissors are smaller and shorter than shears and have round handles. They are used for trimming, grading, clipping seams, and snipping threads.

A *rotary cutter* also cuts pattern pieces from the fabric. It cuts with a round blade as the tool is pushed along the pattern cutting lines. The tool must be used with a mat specially designed for cutting on a table surface.

A *seam ripper* is used to neatly open unwanted seams.

Pinking shears are used to finish the cut edge of seams so they will not ravel. Pinking shears cut a zigzag edge.

Marking Tools

Tracing wheels, tracing paper, tailor's chalk and *tailor's pencil* are types of marking tools. They are used to transfer pattern markings from a pattern piece to the fabric. These markings help you put pattern pieces together for sewing.

Always test your marking tool on a scrap of the actual fabric. If the mark comes off easily without marring the fabric, it is okay to use. If the fabric is marred or the mark is difficult to remove, try a different marking tool.

Pins and Needles

Dressmaker pins are used to hold garment pieces in place until stitched together permanently. These pins have sharp points, **20-8**. *Ballpoint pins* are best for pinning knit fabrics since their rounded points slide between the yarns of the fabric. (Pins with sharp points could cut the yarns and cause snags.)

Needles are used to bring thread through the fabric. They have a small hole, called the eye, which holds the thread. Needles for hand sewing are available in several sizes.

A *pincushion* holds pins and needles when not in use. Pincushions come in many sizes and shapes. Some sewers find a wrist pincushion very convenient to wear while fitting and sewing. Some pincushions have an *emery bag* attached for sharpening pins and needles.

When sewing by hand, you may want to use a *thimble* to prevent the needle from pricking your finger. It should fit snugly on your middle finger. If you are a beginning sewer, a thimble may feel awkward at first. With a little practice, you will see how useful it can be.

Pressing Equipment

When sewing a garment, pressing is as important as stitching. Careful construction alone will not result in a well-made garment. "Press as you sew" is a good rule to follow. Each

20-8

After seams are sewn, dressmaker pins are then used for adjusting fit and holding hemlines.

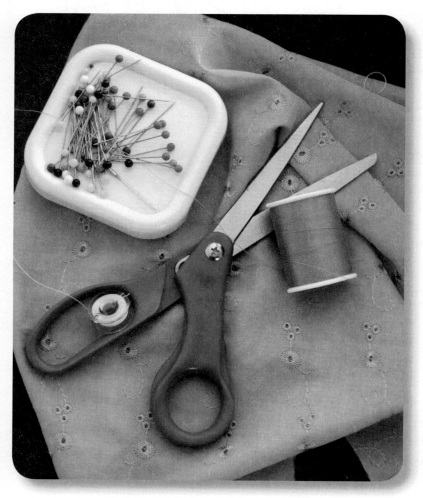

construction line you sew should be pressed before another seam is stitched across it.

Several pieces of pressing equipment are recommended, but an *iron* is the most important. Most irons have a temperature guide that gives the proper heat setting for various types of fabric. A steam iron is more convenient to use for pressing, but a dry iron can also be used.

A *pressing cloth* is used to protect the fabric from overheating and shining when an iron is used. These cloths are made of cheesecloth or muslin.

The *ironing board* needs to be sturdy, level, and tapered to a narrow width at one end. The ironing board should be covered with a pad and cover. A silicone treated cover will prevent scorching and sticking. Keep the cover clean and smooth since a wrinkled cover can cause wrinkles in a garment.

A *tailor's ham* is a firmly stuffed, oval cushion used to shape curved areas while pressing. It is used for pressing a rounded shape into darts, sleeve caps, and curved seams.

The Sewing Machine

Learning how to operate a sewing machine is easier when you have a basic understanding of how it works.

The basic parts of a sewing machine are shown in **20-9**. The job of the sewing machine is to secure pieces of fabric together with a **lockstitch**. This stitch uses thread from both the upper and lower parts of the machine.

20-9

Knowing the names of the parts of the sewing machine is a first step in learning how to operate it.

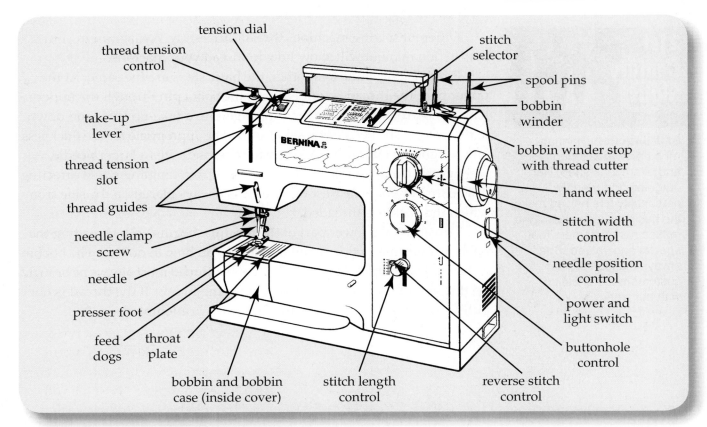

Mental Health Awareness

Creativity and Mental Health

Sewing is a type of art form. You can use this art form as an expression of yourself by creating unique garments and accessories. Building your sewing skills and wearing your finished garments can also positively impact your self-esteem.

Self-direction. Hannah runs her own tailoring and alterations shop. Her outgoing and friendly personality has helped make the business a success. She makes her customers feel special and valued. She always makes sure her customers are satisfied with her work.

Thread from the upper part of the machine is carried by way of the needle down through the fabric to pick up the lower thread. The lower thread comes from the **bobbin**. The two threads lock in the middle of the fabric layers to make a secure stitch.

A knee or foot control sends power to the machine when pressure is applied. The **presser foot** holds the fabric in place as the machine stitches. The **feed dogs** are two small rows of teeth that move the fabric forward under the presser foot. Stitches are made when power is applied. The needle should always be in the highest position before sewing begins.

Two **thread-tension regulators** are found on the sewing machine. The tension, or pull between the upper and lower threads, must be balanced for a proper stitch to form. A perfectly balanced stitch looks identical on the top and bottom of the fabric. Generally, any adjustment can be made with the upper-tension regulator that applies tension to the upper thread. The instruction manual with your machine will show you how to adjust the tension.

Two basic types of sewing machines are in use today—mechanical and computerized machines. With mechanical machines, you dial the stitch you want and adjust the length, width, and tension. With computerized machines, the preferred length, width, and tension are preprogrammed for you. However, you can change the settings and override the computer. Some computerized machines have hundreds of decorative and special stitches programmed into them. Most feature simple, one-step buttonhole operations.

Threading the Machine

Different sewing machines thread differently. A diagram in your instruction manual will show how to thread your machine.

From one machine to another, the basic steps are the same. At the upper part, the thread is guided from the spool pin through the upper tension control. From there the thread goes to a take-up lever and down to the needle. The needle you select should be appropriate for the thickness and weight of your fabric. A larger number indicates a larger needle.

Several thread guides keep the thread from tangling while directing it. The thread guide nearest the needle is always placed on the side from which the needle is threaded.

Threading the lower part of the machine begins with threading the bobbin. Your instruction manual will tell you how to do this. The bobbin is then placed in the bobbin case. The bobbin thread must always be brought up through the needle hole before beginning to sew. If the thread is not pulled up, a knot will form as the first stitch is attempted.

Types of Stitches

Almost all sewing machines make at least two basic types of stitches—the common straight stitch and the frequently used zigzag stitch. Some sewing machines can make a variety of stitches in addition to these two. See **20-10**.

The *straight stitch* is a lockstitch used for holding layers of fabric together. Its length can be adjusted to correspond with different purposes. A typical stitch length is 10 to 15 stitches per inch. A long stitch length, six stitches per inch, can be used for temporarily holding fabric pieces in place, called *machine basting*. A length of 18 to 21 stitches per inch is often used to reinforce stress areas in garments.

The *zigzag stitch* is a sideways stitch. It is often used to overcast seam edges that would otherwise ravel. A short zigzag stitch is used for buttonholes. A variation of the zigzag stitch is also used to sew stretch-knit fabrics. This allows seams to give slightly with the fabric. The zigzag stitch can be adjusted by using the stitch length and stitch-width regulators.

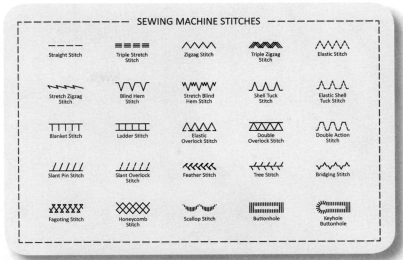

Berezka_Klo/Shutterstock.com

20-10

In addition to the basic straight stitch and zigzag stitch, many sewing machines create other functional (blind hem) and decorative (scallop stitch) stitches such as these.

Caring for the Machine

Regularly cleaning a sewing machine will result in fewer problems. Your instruction manual will have step-by-step directions for cleaning your machine.

Cleaning frequently with a soft cloth and small brush is a must. Use a small brush to remove lint from the bobbin case and under the feed dogs.

Always use the correct type of needle for your machine and the right size for your fabric. Your instruction manual will have guidelines for selecting the correct needle. Replace needles if they become bent or nicked. Needles dull easily and can damage both your fabric and your machine.

Sewing machines should be oiled periodically. Your instruction manual will tell you how often to oil your machine. It will also show where oil should be applied. After oiling your machine, be sure to wipe away any excess oil. Then sew on a scrap of cloth to remove any remaining oil before sewing your good fabric.

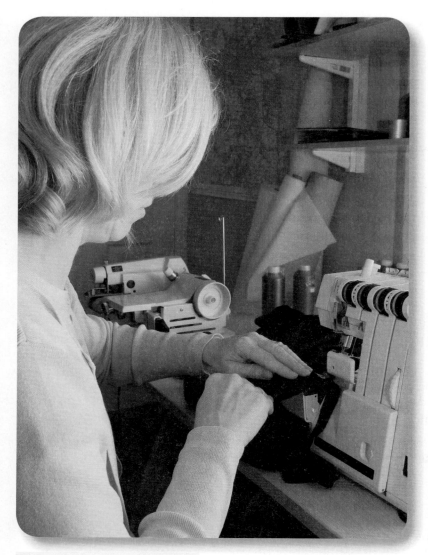

20-11

Learning to use the serger can save you time as you create your own unique fashions.

The Serger

Sergers are high-speed sewing machines that can stitch, trim, and finish seams in one simple step, **20-11**. They were originally designed for the ready-to-wear industry. Now they are available for home use.

The home sewer can obtain professional results by using a serger. The outer edges of garments can be finished without the need for facings, ribbings, or bands. Narrow or rolled hems can be made, such as those found on scarves or tablecloths. Sergers can also produce a blind hemming stitch. Stretch fabrics are easily sewn with a serger. Decorative stitching is popular for embellishing T-shirts, sweatshirts, and similar garments.

Sergers use two, three, four, or five threads and one or two needles. Sergers do not have bobbins. Instead they have one to three **loopers**, both upper and lower. The needle threads intertwine with the looper threads to form stitches. Sergers also have upper and lower knives that trim the seam allowance before the seam is finished.

Though sergers are fast and perform many functions, they cannot replace a conventional sewing machine. A conventional sewing machine is needed for topstitching and buttonholes. Some people also prefer to insert zippers with a conventional machine.

Safety with Sewing Tools

Knowing and using basic safety precautions is important for keeping the sewing area safe for you and others. Follow the safety recommendations pertaining to the tools used in the sewing area, **20-12**. Irons can cause fires and burns. Scissors, pins, and other common tools can cause cuts and wounds. When using electricity, electric shock is always a possibility. In addition, appliance cords can cause people to trip and fall.

Preventing Sewing-Area Hazards

Fires and Burns	• Fill a steam iron with water while unplugged. Let a hot iron cool before emptying it. • Keep your hands and face, especially your eyes, away from steam and heated water. • Rest a hot iron on its heel between uses, and turn it off during periods of nonuse. • Do not allow the electrical cord or any other item to rest against the iron's hot surface. • Let the iron cool before returning it to storage.
Cuts and Wounds	• Keep the blades of scissors and shears closed when not in use. Keep fingers away from moving needles and the serger's cutting blades while sewing. • Use rotary cutters on an appropriate cutting mat, always cutting away from the body. • Avoid placing pins and other tools in your mouth. • Immediately pick up pins and tools that fall to the floor. • Put tools away that are not being used. • Do not point sharp tools at others. When passing a sharp tool to another person, carefully grasp the dangerous end of the tool so the other person can grasp the handle or blunt end.
Electric Shock	• Make sure the switch of an electrical appliance is in the off position before connecting it to, or disconnecting it from, the outlet. • Do not operate an appliance with a damaged electrical cord. • Do not handle electrical appliances with hands that are wet or immersed in any solution. • Unplug an appliance by grasping the plug, not yanking the cord.
Trips and Falls	• Keep paths free of electrical cords. • Unplug and roll up the cord of any appliance not in use.

Reading
Review

20-12

Keep your sewing area safe by removing potential hazards.

1. Explain how the use of dressmaker shears differs from the use of scissors.
2. What is the "press as you sew" rule?
3. If a machine stitch does not look the same on both the top and bottom of the fabric, what needs to be adjusted?
4. What three functions can sergers perform in one fast operation?
5. State four safety hazards that can take place in a sewing area.

Chapter 20 Review

Summary

Knowledge of fabrics—their fiber content, construction, and finishes—will help you select the right fabric for your project.

Before you can select a pattern, you must determine your figure type and size. Taking accurate body measurements is the first step. Your height and body proportions determine your figure type.

The pattern envelope will list recommended fabrics as well as the notions needed to complete the project. Some fabrics are more difficult to sew than others. The pattern sheet also gives a measurement chart and other project details.

Some basic pieces of equipment are needed for sewing. Measuring, cutting, and marking tools are needed, as well as pins, needles, and pressing equipment. The sewing machine is the most important piece of equipment and the most expensive. Learn how the sewing machine operates and give it proper care to keep it running smoothly. As you gain sewing experience, you may decide a serger would be useful. No matter what sewing tools you use, always use them safely.

Critical
Thinking

1. **Compare and contrast.** Which fabric finishes would you like applied to the garments you wear? Which finishes would you like applied to the fabrics you use in your home? Explain your answers.

2. **Identify priorities.** What criteria would you consider when selecting a pattern for yourself? Since trade-offs sometimes need to be made, list your criteria in order of priority.

3. **Recognize value.** In what careers would sewing skills be particularly helpful? somewhat helpful?

4. **Analyze pros and cons.** List some of the advantages of sewing your own clothes. Name some disadvantages.

5. **Analyze trends.** What do you see as the future for home sewing? How have changes in society impacted the home sewing industry?

21st Century
Applications

6. **Global awareness.** For each natural fiber discussed in the text, research which country exports the greatest quantity. Show your findings in a map or table with the information source(s) listed in a footnote.

7. **Flexibility and adaptability.** Research five common mistakes that can occur when using a sewing machine or preparing materials for a sewing project. For each sewing-related mishap, write a brief response for how a beginning sewer could adapt to the situation and correct the problem. Keep your list nearby as you begin sewing projects.

Core
Skills

8. **Science.** Examine swatches of several different fabrics under a microscope. For each, name the type of fabric construction (such as *knit* or *woven*) and make a simple sketch of what you observe. Try to identify the fiber content of each sample.

9. **Reading.** Study the history of sheep in the United States and how sheep influenced the settling of the West. In what regions of the United States are wool-bearing sheep raised? Write a report on your findings.

10. **History, writing.** Prepare a written report on natural sources of dye used in the past. Identify the specific kinds of barks, leaves, berries, and flowers used to create each color.

11. **Math.** Practice determining amounts of fabric to purchase for several hypothetical garment views and fabric widths. You may want to visit a fabric store and find fabrics you like. Identify the yardage required and calculate the total cost of each fabric.

12. **Writing.** Research and prepare a report on Elias Howe. Include his struggle to patent the sewing machine and its impact on the apparel industry.

13. **Speaking.** Choose one of the manufactured fibers to research. Use presentation software to give a class presentation on your findings.

14. **Speaking.** Use the Internet to research one of the finishing processes listed. Give an oral report to the class, including the addresses of the websites on which you found your information.

Leadership
Development

For Fashion Design or Fashion Construction, you can form a panel of FCCLA members and local business owners to research and discuss the effect of world conditions on fabric prices and production. The panel should cover import/export restrictions and taxes, costs of raw materials, price subsidies, and the effect of natural disasters on fiber production.

Portfolio
Builder

Clothes are made from a wide variety of fabrics. The more you know about fabrics, the better choices you will make. Imagine you are in your chosen career and are going to sew or shop for several garments. Write a paper describing your career and the type of fabric that would predominate in your work wardrobe. If possible, obtain samples of the fabric. Place the paper and samples of fabric in your portfolio. Fabric characteristics to keep in mind include: shape retention, comfort, durability, ease of care, and affordability.

Journal
Writing

You have realized that the type of care some fabrics require can be costly. You cannot afford to add the cost of dry cleaning to the price of a garment. You also have little time for washing clothes. While choosing a fabric, you read its care requirements. You will need to wash the garment separately in cold water, avoid chlorine bleach, let it drip-dry, and press with a cool iron.

Write About It: *Would you consider this fabric a good buy? What other factors might prompt you to buy the fabric anyway?*

Chapter 21
Apparel Construction

Reading Prep

Search the Internet for sources of sewing tips and techniques. Record the most helpful sites for future use.

Concept Organizer

Create a spider/web diagram. List the characteristics of basic sewing methods. Include stitching techniques, darts, gathers, seams, fasteners, and hems.

G-WLEARNING.com

Click on the activity icon to visit www.g-wlearning.com/comprehensive/8062 to access online vocabulary activities using key terms from the chapter.

Begin with the Pattern

Objectives

After studying this section, you will be able to

- **explain** the meaning of pattern symbols.
- **adjust** pattern length and width.

Key Terms

cutting line	stitching line	grainline arrow
notch	seam allowance	adjustment line
dot	grain	alteration
multisize pattern		

Like other projects that you complete yourself, sewing projects require instructions. That is why you need a pattern. Sewing patterns include not only the pattern pieces, but also a detailed set of instructions. Most of the instructions are found on the pattern guide sheet.

The Pattern Guide Sheet

Every pattern has a *pattern guide sheet*. See **21-1**. The guide sheet has step-by-step directions that will lead you through each phase of your sewing project. Read and study the guide sheet before beginning your project.

Understanding Pattern Symbols

The pattern guide sheet tells you which pattern pieces are needed for each view you make. From the pattern envelope, remove the pattern pieces you need. If the pieces are wrinkled, press them with a warm, dry iron.

The pattern pieces contain many lines, terms, and symbols. Many of the

21-1

The pattern guide sheet, shown in the right corner, describes and presents step-by-step instructions on how to use the pattern successfully.

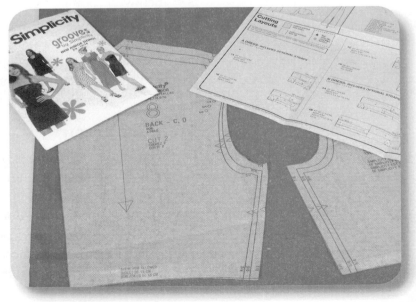

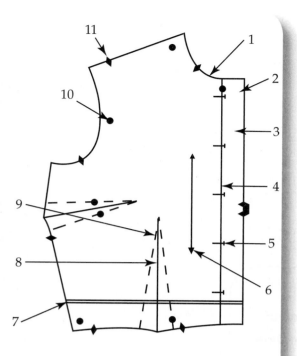

1. cutting line
2. seam allowance
3. stitching line
4. center front
5. buttonhole placement
6. grainline arrow
7. adjustment lines
8. fold line for dart
9. dart stitching line
10. dot
11. notch

21-2

Knowledge of pattern symbols is important to sewing quality.

symbols are used when you lay the pattern pieces on the fabric. Others are used when you sew the pieces together. A pattern with the most common pattern symbols is shown in **21-2**.

Cutting Lines

The **cutting line** borders the pattern piece and is indicated with a bold line. On this line you may see several diamond-shaped symbols called **notches**. There may be single notches, double notches, and even triple notches. Do not cut through them. You will match these notches when you sew the pieces together. **Dots** are also used for matching seams and other construction details.

Practically all patterns available today are multisize. **Multisize patterns** contain three or more sizes on one tissue pattern. You simply cut along the appropriate line for your figure size.

Making adjustments in multisize patterns is easy. Wherever an adjustment is needed, simply cut on the cutting lines for one of the other sizes. For instance, if you need to increase the waistline, gradually angle as you cut to the line for the next larger size.

When making separates, there is another advantage in using multisize patterns. If a person is a different size above the waist than below, there is no need to buy two patterns.

Stitching Lines

The **stitching line** is the seamline, which is ⅝-inch inside the cutting line. On single-size patterns, it appears as a broken line. On multisize patterns, however, the stitching line is not marked. The space between the cutting line and the stitching line is the **seam allowance**. It generally is ⅝-inch wide. Sometimes the pattern guide sheet uses small arrows to indicate the best direction for stitching.

A ⅝-inch gauge is a standard feature at the throat plate of sewing machines. It alerts sewers where to align the edge of the fabric while sewing. When the fabric touches the ⅝-inch mark, the sewing needle is positioned directly over the stitching line.

Grainline Arrows

The two basic directions that yarns run in a woven fabric is called the **grain**. Fabrics have a lengthwise and a crosswise grain. A **grainline arrow** indicates the direction a pattern piece should be placed on the fabric. Usually, this arrow should align the lengthwise grain of the fabric.

Sometimes short arrows point to the edge of a pattern piece. This means the piece must be placed on a fold of the fabric. A cutting line is absent at a fold line to signal that fabric should not be cut.

Adjustment Lines

Lines that indicate where to shorten or lengthen a pattern piece are called **adjustment lines**. These two parallel lines usually extend across the pattern piece. Some pattern pieces will tell you to adjust the length at the hemline.

Altering Your Pattern

A well-fitted garment is comfortable to wear and well proportioned to your body. The garment is neither too big nor too small. It conforms to body contours without binding, pulling, sagging, or hanging unevenly. Proper fit is one of the keys to successful sewing.

Patterns cannot be made to fit every person perfectly. **Alterations** are changes to the size of a pattern or garment to achieve better fit. Carefully selecting a pattern according to your body measurements and figure type will reduce the need for alterations.

If you are using a multisize pattern, alterations to the bust, waist, and hip are easily made. At the point where your size changes, simply draw tapering lines to connect one size to the other.

Alterations should be made on pattern pieces before laying them out on the fabric. To see how well your pattern fits you, you can *pin fit* the pattern. To do this, pin the darts closed. Then pin the pattern pieces together at the seamlines and carefully try on the pattern. Pin the center front and back to your clothing. Then check sleeve, skirt, and pant lengths. You can also check the back and front waist lengths. Check the widths of various pattern pieces, too. Note changes that need to be made.

Adjusting Pattern Length

Adjusting length is one of the most common and least difficult alterations to make. For example, you may be long waisted or short waisted. You may have short arms or long arms. Sometimes length must be adjusted in more than one area of the pattern. Alterations are made where they will not interfere with the lines of the garment.

To shorten a pattern piece, make a fold in the pattern piece between the adjustment lines. The fold should be half the amount to be shortened. Measure the fold to see that it is even. Then tape it in place.

To lengthen a pattern piece, cut between the adjustment lines. Place a piece of paper under the two pattern pieces. Measure the needed distance between the lines. Tape the pattern to the paper. Measure the distance again to check your accuracy. See **21-3**.

21-3

To lengthen a pattern piece, cut between the adjustment lines. Allow room between the pattern pieces for the amount of fabric to be added.

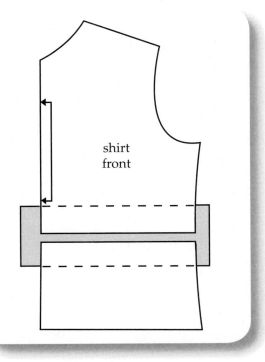

shirt front

Math Connection

Adjusting Pattern Width

Emma wants to adjust the width of the waist on a pants pattern. She needs to decrease the waistline from 26 inches to 24 inches. First, Emma must determine the total decrease.

26 inches − 24 inches = 2 inches

Next, Emma divides the total decrease by 4.

2 inches ÷ 4 = ½ inch

Emma must now measure in from the cutting line ½ inch at the side waistline edge. She then redraws the cutting line, tapering it to the hipline. (If the pants have a waistband, she would shorten it at the same spots by the same amount for a total decrease of 2 inches.)

Adjusting Pattern Width

Width adjustments may need to be made in the sleeve, waist, hips, or thighs. These adjustments should be made in both front and back pieces. Making adjustments to new multisize patterns is easy, as described earlier. With used multisize patterns, however, increasing the width of pattern pieces is more difficult. Waistline alterations in pants and skirts are made at the side seams. See **21-4**. To increase the waistline, tape a strip of paper along the side edges of the front and back pattern pieces. Measure from the side cutting line at the waist edge of the front pattern piece. The width added to this pattern piece should be one-fourth of the total waistline increase. (One-fourth of the increase times four edges—each edge at both side seams—equals the total increase.) Make a dot at the extended point and redraw the cutting line, tapering to the hipline. Do the same with the back pattern piece. To decrease the waistline, measure in from the cutting line one-fourth of the total amount to be removed. Redraw the cutting line, tapering to the hipline. If there is a waistband, lengthen or shorten it the same amount as the total waist adjustment.

If a garment is too small for the hips, wrinkling and pulling will occur around the hipline. If a pants or skirt pattern is too large, there will be extra fullness. Hipline width is altered the same as waistline width. One-fourth the needed fullness is added or removed along the length of the side seams. Taking bigger or smaller darts is another way to adjust waistline width.

21-4

To increase or decrease the width of the waist, measure in or out one-fourth of the needed amount at the side waistline edge. Redraw the cutting lines, tapering to the hipline.

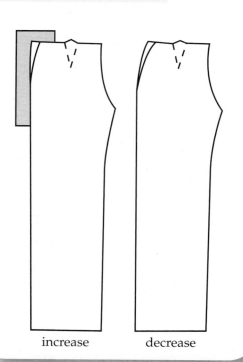

increase   decrease

Reading
Review

1. What pattern symbols are used to match garment pieces when sewing?
2. True or false. To shorten a pattern, make a fold that is half the total amount to be shortened.
3. True or false. To widen a pattern piece, add half of the total alteration needed to the front side seam.

Section 21-2

Pattern Layout, Cutting, and Marking

Objectives

After studying this section, you will be able to

- **choose** the appropriate cutting layout.
- **pin** the pattern pieces to the fabric correctly.
- **cut** the fabric and transfer pattern markings accurately.

Key Terms

cutting layout   selvage

After your pattern and fabric are prepared, you are ready to lay out your pattern. For this step, you will again need to refer to your pattern guide sheet.

The Pattern Layout

The pattern guide sheet shows many cutting layouts, **21-5**. A **cutting layout** is a drawing that shows how to fold fabric and place pattern pieces for cutting. Layouts are shown for different garments, views, sizes, and fabric widths. You will need to find the layout for the pattern version you make. Then look for your size and your fabric width. Circle the layout you will use. This will help you find your layout quickly each time you need to refer to it.

Different layouts are also shown for fabrics with surface texture such as velvet, suede, flannel, velour, and corduroy. When these fabrics are viewed in one direction, they appear light and shiny. When viewed in the opposite direction, they appear darker. To prevent a garment from having a two-tone look, pattern pieces must all be cut in the same direction. The layout for fabrics *with nap* is your guide to placing pattern pieces on these fabrics.

Folding the Fabric

Fold your fabric according to the instructions given for your layout. Fabric is usually folded with the right sides together. The guide sheet may tell you to use a lengthwise fold or a crosswise fold. A *lengthwise fold* brings the two selvages together. A **selvage** is one of two finished

JACKET
use pieces 1 thru 8

58″ 60″ (150cm)
fabric
with nap
size extra-small

sizes small, medium

sizes large, extra-large

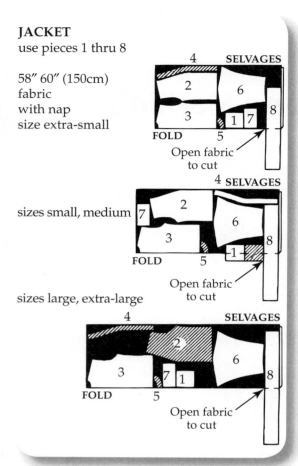

21-5

Several cutting layouts will be shown on a pattern guide sheet.

Adaptability. Bridget works in a busy fabric and craft store. Today, several coworkers have called off sick. Bridget was asked to take on the duties of an absent coworker. Although she is unfamiliar with the coworker's tasks, she does the best she can to keep the department running smoothly by adapting to the situation.

lengthwise edges on a piece of fabric. These edges are stronger than the rest of the fabric and will not ravel.

A *crosswise fold* brings the two cut edges together. Sometimes a *doublefold* is used, which brings each selvage edge toward the center. Measure to be sure you fold the fabric the same amount for the entire length of the fabric. Watch for layout notes, such as the words *selvage, single thickness,* and *double thickness.*

Placing Pattern Pieces

Place pattern pieces on the fabric as pictured in the pattern layout. Most pattern pieces are placed on the fabric with the printed side up. Pattern pieces to be placed with the printed side down will appear shaded on the guide sheet.

Lay all pattern pieces on the fabric before pinning any in place. This allows you to make sure they all fit on the fabric. Plaids, stripes, and checks need special attention during layout so designs will match at seamlines and front openings.

Pinning

Before pinning the pattern pieces to the fabric, they must be placed on the fabric grain. To do this, pin one end of the grainline arrow to the fabric to hold it in place. Measure from the pinned end of the arrow to the fabric selvage. Then measure from the other end of the grainline arrow to the selvage. See **21-6**. If measurements differ, adjust them so the grainline arrow is a uniform distance from the selvage edge or the fold of the fabric. Then pin the pattern piece in place.

Gently smooth the pattern from the grainline. Finish pinning by placing pins every 6 inches inside the cutting lines. Place pins at right angles, perpendicular to the pattern edges. Pin diagonally in corners.

Watch for pattern pieces that must be placed on the fold of the fabric. Pin the fold edge of the pattern piece along the fold first. You will never cut the edge of a fold. Then smooth out the pattern and pin the remaining edges to the fabric.

After pinning each pattern piece, compare your work with the layout guide. Your pattern layout should be accurate before you start to cut.

Cutting the Fabric

Dressmaker shears are best for cutting out pattern pieces. Because the handle is bent, the blades glide along the cutting surface. This allows the fabric to lie flat so cutting lines are obvious.

Find the cutting line on the pattern piece for your size. This is especially important when using multisize patterns since the cutting lines lie close together and occasionally cross one another. Pay attention to any size adjustments you have made to the pattern. Be sure to also cut precisely around any notches on the cutting line.

Marking the Fabric

Markings on the pattern guide you in putting the garment together. Markings for center front, center back, darts, buttons, buttonholes, dots, and pockets all need to be transferred to the fabric. Seamlines do not need to be marked since a ⅝-inch seam is presumed.

When marking, remove only the pins that are in the way. Leave enough pins to hold the pattern and fabric in place.

Using Tracing Paper

Several methods can be used to transfer pattern markings. Tracing paper and a tracing wheel are often used to mark firmly woven and knitted fabrics. Tracing quickly and accurately transfers the marks.

Test the tracing paper on a scrap of your fabric first since it may mark some fabrics permanently. Before marking, place a magazine or piece of cardboard under the fabric. This will protect the cutting surface from the sharp teeth of the tracing wheel. Make sure the marking is visible on the wrong side of your fabric. Also, check to be sure no marking shows on the right side.

Two pieces of tracing paper are needed to mark both fabric layers. Place one piece of paper right side up, under the bottom layer of fabric. Slip the other piece right side down, between the pattern and the top layer of fabric. Make sure both sheets of tracing paper face the wrong sides of the fabric.

Carefully roll the wheel along the markings. To ensure accuracy, use a ruler to help trace straight lines, **21-7.** Use only enough pressure to make the markings visible on the wrong side of the fabric. Too much pressure may mar the fabric with holes or transfer color to the right side of the fabric.

Living Green

After cutting out a garment, save the scraps. They can be repurposed. For example, you can use scraps as pieces in a quilt, for cleaning or paint cloths, or for stuffing toys made of fabric.

21-6

Each end of the grainline arrow should measure the same distance to the selvage.

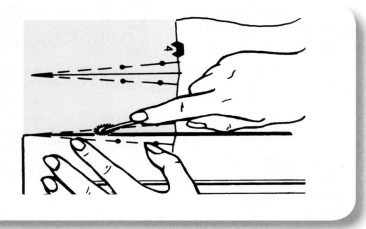

21-7

A ruler will help you trace straight lines when marking with a tracing wheel and tracing paper.

Reading
Review

1. Name five factors that determine which cutting layout you will use.
2. What are you to do with the grainline arrow on a pattern piece?
3. True or false. Notches should be cut inward.
4. Explain the use of a tracing wheel to transfer pattern markings to fabrics.

Section 21-3

Basic Sewing Techniques

Objectives

After studying this section, you will be able to

- **perform** directional stitching and staystitching.
- **construct** darts and gathers.
- **sew** seams.
- **complete** the construction of sewing projects that include fasteners and hems.

Key Terms

directional stitching	gathering	grading
staystitching	seam	clipping
dart	backstitching	notching
easing	trimming	thread shank

Sewing can be both fun and productive. If you follow good sewing techniques, you can make clothes that you will be proud to wear. They will look as good as clothes purchased from stores or even better. Custom-made clothes will probably fit you better, too. Making a good-looking garment requires good sewing techniques from beginning to end.

Stitching Techniques

Before you begin constructing your project, you need to be familiar with basic stitching techniques. These are directional stitching and staystitching.

Directional Stitching

Stitching in the direction of the grain is called **directional stitching**. It makes the yarns lie flat and feel smooth, **21-8**. Directional stitching prevents garments from puckering or stretching along seamlines. It should be used whenever a seam is sewn.

Staystitching

Staystitching is a line of machine stitching that keeps the edges of garment pieces from stretching out of shape as you sew. Staystitching is done through a single layer of fabric ½-inch from the cut edges. Bias and curved edges, such as necklines and armholes, are especially important areas to staystitch. See **21-9**.

Bias means any diagonal direction. Bias edges include all except those aligning the lengthwise or crosswise grain.

Staystitching is needed to stabilize knits, other stretchy fabrics, and loose weaves. Staystitching is not needed on fabrics that do not stretch. Some fabric finishes permanently set yarns in place, preventing the fabric from stretching.

Darts and Gathers

After your garment is staystitched, the guide sheet usually instructs you to make any darts or gathers. These begin to give shape to your garment. Since darts and gathers cross seamlines, they are made before seams are sewn.

21-8

For directional stitching, you sew with the grain so seams lie flat for a smooth appearance.

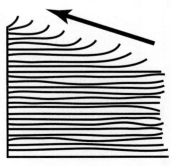
against the grain

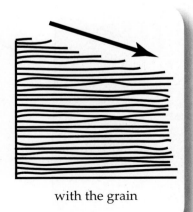
with the grain

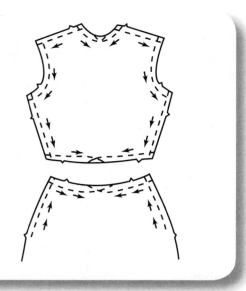

21-9

Staystitch bias and curved edges of garment pieces to prevent them from stretching out of shape as you sew.

21-10

The last three stitches of a dart should be made on the fold to prevent puckering at the point of the dart.

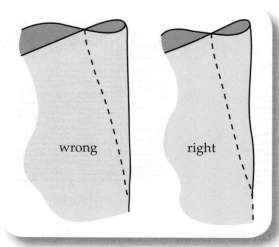

wrong   right

Darts

A **dart** is a construction element used to give shape and fullness to a garment. A dart helps fit a flat piece of fabric to the curves of the body. It is made by stitching to a point through a fold in the fabric, **21-10**. The last three stitches should be made in the fold to prevent the point of the dart from puckering. The larger the body curves, the larger the darts need to be.

All darts point to the fullest part of body curves. On skirts and slacks, darts begin at the waistline and taper to the hipline, allowing fullness around the hips. In jackets, shirts, and blouses, darts taper to the fullest part of the chest.

Gathering and Easing

Gathering and easing are techniques used when two seamlines of unequal length are sewn together. **Easing** involves making a piece of fabric fit a slightly smaller piece of fabric as a flat, curved seam is sewn. Easing provides needed fabric fullness at certain points on the body, usually where sleeves meet front and back sections.

To ease a longer piece of fabric into a shorter one, pin the two ends first. Then distribute the rest of the fullness evenly between these two pins, being sure to match notches, dots, and other markings. Insert additional pins at right angles to the seamline. Stitch the seam with the longer piece on top. Remove the pins only as you come to them. Try to avoid stitching any ripples or puckers into the seam.

When ripples and soft folds are desired at a seamline that joins two different lengths of fabric, **gathering** is used. The ripples and soft folds that result are called *gathers*. They yield a rounded shape. Gathers are often used at waistlines, cuffs, and the shoulder seams of puffy sleeves.

To make gathers, set the stitch length regulator on your machine for 6 to 8 stitches per inch for medium-weight fabrics. Two rows of long stitches are needed to make smooth, even gathers. Place the first row of stitches near the ⅛-inch seamline. Place the second row of stitches ¼-inch from the first row, inside the seam allowance. Do not backstitch. Leave at least three inches of thread at the ends of the stitching lines.

Pin the right sides of the two fabric pieces together, matching notches and other markings. Gently pull both bobbin threads at one end, working toward the center of the edge being gathered. (You will gather one side before the other.) Gather half of the longer fabric piece until it lies flat against half of the shorter one. Fasten the bobbin threads by wrapping them in a figure eight around the pin located where you began gathering. See **21-11**.

Repeat the gathering process at the other end. Distribute the gathers evenly and insert pins across the gathering stitches. Set your machine to a regular stitch length of about 12 stitches per inch. Stitch the two fabric pieces together with the gathered side up. Hold the fabric to prevent any folds from forming in the seam.

Seams

A **seam** is a row of stitching that joins garment pieces together. There are many types of seams used in sewing. The choice of a seam depends on the type and weight of the fabric and the durability desired. Fashion trends in structural and decorative lines may dictate seam choice.

The *plain seam* is the most common seam. A plain seam is made by placing right sides of the fabric together. Sew along the seamline with a ⅝-inch seam allowance, backstitching at both ends. **Backstitching** means to sew backward and forward in the same place for a few stitches to secure the thread ends. Press the seam to one side. Then press the seam open.

Trimming, Grading, Clipping, and Notching

When a curved seam is stitched, such as an armhole or neckline, it will need one of the following treatments to look neat and smooth. Always make sure not to cut the stitching.

Trimming means cutting away part of a seam allowance to reduce bulk in lightweight and medium-weight fabrics. Trimming removes a ⅜-inch strip of fabric along the length of the seam. Trimming is also used to remove bulk from corners and points. See **21-12**.

Grading means trimming each layer of the seam allowance to a different width. This is the best way to treat seams on heavier fabrics or seams with three or more fabric layers. Trim each layer ⅛-inch narrower than the next, keeping the smallest layer at least ¼-inch thick, **21-13**. When all the seams of a heavy fabric are cut alike, they form a noticeable ridge along seam lines.

Clipping is making straight cuts toward the stitching line, usually at ½-inch intervals. Clipping is used on seams that have an inward curve so the seam will not pucker when turned. **Notching** means cutting small wedges from the seam allowance. This removes excess fabric that would create noticeable bulk in seams with an outward curve. Clipping and notching are shown in **21-14**.

Seam Finishes

Seam finishes are treatments done after seams are sewn to prevent the raw edges of the seam allowances from raveling. They also improve the appearance of the

21-11

Secure threads by wrapping them around a pin in a figure eight (right). Then pull the opposite ends to form gathers (left).

21-12

Trim corners and points as shown to reduce bulk when seams are turned to the inside of the garment.

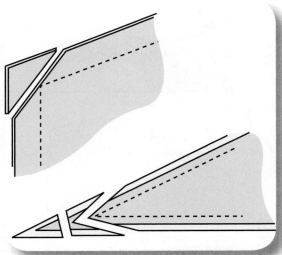

21-13

Grading a seam means trimming each seam allowance to a different width.

inside of the garment. The choice of a seam finish depends on the weight of the fabric and the degree to which it ravels. Some fabrics ravel very little and, therefore, need no further work on the raw edges. Others are loosely woven and require a seam finish.

A *pinked finish* is the easiest finish to do. Simply use pinking shears and cut close to the edge of the seam allowance through both fabric layers. Then press the seam open. Use a pinked finish only on fabrics that ravel slightly. To make a sturdier finish, you can also stitch close to the pinked edge of each seam allowance.

A *zigzag finish* is a quick and easy seam finish used on fabrics that ravel easily. To make a zigzag finish on a seam, press it open before stitching. Stitch through one seam allowance at a time.

Fasteners

Snaps, hooks and eyes, buttons, and hook-and-loop tape are types of fasteners used to close garments. When sewing on fasteners, make sure they are placed correctly. Garment edges should meet evenly and lie smoothly when fasteners are closed. Buttons are the most common fasteners.

The key to sewing on buttons correctly is to allow space for a thread shank. The **thread shank** provides room for the button to lie over the buttonhole fabric. It uses two strands of thread. The length of the shank depends on the thickness of the garment. To make a thread shank, place a toothpick over the button while sewing. Then remove the toothpick and pull the button up. Bring the threaded needle between the button and garment. Wind thread around the stitches several times. Then bring the thread to the wrong side of the garment and fasten with several stitches.

21-14

Clipping is used on inward curves. Notching is used on outward curves.

See **21-15**. Some buttons have shanks already attached. Simply sew these buttons securely in place.

Transfer buttonhole markings from the pattern. Follow the directions for making a buttonhole that came with your sewing machine.

Hems

Hemming is the final step in garment construction. A hem should be flat and unnoticeable on the outside of the garment. Having a neat, level hem is important to the overall appearance of the garment.

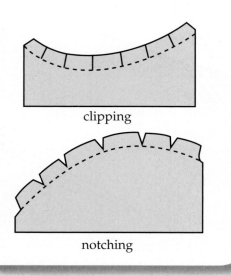

clipping

notching

Marking the Hem

To mark the hem, have someone pin the hem as you stand straight and still. Use a yardstick or hem marker to measure from the floor to the length you like. Mark the hemline with pins, placing them parallel to the floor about 3 inches apart. Now turn up the hem and pin it to the inside of the garment. Match hem and garment seamlines. Press a light crease at the hem edge. Using a ruler, mark the width of the hem with pins or tailor's chalk. Trim along this line, cutting an even hem width.

Finishing the Hem Edge

The hem edge needs to be finished before it is stitched to the garment. Hem finishes are similar to seam finishes. The choice of a finish depends on the fabric and style of the garment. The four methods of finishing hem edges described below are shown in **21-16**.

- The *turned and stitched finish* is used for medium-weight and lightweight fabrics that ravel. Turn the cut hem edge under ¼-inch and stitch close to the fold.

- The *stitched and pinked finish* is used for fabrics that do not ravel, such as knits. Machine stitch ¼-inch from the cut edge. Pink the edge with pinking shears. Be careful not to cut through stitching.

21-15

Make a thread shank as you sew on a button.

21-16

Use one of these hem finishes along the raw edge of your garment.

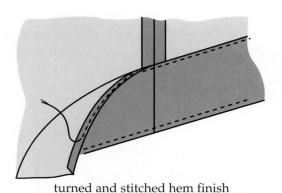

turned and stitched hem finish

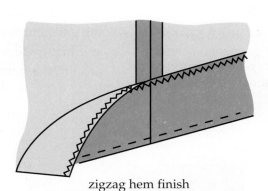

zigzag hem finish

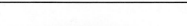
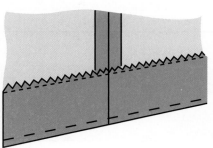

stitched and pinked hem finish

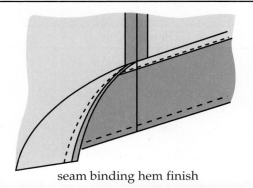

seam binding hem finish

- The *zigzag finish* is used most often for knits where stretch and flexibility are needed. It is also used on bulky fabrics that ravel. To finish, zigzag ¼-inch from the cut edge of the hem.

- *Seam binding tape* is used as a hem finish for medium-weight and heavyweight fabrics that ravel. On the right side of the fabric, lap the tape over the cut edge. Stitch the tape ¼-inch from the cut edge of the hem.

Stretch-lace binding tape is used to finish curved hems and hems of fabrics that stretch. It is applied like seam binding tape.

Stitching the Hem

Most hems are stitched by hand using a single thread. Make stitches somewhat loose to avoid puckers and to allow ease in the hemline. Space stitches evenly and sew neatly. Always begin hemming at a seam and secure the thread knot in the seam allowance. Refer to the diagrams in **21-17** as you read the following descriptions.

Hemming Stitch

This stitch is used for all types of hems, especially those finished with binding tape. Pick up a yarn of the garment with the needle, bring the needle diagonally through the edge of the hem, and pull the thread through. Continue stitching around the hem at ¼-inch intervals, spacing stitches evenly.

Slip Stitch

This nearly invisible stitch is hidden in a fold along the hem edge. A hem with a turned and stitched finish creates the fold. Pick up a yarn of the garment close to the hem, slide the needle into the fold about ¼-inch, and bring the needle out, picking up another garment yarn. Continue around the hem.

21-17

The stitch you use to hem your garment will depend on its hem finish and type of fabric.

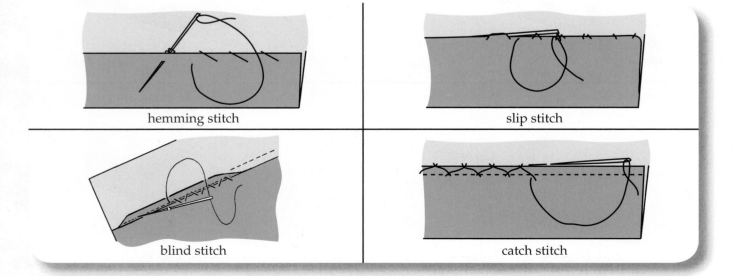

hemming stitch

slip stitch

blind stitch

catch stitch

Blind Stitch

This stitch is often used for hems on coats and suits. The stitch is hidden from view between a finished hem and the garment. The line of machine stitching in the hem's finish serves as a guide for making blind stitches. You will need to hold the hem edge back while hemming. Pick up a yarn from the garment followed by a yarn from the hem in ¼-inch intervals. Continue, making stitches loose so the hem will not pull and pucker.

Catch Stitch

This flexible stitch is good for hemming knit fabrics. You will work from left to right with the needle pointing left. In ¼-inch intervals, pick up a yarn below the hem edge followed by a yarn in the garment diagonally above the edge. Keep the thread loose so the zigzag pattern of stitches will allow some stretch.

Other Hemming Methods

Machine stitching can be used to secure hems. Some machines have a special hemming stitch. Hems can also be topstitched or zigzagged to add a decorative finish. Sergers are particularly good at making hems. Check your sewing machine manual and follow its directions.

Fusible material can also be used to secure hems. The steam heat of an iron causes it to fuse the hem and the garment together. Follow the manufacturer's directions for fusing. The fusible material should be suitable for the garment fabric. Test the material between fabric scraps. Fusing should not change the color or texture of the fabric.

Reading
Review

1. What two stitching techniques are used to prevent stretching of the edges of the seamlines?
2. Explain how to stitch a dart.
3. How does trimming differ from grading?
4. What is the purpose of making a thread shank when sewing on a button?
5. Which hemming stitch is best for knit fabrics?

Section 21-4

Extending the Life of Clothes

Objectives

After studying this section, you will be able to

- **describe** common repairs clothes may need.
- **alter** the seams and hems of clothes.
- **suggest** ways to restyle clothes.
- **identify** ways to recycle clothes you can no longer wear.

Key Term

restyle

Do you have any clothes that you no longer wear? Most people do. Ask yourself why they are not worn. Are you tired of them? Are some clothes too short or too long? Do some have stains that you cannot remove? Do rips and tears need repairing? Are buttons or other fasteners loose or missing? Maybe some clothes seem too plain or too fancy. Others may no longer fit you because your weight or height has changed.

You can probably extend the life of most of these clothes by repairing, altering, or restyling them. If they no longer fit, there are ways to recycle clothes so other people can use them.

Repairing Clothes

Often garments that are not worn just need simple repairs. That is why basic sewing skills are helpful. Even if you never want to sew your own clothes, you can still make repairs for yourself and your family.

To repair a split seam, turn the garment inside out. Pin the seam together and sew on the seamline. If the seam is one that receives a lot of stress, stitch the seam twice, using small stitches.

Buttons and other fasteners often loosen with normal wear. When they become loose, secure them immediately. A lost button cannot always be replaced with an identical one. One lost button may force you to replace them all, which can cost considerable time and money.

Zippers sometimes break with normal wear. They may also be damaged during laundering or dry cleaning. Though you may be able to repair them, some will need to be replaced. Purchase a zipper of the same style and color as the previous one. Replace the zipper using the same application method as the garment originally used.

Hems often come loose in garments. If you need to repair a hem, use one of the hemming stitches described earlier.

Snags detract from the appearance of knitted garments. When left unattended, a small snag can catch and become a large "run." To repair it, slip a needle threader, a needle with a large eye, or a small crochet hook through from the back of the fabric next to the snag. Grasp the snag and pull it to the backside of the garment. Carefully stretch the fabric to smooth the snagged area.

Life Skills

Zipper Applications

The four most common zipper applications are centered, lapped, invisible, and fly front. The location of the zipper and the look you desire will determine which method to use.

When zippers are intended for center front or center back seams, a *centered zipper application* is often used. The zipper coils are centered in the seamline. A row of stitches appears on both sides of the seamline. A *lapped zipper application* has only one row of stitching showing on the outside of the garment. It can be used at front, back, or side openings. An *invisible zipper* looks like a regular seam because no stitches show on the outside of the garment. *Fly front zipper applications* are used on front openings of jeans and slacks.

Holes can be patched in several ways. Iron-on patches are easy to use and appropriate for casual garments. Select a patch that matches the color of the garment. Follow the package directions for ironing the patch onto the garment. If a piece of the garment fabric is available, it can be placed behind the hole. Turn under the torn edges of the garment and secure with small, neat hand stitches.

Altering Clothes

Altering differs from repairing. To repair is to restore something to its original condition. To alter is to change the size. If a garment is too large or small, you may be able to make it fit by altering the seams. If the garment is a little too long or short, you may be able to alter the hem.

Altering Seams

Making the garment smaller is fairly simple. Begin by putting the garment on inside out. Ask someone to pin new seams so the garment will have the snugness you want. Be sure the garment still hangs properly after it is pinned. Take the garment off and baste along the pinned lines, removing pins as you stitch. Try the garment on again to check the fit. Make adjustments as needed. Stitch the new seam with a regular machine stitch. Remove the old stitches. Trim the seam allowance to ⅝-inch and press the new seam open.

Letting out a seam to enlarge a garment is more difficult. First, determine how much wider the garment should be. Then measure the seam allowance to see how much room can be added by letting out one

Host a clothing repair party. Have friends bring items that need minor repairs such as hems or missing buttons, along with sewing supplies and sewing kits. Once clothes are repaired, they can be worn again or donated to a clothing drive.

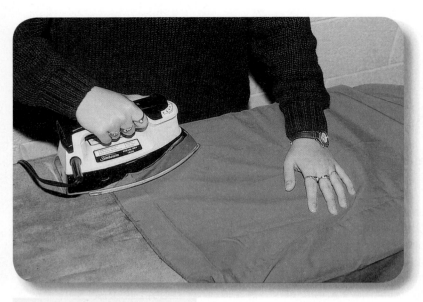

21-18

Thoroughly press the old hem flat before marking a new hem.

or more seams. (The minimum seam allowance is ¼-inch.) If letting out seams will provide the needed space, you can begin.

Altering Hems

Changing a hemline can make a garment fit better or appear more fashionable. Hems can be adjusted on pants, skirts, dresses, sleeves, and jackets.

To shorten a garment, first remove the old hemming stitches. Steam press the crease until it disappears, **21-18**. Put the garment on and have someone mark the desired length. Turn the hem to the inside and pin it in place. Lightly press the hem near the folded edge. Try the garment on again to be sure the length is satisfactory. Then complete the hem as explained earlier. Trim away any excess hem width.

If you want to lengthen a garment, check to see if the existing hem is deep enough to add the desired amount. If so, remove the existing hem and press out the crease. Have someone mark the new hem and complete the hemming of the garment.

Restyling Clothes

You can extend the life of clothes by restyling them. When you **restyle** a garment, you change it to create a different look. Ask yourself why you are not wearing a certain garment. Maybe by restyling you can give it a new look or function. You might try some of the following ideas:

- If a collar is worn and frayed, remove it. You can wear a garment collarless, or you might add a contrasting collar.
- Cover holes or permanent stains with an appliqué or a fancy patch.
- If pants are too short, cut them off. They can be worn as shorts. Sweatshirts can be cut off and made into crop tops.
- If the shape of pant legs is out of fashion, restyle the legs by altering the seams.
- If cuffed pants are out of fashion, shorten the pants to eliminate the cuffs. If the elbows of sweaters or jackets are wearing thin, cover them with elbow patches.
- Give a garment a new look by changing the buttons or adding snap-on button covers. Trims can also be added.
- Try giving an old garment new dazzle with decorative trims or creative additions. See **21-19**.

Mental Health Awareness

Creative Thinking

Thinking creatively to restyle clothes helps improve your problem-solving skills. Creative thinking helps you analyze problems from different perspectives. Developing creativity involves believing in your ideas (self-confidence) and having healthy self-esteem.

- Some dresses can be shortened to make tunic tops.
- If a garment is a light color, you may want to dye it or tie-dye it. Review the literature that comes with the dye so you know what colors to expect. For example, yellow fabric that is dyed blue will result in a green color. Orange fabric that is dyed blue will result in a brown tone.

Recycling Clothes

When you have exhausted the usefulness of a garment, it is time to recycle it. When you recycle a garment, you reuse it in a different way. This may mean passing clothes along to others who can wear them. Have you thought of doing any of the following?

- *Give wearable clothes to someone else.* A family member or a friend may be happy to receive your hand-me-downs.
- *Accept wearable clothes from others.* Friends and family members may have gently used clothes you can use.
- *Have a garage sale.* Then use the money you make to buy new clothes.
- *Take garments in good condition to a consignment shop.* They will try to sell the garments for you and give you a portion of the selling price.
- *Donate unwanted garments to a charitable organization.* Contact such groups as the Red Cross, Salvation Army, or local charities. The garments are repaired and given to people in need. Also consider donating old garments to the craft department of a senior center. They will find many uses for the fabric and trims.

Oleg Gekman/Shutterstock.com

21-19

Adding a fashionable jacket and a new belt can give a piece of clothing a whole new look.

Financial Literacy

Making Extra Money

Even if you hold a part-time job, additional cash is nice to have for your saving or spending goals. One way to make extra money is by selling clothing, shoes, and other accessories/items in good repair that you no longer need or wear. There are several options—using a consignment shop or holding a garage sale.

Consignment shops sell your items for you in exchange for a percentage of the sales price, which tends to run around 50%. You will sign a contract with the store indicating your acceptance of their policies and terms. Most contracts last for 90 days, with the store lowering prices after a given time to sell goods quicker. This means if you gave the local consignment shop an item they priced and sold for $20.00, you would receive $10.00. After the contract ends, you have the option of picking up your unsold items or allowing the store to donate them to charity.

On the other hand, if you and your family or friends hold a garage sale, you will receive 100% of the sales for your items. However, the work of getting zoning permission, marketing the sale, setting it up, pricing and selling, taking it down, and donating unsold items will be up to you and your partners. Garage sales last for one or two weekend days and customers often bargain for lower prices. While you may end up selling items for less than you priced them, all the profit remains yours.

Serving Your Community

Prepare a list of local charitable groups who use recycled clothes, such as religious organizations and community agencies. Arrange to volunteer at the site of one of the organizations or organize a clothing drive.

- *Reuse portions of old clothes to create new items.* Use the fabric in old garments to make crafts, room decorations, or children's toys, such as doll clothes or stuffed animals. Make clothes for children, or let them use old garments to play "dress-up." Remove and save trims, buttons, zippers, and fasteners for future use. Convert soft cotton garments into cleaning and polishing cloths. Cut soft fabrics and nylon hose into small pieces and use as stuffing material in craft projects.

As a last resort, check if your community recycles clothing. In some places, you can drop clothes off at a recycling center along with your paper, glass, and cans.

Reading Review

1. How might time and money be saved by securing loose buttons immediately?
2. How does altering clothes differ from restyling clothes?
3. Name two ways to recycle clothes.
4. How can a consignment shop help you recycle clothes?

Chapter 21 Review

Summary

Studying the pattern guide sheet and knowing the symbols and terms on pattern pieces are important to successful sewing. Common pattern symbols include cutting lines, notches, dots, stitching lines, seam allowances, grainline arrows, and adjustment lines. You can pin-fit your pattern to check for any needed alterations. Making alterations prior to cutting is easier than making them after construction.

Follow the appropriate cutting layout. Lay out the fabric and place pattern pieces as shown. Pin all pattern pieces securely to avoid slipping. Leave the fabric flat on the table as you take long cutting strokes with your shears. After you transfer the pattern markings to the fabric, you can begin sewing.

Sewing involves many different techniques. Two basic stitching techniques are directional stitching and staystitching. Making darts or gathers is often the next step in a sewing project, followed by creating a seam, often with backstitching. Fasteners are added and finally the hem. As you learn and practice these techniques, your skills will develop and you can expand your wardrobe. You can also save money and express your creativity by using sewing skills to extend the life of clothes.

You can save a lot of money by repairing, altering, or restyling clothes. If you can no longer wear a garment, it can be recycled or given to others to wear. You could also sell old clothes at a consignment shop or donate them to a charitable organization. Portions of garments can be reused in other ways. Therefore, consider all your options before throwing old clothes away.

Critical Thinking

1. **Analyze information.** Why is it important to understand the information on the pattern guide sheet and pattern pieces before you begin sewing?

2. **Evaluate decisions.** Why should you pin-fit a pattern and alter pattern pieces before cutting the fabric?

3. **Draw conclusions.** What kind of pattern is best for sewing plaids and stripes?

4. **Recognize value.** Which of the sewing techniques described in this chapter do you think you will use most frequently? Why?

5. **Analyze trends.** Research growing careers including entrepreneurial opportunities that might utilize sewing skills.

6. **Compare and contrast.** Test different seam finishes on different fabrics. Which finishes work best on light, medium, and heavy fabrics?

7. **Recognize alternatives.** Bring an item of clothing to class that can be repaired, altered, or restyled. Explain to the class what you intend to do to make the garment wearable again.

21st Century Applications

8. **Media literacy.** Work on creating a classroom web page that discusses construction techniques. If your school has a website, add a link for the page to the home page.

9. **Financial and economic literacy.** Using reliable print or online sources, research the *hemline index*. According to this concept, when hemlines rise in fashionable garments, the stock market rises, but when hemlines fall, so does the market. Name specific time periods when this was true. Do you think there is any credibility to this theory today? Why or why not?

10. **Civic literacy.** Research local charities or organizations in your area that accept clothing donations. Discover how the organizations sort through the donated items and where the clothing is ultimately sent. Write a report on your findings.

11. **Creativity and innovation.** Imagine you work for an organization that accepts clothing donations. Your supervisor is concerned because the organization is not receiving enough donations. Your team assignment is to develop a creative and innovative plan for solving this problem. Use the following process to produce your plan:
    A. **Analyze the problem.** Look at the problem from all potential angles.
    B. **Brainstorm possible options.** Brainstorm a list of possible solutions without passing judgment on any options. Accept all ideas—including those that seem impossible—and expand the ideas of others. Consider alternatives that stem from any past learning experiences.
    C. **Gather new information for solving the problem.** Examine recent research and data. What costs (both financial and human) are involved in solving the problem?
    D. **Organize data and compare all the options.** What new and unique alternatives can you identify? What risks are involved with each solution? How can each solution benefit the employer and solve the problem? What impact will each solution have on clients?
    E. **Choose an option for solving the problem.** Identify the option that has the best potential value.
    F. **Summarize the actions necessary to solve the problem.** Write a proposal identifying the creative actions your team would take for solving the problem. What is the cost involved in implementing the solution?

Core Skills

12. **Research, writing.** Research the use of CAD software in the design and production of patterns. Prepare a written report of your findings.

13. **Listening.** Ask older family members about whether earlier generations sewed their own clothes. Were commercial patterns available? If they made their own, what did they use for guides? Write your answers and contribute them during a class discussion.

14. **Math.** Research the nonsale price of a store-bought item and compare it to the cost of sewing the item yourself. Include prices for a pattern, fabric, and notions in the cost of sewing the item. Identify the most cost-efficient option as well as the most time-efficient one.

15. **Reading.** Search for sewing blogs online. View various ideas for projects and look for free patterns. Compile a list of the best sewing blogs as a class resource.

16. **Writing.** Investigate the website of Velcro® USA, Inc. Report on products that sewers can use and on the origin of Velcro.

17. **Speaking.** Create a video tutorial demonstrating one of the following sewing techniques:
    - pin-fitting a pattern to determine if any alterations are needed
    - making a pattern alteration
    - pressing darts
    - sewing gathers correctly
    - sewing seams
    - trimming, grading, clipping, and notching
    - sewing on buttons that incorporate a thread shank
    - making the different hemming stitches

Leadership
Development

As part of the Repurpose and Redesign STAR Event, organize a school-wide drive to collect old clothing and home items. Design and create new items from the collected materials. Donate leftover items from the drive to a local charitable organization.

Portfolio
Builder

Sewing is a valuable life skill. Demonstrating your sewing ability may make you a stronger candidate for many careers. You can include samples of your sewing in your portfolio to prove your skill and creativity. Make samples of each sewing technique described in this chapter to create a personal sewing notebook. Label each sample and write a description of the sample. Mount the samples, three-hole punch the pages, and place them in a three-ring binder. Include this in your portfolio.

Journal
Writing

You have an idea to use your sewing skills to start a small business. You want to reuse portions of old clothing creatively to produce unique items to sell. You will be able to get plenty of recycled apparel, including the trims and buttons, by shopping yard sales. Expenses for the business will be minimal. Your imagination and available sewing time are your limits.

Write About It: *What sewing skills will you find most useful? What useful items can you create to sell?*

Housing and Transportation

Unit Eight

Human Services

The Personal Care Services Pathway within the Human Services career cluster includes careers that help people care for their physical needs and appearances. Personal care aides, barbers, and cosmetologists are examples of careers in this pathway.

Human Services Pathways

Early Childhood Development and Services
Counseling and Mental Health Services
Family and Community Services
Personal Care Services
Consumer Services

Stockbyte/ Stockbyte/Thinkstock

Education and Training

Professionals in the Administration and Administrative Support Pathway within the Education and Training career cluster help guide teachers in new methodology. Instructional coordinators and program coordinators are examples of careers that help further train and support teachers.

Education and Training Pathways

Administration and Administrative Support
Professional Support Services
Teaching and Training

Thomas Northcut/ Photodisc/Thinkstock

Career Spotlight: Personal Care Aide

- **Description.** Personal care aides assist people with everyday living tasks. They may work with older adults, people with disabilities, people recovering from illness or surgery, or others who struggle with managing daily activities. Some personal care aides work in care facilities while others travel to clients' homes to provide care. Personal care aides may help clients with health care and hygiene-related tasks, as well as household tasks, such as making beds and preparing meals. They also provide companionship and help clients feel cared for during times of need.

- **Education and training.** Most personal care aides have a high school diploma. They usually receive on-the-job training and learn how to deal with various circumstances. Some states may require postsecondary education or training from programs. Personal care aides may also be required to pass a competency test.

- **Skills and personal qualities.** Personal care aides should be compassionate and have the genuine desire to help others. They should have good physical stamina, as they may be required to lift or help move clients with physical disabilities. Personal care aides should be detail oriented and have good interpersonal and time management skills.

- **Job outlook.** Job growth for personal care aides through 2028 is projected to grow 36 percent, or much faster than average for all occupations. Visit the *Occupational Outlook Handbook* online to learn more about a career as a personal care aide.

Human Services

Career Spotlight: Instructional Coordinator

- **Description.** Instructional coordinators research, create, and organize curricula, or the classes and programs that are taught to students. Instructional coordinators work with school administrations and teachers to implement new courses and teaching practices. They may specialize in one area of study or several areas, such as math, literature, interior design, or automotive repair. They may observe teachers and give feedback on how to strengthen their instructional methods. Instructional coordinators may also be responsible for researching and ordering instructional materials, equipment, and visual aids to support teachers.

- **Education and training.** Requirements vary, but most instructional coordinators are required to have a master's degree in education or curriculum and instruction. They are often required to have several years of experience. Some schools may require licensing.

- **Skills and personal qualities.** Instructional coordinators need excellent analytical, leadership, and decision-making skills. Since they work closely with teachers and school administrators, they should also have strong interpersonal and communication skills.

- **Job outlook.** Job growth for instructional coordinators through 2028 is projected to grow about as fast as average for all occupations. Visit the *Occupational Outlook Handbook* online to learn more about a career as an instructional coordinator.

Education & Training

Sources: States' Career Clusters Initiative, Bureau of Labor Statistics Career Guide to Industries

Chapter 22
Choosing a Place to Live

Sections

Reading Prep

Before reading this chapter, look at the chapter title. What does this title tell you about what you will be learning? Compare the information to be presented with information you already know about the subject matter.

Concept Organizer

+	−	I

Make two PMI (Plus, Minus, and Implications) charts; one for buying housing and the other for renting housing. In the first column of each chart, write all the positive aspects that come to mind. In the second column, write all the negative aspects. In the third column, write interesting facts you learned from this exercise.

G-WLEARNING.com

Click on the activity icon ↗ to visit www.g-wlearning. com/comprehensive/8062 to access online vocabulary activities using key terms from the chapter.

Section 22-1

Housing Options

Objectives

After studying this section, you will be able to

- **give examples** of how housing helps you meet your physical, social, and psychological needs.
- **list** different types of housing.
- **explain** the difference between single-family houses and multifamily dwellings.
- **describe** how cooperatives and condominiums differ.

Key Terms

housing
single-family house
attached house
freestanding house
custom house
tract house
manufactured house
multifamily dwelling
cooperative
condominium

People have many choices to make when choosing a place to live. That is because housing is more than walls and a roof. Housing can affect the way people feel and behave. The housing you choose will reflect your lifestyle and who you are. You may be surprised at the many types of housing available.

Meeting Housing Needs

Housing is any dwelling that provides shelter. Housing should satisfy the needs—physical, social, and psychological—of all residents of the dwelling.

Physical Needs

Shelter, food, and rest are basic physical needs. For protection from bad weather, people turn to housing. The dwelling should also have room for preparing and eating food. It should provide adequate, comfortable space for sleeping and space for personal belongings. When one or more friends or family members share housing, it should meet everyone's physical needs. Individual needs usually change over time.

21st Century Skills

Negotiation. Alicia will be leaving her current job because she will be moving to another city. She uses negotiation skills to make her departure a positive one. She offers to help train her replacement. Her supervisor appreciates this and offers to write a letter of recommendation for Alicia.

Mental Health Awareness

The Psychological Need for Security

According to psychologist Abraham Maslow, feelings of safety and security are psychological needs. When you feel safe and secure, especially in your home, you are more relaxed and less stressed.

22-1

Some people value having enough housing space to gather with a few friends for some fun activities. What needs do you value most for your housing space?

Social Needs

The need to interact with other people is a basic social need. Before you choose a place to live, you should decide which social needs you want to meet. Will you want the space to enjoy friends and family? Do you need indoor or outdoor space for recreation? Do you want to live close to many people or do you prefer a quieter setting? People express their social needs differently, **22-1**.

Psychological Needs

Although psychological needs cannot be measured as accurately as physical and social needs, they have a very strong influence on how you feel about your living space. Sometimes people base their housing choices on their psychological needs before their physical needs. Most people seeking housing consider the following psychological needs important factors when evaluating housing options.

- *Security.* Housing should provide safety from physical harm. Injury and suffering can result from exposure to the dangers of the outside world and destructive forces of nature.

- *Familiarity.* An unfamiliar place makes people feel uneasy. Housing in a familiar place makes people feel comfortable and secure.

- *Beauty.* Almost everyone wants beautiful surroundings, but there are many different standards of beauty.

Prostock-Studio/iStock/Getty Images Plus

- *Privacy.* Most people need to be away from others occasionally. A bedroom or other empty room often fills this need. Sometimes people need an outdoor setting that provides privacy.
- *Self-expression.* People express themselves through the design and location of their homes. A bustling city street, a flower-filled yard, and a river's edge all say something about homeowners in these different locations.

Types of Housing

After determining your housing needs, you can start deciding which type of housing will best meet those needs. A wide variety of housing is available. All housing can be classified as either single-family housing or multifamily housing.

Single-Family Houses

A **single-family house** is designed to shelter one family. The house can be attached to others or a freestanding house.

Attached Houses

Some single-family houses share a common wall with houses on one or more sides. These dwellings are called **attached houses**. *Town houses* and *row houses* are common names for attached houses. The owners possess the dwelling, the land under it, and a yard. They often pay a monthly fee for maintaining the common grounds.

Freestanding Houses

A **freestanding house** is a house that stands alone. The basic types of freestanding houses include custom, tract, and manufactured houses.

Custom houses are specifically designed and built for the new owner. They tend to be very distinctive. The need for an architect and a building contractor also causes them to cost more than other houses in both time and money. See **22-2**.

Tract houses, also called *developer-built houses,* are part of an entire neighborhood built at once. To save money, the houses are generally limited to a few basic designs. The houses are not as distinctive, but are less expensive than custom houses. Landscaping, painting, and additions can give the houses individuality.

Manufactured houses are made in a factory and moved to a site. There are many different kinds, sizes, and prices of factory-built houses. Practically all require assembly at the final site. The use of mass-produced parts saves labor costs. A manufactured house can be less expensive than a same-size custom house or developer-built house.

The smallest manufactured houses, called *mobile homes,* are completely assembled at a factory. They usually come equipped with plumbing, heating, electrical wiring, lights, and furnishings. When wheels are attached, mobile homes can be moved to another location. Be aware that many laws impact how manufactured houses are transported to and secured at a site's foundation.

Serving Your Community

Research the building-preservation activities of your state and local area. Find out what homes are designated as historic landmarks and whether others are being considered.

22-2

A custom house can reflect an owner's particular tastes, but is usually more costly than other types of housing.

Living Green

If you live in a multifamily dwelling or close to your neighbors, remember to keep noise pollution to a minimum. Keep speakers turned down so that you do not disturb your neighbors.

Multifamily Dwellings

Multifamily dwellings are buildings designed to house more than one family. Apartments, cooperative units, and condominiums are common types of multifamily housing. You cannot tell by looking at these buildings which type of housing they provide.

Apartments

Apartments range from small, low-cost units to plush units in expensive high-rises. Some apartment buildings also include laundry rooms, recreational facilities, stores, or parking spaces on lower floors. Residents pay a monthly fee.

Cooperative Units

A **cooperative** is a multiunit building owned by and operated for the benefit of the residents. A person buys stock in the corporation owning the property and receives a housing unit in return. The stockholders decide as a group how the cooperative, or co-op, is run and who can live there. Stockholders pay a monthly fee for upkeep and repairs.

Condominium Units

A **condominium** is an individually-owned housing unit in a multiunit structure. Condominium, or *condo*, owners can sell their units without the approval of other owners. Common areas such as hallways, swimming pools, and parking lots are shared. Each owner has a vote in concerns relating to them and pays a monthly fee for the building's upkeep.

Reading
Review

1. Give examples of how housing helps people meet the physical needs of shelter, food, and rest.
2. List three psychological needs that can be met through housing.
3. List five housing alternatives available for families.
4. Describe the difference between single-family houses and multifamily dwellings.
5. How do cooperatives and condominiums differ?

Section 22-2

Renting or Buying Housing

Objectives

After studying this section, you will be able to

- **discuss** the factors to consider when choosing housing.
- **identify** advantages and disadvantages of renting or buying housing.
- **give examples** of what you need to know before you rent or buy housing.

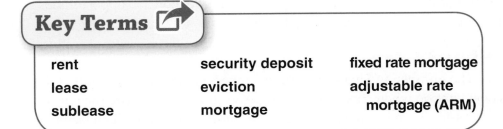

Key Terms

rent	**security deposit**	**fixed rate mortgage**
lease	**eviction**	**adjustable rate**
sublease	**mortgage**	**mortgage (ARM)**

After considering all basic housing options, you will need to decide how to acquire the housing of your choice. You can rent or buy almost all types of housing.

Financial Literacy

Guidelines for Spending on Housing

The housing you can afford depends on your income. One of the following guidelines can help you determine the amount of your income you can spend on housing:

- Allow no more than two and one-half times your gross annual income for the purchase price of a house.
- Budget 28 percent of your gross monthly income for housing costs.

The first guideline refers only to the purchase price of a house. The second guideline can be applied to both renting and buying housing. For this guideline, you should consider other housing expenses as well. These include utility bills, property insurance, taxes, maintenance, and city services.

Living Green

If your family is searching for a place to live, encourage them to consider a place close to school and work. When family members can use mass transit and walk or bike to school and work, it helps cut energy costs and reduces pollution.

Choosing Housing

There are many factors you need to consider as you choose a type of housing. The two main factors are your income and the location of the housing.

Income

Housing prices keep going up, and most people cannot afford to live in their dream house. However, they can decide which housing aspect is most important to them and budget their income to achieve it.

Suppose you dream of living in a large high-rise with a view. You quickly learn that people on your budget cannot afford it. You may then decide that space is more important than a view. However, a roomy high-rise is still out of your price range. You realize that living in a high-rise is not worthwhile without the view. At this point, it is clear that space is the most important aspect of your housing dream. You look for a spacious town house that you can afford.

Location

Where your housing is located has a great impact on the lives of you and your family members. It can affect both the job you have and your family's lifestyle.

Job

Some people choose housing that is close to their jobs or transportation that will take them to their jobs. For instance, doctors need to live close to their offices so they can quickly treat patients in emergencies.

People also choose to live in areas that have jobs available in their fields. For instance, a marine biologist would have more job opportunities living near an ocean than in the desert.

Lifestyle

The number and ages of family members should be taken into consideration when choosing housing. You should make sure the house is accessible to community facilities your lifestyle demands. Such facilities may include shopping centers, entertainment, athletic and cultural attractions, public transportation, and recreational areas, **22-3**.

You should also make sure the house meets the needs of the family. Families with children may want a bigger house with more space. They will need schools and playgrounds, too. Single people and childless couples may want smaller houses that are easy to maintain and are in quiet neighborhoods.

Renting Housing

Rental housing is popular with single people, young married couples, older people, and families with low incomes. Many people think of apartment buildings when they consider rental housing. However, some single-family houses can be rented, too.

Rent is a fee paid to the owner each month. This fee may or may not include utilities, such as heat, water, gas, and electricity.

Advantages and Disadvantages of Renting

Many people rent housing because it is convenient. It lets them get acquainted with a new community before they make a long-term housing commitment. They can move when their leases expire and not worry about selling the property. They also do not have to worry about whether the value of the property is increasing or decreasing.

Renting is economical, too. Renters know how much their housing is going to cost them, and they can budget for it. There also will not be any surprise expenses, such as the cost of a new water heater. The owner of the property is responsible for the maintenance and repair of the building.

Before you rent housing, you need to know what your rights and responsibilities are as a tenant. A *tenant* is the temporary occupant of a rented housing unit. You also need to understand the rights and responsibilities of the owner.

Responsibilities

A lease is written by the property owner to protect the property. A **lease** is a contract between a tenant and a property owner. It lists the rights and responsibilities of both parties. A lease covers a specified rental period, which is often one year.

George Doyle/Stockbyte/Thinkstock

22-3
Some choose housing near parks so they can spend time outdoors.

Responsibility. Kanchan takes responsibility for arriving to work on time. She sets her alarm a few minutes early so that even if there is traffic, she can arrive on time.

Leases identify the amount of rent to be paid each month. In addition, they list what tenants must do and must not do. You must understand everything stated in the lease before you sign it. Once your signature is on the lease, you are responsible for fulfilling all the terms. When you sign a lease, you are saying you will pay your rent promptly. You are agreeing to keep the property clean and free from damage. In turn, the owner agrees to keep the building and grounds in good condition. He or she also promises to obey health and safety laws.

A lease protects you from a rent increase after you move into rental housing. The lease also protects the owner if you want to move out after a short time. If you move, you are still responsible for paying the rent until the lease expires.

Many owners let tenants sublease rental property to someone else. To **sublease**, or sublet, means you have the right to pass the lease over to a second tenant. This person pays rent directly to the owner. If he or she fails to pay, you are still responsible for the rent being paid on time. The owner usually has to approve the new tenant.

A security deposit is commonly required in a lease. A **security deposit** is a sum of money, usually one month's rent, paid by the tenant before moving into the property. It is used to cover possible damages to the property. When the tenant moves out, the owner refunds the security deposit if the terms of the lease have been met. The owner can keep all or part of the deposit if the tenant damages the property. The owner also keeps the deposit if the tenant moves without giving the owner proper notice.

If you are renting property and fail to live up to the terms of the lease, you can be evicted. **Eviction** is a legal procedure that forces a tenant to leave the property before the rental agreement expires. An owner has the right to evict tenants if they fail to uphold the terms of the lease. Failing to pay rent or keeping pets when they are prohibited are grounds for eviction.

Rights

As a tenant, you also have rights. You have the right to housing that is safe and secure. Suppose the owner does not take proper care of the property or follow health and safety laws. You can turn to your local government for help. For instance, if there are fire hazards in the building, you can call the fire department. Your city hall can help you locate the right agency to solve the problem. If your problem cannot be solved through these channels, you can seek legal advice.

Buying Housing

Many people choose to own their own houses instead of renting. They can buy either single-family houses or units in multifamily housing.

Mental Health Awareness

Happiness and Home Buying

Studies have rated people's overall happiness after buying a new home. Many people said their new home did not make them as happy as they had expected. Respondents found that the demands of home ownership forced them to give up some experiences they enjoyed, such as traveling and dining out. These studies indicate that people value rewarding experiences over material goods.

Advantages and Disadvantages of Buying

People buy houses for many different reasons. They may prefer the emotional security of buying a home to the convenience of renting. They may decide to stay in one location for a number of years. Some need the space a single-family house offers.

People may choose to buy houses for financial reasons. Houses sometimes increase in value faster than the rate of inflation. Home ownership improves credit ratings. Money paid for real estate taxes and interest on a home mortgage can be deducted from income taxes.

To buy a house, you will pay a down payment and get a loan to pay the rest. This type of loan is called a **mortgage**. It is usually paid monthly over a set number of years. Two common types of mortgages are fixed rate and adjustable rate.

A **fixed rate mortgage** insures that your monthly mortgage and house payments will stay the same as interest rates go up and down. Those who plan to live in a house for a long time may choose this plan because they like the personal security of knowing what they owe each month.

An **adjustable rate mortgage (ARM)** allows the interest rate to be adjusted up or down periodically. Initially, monthly payments with an ARM may be lower than a fixed rate mortgage. However, if interest rates rise, the mortgage payment will go up. Before choosing an ARM, buyers should make sure they can afford to make monthly payments at the highest possible interest rate.

In addition to the down payment and monthly payments, there are other mortgage expenses. These include closing costs, homeowner's insurance, taxes, and other costs. See **22-4**. Purchasing

Math Connection

Buying a House

Trevor and Nicole both graduated from college. Trevor earns $37,000 per year as a teacher. Nicole earns $45,000 as an accountant. They plan to buy a house. When they met with a Realtor, she told them that they should plan to allow no more than two and one-half times their gross annual income for the purchase price of a house. With this in mind, what is the maximum price Trevor and Nicole should consider spending on a house?

To determine how much they can afford to spend for a house, Trevor and Nicole add their incomes together for their combined gross annual income.

$37,000 + $45,000 = $82,000

They then multiply their gross annual income by 2½ to arrive at the maximum price they should consider spending on a house.

$82,000 × 2.5 = $205,000

22-4

Home buyers need to remember that closing costs must be added to the purchase price of a home.

Expenses Included in Closing Costs

- Appraisal
- Property survey
- Deed
- Title search
- Title insurance
- Tax stamp
- Recording fees
- Notary fee
- Credit report
- Escrow fees

a home and shopping for the best mortgage may become very involved. Be sure to seek the advice of professionals when you are ready to buy. You should get estimates of the costs and be sure to have enough money available to pay for them.

New houses usually need some decorating, furniture, and landscaping. Previously owned houses may need improvements such as painting, new plumbing, or even rewiring. Buying a house usually involves moving expenses, too. Besides the mortgage, all these costs need to be considered when budgeting for a house.

Reading Review

1. Why do you need to consider location when choosing housing?
2. List three advantages of renting housing and two advantages of buying it.
3. What are a tenant's responsibilities after signing a lease?
4. In addition to the down payment and the mortgage, what are three other expenses a home buyer will pay?

Chapter 22 Review

Summary

When choosing a place to live, start by considering your physical, social, and psychological needs. Your physical needs include shelter, food, and rest. Your social needs may require some space for enjoying family, friends, and individual needs like recreation. Your psychological needs are for security, familiarity, beauty, privacy, and self-expression.

Once you identify your needs, you can evaluate how well different types of housing meet these needs. You can choose between a single-family house or a unit in a multifamily dwelling. Single-family houses are either attached or freestanding. Multifamily dwellings include apartments, cooperative units, and condominium units.

After deciding what type of housing meets your needs, decide whether to rent or buy. Both your income and the location of the housing will impact your decision. There are advantages and disadvantages to both options. You need to choose what works best for you.

Critical Thinking

1. **Analyze priorities.** Which of the five psychological needs discussed in this chapter is most important to you when evaluating housing? Why?

2. **Compare and contrast.** Would you rather live in a multifamily dwelling or a freestanding house? Why?

3. **Evaluate decisions.** What would you do if you owned a co-op and you disagreed with a decision made by the other stockholders in the corporation?

4. **Analyze influences.** How does cultural diversity influence your choice of where you would like to live?

5. **Predict outcomes.** Think about how your housing needs will change in the next 5 years and in the next 15 years. Discuss your thoughts in a small group setting.

6. **Draw conclusions.** Suppose you live in a community that was experiencing the closing of a major factory, which was a large area employer. You have a stable job with the potential of promotion. Would this be a good time to purchase housing? Why or why not?

7. **Analyze trends.** One trend in housing is to build the total house or various parts in a factory and move them to the housing site. What are other housing trends? Share your findings with the class.

21st Century Applications

8. **Information literacy.** Look through online real estate listings for your community. Make a list of single-family housing available in your area. Then make a list of multifamily housing available. Compare the two lists to see which type of housing has the most availablities in your area.

9. **Communication and collaboration.** As communities look for ways to improve housing for citizens and protect the environment, opportunities exist for people and their employers to take action. Suppose your employer asks you to work with a team to help

improve living conditions for people in your community. Work in small groups to create a plan using the following steps.

1. *Identify community concerns.* Research housing issues in your community or in a community nearby. Then brainstorm possible ways to address one or more of the problems. Evaluate the list and narrow it down to one project on which the majority of team members agree.

2. *Set a goal.* Select a specific goal. Determine what resources your team will need to meet the goal.

3. *Create a plan for achieving the goal.* Determine who, what, where, when, and how your team will accomplish your goal.

4. *Carry out the team plan.* As a team, work together to implement your plan.

5. *Evaluate the results of the team action.* Was your team able to meet its goal and your employer's goal of getting workers involved in the community? What changes have you seen take place?

Core Skills

10. **Reading, writing.** Locate a recent news article about a problem occurring because physical housing needs were not met. Write a report summarizing the article and housing issue and how this issue could have been prevented.

11. **Reading.** Obtain a copy of a lease. Examine it to see how the tenant's and owner's rights and responsibilities are defined. Highlight terms that are unfamiliar to you. Then research the meaning of each term.

12. **Math.** Research what nearby apartments are charging for rent. Find the cost of rent for three apartments: a one-, two-, and three-bedroom apartment. For each apartment you find, suppose the person renting the apartment would pay exactly 28% of his or her income. Calculate the minimum income a person would need to comfortably afford each housing option. Show your work on a separate sheet of paper.

13. **Listening.** Interview a person who recently bought housing. Write a report on the steps taken before actually buying the house. Then discuss what the owner sees as advantages and disadvantages of owning a house.

14. **Speaking.** Conduct research about the predominant types of housing in one country—from its earliest history to the present day. Make copies or print photos to show the progression of the country's housing types, typical materials, and features for an oral and visual class presentation.

15. **Writing.** Research Ellen Swallow Richards and the impact she had on housing and everyday living concerns, including water sanitation, nutrition, and clothing. Write an informative essay summarizing your research. Create a time line outlining her biography and accomplishments.

16. **Speaking.** Work in small teams to determine what information young people need in order to make the decision to move away from the family

home. Identify the questions that must be answered before moving out and setting up their own homes. Prepare an electronic presentation that could be used to help young people make housing decisions.

17. **Reading.** Research the cost of moving the contents of a three-bedroom home (including all major appliances) within the same town, 100 miles away, and 500 miles away.

18. **Writing.** Of the various types of housing options discussed in this chapter, which type of housing would you prefer to live in as a young adult? as an older adult? Write a brief response explaining your choices.

Leadership
Development

Using local ads, survey available housing and choose the best option for a college graduate who will begin a full-time job and frequently does volunteer work. If you are an FCCLA member working on a Community Service project, you could design a housing booklet for area newcomers based on the data you find.

Portfolio
Builder

Volunteer to work at a homeless shelter. Volunteering can help make a difference in your community and strengthen your résumé. Write a reflection paper to include in your portfolio, describing your experience. Reflect on the role your home plays in your own life. Explain how the shelter meets the following needs of people:
- physical needs
- social needs
- psychological needs

Journal
Writing

Tasha and Bill have been living in an apartment since their marriage. All utilities were included in the monthly payments. They now want to buy a house and have found one they like. The monthly payments will take approximately 33% of their combined incomes. They have no experience in judging the cost of utilities.

Write About It: *Is the cost of the house in keeping with their income? What financial programs help people like Tasha and Bill buy housing? Are they overlooking other important expenses? What might happen if either of them lost their job or developed health problems? What advice would you give them?*

Chapter 23
Maintaining a Home

Reading Prep

What routine tasks do you handle at home? How do they contribute to the home's safety and security?

Concept Organizer

Create a tree chart to help you furnish a home. The main topic will be *Furniture*. Then use the branches to illustrate various choices you have for different rooms.

G-WLEARNING.com

Click on the activity icon to visit www.g-wlearning.com/comprehensive/8062 to access online vocabulary activities using key terms from the chapter.

Applying Design in the Home

Objectives

After studying this section, you will be able to

- **apply** the elements and principles of design to housing.

- **explain** how to choose good furniture.

- **demonstrate** ways to organize living space.

- **give** examples of ways to use accessories.

Key Terms ↗

function	activity center	traffic pattern
universal design	scale floor plan	

In this section, you will learn how the elements and principles of design apply to housing. You will learn how to design a housing interior that helps create a positive atmosphere for its residents.

Furnishing your home involves choosing good-quality furniture that meets your needs. It also involves organizing living space and using accessories to tie the room's design together.

The Elements of Design

The elements of design are color, line, texture, and form. These elements can be used in many different ways to create a variety of designs.

Color

Color is a very important design element. It is one of the first things people notice when they enter a room. Each color reflects certain moods or feelings. See **23-1**. When decorating with color, it is important to follow these basic guidelines:

- Shared areas used by the whole family, such as the kitchen and living room, should be decorated in colors that satisfy everyone. In private areas, such as a bedroom, colors that appeal to individual family members can be used.

- Choose a dominant color when decorating. Smaller amounts of other colors can be used to accent it and add interest and variety.

Moods Created by Color	
Red	Exciting, powerful, courageous, aggressive, dangerous, energetic
Orange	Lively, cheerful, friendly, energetic, warm
Yellow	Cheerful, bright, sympathetic, wise, warm
Green	Natural, friendly, peaceful, refreshing, envious, hopeful
Blue	Calm, serious, reserved, dignified, serene
Violet	Royal, dignified, dominating, mysterious, dramatic
Black	Sophisticated, dignified, somber, desperate, mournful, wise
White	Fresh, innocent, pure, faithful, peaceful

23-1

Each color reflects a different mood or feeling.

- A sharp contrast can emphasize an object. For instance, a dark sofa will stand out against a light background.

- Light colors make items and rooms look larger. Dark colors make items and rooms look smaller.

- Using a variety of color values, especially in unequal amounts, can make a room more interesting.

- Make greater use of low-intensity colors, especially as backgrounds and in large areas. High-intensity colors are better suited for small areas and as accents. Color intensity is more effective when used with variety.

- Using warm colors, shades, and high-intensity colors will make a room appear smaller. Using cool colors, tints, and low-intensity colors will make a room appear larger.

- Warm colors suggest informality, while cool colors suggest formality.

Line

Vertical, horizontal, diagonal, and curved lines are all used in house design. Vertical lines suggest height, confidence, and dignity. They are visible in tall furniture, such as secretaries and armoires; long, narrow draperies; striped wallpaper; and pillars or columns. They can make ceilings seem higher and rooms more spacious.

Horizontal lines suggest relaxation and informality. They are seen in long, low furniture, such as sofas and chests. They can make ceilings seem lower and rooms seem wider.

Diagonal lines suggest activity and movement. They are found in slanted ceilings, staircases, and fabric designs. They provide variety in design, but can be overpowering and tiring unless used in small amounts.

Curved lines can suggest either activity or relaxation, depending on the degree of the curve. Soft curves appear restful and graceful. Upward

Mental Health Awareness

Design Psychology

Interior and building designs that imitate the soothing elements of nature can promote relaxation and other positive mental states. For example, gently waving lines on a bedroom wall may suggest a restful lake or the clouds in a calm sky.

curves give an impression of rising. Small curves look playful. Tight curves look busy and action packed. Curves can be seen in arches, tabletops, ruffled curtains, and rounded furniture.

Using a variety of lines can create interest, but it can also cause confusion. Therefore, when designing a home, one type of line should dominate. For example, vertical lines may dominate a room. Small amounts of curved or diagonal lines can be used in accessories to create interest.

Texture

Texture provides much of a home's character because it strongly stimulates the imagination and affects the senses of touch and sight. Rough textures and bold patterns tend to make a room appear smaller. Uneven surfaces cast small shadows and absorb light. This makes the actual color seem deeper, the room darker, and the objects larger and heavier. In contrast, shiny, smooth textures reflect light and make a room appear brighter and lighter.

Form

Form is three-dimensional. It has length, width, and depth. In housing, it is found in architecture, furniture, equipment, and accessories. Forms should not be chosen only for how they look. They should also be chosen for their **function**, or how they will be used. For example, a lounge chair is designed to let a person stretch out and relax. A dining room chair is designed for eating at a table in an upright position. You could not comfortably stretch out on a dining room chair. Room design works best when the forms are functional and relate to one another while also providing variety.

The Principles of Design

The principles of design are guidelines for working with the elements of design. The principles of design are balance, proportion, rhythm, and emphasis. Harmony is the goal of design.

Balance

Balance gives design a sense of *equilibrium* or a sense of weight on both sides. Balance can be formal or informal.

Formal balance is the arrangement of identical objects on opposite sides of a central point. Formal balance gives a restful, orderly, sophisticated look to a room. However, too much use of formal balance can become dull. With *informal balance,* the two sides are different, but have the same visual impact. Various forms, sizes, and colors can be used together to achieve informal balance.

Combining formal and informal balance in a room creates variety. However, as with other elements and principles of design, balance works best when either formal or informal balance dominates.

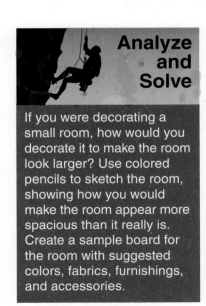

Analyze and Solve

If you were decorating a small room, how would you decorate it to make the room look larger? Use colored pencils to sketch the room, showing how you would make the room appear more spacious than it really is. Create a sample board for the room with suggested colors, fabrics, furnishings, and accessories.

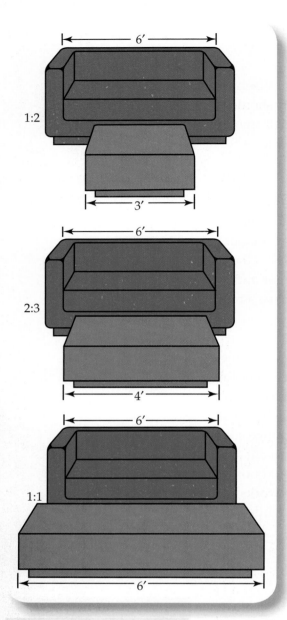

23-2

The table in the middle is in a 2:3 ratio with the sofa. This unequal proportion is considered more pleasing than the 1:2 and 1:1 ratios seen above and below.

Proportion

Proportion is the ratio of one part to another part and to the whole. Unequal proportions, such as 2:3, 3:5, and 5:8, are pleasing to the eye. They are more interesting than equal proportions, such as 2:2 or 2:4. For example, a rectangle is more pleasing in a design than a square. See **23-2** to see how proportion affects furniture and accessories.

Think about proportion when choosing furniture and accessories. If they are too large in proportion to a small room, they will make the room seem crowded.

Rhythm

Rhythm leads the eyes smoothly from one feature to another in a design. The five types of rhythm are repetition, opposition, gradation, radiation, and transition.

By repeating color, line, form, or texture in a design, you can achieve rhythm by *repetition*. The use of the same wood in the furniture pieces creates repetition.

Opposition is rhythm formed by lines meeting at right angles. You can see opposition in the corners of the windows, picture frames, and cabinet doors.

Gradation is rhythm created by a gradual change. The room setting shows gradation in color value from light to dark in the color of the carpeting, furniture, wooden floor, and wallpaper.

In rhythm by *radiation*, lines extend outward from a central point. This is evident in the ornate light fixture.

Transition is rhythm created by curved lines. Transition carries the eyes easily over an architectural feature or piece of furniture. In this case, the rounded backs of the chairs create rhythm.

Emphasis

Emphasis refers to the center of interest, or focal point, in a design. A sense of unity and order in room design is achieved when your eyes are repeatedly drawn to one feature. A fireplace, window, or special piece of artwork or furniture can be a point of emphasis. The special item should blend with other objects in the room.

When using emphasis in design, two guidelines need to be followed. First, the point of emphasis should dominate. No other features should compete with it. Second, the focal point should not overpower the room.

The Goal of Design

Using the elements of design effectively according to the principles of design creates harmony. Unity and variety play an important roll in achieving harmony.

Unity occurs when all of the elements and furnishings in a room are tied together. For example, using a consistent color scheme in adjoining rooms will give a unified effect.

Variety adds interest and excitement to design. One way to achieve variety is by using rough and smooth textures when decorating a room.

Universal Design

Incorporating universal design will make your home more comfortable for yourself and others. **Universal design** is the concept of creating products and living spaces that are easy for everyone to use. People of all ages and abilities benefit from universal design.

Some elements of universal design are structural, such as wide doorways and entrances without steps. However, you can incorporate nonstructural elements by selecting items for your home with the following features:

- cabinets with pull-out shelves
- chairs with raised seats
- lever-style door handles
- touch lamps that operate without switches

Universal design accommodates the needs of all family members throughout the life cycle as well as people with disabilities. Keeping this concept in mind when furnishing your home will increase the comfort and accessibility of your living space both now and in the future.

Choosing Furniture

Your basic furnishings should be comfortable, tasteful, and suitable to your lifestyle. Furniture should also be durable enough to last for several years. The furniture you choose will depend on your preferences for certain materials, styles, and finishes. Your decisions should complement your lifestyle and personal taste.

Factors to Consider

As you select furniture, choose furniture that is functional. Look for pieces that can have multiple uses. For example, a bedroom dresser might be used as a buffet in a dining room. Flexibility of furniture pieces provides more options if you want, or need, to change room arrangements. See **23-3**.

Consider proportion, too. All furniture should be in proportion to the size of the room as well as other furnishings. For instance, select armchairs appropriate for the room. Then choose end tables that are about the height of the arms on the chairs. Finally, choose table lamps that are in proportion to the tables.

You also need to think about who will be using the furniture. Furniture used by children should be sturdy. Its fabrics should be durable and not

Integrity. Kendra is an interior designer. She works very closely with her clients and often visits them in their homes. She is careful not to share personal information she learns about her clients with others.

23-3

The coffee table in this sitting area can be used for storage and as additional seating when needed.

Living Green

Furniture can be restyled. The options are limited only by your imagination. By refinishing wood or reupholstering furniture, you can have a new look to match your décor.

show dirt easily. Choose lighter colors and decorative fabrics for furniture used infrequently.

Furniture Styles

Common furniture styles include traditional, modern, and contemporary. Furnishings in a traditional design are based on popular styles of the past. An example is Early American furniture, which originated in the colonial period. The result was rustic, sturdy furniture often made of pine, birch, or maple.

Modern furniture has simple lines. It reflects the theme of "form follows function." For instance, the basic purpose of a chair is to provide a comfortable place to sit. Unnecessary frills are omitted in the design of modern furniture.

Contemporary furnishings are based on the latest designs and materials. The pieces usually have plain lines and geometric shapes. Contemporary furnishings often use metal, plastics, and glass with or without wood. Textures are emphasized more than decoration.

Judging Quality in Furniture

The type of materials used is one factor to consider when judging furniture quality. The second factor is how well the furniture is made.

When selecting furniture, consider the following guidelines:

- Look for sturdy joints on wood furniture. Quality joints are pricey and usually hidden from view. By comparison, joints held together by glue, screws, or nails are weaker.

- The frame for an upholstered piece should feel sturdy. It should be reinforced with corner blocks or steel plates. The joints should be secure.

- To judge the quality and performance of springs and cushions, sit on the piece of furniture.

- Upholsteries such as silk or loosely woven fabrics are not durable. Soil-repellent and fire-resistant finishes improve safety and durability.

Organizing Living Space

The appearance, convenience, and comfort of a room depend partly on how the living space is organized. How the furniture is arranged should reflect how the room is used. Before arranging furniture, review the space available as well as the activities planned for it. Activities that occur in shared family space will differ from those that take place in personal space.

Shared Space

Most homes have areas where family members can gather and spend time with one another. Kitchens, dining areas, and family rooms are examples of indoor family space. Porches, patios, and yards are examples of outdoor family space.

Family space is shared space. Areas where family members can communicate and enjoy the company of one another are important in fostering family unity. Sharing family space also helps build relationships outside the family. You are more prepared for sharing space with others, such as a roommate or spouse.

Shared space should reflect the needs and tastes of all family members, and also provide a comfortable space for everyone in the home. Having enough furniture to accommodate all family members as well as guests is important, too. Also, arrange the furniture in these areas to make communication easier.

Many families maximize their living space by using it in multiple ways. Examples are a hide-a-bed sofa that converts to sleeping space for an overnight guest and a kitchen table used for homework. See **23-4**.

Shared spaces often contain one or more **activity centers**. This is a grouping of all the furnishings needed for a particular activity. For instance, you might plan an activity center for using a computer or a laptop. It would include a desk or similar surface, chair, lamp, and anything else needed by those who share a computer.

23-4

When shopping for a kitchen table, many families look for a smooth, durable top so children can use it to do homework.

Personal Space

All people need some personal space where they can be alone and store their belongings. Many teens prefer private bedrooms, but it is not always possible. When siblings share a room, they often arrange furniture to achieve greater privacy. They may use bookcases as visual barriers.

Some shared spaces are designed to include quiet sitting or reading areas used as personal spaces. Family members can use these to seek privacy if desired. People may also find private space outdoors.

Making a Scale Floor Plan

As you plan furniture arrangements for your home, you need to consider the space available. A very useful tool for doing this is a scale floor plan. A **scale floor plan** is a drawing that shows the size and shape of a room to scale. Typically, one-fourth of an inch on the scale floor plan is equal to one foot in the room of a home.

To make a scale floor plan for a room, begin by measuring the floor. Draw a scale floor plan on graph paper. Then measure the width and depth of each piece of furniture in the room. Draw the pieces of furniture on graph paper using the same scale as the floor plan. Color the pieces of furniture the color you want the furniture to be. This will help give you a good idea of the color balance in the room. Cut out the furniture pieces. Arrange them on the scale floor plan until you find the best arrangement for your room.

As you arrange furniture pieces on your floor plan, you need to keep traffic patterns in mind. **Traffic patterns** are the paths people follow as they move within and between rooms. These patterns should allow people to walk through a room freely. They should avoid cutting through a conversation area or in front of someone's view. See **23-5**.

After deciding how to arrange furniture on your scale floor plan, you can begin placing furniture in your room. There are several guidelines you should follow.

- Avoid too much furniture in a room.
- Place large pieces first.
- Place large pieces parallel to the walls.
- Allow enough space to use the furniture. For example, you need space in front of a dresser to open drawers.
- Arrange upholstered furniture among pieces of wood furniture.

Computer Programs

Some computer programs, such as those for computer-aided drafting and design (CADD), can help you create floor plans and design interiors. You must input the dimensions of the room and the location of doors, windows, electrical outlets, and other important features. The program will then draw the room to the scale you designate.

Math Connection

Floor Plan

Randy would like to redecorate his bedroom. He decides to start with new carpeting. When Randy visits a carpet website, he is asked what the floor area of the room is. How will Randy determine this? First Randy measures his room. It is 9½ feet by 14 feet. To find the floor area in square feet, Randy multiplies the length of the room by the width of the room using this formula:

length of room × width of room = floor area

9.5 feet × 14 feet = 133 square feet

Next, he converts square feet to square yards.

133 square feet ÷ 9 = 14.8 square yards

Finally, Randy rounds up and places an order for 15 square yards of carpet.

23-5

Using a scale floor plan can save you time when arranging furniture and planning traffic patterns.

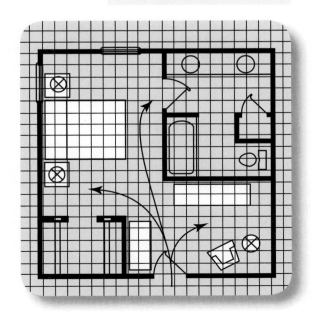

Most programs also have a wide variety of symbols shaped like furniture and appliances. You select the furnishings desired and arrange them. The computer program makes it easy to arrange the symbols and replace those that prove unsuitable. You can keep making changes until you design the scale plan that fits your needs.

By making a floor plan before attempting to arrange furniture, you save a great deal of time and physical effort. You can also avoid mistaken purchases and store returns.

Using Accessories

Accessories can transform an ordinary room into a unique living space. Many accessories, such as pictures, flowers, and statues, are purely decorative. Other accessories are functional, too. For example, clocks display the time and lamps provide lighting.

As you work with accessories, keep these hints in mind:

- Select accessories with textures and colors that go well with the rest of the room.

- Keep proportion in mind. You may choose a tiny vase with one flower for a small shelf, but a large table needs something bigger.

- Consider the design element of line. Some spaces need vertical lines, while others would benefit from horizontal, diagonal, or curved lines.

Living Green

When furnishing your home or room, make your own accessories such as pillows, picture frames, and vases. Recycle fabrics, containers, and other materials to make one-of-a-kind accessories to brighten any room.

Reading Review

1. How do warm colors affect the appearance of a room's size?
2. What are the five types of rhythm?
3. What two rules should be followed when using emphasis in design?
4. Paths people follow as they move within a room are called _____ _____.
5. What is the difference between functional and decorative accessories? Give two examples of each type.

Section 23-2

Home Safety and Security

Objectives

After studying this section, you will be able to

- **explain** how to prevent accidents in the home.
- **identify** ways to provide for personal security.
- **describe** basic emergency procedures.

Key Term

accident

Most people think of their homes and surrounding environments as safe, secure places. However, safety and security cannot be taken for granted, even in familiar settings. You can prevent accidents and protect yourself by following safety precautions and preparing for the unexpected.

Preventing Accidents in the Home

Accidents are unexpected events that cause losses, injuries, and sometimes death. They are the leading cause of death for teenagers. Accidents kill or injure thousands of people in homes annually. Most can be prevented.

What causes accidents? Human error is a major factor. People may become less careful in certain circumstances, especially when ill, tired, in a hurry, or under stress. The most common types of household accidents are falls, fires, poisonings, and electric shock.

Falls

Falling from high places, tripping, or slipping on a wet surface are common accidents in and around the home. Of these accidents, falls are the most common. Older adults and young children are the most frequent victims. Prevent falls and help make your home safer by doing the following:

- Never stand on chairs, tables, or counters instead of a ladder or step stool.
- Use steady ladders or step stools and stay off the top step.
- Do not exceed the weight limit of the ladder. If no label is present, assume the limit is 200 pounds for the person plus any carried items. See **23-6**.

Analyze and Solve

Discuss the importance of securing furniture, appliances, and electronics to walls to prevent these items from tipping over or falling. Cooperatively investigate the use of anchoring kits or restraints to secure items to walls. How do the restraints work? How are they anchored to walls or floors? How do such anchors help keep young children and other family members safe from injury?

23-6

The label on the side of this ladder specifies a weight limit.

- Look for and put away items on the floor, such as toys, shoes, or boxes that may cause someone to trip.
- Wipe up spills on counters and floors immediately.
- Use sturdy, nonskid rugs on wood or tile floors.
- Use nonskid strips in bathtubs and on shower floors.
- Avoid walking on wet floors indoors and slippery surfaces outdoors.
- Place a night-light in hallways and bathrooms to help see at night.
- Keep outdoor walkways clear of ice, snow, and objects.

Fires

Fires are the second leading cause of deaths at home. Careless smoking, kitchen fires, electrical shorts, and mishandled chemicals are common fire hazards.

Kitchen Safety

The kitchen can be a very dangerous place. Safely store matches beyond the reach of children. Keep hot appliances away from materials that can catch fire. Also keep paper towels, pot holders, and kitchen towels away from hot cooking surfaces.

Kitchen fires start suddenly, often without warning. When food is cooking, never leave it unattended. Grease can ignite if it gets too hot. Keep kitchens clean since grease buildup is highly flammable. Pay special attention to the range hood and areas near the range. Always keep a fire extinguisher in the kitchen area and know how to use it.

Another part of kitchen safety is preventing burns. Turn pot handles away from the front of the range when you are cooking. Do not reach over lighted burners. Use dry, heat-resistant oven mitts to remove hot pans from the oven. Lift lids and covers away from your face to prevent steam burns. Turn off appliances and range controls when you finish cooking.

Electrical Hazards

Electrical shorts caused by frayed cords, faulty wiring, or misused appliances start many fires. If electrical cords are frayed or cracked, replace them. Do not run cords or wires under carpets or rugs. Avoid overloading electrical outlets with too many plugs. Use appliances and cords that meet current safety standards. To make sure they do, look for a safety seal such as the Underwriters Laboratories (UL) seal. Use appliances properly, and when finished, unplug them and put them away.

Flammable Chemicals and Heating Equipment

It is important to store flammable chemicals, such as cleaning fluids and aerosol sprays, in safety containers. Always read the label to find out if a product is flammable. Some chemicals, such as glues and nail polish remover, produce flammable vapors that could ignite. Never store or use flammable chemicals near a heat source.

Always follow the instructions for proper use and care of fireplaces, wood-burning stoves, and space heaters. Use a fire screen or glass doors on a fireplace and have the chimney cleaned regularly. Make sure wood-burning stoves are properly installed and maintained. Keep space heaters in top-notch condition and use them away from water and flammable materials.

Smoke and Carbon Monoxide Safety Precautions

Most deaths and injuries from home fires and carbon monoxide (CO) are caused by inhalation. Deadly smoke and gases may be produced before signs appear. More importantly, most fires start at night when people are asleep. This is why having efficient smoke and CO detectors and an escape plan is so important, **23-7**.

23-7

Smoke and carbon monoxide (CO) detectors usually alert residents in enough time for a safe escape. Combination devices are available.

Smoke and CO detectors should be on every level of the home. Hallways, bedrooms, and attics are the best sites. Attach the detector on or near the ceiling according to the manufacturer's instructions. Check each detector once a month to make sure it works properly. Replace dead batteries immediately.

An emergency escape plan can be a lifesaver if a fire strikes. To get prepared, draw a floor plan of your home and map two escape routes. Then conduct a fire drill that involves all family members. Be sure everyone knows the plan perfectly as well as where to meet outdoors.

If a fire occurs, gather everyone and move quickly through the nearest reachable escape route. If the room is filled with smoke, stay close to the floor as you exit. Feel each door before opening it. If a door is hot, take another route. Close all doors behind you when leaving and do not re-enter the home for any reason. If clothing catches on fire, the person should drop to the ground and roll over to smother the flames. When everyone is safely out, call the fire department. If someone cannot get out, leave the home and call the fire department or 911.

Poisoning

Another leading cause of death at home is poisoning. Children are especially in danger because they are curious and tend to put things into their mouths. Store all poisonous chemicals out of children's reach, preferably in locked cabinets. This includes cosmetics, cleaning products, pesticides, fertilizers, and medications. All can be hazardous when improperly used. Securely replace child-resistant caps on products after every use.

Common causes of poisonings among adults include consuming toxic substances from mislabeled containers and overdosing on medications. Store chemicals in their original, properly labeled containers. Chemicals that could be mistaken for food products or seasonings should never be stored in the kitchen. Before taking any medications, labels should be carefully checked for the correct dosage.

Electric Shock

Electricity always presents the potential for hazards. It can spark fires as well as cause electric shock. The shock can range from minor to life threatening. Low-voltage electric current can cause burns by passing through the body, while high-voltage current halts breathing and heart activity. It may even cause death.

Household wiring, electrical outlets, power tools, and appliances should always be used with safety in mind.

- Cover unused outlets with safety covers when children are around. This prevents them from sticking fingers or objects into outlets.

- Keep electrical appliances and cords in good repair. Never use appliances that do not work properly, especially those with damaged cords. Do not use electrical cords with broken plugs or exposed wires.

- Never use electrical appliances near water.

Water and electricity is a deadly combination because water conducts electricity. Sinks, bathtubs, and showers are obvious areas for electrical hazards, but stay alert to unexpected places. For example, do not stand on a damp or wet floor when using an electrical appliance. Do not use power tools on an aluminum ladder near water. In the kitchen, wipe up spills immediately and keep damp cloths away. Always dry your hands before turning power switches on and off or when using electrical appliances or tools. Electrical appliances such as hair dryers, shavers, and radios should not be used around water.

Providing for Security

No home or neighborhood is completely safe from break-ins and attacks. However, certain measures can help make these places safer. You can help prevent break-ins by making it more difficult for intruders. Your best defense against an attack is to be alert and avoid unsafe situations.

In Your Home

Taking extra precautions will help you feel secure when you are home alone. The first step is to identify security hazards that might make your home an easy target. Taking action to reduce or eliminate these hazards is the next step.

Conduct a Home Security Inspection

The main purpose of a security inspection is to identify security hazards in your home. This inspection should include a check of your home's doors, windows, lights, locks, and landscaping. For a complete checklist of items to inspect, contact your local police. Some departments have officers assigned to conduct the inspections. An example of a home security checklist is shown in **23-8**.

Make the Home Secure

Would-be intruders are more likely to strike a home that looks vacant or easy to enter. Increase your home's security by following these tips.

- Create the appearance of activity in your home, even when you are not there. For instance, use timers to turn lights on and off at different times.

- Vary your daily routines slightly so you are not leaving and arriving daily at the same times.

- Keep doors and windows locked at all times—even when at home. Heavy solid wood or metal doors with secure locks offer the best protection against break-ins. Keyed locks on windows provide extra security.

- Leave exterior lights on at night since lighting is the greatest deterrent to intruders. All entrance doors, parking areas, and courtyards should be well lighted. Motion-activated lights are helpful.

Serving Your Community

You can help make your neighborhood safer and more secure by joining a group of neighbors who work together to reduce crime. As part of a watch group, you learn to look for suspicious people, vehicles, or activities. Watch for anything that appears strange and note descriptions of the people and their vehicles. Also, record their license numbers. If they behave suspiciously, immediately call police.

Home Security Inspection Checklist

Front, Side, Rear, and Basement Entrances

- Are the doors of solid wood construction or metal with secure locks?
- Are the door frames strong enough to prevent forced entry?
- Does each entrance have a screen or storm door with a secure lock?
- Are all entrances well lighted?
- Can the entrances be observed from the street?
- Are all entrances clear of landscaping (trees, shrubs, bushes) that could conceal an intruder?

Ground Floor and Upper Floor Windows

- Do all windows have secure locks in working condition?
- Do windows have screens or storm windows that lock from the inside?
- Are window areas well lighted and clear of overgrown landscaping that could conceal an intruder?

Garage Doors and Windows

- Is the overhead door equipped with a secure lock?
- Is the entry door kept closed and locked at all times?
- Are tools and ladders stored in the garage?
- Are all doors well lighted on the outside?

23-8

Law enforcement agencies use this type of checklist to perform home security inspections for residents.

- Consider installing an alarm system for added security, no matter when the home is occupied or empty. A sensory device that sounds an alarm in case of burglary is one type. Prices vary based on the complexity of the system.

Protect Yourself When Home Alone

You need to protect yourself from dangerous situations when you are home alone. You also need to know how to get help in an emergency.

- Leave a spare house key with a trusted neighbor. Never hide extra keys outside. If you come home and find a door unlocked or open, do not go inside. Go to a neighbor's home or another safe place to call the police. Have them check the house first in case an intruder is inside.

- If someone calls or comes to the door, do not tell the person you are alone.

- When the doorbell rings, look through a nearby window or a door peephole to see who is there. Ask the person for identification before you open the door.

- If you must go out for a short time, lock all doors.

- Use night-lights in several rooms. Keep outside areas, especially door entrances, well lighted. If you must go out at night, make sure lights are left on inside and outside for your return.

- If you are returning home at night, ask a friend to accompany you and wait until you are safely indoors. If you must return home alone, have your key ready and get inside quickly.

- Keep a list of emergency telephone numbers posted near the phone. These numbers should include your parents' workplace and cell phone, a neighbor or nearby relative, and police and fire departments.

Away from Home

If you feel a place or a situation is dangerous, avoid it. If you find yourself in a situation that makes you feel uncomfortable, leave as quickly as possible. Whether you are walking or driving, a common-sense approach can help you avoid danger.

As You Walk

Avoid walking alone, especially at night. A lone person is an easier target for attack. If you must walk alone, stay alert to your surroundings and watch for suspicious people. Choose well-lighted, busy streets, not dark paths, vacant lots, alleys, parks, and shortcuts across parking lots.

Walk at a steady pace, appearing calm and confident. The more vulnerable you appear, the more susceptible you are to attack. If you think you are being followed, head for a well-lighted public area. A store or restaurant is a good choice. Use a cell phone or get to a phone in a safe area and call the police.

Avoid wearing jewelry or clothing that looks expensive and draws attention. Keep your valuables in your front pockets. If you carry a purse, keep it tightly tucked under your arm or out of sight. Keep extra money safely hidden (not in your wallet) for an emergency bus fare or cab fare.

If an attacker wants your money or jewelry, let him or her have it. Do not resist, as you could get hurt. It is better to give up the item than to risk your life. Notice the attacker's face and clothing so you can describe the person to police.

In Your Car

Have your keys ready to enter the car quickly. Before opening the door, check to make sure no one is hiding inside. Then, immediately lock the doors. When driving, avoid empty streets and unsafe areas.

If you think a vehicle is following you, drive to a well-lighted public area or the nearest police station. If immediate help is not available, honk the horn nonstop and turn on the emergency signals to grab others' attention. Do not drive home, as the other car may follow. Never stop for the other car.

Keep your car in good running condition with a full tank of gas to lessen the chance of stopping for car problems. If you must stop, raise the car hood and turn on the emergency signals. Use a cell phone to call for

21st Century Skills

Adaptability. Sharon sometimes works the night shift and then is assigned the day shift. Sometimes she is required to work a double shift. Her employer is pleased that she can adapt her schedule to the needs of the company.

Wellness Awareness

Research basic supplies that should be included in a first aid kit. Prepare a first aid kit for your home or classroom.

help. If someone stops, do not roll down your window, open the door, or leave the car. Ask the person to call for help, but stay inside your car with the doors locked until help arrives.

It is important to always park your car in well-lighted areas. If you cannot start your car in a parking lot, call home or the nearest service station for help. Do not accept help from strangers or get into a stranger's car.

Emergency Procedures

An *emergency* is an unexpected event that requires immediate action. Emergencies frequently result from accidents, but are also caused by bad weather and many other factors. In an emergency, you need to remain as calm as possible so you can think clearly. You do not want to upset a scared or injured person.

A well-stocked first aid kit contains basic supplies to care for someone sick or mildly injured. Keep first aid kits at home, in your car, and with camping and hiking gear.

If someone appears seriously injured, call 911 right away. See **23-9**. Some emergency victims require specialized procedures such as *cardiopulmonary resuscitation (CPR)*, a combination of rescue breathing and chest compressions. Hands-Only CPR, or CPR which only uses chest compressions, is an alternative response. The American Red Cross and American Heart Association regularly offer CPR training courses. Learning first aid skills may help you save someone's life.

In a weather emergency, stay tuned to a local news station on a portable radio. You will hear weather updates and important safety instructions. In case you need them, keep a three-day supply of food, water, and other necessities on hand for each family member and pet.

23-9

Knowing how to respond and give first aid in an emergency may help you save someone's life.

Responding to an Emergency

1. In an emergency, while one person gives care, another can call for help.
2. Call 911. Tell the dispatcher the following:
   - Location of the emergency. Include cross streets, room number, and telephone number you are calling from.
   - What happened. For example, motor vehicle crash, sudden illness.
   - What seems to be wrong. For example, victim is bleeding, unconscious.
   - What first aid is being given. For example, control of bleeding.
3. Don't hang up until the dispatcher hangs up. The dispatcher may tell you how to take care of the victim.
4. Remain at the scene. Stay with the victim until help arrives.

Reading
Review

1. True or false. Accidents are the leading cause of death for teenagers.
2. Name the four most common types of household accidents.
3. If you are home alone, what safety precautions should you follow?
4. True or false. When away from home, the best way for people to prevent being attacked is to avoid dangerous situations.
5. What information should you give when calling for help in an emergency?

Section 23-3

Keep It Clean!

Objectives

After studying this section, you will be able to

- **explain** reasons for keeping the home clean.
- **plan** a cleaning schedule that involves everyone in your home.
- **list** measures you can take to help make household cleaning easier.

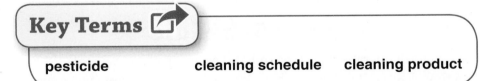

Key Terms

pesticide   cleaning schedule   cleaning product

Cleaning tasks can seem overwhelming and dreary at times, but certain steps can make them less tiresome. Household cleaning becomes easier if you know what products and tools to use. Tasks are more likely to get done on time if the family follows a cleaning schedule that uses the help of all family members.

Why Clean?

There are many reasons for keeping a home neat and clean. A well-kept house provides more than just an attractive appearance. Besides a pleasant living environment, cleaning provides these additional benefits:

- *Health.* Cleanliness reduces harmful bacteria. This helps prevent foodborne illnesses and other disease-causing organisms.

- *Safety.* Residents of a clean, organized home are less prone to the hazards of clutter, such as accidents and injuries.

- *Organization.* Tools and materials are stored in their proper places, so you know where to find them. Work and play areas are free of clutter and ready for use.

- *Efficiency.* Tools and power equipment that are clean and well maintained work more reliably. They have a longer service life, too.

- *Pest control.* Good housekeeping habits help prevent rodents, insects, and other pests. When using **pesticides**, the strong chemicals designed for pest control, carefully follow label directions. Persistent problems may need a professional exterminator.

Routine cleanup keeps household tasks manageable and relatively brief. Putting off small tasks for too long only compounds the workload. It can also jeopardize the family's safety.

How Clean Is Clean?

The people who share a home should decide how it should be kept. There must be agreement on what is important. Do housekeeping tasks and cleanliness standards conflict with other interests and values? Do people sharing the home agree on the importance of the home's appearance?

Together as a family, establish standards for cleaning. Involve all family members in setting the standards. It is hard for one person to set standards acceptable to all. What is clean to one person may fail to meet another's standards. Likewise, what might suggest clutter to one person might be a peaceful, lived-in atmosphere to another. Family members should seek a balance between demanding a spotless home and lowering their standards.

Using a Cleaning Schedule

If all family members understand and agree on cleaning goals, organizing cleaning tasks is much easier. A cleaning schedule helps the family achieve its cleaning goals. A **cleaning schedule** is a written plan identifying what tasks must be done, by whom, and how often. The schedule reminds everyone what to do and when.

Writing the Schedule

Develop a schedule by writing down all cleaning tasks that come to mind. Then separate the tasks by room. Try to determine how long each task should take and how often it needs to be done. Finally, decide who will be responsible for each job.

Unless you live alone, divide the workload among all capable family members. Even small children can handle simple chores. Occasionally rotating tasks can promote understanding and cooperation.

When assigning housekeeping tasks, keep the personalities and lifestyles of family members in mind. If one person enjoys cleaning floors, give the task to that person. If one family member has a busy schedule, he or she might be given less time-consuming tasks. This arrangement makes it much easier for everyone to contribute, **23-10**. Everyone pitches in to make the home a more pleasant place to live.

Performing Cleaning Tasks

Consider the following questions and answers when creating the cleaning schedule and performing cleaning tasks:

- *When is the best time to do them?* This answer depends on the schedule of the person responsible for handling the cleaning task. It also depends on how often an area or item needs to be cleaned.

- *What is the best cleaning method to use?* This is often outlined in use-and-care instructions, on labels, and/or in related booklets or brochures.

- *What is the best order for doing the tasks?* If not immediately apparent, follow this general rule for cleaning a room: Clean from top to bottom, and from outside edges to the center.

As you clean, you will develop methods of your own for making cleaning easier and faster. Remember that a cleaning schedule is not meant to run your life. If it does, the schedule is too rigid. A healthy amount of flexibility should be allowed in the schedule to fit your lifestyle.

23-10
Accepting and maintaining standards of cleanliness is easier when you help define them.

Cleaning Products and Tools

Cleaning products and tools help make the cleaning process more efficient. They also make cleaning easier on all family members. Household cleaners are available as liquids, gels, powders, solids, sheets, and pads. They are used on painted, plastic, metal, porcelain, and other surfaces. Some leave a shiny finish for a polished look. While all-purpose cleaners are designed for general use, many cleaning products work best on specialized jobs. Rug shampoos, glass cleaners, and oven cleaners are some examples.

Cleaning products are the materials used to remove soil. Cleaning products must be selected and used with care. Always read labels to choose the right product for the job. Follow instructions carefully to avoid accidents and health hazards.

Science Connection

Surface Tension and Cleaning Agents

Many cleaning agents are added to water. They are used as *wetting agents* to improve the cleaning ability of water. Cleaning agents reduce water's *surface tension*. This force causes water molecules to cling together and form beads. Surface tension keeps water from penetrating soil.

Planning for Easy Cleaning

Cleaning tools are for fast and efficient removal of soil from floors and other household surfaces. Tools can fill a closet fast, so selecting basic tools is important. By choosing long-handled tools, you can extend your reach and add leverage for efficiency.

Basic tools include a long-handled broom, dustpan, mop, and duster. Microfiber mop heads and cleaning cloths—or other lint-free cloths and mops—are used for wiping surfaces to remove soil and dust. Scrub brushes are needed for soil that is difficult to remove. Use clearly labeled spray bottles for an all-purpose cleaning product, disinfectant, and deodorizer. Finally, a vacuum cleaner with strong, but adjustable, suction and versatile attachments such as nozzles for hard and soft floors, a dusting device, an upholstery attachment, and a crevice tool will help you cover essential cleaning needs.

To prevent big messes and cleanup headaches, you can stop dirt before it enters your home. You can also make cleanup easier by providing storage space for items that cause clutter. With good planning, you can even reduce the size and frequency of certain cleaning tasks.

Use Preventive Measures

Try to prevent dust and dirt from entering the home by focusing on the source. Keep outside walks, steps, and porches swept to reduce the amount of dirt brought indoors. Use doormats and foot scrapers outside each entrance and a small rug just inside. Have boot storage near entrances to prevent the tracking of soil through the home.

Try to keep windows closed on windy days to prevent dust from blowing in. Change furnace filters often to avoid circulating dust indoors during heating and cooling seasons. A furnace humidifier helps keep dust down as it conditions dry air.

Lay out old newspapers before starting projects that create dirt or litter. Debris can be wrapped up in the paper and thrown away when the project is finished. No additional cleanup may be necessary.

You can avoid a lot of future cleaning jobs by choosing easy-care fabrics and durable finishes on your furnishings. For example,

Science Connection

Sustainable Cleaning Products

To be sustainable, people must meet their current needs in ways that will not compromise the environment for others, now and in the future. There are a few basic household products that can be used to create your own sustainable cleaning products. The following items are known to clean well, and save the environment and your money.

- Baking soda—cleans and deodorizes
- Washing soda—cuts grease and removes stains
- Borax—cleans, deodorizes, and disinfects
- Biodegradable soap—a nontoxic cleaner that breaks down into basic substances through normal environmental processes
- Distilled white vinegar—cuts grease and smells fresh
- Oxygen bleach—removes stains as an alternative to chlorine bleach
- Hydrogen peroxide—sanitizes surfaces, including cutting boards
- Rubbing alcohol—disinfects surfaces

Read labels and research the above products. Look for formulas to *safely* combine them as needed.

a family room with light-colored carpeting and upholstery is sure to need constant care and cleaning.

Provide Adequate Storage

Finding a place for everything is not always possible, but clutter can be stopped if most items are organized. Try to store items where they are used. For instance, hanging up coats is easy when a coat closet or coatrack is next to the door.

Each room should have some type of storage space, ideally a closet or built-in area. If not available, furnishings and accessories can be adapted for storage.

Scheduling General Maintenance

Routine maintenance is an important part of caring for your home. Sometimes a drain gets clogged, a faucet leaks, or a fuse blows. These routine problems are usually minor and easy to fix. Occasionally, a more-serious problem occurs. It may involve the building's structure or the plumbing, heating, or electrical systems. Watching for problems and keeping everything in good working condition will make your home safer and more secure.

A plan for regular inspections and maintenance will keep you ahead of costly major repairs. Conduct inspections weekly, monthly, and seasonally.

- *Weekly maintenance* helps you notice minor problems as soon as they occur. Checking for leaky faucets is an example.

- *Monthly maintenance* allows you to take care of necessary tasks before major problems develop. Changing the filters on heating and cooling equipment is an example.

- *Seasonal maintenance* is linked to the onset of hot or cold weather. Actual tasks depend on the climate in which you live. For example, fall maintenance on a home in Florida will differ from that on a home in Minnesota.

You will probably think of other maintenance chores your family performs to keep your home in good repair. Make these chores a part of your cleaning schedule. Repairs made by family members cost less than hiring a professional. Also, most maintenance tasks can be done at the family's convenience.

Mental Health Awareness

Clutter

Clutter in your home environment can interfere with your ability to focus and concentrate. A disorganized, cluttered home can also indicate emotional struggles, such as unresolved fear or grief.

Reading
Review

1. Name and describe four benefits of a clean living environment.
2. A _____ _____ is a written plan identifying what tasks must be done, by whom, and how often.
3. List three preventive measures that will keep soil from entering the home.
4. Name three environmentally friendly cleaning substances.

Chapter 23 Review

Summary

The elements of design are the building blocks for good design. The principles of design are the guidelines for using the elements of design.

Furnishing your home is an important step and should be considered carefully. You will need to determine which areas are shared space or personal space. After choosing furniture from the many styles available, consider how to arrange it. Accessories should coordinate with other furnishings.

Quality of life depends on important factors such as safety, security, and maintaining a healthful environment. Accidents and attackers can threaten your safety and security. To keep them from harming you at home or away from home, you need to identify and eliminate hazards.

While people have different cleaning standards, regular care is needed for safety and comfort. Preventive maintenance, easy-care décor, adequate storage space, and the right cleaning supplies make cleaning tasks easier. Creating a cleaning schedule also helps manage the cleaning process.

Critical Thinking

1. **Recognize alternatives.** Find examples of vertical, horizontal, diagonal, and curved lines in your classroom. Imagine you are given the job of redesigning the room. List ways you would create greater interest through the use of line.

2. **Analyze information.** Visit a furniture showroom. Have a salesperson explain the signs of quality construction.

Study the labels and keep a list of the information they contain.

3. **Evaluate risks.** Develop a safety checklist for each room in your home and use it to conduct a safety inspection. Identify potential hazards and determine how they should be corrected.

4. **Judge actions.** While walking through your neighborhood one evening, you see someone following you. What action would you take to avoid an attack?

21st Century Applications

5. **Global awareness.** Research the Chinese philosophy of Feng Shui, particularly its directions for blending interior design with the forces of nature. Summarize your findings in a presentation to the class.

6. **Information, communications, and technology literacy.** Use drawing software to create a scale floor plan of a room in your home or school. Use basic shapes to represent the furniture in your room and traffic patterns. Rearrange the furniture, keeping activity centers and traffic patterns in mind. Determine the best possible arrangement for the room.

7. **Initiative and self-direction.** Use computer software to make a chart. List the names of each room in your home as main headings. Under each heading, list the cleaning tasks and cleaning supplies needed for each room. Include a short explanation of how each area should be cleaned and which cleaning agents or products are

ideal to use. Discuss your chart with other family members. Consider using this chart as a basis for creating a cleaning schedule.

Core
Skills

8. **Speaking.** Search current interior design and housing magazines and websites for the latest in furniture trends. Give a brief oral report, displaying pictures and identifying your sources in a comprehensive bibliography.

9. **Math.** Estimate the total cost of decorating a one-room apartment that has kitchen cabinets and appliances along one wall. Pick furniture, window coverings, table and/or floor lamps, and any other items you want. List each item and use online retailers to identify costs.

10. **Speaking and listening.** Discuss in class how to prevent electrical fires. What factors can cause them? What steps can be taken to help avoid electrical fires in the home?

11. **Science.** Research the ingredients and the science behind the cleaning action of chemical drain cleaners. Discuss your findings in class.

12. **Reading.** Visit the National Sheriffs' Association neighborhood watch website. Report the type of information found on the site. Also identify the watch groups registered in your state. Create a brief handout outlining these groups and their contact information.

Leadership
Development

As a part of work toward the Power of One National Program or Career Connection, plan a visit to a large furniture manufacturer or retailer or a specialty accessory shop. (The trip could serve as part of your Working on Working project.) The activity will help you learn more about local businesses and the various careers linked to them.

Portfolio
Builder

Design a study area for yourself. Draw a floor plan of the area. Sketch the area and include color samples. Indicate the furniture and accessories you would need. Describe why this would be a good study area and the elements and principles of design you used. Include your study area plans in your portfolio.

Journal
Writing

You are decorating your first apartment. Some of your choices depend on which options are easier to clean and maintain. You need to choose an area rug and other design details. What types of accessories and fabrics do you prefer?

Write About It: *Which options would you select? Are these the easiest options to clean? If not, how will your choices affect your cleaning schedule?*

Chapter 24
Transportation

Reading Prep

The summary at the end of the chapter highlights the most important concepts. Read the summary first. Then make sure you understand those concepts as you read the chapter.

Concept Organizer

Use a sequence chain to illustrate the steps involved in purchasing a car. Include a few details for each step.

G-WLEARNING.com

Click on the activity icon to visit www.g-wlearning.com/comprehensive/8062 to access online vocabulary activities using key terms from the chapter.

kali9/iStock/Getty Images Plus

Types of Transportation

Objectives

After studying this section, you will be able to

- **list** different forms of transportation.
- **evaluate** your transportation options.

Key Terms

mass transit   car pool

Choosing transportation is an important decision. How do you get where you need to go? Right now you may be able to borrow a family car. However, your transportation needs may change over time. Eventually you may want to purchase your own car. You may prefer to rely on public transportation. Identifying and carefully considering all your options can help you choose your best available option.

Your choices for transportation may partly depend on where you live. Cities and suburbs usually have several forms of public transportation. Buses, trains, subways, and taxis may be some of the choices. In other areas, you may only have the option of using transportation you own. Each form of transportation has advantages and disadvantages.

Mass Transit

Mass transit, or public transportation, is usually less expensive than owning a car. People who use public transit may be able to save money by purchasing fare in bulk amounts, such as through a monthly pass.

If mass transit options are safe and reliable, using them can have many advantages over driving yourself. You will not have to fight traffic in crowded rush hours. You will also not have to find a safe, inexpensive place to park your car for the day.

Mass transit can also have disadvantages. You have to plan your day around a set schedule, which may involve reworking your arrangements. You will have to walk or drive to the mass transit station or stop, **24-1**. You may have to pay for parking at the station. Mass transit may be crowded and uncomfortable. In some areas, it may not be safe.

Taxis may be a perfect solution in large cities or for short-term specific needs. Keep in mind, though, that taxis also have disadvantages.

Mental Health Awareness

Public Transportation and Social Awareness

Using mass transit is an opportunity to learn important social skills. You can learn how and when to help others or ask for help, how to respond to offensive behavior, and how to interpret tone of voice and eye contact. Possessing these skills can bring you peace of mind and make the commute more pleasant and safer for everyone.

They can be expensive if used often. In addition, unless you call for a car ahead of time and wait, availability is uncertain. Taxi drivers also expect gratuity.

Cars

Many people enjoy the convenience and pleasure of owning a car. Having a car means having the freedom to go where you want whenever you want. Owning a car may be necessary for people whose other options are limited.

While some people may enjoy owning a car, others may dislike the responsibility. Cars are expensive to buy and maintain. Fuel and insurance are necessary expenses. Some owners may also have to pay for parking.

Some people take turns sharing their car with others through carpooling. A **car pool** is a group of people who commute together in one of the members' vehicles. Each member contributes to the fuel and additional costs such as parking. By sharing the cost of commuting, each member saves money.

Car pools have other benefits. Carpooling reduces the amount of traffic on the road, which is especially beneficial during crowded rush hours in large cities. Less traffic also means less pollution emitted by vehicles. Therefore, carpooling also helps the environment.

Two-Wheelers

Two-wheelers include bicycles, mopeds, and motorcycles. These options may be more economical than cars, but they can also be more dangerous. This type of transportation requires special safety equipment. Two-wheelers are also less convenient than cars for carrying passengers or personal belongings.

Bicycles

Bicycles save energy and do not produce pollutants, so they are good for the environment. Bicycling is also a physical activity that improves a person's health, **24-2**. While basic bicycles are inexpensive, special features add to the cost. Think carefully about what special features you want or need when making a purchase.

24-1

If a bus stop is a short walk from your home, the bus may be a convenient form of transportation for you.

Serving Your Community

Research seat-belt and child-restraint laws in your state. Develop posters to explain these requirements to parents. Obtain permission to display the posters in local malls and other public places.

Mopeds and Motor Scooters

Mopeds and motor scooters can be an inexpensive choice for transportation. However, because they are low-powered vehicles, they are unsuitable for long trips. Laws for scooters vary by city and state. Investigate applicable laws to see what types of permits, licenses, or insurance you need.

Motorcycles

Motorcycles come in many different models and sizes. Consider all the options and your needs before making a choice. If you are looking for a vehicle for short commutes, a basic cycle may be sufficient. More expensive features may be unnecessary for your purposes.

Generally, insurance is more expensive for motorcycles because of the safety risk. Laws vary by state, so research requirements before you make a purchase. Be sure to wear a helmet for safety whether it is required by law in your state or not.

Evaluating Your Choices

Every person has different transportation needs. By answering the following questions, you can begin to evaluate your options. Once you have done a thorough evaluation, you can pick the most logical choice.

- How far and how often do you need to travel?

- What options are available to you? Identify your available choices. Can you use mass transit? Does your family own a vehicle you can use when you need to? Is there someone with whom you could carpool?

- What are the long-term costs, such as car repairs, fuel increases, and mass transit fare increases? Compare the costs involved in each of your options.

- What form of transportation is most convenient to you? Which is closest to your home and work? Is weather an issue?

24-2

Bicycles are a healthful, enjoyable form of transportation.

Healthy Living

Avoid Distracted Driving

According to the Centers for Disease Control and Prevention, motor vehicle accidents are the leading cause of death for all teens. Although talking on a cell phone or texting creates a great accident risk for all drivers, the risk is even greater for teen drivers. These actions, in combination with inexperience, immaturity, and speed, can kill teen drivers or cause them to kill others in traffic accidents. Other distracting behaviors include listening to loud music and drinking alcoholic beverages. The best way to avoid the consequences of distracted driving is to avoid distractions and wear a seat belt.

Living Green

Car pool lanes, also known as high-occupancy vehicle (HOV) lanes, are available in some cities. Cars with two or more occupants are eligible to use car pool lanes. By reducing congestion and encouraging carpooling, these lanes help reduce emissions.

- Which of your options is safest? Are there any that are unsafe?
- Think about what you value most. Do you value time? comfort? the environment?

Reading
Review

1. _____ _____ is another term for public transportation.
2. List two benefits of car pools.

Section 24-2

Buying a Car

Objectives

After studying this section, you will be able to

- **identify** different types of car sellers.
- **evaluate** your transportation options.
- **explain** practices to use when buying a pre-owned car.
- **estimate** costs of buying a car.
- **discuss** criteria for choosing a service center.

Key Terms

certified used car

options

vehicle identification number (VIN)

If you decide to buy a car, you should first learn as much as you can about the process. Determine where you would like to purchase the car. Think about what features you need and desire. Estimate your costs and establish a budget. If you will be financing, do research for your best options.

Shopping for a Car

What is the best way to buy a car? Would you feel most comfortable using a traditional dealership? Would you prefer to use a competitive superstore? Would you ever consider buying a car over the Internet? Any of these options can help you find the best deal for your needs.

Traditional Dealerships

Traditional dealerships sell new and used cars, **24-3**. **Certified used cars** are cars that have been inspected and repaired. After this process, the dealer or manufacturer will often issue a new warranty. Dealerships provide financing for the purchase and have a service department.

The Internet

Use the Internet to find nearby dealers, private sales, and the most up-to-date information on available cars. You can also find information about different features on vehicles and compare prices. When ready to make a purchase, you can also buy a car online; however, it is important to know the pros and cons before making such a purchase.

Auto Superstores

Auto superstores offer new and used cars for fixed prices. You can use the superstore's website to search for attributes you desire in a car. These may include details such as price, model, and options. Superstores will often offer financing and servicing as well.

Communication. Carl is a salesperson at a car dealership. He knows communication skills play an important role in working with customers. He uses these skills to determine what his customers need. His communication skills have helped him develop a loyal customer base.

24-3

The knowledgeable, informative salespeople at traditional dealerships should be able to answer any of your questions.

Private Sellers

Many people buy used cars from private sellers. Unfortunately, buying a car in this way means that there is no warranty unless the original warranty is still in effect. If you plan to buy a car in this way, make sure to have the car checked beforehand by a reliable service technician. When buying a car "as is," you want to be aware of any problems before you commit to the purchase.

Consider Your Needs

Before you begin shopping for a vehicle, think specifically about what you need and want in a car, **24-4**. Consider the following questions:

- How far will you need to travel, and how often?
- What kind of roads will you be traveling?
- What is the vehicle's safety record?
- How large does the vehicle need to be?
- What features do you need? want?
- How important is fuel efficiency?
- What type of warranty would you prefer?
- What make, model, and color would you prefer?

Once you have made your list, determine how many of your criteria you can afford to meet. Since you may not be able to afford everything you need and want, prioritize your list. This way, you will be sure to

24-4

Think carefully about what wants and needs in a vehicle will give you the most satisfaction.

budget for the factors most important to you. Do research that will help you make choices carefully. Resources that will help you include

- *Kelley Blue Book*, which lists the estimated resale value of new and used cars
- *NADA Used Car Guide*, which lists general information on cars by the make, model, and year, as well as information on pricing
- Vehicle Safety Hotline, a toll-free number that gives safety data on various car models from the National Highway Traffic Safety Administration

Size and Style

Think about how much space you will need in a vehicle. You can buy a small compact car, a large sport-utility vehicle, or any size in between. Cars come in all different styles to fit your needs and personality. You can choose from sport cars, sedans, trucks, SUVs, or vans. Your choice may depend on how many passengers you intend to carry on a regular basis. If you plan to transport a lot of cargo, you may need larger trunk space.

Options

The basic features on a car are referred to as *standard equipment*. **Options** are additional features that may be added for appearance, safety, performance, or convenience. Standard equipment is included in the price of the car. Each option costs more, adding to the total price of the car, **24-5.**

Warranty

New cars have warranties. Some parts have full coverage while others have limited coverage. It is likely that the owner will have to meet requirements outlined in the warranty. This usually involves following scheduled maintenance recommendations.

24-5

Many options, while desirable, will add significantly to the price of the car.

Pre-Owned Cars

Used cars, also called *pre-owned cars*, are usually less expensive than a brand-new car. However, the buyer must be sure the car is in good condition before committing to the purchase. If a used car needs many repairs, it can eventually become more costly than buying a new car. There are various ways to check on the status of a car.

Buyers Guide Sticker

To protect consumers, the Federal Trade Commission has rules for used

cars sold by dealers. These rules require that a *Buyers Guide* sticker be displayed on the window of a used car the dealer is selling. The sticker provides helpful information for the consumer, such as any warranty coverage included. It also recommends that an independent automotive technician inspect the car.

VIN

Every car has a **vehicle identification number (VIN)**, which is assigned by the automobile industry. A formula is used to determine a unique VIN for each vehicle. Manufacturers place the VIN on the dashboard and on a sticker on the driver's side doorjamb.

The VIN can be used to find history reports on a particular used car. The records will include important information such as accidents involving the car, theft, and odometer records.

Previous Owner

You may wish to buy a car from its current owner, but remember that this purchase is unlikely to come with warranty coverage. In this case, you will want to ask questions about the reliability of the car, **24-6**. Questions to ask include the following:

- Are you the car's original owner?
- For what type of driving was the car primarily used?
- Do you have service records?

Estimating Car Costs

The purchase price of a car is only the beginning of car ownership expenses. You may only make a down payment on the car. If that is the case, you will be making monthly payments on the loan, which will include interest charges. Other costs to consider include

- taxes and fees
- insurance premiums
- licensing and registration (paid every year)
- fuel and other operating costs
- maintenance costs (oil changes, new tires and tire rotation, battery replacement)
- car repair costs
- parking

24-6

Buying a car from the current owner means you will have the opportunity to ask as many questions as possible.

Making a Final Choice

When you have decided on the details, it is time to test the car itself. You will need to test-drive the car. First, are you comfortable in the driver's seat? Are all controls within reach, and do you have good visibility? When driving the car, how does it handle? Test the car on the open road and in neighborhood driving, **24-7**. Test all the equipment so you understand how everything works.

If you are buying a used car, you will want to have the engine and all fluid levels checked. Check the amount of wear on the tires. When you test-drive, listen for noises and smoothness of the drive. These can help indicate if there are problems.

Financing

Many people use financing when they buy a car. Instead of paying the entire amount in cash, they get a loan and make payments in installments. The length of the repayment period and amount of monthly payments depend on how much you borrow. However, remember that part of the payment is the interest paid on the loan. Learning how financing works can help you make the right choices and learn how much you will really be paying.

Getting dealer financing may be convenient, but you might get better terms from another source. Banks, credit unions, and finance companies all offer loans. Gather as much information as you can so you can compare rates and terms before making a decision.

Financial Literacy

Budgeting for a Car

Most people need to budget carefully to afford a car. To determine your budget, start by figuring how much cash you have for the down payment. (Remember to include the cash you will need for licensing, registration, taxes, and insurance.)

Think about how much you will need to spend each month to cover costs. Consider recurring costs, such as gas, insurance, and parking. It is also wise to set up a fixed monthly allowance for repairs or other unexpected expenses. You may not need this money every month, but if you let it accumulate, you will have a sizable amount when you need it.

Once you have a complete look at your expenses, total your monthly income. Subtract all your monthly expenses. Will your income cover your car expenses as well? If not, you may need to reconsider your options.

24-7

Test-driving the car will help you make a final purchase decision.

Usually, you cannot get a car loan unless you are 18 years old and earn income from a job. Your credit report is also an important factor to creditors.

Cost of Financing

When you finance a loan, you pay back more than just the amount of money you borrow. You also must pay interest. How much you pay is determined by the annual percentage rate (APR) and the length of the repayment period. The more money you borrow, the more interest you will pay over time.

This is why you will want to pay as much cash as you can in the down payment. In addition, if you pay larger monthly payments, you will pay off your loan in less time. This will help you save on interest costs.

Leasing

Many people choose to lease their cars instead of buying. Leasing is generally less expensive than buying a car. The lessee makes a down payment and makes installment payments over time. However, at the end of the lease period, the lessee does not own the car.

When you sign a lease, make sure you know and understand all the terms of the contract. Check the requirements for returning the car, such as the condition of the vehicle. Also check for issues that will incur penalties, such as over-mileage or early termination of the lease.

Maintaining Your Car

You have the responsibility to maintain your car. Your car will perform better and be more reliable. You will also spend less money on fewer repairs.

Part of owning a car is keeping it in good condition. Not only will this save you money on costly repairs, but it will also keep you and your passengers safe. Familiarize yourself with the owner's manual for your vehicle. Some basic maintenance schedules will be outlined in the manual. Maintenance includes oil changes, tire rotation, and other routine servicing, **24-8**.

In newer model cars, warning lights will help notify you of potential problems with your vehicle. Other signs of problems are sounds, leaks, and odors. If you notice a problem with the way the car is driving, get it checked. Watch gauges to make sure they are within normal parameters. Getting a problem checked as soon as it appears may help limit the amount you spend on repairs.

Between trips to the service center for regular maintenance or repairs, there are several things you can learn to do yourself to keep your vehicle in good working order. You can:

- Check the oil. Familiarize yourself with the location of the oil dipstick and check it at least once per month between oil changes. Add oil if needed. Your owner's manual can guide you to the correct location and tell you the type and weight of oil to use.

- Check the tire pressure. Purchase a tire-pressure gauge and check your tire pressure monthly or before extended trips, **24-9**. The tire pressure for your vehicle is listed on the manufacturer's sticker inside the driver's side door. Also, check the tire pressure for your spare tire regularly.

- Check the windshield washer fluid reservoir and make sure it is filled. Also, clean the windows and mirrors on your car regularly for good vision.

- Check the brake lights, headlights, and turn signals at least once per month. You may need assistance from a friend or family member to do this.

Roman R/Shutterstock.com

24-8

Rotating tires regularly helps prevent damage that can lead to blowouts. Likewise, keeping safety equipment in the vehicle can help keep you safe when changing a tire.

Servicing Your Car

When choosing a repair center, you will want to find one that is convenient to you. The location should be close to your home or job. Check to see if you will need appointments or if you can simply bring the car at any time. The hours of operation should also work with your schedule. Keep in mind that you may sometimes have to leave your car for several hours while the repair work is done.

Servicing your car can be very costly. You will want to make sure you are comfortable with your service shop and trust them to make only necessary repairs. You can find mechanics at dealers, independent auto service centers, and chain auto service centers. Before choosing a service shop, you may want to ask friends and family members if they have experience with the shop's services. You can also check with the Better Business Bureau.

Africa Studio/Shutterstock.com

24-9

Checking and maintaining proper tire pressure helps ensure safe travel and extends the life of the tires. Underinflated tires can also lower your gas mileage.

Life Skills

Ride-Hailing: When You Need Another Ride

Although you may own a car, there may be times that you decide to use another form of transportation. One popular form of local public transportation is called *ride-hailing*. Several companies, including Uber and Lyft, offer phone apps through which you can call for a ride and pay by phone as well. You will be picked up where you are and dropped at your specified destination. This service is available in most cities. It is usually less expensive than taxis, and it does not require that you fit your schedule to a bus, train, or carpool schedule.

There are some concerns with the ride-hailing system. You must provide credit card information through the app on your phone, and drivers may not have to pass the more stringent background reviews necessary for taxi drivers. Vehicles also may not be kept up as well as is usual for taxis. To be safe when using ride-hailing services, always do the following:

- Before calling for a ride, be sure your phone has a full charge.
- Call and wait for the driver indoors or other safe place.
- Before getting in the car, have the driver *tell you* your name. Do not give your name first.
- Verify the car, license plate, and driver.
- Ride in the back seat behind the driver and travel with another person or group. Avoid traveling alone.
- Check the door as you get in the vehicle to ensure the child-safety locks are turned off in case you need to exit the vehicle in an emergency.
- Use the maps app on your phone to track your trip, and let the driver know you are doing so. Also, use the trip-sharing feature in the app to let your family and friends know where you are at all times.
- Be sure that your driver knows you have a tight schedule and that others are expecting you at a certain time and place.
- Stay alert! In case of an accident or other emergency, you may need to call 911 or the police.

You may wish to choose a repair center that meets the standards of American Automobile Association and has been endorsed by this organization. You can also check to see that the mechanics are ASE certified. This means they have training and passed the tests of the National Institute for Automotive Service Excellence.

Reading
Review

1. List four places to shop for a car.
2. What are three resources that can help you shop for a car?
3. What items should you keep in mind when estimating car costs?
4. How is leasing a car different from buying a car?

Chapter 24 Review

Summary

Many people have different transportation options from which to choose. These options may include public transportation, cars, or two-wheelers. Public transportation, or *mass transit*, tends to be a more environmentally friendly and cost-effective method of transportation. It can be inconvenient if you live far from a mass-transit stop or have an unusual schedule, though. You might also consider carpooling with other commuters to save money on gas prices. The choice may depend on factors such as cost, convenience, time, safety, and environmental concerns.

If you choose to buy a car, you will have to decide where and how to shop. You may consider dealers, the Internet, auto superstores, or private sellers. Consider your needs for size, style, and make; options; and warranty. You will also need to consider what you can afford.

A pre-owned car may be the best option for some people, as long as the car is in good condition. To check the history of a car, the buyer can use the buyers guide sticker and VIN. Buyers can also question the previous owners.

To estimate the cost, keep in mind costs beyond the purchase price. These include fuel, maintenance, and insurance. If you will need financing, remember to include the interest. Leasing is also an option for people who want to use a car.

Proper maintenance will help keep your car running smoothly. This will save you money in repairs as well as keep you and others safe. In newer cars, warning lights may alert you to necessary car services. Maintenance involves oil changes, tire rotation, and other services that may be recommended depending on the model and age of your car. To keep your car in good repair, find a convenient, reliable service center.

Critical Thinking

1. **Assess options.** Make a list of all the mass-transit options available in your city, including ride-hailing services.. (If you do not have mass transit, use options from a larger city in your state.) Make a list of pros and cons for each option.

2. **Analyze priorities.** What factors are most important to you when choosing transportation?

3. **Evaluate resources.** What transportation resources are available to you? Of these options, which
   - is the least expensive?
   - is most comfortable?
   - is most convenient?
   - takes the least amount of time?

4. **Analyze procedures.** Imagine you are driving and realize you have a flat tire. Research the steps in changing a tire. Then, create an informational sheet explaining how to properly change a tire.

5. **Summarize details.** Find an ad for a new or pre-owned car you might be interested in purchasing. Write a summary of the features that are most interesting to you.

21st Century Applications

6. **Financial literacy.** Suppose you want to borrow $15,000.00 to purchase a new car. Investigate what the credit terms would be if you:
   - obtained credit from the dealership
   - took out a cash loan

- used a credit card
- borrowed from the bank

Find out about finance charges, annual percentage rates, monthly payments, length of repayment period, and late payment charges for each option. Which option gives you the best deal? Why? What benefit would you have from delaying your purchase and paying with cash or a debit card?

7. **Economic literacy.** Explore the *Kelly Blue Book* website. Use the information available to determine the best car choice for you or your family. Report the type of car, manufacturer, and current price. Provide reasons for your choice.

8. **Critical thinking and problem solving.** Before accepting and using information to make transportation decisions, it is important to determine the reliability and validity of sources. Select three websites that give information related to vehicles, such as a car dealership website, car review website, or vehicle safety website. Determine the reliability of each source by analyzing the following factors. Then prepare a report outlining your findings.

    Information: Is the information what you need? Is the information current? Is the information from a *popular source* (magazine, newspaper, Internet) or *scholarly source* (academic institution, trade journal, professional organization journal)? Is the information researched well?

    Author: Who is the author and what are his or her credentials (degree, experience, previous writings)? What is the author's intent for providing the information (to inform, instruct, persuade, entertain, sell)?

    Bias/Objectivity: Does the information address other points of view? Is any important information omitted? Is the writing style emotional or does it promote a certain viewpoint? Is the article or publication sponsored or endorsed by a political entity or special interest group?

    Publisher: Is the publisher known as an educational, commercial, or governmental publisher? What can you find out about the publisher from the website?

    Quality: Is the information presented in a logical sequence or structure? Can you clearly identify key points? Do the key points support a main idea? Does the text use good grammar and correct spelling and punctuation?

Core Skills

9. **Speaking.** Research public transportation systems in three regions, countries, or major cities. What mass transit options does each location have? How are these systems similar? different? Prepare a presentation with images discussing each public transportation system.

10. **Science, writing.** Research the technology used to operate hybrid cars. Write a research paper about the history of hybrid cars, current technology, and future advancements.

11. **Social studies, math.** Compare the price of a gallon of gasoline in 1920, 1950, 1975, 1990, and today. How do the historic prices compare if they were shown in today's dollar?

12. **Math.** Create a transportation budget for yourself based on a transportation option of your choice. Research and include as many items as you can in your budget, such as insurance, maintenance, and fuel.

13. **Reading, writing.** Read a biography of a famous automobile manufacturer and write a short summary of what you learned.

14. **Listening.** Interview someone who has just bought a car. Ask about all the steps the person went through. Also ask about fees that were not included in the price of the car. Report your findings to the class.

15. **Writing.** Research the prevalence of texting while driving. What are the safety risks? How are individual states and city officials responding to texting while driving? Do you believe texting while driving should be banned? Why or why not? Prepare a report outlining your findings.

16. **Speaking and listening.** Have a class debate on whether the minimum driving age should be raised. Is 16 years old too young to be a responsible driver? Practice active listening skills as your classmates articulate their views. Can you follow the speaker's line of reasoning?

Leadership
Development

As part of the Families Acting for Community Traffic Safety (FACTS) National Program, organize a school-wide safety awareness week. Focus on topics such as wearing seat belts, texting while driving, driving under the influence, and safe driving habits. Set up information tables, make announcements on the PA system, and host a pledge wall campaign to raise awareness.

Portfolio
Builder

Join a chapter of Students Against Destructive Decisions (SADD). Take notes at the meetings you attend. Write a feature for your school's newspaper on the group, recounting details of the meetings. Keep the notes and your feature articles in your portfolio.

Journal
Writing

You really want to buy a new car, but when planning your budget, you find that you cannot afford the car you want. You can afford a used car, but it will need some costly repairs within the next few years. Bus fare is inexpensive, and you could continue to save for the car you want. However, you think the bus is crowded and uncomfortable. You could take the train, which is slightly more expensive than the bus, but you would have to be dropped off at the station much earlier than needed.

Write About It: *How would you use the decision-making process to evaluate your choices? Which alternative would you choose?*

Glossary

A

ability. Skill a person learns through practice. (1-2)

abstinence. A choice to refrain from sexual intercourse until marriage. (8-2)

accessory. An item that accents clothing and gives an outfit a finished look. (19-3)

accident. An unexpected event that causes loss, injury, or sometimes death. (23-2)

account statement. A monthly, bimonthly, or quarterly summary of a checking account. (17-1)

acquaintance rape. Rape committed by a person whom the victim knows, such as a friend, someone at school, a coworker, or someone the victim just met. (8-4)

acquired immune deficiency syndrome (AIDS). A deadly sexually transmitted infection caused by the human immunodeficiency virus, which breaks down the immune system, leaving the body vulnerable to disease. (12-3)

active listening. Focusing on the speaker's message and then providing feedback. (2-2)

active-physical play. Play that helps children develop their large-muscle skills. They use their large muscles for movements like walking, running, hopping, jumping, and skipping. (11-1)

activity center. A grouping in a room of all the furnishings needed for a particular activity. (23-1)

addiction. A dependence of the body on a continuing supply of a substance, such as a drug. (7-3)

adjustable rate mortgage (ARM). A mortgage in which the interest rate is adjusted up or down periodically. (22-2)

adjustment lines. Two parallel lines that extend across a pattern piece, indicating where to shorten or lengthen the pattern piece. (21-1)

adolescence. The period of life from when puberty begins until growth ceases and adulthood is reached. (10-4)

adoptive family. Family that forms when a couple chooses to legally adopt and raise another family's child. (6-2)

advertisement. A paid public message about goods and services for sale, which is communicated through various media. (18-3)

à la carte. Items on a restaurant menu that are priced individually. (16-3)

alcoholic. A person who suffers from the disease of alcoholism. (7-3)

alcoholism. A disease in which a person develops a physical and psychological addiction to alcohol. (7-3)

alteration. A change made to the size of a pattern or garment to achieve better fit. (21-1)

Alzheimer's disease. A degenerative brain condition. (10-5)

amino acid. A component of proteins. (13-1)

analogous color scheme. A color scheme that combines three to five hues found next to each other on the color wheel. (19-2)

annual percentage rate (APR). The actual percentage rate of interest paid for an entire year. (17-3)

anorexia nervosa. A complex eating disorder in which a person avoids eating, sometimes to the point of starvation. (13-4)

apprenticeship. Learning program that provides training for a trade or skill on the job under the supervision of a skilled worker. (1-2)

aptitude. A person's natural talent. (1-2)

aseptic packaging. A packaging technique in which foods and containers are sterilized separately before food is packed in the container in a sterilized chamber. (14-4)

Note: The numbers in parentheses following the definitions represent the chapter and section in whicth the terms appear.

attached house. A single-family house that shares a common wall with houses on one or more side; also called a *townhouse* or *rowhouse.* (22-1)

autocratic leadership. A style of leadership in which the leader has full control of the group and makes all the decisions for the group. (3-1)

B

backstitching. Sewing backward and forward in the same place for a few stitches to secure thread ends. (21-3)

bait and switch. A deceptive advertising method in which the advertiser offers a low-priced item as bait to get shoppers in the store. Once shoppers are in the store, the advertiser tries to switch them to a more expensive item. (18-3)

bakeware. Equipment used for baking foods in an oven. (15-1)

balance. Equal visual weight on both sides of a central point. (19-2)

basal metabolism. Life-sustaining activities that account for energy expended when the body is at physical, emotional, and digestive rest. (13-4)

behavioral disorder. Condition that affects the way a person functions emotionally and socially. (10-2)

behaviorism. A theory based on the belief that behavior is the response to stimuli from the environment. (10-1)

beneficiary. A person who receives the death benefit of a life insurance policy. (17-4)

binge-eating disorder. A type of eating disorder in which a person consumes large amounts of food in one sitting without purging the food or attempting to avoid weight gain. (13-4)

biomass. Plant and animal matter that provides energy when burned. (5-3)

biscuit method. A mixing technique used in food preparation in which dry ingredients are mixed together, and then fat is cut into the mixture before liquid ingredients are added. (16-1)

bobbin. A small metal or plastic spool that feeds the lower thread on a sewing machine, which is needed in making a lockstitch. (20-2)

body language. Body movements, such as facial expressions, gestures, and posture, used to send messages to others. (2-2)

body mass index (BMI). A calculation used by health professionals to assess an adult's weight in terms of his or her height. (13-4)

bond. A certificate that represents a promise by a company or government to repay a loan on a given date. (17-2)

brainstorming. A group method of solving problems in which members offer any and all ideas. (3-1)

budget. A plan to help manage money wisely. (4-4)

bulimia nervosa. An eating disorder in which a person consumes large amounts of food and then vomits or takes laxatives or diuretics to avoid weight gain. (13-4)

bylaws. A set of specific rules that expand upon an organization's constitution by giving more information. (3-2)

C

calorie. The unit of measurement of food energy. (13-4)

carbohydrate. A nutrient that serves as the major source of energy in the diet. (13-1)

career. A series of related occupations that show progression in a field of work. (1-2)

caregiver. A person who provides care for someone else. (9-2)

car pool. A group of people who commute together in one of the members' vehicles. (24-1)

cashier's check. A check drawn on a financial institution's own funds and signed by an officer of the institution. (17-1)

cash value. The amount a policyholder can collect if he or she decides to give up a whole-life insurance policy. (17-4)

casual dating. A type of dating, also called *random dating,* that allows people to date more than one person at a time. (8-2)

cereal. A starchy grain used as food, such as wheat, corn, rice, and oats. (14-3)

certificate of deposit (CD). A type of savings account that pays a set rate of interest on money that is deposited for a set period of time. (17-2)

certified check. A personal check for which a financial institution guarantees payment. (17-1)

certified used cars. Cars that have been inspected and repaired. (24-2)

character. Inner traits, such as conscience, moral strength, and social attitudes, that guide a person's conduct and behavior into acceptable standards of right and wrong. (10-1)

child care cooperative. A child care program formed by groups of parents who share in the care of their children, allowing parents more control over the program. (9-2)

childless family. A couple without children. (6-2)

children with special needs. Children with disabilities, and gifted and talented children. (10-2)

cholesterol. A fatty substance found in every body cell. (13-1)

chronological growth. Increase in age, which takes place at the same rate for all people. (10-1)

classic. A fashion that never changes drastically and is therefore worn year after year. (19-3)

classical conditioning. Theory that behaviors can be associated with responses. (10-1)

cleaning products. Materials used to remove soil; often added to water. (23-3)

cleaning schedule. A written plan identifying what household cleaning tasks need to be done, who is responsible for which tasks, and how often the tasks are to be completed. (23-3)

climacteric. Reduced hormone production in middle-aged men, possibly resulting in changes in moods and emotions. (10-5)

clipping. Making straight cuts in a seam allowance toward the stitching line, usually at ½-inch intervals, to prevent puckering. (21-3)

codependency. A pattern of unhealthy behaviors that is used by family members to cover up a problem. (7-1)

cognition. The processes involving thought and knowledge. (10-1)

cognitive disability. A disability that limits the way a person's brain functions, causing a limited learning capacity. (10-2)

coinsurance. An insurance policy provision that requires the policyholder to pay a certain percentage of medical costs. (17-4)

collateral. Something of value a person owns that he or she pledges to a creditor as security for a loan. (17-3)

color wheel. A tool that shows how colors relate to one another. (19-2)

communicable diseases. Illnesses that can be passed on to other people. (11-1)

communication. The process of conveying information so messages are received and understood. (2-2)

community resources. Facilities that are shared by many people, such as parks, schools, and libraries. (4-1)

comparison shopping. Comparing products and prices in different stores before making a purchase. (18-1)

complementary color scheme. A color scheme using colors opposite each other on the color wheel for a strong contrast. (19-2)

compromise. A technique used in negotiating conflicts in which all parties agree to give up something of importance to reach a mutual agreement. (2-4)

computer-aided design (CAD). Graphics software that assists in creating a design. (18-2)

condominium. An individually owned housing unit in a multiunit structure. (22-1)

conflict. A struggle between two people or groups who have opposing views. (2-4)

conflict resolution process. A step-by-step form of communication that allows conflicts to be resolved in a positive manner. (2-4)

consequences. Results that follow an action or behavior. (11-2)

consistency. Enforcing rules the same way each time. (11-2)

constitution. A set of major laws used to govern an organization. (3-2)

Consumer Product Safety Commission (CPSC). A government agency that sets and enforces safety standards for consumer products and handles consumer complaints. (18-4)

convection cooking. A method of cooking that involves circulating hot air over all food surfaces, allowing food to cook quickly and evenly. (15-1)

convenience food. A food product that has some preparation steps finished. (14-1)

cookware. Equipment, including saucepans and skillets, used for cooking on top of a cooktop. (15-1)

cooperative. A multiunit building owned and operated for the benefit of the residents; also called *co-op.* (22-1)

cooperative education. A work-based learning program that prepares students for an occupation immediately after high school through a paid job experience. (1-2)

cooperative play. A stage of play when two or more children play complementary roles and share play activities. (10-2)

copayment. A fixed fee paid by a policyholder for certain insured items or services. (17-4)

cover. The individual place setting and allotted space needed by each person at a table. (16-2)

cover letter. A letter that introduces yourself and your résumé to a potential employer. (1-3)

credit. An arrangement that allows consumers to buy goods or services now and pay for them later. (17-3)

credit contract. A legally binding agreement between creditor and borrower that details the terms of repayment. (17-3)

creditor. A person who gives credit to consumers and to whom debts are owed. (17-3)

credit report. A statement that includes your bill-paying history, loans, current debts, banking, and other financial information. It also includes your name, address, birth date, phone number, credit accounts, and social security number. (17-3)

credit score. A three-digit number between 300 and 850 that rates your credit risk. (17-3)

crisis. An event that greatly influences people's lives and causes them to make difficult changes in their lifestyles. (7-3)

cross-contamination. The spread of bacteria from a contaminated food to other food, equipment, or surfaces. (15-2)

cultural group. A group of people who share common racial and/or cultural characteristics, such as national origin, language, religion, beliefs, and traditions. (10-1)

cultural heritage. Learned behaviors, beliefs, and languages that are passed from generation to generation. (10-1)

custom house. A house specifically designed and built for the new owner. (22-1)

cutting layout. A drawing showing how to fold fabric and place pattern pieces for cutting. (21-2)

cutting line. A bold line on pattern pieces used as a guide for cutting fabric. (21-1)

D

dart. A construction element used to give shape and fullness to a garment made by stitching to a point through a fold in the fabric. (21-3)

date rape. The rape of a dating partner. (8-4)

decision. A conscious or unconscious response to a problem or issue. (4-2)

decision-making process. A logical, step-by-step method people can use to make the decisions that are best for them. (4-2)

deductible. An amount that a policyholder must pay before his or her insurance company will pay on a claim. (17-4)

defense mechanism. A behavior pattern used to protect a person's self-esteem. (12-2)

dehydration. Abnormal loss of body fluids. (13-3)

democratic leadership. A style of leadership that stresses the needs and wishes of individuals and in which members are encouraged to participate in decision making by voting. (3-1)

demographics. Statistical qualities of the human population. (6-2)

depression. An emotional state that ranges from mild, short-lived feelings of sadness to a deep, despairing sense of dejection. (12-2)

developmentally appropriate practices. Techniques suited to the developmental characteristics and needs of the individual child. (11-2)

developmental theories. Explanations of scientists who have studied human growth and development to learn how these processes work and affect individuals. (10-1)

Dietary Guidelines for Americans. Recommendations from the U.S. Departments of Agriculture and Health and Human Services to help people choose healthful diets. (13-2)

Dietary Reference Intakes (DRIs). Five types of reference values that outline nutrient requirements for each sex and for several age groups, including needs for energy, protein, and many vitamins and minerals. (13-1)

direct deposit. A method of transferring money into an account through electronic means. (17-1)

directional stitching. Stitching in the direction of the grain. (21-3)

direct tax. A type of tax that is charged directly to the taxpayer. (5-1)

diverse. Differing from one another. (2-3)

diversified. Term to describe money invested in many different stocks and bonds, so decreases in some are offset by increases in others. (17-2)

diversity. Condition of a group whose members represent many different cultures. (3-1)

dividend. A distribution of a company's profits to a stockholder. (17-2)

dot. A pattern symbol used to match seams and other construction details. (21-1)

dramatic play. A form of play involving role-playing. A child imitates another person or acts out a situation, but does so alone. (11-1)

dress code. A standard of dress that is enforced in a social setting. (19-1)

drug abuse. The use of a drug for a purpose other than it was intended. (7-3)

dry cleaning. The process of cleaning clothes using an organic chemical solvent instead of water. (19-4)

dual-career family. A family in which both spouses are employed. (7-2)

dysfunctional family. A family that provides a negative environment that discourages the growth and development of family members. (7-1)

E

easing. Making a piece of fabric fit a slightly smaller piece of fabric as a flat, curved seam is sewn to provide fabric fullness at certain points on the body. (21-3)

elements of design. Color, line, texture, and form as used in artistic design. (19-2)

emotional abuse. A form of abuse that happens when one person purposely hurts another's self-concept through constant yelling, teasing, or insulting. (7-3)

emotional growth. Development of the ability to express feelings. (10-1)

emotional neglect. The failure to provide loving care and attention to family members. (7-3)

empathy. The quality of understanding how others feel even when personal feelings may differ. (10-4)

emphasis. The center of interest in a design. (19-2)

empty nest syndrome. Feelings of loneliness and depression some parents experience after their children leave home. (10-5)

emulation. The act of imitating the behavior of other people around you. (4-2)

enabler. Someone who unknowingly acts in ways that contribute to an alcoholic's or addict's drug use. (7-3)

endorse. Signing the back, left end of a check before cashing or depositing it. (17-1)

enriched. A term used to describe a food product that has nutrients added back to it that were lost during processing. (13-1)

entrepreneur. A person who starts and manages his or her own business. (1-3)

environment. All the conditions and situations that surround and affect an individual. (10-1)

estate. What a person leaves behind when he or she dies. (17-2)

etiquette. Approved social conduct, or good manners. (16-3)

eviction. A legal procedure that forces a tenant to leave a property before the rental agreement expires if he or she fails to uphold the terms of the lease. (22-2)

expiration date. A date stamped on food products such as yeast and baby formula indicating the last day the product should be used or eaten. (14-2)

extended family. A family structure that includes other relatives, such as grandparents, aunts, uncles, and/or cousins, living with parents and their children. (6-2)

F

fabric. A textile product usually made by weaving or knitting yarns together. (20-1)

fad. A style that is popular for a short time and then disappears. (19-3)

family. Two or more people related by blood, marriage, or adoption; two or more persons who share resources, responsibility for decisions, personal priorities, and goals and who have commitment to one another over time. (6-1)

family life cycle. Basic stages of growth and development experienced by families. (6-3)

family structure. The makeup of a family group based on the relationships of the members in the family. (6-2)

fashion. The manner of dress being worn by the majority of people at a given time. (19-3)

fat. A nutrient that provides a concentrated source of food energy. (13-1)

feedback. A clue that lets the speaker know the message is getting through to the listener and how it is being received. The feedback can be a nod, smile, question, or comment. (2-2)

feed dogs. Two small rows of teeth that move the fabric forward under the presser foot. (20-2).

fiber. The basic unit of all fabrics. (20-1)

filament. Continuous strand of fibers. (20-1)

finance charges. The total amount a borrower must pay a creditor for the use of credit. These charges include interest, service charges, and any other fees. (17-3)

fine-motor skills. The abilities required to use small muscles that control the wrists, hands, thumbs, fingers, and ankles. (10-2, 11-1)

finfish. Fish that have fins and backbones. (14-3)

first aid. Emergency care or treatment given to people right after an accident, which relieves pain and prevents further injury. (11-1).

fixed expense. A set amount of money that a person is committed to pay, such as a monthly car payment. (4-4)

fixed rate mortgage. A mortgage that guarantees a fixed or unchanging interest rate for the life of the loan. (22-2)

flexible expense. A cost that occurs repeatedly, but which varies in amount from one time to the next. (4-4)

flexible workweeks. Work schedules that divide 40 work hours into four 10-hour workdays instead of five eight-hour workdays. (7-2)

flextime. Employees set their own work schedules within certain company terms. (7-2)

follower. A person who supports a group by helping put goals into action. (3-1)

food additive. A substance added to a food for a specific purpose. (14-2)

food allergy. An abnormal reaction of the body's immune system to certain proteins in food. (13-3)

Food and Drug Administration (FDA). A government agency that helps protect consumer safety by regulating the production, packaging, and labeling of foods, drugs, and cosmetics. (18-4)

foodborne illness. A sickness caused by eating contaminated food. (15-2)

food intolerance. An adverse reaction to the consumption of certain foods. (13-3)

food rotation. Storing the freshest food at the back of the shelf in order that the oldest foods, stored at the front of the shelf, will be used first. (14-4)

form. A design element that defines the shape of an object. (19-2)

fortified. A term used to describe a food product that has had nutrients added to improve its nutritional value. (13-1)

fossil fuels. Energy sources, such as oil, coal, and natural gas, derived from the partly decayed plants and animals that lived long ago. (5-2)

foster care. Care provided for a child who needs a home temporarily. (9-2)

foster family. Family that forms when a couple temporarily provides care for another couple's child because the parents cannot provide care. (6-2)

freestanding house. A single-family house that stands alone. (22-1)

freshness date. A date stamped on food products such as baked goods that indicates the end of a product's quality peak. (14-2)

fringe benefits. Employee benefits provided by an employer such as insurance, profit-sharing plans, and paid vacations. (4-4)

function. The way in which architecture, furniture, equipment, and accessories will be used. (23-1)

functional family. A family that provides a positive environment that encourages each family member to grow and develop to his or her fullest potential. (7-1)

G

gathering. Creating ripples and soft folds in a fabric that is attached to a shorter length of fabric. (21-3)

gender roles. Behaviors of males and females, expected by society, and modeled by parents and other adults. (10-3)

gifted and talented. A person who shows outstanding ability in either a general sense or in a specific ability. (10-2)

goal. An aim a person is consciously trying to reach. (4-1)

grading. Trimming each layer of a seam allowance to a different width. (21-3)

grain. The two basic directions that yarns run in a woven fabric. (21-1)

grainline arrow. A pattern symbol indicating that a pattern piece is to be placed on fabric parallel to its lengthwise edge. (21-1)

gratuity. A sum of money left for a waiter in a restaurant as a measure of gratitude for service received, usually ten to twenty percent of the total bill; also called a *tip*. (16-3)

grieve. To feel intense sorrow, usually after the death of a loved one. (10-5)

gross income. The total amount of money an employee earns before deductions. (4-4)

gross-motor skills. The abilities required to control large muscles such as the trunk, arms, and legs. (10-2, 11-1)

group dating. A type of dating in which a number of people of both sexes go out together. (8-2)

growth spurts. Periods of rapid growth. (10-3)

guidance. Everything caregivers do and say to promote socially acceptable behavior in children. (11-2)

H

hangtag. A tag attached to a garment to provide information, such as trademarks, guarantees, style number, size, and price. (19-3)

harmony. A pleasing effect achieved when the elements of design work together. (19-2)

hazardous waste. A by-product of society that poses a danger to human health or the environment when not properly managed. (5-2)

health maintenance organization (HMO). A group of medical professionals and facilities that provides health care services to members. (17-4)

heredity. The sum of all traits passed on through genes from parents to children. (10-1)

homogenized. Subjected to a process by which milk fat is broken up into tiny particles that remain suspended throughout milk. (14-3)

hormone. A substance in the body that triggers cellular activity, such as growth and the development of adult characteristics. (10-4)

hospice. A way of caring for people who are living with a serious illness that cannot be cured. (10-5)

hotline. A telephone number people can call for information or other assistance with a specific problem. (9-2)

hourly wage. A set amount of money paid to an employee for each hour of work. (4-4)

housing. Any dwelling that provides shelter. (22-1)

hue. The name given to a color. (19-2)

human immunodeficiency virus (HIV). The virus that breaks down the immune system, leaving the body vulnerable to disease, and causes AIDS. (12-3)

human resource. A resource, such as knowledge, energy, a skill, or a talent, that comes from within a person. (4-1)

I

identity theft. The unauthorized use of someone's personal data or documents (usually social security number or credit cards) to obtain merchandise, services, or credit. (18-4)

imitative-imaginative play. Form of play in which children use their imaginations as they pretend to be other people or objects; begins at about two years of age. (11-1)

immunizations. Injections or drops given to a person to provide protection against a certain disease. (11-1)

implement. To carry out. (4-2)

impulse buying. Making an unplanned or quick purchase without giving it much thought. (18-1)

inclusion. The placing of students of varying abilities in the same class. (10-2)

indirect tax. A type of tax that is included in the price of taxed items. (5-1)

individual rates of growth. Principle that children grow and develop at different rates based on heredity, environment, and motivation. (10-1)

infant. A baby up to 12 months old. (10-2)

infatuation. An intense feeling of admiration. (8-2)

insomnia. The inability to get the amount of sleep needed when it is needed. (12-1)

intellectual growth. A developing ability to reason and form complex thought patterns. (10-1)

intensity. The brightness or dullness of a color. (19-2)

interest. The price a borrower pays a creditor for the use of money over a period of time. (17-3)

intermediate color. A color produced from equal amounts of one primary color and one secondary color. (19-2)

intermittency of love. When love seems to fade and then reappear. (8-3)

internship. A work-based learning program that offers paid or unpaid practical work experience to learn about a job or industry. (1-2)

interrelated development rates. Interactions between physical, emotional, social, and intellectual aspects of growth. (10-1)

ironing. A process of moving an iron across fabric to smooth wrinkles. (19-4)

J

job. One or more tasks. (1-2)

job shadowing. Exploring career options through observing an experienced professional on the job, usually for one day. (1-2)

job sharing. Two people divide the work responsibilities of one job, each working on a part-time basis. (7-2)

K

kitchen utensil. A handheld kitchen tool used for measuring, cutting, mixing, cooking, or baking tasks. (15-1)

knitting. A process of looping yarns together to form a fabric. (20-1)

L

label. A cloth tag permanently attached to a garment to provide important information usually required by law, such as fiber content, manufacturer, country of origin, and care instructions. (19-3)

lactose intolerance. A form of food intolerance in which the body is unable to digest dairy products that contain lactose. (13-3)

laissez-faire. A style of leadership in which members may do whatever they want to do and leaders are on hand only to serve as resources. (3-1)

leader. A person who has the power to influence the behavior of others. (3-1)

learning disability. A limitation in the way a person's brain sorts and uses certain types of information. (10-2)

lease. A contract between a tenant and a property owner, listing the rights and responsibilities of both parties. (22-2)

leavening agents. Ingredients used to produce carbon dioxide, which causes breads to rise. (16-1)

legumes. Seeds that grow in the pods of some vegetable plants. (14-3)

lifestyle. A person's way of life or style of living. (19-1)

line. A design element that gives direction to a design. (19-2)

liquidity. The degree to which a person will be able to get cash quickly from a savings account or financial investment. (17-2)

loan value. The amount a policyholder can borrow from an insurance company using the cash value of a whole life insurance policy as collateral. (17-4)

lockstitch. A stitch made by a sewing machine with thread coming from both the upper and lower parts of the machine and locking securely in the middle of the fabric layers being sewn. (20-2)

long-term goal. A goal that takes several months or years to achieve. (4-1)

loopers. Serger sewing machine parts that form upper and lower stitches. (20-2)

lumens. A measurement of the amount of light produced by a given source. (5-3)

M

management. Wisely using means to achieve goals. (4-1)

management process. A series of steps that helps people plan how to best use resources to achieve goals. (4-2)

manipulative-constructive play. Play that helps children develop small-muscle skills. The small muscles are those that control the wrists, hands, ankles, fingers, and thumbs. (11-1)

manners. Rules to follow for proper social conduct. (2-2)

manufactured fibers. Fibers that are produced through chemical and technical means from natural cellulose or crude oil products. (20-1)

manufactured house. A house made in a factory, moved to a site, and assembled if not already self-contained. (22-1)

mass transit. Public transportation. (24-1)

material resource. Resources that are not physically or mentally part of a person, including time, money, possessions, and community resources. (4-1)

maturation. The change that occurs between childhood and adulthood, during which physical, personal, and behavioral characteristics become more adult. (10-1)

meal management. Using resources of skills, money, and time to put together nutritious meals. (14-1)

meal service. The way a meal is served. (16-2)

measurement equivalent. An amount that is equal to another amount, such as one-fourth cup equaling four tablespoons. (15-3)

meat. The edible portion of animals, including muscles and organs. (14-3)

meat analog. A plant-based protein product made to resemble various kinds of meat. (14-3)

media. Channels of mass communication, such as magazines, television, radio, and the Internet. (6-2)

mediation. Technique in which a third person is called upon to help reconcile differences between conflicting parties. (2-4)

menopause. Normal stoppage of menstrual cycles in a middle-aged woman, possibly resulting in changes in moods and emotions. (10-5)

microfiber. An extremely thin filament of a manufactured fiber. (20-1)

middle childhood. Stage of children between the ages of 6 and 12 years. (10-3)

midlife crisis. Event caused by difficulty adjusting to the changes that occur during middle adulthood. (10-5)

mineral. An inorganic substance needed for building tissues and regulating body functions. (13-1)

mixed message. A means of communication in which a person's behavior contradicts his or her words or actions. (2-3)

modeling. The act of adults exhibiting behaviors in front of children, which the children then copy. (11-2)

modesty. A standard held by a cultural group about the proper way to cover the body in various settings. (19-1)

money transfer app. A person-to-person app that allows individuals to send and receive money to and from friends and family using a mobile device. (17-1)

monochromatic color scheme. A color scheme based on only one hue, which may be used in various values and intensities for variety. (19-2)

mortgage. A loan used to pay for a home. (22-2)

motivation. A force that gives people a reason to take action. (3-1)

muffin method. A mixing technique used in food preparation in which dry ingredients and liquid ingredients are mixed together in separate bowls, and then the liquid ingredients are poured into a well made in the center of the dry ingredients. (16-1)

multicultural society. People from many different cultures living in the same communities. (8-2)

multifamily dwelling. A building designed to house more than one family. (22-1)

multiple roles. Two or more roles, such as work and family roles, being filled by one person. (7-2)

multisize pattern. A garment pattern designed with three or more sizes on one pattern tissue. (21-1)

multitasking. Combining tasks or working on more than one task at a time. (4-3)

mutual fund. A group of many investments purchased by a company representing many investors. (17-2)

mutual respect. Regard held by two people who each view the other with honor and esteem. (8-1)

MyPlate. The USDA's food guidance system, which features a personalized approach to healthful eating and physical activity. (13-2)

N

nanny. A trained individual who provides quality child care in a parent's home. (9-2)

natural cheese. Cheese made from milk, whey, or cream. (14-3)

natural fibers. Fibers that exist in nature. (20-1)

natural resources. Resources taken from the land, such as agricultural products, forest products, and fossil fuels. (4-1)

needs. Basic items, such as food, clothing, or shelter, that all people require for living. (1-1)

negotiation. Communicating with others in order to reach a mutually satisfying agreement, usually through compromise. (2-4)

net income. The amount of money left after all deductions have been taken from an employee's gross pay. (4-4)

networking. Developing contacts with people who may be able to find you a job. (1-3)

neutrals. Black, white, and gray, which are not true colors but are used as colors in design. (19-2)

newborn. A baby in the first month of life. (10-2)

nonverbal communication. A process of communication that involves sending messages without words. (2-2)

nonwoven fabrics. Fabrics made by bonding or interlocking fibers together directly without using yarns. (20-1)

notch. A diamond-shaped pattern symbol located on the cutting line and used to match garment pieces before sewing them together. (21-1)

notching. Cutting small wedges out of the seam allowance to remove excess fabric. (21-3)

notions. Small items needed to construct a garment, including thread, buttons, trims, fasteners, seam binding, and bias tape. (20-1)

nuclear family. A family group that consists of a man, woman, and their children. (6-2)

nutrient. A chemical substance provided by food and used by the body to function properly. (13-1)

nutrient dense. A term describing foods and beverages that supply vitamins, minerals, and other nutrients that provide positive health with little or no solid fats and added sugars, refined starches, and sodium. (13-2)

nutrition. The science of how nutrients support the body. (13-1)

O

obese. A term used to describe an adult who has a body mass index over 30. (13-4)

object permanence. The concept that objects and people exist even when they cannot be seen. (10-2)

obsolescence. The state of uselessness. (18-2)

occupation. Paid employment involving a job. (1-2)

open communication. A free flow of ideas, opinions, and facts among the people communicating. (2-3)

open dating. A dating process that gives information about the freshness of foods. (14-2)

operant conditioning. A theory that people repeat behaviors that are positively reinforced and discontinue behaviors that are negatively reinforced. (10-1)

opiates. Drugs derived from opium, such as codeine. (12-3)

options. Additional features on a vehicle that may be added for appearance, safety, performance, or convenience. (24-2)

orthorexia nervosa. Similar to anorexia nervosa and shows similar symptoms, however, this eating disorder is characterized by an unhealthy obsession with "healthful eating" that results in severely limiting food choices. (13-4)

overdraft. A check written when there is not enough money in a checking account to cover it. (17-1)

overweight. A term used to describe an adult who has a body mass index of 25 up to 30. (13-4)

P

pack date. A date stamped on food products such as canned goods that tells when the food was processed. (14-2)

parallel play. A stage of play in which a child will play beside other children rather than with them. (10-2)

parenting. The name given to the process of raising a child. (9-1)

parliamentary procedure. Guidelines followed by many organizations to help them conduct meetings in an orderly fashion. (3-2)

passive listening. Hearing the speaker's words, but not the meaning of the words. (2-2)

pasta. Grain products such as spaghetti, macaroni, and noodles. (14-3)

pasteurization. A heating process that destroys harmful bacteria in dairy products. (14-3)

pattern guide sheet. A set of instructions included with every pattern that has step-by-step directions for the sewing project. (21-1)

pattern view. A drawing on the front of a pattern envelope showing a garment design that can be made from the pattern included in the envelope. (20-1)

pediatrician. A doctor who specializes in the care and development of children. (10-2)

peer mediators. Students who are trained in the conflict resolution process and are called upon to act as mediators when conflicts arise among their peers. (2-4)

peer pressure. The influence a person's peers have on him or her. (8-4)

peers. Other people in a person's age group. (1-1)

perseverance. Quality of sticking to an action or belief even when difficult. (1-1)

personality. The total behavioral qualities and traits that make up an individual. (1-1)

personal space. The area surrounding an individual. (2-2)

pesticide. A strong chemical used for pest control. (23-3)

physical abuse. The physical injury of one person by another through such behaviors as hitting, kicking, biting, or throwing objects. (7-3)

physical disability. A disability that limits a person's body or its functions. (10-2)

physical fitness. The condition of the body. (12-1)

physical growth. Changes in body stature influenced by heredity and health habits. (10-1)

physical neglect. Failure to provide proper food, clothing, shelter, medical care, and parental supervision to meet family needs. (7-3)

physical wellness. A state of health in which the body is able to fight illness and infection and repair damage. (12-1)

place setting. The tableware that one person would need, such as a dinner plate, salad plate, cup, and saucer. (16-2)

policy. An insurance contract. (17-4)

policyholder. A person who has an insurance policy. (17-4)

pollution. Harmful changes in the environment that make resources unclean or unsafe to use. (5-2)

portable appliance. A cooking aid that can be easily moved from one place to another. (15-1)

portfolio. An organized collection of your best and most creative work. (1-3) A group of securities purchased by a mutual fund for an investor. (17-2)

positive reinforcement. Rewarding positive behavior as a way to encourage children to repeat the behavior. (11-2)

potential. The capacity to develop, succeed, and make further advances in life. (1-1)

poultry. Any domesticated bird used for meat and/or eggs. (14-3)

preferred provider organization (PPO). A group of doctors and medical facilities that contract to provide services at reduced rates. (17-4)

prejudices. Preconceived ideas or judgments of people or objects that are based on a lack of understanding. (2-3)

premium. A regular payment made for an insurance policy. (17-4)

preschooler. A child who is between the ages of three and five years old. (10-2)

presser foot. A sewing machine part that holds fabric in place as the machine stitches. (20-2)

pressing. The process of lifting an iron up and down to apply pressure in one area of a garment at a time. (19-4)

primary colors. Colors that cannot be created from other colors, such as yellow, blue, and red. (19-2)

principles of design. Balance, proportion, rhythm, and emphasis used as guides for combining the elements of design. (19-2)

priorities. A list of items or tasks that have been ranked in order of importance. (7-2)

process cheese. Cheese made by blending and melting two or more natural cheeses. (14-3)

procreation. The bearing of children. (6-1)

produce. Fresh fruits and vegetables. (14-3)

progressive tax. A type of tax that increases in rate as the price of the item being taxed increases. (5-1)

prompting. Asking questions to prompt children to exhibit desired behavior. (11-2)

proportion. The spatial relationship of the parts of a design to each other and to the whole design. (19-2)

protein. A nutrient that is found in every cell of the body and is needed for growth, maintenance, and repair of body tissues. (13-1)

puberty. A stage of physical growth in which an individual becomes capable of sexual reproduction. (10-4)

pull date. A date stamped on food products such as dairy products and cold cuts that shows the last day a store should sell the product. (14-2)

Q

quality of life. A phrase used to describe many factors that work together to foster personal well-being. (12-4)

R

rape. The crime of forcing another person to submit to sexual relations. (8-4)

rapport. A relationship built on respect and sincerity. (2-2)

recipe. A list of ingredients with a complete set of instructions for preparing a food product. (15-3)

reconciling. The process of comparing the account statement to your check stubs or register to make sure they match. (17-1)

recycle. To reprocess resources so they can be used again. (5-2)

redirection. Focusing the child's attention on something else by providing an appealing substitute. (11-2)

redress. To solve a problem. (18-4)

references. People who know a person well and can vouch for his or her good work. (1-3)

refined grain. Grain that has parts of the kernel removed during the milling process. (13-2)

reflection. The listener repeats in his or her own words what he or she thinks the speaker said. (2-2)

rent. A monthly fee paid to the owner of a property in return for living accommodations. (22-2)

resiliency. The ability to adjust to setbacks and make changes that allow a person to survive and thrive. (1-1)

resource. Time, object, service, or ability used to achieve goals. (4-1)

restyle. To change a garment to give it a different look. (21-4)

résumé. A brief account of a person's education, work experience, and other qualifications for employment. (1-3)

retort packaging. A shelf-stable food packaging method in which foods are sealed in a foil pouch and then sterilized. (14-4)

rhythm. A principle of design that creates a feeling of movement in a design. (19-2)

role expectation. A pattern of socially expected behavior in which people learn to behave the way they think society expects them to behave. (2-3)

S

salary. A set amount of money paid to an employee for a certain period of time. (4-4)

sale. A special selling of goods or services at a reduced price. (18-1)

sandwich generation. Middle-aged adults who provide care for their children and their parents at the same time. (10-5)

sanitation. The process of maintaining a clean and healthful environment. (15-2)

saturated fats. Fats that are solid at room temperature and are often referred to as *solid fats*. (13-1)

scale floor plan. A drawing that shows the size and shape of a room to scale, with one-fourth of an inch equaling one foot in the room of a home. (23-1)

scapegoating. An attempt to resolve conflicts by blaming others. The person blamed for the problem is the scapegoat. (2-4)

school-age children. Children between the ages of 6 and 12 years. (10-3)

seam. A row of stitching that joins garment pieces together. (21-3)

seam allowance. The space between the cutting line on a pattern and the stitching line, usually ⅝-inch wide. (21-1)

secondary colors. Colors created by mixing equal amounts of two primary colors. (19-2)

secondhand smoke. The smoke caused by smoke-producing substances, such as cigarettes, cigars, and pipes, that can be inhaled by people nearby. (12-3)

securities. Proof of debt or ownership of a company or government, often in the form of stocks or bonds. (17-2)

security deposit. A sum of money, usually one month's rent, paid by a tenant before moving into a property to cover possible damages. (22-2)

self-concept. A person's view of himself or herself. (1-1)

self-esteem. The sense of worth a person attaches to himself or herself. (1-1)

self-help feature. A clothing design detail that makes clothes easier for children to put on and take off. (11-1)

selvage. One of two finished lengthwise edges on a piece of fabric. (21-2)

sequential steps. A series of patterns during which children grow and develop. (10-1)

serger. A high-speed sewing machine that can stitch, trim, and finish seams in one simple step. (20-2)

setting limits. Giving children guidelines, or rules, of what they may and may not do. (11-2)

sexual abuse. A form of abuse in which one person forces another to engage in sexual activities. (7-3)

sexual harassment. Unwanted or unwelcome sexual advances, requests for sexual favors, or other verbal or physical sexual conduct. (8-4)

sexually transmitted infection (STI). An infection spread mainly through sexual contact with symptoms and side effects ranging from an outbreak of blisters to blindness to death. (12-3)

shellfish. Fish that have shells instead of backbones. (14-3)

short-term goal. A goal that takes a short time to reach, such as an hour, a day, or a week. (4-1)

sibling. A brother or sister. (8-1)

simulation software. Computer software that imitates an actual experience. (18-2)

single-family house. A house designed to shelter one family. (22-1)

single-parent family. One adult living with one or more children. (6-2)

smokeless tobacco. A product, such as chewing tobacco or snuff, that is placed in the mouth for chewing or dipping. (12-3)

social growth. A developing ability to get along with other people. (10-1)

socialization. The teaching process used to help children learn to conform to social standards. (6-1)

socio-dramatic play. A stage of play in which several children imitate others and act out situations together. (11-1)

solar energy. Energy produced from the sun. (5-3)

solitary play. A stage of play in which a child will play by himself or herself. (10-2)

stages of dying. Clearly defined stages in the acceptance of death. (10-5)

standards. Accepted levels of achievement. (1-1)

starch. The complex carbohydrate part of plants. (16-1)

status. A person's rank within a group. (19-1)

staystitching. A line of machine stitching that keeps the edges of garment pieces from stretching out of shape while being sewn. (21-3)

steady dating. A type of dating in which two people agree to date only each other. (8-2)

stepfamily. A family structure formed when a single parent marries. The husband, wife, or both spouses have children from other marriages. (6-2)

stereotype. A set belief that all members of a group are the same. (2-3)

stitching line. The seamline, which is ⅝-inch inside a pattern's cutting line. It is unmarked in multisize patterns, but marked as a broken line in single-size patterns. (21-1)

stock. A certificate that represents ownership of a small portion of a company. (17-2)

stress. The body's reaction to the events in a person's life. (12-2)

style. Specific construction details that make one garment differ from another garment of the same type. (19-3)

sublease. Passing a lease over from a renter to a second tenant who pays rent directly to the owner. (22-2)

substance abuse. The use of illegal drugs or the misuse of legal drugs such as alcohol. (7-3)

sudden infant death syndrome (SIDS). The sudden death of an apparently healthy baby during sleep. (10-2)

support group. A group of people who share a similar problem or concern. (7-3)

support system. A network of people and organizations family members can turn to during a crisis. (7-3)

T

table d'hôte. A type of menu in which one price is charged for an entire meal. (16-3)

tableware. Dinnerware, flatware, and glassware. (16-2)

tact. Knowledge of what to do or say to avoid offending others. (3-1)

team. A group of people organized around a common goal. (3-1)

telecommuting. An arrangement where an employee works from an office set up at home. The employee is connected to the office through technology. (2-1)

texture. A design element that affects the way a design looks and feels. (19-2)

thread shank. A short stem of thread that provides room for a button to lie over the buttonhole fabric. (21-3)

thread-tension regulator. Two separate controls found on a sewing machine that balance tension or pull between the upper and lower threads to form the proper stitch. (20-2)

time management. The ability to plan and use time well. (4-3)

time-out. Moving a child away from others for a short period of time when a child's disruptive behavior cannot be ignored. The child calms down and gains self-control. (11-2)

toddler. A child who is one or two years old. (10-2)

toxic waste. Waste that can cause injury if inhaled, swallowed, or absorbed through the skin. (5-2)

tract house. A house built by a developer who builds an entire neighborhood at once. (22-1)

traffic pattern. The path people follow as they move within and between rooms. (23-1)

trimming. Cutting away part of a seam allowance to reduce bulk. (21-3)

U

underweight. A term used to describe an adult who has a body mass index below 18.5. (13-4)

uniform. A distinctive outfit that identifies a person who wears it with a specific group. (19-1)

unit pricing. A consumer aid that shows the cost per standard unit of weight or measure for a product. (14-2)

universal design. The concept of creating products and living spaces that are easy for everyone to use. (23-1)

universal product code (UPC). A group of bars and numbers appearing on a product that contains price and product information. (14-2)

unsaturated fats. Fats that are usually liquid at room temperature and often referred to as *oils*. (13-1)

V

value. The lightness or darkness of a color. (19-2)

values. The beliefs, feelings, and experiences a person considers to be important and desirable. (1-1)

vaping. The use of e-cigarettes to inhale vapor through the mouth; most contain nicotine. (12-3)

vegetarian diet. A pattern of eating that is made up largely or entirely of foods from plant sources. (13-3)

vehicle identification number (VIN). A unique number assigned to every vehicle by the automobile industry. (24-2)

verbal communication. A form of communication that involves the use of words. (2-2)

visionary goal. A goal that inspires people to do more than they thought they were capable of achieving. (4-1)

vitamins. Organic substances needed in small amounts for normal growth and the maintenance of good health. (13-1)

volunteers. People who provide valuable services by offering their time, talents, and energy free of charge. (5-1)

W

wants. Items people desire, but do not need to survive. (1-1)

wardrobe. All the clothes and accessories a person has to wear. (19-3)

warranty. A written promise by a manufacturer that a product will meet specified standards of performance. (18-1)

wattage. A measurement of the amount of energy required to operate an electrical device. (5-3)

weaving. The process of interlacing two sets of yarns to produce a fabric. (20-1)

will. A legal document describing how a person intends for property to be distributed after his or her death. (17-2)

work ethic. A standard of conduct for successful job performance. (2-1)

work plan. A detailed list of all the duties that must be completed during a lab experience. (15-4)

Y

yarn. A continuous strand formed from combined fibers. (20-1)

Image Credits

The following images are courtesy of Shutterstock.com:

Feature icons: 21st Century Skills, Analyze and Solve, Financial Literacy, Healthy Living, Life Skills, Living Green, Math Connection, Mental Health Awareness, Science Connection, Serving Your Community, and Wellness Awareness.

Chapter 1: Unit 1 image A (pg. 3) and Figures 1-3, 1-4, 1-7, and 1-8.

Chapter 2: Chapter opener and Figures 2-3, 2-7, 2-8, 2-9, and 2-11.

Chapter 3: Chapter opener and Figure 3-4.

Chapter 4: Unit 2 images (pg. 78), Chapter opener, and Figures 4-1, 4-2, 4-4, 4-5, 4-7, and 4-8.

Chapter 5: Chapter opener and Figures 5-2, 5-3, 5-4, 5-5, 5-6, and 5-9.

Chapter 6: Chapter opener and Figures 6-2, 6-3, 6-4, 6-6, and 6-7.

Chapter 7: Figures 7-3, 7-4, 7-5, 7-6, 7-8, and 7-9.

Chapter 8: Chapter opener and Figures 8-1, 8-2, 8-3, 8-4, 8-8, 8-10, and 8-12.

Chapter 9: Unit 4 image A (pg. 208), Chapter opener, and Figures 9-1, 9-2, 9-3, 9-4, 9-5, and 9-7.

Chapter 10: Chapter opener and Figures 10-1, 10-2, 10-4, 10-5, 10-6, 10-7, 10-8, 10-9, 10-11, 10-12, 10-13, 10-14, 10-16, 10-17, 10-18, 10-19, 10-20, 10-21, 10-22, 10-23, and 10-24.

Chapter 11: Figures 11-3, 11-5, and 11-6.

Chapter 12: Unit 5 image B (pg. 296) and Figure 12-4.

Chapter 13: Chapter opener and Figures 13-1, 13-2, 13-4, 13-7, 13-10, 13-11, 13-12, 13-13, 13-14, 13-15, and 13-16.

Chapter 14: Chapter opener and Figures 14-1, 14-2, 14-11, 14-13, 14-14, 14-16, and 14-17.

Chapter 15: Figures 15-1 and 15-16.

Chapter 16: Chapter opener and Figures 16-3, 16-5, and 16-6.

Chapter 17: Unit 6 images (pg. 448), Chapter opener, and Figures 17-6, 17-8, 17-12, 17-14, and 17-17.

Chapter 18: Figures 18-1, 18-2, 18-3, 18-4, 18-5, 18-7, 18-8, and 18-9.

Chapter 19: Unit 7 images (pg. 516), Chapter opener, and Figures 19-7 and 19-9.

Chapter 20: Chapter opener and Figures 20-3, 20-8, and 20-11.

Chapter 21: Chapter opener.

Chapter 22: Chapter opener.

Chapter 23: Chapter opener and Figures 23-3, 23-7, and 23-10.

Chapter 24: Figures 24-1, 24-2, 24-3, 24-4, 24-5, 24-6, and 24-7.

Index